1 MONTH OF
FREE
READING

at
www.ForgottenBooks.com

By purchasing this book you are eligible for one month membership to ForgottenBooks.com, giving you unlimited access to our entire collection of over 1,000,000 titles via our web site and mobile apps.

To claim your free month visit:
www.forgottenbooks.com/free253772

ISBN 978-0-428-96483-2
PIBN 10253772

Forgotten Books is a registered trademark of FB &c Ltd.
Copyright © 2018 FB &c Ltd.
FB &c Ltd, Dalton House, 60 Windsor Avenue, London, SW19 2RR.
Company number 08720141. Registered in England and Wales.

For support please visit www.forgottenbooks.com

Col. Sir George McLaren Brown, K.B.E.

"Merksworth"

239 McNAB ST. SOUTH
HAMILTON
CANADA

né par le R.P. R. Donovan C.S.B.

h

The House, rue Fortunée, Paris,
in which Balzac died.

HOUSE, RUE FORTUNÉE PARIS,

THE COMÉDIE HUMAINE

OF

HONORÉ DE BALZAC

Edited, with a General Introduction and Prefaces, by

PROF. GEORGE SAINTSBURY, M. A.

By

ANATOLE CERFBERR AND JULES CHRISTOPHE

With an Introduction by
PAUL BOURGET

Translated by
J. WALKER MCSPADDEN

PHILADELPHIA

MCMII

TRANSLATOR'S PREFACE

"Work crowned by the French Academy" is a significant line borne by the title-page of the original edition of Messieurs Cerfberr and Christophe's monumental work. The motto indicates the high esteem in which the French authorities hold this very necessary adjunct to the great Balzacian structure. And even without this word of approval, the intelligent reader needs but a glance within the pages of the *Repertory of the Comédie Humaine* to convince him at once of its utility.

In brief, the purpose of the *Repertory* is to give in alphabetical sequence the names of all the characters forming this Balzacian society, together with the salient points in their lives. It is, of course, well known that Balzac made his characters appear again and again, thus creating out of his distinct novels a miniature world. To cite a case in point, Rastignac, who comes as near being the hero of the *Comédie* as any other single character, makes his first appearance in *Father Goriot*, as a student of law; then appearing and disappearing fitfully in a score of the principal novels, he is finally made a minister and peer of France. Without the aid of the *Repertory* it would be difficult for any save a reader of the entire *Comédie* to trace out his career. But here it is arranged in temporal sequence, thus giving us a concrete view of the man and his relation to this society.

In reading any separate story, when reference is made in passing to a character, the reader will find it helpful and interesting to turn to the *Repertory* and find what manner of man it is that is under advisement. A little systematic reading of this nature will speedily render the reader a "confirmed Balzacian."

A slight confusion may arise in the use of the *Repertory* on account of the subdivision of titles. This is the fault neither of Messieurs Cerfberr and Christophe nor of the translator, but of Balzac himself, who was continually changing titles, dividing and subdividing stories, and revamping and working other changes in his books. *Cousin Betty* and *Cousin Pons* were placed together by him under the general title of *Poor Relations*. Being separate stories, we have retained the separate titles. Similarly, the three divisions of *Lost Illusions* were never published together until 1843—in the first complete edition of the *Comédie;* before assuming final shape its parts had received several different titles. In the present text the editor has deemed it best to retain two of the parts under *Lost Illusions*, while the third, which presents a separate Rubempré episode, is given as *A Distinguished Provincial at Paris.* The three parts of *The Thirteen—Ferragus, The Duchesse de Langeais*, and *The Girl with the Golden Eyes*—are given under the general title. The fourth part of *Scenes from a Courtesan's Life, Vautrin's Last Avatar*, which until the Edition Definitive had been published separately, is here merged into its final place. But the three parts of *The Celibates—Pierrette, The Vicar of Tours* and *A Bachelor's Establishment*, being detached, are given separately. Other minor instances occur, but should be readily cleared up by reference to the Indices, also to the General Introduction given elsewhere.

In the preparation of this English text, great care has been exercised to gain accuracy—a quality not found in other versions now extant. In one or two instances, errors have been discovered in the original French, notably in dates —probably typographical errors—which have been corrected by means of foot-notes. A few unimportant elisions have been made for the sake of brevity and coherence. Many difficulties confront the translator in the preparation of material of this nature, involving names, dates and titles. Opportunities are constantly afforded for error, and the work must necessarily be painstaking in order to be successful. We desire here to express appreciation for the valuable assistance of Mr. Norman Hinsdale Pitman.

To Balzac, more than to any other author, a Repertory of characters is applicable; for he it was who not only created an entire human society, but placed therein a multitude of personages so real, so instinct with vitality, that biographies of them seem no more than simple justice. We can do no more, then, than follow the advice of Balzac—to quote again from the original title-page—and "give a parallel to the civil register."

J. WALKER McSPADDEN

INTRODUCTION

Are you a confirmed *Balzacian?*—to employ a former expression of Gautier in *Jeune France* on the morrow following the appearance of that mystic Rabelaisian epic, *The Magic Skin.* Have you experienced, while reading at school or clandestinely some stray volume of the *Comédie Humaine,* a sort of exaltation such as no other book had aroused hitherto, and few have caused since? Have you dreamed at an age when one plucks in advance all the fruit from the tree of life—yet in blossom—I repeat, have you dreamed of being a Daniel d'Arthez, and of covering yourself with glory by the force of your achievements, in order to be requited, some day, for all the sufferings of your poverty-stricken youth, by the sublime Diane, Duchesse de Maufrigneuse, Princesse de Cadignan?

Or, perchance, being more ambitious and less literary, you have desired to see—like a second Rastignac—the doors of high society opened to your eager gaze by means of the golden key suspended from Delphine de Nucingen's bracelet?

Romancist, have you sighed for the angelic tenderness of a Henriette de Mortsauf, and realized in your dreams the innocent emotions excited by culling nosegays, by listening to tales of grief, by furtive hand-clasps on the banks of a narrow river, blue and placid, in a valley where your friendship flourishes like a fair, delicate lily the ideal, the chaste flower?

Misanthrope, have you caressed the chimera, to ward off the dark hours of advancing age, of a friendship equal to that with which the good Schmucke enveloped even the whims of his poor Pons? Have you appreciated the sovereign power of secret societies, and deliberated with yourself as to which of your acquaintances would be most worthy to enter The Thirteen? In your mind's eye has the map of France ever appeared to be divided up into as many provinces as the *Comédie Humaine* has stories? Has Tours stood for Birotteau, La Gamard, for the formidable Abbé Troubert; Douai, Claës; Limoges, Madame Graslin; Besançon, Savarus and his misguided love; Angouléme, Rubempré; Sancerre, Madame de la Baudraye; Alençon, that touching, artless old maid to whom her uncle, the Abbé de Sponde, remarked with gentle irony: "You have too much wit. You don't need so much to be happy"?

Oh, sorcery ·of the most wonderful magician of letters the world has seen since Shakespeare! If you have come under the spell of his enchantments, be it only for an hour, here is a book that will delight you, a book that would have pleased Balzac himself—Balzac, who was more the victim of his work than his most fanatical readers, and whose dream was to compete with the civil records. This volume of nearly six hundred pages is really the civil record of all the characters in the *Comédie Humaine*, by which you may locate, detail by detail, the smallest adventures of the heroes who pass and repass through the various novels, and by which you can recall at a moment's notice the emotions once awakened by the perusal of such and such a masterpiece. More modestly, it is a kind of table of contents, of a unique type; a table of living contents!

Many Balzacians have dreamed of compiling such a civil record. I myself have known of five or six who attempted this singlar task. To cite only two names out of the many,

the idea of this unusual Vapereau ran through the head of
that keen and delicate critic, M. Henri Meilhac, and of that
detective in continued stories, Emile Gaboriau. I believe
that I also have among the papers of my eighteenth year
some sheets covered with notes taken with the same intention. But the labor was too exhaustive. It demanded
an infinite patience, combined with an inextinguishable
ardor and enthusiasm. The two faithful disciples of the
master who have conjoined their efforts to uprear this monument, could not perhaps have overcome the difficulties of the
undertaking if they had not supported each other, bringing
to the common work, M. Christophe his painstaking method,
M. Cerfberr his accurate memory, his passionate faith in the
genius of the great Honoré, a faith that carried unshakingly
whole mountains of documents.

A pleasing chapter of literary gossip might be written
anent this collaboration; a melancholy chapter, since it brings
with it the memory of a charming man, who first brought
Messieurs Cerfberr and Christophe together, and who has
since died under mournful circumstances. His name was
Albert Allenet, and he was chief editor of a courageous little
review, *La Jeune France*, which he maintained for some years
with a perseverance worthy of the Man of Business in the
Comédie Humaine. I can see him yet, a feverish fellow,
wan and haggard, but with his face always lit up by enthusiasm, stopping me in a theatre lobby to tell me about a plan of
M. Cerfberr's; and almost immediately we discovered that
the same plan had been conceived by M. Christophe. The
latter had already prepared a cabinet of pigeon-holes, arranged and classified by the names of Balzacian characters.
When two men encounter in the same enterprise as compilers,
they will either hate each other or unite their efforts. Thanks

to the excellent Allenet, the two confirmed Balzacians took to each other wonderfully.

Poor Allenet! It was not long afterwards that we accompanied his body to the grave, one gloomy afternoon towards the end of autumn—all of us who had known and loved him. He is dead also, that other Balzacian who was so much interested in this work, and for whom the *Comédie Humaine* was an absorbing thought, Honoré Granoux. He was a merchant of Marseilles, with a wan aspect and already an invalid when I met him. But he became animated when speaking of Balzac; and with what a mysterious, conspirator-like veneration did he pronounce these words: "The Vicomte"—meaning, of course, to the thirty-third degree Balzacolatrites, that incomparable bibliophile to whom we owe the history of the novelist's works, M. de Spoelberch de Lovenjoul!—"The Vicomte will approve—or disapprove." That was the unvarying formula for Granoux, who had devoted himself to the enormous task of collecting all the articles, small or great, published about Balzac since his entry as a writer. And just see what a fascination this *devil of a man*—as Theophile Gautier once called him—exercises over his followers; I am fully convinced that these little details of Balzacian mania will cause the reader to smile. As for me, I have found them, and still find them, as natural as Balzac's own remark to Jules Sandeau, who was telling him about a sick sister: "Let us go back to reality. Who is going to marry Eugénie Grandet?"

Fascination! That is the only word that quite characterizes the sort of influence wielded by Balzac over those who really enjoy him; and it is not to-day that the phenomenon began. Valliés pointed it out long ago in an eloquent page of the *Réfractaires* concerning "book victims."

Sainte Beuve, who can scarcely be suspected of fondness towards the editor-in-chief of the *Revue Parisienne*, tells a story stranger and more significant than every other. At one time an entire social set in Venice, and the most aristocratic, decided to give out among its members different characters drawn from the *Comédie Humaine;* and some of these rôles, the critic adds, mysteriously, were artistically carried out to the very end;—a dangerous experiment, for we are well aware that the heroes and heroines of Balzac often skirt the most treacherous abysses of the social Hell.

All that happened about 1840. The present year is 1887, and there seems no prospect of the sorcery weakening. The work to which these notes serve as an introduction may be taken as a proof. Indeed, somebody has said that the men of Balzac have appeared as much in literature as in life, especially since the death of the novelist. Balzac seems to have observed the society of his day less than he contributed to form a new one. Such and such personages are truer to life in 1860 than in 1835. When one considers a phenomenon of such range and intensity, it does not suffice to employ words like infatuation, fashion, mania. The attraction of an author becomes a psychological fact of prime importance and subject to analysis. I think I can see two reasons for this particular strength of Balzac's genius. One dwells in the special character of his vision, the other in the philosophical trend which he succeeded in giving to all his writing.

As to the scope of his vision, this *Repertory* alone will suffice to show. Turn over the leaves at random and estimate the number of fictitious deeds going to make up these two thousand biographies, each individual, each distinct, and

most of them complete—that is to say, taking the character
at his birth and leaving him only at his death. Balzac not
only knows the date of birth or of death, he knows as well
the local coloring of the time and the country and profession
to which the man belongs. He is thoroughly conversant
with questions of taxation and income and the agricultural
conditions. He is not ignorant of the fact that Grandet
cannot make his fortune by the same methods employed by
Gobseck, his rival in avarice; nor Ferdinand du Tillet, that
jackal, with the same magnitude of operations worked out
by that elephant of a Nucingen. He has outlined and
measured the exact relation of each character to his environment in the same way that he has outlined and measured
the bonds uniting the various characters; so well that each
individual is defined separately as to his personal and his
social side, and in the same manner each family is defined.
It is the skeleton of these individuals and of these families
that is laid bare for your contemplation in these notes of
Messieurs Cerfberr and Christophe. But this structure of
facts, dependent one upon another by a logic equal to that
of life itself, is the smallest effort of Balzac's genius. Does
a birth-certificate, a marriage-contract or an inventory of
wealth represent a person? Certainly not. There is still
lacking, for a bone covering, the flesh, the blood, the muscles
and the nerves. A glance from Balzac, and all these tabu-
lated facts become imbued with life; to this circumstantial
view of the conditions of existence with certain beings is added
as full a view of the beings themselves.

And first of all he knows them physiologically. The inner
workings of their corporeal mechanism is no mystery for him.
Whether it is Birotteau's gout, or Mortsauf's nervousness,
or Fraisier's skin trouble, or the secret reason for Rouget's
subjugation by Flore, or Louis Lambert's catalepsy, he is as

conversant with the case as though he were a physician; and he is as well informed, also, as a confessor concerning the spiritual mechanism which this animal machine supports. The slightest frailties of conscience are perceptible to him. From the portress Gibot to the Marquise d'Espard, not one of his women has an evil thought that he does not fathom. With what art, comparable to that of Stendhal, or Laclos, or the most subtle analysts, does he note—in *The Secrets of a Princess*—the transition from comedy to sincerity! He knows when a sentiment is simple and when it is complex, when the heart is a dupe of the mind and when of the senses. And through it all he hears his characters speak, he distinguishes their voices, and we ourselves distinguish them in the dialogue. The growling of Vautrin, the hissing of La Gamard, the melodious tones of Madame de Mortsauf still linger in our ears. For such intensity of evocation is as contagious as an enthusiasm or a panic.

There is abundant testimony going to show that with Balzac this evocation is accomplished, as in the mystic arts, by releasing it, so to speak, from the ordinary laws of life. Pray note in what terms M. le Docteur Fournier, the real mayor of Tours, relates incidents of the novelist's method of work, according to the report of a servant employed at the château of Saché: "Sometimes he would shut himself up in his room and stay there several days. Then it was that, plunged into a sort of ecstasy and armed with a crow quill, he would write night and day, abstaining from all food and merely contenting himself with decoctions of coffee which he himself prepared."[1]

[1] Brochure of M. le Docteur Fournier in regard to the statue of Balzac, that statue a piece of work to which M. Henry Renault—another devotee who had established *Le Balzac*—had given himself so ardently. In this brochure is found a very curious portrait of Balzac, after a sepia by Louis Boulanger belonging to M. le Baron Larrey.

In the opening pages of *Facino Cane* this phenomenon is thus described: "With me observation had become intuitive from early youth. It penetrated the soul without neglecting the body, or rather it seized so completely the external details that it went beyond them. It gave me the faculty of living the life of the individual over whom it obtained control, and allowed me to substitute myself for him like the dervish in *Arabian Nights* assumed the soul and the body of persons over whom he pronounced certain words." And he adds, after describing how he followed a workman and his wife along the street: "I could espouse their very life, I felt their rags on my back. I trod in their tattered shoes. Their desires, their needs, all passed into my soul, or my soul passed into them. It was the dream of a man awakened." One day while he and a friend of his were watching a beggar pass by, the friend was astonished to see Balzac touch his own sleeve; he seemed to feel the rent which gaped at the elbow of the beggar.

Am I wrong in connecting this sort of imagination with that which one witnesses in fanatics of religious faith? With such a faculty Balzac could not be, like Edgar Poe, merely a narrator of nightmares. He was preserved from the fantastic by another gift which seems contradictory to the first. This visionary was in reality a philosopher, that is to say, an experimenter and a manipulator of general ideas. Proof of this may be found in his biography, which shows him to us, during his college days at Vendôme, plunged into a whirl of abstract reading. The entire theological and occult library which he discovered in the old Oratorian institution was absorbed by the child, till he had to quit school sick, his brain benumbed by this strange opium. The story of Louis Lambert is a monograph of his own mind. During his youth and in the moments snatched from his profession, to what did he turn his attention? Still to general ideas. We find him an interested onlooker at the quarrel of Geoffroy Saint-Hilaire and Cuvier, troubling himself about the hypothesis of the unity of creation, and still dealing with mysticism; and, in fact, his romances abound in theories. There is not one of his works from which you cannot obtain abstract thoughts by the hundreds. If he describes, as in *The Vicar of Tours*, the woes of an old priest, he profits by the opportunity to exploit a theory concerning the development of sensibility, and a treatise on the future of Catholicism. If he describes, as in *The Firm of Nucingen*, a supper given to Parisian *blasés*, he introduces a system of credit, reports of the Bank and Bureau of Finance, and—any number of other things! Speaking of Daniel d'Arthez, that one of his heroes who, with Albert Savarus and Raphaël, most nearly resembles himself, he writes: "Daniel would not admit the existence of talent without profound metaphysical knowledge. At this moment he was in the act of despoiling both ancient and modern philosophy of all their wealth in order to assimilate it. He desired, like Moliére, to become a profound philosopher first of all, a writer of comedies afterwards." Some readers there are, indeed, who think that philosophy superabounds with Balzac, that the surplus of general hypotheses overflows at times, and that the novels are too prone to digressions. Be that as it may, it seems incontestible that this was his master faculty, the virtue and vice of his thought. Let us see, however, by what singular detour this power of generalization—the antithesis, one might say, of the creative power—increased in him the faculty of the poetic visionary.

It is important, first of all, to note that this power of the visionary could not be put directly into play. Balzac had not long enough to live. The list of his works, year by year, prepared by his sister, shows that from the moment he achieved his reputation till the day of his death he never took time for rest or observation or the study of mankind by daily and close contact, like Moliére or Saint-Simon. He cut his life in two, writing by night, sleeping by day, and after sparing not a single hour for calling, promenades or sentiment. Indeed, he would not admit this troublesome factor of sentiment, except at a distance and through letters— "because it forms one's style"! At any rate, that is the kind of love he most willingly admitted—unless an exception be made of the mysterious intimacies of which his correspondence has left traces. During his youth he had followed this same habit of heavy labor, and as a result the experience of this master of exact literature was reduced to a minimum; but this minimum sufficed for him, precisely because of the philosophical insight which he possessed to so high a degree. To this meagre number of positive faculties furnished by observation, he applied an analysis so intuitive that he discovered, behind the small facts amassed by him in no unusual quantity, the profound forces, the generative influences, so to speak.

He himself describes—once more in connection with Daniel d'Arthez—the method pursued in this analytical and generalizing work. He calls it a "retrospective penetration." Probably he lays hold of the elements of experience and casts them into a seeming retort of reveries. Thanks to an alchemy somewhat analogous to that of Cuvier, he was enabled to reconstruct an entire temperament from the smallest detail, and an entire class from a single individual; but that which guided him in this work of reconstruction was always and everywhere the habitual process of philosophers: the quest and investigation of causes.

It is due to this analysis that this dreamer has defined almost all the great principles of the psychological changes incident to our time. He saw clearly, while democracy was establishing itself with us on the ruins of the ancient régime, the novelty of the sentiments which these transfers from class to class were certain to produce. He fathomed every complication of heart and mind in the modern woman by an intuition of the laws which control her development. He divined the transformation in the lives of artists, keeping pace with the change in the national situation; and to this day the picture he has drawn of journalism in *Lost Illusions*[1] remains strictly true. It seems to me that this same power of locating causes, which has brought about such a wealth of ideas in his work, has also brought about the magic of it all. While other novelists describe humanity from the outside, he has shown man to us both from within and without. The characters which crowd forth from his brain are sustained and impelled by the same social waves which sustain and impel us. The generative facts which created them are the same which are always in operation about us. If many young men have taken as a model a Rastignac, for instance, it is because the passions by which this ambitious pauper was consumed are the same which our age of unbridled greed multiplies around disinherited youth. Add to this that Balzac was not content merely to display the fruitful sources of a modern intellect, but that he cast upon them the glare of the most ardent imagination the world has ever known. By a rare combination this philosopher was also a man, like the story-tellers of the Orient, to whom solitude and the over-excitement of night-work had communicated a brilliant and unbroken hallucination. He was able to impart this

[1] "A Distinguished Provincial at Paris."

fever to his readers, and to plunge them into a sort of *Arabian Nights* country, where all the passions, all the desires of real life appear, but expanded to the point of fantasy, like the dreams brought on by laudanum or hasheesh. Why, then, should we not understand the reason that, for certain readers, this world of Balzac's is more real than the actual world, and that they devoted their energies to imitating it?

It is possible that to-day the phenomenon is becoming rarer, and that Balzac, while no less admired, does not exercise the same fascinating influence. The cause for this is that the great social forces which he defined have almost ended their work. Other forces now shape the oncoming generations and prepare them for further sensitive influences. It is none the less a fact that, to penetrate the central portions of the nineteenth century in France, one must read and re-read the *Comédie Humaine*. And we owe sincere thanks to Messieurs Cerfberr and Christophe for this *Repertory*. Thanks to them, we shall the more easily traverse the long galleries, painted and frescoed, of this enormous palace—a palace still unfinished, inasmuch as it lacks those Scenes of Military Life whose titles awaken dreams within us: *Forced Marches; The Battle of Austerlitz; After Dresden.* Incontestably, Tolstoy's *War and Peace* is an admirable book, but how can we help regretting the loss of the painting of the Grand Army and of our Great Emperor, by Balzac, our Napoleon of letters ?

PAUL BOURGET.

REPERTORY OF THE COMEDIE HUMAINE

A

Abramko, Polish Jew of gigantic strength, thoroughly devoted to the broker, Elie Magus, whose porter he was, and whose daughter and treasures he guarded with the aid of three fierce dogs, in 1844, in an old house on the Minimes road hard by the Palais Royale, Paris. Abramko had allowed himself to be compromised in the Polish insurrection and Magus was interested in saving him. [Cousin Pons.]

Adèle, sturdy, good-hearted Briarde servant of Denis Rogron and his sister, Sylvie, from 1824 to 1827 at Provins. Contrary to her employers, she displayed much sympathy and pity for their youthful cousin, Pierrette Lorrain. [Pierrette.]

Adèle, chambermaid of Madame du Val-Noble at the time when the latter was maintained so magnificently by the stockbroker, Jacques Falleix, who failed in 1829. [Scenes from a Courtesan's Life.]

Adolphe, slight, blonde young man employed at the shop of the shawl merchant, Fritot, in the Bourse quarter, Paris, at the time of the reign of Louis Philippe. [Gaudissart II.]

Adolphus, head of the banking firm of Adolphus & Company of Manheim, and father of the Baroness Wilhelmine d'Aldrigger. [The Firm of Nucingen.]

Agathe (Sister), née Langeais, nun of the convent of Chelles, and, with her sister Martha and the Abbé de Marolles, a refugee under the Terror in a poor house of the Faubourg Saint-Martin, Paris. [An Episode Under the Terror.]

Aiglemont (Général, Marquis Victor d'), heir of the Marquis d'Aiglemont and nephew of the dowager Comtesse de Listomère-Landon; born in 1783. After having been the lover of the Maréchale de Carigliano, he married, in the latter part of 1813 (at which time he was one of the youngest and most dashing colonels of the French cavalry), Mlle. Julie de Chatillonest, his cousin, with whom he resided successively at Touraine, Paris and Versailles.[1] He took part in the great struggle of the Empire; but the Restoration freed him from his oath to Napoleon, restored his titles, entrusted to him a station in the Body Guard, which gave him the rank of general, and later made him a peer of France. Gradually he forsook his wife, whom he deceived on account of Madame de Sérizy. In 1817 the Marquis d'Aiglemont became the father of a daughter (See Héléne d'Aiglemont) who was his image physically and morally; his last three children came into the world during a *liaison* between the Marquise d'Aiglemont and the brilliant diplomat, Charles de Vandenesse. In 1827 the general, as well as his protégé and cousin, Godefroid de Beaudenord, was hurt by the fraudulent failure of the Baron de Nucingen. Moreover, he sank a million in the Wortschin mines where he had been speculating with hypothecated securities of his wife's. This completed his ruin. He went to America, whence he returned, six years later, with a new fortune. The Marquis d'Aiglemont died, overcome by his exertions, in 1833.[2] [At the Sign of the Cat and Racket. The Firm of Nucingen. A Woman of Thirty.]

Aiglemont (Générale, Marquise Julie d'), wife of the preceding; born in 1792. Her father, M. de Chatillonest, advised her against, but gave her in marriage to her cousin, the attractive Colonel Victor d'Aiglemont, in 1813. Quickly disillusioned and attacked from another source by an "inflammation very often fatal, and which is spoken of by women only in confidence," she sank into a profound melancholy. The death of the Comtesse de Listomère-Landon, her aunt by marriage, deprived her of valuable protection and advice.

---

[1] It appears that the residence of the Marquis d'Aiglemont at Versailles was located at number 57, on the present Avenue de Paris ; until recently it was occupied by one of the authors of this work.

[2] Given erroneously in the original as 1835.

Shortly thereafter she became a mother and found, in the re-
alization of her new duties, strength to resist the mutual attachment between herself and the young and romantic Englishman, Lord Arthur Ormond Grenville, a student of medicine
who had nursed her and healed her bodily ailments, and
who died rather than compromise her. Heart-broken, the
marquise withdrew to the solitude of an old château situated
between Moret and Montereau in the midst of a neglected
waste. She remained a recluse for almost a year, given
over utterly to her grief, refusing the consolations of the
Church offered her by the old curé of the village of Saint-
Lange. Then she re-entered society at Paris. There, at
the age of about thirty, she yielded to the genuine passion
of the Marquis de Vandenesse. A child, christened Charles,
was born of this union, but he perished at an early age under
very tragic circumstances. Two other children, Moïna
and Abel, were also the result of this love union. They
were favored by their mother above the two eldest children,
Héléne and Gustave, the only ones really belonging to the
Marquis d'Aiglemont. Madame d'Aiglemont, when nearly
fifty, a widow, and having none of her children remaining
alive save her daughter Moïna, sacrificed all her own fortune
for a dower in order to marry the latter to M. de Saint-
Hércen, heir of one of the most famous families of France.
She then went to live with her son-in-law in a magnificent
mansion overlooking the Esplanade des Invalides. But
her daughter gave her slight return for her love. Ruffled
one day by some remarks made to her by Madame d'Aiglemont
concerning the suspicious devotion of the Marquis de Vandenesse, Moïna went so far as to fling back at her mother
the remembrance of the latter's own guilty relations with
the young man's father. Terribly overcome by this attack,
the poor woman, who was a physical wreck, deaf and subject to heart disease, died in 1844. [A Woman of Thirty.]

Aiglemont (Héléne d'), eldest daughter of the Marquis
and Marquise Victor d'Aiglemont; born in 1817. She and
her brother Gustave were neglected by her mother for Charles,

Abel and Moïna.   On this account Héléne became jealous and defiant.   When about eight years old, in a paroxysm of ferocious hate, she pushed her brother Charles into the Biévre, where he was drowned.   This childish crime always passed for a terrible accident.   When a young woman —one Christmas night—Héléne eloped with a mysterious adventurer who was being tracked by justice and who was, for the time being, in hiding at the home of the Marquis Victor d'Aiglemont, at Versailles.   Her despairing father sought her vainly.   He saw her no more till seven years later, and then only once, when on his return from America to France.   The ship on which he returned was captured by pirates, whose captain, "The Parisian," the veritable abductor of Héléne, protected the marquis and his fortune.   The two lovers had four beautiful children and lived together in the most perfect happiness, sharing the same perils.   Héléne refused to follow her father.   In 1835, some months after the death of her husband, Madame d'Aiglemont, while taking the youthful Moïna to a Pyrenees watering-place, was asked to aid a poor sufferer.   It was her daughter, Héléne, who had just escaped shipwreck, saving only one child.   Both presently succumbed before the eyes of Madame d'Aiglemont.   [A Woman of Thirty.]

Aiglemont (Gustave d'), second child of the Marquis and Marquise Victor d'Aiglemont, and born under the Restoration. His first appearance is while still a child, about 1827 or 1828, when returning in company with his father and his sister Héléne from the presentation of a gloomy melodrama at the Gaîté theatre.   He was obliged to flee hastily from a scene, which violently agitated Héléne, because it recalled the circumstances surrounding the death of his brother, some two or three years earlier.   Gustave d'Aiglemont is next found in a Lyceum garb reading "Arabian Nights" in the drawing-room at Versailles, where the family is assembled, on the same evening of the abduction of Héléne.   He died at an early age of the cholera, leaving a widow and children for whom the Dowager Marquise d'Aiglemont showed little love.   [A Woman of Thirty.]

Aiglemont (Charles d'), third child of the Marquis and the Marquise d'Aiglemont, born at the time of the intimacy of Madame d'Aiglemont with the Marquis de Vandenesse. He appears but a single time, one spring morning about 1824 or 1825, then being four years old. He was out walking with his sister Héléne, his mother and the Marquis de Vandenesse. In a sudden outburst of jealous hate, Héléne pushed the little Charles into the Biévre, where he was drowned. [A Woman of Thirty.]

Aiglemont (Moïna d'), fourth child and second daughter of the Marquis and Marquise Victor d'Aiglemont. (*See* Comtesse de Saint-Héreen.) [A Woman of Thirty.]

Aiglemont (Abel d'), fifth and last child of the Marquis and Marquise Victor d'Aiglemont, born during the relations of his mother with M. de Vandenesse. Moïna and he were the favorites of Madame d'Aiglemont. Killed in Africa before Constantine. [A Woman of Thirty.]

Ajuda-Pinto (Marquis Miguel d'), Portuguese belonging to a very old and wealthy family, the oldest branch of which was connected with the Bragance and the Grandlieu houses. In 1819 he was enrolled among the most distinguished dandies who graced Parisian society. At this same period he began to forsake Claire de Bourgogne, Vicomtesse de Beauséant, with whom he had been intimate for three years. After having caused her much uneasiness concerning his real intentions, he returned her letters, on the intervention of Eugéne de Rastignac, and married Mlle. Berthe de Rochefide. [Father Goriot. Scenes from a Courtesan's Life.] In 1832 he was present at one of Madame d'Espard's receptions, where every one there joined in slandering the Princesse de Cadignan before Daniel d'Arthez, then violently enamored of her. [The Secrets of a Princess.] Towards 1840, the Marquis d'Ajuda-Pinto, then a widower, married again—this time Mlle. Joséphine de Grandlieu, third daughter of the last duke of this name. Shortly thereafter, the marquis was accomplice in a plot hatched by the friends of the Duchesse de Grandlieu and Madame du Guénie to rescue Calyste du Guénie from the clutches of the Marquise de Rochefide. [Béatrix.]

Ajuda-Pinto (Marquise Berthe d'), *née* Rochefide. Married to the Marquis Miguel d'Ajuda-Pinto in 1820. Died about 1840. [Béatrix.]

Ajuda-Pinto (Marquise Joséphine d'), daughter of the Duc and Duchesse Ferdinand de Grandlieu; second wife of the Marquis Miguel d'Ajuda-Pinto, her kinsman by marriage. Their marriage was celebrated about 1840. [Scenes from a Courtesan's Life.]

Alain (Frédéric), born about 1767. He was clerk in the office of Bordin, procureur of Châtelet. In 1798 he lent one hundred crowns in gold to Monegod his life-long friend. This sum not being repaid, M. Alain found himself almost insolvent, and was obliged to take an insignificant position at the Mont-de-Piété. In addition to this he kept the books of César Birotteau, the well-known perfumer. Monegod became wealthy in 1816, and he forced M. Alain to accept a hundred and fifty thousand francs in payment of the loan of the hundred crowns. The good man then devoted his unlooked-for fortune to philanthropies in concert with Judge Popinot. Later, at the close of 1825, he became one of the most active aides of Madame de la Chanterie and her charitable association. It was M. Alain who introduced Godefroid into the Brotherhood of the Consolation. [The Seamy Side of History.]

Albertine, Madame de Bargeton's chambermaid, between the years 1821 and 1824. [Lost Illusions.]

Albon (Marquis d'), court councillor and ministerial deputy under the Restoration. Born in 1777. In September, 1819, he went hunting in the edge of the forest of l'Isle-Adam with his friend Philippe de Sucy, who suddenly fell senseless at the sight of a poor madwoman whom he recognized as a former mistress, Stéphanie de Vandiéres. The Marquis d'Albon, assisted by two passers by, M. and Mme. de Granville, resuscitated M. de Sucy. Then the marquis returned, at his friend's entreaty, to the home of Stéphanie, where he learned from the uncle of this unfortunate one the sad story of the love of his friend and Madame de Vandiéres. [Farewell.]

Albrizzi (Comtesse), a friend, in 1820, at Venice, of the celebrated melomaniac, Capraja. [Massimilla Doni.]

Aldrigger (Jean-Baptiste, Baron d'), born in Alsace in 1764. In 1800 a banker at Strasbourg, where he was at the apogee of a fortune made during the Revolution, he wedded, partly through ambition, partly through inclination, the heiress of the Adolphuses of Manheim. The young daughter was idolized by every one in her family and naturally inherited all their fortune after some ten years. Aldrigger, created baron by the Emperor, was passionately devoted to the great man who had bestowed upon him his title, and he ruined himself, between 1814 and 1815, by believing too deeply in "the sun of Austerlitz." At the time of the invasion, the trustworthy Alsatian continued to pay on demand and closed up his bank, thus meriting the remark of Nucingen, his former head-clerk: "Honest, but stoobid." The Baron d'Aldrigger went at once to Paris. There still remained to him an income of forty-four thousand francs, reduced at his death, in 1823, by more than half on account of the expenditures and carelessness of his wife. The latter was left a widow with two daughters, Malvina and Isaure. [The Firm of Nucingen.]

Aldrigger (Théodora-Marguerite-Wilhelmine, Baronne d'), *née* Adolphus. Daughter of the banker Adolphus of Manheim, greatly spoiled by her parents. In 1800 she married the Strasbourg banker, Aldrigger, who spoiled her as badly as they had done and as later did the two daughters whom she had by her husband. She was superficial, incapable, egotistic, coquettish and pretty. At forty years of age she still preserved almost all her freshness and could be called "the little Shepherdess of the Alps." In 1823, when the baron died, she came near following him through her

violent grief. The following morning at breakfast she
was served with small pease, of which she was very fond,
and these small pease averted the crisis. She resided in
the rue Joubert, Paris, where she held receptions until the
marriage of her younger daughter. [The Firm of Nucingen.]

Aldrigger (Malvina d'), elder daughter of the Baron and
Baroness d'Aldrigger, born at Strasbourg in 1801, at the
time when the family was most wealthy. Dignified, slender,
swarthy, sensuous, she was a good type of the woman "you
have seen at Barcelona." Intelligent, haughty, whole-
souled, sentimental and sympathetic, she was nevertheless
smitten by the dry Ferdinand du Tillet, who sought her
hand in marriage at one time, but forsook her when he
learned of the bankruptcy of the Aldrigger family. The
lawyer Desroches also considered asking the hand of Malvina,
but he too gave up the idea. The young girl was counseled
by Eugéne de Rastignac, who took it upon himself to see
that she got married. Nevertheless, she ended by being
an old maid, withering day by day, giving piano lessons,
living rather meagrely with her mother in a modest flat
on the third floor, in the rue du Mont-Thabor. [The Firm
of Nucingen.]

Aldrigger (Isaure d'), second daughter of the Baron and
Baroness d'Aldrigger, married to Godefroid de Beaudenord.
(*See* that name.) [The Firm of Nucingen.]

Aline, a young Auvergne chambermaid in the service of
Madame Véronique Graslin, to whom she was devoted body
and soul. She was probably the only one to whom was
confided all the terrible secrets pertaining to the life of
Madame Graslin. [The Country Parson.]

Allegrain[1] (Christophe-Gabriel), French sculptor, born in
1710. With Lauterbourg and Vien, at Rome, in 1758, he
assisted his friend Sarrasine to abduct Zambinella, then a famous singer. The prima-donna was a eunuch. [Sarrasine.]

[1] To the sculptor Allegrain who died in 1795, the Louvre Museum is indebted for
a " Narcisse," a " Diana," and a " Venus entering the Bath."

Alphonse, a friend of the ruined orphan, Charles Grandet, tarrying temporarily at Saumur. In 1819 he acquitted himself most creditably of a mission entrusted to him by that young man. He wound up Charles' business at Paris, paying all his debts by a single little sale. [Eugénie Grandet.]

Al-Sartchild, name of a German banking-house, where Gédéon Brunner was compelled to deposit the funds belonging to his son Frédéric and inherited from his mother. [Cousin Pons.]

Althor (Jacob), a Hambourg banker, who opened up a business at Havre in 1815. He had a son, whom in 1829 M. and Mme. Mignon desired for a son-in-law. [Modeste Mignon.]

Althor (Francisque), son of Jacob Althor. Francisque was the dandy of Havre in 1829. He wished to marry Modeste Mignon, but forsook her quickly enough when he found out that her family was bankrupt. Not long afterwards he married Mlle. Vilquin the elder. [Modeste Mignon.]

Amanda, Parisian modiste at the time of Louis Philippe. Among her customers was Marguerite Turquet, known as Malaga, who was slow in paying bills. [A Man of Business.]

Amaury (Madame), owner, in 1829, of a pavilion at Sanvic, near Ingouville, which Canalis leased when he went to Havre to see Mlle. Mignon. [Modeste Mignon.]

Ambermesnil (Comtesse de l') went in 1819, when about thirty-six years old, to board with the widow, Mme. Vauquer, rue Neuve Sainte-Genevieve, now Tournefort, Paris. Mme. de l'Ambermesnil gave it out that she was awaiting the settlement of a pension which was due her on account of being the widow of a general killed "on the battlefield." Mme. Vauquer gave her every attention, confiding all her own affairs to her. The comtesse vanished at the end of six months, leaving a board bill unsettled. Mme. Vauquer sought her eagerly, but was never able to obtain a trace of this adventuress. [Father Goriot.]

Amédée, nickname bestowed on Félix de Vandenesse by Lady Dudley when she thought she saw a rival in Madame de Mortsauf. [The Lily of the Valley.]

Anchise (Pére), a surname given by La Palférine to a little Savoyard of ten years who worked for him without pay. "I have never seen such silliness coupled with such intelligence," the Prince of Bohemia said of this child; "he would go through fire for me, he understands everything, and yet he does not see that I cannot help him." [A Prince of Bohemia.]

Angard—At Paris, in 1840, the "professor" Angard was consulted, in connection with the Doctors Bianchon and Larabit, on account of Mme. Hector Hulot, who it was feared was losing her reason. [Cousin Betty.]

Angélique (Sister), nun of the Carmellite convent at Blois under Louis XVIII. Celebrated for her leanness. She was known by Renée de l'Estorade (Mme. de Maucombe) and Louise de Chaulieu (Mme. Marie Gaston), who went to school at the convent. [Letters of Two Brides.]

Anicette, chambermaid of the Princesse de Cadignan in 1839. The artful and pretty Champagne girl was sought by the sub-prefect of Arcis-sur-Aube, by Maxime de Trailles, and by Mme. Beauvisage, the mayor's wife, each trying to bribe and enlist her on the side of one of the various candidates for deputy. [The Member for Arcis.]

Annette, Christian name of a young woman of the Parisian world, under the Restoration. She had been brought up at Ecouen, where she had received the practical counsels of Mme. Campan. Mistress of Charles Grandet before his father's death. Towards the close of 1819, a prey to suspicion, she must needs sacrifice her happiness for the time being, so she made a weary journey with her husband into Scotland. She made her lover effeminate and materialistic, advising with him about everything. He returned from the Indies in 1827, when she quickly brought about his engagement with Mlle. d'Aubrion. [Eugénie Grandet.]

Annette, maid servant of Rigou at Blangy, Burgundy. She was nineteen years old, in 1823, and had held this place for more than three years, although Grégoire Rigou never kept servants for a longer period than this, however much he might and did favor them. Annette, sweet, blonde, delicate, a true masterpiece of dainty, piquant loveliness, worthy to wear a duchess' coronet, earned nevertheless only thirty francs a year. She kept company with Jean-Louis Tonsard without letting her master once suspect it; ambition had prompted this young woman to flatter her employer as a means of hoodwinking this lynx. [The Peasantry.]

Anselme, Jesuit, living in rue des Postes (now rue Lhomond). Celebrated mathematician. Had some dealings with Félix Phellion, whom he tried to convert to his religious belief. This rather meagre information concerning him was furnished by a certain Madame Komorn. [The Middle Classes.]

Antoine, born in the village of Echelles, Savoy. In 1824 he had served longest as clerk in the Bureau of Finance, where he had secured positions, still more modest than his own, for a couple of his nephews, Laurent and Gabriel, both of whom were married to lace laundresses. Antoine meddled with every act of the administration. He elbowed, criticised, scolded and toadied to Clément Chardin des Lupeaulx and other office-holders. He doubtless lived with his nephews. [The Government Clerks.]

Antoine, old servant of the Marquise Béatrix de Rochefide, in 1840, on the rue de Chartres-du-Roule, near Monceau Park, Paris. [Béatrix.]

Antonia—*See* Chocardelle, Mlle.

Aquilina, a Parisian courtesan of the time of the Restoration and Louis Philippe. She claimed to be a Piedmontese. Of her true name she was ignorant. She had appropriated this *nom de guerre* from a character in the well-known tragedy by Otway, "Venice Preserved," that she had chanced to read. At sixteen, pure and beautiful, at the time of her downfall, she had met Castanier, Nucingen's cashier, who resolved to save her from evil for his own gain, and live maritally with her in the rue Richter. Aquilina then took the name of Madame de la Garde. At the same time of her relations with Castanier, she had for a lover a certain Léon, a petty officer in a regiment of infantry, and none other than one of the sergeants of Rochelle to be executed on the Place de Gréve in 1822. Before this execution, in the reign of Louis XVIII., she attended a performance of "Le Comédien d'Etampes," one evening at the Gymnase, when she laughed immoderately at the comical part played by Perlet. At the same time, Castanier, also present at this mirthful scene, but harassed by Melmoth, was experiencing the insufferable doom of a cruel hidden drama. [Melmoth Reconciled.] Her next appearance is at a famous orgy at the home of Frédéric Taillefer, rue Joubert, in company with Emile Blondet, Rastignac, Bixiou and Raphael de Valentin. She was a magnificent girl of good figure, superb carriage, and striking though irregular features. Her glance and smile startled one. She always included some red trinket in her attire, in memory of her executed lover. [The Magic Skin.]

Arcos (Comte d'), a Spanish grandee living in the Peninsula at the time of the expedition of Napoleon I. He would probably have married Maria-Pepita-Juana Marana de Mancini, had it not been for the peculiar incidents which brought about her marriage with the French officer, François Diard. [The Maranas.]

Argaïolo (Duc d'), a very rich and well-born Italian, the respected though aged husband of her who later became the Duchesse de Rhétoré, to the perpetual grief of Albert Savarus. Argaïolo died, almost an octogenarian, in 1835. [Albert Savarus.]

Argaïolo (Duchesse d'), née Soderini, wife of the Duc d'Argaïolo. She became a widow in 1835, and took as her second husband the Duc de Rhétoré. (See Duchesse de Rhétoré.) [Albert Savarus.]

Arrachelaine, surname of the rogue, Ruffard. (*See* that name.) [Scenes from a Courtesan's Life.]

Arthez (Daniel d'), one of the most illustrious authors of the nineteenth century, and one of those rare men who display "the unity of excellent talent and excellent character." Born about 1794 or 1796. A Picard gentleman. In 1821, when about twenty-five, he was poverty-stricken and dwelt on the fifth floor of a dismal house in the rue des Quatre-Vents, Paris, where had also resided the illustrious surgeon Desplein, in his youth. There he fraternized with: Horace Bianchon, then house-physician at Hotêl-Dieu; Léon Giraud, the profound philosopher; Joseph Bridau, the painter who later achieved so much renown; Fulgence Ridal, comic poet of great sprightliness; Meyraux, the eminent physiologist who died young; lastly, Louis Lambert and Michel Chrestien, the Federalist Republican, both of whom were cut off in their prime. To these men of heart and of talent Lucien de Rubempré, the poet, sought to attach himself. He was introduced by Daniel d'Arthez, their recognized leader. This society had taken the name of the "Cénacle." D'Arthez and his friends advised and aided, when in need, Lucien the "Distinguished Provincial at Paris" who ended so tragically. Moreover, with a truly remarkable disinterestedness d'Arthez corrected and revised "The Archer of Charles IX.," written by Lucien, and the work became a superb book, in his hands. Another glimpse of d'Arthez is as the unselfish friend of Marie Gaston, a young poet of his stamp, but "effeminate." D'Arthez was swarthy, with long locks, rather small and bearing some resemblance to Bonaparte. He might be called the rival of Rousseau, "the Aquatic," since he was very temperate, very pure, and drank water only. For a long time he ate at Flicoteaux's in the Latin Quarter. He had grown famous in 1832, besides enjoying an income of thirty thousand francs bequeathed by an uncle who had left him a prey to the most biting poverty so long as the author was unknown. D'Arthez then resided in a pretty house of his own in the rue de Bellefond, where he lived in other respects as formerly, in the rigor

of work.   He was a deputy sitting on the right and upholding
the Royalist platform of Divine Right.   When he had
acquired a competence, he had a most vulgar and incom-
prehensible *liaison* with a woman tolerably pretty, but
belonging to a lower society and without either education
or breeding.   D'Arthez maintained her, nevertheless, carefully concealing her from sight; but, far from being a pleas-
urable manner of life, it became odious to him.   It was
at this time that he was invited to the home of Diane de
Maufrigneuse, Princesse de Cadignan, who was then thirty-
six, but did not look it.   The famous "great coquette"
told him her (so-called) "secrets," offered herself outright
to this man whom she treated as a "famous simpleton,"
and whom she made her lover.   After that day there was
no doubt about the relations of the princesse and Daniel
d'Arthez.   The great author, whose works became very
rare, appeared only during some of the winter months at
the Chamber of Deputies. [A Distinguished Provincial
at Paris. Letters of Two Brides. The Member for Arcis.
The Secrets of a Princess.]

Asie, one of the pseudonyms of Jacqueline Collin.   (*See*
that name.)   [Scenes from a Courtesan's Life.]

Athalie, cook for Mme. Schontz in 1836.   According
to her mistress, she was specially gifted in preparing venison.
[The Muse of the Department.]

Aubrion (Marquis d'), a gentleman-in-waiting of the
Bedchamber, under Charles X.   He was of the house of
Aubrion de Buch, whose last head died before 1789.   He
was silly enough to wed a woman of fashion, though he was
already an old man of but twenty thousand francs income,
a sum hardly sufficient in Paris.   He tried to marry his
daughter without a dowry to some man who was intoxicated
with nobility.   In 1827, to quote Mme. d'Aubrion, this
ancient wreck was madly devoted to the Duchesse de
Chaulieu. [Eugénie Grandet.]

Aubrion (Marquise d'), wife of the preceding.   Born in
1789.   At thirty-eight she was still pretty, and, having

always been somewhat aspiring, she endeavored (in 1827), by hook or by crook, to entangle Charles Grandet, lately returned from the Indies. She wished to make a son-in-law out of him, and she succeeded. [Eugénie Grandet.]

Aubrion (Mathilde d'), daughter of the Marquis and Marquise d'Aubrion; born in 1808; married to Charles Grandet. (*See* that name.) [Eugénie Grandet.]

Aubrion (Comte d'), the title acquired by Charles Grandet after his marriage to the daughter of the Marquis d'Aubrion. [The Firm of Nucingen.]

Auffray, grocer at Provins, in the period of Louis XV., Louis XVI. and the Revolution. M. Auffray married the first time when eighteen, the second time at sixty-nine. By his first wife he had a rather ugly daughter who married, at sixteen, a landlord of Provins, Rogron by name. Auffray had another daughter, by his second marriage, a charming girl, this time, who married a Breton captain in the Imperial Guard. Pierrette Lorrain was the daughter of this officer. The old grocer Auffray died at the time of the Empire without having had time enough to make his will. The inheritance was so skillfully manipulated by Rogron, the first son-in-law of the deceased, that almost nothing was left for the goodman's widow, then only about thirty-eight years old. [Pierrette.]

Auffray (Madame), wife of the preceding. (*See* Néraud, Mme.) [Pierrette.]

Auffray, a notary of Provins in 1827. Husband of Mme. Guénée's third daughter. Great-grand-nephew of the old grocer, Auffray. Appointed a guardian of Pierrette Lorrain. On account of the ill-treatment to which this young girl was subjected at the home of her guardian, Denis Rogron, she was removed, an invalid, to the home of the notary Auffray, a designated guardian, where she died, although tenderly cared for. [Pierrette.]

Auffray (Madame), born Guénée. Wife of the preceding. The third daughter of Mme. Guénée, born Tiphaine. She exhibited the greatest kindness for Pierrette Lorrain, and nursed her tenderly in her last illness. [Pierrette.]

Auguste, name borne by Boislaurier, as chief of "brigands," in the uprisings of the West under the Republic and under the Empire. [The Seamy Side of History.]

Auguste, *valet de chambre* of the Général Marquis Armand de Montriveau, under the Restoration, at the time when the latter dwelt in the rue de Seine hard by the Chamber of Peers, and was intimate with the Duchesse Antoinette de Langeais. [The Thirteen.]

Auguste, notorious assassin, executed in the first years of the Restoration. He left a mistress, surnamed Rousse, to whom Jacques Collin had faithfully remitted (in 1819) some twenty odd thousands of francs, on behalf of her lover, after his execution. This woman was married in 1821, by Jacques Collin's sister, to the head clerk of a rich, whole-sale hardware merchant. Nevertheless, though once more in respectable society, she remained bound, by a secret compact, to the terrible Vautrin and his sister. [Scenes from a Courtesan's Life.]

Auguste (Madame), dressmaker of Esther Gobseck, and her creditor in the time of Louis XVIII. [Scenes from a Courtesan's Life.]

Augustin, *valet de chambre* of M. de Sérizy in 1822. [A Start in Life.]

Aurélie, a Parisian courtesan, under Louis Philippe, at the time when Mme. Fabien du Roncerct commenced her conquests. [Béatrix.]

Aurélie (La Petite), one of the nicknames of Joséphine Schiltz, also called Schontz, who became, later, Mme. Fabien du Roncerct. [Béatrix.]

Auvergnat (L'), one of the assumed names of the rogue Sélérier, alias Père Ralleau, alias Rouleur, alias Fil-de-soie. (*See* Sélérier.) [Scenes from a Courtesan's Life.]

B

Babylas, groom or "tiger" of Amédée de Soulas, in 1834, at Besançon. Was fourteen years old at this time. The son of one of his master's tenants. He earned thirty-six francs a month by his position to support himself, but he was neat and skillful. [Albert Savarus.]

Baptiste, *valet de chambre* to the Duchesse de Lenoncourt-Chaulieu in 1830. [Scenes from a Courtesan's Life.]

Barbanchu, Bohemian with a cocked hat, who was called into Véfour's by some journalists who breakfasted there at the expense of Jérôme Thuillier, in 1840, and invited by them to "sponge" off of this urbane man, which he did. [The Middle Classes.]

Barbanti (The), a Corsican family who brought about the reconciliation of the Piombos and the Portas in 1800. [The Vendetta.]

Barbet, a dynasty of second-hand book-dealers in Paris under the Restoration and Louis Philippe. They were Normans. In 1821 and the years following, one of them ran a little shop on the quay des Grands-Augustins, and purchased Lousteau's books. In 1836, a Barbet, partner in a book-shop with Métivier and Morand, owned a wretched house on the rue Notre-Dame-des-Champs and the boulevard du Mont-Parnasse, where dwelt the Baron Bourlac with his daughter and grandson. In 1840 the Barbets had become regular usurers dealing in credits with the firm of Cérizet and Company. The same year a Barbet occupied, in a house belonging to Jérôme Thuillier, rue Saint-Dominique-d'Enfer (now rue Royer-Collard), a room on the first flight up and a shop on the ground floor. He was then a "publisher's shark." Barbet junior, a nephew of the foregoing, and editor in the alley des Panoramas, placed on the market at this time a brochure composed by Th. de la Peyrade, but signed by Thuillier and having the title "Capital and Taxes." [A Distinguished Provincial at Paris. A Man of Business. The Seamy Side of History. The Middle Classes.]

Barbette, wife of the great Cibot, known as Galope-Chopine. (*See* Cibot, Barbette.) [Les Chouans.]

Barchou de Penhoen (Auguste-Théodore-Hilaire), born at Morlaix (Finistère), April 28, 1801, died at Saint-Germain-en-Laye, July 29, 1855. A school-mate of Balzac, Jules Dufaure and Louis Lambert, and his neighbors in the college dormitory of Vendôme in 1811. Later he was an officer, then a writer of transcendental philosophy, a translator of Fichte, a friend and interpreter of Ballanche. In 1849 he was elected, by his fellow-citizens of Finistère, to the Legislative Assembly where he represented the Legitimists and the Catholics. He protested against the *coup d'étât* of December 2, 1851 (*See* "The Story of a Crime," by Victor Hugo). When a child he came under the influence of Pyrrhonism. He once gainsaid the talent of Louis Lambert, his Vendôme school-mate. [Louis Lambert.]

Bargeton (De), born between 1761 and 1763. Great-grandson of an Alderman of Bordeaux named Mirault, ennobled during the reign of Louis XIII., and whose son, under Louis XIV., now Mirault de Bargeton, was an officer of the Guards de la Porte. He owned a house at Angoulême, in the rue du Minage, where he lived with his wife, Marie-Louise-Anaïs de Négrepelisse, to whom he was entirely obedient. On her account, and at her instigation, he fought with one of the habitues of his salon, Stanislas de Chandour, who had circulated in the town a slander on Mme. de Bargeton. Bargeton lodged a bullet in his opponent's neck. He had for a second his father-in-law, M. de Nègrepelisse. Following this, M. de Bargeton retired into his estate at Escarbas, near Barbezieux, while his wife, as a result of the duel, left Angoulême for Paris. M. de Bargeton had been of good physique, but "injured by youthful excesses." He was commonplace, but a great gourmand. He died of indigestion towards the close of 1821. [Lost Illusions.]

Bargeton (Madame de), *née* Marie-Louise-Anaïs Négrepelisse, wife of the foregoing. Left a widow, she married again, this time the Baron Sixte du Chatelet. (*See* that name.)

Barillaud, known by Frédérie Alain whose suspicion he aroused with regard to Monegod. [The Seamy Side of History.]

Barimore (Lady), daughter of Lord Dudley, and apparently the wife of Lord Barimore, although it is a disputed question. Just after 1830, she helped receive at a function of Mlle. des Touches, rue de la Chaussée-d'Antin, where Marsay told about his first love affair. [Another Study of Woman.]

Barker (William), one of Vautrin's "incarnations." In 1824 or 1825, under this assumed name, he posed as one of the creditors of M. d'Estourny, making him endorse some notes of Cérizet's, the partner of this M. d'Estourny. [Scenes from a Courtesan's Life.]

Barnheim, family in good standing at Bade. On the maternal side, the family of Mme. du Ronceret, *née* Schiltz, alias Schontz. [Béatrix.]

Barniol, Phellion's son-in-law. Head of an academy (in 1840), rue Saint-Hyacinthe-Saint-Michel (now, rue Le Goff and rue Malebranche). A rather influential man in the Faubourg Saint-Jacques. Visited the salon of Thuillier. [The Middle Classes.]

Barniol (Madame), *née* Phellion, wife of the preceding. She had been under-governess in the boarding school of the Mlles. Lagrave, rue Notre-Dame des Champs. [The Middle Classes.]

Barry (John), a young English huntsman, well known in the district whence the Prince of Loudon brought him to employ him at his own home. He was with this great lord in 1829, 1830. [Modeste Mignon.]

Bartas (Adrien de), of Angoulême. In 1821, he and his wife were very devoted callers at the Bargetons. M. de Bartas gave himself up entirely to music, talking about this subject incessantly, and courting invitations to sing with his heavy bass voice. He posed as the lover of Mme. de Brébion, the wife of his best friend. M. de Brébion became the lover of Mme. de Bartas. [Lost Illusions.]

Bartas (Madame Joséphine de), wife of the preceding, always called Fifine, "for short." [Lost Illusions.]

Bastienne, Parisian modiste in 1821. Finot's journal vaunted her hats, for a pecuniary consideration, and derogated those of Virginie, formerly praised. [Lost Illusions.]

Batailles (The), belonging to the bourgeoisie of Paris, traders of Marais, neighbors and friends of the Baudoyers and the Saillards in 1824. M. Bataille was a captain in the National Guard, a fact which he allowed no one to ignore. [The Government Clerks.]

Baudenord (Godefroid de), born in 1800. In 1821 he was one of the kings of fashion, in company with Marsay, Vandenesse, Ajuda-Pinto, Maxime de Trailles, Rastignac, the Duc de Maufrigneuse and Manerville. [A Distinguished Provincial at Paris.] His nobility and breeding were perhaps not very orthodox. According to Mlle. Emilie de Fontaine, he was of bad figure and stout, having but a single advantage —that of his brown locks. [The Ball at Sçeaux.] A cousin, by marriage, of his guardian, the Marquis d'Aiglemont, he was, like him, ruined by the Baron de Nucingen in the Wortschin mine deal. At one time Beaudenord thought of paying court to his pretty cousin, the Marquise d'Aigle-mont. In 1827 he wedded Isaure d'Aldrigger and, after having lived with her in a cosy little house on the rue de le Planche, he was obliged to solicit employment of the Minister of Finance, a position which he lost on account of the Revolution of 1830. However, he was reinstated through the influence of Nucingen, in 1836. He now lived modestly with his mother-in-law, his unmarried sister-in-law Malvina, his wife and four children which she had given him, on the third floor, over the entresol, rue du Mont-Thabor. [The Firm of Nucingen.]

Baudoyer (Monsieur and Madame), formerly tanners at Paris, rue Censier. They owned their house, besides having a country seat at l'Isle Adam. They had but one child, Isidore, whose sketch follows. Mme. Baudoyer, born Mitral, was the sister of the bailiff of that name. [The Government Clerks.]

Baudoyer (Isidore), born in 1788; only son of M. and Mme. Baudoyer, tanners, rue Censier, Paris. Having finished a course of study, he obtained a position in the Bureau of Finance, where, despite his notorious incapacity—and through "wire-pulling"—he became head of the office. In 1824, a head of the division, M. de La Billardière died, when the meritorious clerk, Xavier Rabourdin, aspired to succeed him; but the position went to Isidore Baudoyer, who was backed by the power of money and the influence of the Church. He did not retain this post long; six months thereafter he became a preceptor at Paris. Isidore Baudoyer lived with his wife and her parents in a house on Palais Royale (now Place des Vosges), of which they were joint owners. [The Government Clerks.] He dined frequently, in 1840, at Thuillier's, an old employé of the Bureau of Finance, then domiciled at the rue Saint-Dominique-d'Enfer, who had renewed his acquaintance with his old-time colleagues. [The Middle Classes.] In 1845, this man, who had been a model husband and who made a great pretence of religion maintained Héloïse Brisetout. He was then mayor of the arrondissement of the Palais Royale. [Cousin Pons.]

Baudoyer (Madame), wife of the preceding and daughter of a cashier of the Minister of Finance; born Elisabeth Saillard in 1795. Her mother, an Auvergnat, had an uncle, Bidault, alias Gigonnet, a short-time money lender in the Halles quarter. On the other side, her mother-in-law was the sister of the bailiff Mitral. Thanks to these two men of means, who exercised a veritable secret power, and through her piety, which put her on good terms with the clergy, she succeeded in raising her husband up to the highest official positions—profiting also by the financial straits of Clément Chardin des Lupeaulx, Secretary General of Finance. [The Government Clerks.]

Baudoyer (Mademoiselle), daughter of Isidore Baudoyer and Elisabeth Saillard, born in 1812. Reared by her parents with the idea of becoming the wife of the shrewd and energetic speculator Martin Falleix, brother of Jacques Falleix the stock-broker. [The Government Clerks.]

Baudrand, cashier of a boulevard theatre, of which Gaud-issart became the director about 1834. In 1845 he was succeeded by the proletariat Topinard. [Cousin Pons.]

Baudry (Planat de), Receiver General of Finances under the Restoration. He married one of the daughters of the Comte de Fontaine. He usually passed his summers at Sçeaux, with almost all his wife's family. [The Ball at Sçeaux.]

Bauvan (Comte de), one of the instigators of the Chouan insurrection in the department d'Ille-et-Vilaine, in 1799. Through a secret revelation made to his friend the Marquis de Montauran on the part of Mlle. de Varneuil, the Comte de Bauvan caused, indirectly, the Massacre des Bleus at Vivetière. Later, surprised in an ambuscade by soldiers of the Republic, he was made prisoner by Mlle. de Verneuil and owed his life to her; for this reason he became entirely devoted to her, assisting as a witness at her marriage with Montauran. [The Chouans.]

Bauvan (Comtesse de), ·in all likelihood the wife of the foregoing, whom she survived. In 1822 she was manager of a Parisian lottery bureau which employed Madame Agatha Bridau, about the same time. [A Bachelor's Establishment.]

. **Bauvan** (Comte and Comtesse de), father and mother of Octave de Bauvan. Relics of the old Court, living in a tumble-down house on the rue Payenne at Paris, where they died, about 1815, within a few months of each other, and before the conjugal infelicity of their son. (*See* Octave de Bauvan.) Probably related to the two preceding. [Honorine.]

Bauvan (Comte Octave de), statesman and French magistrate. Born in 1787. When twenty-six he married Honorine, a beautiful young heiress who had been reared carefully at the home of his parents, M. and Mme. de Bauvan, whose ward she was. Two or three years afterwards she left the conjugal roof, to the infinite despair of the comte, who gave himself over entirely to winning her back 'again. At the end of several years he succeeded in getting her to return to him through pity, but she died soon after this reconciliation, leaving one son born of their reunion. The Comte de Bauvan, completely broken, set out for Italy about 1836. He had two residences at Paris, one on rue Payenne, an heirloom, the other on Faubourg Saint-Honoré, which was the scene of the domestic reunion. [Honorine.] In 1830, the Comte de Bauvan, then president of the Court of Cassation, with MM. de Granville and de Sérizy, tried to save Lucien de Rubempré from a criminal judgment, and, after the suicide of that unhappy man, he followed his remains to the grave. [Scenes from a Courtesan's Life.]

Bauvan (Comtesse Honorine de), wife of the preceding. Born in 1794. Married at nineteen to the Comte Octave de Bauvan. After having abandoned her husband, she was in turn, while expecting a child, abandoned by her lover, some eighteen months later. She then lived a very retired life in the rue Saint-Maur, yet all the time being under the secret surveillance of the Comte de Bauvan who paid exorbitant prices for the artificial flowers which she made. She thus derived from him a rather large part of the sustenance which she believed she owed only to her own efforts. She died, reunited to her husband, shortly after the Revolution of July, 1830. Honorine de Bauvan lost her child born out of wedlock, and she always mourned it. During her years of toilsome exile in the Parisian faubourg, she came in contact successively with Marie Gobain, Jean-Jules Popinot, Félix Gaudissart, Maurice de l'Hostal and Abbé Loraux. [Honorine.]

Beaudenord (Madame de), wife of the preceding. Born Isaure d'Aldrigger, in 1807, at Strasbourg. An indolent blonde, fond of dancing, but a nonentity from both the moral and the intellectual standpoints. [The Firm of Nucingen.]

Beaumesnil (Mademoiselle), a celebrated actress of the Théâtre-Français, Paris. Mature at the time of the Restora-

tion. She was the mistress of the police-officer Peyrade,
by whom she had a daughter, Lydie, whom he acknowledged.
The last home of Mlle. Beaumesnil was on rue de Tournon.
It was there that she suffered the loss by theft of her valuable
diamonds, through Charles Crochard, her real lover. This
was at the beginning of the reign of Louis Philippe. [The
Middle Classes.   Scenes from a Courtesan's Life.   A Second
Home.]

Beaupied, or Beau-Pied, an alias of Jean Falcon. (*See*
that name.)

Beaupré (Fanny), an actress at the Théâtre de la Porte-
Saint-Martin, Paris, time of Charles X.   Young and beautiful,
in 1825, she made a name for herself in the rôle of marquise
in a melodrama entitled "La Famille d'Anglade."   At
this time she had replaced Coralie, then dead, in the affections
of Camusot the silk-merchant.   It was at Fanny Beaupré's
that Oscar Husson, one of the clerks of lawyer Desroches,
lost in gaming the sum of five hundred francs belonging
to his employer, and that he was discovered lying dead-
drunk on a sofa by his uncle Cardot. [A Start in Life.]
In 1829 Fanny Beaupré, for a money consideration, posed
as the best friend of the Duc d'Hérouville.   [Modeste Mignon.]
In 1842, after his liaison with Mme. de la Baudraye, Lousteau
lived maritally with her. [The Muse of the Department.]
A frequent inmate of the mansion magnificently fitted
up for Esther Gobseck by the Baron de Nucingen, she knew
all the fast set of the years 1829 and 1830. [Scenes from
a Courtesan's Life.]

Beauséant (Marquis and Comte de), the father and eldest
brother of the Vicomte de Beauséant, husband of Claire
de Bourgogne. [The Deserted Woman.]   In 1819, the
marquis and the comte dwelt together in their house, rue
Saint-Dominique, Paris. [Father Goriot.]   While the Revolution was on, the marquis had emigrated.   The Abbé
de Marolles had dealings with him. [An Episode under
the Terror.]

Beauséant (Marquise de). In 1824 a Marquise de Beau-séant, then rather old, is found to have dealings with the Chaulieus. It was probably the widow of the marquis of this name, and the mother of the Comte and Vicomte de Beauséant. [Letters of Two Brides.] The Marquise de Beauséant was a native of Champagne, coming of a very old family. [The Deserted Woman.]

Beauséant (Vicomte de), husband of Claire de Bourgogne. He understood the relations of his wife with Miguel d'Ajuda-Pinto, and, whether he liked it or not, he respected this species of morganatic alliance recognized by society. The Vicomte de Beauséant had his residence in Paris on the rue de Grenelle in 1819. At that time he kept a dancer and liked nothing better than high living. He became a marquis on the death of his father and eldest brother. He was a polished man, courtly, methodical, and ceremonious. He insisted upon living selfishly. His death would have allowed Mme. de Beauséant to wed Gaston de Nueil. [Father Goriot. The Deserted Woman.]

Beauséant (Vicomtesse de), born Claire de Bourgogne, in 1792. Wife of the preceding and cousin of Eugéne de Rastignac. Of a family almost royal. Deceived by her lover, Miguel d'Ajuda-Pinto, who, while continuing his intimacy with her, asked and obtained the hand of Berthe de Roche-fide, the vicomtesse left Paris secretly before this wedding and on the morning following a grand ball was given at her home where she shone in all her pride and splendor. In 1822 this "deserted woman" had lived for three years in the most rigid seclusion at Courcelles near Bayeux. Gaston de Nueil, a young man of three and twenty, who had been sent to Normandy for his health, succeeded in making her acquaintance, was immediately smitten with her and, after a long siege, became her lover. This was at Geneva, whither she had fled. Their intimacy lasted for nine years, being broken by the marriage of the young man. In 1819 the Vicomtesse de Beauséant received at Paris the most famous "high-rollers" of the day—Malincour, Ronquerolles,

Maxime de Trailles, Marsay, Vandenesse, together with an intermingling of the most elegant dames, as Lady Brandon, the Duchesse de Langeais, the Comtesse de Kergarouët, Mme. de Sérizy, the Duchesse Carigliano, the Comtesse Ferraud, Mme. de Lantry, the Marquise d'Aiglemont, Mme. Firmiani, the Marquise de Listomère, the Marquise d'Espard and the Duchesse de Maufrigneuse. She was equally intimate with Grandlieu, and the Général de Montriveau. Rastignac, then poor at the time of his start in the world, also received cards to her receptions. [Father Goriot. The Deserted Woman. Albert Savarus.]

Beaussier, a bourgeois of Issoudun under the Restoration. Upon seeing Joseph Bridau in the diligence, while the artist and his mother were on a journey in 1822, he remarked that he would not care to meet him at night in the corner of a forest—he looked so much like a highwayman. That same evening Beaussier, accompanied by his wife, came to call at Hochon's in order to get a nearer view of the painter. [A Bachelor's Establishment.]

Beaussier the younger, known as Beaussier the Great; son of the preceding and one of the Knights of Idlesse at Issoudun, commanded by Maxence Gilet, under the Restoration. [A Bachelor's Establishment.]

Beauvisage, physician of the Convent des Carmélites at Blois, time of Louis XVIII. He was known by Louise de Chaulieu and by Renée de Maucombe, who were reared in the convent. According to Louise de Chaulieu, he certainly belied his name. [Letters of Two Brides.]

Beauvisage, at one time tenant of the splendid farm of Bellache, pertaining to the Gondreville estate at Arcis-sur-Aube. The father of Philéas Beauvisage. Died about the beginning of the nineteenth century. [The Gondreville Mystery. The Member for Arcis.]

Beauvisage (Madame), wife of the preceding. She survived him for quite a long period and helped her son Philéas win his success. [The Member for Arcis.]

Beauvisage (Philéas), son of Beauvisage the farmer. Born in 1792. A hosier at Arcis-sur-Aube during the Restoration. Mayor of the town in 1839. After a preliminary defeat he was elected deputy at the time when Sallenauve sent in his resignation, in 1841. An ardent admirer of Crevel whose affectations he aped. A millionaire and very vain, he would have been able, according to Grevel, to advance Mme. Hulot, for a consideration, the two hundred thousand francs of which that unhappy lady stood in so dire a need about 1842. [Cousin Betty. The Member for Arcis.]

Beauvisage (Madame), born Séverine Grévin in 1795. Wife of Philéas Beauvisage, whom she kept in complete subjugation. Daughter of Grévin the notary of Arcis-sur-Aube, Senator Malin de Gondreville's intimate friend. She inherited her father's marvelous faculty of discretion; and, though diminutive in stature, reminded one forcibly, in her face and ways, of Mlle. Mars. [The Member for Arcis.]

Beauvisage (Cécile-Renée), only daughter of Philéas Beauvisage and Séverine Grévin. Born in 1820. Her natural father was the Vicomte Melchior de Chargeboeuf who was sub-prefect of Arcis-sur-Aube at the commencement of the Restoration. She looked exactly like him, besides having his aristocratic airs. [The Member for Arcis.]

Beauvoir (Charles-Félix-Theodore, Chevalier de), cousin of the Duchesse de Maillé. A Chouan prisoner of the Republic in the château de l'Escarpe in 1799. The hero of a tale of marital revenge related by Lousteau, in 1836, to Mme. de la Baudraye, the story being obtained—so the narrator said—from Charles Nodier. [The Muse of the Department.]

Bécanière (La), surname of Barbette Cibot. (*See* that name.)

Becker (Edme), a student of medicine who dwelt in 1828 at number 22, rue de la Montagne-Sainte-Geneviève—the residence of the Marquis d'Espard. [The Commission in Lunacy.]

Bedeau, office boy and roustabout for Maitre Bordin, attorney to the Châtelet in 1787. [A Start in Life.]

Béga, surgeon in a French regiment of the Army of Spain in 1808. After having privately accouched a Spaniard under the espionage of her lover, he was assassinated by her husband, who surprised him in the telling of this clandestine operation. The foregoing adventure was told Mme. de la Baudraye, in 1836, by the Receiver of Finances, Gravier, former paymaster of the Army. [The Muse of the Department.]

Bégrand (La), a dancer at the theatre of Porte-Saint-Martin, Paris, in 1820.[1] Mariette, who made her début at this time, also scored a success. [A Bachelor's Establishment.]

Bellefeuille (Mademoiselle de), assumed name of Caroline Crochard.

Bellejambe, servant of Lieutenant-Colonel Husson in 1837. [A Start in Life.]

Belor (Mademoiselle de), young girl of Bordeaux living there about 1822. She was always in search of a husband, whom, for some cause or other, she never found. Probably intimate with Evangelista. [A Marriage Settlement.]

Bemboni (Monsignor), attaché to the Secretary of State at Rome, who was entrusted with the transmission to the Duc de Soria at Madrid of the letters of Baron de Macumer his brother, a Spanish refugee at Paris in 1823, 1824. [Letters of Two Brides.]

Bénard (Pieri). After corresponding with a German for two years, he discovered an engraving by Muller entitled the "Virgin of Dresden." It was on Chinese paper and made before printing was discovered. It cost César Birotteau fifteen hundred francs. The perfumer destined this engraving for the savant Vauquelin, to whom he was under obligations. [César Birotteau.]

---

[1] She shone for more than sixty years as a famous chorographical artist in the boulevards.

Benassis (Doctor), born about 1779 in a little town of Languedoc. He received his early training at the College of Soréze, Tarn, which was managed by the Oratorians. After that he pursued his medical studies at Paris, residing in the Latin quarter. When twenty-two he lost his father, who left him a large fortune; and he deserted a young girl by whom he had had a son, in order to give himself over to the most foolish dissipations. This young girl, who was thoroughly well meant and devoted to him, died two years after the desertion despite the most tender care of her now contrite lover. Later Benassis sought marriage with another young girl belonging to a Jansenist family. At first the affair was settled, but he was thrown over when the secret of his past life, hitherto concealed, was made known. He then devoted his whole life to his son, but the child died in his youth. After wavering between suicide and the monastery of Grande-Chartreuse, Doctor Benassis stopped by chance in the poor village of l'Isère, five leagues from Grenoble. He remained there until he had transformed the squalid settlement, inhabited by good-for-nothing Cretins, into the chief place of the Canton, bustling and prosperous. Benassis died in 1829, mayor of the town. All the populace mourned the benefactor and man of genius. [The Country Doctor.]

Benedetto, an Italian living at Rome in the first third of the nineteenth century. A tolerable musician, and a police spy, "on the side." Ugly, small and a drunkard, he was nevertheless the lucky husband of Luigia, whose marvelous beauty was his continual boast. After an evening spent by him over the wine-cups, his wife in loathing lighted a brasier of charcoal, after carefully closing all the exits of the bedchamber. The neighbors rushing in succeeded in saving her alone; Benedetto was dead. [The Member for Arcis.]

Bérénice, chambermaid and cousin of Coralie the actress of the Panorama and Gymnase Dramatique. A large Norman woman, as ugly as her mistress was pretty, but tender and sympathetic in direct proportion to her corpulence.

She had been Coralie's childhood playmate and was absolutely bound up in her. In October, 1822, she gave Lucien de Rubempré, then entirely penniless, four five-franc pieces which she undoubtedly owed to the generosity of chance lovers met on the boulevard Bonne-Nouvelle. This sum enabled the unfortunate poet to return to Angoulême. [Lost Illusions. A Distinguished Provincial at Paris.]

Bergerin was the best doctor at Saumur during the Restoration. He attended Félix Grandet in his last illness. [Eugénie Grandet.]

Bergmann (Monsieur and Madame), Swiss. Venerable gardeners of a certain Comte Borromeo, tending his parks located on the two famous isles in Lake Major. In 1823 they owned a house at Gersau, near Quatre-Canton Lake, in the Canton of Lucerne. For a year back they had let one floor of this house to the Prince and Princess Gandolphini,—personages of a novel entitled, "L'Ambitieux par Amour," published by Albert Savarus in the Revue de l'Est, in 1834. [Albert Savarus.]

Bernard. (*See* Baron de Bourlac.)

Bernus, diligence messenger carrying the passengers, freight and, perhaps, the letters of Saint-Nazaire to Guérande, during the times of Charles X. and Louis Philippe. [Béatrix.]

Berquet, workman of Besançon who erected an elevated kiosk in the garden of the Wattevilles, whence their daughter Rosalie could see every act and movement of Albert Savarus, a near neighbor. [Albert Savarus.]

Berthier (Alexandre), marshal of the Empire, born at Versailles in 1753, dying in 1815. He wrote, as Minister of War at the close of 1799, to Hulot, then in command of the Seventy-second demi-brigade, refusing to accept his resignation and giving him further orders. [The Chouans.] On the evening of the battle of Jéna, October 13, 1806, he accompanied the Emperor and was present at the latter's interview with the Marquis de Chargeboeuf and Laurence de Cinq-Cygne, special envoys to France to implore pardon for the Simeuses, the Hauteserres, and Michu who had been condemned as abductors of Senator Malin de Gondreville. [The Gondreville Mystery.]

Berthier, Parisian notary, successor of Cardot, whose assistant head-clerk he had been and whose daughter Félicité (or Félicie) he married. In 1843 he was Mme. Marneffe's notary. At the same time he had in hand the affairs of Camusot de Marville; and Sylvain Pons often dined with him. Master Berthier drew up the marriage settlement of Wilhelm Schwab with Emilie Graff, and the copartnership articles between Fritz Brunner and Wilhelm Schwab. [Cousin Betty. Cousin Pons.]

Berthier (Madame), *née* Félicie Cardot, wife of the preceding. She had been wronged by the chief-clerk in her father's office. This young man died suddenly, leaving her enceinte. She then espoused the second clerk, Berthier, in 1837, after having been on the point of accepting Lousteau. Berthier was cognizant of all the head-clerk's doings. In this affair both acted for a common interest. The marriage was measurably happy. Madame Berthier was so grateful to her husband that she made herself his slave. About the end of 1844 she welcomed very coldly Sylvain Pons, then in disgrace in the family circle. [The Muse of the Department. Cousin Pons.]

Berton, tax-collector at Arcis-sur-Aube in 1839. [The Member for Arcis.]

Berton (Mademoiselle), daughter of the tax-collector of Arcis-sur-Aube. A young, insignificant girl who acted the satellite to Cécile Beauvisage and Ernestine Mollot. [The Member for Arcis.]

Berton (Doctor), physician of Paris. In 1836 he lived on rue d'Enfer (now rue Denfert-Rochereau). An assistant in the benevolent work of Mme. de la Chanterie, he visited the needy sick whom she pointed out. Among others he attended Vanda de Mergi, daughter of the Baron de Bourlac— M. Bernard. Doctor Berton was gruff and frigid. [The Seamy Side of History.]

Béthune (Prince de), the only man of fashion who knew "what a hat was"—to quote a saying of Vital the hatter, in 1845. [The Unconscious Humorists.]

Beunier & Co., the firm Bixiou inquired after in 1845, near Mme. Nourrisson's. [The Unconscious Humorists.]

Bianchi. Italian. During the first Empire a captain in the sixth regiment of the French line, which was made up almost entirely of men of his nationality. Celebrated in his company for having bet that he would eat the heart of a Spanish sentinel, and winning the bet. Captain Bianchi was first to plant the French colors on the wall of Tarragone, Spain, in the attack of 1808. But a friar killed him. [The Maranas.]

Bianchon (Doctor), a physician of Sancerre, father of Horace Bianchon, brother of Mme. Popinot, the wife of Judge Popinot. [The Commission in Lunacy.]

Bianchon (Horace), a physician of Paris, celebrated during the times of Charles X. and Louis Philippe; an officer of the Legion of Honor, member of the Institute, professor of the Medical Faculty, physician-in-charge, at the same time, of a hospital and the Ecole Polytechnique. Born at Sancerre, Cher, about the end of the eighteenth century. He was "interne" at the Cochin Hospital in 1819, at whicn time he boarded at the Vauquer Pension where he knew Eugéne de Rastignac, then studying law, and Goriot and Vautrin. [Father Goriot.] Shortly thereafter, at Hotel Dieu, he became the favored pupil of the surgeon Desplein, whose last days he tended. [The Atheist's Mass.] Nephew of Judge Jean-Jules Popinot and relative of Anselme Popinot, he had dealings with the perfumer César Birotteau, who acknowledged indebtedness to him for a prescription of his famous hazelnut oil, and who invited him to the grand ball which precipitated Birotteau's bankruptcy. [César Birotteau. The Commission in Lunacy.] Member of the "Cénacle" in rue des Quatre-Vents, and on intimate terms with all the young fellows composing this clique, he was consequently enabled, to an extent, to bring Daniel d'Arthez to the notice of Rastignac, now Under-Secretary of State. He nursed Lucien de Rubempré who was wounded in a duel with Michel Chrestien in 1822; also Coralie, Lucien's mistress, and Mme. Bridau in their last illnesses. [Lost Illusions. A Distinguished Provincial at Paris. A Bachelor's Establishment. The Secrets of a Princess.] In 1824 the young Doctor Bianchon accompanied Desplein, who was called in to attend to the dying Flamet de la Billardière. [The Government Clerks.] In Provins in 1828, with the same Desplein and Dr. Martener, he gave the most assiduous attention to Pierrette Lorrain. [Pierrette.] In this same year of 1828 he had a momentary desire to become one of an expedition to Morea. He was then physician to Mme. de Listomère, whose misunderstanding with Rastignac he learned and afterwards related. [A Study of Woman.] Again in company with Desplein, in 1829, he was called in by Mme. de Nucingen with the object of studying the case of Baron de Nucingen, her husband, love-sick for Esther Gobseck. In 1830, still with his celebrated chief, he was cited by Corentin to express opinion on the death of Peyrade and the lunacy of Lydie his daughter. Then, with Desplein and with Dr. Sinard, to attend Mme. de Sérizy, who it was feared would go crazy over the suicide of Lucien de Rubempré. [Scenes from a Courtesan's Life.] Associated with Desplein, at this same time, he cared for the dying Honorine, wife of Comte de Bauvan [Honorine], and examined the daughter of Baron de Bourlac—M. Bernard —who was suffering from a peculiar Polish malady, the plica. [The Seamy Side of History.] In 1831 Horace Bianchon was the friend and physician of Raphaël de Valentin. [The Magic Skin.] In touch with the Comte de Granville in 1833, he attended the latter's mistress, Caroline Crochard. [A Second Home.] He also attended Mme. du Bruel, then mistress of La Palférine, who had injured herself by falling and striking her head against the sharp corner of a fireplace. [A Prince of Bohemia.] In 1835 he attended Mme. Marie Gaston—Louise de Chaulieu—though a hopeless case. [Letters of Two Brides.] In 1837 at Paris he accouched

Mme. de la Baudraye who had been intimate with Lousteau; he was assisted by the celebrated accoucheur Duriau. [The Muse of the Department.] In 1838 he was Comtc Laginski's physician. [The Imaginary Mistress.] In 1840 Horace Bianchon resided on rue de la Montagne-Sainte-Geneviéve, in the house where his uncle, Judge Popinot, died, and he was asked to become one of the Municipal Council, in place of that upright magistrate. But he declined, declaring in favor of Thuillier. [The Middle Classes.] The physician of Baron Hulot, Crevel and Mme. Marneffe, he observed, with seven of his colleagues, the terrible malady which carried off Valerie and her second husband in 1842. In 1843 he also visited Lisbeth Fischer in her last illness. [Cousin Betty.] Finally, in 1844, Dr. Bianchon was consulted by Dr. Roubaud regarding Mme. Graslin at Montégnac. [The Country Parson.] Horace Bianchon was a brilliant and inspiring conversationalist. He gave to society the adventures known by the following titles: A Study of Woman; Another Study of Woman; La Grande Bretéche.

Bibi-Lupin, chief of secret police between 1819 and 1830; a former convict. In 1819 he personally arrested at Mme. Vauquer's boarding-house Jacques Collin, alias Vautrin, his old galley-mate and personal enemy. Under the name of Gondureau, Bibi-Lupin had made overtures to Mlle. Michonneau, one of Mme. Vauquer's guests, and through her he had obtained the necessary proofs of the real identity of Vautrin who was then without the pale of the law, but who later, May, 1830, became his successor as chief of secret police. [Father Goriot. Scenes from a Courtesan's Life.]

Bidault (Monsieur and Madame), brother and sister-in-law of Bidault, alias Gigonnet; father and mother of M. and Mme. Saillard, furniture-dealers under the Central Market pillars during the latter part of the eighteenth and perhaps the beginning of the nineteenth centuries. [The Government Clerks.]

Bidault, known as Gigonnet, born in 1755; originally an Auvergnat; uncle of Mme. Saillard on the paternal side.

A paper-merchant at one time, retired from business since the year II of the Republic, he opened an account with a Dutchman called Sieur Werbrust, who was a friend of Gobseck. In business relations with the latter, he was one of the most formidable usurers in Paris, during the Empire, the Restoration and the first part of the July Government. He dwelt in rue Greneta. [The Government Clerks. Gobseck.] Luigi Porta, a ranking officer retired under Louis XVIII., sold all his back pay to Gigonnet. [The Vendetta.] Bidault was one of the syndicate that engineered the bankruptcy of Birotteau in 1819. At this time he persecuted Mme. Madou, a market dealer in filberts, who was his debtor. [César Birotteau.] In 1824 he succeeded in making his grand-nephew, Isidore Baudoyer, chief of division under the Minister of Finance; in this he was aided by Gobseck and Mitral, and worked on the General Secretary, Chardin des Lupeaulx, through the medium of the latter's debts and the fact of his being candidate for deputy. [The Government Clerks.] Bidault was shrewd enough; he saw through —and much to his profit—the pretended speculation involved in the third receivership which was operated by Nucingen in 1826. [The Firm of Nucingen.] In 1833 M. du Tillet advised Nathan, then financially stranded, to apply to Gigonnet, the object being to involve Nathan. [A Daughter of Eve.] The nick-name of Gigonnet was applied to Bidault on account of a feverish, involuntary contraction of a leg muscle. [The Government Clerks.]

Biddin, goldsmith, rue de l'Arbe-Sec, Paris, in 1829; one of Esther Gobseck's creditors. [Scenes from a Courtesan's Life.]

Biffe (La), concubine of the criminal Riganson, alias Le Biffon. This woman, who was a sort of Jacques Collin in petticoats, evaded the police, thanks to her disguises. She could ape the marquise, the baronne and the comtesse to perfection. She had her own carriage and footmen. [Scenes from a Courtesan's Life.]

Biffon (Le), an alias of Riganson.

Bigorneau, sentimental clerk of Fritot's, the shawl merchant in the Bourse quarter, Paris, time of Louis Philippe. [Gaudissart II.]

Bijou (Olympe). (*See* Grenouville, Madame.)

Binet, inn-keeper in the Department of l'Orne in 1809. He was concerned in a trial which created some stir, and cast a shadow over Mme. de la Chanterie, striking at her daughter, Mme. des Tours-Miniéres. Binet harbored some brigands known as "chauffeurs." He was brought to trial for it and sentenced to five years' imprisonment. [The Seamy Side of History.]

Birotteau (Jacques), a gardener hard by Chinon. He married the chambermaid of a lady on whose estate he trimmed vines. Three boys were born to them: François, Jean and César. He lost his wife on the birth of the last child (1779), and himself died shortly after. [César Birotteau.]

Birotteau (Abbé François), eldest son of Jacques Birotteau; born in 1766; vicar of the church of Saint-Gatien at Tours, and afterwards curé of Saint-Symphorien in the same city. After the death of the Abbé de la Berge, in 1817, he became confessor of Mme. de Mortsauf, attending her last moments. [The Lily of the Valley.] His brother César, the perfumer, wrote him after his—César's—business failure in 1819, asking aid. Abbé Birotteau, in a touching letter, responded with a sum of one thousand francs which represented all his own little hoard and, in addition, a loan obtained from Mme. de Listomère. [César Birotteau.] Accused of having inveigled Mme. de Listomére to leave him the income of fifteen hundred francs, which she bequeathed him on her death, Abbé Birotteau was placed under interdiction, in 1826, the victim of the terrible hatred of the Abbé Troubert. [The Vicar of Tours.]

Birotteau (Jean), second son of Jacques Birotteau. A captain in the army, killed in the historic battle of La Trebia which lasted three days, June 17-19, 1799. [César Birotteau.]

Birotteau (César), third son of Jacques Birotteau, born in 1779; dealer in perfumes in Paris at number 397 rue Saint-Honoré, near the Place Vendome, in the old shop once occupied by the grocer Descoings, who was executed with André Chénier in 1794. After the eighteenth Brumaire, César Birotteau succeeded Sieur Ragon, and moved the source of the "Queen of Roses" to the above address. Among his customers were the Georges, the La Billardières, the Montaurans, the Bauvans, the Longuys, the Mandas, the Berniers, the Guénics, and the Fontaines. These relations with the militant Royalists implicated him in the plot of the 13th Vendémaire, 1795, against the Convention; and he was wounded, as he told over and over, "by Bonaparte on the borders of Saint-Roch." In May, 1800, Birotteau the perfumer married Constance-Barbe-Joséphine Pillerault. By her he had an only daughter, Césarine, who married Anselme Popinot in 1822. Successively captain, then chief of battalion in the National Guard and adjunct-mayor of the eleventh arrondissement, Birotteau was appointed Chevalier of the Legion of Honor in 1818. To celebrate his nomination in the Order, he gave a grand ball[1] which, on account of the very radical changes necessitated in his apartments, and coupled with some bad speculations, brought about his total ruin; he filed a petition in bankruptcy the year following. By stubborn effort and the most rigid economy, Birotteau was able to indemnify his creditors completely, three years later (1822). But he died soon after the formal court reinstating. He numbered among his patrons in 1818 the following: the Duc and Duchesse de Lenoncourt, the Princesse de Blamont-Chauvry, the Marquise d'Espard, the two Vandenesses, Marsay, Ronquerolles, and the Marquis d'Aiglemont. [César Birotteau. A Bachelor's Establishment.] César Birotteau was likewise on friendly terms with the Guillaumes, clothing dealers in the rue Saint-Denis. [At the Sign of the Cat and Racket.]

[1] The 17th of December was really Thursday and not Sunday, as erroneously given.

Birotteau (Madame), born Constance-Barbe-Joséphine Pillerault in 1782. Married César Birotteau in May, 1800. Previous to her marriage she was head "saleslady" at the "Little Sailor"[1] novelty shop, corner of Quai Anjou and rue des Deux Ponts, Paris. Her surviving relative and guardian was her uncle, Claude-Joseph Pillerault. [César Birotteau.]

Birotteau (Césarine). (*See* Popinot, Madame Anselme.)

Bixiou,[2] Parisian grocer, in rue Saint-Honoré, before the Revolution in the eighteenth century. He had a clerk called Descoings, who married his widow. The grocer Bixiou was the grandfather of Jean-Jacques Bixiou, the celebrated cartoonist. [A Bachelor's Establishment.]

Bixiou, son of the preceding and father of Jean-Jacques Bixiou. He was a colonel of the Twenty-first Regiment; killed at the battle of Dresden, on the 26th or 27th of August, 1813. [A Bachelor's Establishment.]

Bixiou (Jean-Jacques), famous artist; son of Colonel Bixiou who was killed at Dresden; grandson of Mme. Descoings, whose first husband was the grocer Bixiou. Born in 1797, he pursued a course of study at the Lyceum, to which he had obtained a scholarship. He had for friends Philippe and Joseph Bridau, and Master Desroches. Later he entered the painter Gros's studio. Then in 1819, through the influence of the Ducs de Maufrigneuse and de Rhétoré, whom he met at some dancer's, he obtained a position with the Minister of Finance. He remained with this administration until December, 1824, when he resigned. In this same year he was one of the best men for Philippe Bridau, who married Flore Brazier, known as La Rabouilleuse, the widow of J.-J. Rouget. After this woman's death, in 1828, he was led, disguised as a priest, to the residence of the Soulanges, where he told the comte about the scandal connected with her death, knowingly caused by her husband; he told, also, about the bad habits and vulgarities of Philippe Bridau,

---

[1] This shop still exists at the same place, No. 43 Quai d'Anjou and 40 rue des Deux-Fonts, being run by M. L. Bellevaut.

[2] Pronounced "Bissiou."

and thus caused the breaking off of the marriage of this weather-beaten soldier with Mlle. Amélie de Soulanges. A talented cartoonist, distinguished practical joker, and recognized as one of the kings of *bon mot,* he led a free and easy life. He was on speaking terms with all the artists and all the lorettes of his day. Among others he knew the painter, Hippolyte Schinner. He turned a pretty penny, during the trial of De Fualdès and De Castaing, by illustrating in a fantastic way the account of this trial. [A Bachelor's Establishment. The Government Clerks. The Purse.] He designed some vignettes for the writing of Canalis. [Modeste Mignon.] With Blondet, Lousteau and Nathan he was a habitue of the house of Esther Gobseck, rue Saint-Georges, in 1829, 1830. [Scenes from a· Courtesan's Life.] In a private room of a well-known restaurant, in 1836, he wittily related to Finot, Blondet and Couture the source of Nucingen's fortune. [The Firm of Nucingen.] In January, 1837, his friend Lousteau had him come especially to upbraid him, Lousteau, on account of the latter's irregular ways with Mme. de la Baudraye, while she, concealed in an ante-room, heard it all. This scene had been arranged beforehand; its object was to give Lousteau a chance to declare, apparently, his unquenchable attachment for his mistress. [The Muse.of the Department.] In 1838 he attended the house-warming of Héloïse Brisetout in rue Chauchat. In the same year he was attendant at the marriage of Steinbock with Hortense Hulot, and of Grevel with the widow Marneffe. [Cousin Betty.] In 1839 the sculptor Dorlange-Sallenauve knew of Bixiou and complained of his slanders. [The Member for Arcis.] Mme. Schontz treated him most cordially in 1838, and he had to pass for her "special," although their relations, in fact, did not transcend the bounds of friendship. [Béatrix.] In 1840, at the home of Marguerite Turquet, maintained by the notary Cardot, when Lousteau, Nathan and La Palférine were also present, he heard a story by Desroches. [A Man of Business.] About 1844, Bixiou helped in a high comedy relative to a Selim shawl sold by Fritot to Mistress Noswell. Bixiou himself had purchased,

in a shop with M. du Ronceret, a shawl for Mme. Schontz.
[Gaudissart II.] In 1845 Bixiou showed Paris and the
"Unconscious Humorists" to a Pyrrenean named Gazonal,
in company with Léon de Lora, a cousin of the countryman.
At this time Bixiou dwelt at number 112 rue Richelieu,
sixth floor; when he had a regular position he had lived
in rue de Ponthieu. [The Unconscious Humorists.] In
the rue Richelieu period he was the lover of Héloïse Brïsetout.
[Cousin Pons.]

Blamont-Chauvry (Princesse de), mother of Mme. d'Espard;
aunt of the Duchesse de Langeais; great aunt of Mme.
de Mortsauf; a veritable d'Hozier in petticoats. Her drawing-
room set the fashion in Faubourg Saint-Germain, and the
sayings of this feminine Talleyrand were listened to as
oracles. Very aged at the beginning of the reign of Louis
XVIII., she was one of the most poetic relics of the reign
of Louis XV., the "Well-Beloved;" and to this nick-name—
as the records had it—she had contributed her full share.
[The Thirteen.] Mme. Firmiani was received by the princess
on account of the Cadignans, to whom she was related on
her mother's side. [Madame Firmiani.] Félix de Vandenesse
was admitted to her "At Homes," on the recommendation
of Mme. de Mortsauf; nevertheless he found in this old lady
a friend whose affection had a quality almost maternal.
The princess was in the family conclave which met to consider
an amorous escapade of the Duchesse Antoinette de Langeais.
[The Lily of the Valley. The Thirteen.]

Blandureaus (The), wealthy linen merchants at Alençon,
time of the Restoration. They had an only daughter, to
whom the President du Ronceret wished to marry his son.
She, however, married Joseph Blondet, the oldest son of
Judge Blondet. This marriage caused secret hostility
between the two fathers, one being the other's superior in
office. [Jealousies of a Country Town.]

Blondet, judge at Alençon in 1824; born in 1758; father
of Joseph and Émile Blondet. At the time of the Revolution
he was public prosecutor. A botanist of note, he had a

remarkable conservatory where he cultivated geraniums only. This conservatory was visited by the Empress Marie-Louise, who spoke of it to the Emperor and obtained for the judge the décoration of the Legion òf Honor. Following the Victurien d'Esgrignon episode, about 1825, Judge Blondet was made an officer in the Order and chosen councillor at the Royal Court. Here he remained in office no longer than absolutely necessary, retreating to his dear Alençon home. He married in 1798, at the age of forty, a young girl of eighteen, who in consequence of this disparity was unfaithful to him. He knew that his second son, Emile, was not his own; he therefore cared only for the elder and sent the younger elsewhere as soon as possible. [Jealousies of a Country Town.] About 1838 Fabien du Ronceret obtained credit in an agricultural convention for a flower which the old Blondet had given him, but which he exhibited as a product of his own green-house. [Béatrix.]

Blondet (Madame), wife of the preceding; born in 1780; married in 1798. She was intimate with a prefect of Orne, who was the natural father of Emile Blondet. Distant ties bound her to the Troisville family, and it was to them that she sent Emile, her favored son. Before her death, in 1818, she commended him to her old-time lover and also to the future Madame de Montcornet, with whom he had been reared. [Jealousies of a Country Town.]

Blondet (Joseph), elder son of Judge Blondet of Alençon; born in that city about 1799. In 1824 he practiced law and aspired to become a substitute judge. Meanwhile he succeeded his father, whose post he filled till his death. He was one of the numerous men of ordinary talent. [Jealousies of a Country Town.]

Blondet (Madame Joseph), *née* Claire Blandureau, wife of Joseph Blondet, whom she married when he was appointed judge at Alençon. She was the daughter of wealthy linen, dealers in the city. [Jealousies of a Country Town.]

Blondet (Emile), born at Alençon about 1800; legally the younger son of Judge Blondet, but really the son of a prefect of Orne. Tenderly loved by his mother, but hated by Judge Blondet, who sent him, in 1818, to study law in Paris. Emile Blondet knew the noble family of d'Esgrignon in Alençon, and for the youngest daughter of this illustrious house he felt an esteem that was really admiration. [Jealousies of a Country Town.] In 1821 Emile Blondet was a remarkably handsome young fellow. He made his first appearance in the "Débats" by a series of masterly articles which called forth from Lousteau the remark that he was "one of the princes of criticism." [A Distinguished Provincial at Paris.] In 1824 he contributed to a review edited by Finot, where he collaborated with Lucien de Rubempré and where he was allowed full swing by his chief. Emile Blondet had the most desultory of habits; one day he would be a boon companion, without compunction, with those destined for slaughter on the day following. He was always "broke" financially. In 1829, 1830, Bixiou, Lousteau, Nathan and he were frequenters of Esther's house, rue Saint-Georges. [Scenes from a Courtesan's Life.] A cynic was Blondet, with little regard for glory undefiled. He won a wager that he could upset the poet Canalis, though the latter was full of assurance. He did this by staring fixedly at the poet's curls, his boots, or his coat-tails, while he recited poetry or gesticulated with proper emphasis, fixed in a studied pose. [Modeste Mignon.] He was acquainted with Mlle. des Touches, being present at her home on one occasion, about 1830, when Henri de Marsay told the story of his first love affair. He took part in the conversation and depicted the "typical woman" to Comte Adam Laginski. [Another Study of Woman.] In 1832 he was a guest at Mme. d'Espard's, where he met his childish flame, Mme. de Montcornet, also the Princesse de Cadignan, Lady Dudley, d'Arthez, Nathan, Rastignac, the Marquis d'Ajuda-Pinto, Maxime de Trailles, the Marquis d'Esgrignon, the two Vandenesses, du Tillet, the Baron Nucingen and the Chevalier d'Espard, brother-in-law of the marquise. [The Secrets of a Princess.] About 1833 Blondet presented Nathan to Mme. de Montcornet, at whose home the young Countess Félix de Vandenesse made the acquaintance of the poet and was much smitten with him for some time. [A Daughter of Eve.] In 1836 he and Finot and Couture chimed in on the narrative of the rise of Nucingen, told with much zest by Bixiou in a private room of a famous restaurant. [The Firm of Nucingen.] Eight or ten years prior to February, 1848, Emile Blondet, on the brink of suicide, witnessed an entire transition in his affairs. He was chosen a prefect, and he married the wealthy widow of Comte de Montcornet, who offered him her hand when she became free. They had known and loved each other since childhood. [The Peasantry.]

Blondet (Virginie), wife by second marriage of Emile Blondet; born in 1797; daughter of the Vicomte de Troisville; granddaughter of the Russian Princesse Scherbelloff. She was brought up at Alençon, with her future husband. In 1819 she married the Général de Montcornet. Twenty years later, a widow, she married the friend of her youth, who this long time had been her lover. [Jealousies of a Country Town. The Secrets of a Princess. The Peasantry.] She and Mme. d'Espard tried to convert Lucien de Rubempré to the monarchical side in 1821. [A Distinguished Provincial at Paris.] She was present at Mlle. des Touches', about 1830, when Marsay told about his first love, and she joined in the conversation. [Another Study of Woman.] She received a rather mixed set, from an aristocratic standpoint, but here might be found the stars of finance, art and literature. [The Member for Arcis.] Mme. Félix de Vandenesse saw Nathan the poet for the first time and noticed him particularly at Mme. de Montcornet's, in 1834, 1835. [A Daughter of Eve.] Mme. Emile Blondet, then Madame la Générale de Montcornet, passed the summer and autumn of 1823 in Burgundy, at her beautiful estate of Aigues, where she lived a burdened and troubled life among the many and varied types of peasantry. Remarried, and now the wife of a prefect, eight years or so before February, 1848, time of Louis Philippe, she visited her former properties. [The Peasantry.]

Bluteau (Pierre), assumed name of Genestas. [The Country Doctor.]

Bocquillon, an acquaintance of Mme. Etienne Gruget. In 1820, rue des Enfants-Rouges, Paris, she mistook for him the stock-broker, Jules Desmarets, who was entering her door. [The Thirteen.]

Bogseck (Madame van), name bestowed by Jacques Collin on Esther van Gobseck when, in 1825, he gave her, transformed morally and intellectually, to Lucien de Rubempré, in an elegant flat on rue Taitbout. [Scenes from a Courtesan's Life.]

Boirouge, president of the Sancerre Court at the time when the Baronne de la Baudraye held social sway over that city. Through his wife, he was related to the Popinot-Chandiers, to Judge Popinot of Paris, and to Anselme Popinot. He was hereditary owner of a house which he did not need, and which he very gladly leased to the baronne for the purpose of starting a literary society that, however, degenerated very soon into an ordinary clique. Actuated by jealousy, President Boirouge was one of the principals in the defeat of Procureur Clagny for deputy. He was reputed to be unchaste at repartee. [The Muse of the Department.]

Boirouge (Madame), *née* Popinot-Chandier, wife of President Boirouge; stood well among the middle-class of Sancerre. After having been leader in the opposition to Mme. de la Baudraye for nine years, she induced her son Gatien to attend the Baudraye receptions, persuading herself that he would soon make his way. Profiting by the visit of Bianchon to Sancerre, Mme. Boirouge obtained of the famous physician, her relative, a gratuitous consultation by giving him full particulars regarding some pretended nervous trouble of the stomach, in which complaint he recognized a periodic dyspepsia. [The Muse of the Department.]

Boirouge (Gatien), son of President Boirouge; born in 1814; the junior "patito" of Mme. de la Baudraye, who employed him in all sorts of small ways. Gatien Boirouge was made game of by Lousteau, to whom he had confessed his love for that masterful woman. [The Muse of the Department.]

Boisfranc (De), procureur-general, then first president of a royal court under the Restoration. (*See* Dubut.)

Boisfranc (Dubut de), president of the Aides court under the old régime; brother of Dubut de Boisfrelon and of Dubut de Boislaurier. [The Seamy Side of History.]

Boisfrelon (Dubut de), brother of Dubut de Boisfranc and of Dubut de Boislaurier; at one time councillor in Parliament; born in 1736; died in 1832 in the home of his niece, the Baronne de la Chanterie. Godefroid succeeded him. M. de Boisfrelon had been one of the "Brotherhood of Consolation." He was married, but his wife probably died before him. [The Seamy Side of History.]

Boislaurier (Dubut de), junior brother of Dubut de Boisfranc and of Dubut de Boisfrelon. Commander-in-chief of the Western Rebellion in 1808-1809, and designated then by the surname of Augustus. With Rifoël, Chevalier du Vissard, he plotted the organization of the "Chauffeurs" of Mortagne. Then, in the trial of the "brigands," he was condemned to death by default. [The Seamy Side of History.]

Bois-Levant, chief of division under the Minister of Finance in 1824, at the time when Xavier Rabourdin and Isidore Baudoyer contested the succession of office in another division, that of F. de la Billardière. [The Government Clerks.]

Boleslas, Polish servant of the Comte and Comtesse Laginski, in rue de la Pépiniére, Paris, between 1835 and 1842. [The Imaginary Mistress.]

Bonamy (Ida), aunt of Mlle. Antonia Chocardellc. At the time of Louis Philippe, she conducted, on rue Coquenard (since 1848 rue Lamartine), "just a step· or two from rue Pigalle," a reading-room given to her niece by Maxime de Trailles. [A Man of Business.]

Bonaparte (Napoleon), Emperor of the French; born at Ajaccio, August 15, 1768, or 1769, according to varying accounts; died at St. Helena May 5, 1821. As First Consul in 1800 he received at the Tuileries the Corsican, Bartholomeo di Piombo, and disentangled his countryman from the latter's implication in a vendetta. [The Vendetta.] On the evening of the battle of Jena, October 13, 1806, he was met on that ground by Laurence de Cinq-Cygne, who had come post haste from France, and to whom he accorded pardon for the Simeuses and the Hauteserres, compromised in the abduction of Senator Malin de Gondreville. [The Gondreville Mystery.] Napoleon Bonaparte was strongly concerned in the welfare of his lieutenant, Hyacinthe Chabert, during the battle of Eylau. [Colonel Chabert.] In November, 1809, he was to have attended a grand ball given by Senator Malin de Gondreville; but he was detained at the Tuileries by a scene—noised abroad that same evening—between Joséphine and himself, a scene which disclosed their impending divorce. [Peace in the House.] He condoned the infamous conduct of the police officer Contenson. [The Seamy Side of History.] In April, 1813, during a dress-parade on the Place du Carrousel, Paris, Napoleon noticed Mlle. de Chatillonest, who had come with her father to see the handsome Colonel d'Aiglemont, and leaning towards Duroc he made a brief remark which made the Grand Marshal smile. [A Woman of Thirty.]

Bonaparte (Lucien), brother of Napoleon Bonaparte; born in 1775; died in 1840. In June, 1800, he went to the house of Talleyrand, the Foreign Minister, and there announced to him and also to Fouché, Sieyés and Carnot, the victory of his brother at Montebello. [The Gondreville Mystery.] In the month of October of the same year he was encountered by his countryman, Bartholomeo di Piombo, whom he introduced to the First Consul; he also gave his purse to rhe Corsican and afterwards contributed towards relieving his difficulties. [The Vendetta.]

Bonfalot, or **Bonvalot** (Madame), an aged relative of F. du Bruel at Paris. La Palferine first met Mme. du Bruel in 1834 on the boulevard, and boldly followed her all the way to Mme. de Bonfalot's, where she was calling. [A Prince of Bohemia.]

Bonfons (Cruchot de), nephew of Cruchot the notary and Abbé Cruchot; born in 1786; president of the Court of First Instance of Saumur in 1819. The Cruchot trio, backed by a goodly number of cousins and allied to twenty families in the city, formed a party similar to that of the olden-time Medicis at Florence; and also, like the Medicis, the Cruchots had their Pazzis in the persons of the Grassins. The prize contested for between the Cruchots and the Grassins was the hand of the rich heiress, Eugénie Grandet. In 1827, after nine years of suing, the President Cruchot de Bonfons married the young woman, now left an orphan. Previous to this he had been commissioned by her to settle in full, both principal and interest, with the creditors of Charles Grandet's father. Six months after his marriage, Bonfons was elected councillor to the Royal Court of Angers. Then after some years signalized by devoted service he became first president. Finally chosen deputy for Saumur in 1832, he died within a week, leaving his widow in possession •of an immense fortune, still further augmented by the bequests of the Abbé and the notary Cruchot. Bonfons was the name of an estate of the magistrate. He married Eugénie only through cupidity. He looked like "a big, rusty nail." [Eugénie Grandet.]

Bonfons (Eugénie Cruchot de), only daughter of M. and Mme. Félix Grandet; born at Saumur in 1796. Strictly reared by a mother gentle and devout, and by a father hard and avaricious. The single bright ray across her life was an absolutely platonic love for her cousin Charles Grandet. But, once away from her, this young man was forgetful of her; and, on his return from the Indies in 1827, a rich man, he married the young daughter of a nobleman. Upon this occurrence, Eugénie Grandet, now an orphan, settled in full with the creditors of Charles' father, and then bestowed her hand upon the President Cruchot de Bonfons, who had paid her court for nine years. At the age of thirty-six she was left a widow without having ceased to be a virgin, following her expressed wish. Sadly she secluded herself in the gloomy home of her childhood at Saumur, where she devoted the rest of her life to works of benevolence and charity. After her father's death, Eugénie was often alluded to, by the Cruchot faction, as Mlle. de Froidfond, from the name of one of her holdings. In 1832 an effort was made to induce Mme. de Bonfons to wed with Marquis de Froidfond, a bankrupt widower of fifty odd years and possessed of numerous progeny. [Eugénie Grandet.]

Bongrand, born in 1769; first an advocate at Melun, then justice of the peace at Nemours from 1814 to 1837. He was a friend of Doctor Mirouët's and helped educate Ursule Mirouët, protecting her to the best of his ability after the death of the old physician, and aiding in the restitution of her fortune which Minoret-Levrault had impaired by the theft of the doctor's will. M. Bongrand had wanted to make a match between Ursule Mirouët and his son, but she loved Savinien de Portenduère. The justice of the peace became president of the court at Melun, after the marriage of the young lady with Savinien. [Ursule Mirouët.]

Bongrand (Eugéne), son of Bongrand the justice of the peace. He studied law at Paris under Derville the attorney, this constituting all his course. He became public prosecutor at Melun after the Revolution of 1830, and general prosecutor in 1837. Failing in his love suit with Ursule Mirouët, he probably married the daughter of M. Levrault, former mayor of Nemours. [Ursule Mirouët].

Bonnac, a rather handsome young fellow, who was head clerk for the notary Lupin at Soulanges in 1823. His accomplishments were his only dowry. He was loved in platonic fashion by his employer's wife, Mme. Lupin, otherwise known as Bébelle, a fat ridiculous female without education. [The Peasantry.]

Bonnébault, retired cavalry soldier, the Lovelace of the village of Blangy,. Burgundy, and its suburbs in 1823.

Bonnébault was the lover of Marie Tonsard who was perfectly foolish about him. He had still other "good friends" and lived at their expense. Their generosity did not suffice for his dissipations, his café bills and his unbridled taste for billiards. He dreamed of marrying Aglaé Socquard, only daughter of Pére Socquard, proprietor of the "Café de la Paix" at Soulanges. Bonnébault obtained three thousand francs from General de Montcornet by coming to him to confess voluntarily that he had been commissioned to kill him for this price. This revelation, with other things, led the general to weary of his fierce struggle with the peasantry, and to put up for sale his property at Aigues, which became the prey of Gaubertin, Rigou and Soudry. Bonnébault was squint-eyed and his physical appearance did not belie his depravity. [The Peasantry.]

Bonnébault (Mére), grandmother of Bonnébault the veteran. In 1823, at Conches, Burgundy, where she lived, she owned a cow which she did not hesitate to pasture in the fields belonging to General de Montcornet. The numerous depredations of the old woman, added to convictions for many similar offences, caused the general to decide to confiscate the cow. [The Peasantry.]

Bonnet (Abbé), Curé of Montégnac near Limoges from 1814 on. In this capacity, he assisted at the public confession of his penitent, Mme. Graslin, in the summer of 1844. Upon leaving the seminary of Saint-Sulpice, Paris, he was sent to this village of Montégnac, which he never after wished to leave. Here, sometimes unaided, sometimes with the help of Mme. Graslin, he toiled for a material and moral betterment, bringing about an entire regeneration of a wretched country. It was he who brought the outlawed Tascheron back into the Church, and who accompanied him to the very foot of the scaffold, with a devotion which caused his own very sensitive nature much cringing. Born in 1788, he had embraced the ecclesiastical calling through choice, and all his studies had been to that end. He belonged to a family of more than easy circumstances. His father was a self-made man, stern and unyielding. Abbé Bonnet had an older brother, and a sister whom he counseled with his mother to marry as soon as possible, in order to release the young woman from the terrible paternal yoke. [The Country Parson.]

Bonnet, older brother of Abbé Bonnet, who enlisted as a private about the beginning of the Empire. He became a general in 1813; fell at Leipsic. [The Country Parson.]

Bonnet (Germain), *valet de chambre* of Canalis in 1829, at the time when the poet went to Havre to contest the hand of Modeste Mignon. A servant full of *finesse* and irreproachable in appearance, he was of the greatest service to his master. He courted Philoxène Jacmin, chambermaid of Mme. de Chaulieu. Here the pantry imitated the parlor, for the academician's mistress was the great lady herself. [Modeste Mignon.]

Bontems, a country landowner in the neighborhood of Bayeux, who feathered his nest well during the Revolution, by purchasing government confiscations at his own terms. He was a pronounced "red cap," and became president of his district. His daughter, Angélique Bontems, married Granville during the Empire; but at this time Bontems was dead. [A Second Home.]

Bontems (Madame), wife of the preceding; outwardly pious, inwardly vain; mother of Angélique Bontems, whom she had reared in much the same attitude, and whose marriage with a Granville was, in consequence, so unhappy. [A Second Home.]

Bontems (Angélique). (*See* Granville, Madame de.)

Borain (Mademoiselle), the most stylish costumer in Provins, at the time of Charles X. She was commissioned by the Rogrons to make a complete wardrobe for Pierrette Lorrain, when that young girl was sent them from Brittany. [Pierrette.]

Bordevin (Madame), Parisian butcher in rue Charlot, at the time when Sylvain Pons dwelt hard by in rue de Normandie. Mme. Bordevin was related to Mme. Sabatier. [Cousin Pons.]

Bordin, procureur at the Châtelet before the Revolution; then advocate of the Court of First Instance of the Seine, under the Empire. In 1798 he instructed and advised with M. Alain, a creditor of Monegod's. Both had been ·clerks at the procureur's. In 1806, the Marquis de Charge-boeuf went to Paris to hunt for Master Bordin, who defended the Simeuses before the Criminal Court of Troyes in the trial regarding the abduction and sequestration of Senator Malin. In 1809 he also defended Henriette Bryond des Tours-Mimères, *née* La Chanterie, in the trial docketed as the "Chauffeurs of Mortagne." [The Gondreville Mystery. The Seamy Side of History.] In 1816 Bordin was consulted by Mme. d'Espard regarding her husband. [The Commission in Lunacy.] During the Restoration a banker at Alençon made quarterly payments of one hundred and fifty livres to the Chevalier de Valois through the Parisian medium of Bordin. [Jealousies of a Country Town.] For ten years Bordin represented the nobility. Derville succeeded him. [The Gondreville Mystery.]

Bordin (Jérome-Sebastien), was also procureur at the Châtelet, and, in 1806, advocate of the Seine Court. He succeeded Master Guerbet, and sold his practice to Sauvagn-est, who disposed of it to Desroches. [A Start in Life.]

Born (Comte de), brother of the Vicomtesse de Grandlieu. In the winter of 1829-1830, he is discovered at the home of his sister, taking part in a conversation in which the advocate Derville related the marital infelicities of M. de Res-taud, and the story of his will and his death. The Comte de Born seized the chance to exploit the character of Maxime de Trailles, the lover of Mme. de Restaud. [Gobseck.]

Borniche, son-in-law of M. Hochon, the old miser of Issou-dun. He died of chagrin at business failures, and at not having received any assistance from his father or mother. His wife preceded him but a short time to the tomb. They left a son and a daughter, Baruch and Adolphine, who were brought up by their maternal grandfather, with François Hochon, another grandchild of the goodman's. Borniche was probably a Calvinist. [A Bachelor's Establishment.]

Borniche (Monsieur and Madame), father and mother of the preceding. They were still living in 1823, when their son and their daughter-in-law had been deceased some time. In April of this year, old Mme. Borniche and her friend Mme. Hochon, who ruled socially in Issoudun, assisted àt the wedding of La Rabouilleuse with Jean-Jacques Rouget. [A Bachelor's Establishment.]

Borniche (Baruch), grandson of the preceding, and of M. and Mme. Hochon. Born in 1800. Early left an orphan, he and his sister were reared by his grandfather on the maternal side. He had been one of the accomplices of Maxence Gilet, and took part in the nocturnal raids of the "Knights of Idlesse." When his conduct became known to his grandfather, in 1822, the latter lost no time in removing him from Issoudun, sending him to Monegod's .office, Paris, to study law. [A Bachelor's Establishment.]

Borniche (Adolphine), sister of Baruch Borniche; born in 1804. Brought up almost a recluse in the frigid, dreary house of her grandfather, Hochon, she spent most of her time peering through the windows, in the hope of discovering some of the terrible things which—as Dame Rumor had it—occurred in the home of Jean-Jacques Rouget, next door. She likewise awaited with some impatience the arrival of Joseph Bridau in Issoudun, wishing to inspire some sentiment in him, and taking the liveliest interest in the painter, on account of the monstrosities which were attributed to him because of his being an artist. [A Bachelor's Establishment.]

Boucard, head-clerk of the attorney Derville in 1818, at the time when Colonel Chabert sought to recover his rights with his wife who had been remarried to Comte Ferraud. [Colonel Chabert.]

Boucher, Besançon merchant in 1834, who was the first client of Albert Savarus in that city. He assumed financial control of the " Revue de l'Est," founded by the lawyer. M. Boucher was related by marriage to one of the ablest editors of great theological works. [Albert Savarus.]

Boucher (Alfred), eldest son of the preceding. Born in 1812. A youth, eager for literary fame, whom Albert Savarus put on the staff of his "Revue de l'Est," giving him his themes and subjects. Alfred Boucher conceived a strong admiration for the managing editor, who treated him as a friend. The first number of the "Revue" contained a "Meditation" by Alfred. This Alfred Boucher believed he was exploiting Savarus, whereas the contrary was the case. [Albert Savarus.]

Bouffé (Marie), alias Vignol, actor born in Paris, September 4, 1800. He appeared about 1822 at the Panorama-Dramatique theatre, on the Boulevard du Temple, Paris, playing the part of the Alcade in a three-act imbroglio by Raoul Nathan and Du Bruel entitled "L'Alcade dans l'embarras." At the first night performance he announced that the authors were Raoul and Cursy. Although very young at the time, this artist made his first great success in this rôle, and revealed his talent for depicting an old man. The critique of Lucien de Rubempré established his position. [A Distinguished Provincial at Paris.]

Bougival (La). (See Cabirolle, Madame.)

Bougniol (Mesdemoiselles), proprietors of an inn at Guérande (Loire-Inférieure), at the time of Louis Philippe. They had as guests some artist friends of Félicité des Touches —Camille Maupin—who had come from Paris to see her. [Béatrix.]

Bourbonne (De), wealthy resident of Tours, time of Louis XVIII. and Charles X. An uncle of Octave de Camps. In 1824 he visited Paris to ascertain the cause of the ruin of his nephew and sole heir, which ruin was generally credited to dissipations with Mme. Firmiani. M. de Bourbonne, a retired musketeer in easy circumstances, was well connected. He had entry into the Faubourg Saint-Germain through the Listomères, the Lenoncourts and the Vandenesses. He caused himself to be presented at Mme. Firmiani's as M. de Rouxellay, the name of his estate. The advice of Bourbonne, which was marked by much perspicacity, if followed, would have extricated François Birotteau from Troubert's clutches; for the uncle of M. de Camps fathomed the plottings of the future Bishop of Troyes. Bourbonne saw a great deal more than did the Listomères of Tours. [Madame Firmiani. The Vicar of Tours.]

Bourdet (Benjamin) old soldier of the Empire, formerly serving under Philippe Bridau's command. He lived quietly in the suburbs of Vatan, in touch with Fario. In 1822 he placed himself at the entire disposal of the Spaniard, and also of the officer who previously had put him under obligations. Secretly he served them in their hatred of and plots against Maxence Gilet. [A Bachelor's Establishment.]

Bourgeat, foundling of Saint-Flour. Parisian water-carrier about the end of the eighteenth century. The friend and protector of the young Desplein, the future famous surgeon. He lived in rue Quatre-Vents in an humble house rendered doubly famous by the sojourn of Desplein and by that of Daniel d'Arthez. A fervent Churchman of unswerving faith. The future famous savant (Desplein) watched by his bedside at the last and closed his eyes. [The Atheist's Mass.]

Bourget, uncle of the Chaussard brothers. An old man who became implicated in the trial of the Chauffeurs of Mortagne in 1809. He died during the taking of the testimony, while making some confessions. His wife, also apprehended, appeared before the court and was sentenced to twenty-two years' imprisonment. [The Seamy Side of History.]

Bourgneufs (The), a family ruined by the De Camps and living in poverty and seclusion at Saint-Germain en Laye, during the early part of the nineteenth century. This family consisted of: the aged father, who ran a lottery-office; the mother, almost always sick; and two delightful daughters, who took care of the home and attended to the correspondence. The Bourgneufs were rescued from their troubles by Octave

de Camps who, prompted by Mme. Firmiani, and at the cost
of his entire property, restored to them the fortune made
away with by his father. [Madame Firmiani.]

Bourgnier (Du). (*See* Bousquier, Du.)

Bourignard (Gratien-Henri-Victor-Jean-Joseph), father of
Mme. Jules Desmarets. One of the "Thirteen" and the
former chief of the Order of the Devorants under the title
of **Ferragus XXIII.** He had been a laborer, but afterwards
was a contractor of buildings. His daughter was born
to an abandoned woman. About 1807 he was sentenced
to twenty years of hard labor, but he managed to escape
during a journey of the chain-gang from Paris to Toulon,
and he returned to Paris. In 1820 he lived there under
diverse names and disguises, lodging successively on rue
des Vieux Augustins (now rue d'Argout), corner of rue
Soly (an insignificant street which disappeared when the
Hotel des·Postes was rebuilt); then at number seven rue
Joquelet; finally at Mme. E. Gruget's, number twelve rue
des Enfants-Rouges (now part of the rue des Archives running
from rue Pastourelle to rue Portefoin), changing lodgings
at this time to evade the investigations of Auguste de Maulincour. Stunned by the death of his daughter, whom he
adored and with whom he held secret interviews to prevent
her becoming amenable to the law, he passed his last days
in an indifferent, almost idiotic way, idly watching match
games at bowling on the Place de l'Observatoire; the ground
between the Luxembourg and the Boulevard de Montparnasse
was the scene of these games. One of the assumed names
of Bourignard was the Comte de Funcal. In 1815, Bourignard,
alias Ferragus, assisted Henri de Marsay, another member
of the "Thirteen," in his raid on Hotel San-Réal, where
dwelt Paquita Valdés. [The Thirteen.]

Bourlac (Bernard-Jean-Baptiste-Macloud, Baron de), former procureur-general of the Royal Court of Rouen, grand
officer of the Legion of Honor. Born in 1771. He fell
in love with and married the daughter of the Pole, Tarlowski,
a colonel in the French Imperial Guard. By her he had a

daughter, Vanda, who became the Baronne de Mergi. A widower and reserved by nature, he came to Paris in 1829 to take care of Vanda, who was seized by a strange and very dangerous malady. After having lived in the Quartier du Roule in 1838, with his daughter and grandson, he dwelt for several years, in very straitened circumstances, in a tumble-down house on the Boulevard du Montparnasse, where Godefroid, a recent initiate into the "Brotherhood of the Consolation" and under the direction of Mme. de la Chanterie and her associates, came to his relief. Afterwards it was discovered that the Baron de Bourlac was none other than the terrible magistrate who had pronounced judgment on this noble woman and her daughter during the trial of the Chauffeurs of Mortagne in 1809. Nevertheless, the aiding of the family was not abated in the least. Vanda was cured, thanks to a foreign physician, Halpersohn, procured by Godefroid. M. de Bourlac was enabled to publish his great work on the "Spirit of Modern Law." At Sorbonne a chair of comparative legislation was created for him. At last he obtained forgiveness from Mme. de la Chanterie, at whose feet he flung himself. [The Seamy Side of History.] In 1817 the Baron de Bourlac, then procureur-general, and superior of Soudry the younger, royal procureur, helped, with the assistance also of the latter, to secure for Sibilet the position of estate-keeper to the General de Montcornet at Aigues. [The Peasantry.]

Bournier, natural son of Gaubertin and of Mme. Socquard, the wife of the café manager of Soulanges. His existence was unknown to Mme. Gaubertin. He was sent to Paris where, under Leclercq, he learned the printer's trade and finally became a foreman. Gaubertin then brought him to Ville-aux-Fayes where he established a printing office and a paper known as "Le Courrier de l'Avonne", entirely devoted to the interests of the triumvirate, Rigou, Gaubertin and Soudry. [The Peasantry.]

Bousquier (Du), or Croisier (Du), or Bourguier (Du), a descendant of an old Alençon family. Born about 1760.

He had been commissary agent in the army from 1793 to 1799; had done business with Ouvrard, and kept a running account with Barras, Bernadotte and Fouché. He was at that time one of the great folk of finance. Discharged by Bonaparte in 1800, he withdrew to his natal town After selling the Beauséant house, which he owned, for the benefit of his creditors, he had remaining an income of not more than twelve hundred francs. About 1816 he married Mlle. Cormon, a spinster who had been courted also by the Chevalier de Valois and Athanase Granson. This marriage set him on his feet again financially. He took the lead in the party of the opposition, established a Liberal paper called "Le Courrier de l'Orne," and was elected Receiver-General of the Exchequer, after the Revolution of 1830. He waged bitter war on the white flag Royalists, his hatred of them causing him secretly to condone the excesses of Victurnien d'Esgrignon, until the latter involved him in an affair, when Bousquier had him arrested, thinking thus to dispose of him summarily. The affair was smoothed over only by tremendous pressure. But the young nobleman provoked Du Bousquier into a duel where the latter dangerously wounded him. Afterwards Bousquier gave him in marriage the hand of his niece, Mlle. Duval, dowered with three millions. [Jealousies of a Country Town.] Probably he was the father of Flavie Minoret, the daughter of a celebrated Opéra danseuse. But he never acknowledged this child, and she was dowered by Princesse Galathionne and married Colleville. [The Middle Classes.]

Bousquier (Madame du), born Cormon (Rose-Marie-Victoire) in 1773. She was a very wealthy heiress, living with her maternal uncle, the Abbé de Sponde, in an old house of Alençon (rue du Val-Noble), and receiving, in 1816, the aristocracy of the town, with which she was related through marriage. Courted simultaneously by Athanase Cranson, the Chevalier de Valois and Du Bousquier, she gave her hand to the old commissariat, whose athletic figure and *passé* libertinism had impressed her vaguely. But her secret desires were uttely dashed by him; she confessed later that she couldn't endure the idea of dying a maid. Mme. du Bousquier was very devout. She was descended from the stewards of the ancient Ducs d'Alencon. In this same year of 1816, she hoped in vain to wed a Troisville, but he was already married. She found it difficult to brook the state of hostility declared between M. du Bousquier and the Esgrignons. [Jealousies of a Country Town.]

Boutin, at one time sergeant in the cavalry regiment of which Chabert was colonel. He lived at Stuttgart in 1814, exhibiting white bears very well trained by him. In this city he encountered his former ranking officer, shorn of all his possessions, and just emerging from an insane asylum. Boutin aided him as best he could and took it upon himself to go to Paris and inform Mme. Chabert of her husband's whereabouts. But Boutin fell on the field of Waterloo, and could hardly have accomplished his mission. [Colonel Chabert.]

Bouvard (Doctor), physician of Paris, born about 1758. A friend of Dr. Minoret, with whom he had some lively tilts about Mesmer. He had adopted that system, while Minoret gainsaid the truth thereof. These discussions ended in an estrangement, for some time, between the two cronies. Finally, in 1829, Bouvard wrote Minoret asking him to come to Paris to assist in some conclusive tests of magnetism. As a result of these tests, Dr. Minoret, materialist and atheist that he was, became a devout Spiritualist and Catholic. In 1829 Dr. Bouvard lived on rue Férou. [Ursule Mirouët.] He had been as a father to Dr. Lebrun, physician of the Conciergerie in 1830, who, according to his own avowal, owed to him his position, since he often drew from his master his own ideas regarding nervous energy. [Scenes from a Courtesan's Life.]

Bouyonnet, a lawyer at Mantes, under Louis Philippe, who, urged by his confreres and stimulated by the public prosecutor, "showed up" Fraisier, another lawyer in the town, who had been retained in a suit for both parties at once. The result of this denunciation was to make Fraisier sell his office and leave Mantes. [Cousin Pons.]

Brambourg (Comte de), title of Philippe Bridau to which his brother Joseph succeeded. [A Bachelor's Establishment. The Unconscious Humorists.]

Brandon (Lady Marie-Augusta), mother of Louis and Marie Gaston, children born out of wedlock. Together with the Vicomtesse de Beauséant she assisted, in company with Colonel Franchessini, probably her lover, at the famous ball on the morning following which the duped mistress of D'Ajuda-Pinto secretly left Paris. [The Member for Arcis.] In 1820, while living with her two children in seclusion at La Grenadiére, in the neighborhood of Tours, she saw Félix de Vandenesse, at the time when Mme. de Mortsauf died, and charged him with a pressing message to Lady Arabelle Dudley. [The Lily of the Valley.] She died, aged thirty-six, during the Restoration, in the house at La Grenadiére, and was buried in the Saint-Cyr Cemetery. Her husband, Lord Brandon, who had abandoned her, lived in London, Brandon Square, Hyde Park, at this time. In Touraine Lady Brandon was known only by the assumed name of Mme. Willemsens. [La Grenadiére.]

Braschon, upholsterer and cabinet-maker in the Faubourg Saint-Antoine, famous under the Restoration. He did a considerable amount of work for César Birotteau and figured among the creditors in his bankruptcy. [César Birotteau. Scenes from a Courtesan's Life.]

Braulard, born in 1782. The head *claquer* at the theatre of the Panorama-Dramatique, and then at the Gymnase, about 1822. The lover of Mlle. Millot. At this time he lived on rue Faubourg du Temple, in a rather comfortable flat where he gave fine dinners to actresses, managing editors and authors—among others, Adéle Dupuis, Finot, Ducange and Frédéric du Petit-Méré. He was credited with having gained an income of twenty thousand francs by discounting authors' and other complimentary tickets. [A Distinguished

Provincial at Paris.] When chief *claquer*, about 1843, he had in his following Chardin, alias Idamore [Cousin Betty], and commanded his "Romans" at the Boulevard theatre, which presented operas, spectaculars and ballets at popular prices, and was run by Félix Gaudissart. [Cousin Pons.]

Brazier, this family included the following:
A peasant of Vatan (Indre), the paternal uncle and guardian of Mlle. Flore Brazier, known as "La Rabouilleuse." In 1799 he placed her in the house of Dr. Rouget on very satisfactory conditions for himself, Brazier. Rendered comparatively rich by the doctor, he died two years before the latter, in 1805, from a fall received on leaving an inn where he spent his time after becoming well-to-do.
His wife, who was a very harsh aunt of Flore's.
Lastly the brother and brother-in-law of this girl's guardians, the real father of "La Rabouilleuse," who died in 1799, a demented widower, in the hospital of Bourges. [A Bachelor's Establishment.]

Brazier (Flore). (*See* Bridau, Madame Philippe.)

Breautey (Comtesse de), a venerable woman of Provins, who maintained the only aristocratic salon in that city, in 1827-1828. [Pierrette.]

Brébian (Alexandre de), member of the Angoulême aristocracy in 1821. He frequented the Bargeton receptions. An artist like his friend Bartas, he also was daft over drawing and would ruin every album in the department with his grotesque productions. He posed as Mme. de Bartas' lover, since Bartas paid court to Mme. de Brébian. [Lost Illusions.]

Brébian (Charlotte de), wife of the preceding. Currently called "Lolotte." [Lost Illusions.]

Breintmayer, a banking house of Strasbourg, entrusted by Michu in 1803 with the transmission of funds to the De Simeuses, young officers of the army of Condé. [The Gondreville Mystery.]

Brézacs (The), Auvergnats, dealers in general merchandise and the furnishings of châteaux during the Revolution, the Empire and the Restoration. They had business dealings with Pierre Graslin, Jean-Baptiste Sauviat and Martin Falleix. [The Country Parson. The Government Clerks.]

Bridau, father of Philippe and Joseph Bridau; one of the secretaries of Roland, Minister of the Interior in 1792, and the right arm of succeeding ministers. He was attached fanatically to Napoleon, who could appreciate him, and who made him chief of division in 1804. He died in 1808, at the moment when he had been promised the offices of director general and councillor of state with the title of comte. He first met Agathe Rouget, whom he made his wife, at the home of the grocer Descoings, the man whom he tried to save from the scaffold. [A Bachelor's Establishment.]

Bridau (Agathe Rouget, Madame), wife of the preceding; born in 1773. Legal daughter of Dr. Rouget of Issoudun, but possibly the natural daughter of Sub-delegate Lousteau. The doctor did not waste any affection upon her, and lost no time in sending her to Paris, where she was reared by her uncle, the grocer Descoings. She died at the close of 1828. Of her two sons, Philippe and Joseph, Mme. Bridau always preferred the elder, though he caused her nothing but grief. [A Bachelor's Establishment.]

Bridau (Philippe), elder son of Bridau and Agathe Rouget. Born in 1796. Placed in the Saint-Cyr school in 1813, he remained but six months, leaving it to become under-lieutenant of the cavalry. On account of a skirmish of the advance guard he was made full lieutenant, during the French campaign, then captain after the battle of La Fére-Champenoise, where Napoleon made him artillery officer. He was decorated at Montereau. After witnessing the farewell at Fontainebleu, he came back to his mother in July, 1814, being then hardly nineteen. He did not wish to serve the Bourbons. In March, 1815, Philippe Bridau rejoined the Emperor at Lyons, accompanying him to the Tuileries. He was promised a captaincy in a squadron of dragoons of the Guard, and made officer of the Legion of Honor at Waterloo. Reduced to half-pay, during the Restoration, he nevertheless preserved his rank and officer's cross. He rejoined General Lallemand in Texas, returning from America in October, 1819, thoroughly degenerated. He ran an opposition newspaper in Paris in 1820-1821. He led a most dissolute life; was the lover of Mariette Godeschal; and attended all the parties of Tullia, Florentine, Florine, Coralie, Matifat and Camusot. Not content with using the income of his brother Joseph, he stole a coffer entrusted to him, and despoiled of her last savings Mme. Descoings, who died of grief. Involved in a military plot in 1822, he was sent to Issoudun, under the surveillance of the police. There he created a disturbance in the "bachelor's establishment" of his uncle, Jean-Jacques Rouget; killed in a duel Maxence Gilet, the lover of Flore Brazier; brought about the girl's marriage with his uncle; and married her himself when she became a widow in 1824. When Charles X. succeeded to the throne, Philippe Bridau re-entered the army as lieutenant-colonel of the Duc de Maufrigneuse's regiment. In 1827 he passed with this grade into a regiment of cavalry of the Royal Guard, and was made Comte de Brambourg from the name of an estate which he had purchased. He was promised further the office of commander in the Legion of Honor, as well as in the Order of Saint-Louis. After having consciously caused the death of his wife, Flore Brazier, he tried to marry Amélie de Soulanges, who belonged to a great family. But his manœuvres were frustrated by Bixiou. The Revolution of 1830 resulted in the loss to Philippe Bridau of a portion of the fortune which he had obtained from his uncle by his marriage. Once more he entered military service, under the July Government, which made him a colonel. In 1839 he fell in an engagement with the Arabs in Africa. [A Bachelor's Establishment. Scenes from a Courtesan's Life.]

Bridau (Joseph), painter; younger brother of Philippe Bridau; born in 1799. He studied with Gros, and made his first exhibit at the Salon of 1823. He received great stimulus from his fellow-members of the "Cénacle," in rue Quatre-Vents, also from his master, from Gérard and from Mlle. des Touches. Moreover he was a hard-worker and an artist of genius. He was decorated in 1827, and about 1839, through the interest of the Comte de Sérizy, for whose home he had formerly done some work, he married the only daughter of a retired farmer, now a millionaire. On the death of his brother Philippe, he inherited his house in rue de Berlin, his estate of Brambourg, and his title of comte. [A Bachelor's Establishment. A Distinguished Provincial at Paris. A Start in Life.] Joseph Bridau made some vignettes for the works of Canalis. [Modeste Mignon.] He was intimate with Hippolyte Schinner, whom he had known at Gros' studio. [The Purse.] Shortly after 1830, he was present at an "at home" at Mlle. des Touches, when Henri de Marsay told about his first love affair. [Another Study of Woman.] In 1832 he rushed in to see Pierre Grassou, borrowed five hundred francs of him, and told him to "cater to his talent" and even to plunge into literature since he was nothing more than a poor painter. At this same time, Joseph Bridau painted the dining-hall in the D'Arthez château. [Pierre Grassou.] He was a friend of Marie Gaston, and was attendant at his marriage with Louise de Chaulieu, widow of Macumer, in 1833. [Letters of Two Brides.] He also assisted at the wedding of Steinbock with Hortense Hulot, and in 1838, at the instigation of Stidmann, clubbed in with Léon de Lora to raise four thousand francs for the Pole, who was imprisoned for debt. He had made the portrait of Josépha Mirah. [Cousin Betty.] In 1839, at Mme. Montcornet's, Joseph Bridau praised the talent and character displayed by Dorlange, the sculptor. [The Member for Arcis.]

Bridau (Flore Brazier, Madame Philippe), born in 1787 at Vatan Indre, known as "La Rabouilleuse," on account of her uncle having put her to work, when a child, at stirring up (to "rabouiller") the streamlets, so that he might find crayfishes. She was noticed on account of her great beauty by Dr. Rouget of Issoudun, and taken to his home in 1799. Jean-Jacques Rouget, the doctor's son, became much enamored of her, but obtained favor only through his money. On her part she was smitten with Maxence Gilet, whom she entertained in the house of the old bachelor at the latter's expense. But everything was changed by the arrival of Philippe Bridau at Issoudun. Gilet was killed in a duel, and Rouget married La Rabouilleuse in 1823. Left a widow soon after, she married the soldier. She died in Paris in 1828, abandoned by her husband, in the greatest distress, a prey to innumerable terrible complaints, the products of the dissolute life into which Philippe Bridau had designedly thrown her. She dwelt then on rue du Houssay, on the fifth floor. She left here for the Dubois Hospital in Faubourg Saint-Denis. [A Bachelor's Establishment.]

Bridau (Madame Joseph), only daughter of Leger, an old farmer, afterwards a multi-millionaire at Beaumont-sur-Oise; married to the painter Joseph Bridau about 1839. [A Bachelor's Establishment.]

Brigaut (Major), of Pen-Hoël, Vendée; retired major of the Catholic Army which contested with the French Republic. A man of iron, but devout and entirely unselfish. He had served under Charette, Mercier, the Baron du Guénie and the Marquis de Montauran. He died in 1819, six months after Mme. Lorrain, the widow of a major in the Imperial Army, whom he was said to have consoled on the loss of her husband. Major Brigaut had received twenty-seven wounds. [Pierrette. The Chouans.]

Brigaut (Jacques), son of Major Brigaut; born about 1811. Childhood companion of Pierrette Lorrain, whom he loved in innocent fashion similar to that of Paul and Virginia, and whose love was reciprocated in the same way. When Pierrette was sent to Provins, to the home of the Rogrons, her relatives, Jacques also went to this town and worked at the carpenter's trade. He was present at the death-bed of the young girl and immediately thereafter enlisted as a soldier; he became head of a battalion, after having several times sought death vainly. [Pierrette.]

Brigitte. (*See* Cottin, Madame.)

Brigitte, servant of Chesnel from 1795 on. In 1824 she was still with him in rue du Bercail, Alençon, at the time of the pranks of the young D'Esgrignon. Brigitte humored the gormandizing of her master, the only weakness of the goodman. [Jealousies of a Country Town.]

Brignolet, clerk with lawyer Bordin in 1806. [A Start in Life.]

Brisetout (Héloïse), mistress of Célestin Crevel in 1838, at the time when he was elected mayor. She succeeded Josépha Mirah, in a little house on rue Chauchat, after having lived on rue Notre-Dame-de Lorette. [Cousin Betty.] In 1844-1845 she was *première danseuse* in the Théâtre du Boulevard, when she was claimed by both Bixiou and Gaudissart, her manager. She was a very literary young woman, much spoken of in Bohemian circles for elegance and graciousness. She knew all the great artists, and favored her kinsman, the musician Garangeot. [Cousin Pons.] Towards the end of the reign of Louis Philippe, she had Isidore Baudoyer for a "protector"; he was then mayor of the arrondissement of Paris, which included the Palais Royale. [The Middle Classes.]

Brisset, a celebrated physician of Paris, time of Louis Philippe. A materialist and successor to Bichat, and Cabanis. At the head of the "Organists," opposed to Caméristus head of the "Vitalists." He was called in consultation regarding Raphaël de Valentin, whose condition was serious. [The Magic Skin.]

Brochon, a half-pay soldier who, in 1822, tended the horses and did chores for Moreau, manager of Presles, the estate of the Comte de Sérizy. [A Start in Life.]

Brossard (Madame), widow received at Mme. de Bargeton's, at Angoulême in 1821. Poor but well-born, she sought to marry her daughter, and in the end, despite her precise dignity and "sour-sweetness," she got along fairly well with the other sex. [Lost Illusions.]

Brossard (Camille du), daughter of the preceding. Born in 1794. Fleshy and imposing. Posed as a good pianist. Not yet married at twenty-seven. [Lost Illusions.]

Brossette (Abbé), born about 1790; curé of Blangy, Burgundy, in 1823, at the time when General de Montcornet was struggling with the peasantry. The abbé himself was an object of their defiance and hatred. He was the fourth son of a good bourgeoisie family of Autun, a faithful prelate, an obstinate Royalist and a man of intelligence. [The Peasantry.] In 1840 he became a curé at Paris, in the Faubourg Saint-Germain, and at the request of Mme. de Grandlieu, he interested himself in removing Calyste du Guénie from the clutches of Mme. de Rochefide and restoring him to his wife. [Béatrix.]

Brouet (Joseph), a Chouan who died of wounds received in the fight of La Pélerine or at the siege of Fougéres, in 1799. [The Chouans.]

Brousson (Doctor), attended the banker Jean-Frédéric Taillefer, a short time before the financier's death. [The Red Inn.]

Bruce (Gabriel), alias Gros-Jean, one of the fiercest Chouans of the Fontaine division. Implicated in the affair of the "Chauffeurs of Mortagne" in 1809. Condemned to death for contumacy. [The Seamy Side of History.]

Bruel (Du), chief of division to the Ministers of the Interior, under the Empire. A friend of Bridau senior, retired on the advent of Restoration. He was on very friendly terms with the widow Bridau, coming each evening for a game of cards at her house, on rue Mazarine, with his old-time colleagues, Claparon and Desroches. These three old employés were called the "Three Sages of Greece" by Mmes. Bridau and Descoings. M. du Bruel was descended of a contractor ennobled at the end of the reign of Louis XIV. He died about 1821. [A Bachelor's Establishment.]

Bruel (Madame du), wife of the preceding. She survived him. She was the mother of the dramatic author Jean-François du Bruel, christened Cursy on the Parisian billboards. Although a bourgeoisie of strict ideas, Mme. du Bruel welcomed the dancer Tullia, who became her daughter-in-law. [A Prince of Bohemia.]

Bruel (Jean-François du), son of the preceding; born about 1797. In 1816 he obtained a place under the Minister of Finance, thanks to the favor of the Duc de Navarreins. [A Bachelor's Establishment.] He was sub-chief of Rabourdin's office when the latter, in 1824, contested with M. Baudoyer for a place of division chief. [The Government Clerks.] In November, 1825, Jean-François du Bruel assisted at a breakfast given at the "Rocher de Cancale" to the clerks of Desroches' office by Frédéric Marest who was treating to celebrate his incoming. He was present also at the orgy which followed at Florentine's home. [A Start in Life.] M. du Bruel successively rose to be chief of bureau, director, councillor of state, deputy, peer of France and commander of the Legion of Honor; he received the title of count and entered one of the classes in the Institute. All this was accomplished through his wife, Claudine Chaffaroux, formerly the dancer, Tullia, whom he married in 1829. [A Prince of Bohemia. The Middle Classes.] For a long time he wrote vaudeville sketches over the name of Cursy. Nathan, the poet, found it necessary to unite with him. Du Bruel would make use of the author's ideas, condensing them into small, sprightly skits which always scored successes for the actors. Du Bruel and Nathan discovered the actress Florine. They were the authors of "L'Alcade dans l'embarras," an imbroglio in three acts, played at the Théâtre du Panorama-Dramatique about 1822, when Florine made her début, playing with Coralie and Bouffé, the latter under the name of Vignol. [A Distinguished Provincial at Paris. A Daughter of Eve.]

Bruel (Claudine Chaffaroux, Madame du), born at Nanterre in 1799. One of the *première danseuses* of the Opéra from 1817 to 1827. For several years she was the mistress of the Duc de Rhétoré [A Bachelor's Establishment], and afterwards of Jean-François du Bruel, who was much in love with her in 1823, and married her in 1829. She had then left the stage. About 1834 she met Charles Edouard de la Palférine and formed a violent attachment for him. In order to please him and pose in his eyes as a great lady, she urged her husband to the constant pursuit of honors, and finally achieved the title of countess. Nevertheless she continued to play the lady of propriety and found entrance into bourgeoisie society. [A Prince of Bohemia. A Distinguished Provincial at Paris. Letters of Two Brides.] In 1840, to please Mme. Colleville, her friend, she tried to obtain a decoration for Thuillier. [The Middle Classes.] Mme. du Bruel bore the name of Tullia on the stage and in the "gallant" circle. She lived then in rue Chauchat, in a house afterwards occupied by Mmes. Mirah and Brisetout, when Claudine moved after her marriage to rue de la Victoire.

Brunet, bailiff at Blangy, Burgundy, in 1823. He was also councillor of the Canton during the Terror, having for practitioners Michel Vert alias Vermichel and Fourchon the elder. [The Peasantry.]

Brunner (Gédéon), father of Frédéric Brunner. At the time of the French Restoration and of Louis Philippe he owned the great Holland House at Frankford-on-the-Main. One of the early railway projectors. He died about 1844, leaving four millions. Calvinist. Twice married. [Cousin Pons.]

Brunner (Madame), first wife of Gédéon Brunner, and mother of Frédéric Brunner. A relative of the Virlaz family, well-to-do Jewish furriers of Leipsic. A converted Jew. Her dowry was the basis of her husband's fortune. She died young, leaving a son aged but twelve. [Cousin Pons.]

Brunner (Madame), second wife of Gédéon Brunner. The only daughter of a German inn-keeper. She had been very badly spoiled by her parents. Sterile, dissipated and prodigal, she made her husband very unhappy, thus avenging the first Mme. Brunner. She was a step-mother of the most abominable sort, launching her stepson into an unbridled life, hoping that debauchery would devour both the child and the Jewish fortune. After ten years of wedded life she died before her parents, having made great inroads upon Gédéon Brunner's property. [Cousin Pons.]

Brunner (Frédéric), only son of Gédéon Brunner, born within the first four years of the century. He ran through his maternal inheritance by silly dissipations, and then helped his friend Wilhelm Schwab to make away with the hundred thousand francs his parents had left him. Without resources and cast adrift by his father he went to Paris in 1835, where, upon the recommendation of Graff, the inn-keeper, he obtained a position with Keller at six hundred francs per annum. In 1843 he was only two thousand francs ahead; but Gédéon Brunner having died, he became a multi-millionaire. Then for friendship's sake he founded, with his chum Wilhelm, the banking house of "Brunner, Schwab & Co.," on rue Richelieu, between rue Neuve-des-Petits-Champs and rue Villedo, in a magnificent building belonging to the tailor, Wolfgang Graff. Frédéric Brunner had been presented by Sylvain Pons to the Camusots de Marville; he would have married their daughter had she not been the only child. The breaking off of this match involved also the relations of Pons with the De Marville family and resulted in the death of the musician. [Cousin Pons.]

Bruno, *valet de chambre* of Corentin at Passy, on rue des Vignes, in 1830. [Scenes from a Courtesan's Life.] About 1840 he was again in the service of Corentin, who was now known as M. du Portail and lived on rue Honoré-Chevalier, at Paris. [The Middle Classes.] This name is sometimes spelled Bruneau.

Brutus, proprietor of the Hôtel des Trois-Maures in the Grande-Rue, Alençon, in 1799, where Alphonse de Montauran met Mlle. de Verneuil for the first time. [The Chouans.]

Buneaud (Madame) ran a bourgeoisie boarding-house in opposition to Mme. Vauquer on the heights of Sainte-Geneviéve, Paris, in 1819. [Father Goriot.]

Butifer, noted hunter, poacher and smuggler, living in the village hard by Grenoble, where Dr. Benassis located, during the Restoration. When the doctor arrived in the country, Butifer drew a bead on him, in a corner of the forest. Later, however, he became entirely devoted to him. He was charged by Genestas with the physical education of this officer's adopted son. It may be that Butifer enlisted in Genestas' regiment, after the death of Dr. Benassis. [The Country Doctor.]

Butscha (Jean), head-clerk of Maitre Latournelle, a notary at Havre in 1829. Born about 1804. The natural son of a Swedish sailor and a Demoiselle Jacmin of Honfleur. A hunchback. A type of intelligence and devotion. Entirely subservient to Modeste Mignon, whom he loved without hope; he aided, by many adroit methods, to bring about her marriage with Ernest de la Briére. Butscha decided that this union would make the young lady happy. [Modeste Mignon.]

C

Cabirolle, in charge of the stages of Minoret-Levrault, postmaster of Nemours. Probably a widower, with one son. About 1837, a sexagenarian, he married Antoinette Patris, called La Bougival, who was over fifty, but whose income amounted to twelve hundred francs. [Ursule Mirouët.]

Cabirolle, son of the preceding. In 1830 he was Dr. Minoret's coachman at Nemours. Later he was coachman for Savinien de Portenduère, after the vicomte's marriage with Ursule Mirouët. [Ursule Mirouët.]

Cabirolle (Madame), wife of Cabirolle senior. Born Antoinette Patris in 1786, of a poor family of La Bresse. Widow of a workman named Pierre alias Bougival; she was usually designated by the latter name. After having been Ursule

Mirouët's nurse, she became Dr. Minoret's servant, marrying Cabirolle about 1837. [Ursule Mirouët.]

Cabirolle (Madame), mother of Florentine, the *danseuse*. Formerly janitress on rue Pastourelle, but living in 1820 with her daughter on rue de Crussol in a modest affluence assured by Cardot the old silk-dealer, since 1817. According to Girondeau, she was a woman of sense. [A Start in Life. A Bachelor's Establishment.]

Cabirolle (Agathe-Florentine), known as Florentine; born in 1804. In 1817, upon leaving Coulon's class, she was discovered by Cardot, the old silk-merchant, and established by him with her mother in a relatively comfortable flat on rue de Crussol. After having been featured at the Gaité theatre, in 1820, she danced for the first time in a spectacular drama entitled "The Ruins of Babylon."[1] Immediately afterwards she succeeded Mariette as *première danseuse* at the theatre of the Porte-Saint-Martin. Then in 1823 she made her début at the Opéra in a trio skit with Mariette and Tullia. At the time when Cardot "protected" her, she had for lover the retired Captain Girondeau, and was intimate with Philippe Bridau, to whom she gave money when in need. In 1825 Florentine occupied Coralie's old flat, now for some three years, and it was at this place that Oscar Husson lost at play the money entrusted to him by his employer, Desroches the attorney, and was surprised by his uncle, Cardot. [A Start in Life. Lost Illusions. A Distinguished Provincial at Paris. A Bachelor's Establishment.]

Cabot (Armand-Hippolyte), a native of Toulouse who, in 1800, established a hair-dressing salon on the Place de la Bourse, Paris. On the advice of his customer, the poet Parny, he had taken the name of Marius, a sobriquet which stuck to the establishment. In 1845 Cabot had earned an income of twenty-four thousand francs and lived at Libourne, while a fifth Marius, called Mougin, managed the business founded by him. [The Unconscious Humorists.]

---

[1] By Renée-Charles Guilbert de Pixérécourt; played for the first time at Paris in 1810.

Cabot (Marie-Anne), known as Lajeunesse, an old servant of Marquis Carol d'Esgrignon. Implicated in the affair of the "Chauffeurs of Mortagne" and executed in 1809. [The Seamy Side of History.]

Cachan, attorney at Angoulême under the Restoration. He and Petit-Claud had similar business interests and the same clients. In 1830 Cachan, now mayor of Marsac, had dealings with the Séchards. [Lost Illusions. Scenes from a Courtesan's Life.]

Cadenet, Parisian wine-merchant, in 1840, on the ground-floor of a furnished lodging-house, corner of rue des Postes and rue des Poules. Cérizet also dwelt there at that time. Cadenet, who was proprietor of the house, had something to do with the transactions of Cérizet, the "banker of the poor." [The Middle Classes.]

Cadignan (Prince de), a powerful lord of the former régime, father of the Duc de Maufrigneuse, father-in-law of the Duc de Navarreins. Ruined by the Revolution, he had regained his properties and income on the accession of the Bourbons. But he was a spendthrift and devoured everything. He also ruined his wife. He died at an advanced age some time before the Revolution of July. [The Secrets of a Princess.] At the end of 1829, the Prince de Cadignan, then Grand Huntsman to Charles X., rode in a great chase where were also found, amid a very aristocratic throng, the Duc d'Hérouville, organizer of the jaunt, Canalis and Ernest de la Briére, all three of whom were suitors for the hand of Modeste Mignon. [Modeste Mignon.]

Cadignan (Prince and Princesse de), son and daughter-in-law of the preceding. (*See* Maufrigneuse, Duc and Duchesse de.)

Cadine (Jenny), actress at the Gymnase theatre, times of Charles X. and Louis Philippe. The most frolicsome of women, the only rival of Déjazet. Born in 1814. Discovered, trained and "protected" from thirteen years old on, by Baron Hulot. Intimate friend of Josépha Mirah. [Cousin Betty.] Between 1835 and 1840, while maintained by Couture, she lived on rue Blanche in a delightful little ground-floor flat with its own garden. Fabien du Ronceret and Mme. Schontz succeeded her here. [Béatrix.] In 1845 she was Massol's mistress and lived on rue de la Victoire. At this time, she apparently led astray in short order Palafox Gazonal, who had been taken to her home by Bixiou and Léon de Lora. [The Unconscious Humorists.] About this time she was the victim of a jewelry theft. After the arrest of the thieves her property was returned by Saint-Estéve ---Vautrin—who was then chief of the special service. [The Member for Arcis.]

Cadot (Mademoiselle), old servant-mistress of Judge Blondet at Alençon, during the Restoration. She pampered her master, and, like him, preferred the elder of the magistrate's two sons. [Jealousies of a Country Town.]

Calvi (Théodore), alias Madeleine. Born in 1803. A Corsican condemned to the galleys for life on account of eleven murders committed by the time he was eighteen. A member of the same gang with Vautrin from 1819 to 1820. Escaped with him. Having assassinated the widow Pigeau of Nanterre, in May, 1830, he was rearrested and this time sentenced to death. The plotting of Vautrin, who bore for him an unnatural affection, saved his life; the sentence was commuted. [Scenes from a Courtesan's Life.]

Cambon, lumber merchant, a deputy mayor to Benassis, in 1829, in a community near Grenoble, and a devoted assistant in the work of regeneration undertaken by the doctor. [The Country Doctor.]

. Cambremer (Pierre), fisherman of Croisic on the Lower-Loire, time of Louis Philippe, who, for the honor of a jeopardized name, had cast his only son into the sea and afterwards remained desolate and a widower on a cliff near by, in expiation of his crime induced by paternal justice. [A Seaside Tragedy. Béatrix.]

Cambremer (Joseph), younger brother of Pierre **Cam**-bremer, father of Pierrette, called Perotte. [A Seaside Tragedy.]

Cambremer (Jacques), only son of Pierre Cambremer and Jacquette Brouin. Spoiled by his parents, his mother especially, he became a rascal of the worst type. Jacques Cambremer evaded justice only by reason of the fact that his father gagged him and cast him into the sea. [A Seaside Tragedy.]

Cambremer (Madame), born Jacquette Brouin, wife of Pierre Cambremer and mother of Jacques. She was of Guérande; was educated; could write "like a clerk"; taught her son to read and this brought about his ruin. She was usually spoken of as the beautiful Brouin. She died a few days after Jacques. [A Seaside Tragedy.]

Cambremer (Pierrette), known as Perotte; daughter of Joseph Cambremer; niece of Pierre and his goddaughter. Every morning the sweet and charming creature came to bring her uncle the bread and water upon which he subsisted. [A Seaside Tragedy.]

Caméristus, celebrated physician of Paris under Louis Philippe; the Ballanche of medicine and one of the defenders of the abstract doctrines of Van Helmont; chief of the "Vitalists" opposed to Brisset who headed the "Organists." He as well as Brisset was called in consultation regarding a very serious malady afflicting Raphaël de Valentin. [The Magic Skin.]

Camps (Octave de), lover then husband of Mme. Firmiani. She made him restore the entire fortune of a family named Bourgneuf, ruined in a lawsuit by Octave's father, thus reducing him to the necessity of making a living by teaching mathematics. He was only twenty-two years old when he met Mme. Firmiani. He married her first at Gretna Green. The marriage at Paris took place in 1824 or 1825. Before marriage, Octave de Camps lived on rue de l'Observance. He was a descendant of the famous Abbé de Camps, so well known among bookmen and savants. [Madame Firmiani.] Octave de Camps reappears as an ironmaster, during the reign of Louis Philippe. At this time he rarely resided at Paris. [The Member for Arcis.]

Camps (Madame Octave de), *née* Cadignan; niece of the old Prince de Cadignan; cousin of the Duc de Maufrigneuse. In 1813, at the age of sixteen, she married M. Firmiani, receiver-general in the department of Montenotte. M. Firmiani died in Greece about 1822, and she became Mme. de Camps in 1824 or 1825. At this time she dwelt on rue du Bac and had entrée into the home of Princesse de Blamont-Chauvry, the oracle of Faubourg Saint-Germain. An accomplished and excellent lady, loved even by her rivals, the Duchesse de Maufrigneuse, her cousin, Mme. de Macumer —Louise de Chaulieu—and the Marquise d'Espard. [Madame Firmiani.] She welcomed and protected Mme. Xavier Rabourdin. [The Government Clerks.] At the close of 1824 she gave a ball where Charles de Vandenesse made the acquaintance of Mme. d'Aiglemont whose lover he became. [A Woman of Thirty.] In 1834 Mme. Octave de Camps tried to check the slanders going the rounds at the expense of Mme. Félix de Vandenesse, who had compromised herself somewhat on account of the poet Nathan; and Mme. de Camps gave the young woman some good advice. [A Daughter of Eve.] On another occasion she gave exceedingly good counsel to Mme. de l'Estorade, who was afraid of being smitten with Sallenauve. [The Member for Arcis.] Mme. Firmiani, "that was," shared her time between Paris and the furnaces of M. de Camps; but she gave the latter much the preference—at least so said one of her intimate friends, Mme. de l'Estorade. [The Member for Arcis.]

Camuset, one of Bourignard's assumed names.

Camusot, silk-merchant, rue des Bourdonnais, Paris, under the Restoration. Born in 1765. Son-in-law and successor of Cardot, whose eldest daughter he had married. At that time he was a widower, his first wife being a Demoiselle Pons, sole heiress of the celebrated Pons family, embroiderers to the Court during the Empire. About 1834 Camusot retired from business, and became a member of the Manufacturers' Council, deputy, peer of France and baron. He had four children. In 1821-1822 he maintained Coralie, who became so violently enamored of Lucien de Rubempré. Although she abandoned him for Lucien, he promised the poet, after the actress' death, that he would purchase for her a permanent plot in the cemetery of Pére-Lachaise. [A Distinguished Provincial at Paris. A Bachelor's Establishment. Cousin Pons.] Later he was intimate with Fanny Beaupré for some time. [The Muse of the Department.] He and his wife were present at César Birotteau's big ball in December, 1818; he was also chosen commissary-judge of the perfumer's bankruptcy, instead of Gobenheim-Keller, who was first designated. [César Birotteau.] He had dealings with the Gillaumes, clothing merchants, rue Saint-Denis. [At the Sign of the Cat and Racket.]

Camusot de Marville, son of Camusot the silk-merchant by his first marriage. Born about 1794. During Louis Philippe's reign he took the name of a Norman estate and green, Marville, in order to distinguish between himself and a half-brother. In 1824, then a judge at Alençon, he helped render an alibi decision in favor of Victurnien d'Esgrignon, who really was guilty. [Cousin Pons. Jealousies of a Country Town.] He was judge at Paris in 1828, and was appointed to replace Popinot in the court which was to render a decision concerning the appeal for interdiction presented by Mme. d'Espard against her husband. [The Commission in Lunacy.] In May, 1830, in the capacity of judge of instruction, he prepared a report tending to the liberation of Lucien de Rubempré, accused of assassinating Esther Gobseck. But the suicide of the poet rendered the proposed measure useless, besides upsetting, momentarily, the ambitious projects of the magistrate. [Scenes from a Courtesan's Life.] Camusot de Marville had been president of the Court of Nantes. In 1844 he was president of the Royal Court of Paris and commander of the Legion of Honor. At this time he lived in a house on rue de Hanovre, purchased by him in 1834, where he received the musician Pons, a cousin of his. The President de Marville was elected deputy in 1846. [Cousin Pons.]

Camusot de Marville (Madame), born Thirion, Marie-Cécile-Amélie, in 1798. Daughter of an usher of the Cabinet of Louis XVIII. Wife of the magistrate. In 1814 she frequented the studio of the painter Servin, who had a class for young ladies. This studio contained two factions; Mlle. Thirion headed the party of the nobility, though of ordinary birth, and persecuted Ginevra di Piombo, of the Bonapartist party. [The Vendetta.] In 1818 she was invited to accompany her father and mother to the famous ball of César Birotteau. It was about the time her marriage with Camusot de Marville was being considered. [César Birotteau.] This wedding took place in 1819, and immediately the imperious young woman gained the upper hand with the judge, making him follow her own will absolutely and in the interests of her boundless ambition. It was she who brought about the discharge of the young d'Esgrignon in 1824, and the suicide of Lucien de Rubempré in 1830. Through her, the Marquis d'Espard failed of interdiction. However, Mme. de Marville had no influence over her father-in-law, the senior Camusot, whom she bored dreadfully and importuned excessively. She caused, also, by her evil treatment, the death of Sylvain Pons "the poor relation," inheriting with her husband his fine collection of curios. [Jealousies of a Country Town. Scenes from a Courtesan's Life. Cousin Pons.]

Camusot (Charles), son of the preceding couple. He died young, at a time when his parents had neither land nor title of Marville, and when they were in almost straitened circumstances. [Cousin Pons.]

Camusot de Marville (Cécile). (See Popinot, Vicomtesse.)

Canalis (Constant-Cyr-Melchior, Baron de), poet—chief of the "Angelic" school—deputy minister, peer of France,

member of the French Academy, commander of the Legion
of Honor. Born at Canalis, Corréze, in 1800. About 1821
he became the lover of Mme. de Chaulieu, who was constantly
aiding him to high positions, but who, at the same time,
was always very exacting. Not long after, Canalis is seen
at the opera in Mme. d'Espard's box, being presented to
Lucien de Rubempré. From 1824 he was the fashionable
poet. [Letters of Two Brides. A Distinguished Provincial
at Paris.] In 1829 he lived at number 29 rue Paradis-
Poissonière (now simply rue Paradis) and was master of
requests in the Council of State. This is the time when
he was in correspondence with Modeste Mignon and wished
to espouse that rich heiress. [Modeste Mignon.] Shortly
after 1830, now a great man, he was present at Mlle. des
Touches', when Henri de Marsay told of his first love affair.
Canalis took part in the conversation and uttered a most
vigorous tirade against Napoleon. [The Magic Skin. Another
Study of Woman.] In 1838 he married the daughter of
Moreau (de l'Oise), who brought him a very large dowry.
[A Start in Life.] In October, 1840, he and Mme. de Rochefide
were present at a performance at the Variétés theatre,
where that dangerous woman was encountered again after
a lapse of three years by Calyste du Guénie. [Béatrix.]
In 1845 Canalis was pointed out in the Chamber of Deputies
by Léon de Lora to Palefox Gazonal. [The Unconscious
Humorists.] In 1845, he consented to act as second to Sallenauve in his duel with Maxime de Trailles. [The Member
for Arcis.]

Canalis (Baronne Melchior de), wife of the preceding
and daughter of M. and Mme. Moreau (de l'Oise). About
the middle of the reign of Louis Philippe, she being then
recently married, she made a journey to Seine-et-Oise. She
went first to Beaumont and Presles. Mme. de Canalis
with her daughter and the Academician, occupied Pierrotin's
stage-coach. [A Start in Life.]

Cane (Marco-Facino), known as Pére Canet, a blind old
man, an inmate of the Hospital des Quinze-Vingts, who

during the Restoration followed the vocation of musician, at Paris. He played the clarionet at a ball of the working-people of rue de Charenton, on the occasion of the wedding of Mme. Vaillant's sister. He said he was a Venetian, Prince de Varése, a descendant of the *condottiere* Facino Cane, whose conquests fell into the hands of the Duke of Milan. He told strange stories regarding his patrician youth. He died in 1820, more than an octogenarian. He was the last of the Canes on the senior branch, and he transmitted the title of Prince de Varése to a relative, Emilio Memmi. [Facino Cane. Massimilla Doni.]

Cante-Croix (Marquis de), under-lieutenant in one of the regiments which tarried at Angouléme from November, 1807, to March, 1808, while on its way to Spain. He was a Colonel at Wagram on July 6, 1809, although only twenty-six years old, when a shot crushed over his heart the picture of Mme. de Bargeton, whom he loved. [Lost Illusions.]

Cantinet, an old glass-dealer, and beadle of Saint-François church, Marais, Paris, in 1845; dwelt on rue d'Orléans. A drunken idler. [Cousin Pons.]

Cantinet (Madame), wife of preceding ; renter of seats in Saint-François. Last nurse to Sylvain Pons, and a tool to the interests of Fraisier and Poulain. [Cousin Pons.]

Cantinet, Junior, would have been made beadle of Saint-François, where his father and mother were employed, but he preferred the theatre. He was connected with the Cirque-Olympique in 1845. He caused his mother sorrow, by a dissolute life and by forcible inroads on the maternal purse. [Cousin Pons.]

Capraja, a noble Venetian, a recognized dilettante, living only by and through music. Nicknamed "Il Fanatico." Known by the Duke and Duchess Catanco and their friends. [Massimilla Doni.]

Carabine, assumed name of Séraphine Sinet, which name see.

Carbonneau, physician whom the Comte de Mortsauf spoke of consulting about his wife, in 1820, instead of Dr. Origet, whom he fancied to be unsatisfactory. [The Lily of the Valley.]

Carcado (Madame de), founder of a Parisian benevolent society, for which Mme. de la Baudraye was appointed collector, in March, 1843, on the request of some priests, friends of Mme. Piédefer. This choice resulted, noteworthily, in the re-entrance into society of the "muse," who had been beguiled and compromised by her relations with Lousteau. [The Muse of the Department.]

Cardanet (Madame de), grandmother of Mme. de Senonches. [Lost Illusions.]

Cardinal (Madame), Parisian fish-vender, daughter of one Toupillier, a carrier. Widow of a well-known marketman. Niece of Toupillier the pauper of Saint-Sulpice, from whom in 1840, with Cérizet's assistance, she tried to capture the hidden treasure. This woman had three sisters, four brothers and three uncles, who would have shared with her the pauper's bequest. The scheming of Mme. Cardinal and Cérizet was frustrated by M. du Portail—Corentin. [The Middle Classes.]

Cardinal (Olympe). (*See* Cérizet, Madame.)

Cardot (Jean-Jérôme-Séverin), born in 1755. Head-clerk in an old silk-house, the "Golden Cocoon," rue des Bour-. donnais. He bought the establishment in 1793, at the "maximum" moment, and in ten years had made a large fortune, thanks to the dowry of one hundred thousand francs brought him by his wife; she was a Demoiselle Husson, and gave him four children. Of these, the elder daughter married Camusot, who succeeded his father-in-law; the second, Marianne, married Protez, of the firm of Protez & Chiffreville; the elder son became a notary; the younger son, Joseph, took an interest in Matifat's drug business. Cardot was the "protector" of the actress, Florentine, whom he discovered and started.. In 1822 he lived at Belleville in one of the first houses above Courtille; he had then been a widower for six years. He was an uncle of Oscar Husson, and had taken some interest in and helped the dolt, until an incident occurred that changed everything: the old man discovered the young fellow asleep one morning, on one of Florentine's divans, after an orgy wherein he had squandered the money entrusted to him by his employer, Desroches the attorney. [A Start in Life. Lost Illusions. A Distinguished Provincial at Paris. A Bachelor's Establishment.] Cardot had dealings with the Gillaumes, clothiers, rue Saint-Denis. [At the Sign of the Cat and Racket.] He and his entire family were invited to the great ball given by César Birotteau, December 17, 1818. [César Birotteau.]

Cardot, elder son of the preceding. Parisian notary, successor of Sorbier. Born in 1794. Married to a Demoiselle Chiffreville, of a family of celebrated chemists. Three children were born to them: a son who in 1836 was fourth clerk in his father's business, and should have succeeded him, but dreamed instead of literary fame; Félicie, who married Berthier; and another daughter, born in 1824. The notary Cardot maintained Malaga, during the reign of Louis Philippe. [The Muse of the Department. A Man of Business. Jealousies of a Country Town.] He was attorney for Pierre Grassou, who deposited his savings with him every quarter. [Pierre Grassou.] He was also notary to the Thuilliers, and, in 1840, had presented in their drawing-rooms, on rue Saint-Dominique d'Enfer, Godeschal an aspirant for the hand of Celeste Colleville. After living on Place du Châtelet, Cardot became one of the tenants of the house purchased by the Thuilliers, near the Madeleine. [The Middle Classes.] In 1844 he was mayor and deputy of Paris. [Cousin Pons.]

Cardot (Madame) née Chiffreville, wife of Cardot the notary. Very devoted, but a "wooden" woman, a "veritable penitential brush." About 1840 she lived on Place du Châtelet, Paris, with her husband. At this time, the notary's wife took her daughter Félicie to rue des Martyrs, to the home of Etienne Lousteau, whom she had planned to have for a son-in-law, but whom she finally threw over on account of the journalist's dissipated ways. [The Muse of the Department.]

Cardot (Félicie or Félicité). (*See* Berthier, Madame.)

Carigliano (Maréchal, Duc de), one of the illustrious soldiers of the Empire; husband of a Demoiselle Malin de Gondreville, whom he worshiped, obeyed and stood in awe of, but who deceived him. [At the Sign of the Cat and Racket.] In 1819, Maréchal de Carigliano gave a ball where Eugéne de Rastignac was presented by his cousin, the Vicomtesse de Beauséant, at the time he entered the world of fashion. [Father Goriot.] During the Restoration he owned a beautiful house near the Elysée-Bourbon, which he sold to M. de Lanty. [Sarrasine.]

Carigliano (Duchesse de), wife of the preceding, daughter of Senator Malin de Gondreville. At the end of the Empire, when thirty-six years of age, she was the mistress of the young Colonel d'Aiglemont, and of Sommervieux, the painter, almost at the same time; the latter had recently wedded Augustine Guillaume. The Duchesse de Carigliano received a visit from Mme. de Sommervieux, and gave her very ingenious advice concerning the method of reconquering her husband, and binding him forever to her by her coquetry. [At the Sign of the Cat and Racket.] In 1821-1822 she had an opera-box near Mme. d'Espard. Sixte du Châtelet came to her to make his acknowledgments on the evening when Lucien de Rubempré, a newcomer in Paris, cut such a sorry figure at the theatre in company with Mme. de Bargeton. [A Distinguished Provincial at Paris.] 'Twas the Duchesse de‧ Carigliano who, after great effort, found a wife suited to General de Montcornet, in the person of Mlle. de Troisville. [The Peasantry.] Mme. de Carigliano, although a Napoleonic duchesse, was none the less devoted to the House of the Bourbons, being attached especially to the Duchesse de Berry. Becoming imbued also with a high degree of piety, she visited nearly every year a retreat of the Ursulines of Arcis-sur-Aube. In 1839 Sallenauve's friends counted on the duchesse's support to elect him deputy. [The Member for Arcis.]

Carmagnola (Giambattista), an old Venetian gondolier, entirely devoted to Emilio Memmi, in 1820. [Massimilla Doni.]

Carnot (Lazare-Nicolas-Marguerite), born at Nolay—Cote-d'Or—in 1753; died in 1823. In June, 1800, while Minister of War, he was present in company with Talleyrand, Fouché and Siéyés, at a council held at the home of the Minister of Foreign Affairs, rue du Bac, when the overthrow of First Consul Bonaparte was discussed. [The Gondreville Mystery.]

Caroline (Mademoiselle), governess, during the Empire, of the four children of M. and Mme. de Vandenesse. "She was a terror." [The Lily of the Valley.]

Caroline, chambermaid of the Marquis de Listomère, in 1827-1828, on rue Saint-Dominique-Saint-Germain, Paris, when the marquis received a letter from Eugéne de Rastignac intended for Delphine de Nucingen. [A Study of Woman.]

Caroline, servant of the Thuilliers in 1840. [The Middle Classes.]

Caron, lawyer, in charge of the affairs of Mlle. Gamard at Tours in 1826. He acted against Abbé François Birotteau. [The Vicar of Tours.]

Carpentier, formerly captain in the Imperial Army, retired at Issoudun during the Restoration. He had a position in the mayor's office. He was allied by marriage to one of the strongest families of the city, the Borniche-Héreaus. ·He was an intimate friend of the artillery captain, Mignonnet, sharing with him his aversion for Commandant Maxence Gilet. Carpentier and Mignonnet were seconds of Philippe Bridau in his duel with the chief of the "Knights of Idlesse." [A Bachelor's Establishment.]

Carpi (Benedetto), jailer of a Venetian prison, where Facino Cane was confined between the years 1760 and 1770. Bribed by the prisoner, he fled with him, carrying a portion of the hidden treasure of the Republic. But he perished soon after, by drowning, while trying to cross the sea. [Facino Cane.]

Carthagenova, a superb basso of the Fenice theatre at Venice. In 1820 he sang the part of Moses in Rossini's opera, with Genovese and La Tinti. [Massimilla Doni.]

Cartier, gardener in the Montparnasse quarter, Paris, during the reign of Louis Philippe. In 1838 he supplied flowers to M. Bernard—Baron de Bourlac—for his daughter Vanda. [The Seamy Side of History.]

Cartier (Madame), wife of the preceding; vender of milk, eggs and vegetables to Mme. Vauthier, landlady of a miserable boarding-house on Boulevard Montparnasse, and also to M. Bernard, lessee of real estate. [The Seamy Side of History.]

Casa-Réal (Duc de), younger brother of Mme. Balthazar Claés; related to the Evangelistas of Bordeaux; of an illus-- trious family under the Spanish monarchy; his sister had renounced the paternal succession in order to procure for him a marriage worthy of a house so noble. He died young, in 1805, leaving to Mme. Claés, a considerable fortune in money. [The Quest of the Absolute. A Marriage Settlement.]

Castagnould, mate of the "Mignon," a pretty, hundred-ton vessel owned by Charles Mignon, the captain. In this he made several important and prosperous voyages, from 1826 to 1829. Castagnould was a Provençal and an old servant of the Mignon family. [Modeste Mignon.]

Castanier (Rodolphe), retired chief of squadron in the dragoons, under the Empire. Cashier of Baron de Nucingen during the Restoration. Wore the decoration of the Legion of Honor. He maintained Mme. de la Garde—Aquilina—

and on her account, in 1821, he counterfeited the banker's name on a letter of credit for a considerable amount. John Melmoth, an Englishman, got him out of this scrape by exchanging his own individuality for that of the old officer. Castanier was thus all-powerful, but becoming promptly at outs with the proceeding, he adopted the same tactics of exchange, transferring his power to a financier named Claparon. Castanier was a Southerner. He had seen service from sixteen till nearly forty. [Melmoth Reconciled.]

Castanier (Madame), wife of the preceding, married during the first Empire. Her family—that of the bourgeoisie of Nancy—fooled Castanier about the size of her dowry and her "expectations." Mme. Castanier was honest, ugly and sour-tempered. She was separated from her husband, to his relief, and for several years previous to 1821 lived in the suburbs of Strasbourg. [Melmoth Reconciled.]

Casteran (De), a very ancient aristocracy of Normandy; related to William the Conqueror; allied with the Verneuils, the Esgrignons and the Troisvilles. The name is pronounced "Cateran." A Demoiselle Blanche de Casteran was the mother of Mlle. de Verneuil, and died Abbess of Notre-Dame de Séez. [The Chouans.] In 1807 Mme. de la Chanterie, then a widow, was hospitably received in Normandy by the Casterans. [The Seamy Side of History.] In 1822 a venerable couple, Marquis and Marquise de Casteran visited the drawing-room of Marquis d'Esgrignon at Alençon. [Jealousies of a Country Town.] The Marquise de Rochefide, *née* Béatrix-Maximilienne-Rose de Casteran, was the younger daughter of a Marquis de Casteran who wished to marry off both his daughters without dowries, and thus save his entire fortune for his son, the Comte de Casteran. [Béatrix.] A Comte de Casteran, son-in-law of the Marquis de Troisville, relative of Mme. de Montcornet, was prefect of a department of Burgundy between 1820 and 1825. [The Peasantry.]

Cataneo (Duke), noble Sicilian, born in 1773; first husband of Massimilla Doni. Physically ruined by early debaucheries, he was a husband only in name, living only by and through the influence of music. Very wealthy, he had educated Clara Tinti, discovered by him when still a child and a simple tavern servant. The young girl became, thanks to him, the celebrated prima donna of the Fenice theatre, at Venice in 1820. The wonderful tenor Genovese, of the same theatre, was also a protégé of Duke Cataneo, who paid him a high salary to sing only with La Tinti. The Duke Cataneo cut a sorry figure. [Massimilla Doni.]

Cataneo (Duchess), *née* Massimilla Doni, wife of the preceding; married later to Emilio Memmi, Prince de Varése. (*See* Princesse de Varése.)

Catherine, an old woman in the service of M. and Mme. Saillard, in 1824. [The Government Clerks.]

Catherine, chambermaid and foster sister of Laurence de Cinq-Cygne in 1803. A handsome girl of nineteen. According to Gothard, Catherine was in all her mistress' secrets and furthered all her schemes. [The Gondreville Mystery.]

Cavalier, Fendant's partner; both were book-collectors, publishers and venders in Paris, on rue Serpente in 1821. Cavalier traveled for the house, whose firm name appeared as "Fendant and Cavalier." The two associates failed shortly after having published, without success, the famous romance of Lucien de Rubempré, "The Archer of Charles IX.," which title they had changed for one more fantastic. [A Distinguished Provincial at Paris.] In 1838, a firm of Cavalier published "The Spirit of Modern Law" by Baron Bourlac, sharing the profits with the author. [The Seamy Side of History.]

Cayron, of Languedoc, a vender of parasols, umbrellas and canes, on rue Saint-Honoré in a house adjacent to that inhabited by Birotteau the perfumer in 1818. With the consent of the landlord, Molineux, Cayron sublet two apartments over his shop to his neighbor. He fared badly in business, suddenly disappearing a short time after the grand ball given by Birotteau. Cayron admired Birotteau. [César Birotteau.]

Célestin, *valet de chambre* of Lucien de Rubempré, on the Malaquais quai, in the closing years of the reign of Charles X. [Scenes from a Courtesan's Life.]

Cérizet, orphan from the Foundling Hospital, Paris; born in 1802; an apprentice of the celebrated printers Didot, at whose office he was noticed by David Séchard, who took him to Angouléme and employed him in his own shop, where Cérizet performed triple duties of form-maker, compositor and proof-reader. Presently he betrayed his master, and by leaguing with the Cointet Brothers, rivals of David Séchard, he obtained possession of his property. [Lost Illusions.] Following this he was an actor in the provinces; managed a Liberal paper during the Restoration; was sub-prefect at the beginning of the reign of Louis Philippe; and finally was a "man of business." In the latter capacity he was sentenced to two years' imprisonment for swindling. After business partnership with Georges d'Estourny, and later with Claparon, he stranded and was reduced to transcrib-ing for a justice of the peace in the quartier Saint-Jacques. At the same time he began lending money on short time, and by speculating with the poorer class he acquired a certain competence. Although thoroughly debauched, Cérizet mar-ried Olympe Cardinal about 1840. At this time he was implicated in the intrigues of Théodose de la Peyrade and in the interests of Jérôme Thuillier. Becoming possessed of a note of Maxime de Trailles in 1833, he succeeded by Scapinal tactics in obtaining face value of the paper. [A Man of Business. Scenes from a Courtesan's Life. The Middle Classes.]

Cérizet (Olympe Cardinal, Madame), wife of foregoing; born about 1824; daughter of Mme. Cardinal the fish-dealer. Actress at the Bobino, Luxembourg, then at the Folies-Dramatiques, where she made her début in "The Telegraph of Love." At first she was intimate with the first comedian.

Afterwards she had Julien Minard for lover. From the father of the latter she received thirty thousand francs to renounce his son. This money she used as a dowry and it aided in consummating her marriage with Cérizet. [The Middle Classes.]

Césarine, laundry girl at Alençon. Mistress of the Chevalier de Valois, and mother of a child that was attributed to the old aristocrat. It was also said in the town, in 1816, that he had married Césarine clandestinely. These rumors greatly annoyed the chevalier, since he had hoped at this time to wed Mlle. Cormon. Césarine, the sole legatee of her lover, received an income of only six hundred livres. [Jealousies of a Country Town.]

Césarine, dancer at the Opéra de Paris in 1822; an acquaintance of Philippe Bridau, who at one time thought of breaking off with her on account of his uncle Rouget at Issoudun. [A Bachelor's Establishment.]

Chabert (Hyacinthe), Count, grand officer of the Legion of Honor, colonel of a cavalry regiment. Left for dead on the battlefield of Eylau (February 7-8, 1807). He was healed at Heilsberg, then locked up in an insane asylum at Stuttgart. Returning to France after the downfall of the Empire, he lived, in 1818, in straitened circumstances, with the herdsman Vergniaud, an old lieutenant of his regiment, on rue du Petit-Banquier, Paris. After having sought without arousing scandal to make good his rights with Rose Chapotel, his wife, now married to Count Ferraud, he sank again into poverty and was convicted of vagrancy. He ended his days at the Hospital de Bicétre; they had begun at the Foundling Hospital. [Colonel Chabert.]

Chabert (Madame), *née* Rose Chapotel. (*See* Ferraud Comtesse.)

Chaboisseau, an old bookseller , book-lender, something of a usurer, a millionaire living in 1821-1822 on quai Saint-Michel, where he discussed a business deal with Lucien de Rubempré, who had been piloted there by Lousteau.

[A Distinguished Provincial at Paris.] He was a friend of Gobseck and of Gigonnet and with them he frequented, in 1824, the Café Thémis. [The Government Clerks.] During the reign of Louis Philippe he had dealings with the Cérizet-Claparon Company. [A Man of Business.]

Chaffaroux, building-contractor, one of César Birotteau's creditors [César Birotteau]; uncle of Claudine Chaffaroux who became Mme. du Bruel. Rich and a bachelor, he showered much affection upon his niece; she had helped him to launch into business. He died in the second half of the reign of Louis Philippe, leaving an income of forty thousand francs to the former *danseuse*. [A Prince of Bohemia.] In 1840 he did some work on an unfinished house in the suburbs of the Madeleine, purchased by the Thuilliers. [The Middle Classes.]

Chamarolles (Mesdemoiselles), conducted a boarding-school for young ladies at Bourges, at the beginning of the century. This school enjoyed a great reputation in the department. Here was educated Anna Grosetête, who later married the third son of Comte de Fontaine; also Dinah Piédefer who became Mme. de la Baudraye. [The Muse of the Department.]

Champagnac, charman of Limoges, a widower, native of Auvergne. In 1797 Jérôme-Baptiste Sauviat married Champagnac's daughter, who was at least thirty. [The Country Parson.]

Champignelles (De), an illustrious Norman family. In 1822 a Marquis de Champignelles was the head of the leading house of the country at Bayeux. Through marriage this family was allied with the Navarreins, the Blamont-Chauvries, and the Beauséants. Marquis de Champignelles introduced Gaston de Nueil to Mme. de Beauséant's home. [The Deserted Woman.] A M. de Champignelles presented Mme. de la Chanterie to Louis XVIII., at the beginning of the Restoration. The Baronne de la Chanterie was formerly a Champignelles. [The Seamy Side of History.]

Champion (Maurice), a young boy of Montégnac, Haute-Vienne, son of the postmaster of that commune; employed as stable-boy at Mme. Graslin's, time of Louis Philippe. [The Country Parson.]

Champlain (Pierre), vine-dresser, a neighbor of the crazy Margaritis, at Vouvray in 1831. [Gaudissart the Great.]

Champy (Madame de), name given to Esther Gobseck.

Chandour (Stanislas de), born in 1781; one of the habitues of the Bargeton's drawing-room at Angouléme, and the "beau" of that society. In 1821 he was decorated. He obtained some success with the ladies by his sarcastic pleasantries in the fashion of the eighteenth century. Having spread about town a slander relating to Mme. de Bargeton and Lucien de Rubempré, he was challenged by her husband and was wounded in the neck by a bullet, which wound brought on him a kind of chronic twist of the neck. [Lost Illusions.]

Chandour (Amélie de), wife of the preceding; charming conversationalist, but troubled with an unacknowledged asthma. In Angouléme she posed as the antagonist of her friend, Mme. de Bargeton. [Lost Illusions.]

Chanor, partner of Florent, both being workers and dealers in bronze, rue des Tournelles, Paris, time of Louis Philippe. Wenceslas Steinbock was at first an apprentice and afterwards an employe of the firm. [Cousin Betty.] In 1845, Frédéric Brunner obtained a watch-chain and a cane-knob from the firm of Florent & Chanor. [Cousin Pons.]

Chantonnit, mayor of Riceys, near Besançon, between 1830 and 1840. He was a native of Neufchatel, Switzerland, and a Republican. He was involved in a lawsuit with the Wattevilles. Albert Savarus pleaded for them against Chantonnit. [Albert Savarus.]

Chapeloud (Abbé), canon of the Church of Saint-Gatien at Tours. Intimate friend of the Abbé Birotteau, to whom he bequeathed on his death-bed, in 1824, a set of furniture and a library of considerable value which had been ardently coveted by the naïve priest. [The Vicar of Tours.]

Chaperon (Abbé), Curé of Némours, Seine-et-Marne, after the re-establishment of religious worship following the Revolution. Born in 1755, died in 1841, in that city. He was a friend of Dr. Minoret and helped educate Ursule Mirouët, a niece of the physician. He was nicknamed "the Fenélon of Gâtinais." His successor was the curé of Saint-Lange, the priest who tried to give religious consolation to Mme. d'Aiglemont, a prey to despair. [Ursule Mirouët.]

Chapotel (Rose), family name of Mme. Chabert, who afterwards became Comtesse Ferraud, which name see.

Chapoulot (Monsieur and Madame), formerly lace-dealers of rue Saint-Denis in 1845. Tenants of the house, rue de Normandie, where lived Pons and Schmucke. One evening, when M. and Mme. Chapoulot accompanied by their daughter Victorine were returning from the Théâtre de l'Ambigu-Comique, they met Héloïse Brisetout on the landing, and a little conjugal scene resulted. [Cousin Pons.]

Chapuzot (Monsieur and Madame), porters of Marguerite Turquet, known as Malaga, rue des Fosses-du-Temple at Paris in 1836; afterwards her servants and her confidants when she was maintained by Thaddée Paz. [The Imaginary Mistress.]

Chapuzot, chief of division to the prefecture of police in the time of Louis Philippe. Visited and consulted in 1843 by Victorin Hulot on account of Mme. de Saint-Estéve. [Cousin Betty.]

Chardin (Pére), old mattress-maker, and a sot. In 1843 he acted as a go-between for Baron Hulot under the name of Pére Thoul, and Cousin Betty, who concealed from the family the infamy of its head. [Cousin Betty.]

Chardin, son of the preceding. At first a watchman for Johann Fischer, commissariat for the Minister of War in the province of Oran from 1838 to 1841. Afterwards *claqueur* in a theatre under Braulard, and designated at that time by the name of Idamore. A brother of Elodie Chardin whom he procured for Pére Thoul in order to release Olympe Bijou whose lover he himself was. After Olympe Bijou, Chardin paid court in 1843 to a young *première* of the Théâtre des Funambules. [Cousin Betty.]

Chardin (Elodie), sister of Chardin alias Idamore; lace-mender; mistress of Baron Hulot—Pére Thoul—in 1843. She lived then with him at number 7 rue des Bernardins. She had succeeded Olympe Bijou in the old fellow's affections. [Cousin Betty.]

Chardon, retired surgeon of the army of the Republic; established as a druggist at Angoulême during the Empire. He was engrossed in trying to cure the gout, and he also dreamed of replacing rag-paper with paper made from vege-table fibre, after the manner of the Chinese. He died at the beginning of the Restoration at Páris, where he had come to solicit the sanction of the Academy of Science, in despair at the lack of result, leaving a wife and two children poverty-stricken. [Lost Illusions.]

Chardon (Madame), *née* Rubempré, wife of the preceding. The final branch of an illustrious family. Saved from the scaffold in 1793 by the army surgeon Chardon who declared her enceinte by him and who married her despite their mutual poverty. Reduced to suffering by the sudden death of her husband, she concealed her misfortunes under the name of Mme. Charlotte. She adored her two children, Eve and Lucien. Mme. Chardon died in 1827. [Lost Illusions. Scenes from a Courtesan's Life.]

Chardon (Lucien). (*See* Rubempré, Chardon de.)

Chardon (Eve). (*See* Séchard, Madame David.)

Charels (The), worthy farmers in the outskirts of Alençon; the father and mother of Olympe Charel who became the wife of Michaud, the head-keeper of General de Montcornet's estate. [The Peasantry.]

Chargeboeuf (Marquis de), a Champagne gentleman, born in 1739, head of the house of Chargeboeuf in the time of the Consulate and the Empire. His lands reached from the department of Seine-et-Marne into that of the Aube. A relative of the Hauteserres and the Simeuses whom he sought to erase from the emigrant list in 1804, and whom he assisted in the lawsuit in which they were implicated after the abduction of Senator Malin. He was also related to Laurence de Cinq-Cygne. The Chargeboeufs and the Cinq-Cygnes had the same origin, the Frankish namé of Duineff being their joint property. Cinq-Cygne became the name of the junior branch of the Chargeboeufs. The Marquis de Chargeboeuf was acquainted with Talleyrand, at whose instance he was enabled to transmit a petition to First-Consul Bonaparte. M. de Chargeboeuf was apparently reconciled to the new order of things springing out of the year '89; at any rate he displayed much politic prudence. His family reckoned their ancient titles from the Crusades; his name arose from an equerry's exploit with Saint Louis in Egypt. [The Gondreville Mystery.]

Chargeboeuf (Madame de), mother of Bathilde de Chargeboeuf who married Denis Rogron. She lived at Troyes with her daughter during the Restoration. She was poor but haughty. [Pierrette.]

Chargeboeuf (Bathilde de), daughter of the preceding; married Denis Rogron. (*See* Rogron, Madame.)

Chargeboeuf (Melchior-René, Vicomte de), of the poor branch of the Chargeboeufs. Made sub-prefect of Arcis-sur-Aube in 1815, through the influence of his kinswoman, Mme. de Cinq-Cygne. It was there that he met Mme. Séverine Beauvisage. A mutual attachment resulted, and a daughter called Cécile-Renée was born of their intimacy. [The Member for Arcis.] In 1820 the Vicomte de Chargeboeuf removed to Sancerre where he knew Mme. de la Baudraye. She would probably have favored him, had he not been made prefect and left the city. [The Muse of the Department.]

Chargeboeuf (De), secretary of attorney-general Granville at Paris in 1830; then a young man. Entrusted by the magistrate with the details of Lucien de Rubempré's funeral, which was carried through in such a way as to make one believe that he had died a free man and in his own home, on quai Malaquais. [Scenes from a Courtesan's Life.]

Chargegrain (Louis), inn-keeper of Littray, Normandy. He had dealings with the brigands and was arrested in the suit of the Chauffeurs of Mortagne, in 1809, but acquitted. [The Seamy Side of History.]

Charles, first name of a rather indifferent young painter, who in 1819 boarded at the Vauquer pension. A tutor at college and a Museum attaché; very jocular; given to personal witticisms, which were often aimed at Goriot. [Father Goriot.]

Charles, a young prig who was killed in a duel of small arms with Raphaél de Valentin at Aix, Savoy, in 1831. Charles had boasted of having received the title of "Bachelor of shooting" from Lepage at Paris, and that of doctor from Lozés the "King of foils." [The Magic Skin.]

Charles, *valet de chambre* of M. d'Aiglemont at Paris in 1823. The marquis complained of his servant's carelessness. [A Woman of Thirty.]

Charles, footman to Comte de Montcornet at Aigues, Burgundy, in 1823. Through no good motive he paid court to Catherine Tonsard, being encouraged in his gallantries by Fourchon the girl's maternal grandfather, who desired to have a spy in the château. In the peasants' struggle against the people of Aigues, Charles usually sided with the peasants: "Sprung from the people, their livery remained upon him." [The Peasantry.]

Charlotte, a great lady, a duchess, and a widow without children. She was loved by Marsay then only sixteen and some six years younger than she. She deceived him and he resented by procuring her a rival. She died young of consumption. He husband was a statesman. [Another Study of Woman.]

Charlotte (Madame), name assumed by Mme. Chardon, in 1821 at Angoulême, when obliged to make a living as a nurse. [Lost Illusions.]

Châtelet (Sixte, Baron du), born in 1776 as plain Sixte Châtelet. About 1806 he qualified for and later was made baron under the Empire. His career began with a secretary-ship to an Imperial princess. Later he entered the diplo-matic corps, and finally, under the Restoration, M. de Barante selected him for director of the indirect taxes at Angouléme. Here he met and married Mme. de Bargeton when she became a widow in 1821. He was the prefect of the Charente. [Lost Illusions. A Distinguished Provincial at Paris.] In 1824 he was count and deputy. [Scenes from a Courtesan's Life.] Châtelet accompanied General Marquis Armand de Montriveau in a perilous and famous excursion into Egypt. [The Thirteen.]

Châtelet (Marie-Louise-Anaïs de Négrepelisse, Baronne du), born in 1785; cousin by marriage of the Marquise d'Espard; married in 1803 to M. de Bargeton of Angoulême; widow in 1821 and married to Baron Sixte du Châtelet, prefect of the Charente. Temporarily enamored of Lucien de Rubempré, she attached him to her party in a journey to Paris made necessary by provincial slanders and ambition. There she abandoned her youthful lover at the instigation of Châtelet and of Mme. d'Espard. [Lost Illusions. A Dis-tinguished Provincial at Paris.] In 1824, Mme. du Châtelet attended Mme. Rabourdin's evening reception. [The Gov-ernment Clerks.] Under the direction of Abbé Niolant (or Niollant), Madame du Châtelet, orphaned of her mother, had been reared a little too boyishly at l'Escarbas, a small paternal estate situated near Barbezieux. [Lost Illu-sions.]

Chatillonest (De), an old soldier; father of Marquise d'Aigle-mont. He was hardly reconciled to her marriage with her cousin, the brilliant colonel. [A Woman of Thirty.] The device of the house of Chatillonest (or Chastillonest) was:

Fulgens, sequar ("Shining, I follow thee"). Jean Butscha had put this device beneath a star on his seal. [Modeste Mignon.]

Chaudet (Antoine-Denis), sculptor and painter, born in Paris in 1763, interested in the birth of Joseph Bridau's genius. [A Bachelor's Establishment.]

Chaulieu (Henri, Duc de), born in 1773; peer of France; one of the gentlemen of the Court of Louis XVIII. and of that of Charles X., principally in favor under the latter. After having been ambassador from France to Madrid, he became Minister of Foreign Affairs at the beginning of 1830. He had three children: the eldest was the Duc de Rhétoré; the second became Duc de Lenoncourt-Givry through his marriage with Madeleine de Mortsauf; the third, a daughter, Armande-Louise-Marie, married Baron de Macumer and, left a widow, afterwards married the poet Marie Gaston. [Letters of Two Brides. Modeste Mignon. A Bachelor's Establishment.] The Duc de Chaulieu was on good terms with the Grandlieus and promised them to obtain the title of marquis for Lucien de Rubempré, who was aspiring to the hand of their daughter Clotilde. The Duc de Chaulieu resided in Paris in very close relations with these same Grandlieus of the elder branch. More than once he took particular interest in the family's affairs. He employed Corentin to clear up the dark side of the life of Clotilde's fiancé. [Scenes from a Courtesan's Life.] Some time before this M. de Chaulieu made one of a portentous conclave assembled to extricate Mme. de Langeais, a relative of the Grandlieus, from a serious predicament. [The Thirteen.]

Chaulieu (Eléonore, Duchesse de), wife of the preceding. She was a friend of M. d'Aubrion and sought to influence him to bring about the marriage of Mlle. d'Aubrion with Charles Grandet. [Eugénie Grandet.] For a long time she was the mistress of the poet Canalis, several years her junior. She protected him, helping him on in the world, and in public life, but she was very jealous and kept him under strict surveillance. She still retained her hold of him at fifty years. Mme. de Chaulieu gave her husband the three children designated in the duc's biography. Her hauteur and coquetry subdued most of her maternal sentiments. During the last year of the second Restoration, Eléonore de Chaulieu followed on the way to Normandy, not far from Rosny, a chase almost royal where her sentiments were fully occupied. [Letters of Two Brides.]

Chaulieu (Armande-Louise-Marie de), daughter of Duc and Duchesse de Chaulieu. (*See* Marie Gaston, Madame.)

Chaussard (The Brothers), inn-keepers at Louvigny, Orne; old game-keepers of the Troisville estate, implicated in a trial known as the "Chauffeurs of Mortagne" in 1809. Chaussard the elder was condemned to twenty years' hard labor, was sent to the galleys, and later was pardoned by the Emperor. Chaussard junior was contumacious, and therefore received sentence of death. Later he was cast into the sea by M. de Boislaurier for having been traitorous to the Chouans. A third Chaussard, enticed into the ranks of the police by Contenson, was assassinated in a nocturnal affair. [The Seamy Side of History.]

Chavoncourt (De), Besançon gentleman, highly thought of in the town, representing an old parliamentary family. A deputy under Charles X., one of the famous 221 who signed the address to the King on March 18, 1830. He was re-elected under Louis Philippe. Father of three children but possessing a rather slender income. The family of Chavoncourt was acquainted with the Wattevilles. [Albert Savarus.]

Chavoncourt (Madame de), wife of the preceding and one of the beauties of Besançon. Born about 1794; mother of three children; managed capably the household with its slender resources. [Albert Savarus.]

Chavoncourt (De), born in 1812. Son of M. and Mme. de Chavoncourt of Besançon. College-mate and chum of M. de Vauchelles. [Albert Savarus.]

Chavoncourt (Victoire de), second child and elder daughter of M. and Mme. de Chavoncourt. Born between 1816 and 1817. M. de Vauchelles desired to wed her in 1834. [Albert Savarus.]

Chavoncourt (Sidonie de), third and last child of M. and Mme. de Chavoncourt of Besançon. Born in 1818. [Albert Savarus.]

Chazelle, clerk under the Minister of Finance, in Baudoyer's bureau, in 1824. A benedict and wife-led, although wishing to appear his own master. He argued without ceasing upon subjects and through causes the idlest with Paulmier the bachelor. The one smoked, the other took snuff; this different way of taking tobacco was one of the endless themes between the two. [The Government Clerks.]

Chelius, physician of Heidelberg with whom Halpersohn corresponded, during the reign of Louis Philippe. [The Seamy Side of History.]

Chervin, a police-corporal at Montégnac near Limoges in 1829. [The Country Parson.]

Chesnel, or Choisnel, notary at Alençon, time of Louis XVIII. Born in 1753. Old attendant of the house of Gordes, also of the d'Esgrignon family whose property he had protected during the Revolution. A widower, childless, and possessed of a considerable fortune, he had an aristocratic clientele, notably that of Mme. de la Chanterie. On every hand he received that attention which his good points merited. M. du Bousquier held him in profound hatred, blaming him with the refusal which Mlle. d'Esgrignon had made of Du Bousquier's proffered hand in marriage, and another check of the same nature which he experienced at first from Mlle. Cormon. By a dexterous move in 1824 Chesnel succeeded in rescuing Victurnien d'Esgrignon, though guilty, from the Court of Assizes. The old notary succumbed soon after this event. [The Seamy Side of History. Jealousies of a Country Town.]

Chessel (De), owner of the château and estate of Frapesle near Saché in Touraine. Friend of the Vandenesscs; he introduced their son Félix to his neighbors, the Mortsaufs. The son of a manufacturer named Durand who became very rich during the Revolution, but whose plebeian name he had entirely dropped; instead he adopted that of his wife, the only heiress of the Chessels, an old parliamentary family. M. de Chessel was director-general and twice deputy. He received the title of count under Louis XVIII. [The Lily of the Valley.]

Chessel (Madame de), wife of the preceding. She made up elaborate toilettes. [The Lily of the Valley.] In 1824 she frequented Mme. Rabourdin's Paris home. [The Government Clerks.]

Chevrel (Monsieur and Madame), founders of the house of the "Cat and Racket," rue Saint-Denis, at the close of the eighteenth century. Father and mother of Mme. Guillaume, whose husband succeeded to the management of the firm. [At the Sign of the Cat and Racket.]

Chevrel, rich Parisian banker at the beginning of the nineteenth century. Probably brother and brother-in-law of the foregoing. He had a daughter who married Maître Roguin. [At the Sign of the Cat and Racket.]

Chiavari (Prince de), brother of the Duke of Vissembourg; son of Maréchal Vernon. [Béatrix.]

Chiffreville (Monsieur and Madame), ran a very prosperous drug-store and laboratory in Paris during the Restoration. Their partners were MM. Protcz and Cochin. This firm had frequent business dealings with César Birotteau's "Queen of Roses"; it also supplied Balthazar Claés. [César Birotteau. The Quest of the Absolute.]

Chigi (Prince), great lord of Rome in 1758. He boasted of having "made a soprano out of Zambinella" and disclosed the fact to Sarrasine that this creature was not a woman. [Sarrasine.]

Chissé (Madame de), great aunt of M. du Bruel; a grasping old Provincial at whose home the retired dancer Tullia, now Mme. du Bruel, was fortunate to pass a summer in a rather hypocritical religious penance. [A Prince of Bohemia.]

Chocardelle (Mademoiselle), known as Antonia; a Parisian courtesan during the reign of Louis Philippe; born in 1814. Maxime de Trailles spoke of her as a woman of wit; "She's a pupil of mine, indeed," said he. About 1834 she lived on rue Helder and for fifteen days was the mistress of M. de la Palférine. [Béatrix. A Prince of Bohemia.] For a time she operated a reading-room that M. de Trailles had established for her on rue Coquenard. Like Marguerite Turquet she had "well soaked the little d'Esgrignon." [A Man of Business.] In 1838 she was present at the "house-warming" to Josépha Mirah on rue de la Ville-l'Evêque. [Cousin Betty.] In 1839 she accompanied her lover Maxime de Trailles to Arcis-sur-Aube to aid him in his official transactions relating to the legislative elections. [The Member for Arcis.]

Choin (Mademoiselle), good Catholic who built a parsonage on some land at Blangy bought expressly by her in the eighteenth century; the property was acquired later by Rigou. [The Peasantry.]

Chollet (Mother), janitress of a house on rue du Sentier occupied by Finot's paper in 1821. [A Distinguished Provincial at Paris.]

Chrestien (Michel), Federalist Republican; member of the "Cénacle" of rue des Quatre-Vents. In 1819 he and his friends were invited by the widow Bridau to her home to celebrate the return of her elder son Philippe from Texas. He posed as a Roman senator in a historic picture. The painter Joseph Bridau was a friend of his. [A Bachelor's Establishment.] About 1822 Chrestien fought a duel with Lucien Chardon de Rubempré on account of Daniel d'Arthez. He was a great though unknown statesman. He was killed at the Saint-Merri cloister on June 6, 1832, where he was defending ideas not his own. [A Distinguished Provincial at Paris.] He became foolishly enamored of Diane de Maufrigneuse, but did not confess his love save by a letter addressed to her just before he went to his death at the barricade. He had saved the life of M. de Maufrigneuse in the Revolution of July, 1830, through love for the duchesse. [The Secrets of a Princess.]

Christemio, creole and foster-father of Paquita Valdés, whose protector and body-guard he constituted himself. The Marquis de San-Réal caused his death for having abetted the intimacy between Paquita and Marsay. [The Thirteen.]

Christophe, native of Savoy; servant of Mme. Vauquer on rue Neuve-Saint-Geneviéve, Paris, in 1819. He alone was with Rastignac at the funeral of Goriot, accompanying the body as far as Pére-Lachaise in the priest's carriage. [Father Goriot.]

Cibot, alias Galope-Chopine, also called Cibot the Great. A Chouan implicated in the Breton insurrection of 1799. Decapitated by his cousin Cibot, alias Pille-Miche, and by Marche-à-Terre for having unthinkingly betrayed the brigand position to the "Blues." [The Chouans.]

Cibot (Barbette), wife of Cibot, alias Galope-Chopine. She went over to the "Blues" after her husband's execution, and vowed through vengeance to devote her son, who was still a child, to the Republican cause. [The Chouans.]

Cibot (Jean), alias Pille-Miche; one of the Chouans of the Breton insurrection of 1799; cousin of Cibot, alias Galope-Chopine, and his murderer. Pille-Miche it was, also, who shot and killed Adjutant Gerard of the 72d demibrigade at the Vivetièrc. [The Chouans.] Signalized as the hardiest of the indirect allies of the brigands in the affair of the "Chauffeurs of Mortagne." Tried and executed in 1809. [The Seamy Side of History.]

Cibot, born in 1786. From 1818 to 1845 he was tailorjanitor in a house in rue de Normandie, belonging to Claude-

Joseph Pillerault, where dwelt Pons and Schmucke, the two musicians, time of Louis Philippe. Poisoned by the pawn-broker Rémonencq, Cibot died at his post in April, 1845, on the same day of Sylvain Pons' demise. [Cousin Pons.]

Cibot (Madame). (*See* Rémonencq, Madame.)

Cicognara, Roman Cardinal in 1758; protector of Zam-binella. He caused the assassination of Sarrasine who otherwise would have slain Zambinella. [Sarrasine.]

Cinq-Cygne, the name of an illustrious family of Champagne, the younger branch of the house of Chargeboeuf. These two branches of the same stock had a common origin in the Duineffs of the Frankish people. The name of Cinq-Cygne arose from the defence of a castle made, in the absence of their father, by five (*cinq*) daughters all remarkably fair. On the blazon of the house of Cinq-Cygne is placed for device the response of the eldest of the five sisters when summoned to surrender: "We die singing!". [The Gondreville Mystery.]

Cinq-Cygne (Comtesse de), mother of Laurence de Cinq-Cygne. Widow at the time of the Revolution. She died in the height of a nervous fever induced by an attack on her château at Troyès by the populace in 1793. [The Gondreville Mystery.]

Cinq-Cygne (Marquis de), name of Adrien d'Hauteserre after his marriage with Laurence de Cinq-Cygne. (*See* Hauteserre, Adrien d'.)

Cinq-Cygne (Laurence, Comtesse, afterwards Marquise de), born in 1781. Left an orphan at the age of twelve, she lived, at the last of the eighteenth and first of the nineteenth century, with her kinsman and tutor M. d'Hauteserre at Cinq-Cygne, Aube. She was loved by both her cousins, Paul-Marie and Marie-Paul de Simeuse, and also by the younger of her tutor's two sons, Adrien d'Hauteserre, whom she married in 1813. Laurence de Cinq-Cygne struggled valiantly against a cunning and redoubtable police-agency, the soul of which was Corentin. The King of France approved the charter of the Count of Champagne, by virtue of which, in the family of Cinq-Cygne, a woman might "ennoble and succeed"; therefore the husband of Laurence took the name and the arms of his wife. Although an ardent Royalist she went to seek the Emperor as far as the battlefield of Jéna, in 1806, to ask pardon for the two Simeuses and the two Hauteserres involved in a political trial and condemned to hard labor, despite their innocence. Her bold move succeeded. The Marquise de Cinq-Cygne gave her husband two children, Paul and Berthe. This family passed the winter season at Paris in a magnificent mansion on Faubourg du Roule. [The Gondreville Mystery.] In 1832 Mme. de Cinq-Cygne, at the instance of the Archbishop of Paris, consented to call on the Princesse de Cadignan who had reformed. [The Secrets of a Princess.] In 1836 Mme. de Cinq-Cygne was intimate with Mme. de la Chanterie. [The Seamy Side of History.] Under the Restoration, and principally during Charles X.'s reign, Mme. de Cinq-Cygne exercised a sort of sovereignty over the Department of the Aube which the Comte de Gondreville counterbalanced in a measure by his family connections and through the generosity of the department. Some time after the death of Louis XVIII. she brought about the election of François Michu as president of the Arcis Court. [The Member for Arcis.]

Cinq-Cygne (Jules de), only brother of Laurence de Cinq-Cygne. He emigrated at the outbreak of the Revolution and died for the Royalist cause at Mayence. [The Gondreville Mystery.]

Cinq-Cygne (Paul de), son of Laurence de Cinq-Cygne and of Adrien d'Hauteserre; he became marquis after his father's death. [The Gondreville Mystery.]

Cinq-Cygne (Berthe de). (See Maufrigneuse, Mme. Georges de.)

Ciprey of Provins, Seine-et-Marne; nephew of the maternal grandmother of Pierrette Lorrain. He formed one of the

family council called together in 1828 to decide whether
or not the young girl should remain underneath Denis Rogron's
roof. This council replaced Rogron with the notary Auffray
and chose Ciprey for vice-guardian. [Pierrette.]

Claës-Molina (Balthazar), Comte de Nourho; born at
Douai in 1761 and died in the same town in 1832; sprung
from a famous family of Flemish weavers, allied to a very
noble Spanish family, time of Philip II. In 1795 he married
Joséphine de Temninck of Brussels, and lived happily
with her until 1809, at which time a Polish officer, Adam
de Wierzchownia, seeking shelter at the Claës mansion,
discussed with him the subject of chemical affinity. From
that time on Balthazar, who formerly had worked in Lavoi-
sier's laboratory, buried himself exclusively in the "quest
of the absolute." He expended seven millions in experiments,
leaving his wife to die of neglect. From 1820 to 1825[1] he
was tax-collector in Brittany—duties performed by his
elder daughter who had secured the position for him in order
to divert him from his barren labors. During this time
she rehabilitated the family fortunes. Balthazar died,
almost insane, crying "Eureka!" [The Quest of the Absolute.]

Claës (Joséphine de Temninck, Madame), wife of Balthazar
Claës; born at Brussels in 1770, died at Douai in 1816; a
native Spaniard on her mother's side; commonly called
Pepita. She was small, crooked and lame, with heavy
black hair and glowing eyes. She gave her husband four
children: Marguerite, Félicie, Gabriel (or Gustave) and
Jean-Balthazar. She was passionately devoted to her husband, and died of grief over his neglect of her for the scientific
experiments which never came to an end. [The Quest
of the Absolute.] Mme. Claés counted among her kin the
Evangelistas of Bordeaux. [A Marriage Settlement.]

Claës (Marguerite), elder daughter of Balthazar Claës
and Joséphine de Temninck. (*See* Solis, Madame de.)

---

[1] Given erroneously in original text as 1852.— J. W. M.

Claës (Félicie), second daughter of Balthazar Claës and of Joséphine de Temninck; born in 1801. (*See* Pierquin, Madame.)

Claës (Gabriel or Gustave), third child of Balthazar Claës and of Joséphine de Temninck; born about 1802. He attended the College of Douai, afterwards entering the Ecole Polytechnique, becoming an · engineer of roads and bridges. In 1825 he married Mlle. Conyncks of Cambrai. [The Quest of the Absolute.]

Claës (Jean-Balthazar) last child of Balthazar Claës and Joséphine de Temninck; born in the early part of the nineteenth century. [The Quest of the Absolute.]

Clagny (J.-B. de), public prosecutor at Sancerre in 1836. A passionate admirer of Dinah de la Baudraye. He got transferred to Paris when she returned there, and became successively the substitute for the general prosecutor, attorney-general and finally attorney-general to the Court of Cassation. He watched over and protected the misguided woman, consenting to act as godfather to the child she had by Lousteau. [The Muse of the Department.]

Clagny (Madame de), wife of the preceding. To use an expression of M. Gravier's, she was "ugly enough to chase a young Cossack" in 1814. Mme. de Clagny associated with Mme. de la Baudraye. [The Muse of the Department.]

Claparon, clerk for the Minister of the Interior under the Republic and Empire. Friend of Bridau, Sr., after whose death he continued his cordial relations with Mme. Bridau. He gave much attention to Philippe and Joseph on their mother's account. Claparon died in 1820. [A Bachelor's Establishment.]

Claparon (Charles), son of the preceding; born about 1790. Business man and banker (rue de Provence); at first a commercial traveler; an aide of F. du Tillet in transactions of somewhat shady nature. He was invited to the famous ball given by César Birotteau in honor of César's nomination to the Legion of Honor and the release of French possessions.

[A Bachelor's Establishment. César Birotteau.] In 1821, at the Bourse in Paris, he made a peculiar bargain with the cashier Castanier, who transferred to him, in exchange for his own individuality, the power which he had received from John Melmoth, the Englishman. [Melmoth Reconciled.] He was interested in the third liquidation of Nucingen in 1826, a settlement which made the fortune of the Alsatian banker whose "man of straw" he was for some time. [The Firm of Nucingen.] He was associated with Cérizet who deceived him in a deal about a house sold to Thuillier. Becoming bankrupt he embarked for America about 1840. He was probably condemned for contumacy on account of swindling. [A Man of Business. The Middle Classes.]

Clapart, employé to the prefecture of the Seine during the Restoration, at a salary of twelve hundred francs. Born about 1776. About 1803 he married a widow Husson, aged twenty-two. At that time he was employed in the Bureau of Finance, at a salary of eighteen hundred francs and a promise of more. But his known incapacity held him down to a secondary place. At the fall of the Empire he lost his position, obtaining his new one on the recommendation of the Comte de Sérizy. Mme. Husson had by her first husband a child that was Clapart's evil genius. In 1822 his family occupied an apartment renting for two hundred and fifty francs at number seven rue de la Cerisaie. There he saw much of the old pensioner Poiret. Clapart was killed by the Fieschi attack of July 28, 1835. [A Start in Life.]

Clapart (Madame), wife of the preceding; born in 1780; one of the "Aspasias" of the Directory, and famous for her acquaintance with one of the "Pentarques." He married her to Husson the contractor, who made millions but who became bankrupt suddenly through the First Consul, and suicided in 1802. At that time she was mistress of Moreau, steward of M. de Sérizy. Moreau was in love with her and would have made her his wife, but just then was under sentence of death and a fugitive. Thus it was that in her distress she married Clapart, a clerk in the Bureau of Finance. By her first husband Mme. Clapart had a son, Oscar Husson, whom she was bound up in, but whose boyish pranks caused her much trouble. During the first Empire Mme. Clapart was a lady-in-waiting to Mme. Mére—Letitia Bonaparte. [A Start in Life.]

Clarimbault (Maréchal de), maternal grandfather of Mme. de Beauséant. He had married the daughter of Chevalier de Rastignac, great-uncle of Eugéne de Rastignac. [Father Goriot.]

Claude, an idiot who died in the village of Dauphiné in 1829, nursed and metamorphosed by Dr. Benassis. [The Country Doctor.]

Cleretti, an architect of Paris who was quite the fashion in 1843. Grindot, though decadent at this time, tried to compete with him. [Cousin Betty.]

Clerget (Basine), laundress at Angouléme during the Restoration, who succeeded Mme. Prieur with whom Eve Chardon had worked. Basine Clerget concealed David Séchard and Kolb when Séchard was pursued by the Cointet brothers. [Lost Illusions.]

Clousier, retired attorney of Limoges; justice of the peace at Montégnac after 1809. He was in touch with Mme. Graslin when she moved there about 1830. An upright, phlegmatic man who finally led the contemplative life of one of the ancient hermits. [The Country Parson.]

Cochegrue (Jean), a Chouan who died of wounds received at the fight of La Pélerine or at the siege of Fougéres in 1799. Abbé Gudin said a mass, in the forest, for the repose of Jean Cochegrue, and others slain by the "Blues." [The Chouans.]

Cochet (Françoise), chambermaid of Modesto Mignon at Havre in 1829. She received the answers to the letters addressed by Modeste to Canalis. She had also faithfully served Bettina-Caroline, Modeste's elder sister who took her to Paris. [Modeste Mignon.]

Cochin (Emile-Louis-Lucien-Emmanuel), employé in Clergeot's division of the Bureau of Finance during the Restoration. He had a brother who looked after him in the administration. At this time Cochin was also a silent partner in Matifat's drug-store. Colleville invented an anagram on Cochin's name; with his given names it made up "Cochenille." Cochin and his wife were in **Birotteau's** circle, being present with their son at the famous ball given by the perfumer. In 1840, Cochin, now a baron, was spoken of by Anselme **Popinot** as the oracle of the Lombard and Bourdonnais quarters. [César Birotteau. The Government Clerks. The Firm of Nucingen. The Middle Classes.]

Cochin (Adolphe), son of the preceding; an employé of the Minister of Finance as his father had been for some years. In 1826 his parents tried to obtain for him the hand of Mlle. Matifat. [César Birotteau. The Firm of Nucingen.]

Coffinet, porter of a house belonging to **Thuillier** on rue Saint-Dominique-d'Enfer, Paris, in 1840. His employer put him to work in connection with the "Echo de la Biévre," when Louis-Jérôme Thuillier became editor-in-chief of this paper. [The Middle Classes.]

Coffinet (Madame), wife of the preceding. She looked after Théodose de la **Peyrade's** establishment. [The Middle Classes.]

Cognet, inn-keeper at Issoudun during the Restoration. House of the "Knights of Idlesse" captained by Maxence Gilet. A former groom; born about 1767; short, thickset, wife-led; one-eyed. [A Bachelor's Establishment.]

Cognet (Madame), known as Mother Cognet, wife of the preceding; born about 1783. A retired cook of a good house, who on account of her "Cordon blue" talents, was chosen to be the Léonarde of the Order which had Maxence Gilet for chief. A tall, swarthy woman of intelligent and pleasant demeanor. [A Bachelor's Establishment.]

Cointet (Boniface), and his brother Jean, ran a thriving printing-office at Angouléme during the Restoration. He ruined David Séchard's shop by methods hardly honorable. Boniface Cointet was older than Jean, and was usually called Cointet the Great. He put on the devout. Extremely wealthy, he became deputy, was made a peer of France and Minister of Commerce in Louis Philippe's coalition ministry. In 1842 he married Mlle. Popinot, daughter of Anselme Popinot. [Lost Illusions. The Firm of Nucingen.] On May 28, 1839, he presided at the sitting of the Chamber of Deputies when the election of Sallenauve was ratified. [The Member for Arcis.]

Cointet (Jean), younger brother of the preceding; known as "Fatty" Cointet; was foreman of the printing-office, while his brother ran the business end. Jean Cointet passed for a good fellow and acted the generous part. [Lost Illusions.]

Colas (Jacques), a consumptive child of a village near Grenoble, who was attended by Dr. Benassis. His passion was singing, for which he had a very pure voice. Lived with his mother who was poverty-stricken. Died in the latter part of 1829 at the age of fifteen, shortly after the death of his benefactor, the physician. A nephew of Moreau, the old laborer. [The Country Doctor.]

Colleville, son of a talented musician, once leading violin of the Opéra under Francœur and Rebel. He himself was first clarionet at the péra-Comique, and at the same time chief clerk under the Minister of Finance, and, in addition, book-keeper for a merchant from seven to nine in the mornings. Great on anagrams. Made deputy-chief clerk in Baudoyer's bureau when the latter was promoted to division chief. He was preceptor at Paris six months later. In 1832 he became secretary to the mayor of the twelfth Arrondissement and officer of the Legion of Honor. At that time Colleville lived with his wife and family on rue d'Enfer. He was Thuillier's most intimate friend. [The Government Clerks. The Middle Classes.]

Colleville (Flavie Minoret, Madame), born in 1798; wife of the preceding; daughter of a celebrated dancer and, supposedly, of M. du Bourguier. She made a love match, and between 1816 and 1826 bore five children, each of whom resembled and may actually have had a different father:

1st. A daughter born in 1816, who favored Colleville.

2d. A son, Charles, cut out for a soldier, born during his mother's acquaintance with Charles de Gondreville, under-lieutenant of the dragoons of Saint-Chamans.

3d. A son, François, destined for business, born during Mme. Colleville's intimacy with François Keller, the banker.

4th. A daughter, Céleste, born in 1821, of whom Thuillier, Colleville's best friend, was the godfather—and father *in partibus*. (*See* Phellion, Mme. Félix.)

5th. A son, Théodore, or Anatole, born at a period of religious zeal.

Madame Colleville was a Parisian, piquant, winning and pretty, as well as clever and ethereal. She made her husband very happy. He owed all his advancement to her. In the interests of their ambition she granted momentary favor to Chardin des Lupeaulx, the Secretary-General. On Wednesdays she was at home to artists and distinguished people. [The Government Clerks. Cousin Betty. The Middle Classes.]

Collin (Jacques), born in 1779. Reared by the Fathers of the Oratory. He went as far as rhetoric, at school, and was then put in a bank by his aunt, Jacqueline Collin. Accused, however, of a crime probably committed by Franchessini, he fled the country. Later he was sent to the galleys where he remained from 1810 to 1815, when he escaped and came to Paris, stopping under the name of Vautrin at the Vauquer pension. There he knew Rastignac, then a young man, became interested in him, and tried to bring about his marriage with Victorine Taillefer, for whom he procured a rich dowry by causing her brother to be slain in a duel with Franchessini. Bibi-Lupin, chief of secret police, arrested him in 1819 and returned him to the bagne, whence he escaped again in 1820, reappearing in Paris as Carlos Herrera, honorary canon of the Chapter of Toledo. At this time he rescued Lucien de Rubempré from suicide, and took charge of the young poet. Accused, with the latter, of having murdered Esther Gobseck, who in truth was poisoned, Jacques Collin was acquitted of this charge, and ended by becoming chief of secret police under the name of Saint-Estéve, in 1830. He held this position till 1845. He finally became wealthy, having an income of twelve thousand francs, three hundred thousand francs inherited from Lucien de Rubempré, and the profits of a green-leather manufactory at Gentilly. [Father Goriot. Lost Illusions. A Distinguished Provincial at Paris. Scenes from a Courtesan's Life. The Member for Arcis.] In addition to the pseudonym of M. Jules, under which he was known by Catherine Goussard, Jacques Collin also took for a time the English name of William Barker, creditor for Georges d'Estourny. Under this name he hoodwinked the cunning Cérizet, inducing that "man of business" to endorse some notes for him. [Scenes from a Courtesan's Life.] He was also nick-named "Trompe-la-Mort."

Collin (Jacqueline), aunt of Jacques Collin, whom she had reared; born at Java. In her youth she was Marat's mistress, and afterwards had relations with the chemist, Duvignon, who was condemned to death for counterfeiting in 1799. During this intimacy she attained a dangerous knowledge of toxicology. From 1800 to 1805 she was a clothing dealer; and from 1806 to 1808 she spent two years in prison for having influenced minors. From 1824 to 1830 Mlle. Collin exerted a strong influence over Jacques, alias Vautrin, toward his life of adventure without the pale of the law. Her strong point was disguises. In 1839 she ran a matrimonial bureau on rue de Provence, under the name of Mme. de Saint-Estève. She often borrowed the name of her friend Mme. Nourrisson, who, during the time of Louis Philippe, made a pretence of business more or less dubious on rue Neuve-Saint-Marc. She had some dealings with Victorin Hulot, at whose instance she brought about the overthrow of Mme. Marneffe, mistress, and afterwards wife, of Crevel. Under the name of Asie, Jacqueline Collin made an excellent cook for Esther Gobseck, whom she was ordered by Vautrin to watch. [Scenes from a Courtesan's Life. Cousin Betty. The Unconscious Humorists.]

Collinet, grocer at Arcis-sur-Aube, time of Louis Philippe. Elector for the Liberals headed by Colonel Giguet. [The Member for Arcis.]

Collinet (François-Joseph), merchant of Nantes. In 1814 the political changes brought about his business failure. He went to America, returning in 1824 enriched, and re-established. He had caused the loss of twenty-four thousand francs to M. and Mme. Lorrain, small retailers of Pen-Hoël, and father and mother of Major Lorrain. But, on his return to France, he restored to Mme. Lorrain, then a widow and almost a septuagenarian, forty-two thousand francs, being capital and interest of his indebtedness to her. [Pierrette.]

Colonna, an aged Italian at Genoa, during the latter part of the eighteenth century. He had reared Luigia Porta under the name of Colonna and as his own son, from the age of six until the time when the young man enlisted in the French army. [The Vendetta.]

Coloquinte, given name of a pensioner who was "office boy" in Finot's newspaper office in 1820. He had been through the Egyptian campaign, losing an arm at the Battle of Montmirail. [A Bachelor's Establishment. A Distinguished Provincial at Paris.]

Colorat (Jérôme), estate-keeper for Mme. Graslin at Montégnac; born at Limoges. Retired soldier of the Empire; ex-sergeant in the Royal Guard; at one time estate-keeper for M. de Navarreins, before entering Mme. Graslin's service. [The Country Parson.]

Constance, chambermaid for Mme. de Restaud in 1819. Through her old Goriot knew about everything that was going on at the home of his elder daughter. This Constance, sometimes called Victorie, took money to her mistress when the latter needed it. [Father Goriot.]

Constant de Rebecque (Benjamin), born at Lausanne in 1767, died at Paris, December 8, 1830. About the end of 1821 he is discovered in Dauriat's book-shop at Palais-Royal, where Lucien de Rubempré noticed his splendid head and spiritual eyes. [A Distinguished Provincial at Paris.]

Conti (Gennaro), musical composer; of Neapolitan origin, but born at Marseilles. Lover of Mlle. des Touches—Camille Maupin—in 1821-1822. Afterwards he paid court to Marquise Béatrix de Rochefide. [Lost Illusions. Béatrix.]

Conyncks, family of Bruges, who were maternal ancestors of Marguerite Claës. In 1812 this young girl at sixteen was the living image of a Conyncks, her grandmother, whose portrait hung in Balthazar Claés' home. A Conyncks, also of Bruges but later established at Cambrai, was granduncle of the children of Balthazar Claës, and was appointed their vice-guardian after the death of Mme. Claés. He had a daughter who married Gabriel Claés. [The Quest of the Absolute.]

Coquelin (Monsieur and Madame), hardware dealers, successors to Claude-Joseph Pillerault in a store on quai de la Ferraille, sign of the Golden Bell. Guests at the big ball given by César Birotteau. After getting the invitation, Mme. Coquelin ordered a magnificent gown for the occasion. [César Birotteau.]

Coquet, chief of bureau to the Minister of War, in Lebrun's division in 1838. Marneffe was his successor. Coquet had been in the service of the administration since 1809, and had given perfect satisfaction. He was a married man and his wife was still living at the time when he was displaced. [Cousin Betty.]

Coralie (Mademoiselle), actress at the Panorama-Dramatique and at the Théâtre du Gymnase, Paris, time of Louis

XVIII. Born in 1803 and brought up a Catholic, she was nevertheless of distinct Jewish type. She died in August, 1822. Her mother sold her at fifteen to young Henri de Marsay, whom she abhorred and who soon deserted her. She was then maintained by Camusot, who was not obnoxious. She fell in love with Lucien de Rubempré at first sight, surrendering to him immediately and being faithful to him until her dying breath. The glory and downfall of Coralie dated from this love. An original criticism of the young Chardon established the success of " L'Alcade dans l' Embarras," at the Marais, and brought to Coralie, one of the principals in the play, an engagement at Boulevard Bonne-Nouvelle, with a salary of twelve thousand francs. But here the artist stranded, the victim of a cabal, despite the protection of Camille Maupin. At first she was housed on rue de Vendôme, afterwards in a more modest lodging where she died, attended and nursed by her cousin, Berenice. She had sold her elegant furniture to Cardot, Sr., on leaving the apartment on rue de Vendôme, and in order to avoid moving it, he installed Florentine there. Coralie was the rival of Mme. Perrin and of Mlle. Fleuriet, whom she resembled and whose destiny should have been her own. The funeral service of Coralie took place at noon in the little church of Notre-Dame de Bonne-Nouvelle. Camusot promised to purchase a permanent plot of ground for her in the cemetery of Pére-Lachaise. [A Start in Life. A Distinguished Provincial at Paris. A Bachelor's Establishment.]

Corbigny (De), prefect of Loire-et-Cher, in 1811. Friend of Mme. de Staël who authorized him to place Louis Lambert, at her expense, in the College of Vendôme. He probably died in 1812. [Louis Lambert.]

Corbinet, notary at Soulanges, Burgundy, in 1823, and at one time an old patron of Sibilet's. The Gravelots, lumber dealers, were clients of his. Commissioned with the sale of Aigues, when General de Montcornet became wearied with developing his property. At one time known as Corbineau. [The Peasantry.]

Corbinet, court-judge at Ville-aux-Fayes in 1823; son of Corbinet the notary. He belonged, body and soul, to Gaubertin, the all-powerful mayor of the town. [The Peasantry.]

Corbinet, retired captain, postal director at Ville-aux-Fayes in 1823; brother of Corbinet, the notary. The last daughter of Sibilet, the copy-clerk, was engaged to him when she was sixteen. [The Peasantry.]

Corentin, born at Vendôme in 1777; a police-agent of great genius, trained by Peyrade as Louis David was by Vien. A favorite of Fouché's and probably his natural son. In 1799 he accompanied Mlle. de Verneuil sent to lure and betray Alphonse de Montauran, the young chief of the Bretons who were risen against the Republic. For two years Corentin was attached to this strange girl as a serpent to a tree. [The Chouans.] In 1803 he and his chief, Peyrade, were entrusted with a difficult mission in the department of Aube, where he had to search the home of Mlle. de Cinq-Cygne. She surprised him at the moment when he was forcing open a casket, and struck him a blow with her riding whip. This he avenged cruelly, involving, despite their innocence, the Hauteserres and the Simeuses, friends and cousins of the young girl. This was during the affair of the abduction of Senator Malin. About the same time he concluded another delicate mission to Berlin to the satisfaction of Talleyrand, the Minister of Foreign Affairs. [The Gondreville Mystery.] From 1824 to 1830, Corentin was pitted against the terrible Jacques Collin, alias Vautrin, whose friendly plans in behalf of Lucien de Rubempré he thwarted so cruelly. Corentin it was who rendered futile the contemplated marriage of the aspirant with Clotilde de Grandlieu, bringing about as a consequence the absolute ruin of the "distinguished provincial at Paris." He rusticated at Passy, rue des Vignes, about May, 1830. Under Charles X., Corentin was chief of the political police of the château. [Scenes from a Courtesan's Life.] For more than thirty years he lived on rue Honoré-Chevalier under the name of M. du Portail. He sheltered Lydie, daughter of his friend,

Peyrade, after the death of the old police-agent. About 1840 he brought about her marriage with Théodose de la Peyrade, nephew of Peyrade, after having upset the plans of the very astute young man, greatly in love with Céleste Colleville's dowry. Corentin—M. du Portail—then installed the chosen husband of his adopted child into his own high official duties. [The Middle Classes.]

Cormon (Rose-Marie-Victoire). (*See* Bousquier, Madame du.)

Cornevin, an old native of Perche; foster-father of Olympe Michaud. He was with the Chouans in 1794 and 1799. In 1823 he was a servant at Michaud's. [The Peasantry.]

Cornoiller (Antoine), game-keeper at Saumur ; married the sturdy Nanon then fifty-nine years old, after the death of Grandet, about 1827, and became general overseer of lands and properties of Eugénie Grandet. [Eugénie Grandet.]

Cornoiller (Madame). (*See* Nanon.)

Cottereau, well-known smuggler, one of the heads of the Breton insurrection. In 1799 he was principal in a rather stormy scene at the Vivetière, when he threatened the Marquis de Montauran with swearing allegiance to the First Consul if he did not immediately obtain noteworthy advantages in payment of seven years of devoted service to "the good cause." " My men and I have a devilish importunate creditor," said he, slapping his stomach. One of the brothers of Jean Cottereau, was nick-named the "Chouan," a title used by all the Western rebels against the Republic. [The Chouans.]

Cottin (Maréchal), Prince of Wissembourg; Duke of Orfano; old soldier of the Republic and the Empire; Minister of War in 1841; born in 1771. He was obliged to bring great shame upon his old friend and companion-in-arms, Marshal Hulot, by advising him of the swindling of the commissariat, Hulot d'Ervy. Marshal Cottin and Nucingen were witnesses at the wedding of Hortense Hulot and Wenceslas Steinbock. [Cousin Betty.]

Cottin (Francine), a Breton woman, probably born at Fougères in 1773; chambermaid and confidante of Mlle. de Verneuil, who had been reared by Francine's parents. Childhood's friend of Marche-à-Terre, with whom she used her influence to save the life of her mistress during the massacre of the "Blues" at the Vivitière in 1799. [The Chouans.]

Coudrai (Du), register of mortgages at Alençon, time of Louis XVIII. A caller at the home of Mlle. Cormon, and afterwards at that of M. du Bousquier, who married "the old maid." One of the town's most open-hearted men; his only faults were having married a rich old lady who was unendurable, and the habit of making villainous puns at which he was first to laugh. In 1824 M. du Coudrai was poverty-stricken; he had lost his place on account of voting the wrong way. [Jealousies of a Country Town.]

Coupiau, Breton courier from Mayenne to Fougéres in 1799. In the struggle between the "Blues" and the Chouans he took no part, but acted as circumstances demanded and for his own interests. Indeed he offered no resistance when the "Brigands" stole the government chests. Coupiau was nick-named Méne-à-Bien by Marche-à-Terre the Chouan. [The Chouans.]

Coupiau (Sulpice), Chouan and probably the father of Coupiau the messenger. Killed in 1799 in the battle of La Pélerine or at the siege of Fougéres. [The Chouans.]

Courand (Jenny), florist; mistress of Félix Gaudissart in 1831. At that time she lived in Paris on rue d'Artois. [Gaudissart the Great.]

Courceuil (Félix), of Alençon, retired army surgeon of the Rebel forces of the Vendée. In 1809 he furnished arms to the "Brigands." Involved in the trial known as "Chauffeurs of Mortagne." Condemned to death for contumacy. [The Seamy Side of History.]

Cournant, notary at Provins in 1827; rival of Auffray, the notary; of the Opposition; one of the few public-spirited men of the little town. [Pierrette.]

Courtecuisse, game-keeper of the Aigues estate in Burgundy under the Empire and Restoration until 1823. Born about 1777; at first in the service of Mlle. Laguerre; discharged by General de Montcornet for absolute incapacity, and replaced by keepers who were trusty and true. Courtecuisse was a little fellow with a face like a full moon. He was never so happy as when idle. On leaving he demanded a sum of eleven hundred francs which was not due him. His master indignantly denied his claim at first, but yielded the point, however, on being threatened with a lawsuit, the scandal of which he wished to avoid. Courtecuisse, out of a job, purchased from Rigou for two thousand francs the little property of La Bâchelerie, enclosed in the Aigues estate, and wearied himself, without gain, in the management of his land. He had a daughter who was tolerably pretty and eighteen years old in 1823. At this time she was in the service of Mme. Mariotte the elder, at Auxerre. Courtecuisse was given the sobriquet of "Courtebotte" —short-boot. [The Peasantry.]

Courtecuisse (Madame), wife of the preceding; in abject fear of the miser, Grégoire Rigou, mayor of Blangy, Burgundy. [The Peasantry.]

Courteville (Madame de), cousin of Comte de Bauvan on the maternal side; widow of a judge of the Seine Court. She had a very beautiful daughter, Amélie, whom the comte wished to marry to his secretary, Maurice de l'Hostal. [Honorine.]

Courtois, Marsac miller, near Angoulême during the Restoration. In 1821 rumor had it that he intended to wed a miller's widow, his patroness, who was thirty-two years old. She had one hundred thousand francs in her own right. David Séchard was advised by his father to ask the hand of this rich widow. At the end of 1822 Courtois, now married, sheltered Lucien de Rubempré, returning almost dead from Paris. [Lost Illusions.]

Courtois (Madame), wife of the preceding, who cared sympathetically for Lucien de Rubempré, on his return. [Lost Illusions.]

Coussard (Laurent). (*See* Goussard, Laurent.)   .

Coutelier, a creditor of Maxime de Trailles. The Coutelier credit, purchased for five hundred francs by the Claparon-Cérizet firm, came to thirty-two hundred francs, seventy-five centimes, capital, interest and costs. It was recovered by Cérizet by means of strategy worthy of a Scapin. [A Man of Business.]

Couture, a kind of financier-journalist of an equivocal reputation; born about 1797. One of Mme. Schontz's earliest friends; and she alone remained faithful to him when he was ruined by the downfall of the ministry of March 1st, 1840. Couture was always welcome at the home of the courtesan, who dreamed, perhaps, of making him her husband. But he presented Fabien du Ronceret to her and the "lorette" married him. In 1836, in company with Finot and Blondet, he was present in a private room of a well-known restaurant, when Jean-Jacques Bixiou related the origin of the Nucingen fortune. At the time of his transient wealth Couture splendidly maintained Jenny Cadine. At one time he was celebrated for his waistcoats. He had no known relationship with the widow Couture. [Béatrix. * The Firm of Nucingen.] The financier drew upon himself the hatred of Cérizet for having deceived him in a deal about the purchase of lands and houses situated in the suburbs of the Madeleine, an affair in which Jérôme Thuillier was afterwards concerned. [The Middle Classes.]

Couture (Madame), widow of an ordonnance-commissary of the French Republic. Relative and protectress of Mlle. Victorine Taillefer with whom she lived at the Vauquer pension, in 1819. [Father Goriot.]

Couturier (Abbé), curate of Saint-Leonard church at Alençon, time of Louis XVIII. Spiritual adviser of Mlle. Cormon, remaining her confessor after her marriage with Du Bousquier, and influencing her in the way of excessive penances. [Jealousies of a Country Town.]

Crémière, tax-collector at Nemours during the Restoration. Nephew by marriage of Dr. Minoret, who had secured the position for him, furnishing his security. One of the three collateral heirs of the old physician, the two others being Minoret-Levrault, the postmaster, and Massin-Levrault, copy-clerk to the justice of the peace. In the curious branching of these four Gâtinais bourgeois families—the Minorets, the Massins, the Levraults and the Crémières—the tax-collector belonged to the Crémière-Crémière branch. He had several children, among others a daughter named Angélique. After the Revolution of July, 1830, he became municipal councillor. [Ursule Mirouët.]

Crémière (Madame), *née* Massin-Massin, wife of the tax-collector, and niece of Dr. Minoret—that is, daughter of the old physician's sister. A stout woman with a muddy blonde complexion splotched with freckles. Passed for an educated person on account of her novel-reading. Her *lapsi linguæ* were maliciously spread abroad by Goupil, the notary's clerk, who labelled them "Capsulinguettes"; indeed, Mme. Crémière thus translated the two Latin words. [Ursule Mirouët.]

Crémière-Dionis, always called Dionis, which name see.

Crevel (Célestin), born between 1786 and 1788; clerked for César Birotteau the perfumer—first as second clerk, then as head-clerk when Popinot left the house to set up in business for himself. After his patron's failure in 1819, he purchased for five thousand seven hundred francs, "The Queen of Roses," making his own fortune thereby. During the reign of Louis Philippe he lived on his income. Captain, then chief of battalion in the National Guard; officer of the Legion of Honor; mayor of one of the arrondissements of Paris, he ended up by being a very great personage. He had married the daughter of a farmer of Brie; became a widower in 1833, when he gave himself over to a life of pleasure. He maintained Josépha, who was taken away from him by his friend, Baron Hulot. To avenge himself he tried to win Mme. Hulot. He "protected" Heloïse Brisetout. Finally he was smitten with Mme. Marneffe, whom he had for mistress and afterwards married when she became a widow in 1843. In May of this same year, Crevel and his wife died of a horrible disease which had been communicated to Valérie by a negro belonging to Montés the Brazilian. In 1838 Crevel lived on rue des Saussaies; at the same time he owned a little house on rue du Dauphin, where he had prepared a secret chamber for Mme. Marneffe; this last house he leased to Maxime de Trailles. Besides these Crevel owned: a house on rue Barbet de Jouy; the Presles property bought of Mme. de Sérizy at a cost of three million francs. He caused himself to be made a member of the General Council of Seine-et-Oise. By his first marriage he had an only daughter, Célestine, who married Victorin Hulot. [César Birotteau. Cousin Betty.] In 1844-1845 Crevel owned a share in the management of the theatre directed by Gaudissart. [Cousin Pons.]

Crevel (Célestine), only child of the first marriage of the preceding. (See Hulot, Mme. Victorin.)

Crevel (Madame Célestin), born Valérie Fortin in 1815; natural daughter of the Comte de Montcornet, marshal of France; married, first Marneffe, an employé in the War Office, with whom she broke faith by agreement with the clerk; and second, Célestin Crevel. She bore Marneffe a child, a stunted, scrawny urchin named Stanislas. An intimate friend of Lisbeth Fischer who utilized Valérie's irresistible attractions for the satisfying of her hatred towards her rich relatives. At this time Mme. Marneffe belonged jointly to Marneffe, to the Brazilian Montés, to Steinbock the Pole, to Célestin Crevel and to Baron Hulot. Each of these she held responsible for a child born in 1841, and which died on coming into the world. By prearrangement, she was surprised with Hulot by the police-commissioners, during this period, in Grevel's cottage on rue du Dauphin. After having lived with Marneffe on rue du Doyenné in the house occupied by Lisbeth Fischer—"Cousin Betty"—she was installed by Baron Hulot on rue Vaneau; then by Crevel in a mansion on rue Barbet-de-Jouy. She died in 1843, two days prior to Célestin. She perished while trying to "cajole God"—to use her own expression. She bequeathed, as a restitution, 300,000 francs to Hector Hulot. Valérie Marneffe did not lack spirit. Claude Vignon, the great critic, especially appreciated this woman's intellectual depravity. [Cousin Betty.]

Crochard, Opera dancer in the second half of the eighteenth century. Director of theatrical evolutions. He commanded a band of assailants upon the Bastile, July 14, 1789; became an officer, a colonel, dying of wounds received at Lutzen, May 2, 1813. [A Second Home.]

Crochard (Madame), widow of the preceding. Before the Revolution she had sung with her husband in the chorus. In 1815 she lived wretchedly with her daughter Caroline, following the embroiderer's trade, in a house on rue du Tourniquet-Saint-Jean, which belonged to Molineux. Wishing to find a protector for her daughter, Caroline, Mme. Crochard favored the attentions of the Comte de Granville. He rewarded her with a life-annuity of three thousand francs. She died, in 1822, in a comfortable lodging on rue Saint-Louis at Marais. She constantly wore on her breast the cross of chevalier of the Legion of Honor conferred on her husband by the Emperor. The widow Crochard, watched by an eager circle, received, at her last moments, a visit from Abbé Fontanon, confessor of the Comtesse de Granville, and was greatly troubled by the prelate's proceedings. [A Second Home.]

Crochard (Caroline), daughter of the preceding; born in 1797. For several years during the Restoration she was the mistress of Comte de Granville; at that time she was known as Mlle. de Bellefeuille, from the name of a small piece of property at Gâtinais given to the young woman by an uncle of the comte who had taken a liking to her. Her lover installed her in an elegant apartment on rue Taitbout, where Esther Gobseck afterwards lived. Caroline

Crochard abandoned M. de Granville and a good position for a needy young fellow named Solvet, who ran through with all her property. Sick and poverty-stricken in 1833, she lived in a wretched two-story house on rue Gaillon. She gave the Comte de Granville a son, Charles, and a daughter, Eugénie. [A Second Home.]

Crochard (Charles), illegitimate child of Comte de Granville and Caroline Crochard. In 1833 he was apprehended for a considerable theft, when he appealed to his father through the agency of Eugéne de Granville, his half-brother. The comte gave the latter money enough to clear up the miserable business, if such were possible. [A Second Home.] The theft in question was committed at the home of Mlle. Beaumesnil. He carried off her diamonds. [The Middle Classes.]

Croisier (Du). (*See* Bousquier, Du.)

Croizeau, former coachmaker to Bonaparte's Imperial Court; had an income of about forty thousand francs; lived on rue Buffault; a widower without children. He was a constant visitor at Antonia Chocardelle's reading-room on rue Coquenard, time of Louis Philippe, and he offered to marry the "charming woman." [A Man of Business.]

Crottat (Monsieur and Madame), retired farmers; parents of the notary Crottat, assassinated by some thieves, among them being the notorious Dannepont, alias La Pouraille. the trial of this crime was called in May, 1830. [Scenes from a Courtesan's Life.] They were well-to-do folk and, according to César Birotteau who knew them, old man Crottat was as "close as a snail." [César Birotteau.]

Crottat (Alexandre), head-clerk of Maitre Roguin, and his successor in 1819, after the flight of the notary. He married the daughter of Lourdois, the painting-contractor. César Birotteau thought for a time of making him his son-in-law. He called him, familiarly, " Xandrot." Alexandre Crottat was a guest at the famous ball given by the perfumer in December, 1818. He was in friendly relations with Derville, the attorney, who commissioned him with a sort of half-pay for Colonel Chabert. He was also Comtesse Ferraud's notary at this time. [César Birotteau. Colonel Chabert.] In 1822 he was notary to Comte de Sérizy. [A Start in Life.] He was also notary to Charles de Vandenesse; and one evening, at the home of the marquis, he made some awkward allusions which undoubtedly recalled unpleasant memories to his client and Mme. d'Aiglemont. Upon his return home he narrated the particulars to his wife, who chided him sharply. [A Woman of Thirty.] Alexandre Crottat and Leopold Hannequin signed the will dictated by Sylvain Pons on his death-bed. [Cousin Pons.]

Cruchot (Abbé), priest of Saumur; dignitary of the Chapter of Saint-Martin of Tours; brother of Cruchot, the notary; uncle of President Cruchot de Bonfons; the Talleyrand of his family; after much angling he induced Eugénie Grandet to wed the president in 1827. [Eugénie Grandet.]

Cruchot, notary at Saumur during the Restoration; brother of Abbé Cruchot; uncle of President Cruchot de Bonfons. He as well as the prelate was much concerned with making the match between his nephew and Eugénie Grandet. The young girl's father entrusted M. Cruchot with his usurious dealings and probably with all his money matters. [Eugénie Grandet.]

Curieux (Catherine). (*See* Farrabesche, Madame.)

Cydalise, magnificent woman of Valognes, Normandy, who launched out in Paris in 1840 to make capital out of her beauty. Born in 1824, she was then only sixteen. She served as an instrument for Montés the Brazilian who, in order to avenge himself on Mme. Marnéffe—now Mme. Crevel—inoculated the young girl with a terrible disease through one of his negroes. He in turn obtained it from Cydalise and transmitted it to the faithless Valérie who died, as also did her husband. Cydalise probably accompanied Montés to Brazil, the only place where this horrible ailment is curable. [Cousin Betty.]

D

Dallot, mason in the suburbs of l'Isle-Adam in the early days of the Restoration, who was to marry a peasant woman of small wit named Geneviéve. After having courted her for the sake of her little property, he deserted her for a woman of more means and also of a sharper intelligence. This separation was so cruel a blow to Geneviéve that she became idiotic. [Farewell.]

Dannepont, alias La Fouraille, one of the assassins of M. and Mme. Crottat. Imprisoned for his crime in 1830 at the Conciergerie, and under sentence of capital punishment; an escaped convict who had been sought on account of other crimes by the police for five years past. Born about 1785 and sent to the galleys at the age of nineteen. There he had known Jacques Collin—Vautrin. Riganson, Sélérier and he formed a sort of triumvirate. A short, skinny, dried-up fellow with a face like a marten. [Scenes from a Courtesan's Life.]

Dauphin, pastry-cook of Arcis-sur-Aube; well-known Republican. In 1830, in an electoral caucus, he questioned Sallenauve, a candidate for deputy, about Danton. [The Member for Arcis.]

Dauriat, editor and bookman of Paris, on Palais-Royale, Galleries de Bois during the Restoration. He purchased for three thousand francs a collection of sonnets "Marguerites" from Lucien de Rubempré, who had scored a book of Nathan's. But he did not publish the sonnets until a long time afterwards, and with a success that the author declared to be posthumous. Dauriat's shop was the rendezvous of writers and politicians of note at this time. [A Distinguished Provincial at Paris. Scenes from a Courtesan's Life.] Dauriat, who was Canalis' publisher, was asked in 1829 by Modeste Mignon for personal information concerning the poet, to which he made a rather ironical reply. In speaking of celebrated authors Dauriat was wont to say, "I have made Canalis. I have made Nathan." [Modeste Mignon.]

David (Madame), woman living in the outskirts of Brives, who died of fright on account of the Chauffeurs, time of the Directory. [The Country Parson.]

Delbecq, secretary and steward of Comte Ferraud during the Restoration. Retired attorney. A capable, ambitious man in the service of the countess, whom he aided to rid herself of Colonel Chabert when that officer claimed his former wife. [Colonel Chabert.]

Denisart, name assumed by Cérizet.

Derville, attorney at Paris, rue Vivienne, from 1819 to 1840. Born in 1794, the seventh child of an insignificant bourgeois of Noyon. In 1816 he was only second clerk and dwelt on rue des Grés, having for a neighbor the well-known usurer Gobseck, who later advanced him one hundred and fifty thousand francs at 15 per cent., with which he purchased the practice of his patron, a man of pleasure now somewhat short of funds. Through Gobseck he met his future wife, Jenny Malvaut; through the same man he learned the Restand secrets. In the winter of 1829-30 he told of their troubles to the Vicomtesse de Grandlieu. Derville had re-established the fortune of the feminine representative of the Grandlieu's younger branch, at the time of the Bourbon's re-entry, and therefore was on a friendly footing at her home. [Gobseck.] He had been a clerk at Bordin's. [A Start in Life. The Gondreville Mystery.] He was attorney for Colonel Chabert who sought his conjugal rights with Comtesse Ferraud. He became keenly interested in the old officer, aiding him and being greatly grieved when, some years later, he found him plunged into idiocy in the Bicétre hospital. [Colonel Chabert.] Derville was also attorney for Comte de Sérizy, Mme. de Nucingen and the Ducs de Grandlieu and de Chaulieu, whose entire confidence he possessed. In 1830, under the name of Saint-Denis, he and Corentin inquired of the Séchards at Angouléme concerning the real resources of Lucien de Rubempré. [Father Goriot. Scenes from a Courtesan's Life.]

Derville (Madame), born Jenny Malvaut; wife of Derville the attorney; young Parisian girl, though born in the country. In 1826 she lived alone, but maintaining a virtuous life, supported by her work. She was on the fifth floor of a gloomy house on rue Montmartre, where Gobseck had called to collect a note signed by her. He pointed her out to Derville, who married her without dowry. Later she inherited from an uncle, a farmer who had become wealthy, seventy thousand francs with which she aided her husband to cancel his debt with Gobseck. [Gobseck.] Being anxious for an invitation to the ball given by Birotteau, she paid a rather unexpected visit to the perfumer's wife. She made much of the latter and of Mlle. Birotteau, and was invited with her husband to the festivities. It appears that some years before her marriage she had worked as dressmaker for the Birotteaus. [César Birotteau.]

Descoings (Monsieur and Madame), father-in-law and mother-in-law of Dr. Rouget of Issoudun. Dealers in wool, acting as selling agents for owners, and buying agents for fleece merchants of Berry. They also bought state lands. Rich and miserly. Died during the Republic within two years of each other and before 1799. [A Bachelor's Establishment.]

Descoings, son of. the preceding; younger brother of Mme. Rouget, the doctor's wife; grocer at Paris, on rue Saint-Honoré, not far from Robespierre's quarters. Descoings had married for love the widow of Bixiou, his predecessor. She was twelve years his senior but well preserved and "plump as a thrush after harvest." Accused of foreclosing, he was sent to the scaffold, in company with André Chénier, on the seventh Thermidor of year 2, July 25, 1794. The death of the grocer caused a greater sensation than did that of the poet. César Birotteau moved the plant of the perfumery "Queen of Roses" into Descoings' shop about 1800. The successor of the executed man managed his business badly; the inventor of the "Eau Carminative" went bankrupt. [A Bachelor's Establishment.]

Descoings (Madame), born in 1744; widow of two husbands, Bixiou and Descoings, the latter succeeding the former in the grocer shop on rue Saint-Honoré, Paris. Grandmother of Jean-Jacques Bixiou, the cartoonist. After the death of M. Bridau, chief of division in the Department of the Interior, Mme. Descoings, now a widow, came in 1819 to live with her niece, the widow Bridau, *née* Agathe Rouget, bringing to the common fund an income of six thousand francs. An excellent woman, known in her day as "the pretty grocer." She ran the household, but had likewise a decided mania for lottery, and always for the same numbers; she "nursed a trey." She ended by ruining her niece who had blindly entrusted her interests to her, but Mme. Descoings repaid for her foolish doings by an absolute devotion,—all the while continuing to place her money on the evasive combinations. One day her hoardings were stolen from her mattress by Philippe Bridau. On this account she was unable to renew her lottery tickets. Then it was that the famous trey turned up. Madame Descoings died of grief, December 31, 1821. Had it not been for the theft she would have become a millionaire. [A Bachelor's Establishment.]

Desfondrilles, substitute judge at Provins during the Restoration; made president of the court of that town, time of Louis Philippe. An old fellow more archæologist than judge, who found delight in the petty squabbles under his eyes. He forsook Tiphaine's party for the Liberals headed by lawyer Vinet. [Pierrette.]

Deslandes, surgeon of Azay-le-Rideau in 1817. Called in to bleed Mme. de Mortsauf, whose life was saved by this operation. [The Lily of the Valley.]

Desmarets (Jules), Parisian stock-broker under the Restoration. Hardworking and upright, being reared in sternness and poverty. When only a clerk he fell in love with a charming young girl met at his patron's home, and he married her despite the irregularity connected with her birth. With the money obtained by his wife's mother he was able to purchase the position of the stock-broker for whom he had clerked; and for several years he was very happy in a mutual love and a liberal competence—an income of two hundred and fifty thousand francs. In 1820 he and his wife lived in a large mansion on rue Ménars. In the early years of his wedded life he killed in a duel—though unknown to his wife—a man who had villified Mme. Desmarets. The flawless happiness which abode with this well-mated couple was cut short by the death of the wife, mortally wounded by a doubt, held for a moment only by her husband, concerning her faithfulness. Desmarets, bereaved, sold his place to Martin Falleix's brother and left Paris in despair. [The Thirteen.] M. and Mme. Desmarets were invited to the famous ball given by César Birotteau in 1818. After the bankruptcy of the perfumer, the broker kindly gave him useful tips about placing funds laboriously scraped together towards the complete reimbursing of the creditors. [César Birotteau.]

Desmarets (Madame Jules), wife of the preceding; natural daughter of Bourignard alias Ferragus, and of a married woman who passed for her godmother. She had no civil status, but when she married Jules Desmarets her name, Clémence, and her age .were publicly announced. Despite herself, Mme. Desmarets was loved by a young officer of the Royal Guard, Auguste de Maulincour. Mme. Desmaret's secret visits to her father, a man of mystery, unknown to her husband, caused the downfall of their absolute happiness. Desmarets thought himself deceived, and she died on account of his suspicions, in 1820 or 1821. The remains of Clémence were placed at first in Pére Lachaise, but afterwards were disinterred, incinerated and sent to Jules Desmarets by Bourignard, assisted by twelve friends who thus thought to dull the edge of the keenest of conjugal sorrows. [The Thirteen.] M. and Mme. Desmarets were oftén alluded to as M. and Mme. Jules. At the ball given by César Birotteau, Mme. Desmarets shone as the most beautiful woman, according to the perfumer's wife herself. [César Birotteau.]

Desmarets, Parisian notary during the Restoration; elder brother of the broker, Jules Desmarets. The notary was set up in business by his younger brother and grew rich rapidly. He received his brother's will. He accompanied him to Mme. Desmarets' funeral. [The Thirteen.]

Desplein, famous surgeon of Paris, born about the middle of the eighteenth century. Sprung of a poor provincial family, he spent a youth full of suffering, being enabled to pass his examinations only through assistance rendered him by his neighbor in poverty, Bourgeat the water-carrier. For two years he lived with him on the sixth floor of a wretched house on rue des Quatre-Vents, where later was established the "Cénacle" with Daniel d'Arthez as host—on which account the house came to be spoken of as the "bowl for great men." Desplein, evicted by his landlord whom he could not pay, lodged next with his friend the Auvergnat in the Court de Rohan, Passage du Commerce. Afterwards, when an "intern" at Hôtel-Dieu, he remembered the good deeds of Bourgeat, nursed him as a devoted son, and, in the time of the Empire, established in honor of this simple man who professed religious sentiments a quarterly mass at Saint-Sulpice, at which he piously assisted, though himself an outspoken atheist. [The Atheist's Mass.] In 1806 Desplein had predicted speedy death for an old fellow then fifty-six years old, but who was still alive in 1846. [Cousin Pons.] The surgeon was present at the death caused by despair of M. Chardon, an old military doctor. [Lost Illusions.] Desplein attended the last hours of Mme. Jules Desmarets, who died in 1820 or 1821; also of the chief of division, Flamet de la Billardière, who died in 1824. [The Thirteen. The Government Clerks.] In March, 1828, at Provins, he performed an operation of trepanning on Pierrette Lorrain. [Pierrette.] In the same year he undertook a bold operation upon Mme. Philippe Bridau whose abuse of strong drink had induced a "magnificent malady" that he believed had disappeared. This operation was reported in the "Gazette des Hôpitaux;" but the patient died. [A

Bachelor's Establishment.]   In 1829 Desplein was summoned on behalf of Vanda de Mergi, daughter of Baron de Bourlac. [The Seamy Side of History.]   In the latter part of the same year he operated successfully upon Mme. Mignon for blindness. In February, 1830, on account of the foregoing, he was a witness at Modeste Mignon's wedding with Ernest de la Briére. [Modeste Mignon.]   In the beginning of the same year, 1830, he was called by Corentin to visit Baron de Nucingen, love-sick for Esther Gobseck; and Mme. de Sérizy ill on account of the suicide of Lucien de Rubempré.   [Scenes from a Courtesan's Life.]   He and his assistant, Bianchon, waited on Mme. de Bauvan, who was on the verge of death at the close of 1830 and beginning of 1831.   [Honorine.] Desplein had an only daughter whose marriage in 1829 was arranged with the Prince of Loudon.

Desroches, clerk of the Minister of the Interior under the Empire; friend of Bridau Senior, who had procured him the position.   He was also on friendly terms with the chief's widow, at whose home he met, nearly every evening, his colleagues Du Bruel and Claparon.   A dry, crusty man, who would never become sub-chief, despite his ability. He earned only one thousand eight hundred francs, and his wife one thousand two hundred francs by running a department for stamped paper.   Retired after the second return of Louis XVIII., he talked of entering as chief of bureau into an insurance company with a graduated salary. In 1821, despite his scarcely tender disposition, Desroches undertook with much discretion and confidence to extricate Philippe Bridau out of a predicament—the latter having made a "loan" on the cash-box of the newspaper for which he was working; he brought about his resignation without any scandal.   Desroches was a man of good "judgment." He remained to the last a friend of the widow Bridau after the death of MM. du Bruel and Claparon.   He was a persistent fisherman.   [A Bachelor's Establishment.]·

Desroches (Madame), wife of the preceding.   A widow, in 1826, she sought the hand of Mlle. Matifat for her son, Desroches the attorney.   [The Firm of Nucingen.]

Desroches, son of the two foregoing; born about 1795; reared strictly by a very harsh father. He went into Derville's office as fourth clerk in 1818, and on the following year passed to the second clerkship. He saw Colonel Chabert at Derville's. In 1821 or 1822 he purchased a lawyer's office with bare title on rue de Béthizy. He was shrewd and quick and therefore was not long in finding a clientele composed of littérateurs, artists, actresses, famous lorettes and elegant Bohemians. He was counsellor for Agathe and Joseph Bridau, and also gave excellent advice to Philippe Bridau who was setting out for Issoudun about 1822. [A Bachelor's Establishment. Colonel Chabert. A Start in Life.] Desroches was advocate for Charles de Vandenesse, pleading against his brother Félix; for the Marquise d'Espard, seeking interdiction against her husband; and for the Secretary-General Chardin des Lupeaulx, with whom he counseled astutely. [A Woman of Thirty. The Commission in Lunacy. The Government Clerks.] Lucien de Rubempré consulted Desroches about the seizure of the furniture of Coralie, his mistress, in 1822. [A Distinguished Provincial at Paris.] Vautrin appreciated the attorney; he said that the latter would be able to "recover" the Rubempré property, to improve it and make it capable of yielding Lucien an income of thirty thousand francs, which would probably have allowed him to wed Clotilde de Grandlieu. [Scenes from a Courtesan's Life.] In 1826 Desroches made a short-lived attempt to marry Malvina d'Aldrigger. [The Firm of Nucingen.] About 1840 he related, at Mlle. Turquet's—Malaga's—home, then maintained by Cardot the notary, and in the presence of Bixiou, Lousteau and Nathan, who were invited by the tabellion, the tricks employed by Cérizet to obtain the face value of a note out of Maxime de Trailles. [A Man of Business.] Indeed, Desroches was Cérizet's lawyer when the latter had a quarrel with Théodose de la Peyrade in 1840. He also looked after the interests of the contractor, Sauvaignou, at this same time. [The Middle Classes.] Desroches' office was probably located for a time on rue de Buci. [A Bachelor's Establishment.]

Desroys, clerk with the Minister of Finance in Baudoyer's bureau, under the Restoration. The son of a Conventionalist who had not favored the King's death. A Republican; friend of Michel Chrestien. He did not associate with any of his colleagues, but kept his manner of life so concealed that none knew where he lived. In December, 1824, he was discharged because of his opinions concerning the denunciation of Dutocq. [The Government Clerks.]

Desroziers, musician; prize-winner at Rome; died in that city through typhoid fever in 1836. Friend of the sculptor Dorlange, to whom he recounted the story of Zambinella, the death of Sarrasine and the marriage of the Count of Lanty. Desroziers gave music lessons to Marianina, daughter of the count. The musician employed his friend, who was momentarily in need of money, to undertake a copy of a statue of Adonis, which reproduced Zambinella's features. This copy he sold to M. de Lanty. [The Member for Arcis.]

Desroziers, printer at Moulins, department of the Allier. After 1830 he published a small volume containing the works of "Jan Diaz, son of a Spanish prisoner, and born in 1807 at Bourges." This volume had an introductory sketch on Jan Diaz by M. de Clagny. [The Muse of the Department.]

Dey (Comtesse de), born about 1755. Widow of a lieutenant-general retired to Carentan, department of the Manche, where she died suddenly in November, 1793, through a shock to her maternal sensibilities. [The Conscript.]

Dey (Auguste, Comte de), only son of Mme. de Dey. Made lieutenant of the dragoons when only eighteen, and followed the princes in emigration as a point of honor. He was idolized by his mother, who had remained in France in order to preserve his fortune for him. He participated in the Granville expedition. Imprisoned as a result of this affair, he wrote Mme. de Dey that he would arrive at her home, disguised and a fugitive, within three days' time. But he was shot in the Morbihan at the exact moment when his .

mother expired from the shock of having received instead of her son the conscript Julien Jussieu. [The Conscript.]

Diard (Pierre-François), born in the suburbs of Nice; the son of a merchant-provost; quartermaster of the Sixth regiment of the line, in 1808, then chief of battalion in the Imperial Guard; retired with this rank on account of a rather severe wound received in Germany; afterwards an administrator and business man; excessive gambler. Husband of Juana Mancini who had been the mistress of Captain Montefiore, Diard's most intimate friend. In 1823, at Bordeaux, Diard killed and robbed Montefiore, whom he met by accident. Upon his return home he confessed his crime to his wife who vainly besought him to commit suicide; and she herself finally blew out his brains with a pistol shot. [The Maranas.]

Diard (Maria-Juana-Pepita), daughter of La Marana, a Venetian courtesan, and a young Italian nobleman, Mancini, who acknowledged her. Wife of Pierre-François Diard whom she accepted on her mother's request, after having given herself to Montefiore who did not wish to marry her. Juana had been reared very strictly in the Spanish home of Perez de Lagounia, at Tarragone, and she bore her father's name. She was the descendant of a long line of courtesans, a feminine branch that had never made legal marriages. The blood of her ancestors was in her veins; she showed this involuntarily by the way in which she yielded to Montefiore. Although she did not love her husband, yet she remained entirely faithful to him, and she killed him for honor's sake. She had two children. [The Maranas.]

Diard (Juan), first child of Mme. Diard. Born seven months after his mother's marriage, and perhaps the son of Montefiore. He was the image of Juana, who secretly petted him extravagantly, although she pretended to like her younger son the better. By a "species of admirable flattery" Diard had made Juan his choice. [The Maranas.]

Diard (Francisque), second son of M. and Mme. Diard; born in Paris. A counterpart of his father, and the favorite—only outwardly—of his mother. [The Maranas.]

Diaz (Jan), assumed name of Mme. Dinah de la Baudraye.

Diodati, owner of a villa on Lake Geneva in 1823-1824.— Character in a novel called "L'Ambitieux par Amour" published by Albert Savarus in the "Revue de l'Est" in 1834. [Albert Savarus.]

Dionis, notary at Nemours from about 1813 till the early part of the reign of Louis Philippe. He was a Crémière-Dionis, but was always known by the latter name. A shrewd, double-faced individual, who was secretly a partner with Massin-Levrault the money-lender. He concerned himself with the inheritance left by Dr. Minoret, giving advice to the three legatees of the old physician. After the Revolution of 1830, he was elected mayor of Nemours, instead of M. Levrault, and about 1837 he became deputy. He was then received at court balls, in company with his wife, and Mme. Dionis was "enthroned" in the village because of her "ways of the throne." The couple had at least one daughter. [Ursule Mirouët.] Dionis breakfasted familiarly with Rastignac, Minister of Public Works, from 1839 to 1845. [The Member for Arcis.]

Doguereau, publisher on rue de Coq, Paris, in 1821, having been established since the first of the century; retired professor of rhetoric. Lucien de Rubempré offered him his romance, "The Archer of Charles IX.," but the publisher would not give him more than four hundred francs for it, so the trade was not concluded. [A Distinguished Provincial at Paris.]

Doisy, porter of the Lepitre Institution, quarter du Marais, Paris, about 1814, at the time when Félix de Vandenesse came there to complete his course of study. This young man contracted a debt of one hundred francs on Doisy's account, which resulted in a very severe reprimand from his mother. [The Lily of the Valley.]

Dominis (Abbé de), priest of Tours during the Restoration; preceptor of Jacques de Mortsauf. [The Lily of the Valley.]

Dommanget, an accoucheur-physician, famous in Paris

at the time of Louis Philippe. In 1840 he was called in to visit Mme. Calyste du Guénic, whom he had accouched, and who had taken a dangerous relapse on learning of her husband's infidelity. She was nursing her son at this time. On being taken into her confidence, Dommanget treated and cured her ailment by purely moral methods. [Béatrix.]

Doni (Massimilla). (*See* Varèse, Princesse de.)

Dorlange (Charles), first name of Sallenauve, which name see.

Dorsonval (Madame), bourgeoise of Saumur, acquainted with M. and Mme. de Grassins at the time of the Restoration. [Eugénie Grandet.]

Doublon (Victor-Ange-Herménégilde), bailiff at Angoulême during the Restoration. He acted against David Séchard on behalf of the Cointet brothers. [Lost Illusions.]

Duberghe, wine-merchant of Bordeaux from whom Nucingen purchased in 1815, before the battle of Waterloo, 150,000 bottles of wine, averaging thirty sous to the bottle. The financier sold them for six francs each to the allied armies, from 1817 to 1819. [The Firm of Nucingen.]

Dubourdieu, born about 1805; a symbolic painter of the Fouierist school; decorated. In 1845 he was met at the corner of rue Neuve-Vivienne by his friend Léon de Lora, when he expressed his ideas on art and philosophy to Gazonal and Bixiou, who were with the famous landscape-painter. [The Unconscious Humorists.]

Dubut of Caen, merchant connected with MM. de Boisfranc, de Boisfrelon and de Boislaurier who were also Dubuts, and whose grandfather was a dealer in linens. Dubut of Caen was involved in the trial of the Chauffeurs of Mortagne, in 1809, and sentenced to death for contumacy. During the Restoration, on account of his devotion to the Royal cause, he had hoped to obtain the succession to the title of M. de Boisfranc. Louis XVIII. made him grand provost, in 1815, and later public prosecutor under the coveted name; finally he died as first president of the court. [The Seamy Side of History.]

Ducange (Victor), novelist and playwright of France; born in 1783 at La Haye; died in 1833; one of the collaborators in "Thirty Years," or "A Gambler's Life," and the author of "Léonide." Victor Ducange was present at Braulard's, the head-claquer's, in 1821, at a dinner where were also Adéle Dupois, Frédéric Dupetit-Méré and Mlle. Millot, Braulard's mistress. [A Distinguished Provincial at Paris.]

Dudley (Lord), statesman; one of the most distinguished of the older English peers living in Paris after 1816; husband of Lady Arabella Dudley; natural father of Henri de Marsay, to whom he paid small attention, and who became the lover of Arabella. He was "profoundly immoral." He reckoned among his illegitimate progeny, Euphémia Porrabéril, and among the women he maintained a certain Hortense who lived on rue Tronchet. Before removing to France, Lord Dudley lived in his native land with two sons born in wedlock, but who were astonishingly like Marsay. [The Lily of the Valley. The Thirteen. A Man of Business.] Lord Dudley was present at Mlle. des Touches, shortly after 1830, when Marsay, then prime minister, told of his first love affair; these two statesmen exchanged philosophical reflections. [Another Study of Woman.] In 1834 he chanced to be present at a grand ball given by his wife, when he gambled in a salon with bankers, ambassadors and retired ministers. [A Daughter of Eve.]

Dudley (Lady Arabella), wife of the preceding; member of an illustrious English family that was free of any *mésalliance* from the time of the Conquest; exceedingly wealthy; one of those almost regal ladies; the idol of the highest French society during the Restoration. She did not live with her husband to whom she had left two sons who resembled Marsay, whose mistress she had been. In some way she succeeded in taking Félix de Vandenesse away from Mme. de Mortsauf, thus causing that virtuous woman keen anguish. She was born, so she said, in Lancashire, where women die of love. [The Lily of the Valley.] In the early years of the reign of Charles X., at least during the summers, she lived at

the village of Châtenay, near Sçeaux.   [The Ball at Sçeaux.]
Raphaël de Valentin desired her and would have sought her
but for the fear of exhausting the "magic skin." [The Magic
Skin.] In 1832 she was among the guests at a soirée given by
Mme. d' Espard, where the Duchesse de Maufrigneuse was
maligned in the presence of Daniel d'Arthez, in love with her.
[The Secrets of a Princess.] She was quite jealous of Mme.
Félix de Vandenesse, the wife of her old-time lover, and in
1834-35 she monœuvred, with Mme. de Listomère and Mme.
d'Espard to make the young woman fall into the arms of the
poet Nathan, whom she wished to be even homelier than he
was. She said to Mme. Félix de Vandenesse: "Marriage, my
child, is our purgatory; love our paradise." [A Daughter of
Eve.] Lady Dudley, vengeance-bent, caused Lady Brandon
to die of grief. [Letters of Two Brides.]

Dufau, justice of the peace in a commune in the outskirts
of Grenoble, where Dr. Benassis was mayor under the Restoration. Then a tall, bony man with gray locks and clothed in
black. He aided materially in the work of regeneration
accomplished by the physician in the village. [The Country
Doctor.]

Dufaure (Jules-Armand-Stanislaus), attorney and French
politician; born December 4, 1798, at Saujon, Charente-
Inférieure; died an Academician at Rueil in the summer of
1881; friend and co-disciple of Louis Lambert and of
Barchou de Penhoën at the college of Vendôme in 1811.
[Louis Lambert.]

Dumay (Anne-François-Bernard), born at Vannes in 1777;
son of a rather mean lawyer, the president of a revolutionary
tribunal under the Republic, and a victim of the guillotine
subsequent to the ninth Thermidor. His mother died of
grief. In 1799 Anne Dumay enlisted in the army of Italy.
On the overthrow of the Empire, he retired with the rank of
lieutenant, and came in touch with Charles Mignon, with
whom he had become acquainted early in his military career.
He was thoroughly devoted to his friend, who had once saved
his life at Waterloo. He gave great assistance to the commer-

cial enterprises of the Mignon house, and faithfully looked after the interests of Mme. and Mlle. Mignon during the protracted absence of the head of the family, who was suddenly ruined. Mignon came back from America a rich man, and he made Dumay share largely in his fortune. [Modeste Mignon.]

Dumay (Madame), *née* Grummer, wife of the foregoing; a pretty little American woman who married Dumay while he was on a journey to America on behalf of his patron and friend Charles Mignon, during the Restoration. Having had the misfortune to lose several children at birth, and deprived of the hope of others, she became entirely devoted to the two Mignon girls. She as well as her husband was thoroughly attached to that family. [Modeste Mignon.]

Dupetit-Méré (Frédéric), born at Paris in 1785 and died in 1827; dramatic author who enjoyed his brief hour of fame. Under the name of Frédéric he constructed either singly, or in collaboration with Ducange, Rougemont, Brazier and others, a large number of melodramas, vaudevilles, and fantasies. In 1821 he was present with Ducange, Adéle Dupuis and Mlle. Millot at a dinner at Braulard's, the head-claquer. [A Distinguished Provincial at Paris.]

Duplanty (Abbé), vicar of Saint-François church at Paris; at Schmucke's request he administered extreme unction to the dying Pons, in April, 1845, who understood and appreciated his goodness. [Cousin Pons.]

Duplay (Madame), wife of a carpenter of rue Honoré at whose house Robespierre lived; a customer of the grocer Descoings, whom she denounced as a forestaller. This accusation led to the grocer's imprisonment and execution. [A Bachelor's Establishment.]

Dupotet, a sort of banker established at Croisic under the Restoration. He had on deposit the modest patrimony of Pierre Cambremer. [A Seaside Tragedy.]

Dupuis, notary of the Saint-Jacques quarter, time of Louis Philippe; affectedly pious; beadle of the parish. He kept the savings of a lot of servants. Théodose de la Peyrade, who drummed up trade for him in this special line, induced Mme. Lambert, the housekeeper of M. Picot, to place two thousand five hundred francs, saved at her employer's expense, with this virtuous man, who immediately went into bankrutpcy. [The Middle Classes.]

Dupuis (Adéle), Parisian actress who for a long time and brilliantly held the leading rôles and creations at the Gâité theatre.   In 1821 she dined with the chief claquer, Braulard, in company with Ducange, Frédéric Dupetit-Méré and Mlle. Millot. [A Distinguished Provincial at Paris.]

Durand, real name of the Chessels. This name of Chessel had been borrowed by Mme. Durand, who was born a Chessel.

Duret (Abbé), curé of Sancerre during the Restoration; aged member of the old clerical school.   Excellent company; a frequenter of the home of Mme. de la Baudraye, where he satisfied his penchant for gaming. With much *finesse* Duret showed this young woman the character of M. de la Baudraye in its true light.   He counseled her to seek in literature relief from the bitterness of her wedded life. [The Muse of the Department.]

Duriau, a celebrated accoucheur of Paris. Assisted by Bianchon he delivered Mme. de la Baudraye of a child at the home of Lousteau, its father, in 1837. [The Muse of the Department.]

Durieu, cook and house servant at the château de Cinq-Cygne, under the Consulate. An old and trusted servant, thoroughly devoted to his mistress, Laurence de Cinq-Cygne, whose fortunes he had always followed. He was a married man, his wife being general housekeeper in the establishment. [The Gondreville Mystery.]

Duroc (Gérard-Christophe-Michel), Duc de Frioul; grand marshal of the palace of Napoleon; born at Pont-à-Mousson, in 1772; killed on the battlefield in 1813. On October 13, 1806, the eve of the battle of Jéna, he conducted the Marquis de Chargeboeuf and Laurence de Cinq-Cygne to the Emperor's presence. [The Gondreville Mystery.] In April, 1813, he was at a dress-parade at the Carrousel, Paris, when Napoleon addressed him, regarding Mlle. de Chatillonest, noted by him in the throng, in language which made the grand marshal smile. [A Woman of Thirty.]

Durut (Jean-François), a criminal whom Prudence Servien helped convict to hard labor by her testimony in the Court of Assizes. Durut took oath to Prudence, before the same tribunal, that, once free, he would kill her. However, he was executed at the bagne of Toulon four years later (1829). Jacques Collin, alias Vautrin, to obtain Prudence's affections, boasted of having freed her from Durut, whose threat held her in perpetual terror. [Scenes from a Courtesan's Life.]

Dutheil (Abbé), one of the two vicars-general of the Bishop of Limoges during the Restoration. One of the lights of the Gallican clergy. Made a bishop in August, 1831, and promoted to archbishop in 1840. He presided at the public confession of Mme. Graslin, whose friend and adviser he was, and whose funeral procession he followed in 1844. [The Country Parson.]

Dutocq, born in 1786. In 1814 he entered the Department of Finance, succeeding Poiret senior who was displaced in the bureau directed by Rabourdin. He was order clerk. Idle and incapable, he hated his chief and caused his overthrow. Very despicable and very prying, he tried to make his place secure by acting as spy in the bureau. Chardin des Lupeaulx, the secretary-general, was advised by him of the slightest developments. After 1816, Dutocq outwardly affected very pronounced religious tendencies because he believed them useful to his advancement. He eagerly collected old engravings, possessing complete "his Charlet," which he desired to give or lend to the minister's wife. At this time he dwelt on rue Saint-Louis-Saint-Honoré (in 1854 this street disappeared) near Palais Royal, on the fifth floor of an enclosed house, and boarded in a pension of rue de Beaune. [The Government Clerks.] In 1840, retired, he clerked for a justice of the peace of the Pantheon municipality, and lived in Thuillier's house, rue Saint-Dominique d'Enfer. He was a bachelor and had all the vices which, however, he religiously concealed. He kept in with his superiors by fawning. He was concerned with the villainous intrigues of Cérizet, his copy-clerk, and with Théodose de la Peyrade, the tricky lawyer. [The Middle Classes.]

Duval, wealthy forge-master of Alençon, whose daughter, the grand-niece of M. du Croisier (du Bousquier), was married in 1830 to Victurnien d'Esgrignon. Her dowry was three million francs. [Jealousies of a Country Town.]

Duval, famous professor of chemistry at Paris in 1843. A friend of Dr. Bianchon, at whose instance he analyzed the blood of M. and Mme Crevel, who were infected by a peculiar cutaneous disease of which they died. [Cousin Betty.]

Duvignon. (*See* Lanty, de.)

Duvivier, jeweler at Vendôme during the Empire. Mme. de Merret declared to her husband that she had purchased of this merchant an ebony crucifix encrusted with silver; but in truth she had obtained it of her lover, Bagos de Férédia. She swore falsely on this very crucifix. [La Grande Bretéche.]

E

Emile, a "lion of the most triumphant kind," of the acquaintance of Mme. Komorn—Comtesse Godollo. One evening in 1840 or 1841 this woman, in order to avoid Théodose de la Peyrade, on the Boulevard des Italiens, took the dandy's arm and requested him to take her to Mabille. [The Middle Classes.]

Esgrignon (Charles-Marie-Victor-Ange-Carol, Marquis d'), or, Des Grignons—following the earlier name—commander of the Order of Saint-Louis; born about 1750, died in 1830. Head of a very ancient family of the Francs, the Karawls who came from the North to conquer the Gauls, and who were entrusted with the defence of a French highway. The Esgrignons, quasi-princes under the House of Valois and all-powerful under Henry IV., were very little known at the court of Louis XVIII.; and the marquis, ruined by the Revolution, lived in rather reduced circumstances at Alençon in an old gable-roofed house formerly belonging to him, which had been sold as common property, and which the faithful notary

Chesnel had repurchased, together with certain portions of his other estates. The Marquis d'Esgrignon, though not having to emigrate, was still obliged to conceal himself. He participated in the Vendean struggle against the Republic, and was one of the members of the Committee Royal of Alençon. In 1800, at the age of fifty, in the hope of perpetuating his race, he married Mlle. de Nouastre, who died in child-birth, leaving the marquis an only son. M. d'Esgrignon always overlooked the escapades of this child, whose reputation was preserved by Chesnel; and he passed away shortly after the downfall of Charles X., saying: "The Gauls triumph." [The Chouans. Jealousies of a Country Town.]

Esgrignon (Madame d'), *née* Nouastre; of blood the purest and noblest; married at twenty-two, in 1800, to Marquis Carol d'Esgrignon, a man of fifty. She soon died at the birth of an only son. She was "the prettiest of human beings; in her person were reawakened the charms—now fanciful—of the feminine figures of the sixteenth century." [Jealousies of a Country Town.]

Esgrignon (Victurnien, Comte, then Marquis d'), only son of Marquis Carol d'Esgrignon; born about 1800 at Alençon. Handsome and intelligent, reared with extreme indulgence and kindness by his aunt, Mlle. Armande d'Esgrignon, he gave himself over without restraint to all the whims usual to the ingenuous egoism of his age. From eighteen to twenty-one he squandered eighty thousand francs without the knowledge of his father and his aunt; the devoted Chesnel footed all the bills. The youthful d'Esgrignon was systematically urged to wrong-doing by an ally of his own age, Fabien du Ronceret, a perfidious fellow of the town whom M. du Croisier employed. About 1823 Victurnien d'Esgrignon was sent to Paris. There he had the misfortune to fall into the society of the Parisian *roués*—Marsay, Ronquerolles, Trailles, Chardin des Lupeaulx, Vandenesse, Ajuda-Pinto, Beaudenord, Martial de la Roche-Hugon, Manerville, people met at the homes of Marquise d'Espard, the Duchesses de Grandlieu, de Carigliano, de Chaulieu, the Marquises d'Aigle-

mont and de Listomère, Mme. Firmiani and the Comtesse de
Sérizy; at the opera and at the embassies—being welcomed
on account of his good name and seeming fortune. It was
not long until he became the lover of the Duchesse de Maufrigneuse, ruined himself for her and ended by forging a note
against M. du Croisier for one hundred thousand francs.   His
aunt took him back quickly to Alençon, and by a great effort
he was rescued from legal proceedings. Following this he
fought a duel with M. du Croisier, who wounded him dangerously.   Nevertheless, shortly after the death of his father,
Victurnien d'Esgrignon married Mlle. Duval, niece of the
retired contractor.   He did not give himself over to his wife,
but instead betook himself to his former gay life of a bachelor.
[Jealousies of a Country Town. Letters of Two Brides.]
According to Marguerite Turquet "the little D'Esgrignon was
well soaked" by Antonia. [A Man of Business.] In 1832
Victurnien d'Esgrignon declared before a numerous company
at Mme. d'Espard's that the Princesse de Cadignan—Mme.
de Maufrigneuse—was a dangerous woman.   "To her I owe
the disgrace of my marriage," he added.   Daniel d'Arthez,
who was then in love with this woman, was present at the
conversation. [The Secrets of a Princess.] In 1838 Victurnien d'Esgrignon was present with some artists, lorettes and
men about town, at the opening of the house on rue de la
Ville-Evéque given to Josépha Mirah, by the Duc d'Hérouville.   The young marquis himself had been Josépha's lover;
Baron Hulot and he had been rivals for her on another occasion. [Cousin Betty.]

Esgrignon (Marie-Armande-Claire d'), born about 1775;
sister of Marquis Carol d'Esgrignon and aunt of Victurnien
d'Esgrignon to whom she had been as a mother, with an
absolute tenderness.   In his old age her father had married
for a second time, and to the young daughter of a tax collector,
ennobled by Louis XIV. She was born of this union which
was looked upon as a horrible *mésalliance*, and although the
marquis loved her dearly he regarded her as an alien.   He
made her weep for joy, one day, by saying solemnly: "You
are an Esgrignon, my sister." Emile Blondet, reared at

Alençon, had known and loved her in his childhood, and often later he praised her beauty and good qualities. On account of her devotion to her nephew she refused M. de la Roche-Guyon and the Chevalier de Valois, also M. du Bousquier. She gave the fullest proof of her genuinely maternal affection for Victurnien, when the latter committed the crime at Paris, which would have placed him on the prisoner's bench of the Court of Assizes, but for the clever work of Chesnel. She outlived her brother, given over "to her religion and her over-thrown beliefs." About the middle of Louis Philippe's reign Blondet, who had come to Alençon to obtain his marriage license, was again moved on the contemplation of that noble face. [Jealousies of a Country Town.]

Espard (Charles-Maurice-Marie-Andoche, Comte de Négre-pelisse, Marquis d'), born about 1789; by name a Négrepelisse, of an old Southern family which acquired by a marriage, time of Henry IV., the lands and titles of the family of Espard, of Béarn, which was allied also with the Albret house. The device of the d'Espards was: "Des partem leonis." The Négrepelisses were militant Catholics, ruined at the time of the Church wars, and afterwards considerably enriched by the despoiling of a family of Protestant merchants, the Jeanrenauds whose head had been hanged after the revocation of the Edict of Nantes. This property, so badly acquired, became won-drously profitable to the Négrepelisses-d'Espards. Thanks to his fortune, the grandfather of the marquis was enabled to wed a Navarreins-Lansac, an extremely wealthy heiress; her father was of the younger branch of the Grandlieus. In 1812 the Marquis d'Espard married Mlle. de Blamont-Chauvry, then sixteen years of age. He had two sons by her, but discord soon arose between the couple. Her silly extravagances forced the marquis to borrow. He left her in 1816, going with his two children to live on rue de la Mon-tagne-Sainte-Geneviéve. Here he devoted himself to the education of his boys and to the composition of a great work: "The Picturesque History of China," the profits of which, combined with the savings resultant from an austere manner of living, allowed him to pay in twelve years' time to the legatees of the suppliant Jeanrenauds eleven hundred thousand francs, representing the value—time of Louis XIV.—of the property confiscated from their ancestors. This book was written, so to speak, in collaboration with Abbé Crozier, and its financial results aided greatly in comforting the declining years of a ruined friend, M. de Nouvion. In 1828 Mme. d'Espard tried to have a guardian appointed for her husband, by ridiculing the noble conduct of the marquis. But the defendant won his rights at court. [The Commission in Lunacy.] Lucien de Rubempré, who entertained Attorney-General Granville with an account of this suit, probably was instrumental in causing the judgment to favor M. d'Espard. Thus he drew upon himself the hatred of the marquise. [Scenes from a Courtesan's Life.

Espard (Camille, Vicomte d'), second son of Marquis d'Espard; born in 1815; pursued his studies at the college of Henri IV., in company with his elder brother, the Comte Clément de Négrepelisse. He studied rhetoric in 1828. [The Commission in Lunacy.]

Espard (Chevalier d'), brother of Marquis d'Espard, whom he wished to see interdicted, in order that he might be made curator. His face was thin as a knife-blade, and he was frigid and severe. Judge Popinot said he reminded him somewhat of Cain. He was one of the deepest personages to be found in the Marquise d'Espard's drawing-room, and was the political half of that woman. [The Commission in Lunacy. Scenes from a Courtesan's Life. The Secrets of a Princess.]

Espard (Jeanne-Clémentine-Athenaïs de Blamont-Chauvry, Marquise d'), born in 1795; wife of Marquis d'Espard; of one of the most illustrious houses of Faubourg Saint-Germain. Deserted by her husband in 1816, she was at the age of twenty-two mistress of herself and of her fortune, an income of twenty-six thousand francs. At first she lived in seclusion; then in 1820 she appeared at court, gave some receptions at her own home, and did not long delay about becoming a society woman. Cold, vain and coquettish she knew neither love nor hatred; her indifference for all that did not directly concern her was profound. She never showed emotion. She had certain scientific formulas for preserving her beauty. She never wrote but spoke instead, believing that two words from a woman were sufficient to kill three men. More than once she made epigrams to peers or deputies which the courts of Europe treasured. In 1828 she still passed with the men for youthful. Mme. d'Espard lived at number 104 rue du Faubourg Saint-Honoré. [The Commission in Lunacy.] She was a magnificent Célimène. She displayed such prudence and severity on her separation from her husband that society was at a loss to account for this disagreement. She was surrounded by her relatives, the Navarreins, the Blamont-Chauvrys and the Lenoncourts; ladies of the highest social position claimed her acquaintance. She was a cousin of Mme. de Bargeton, who was rehabilitated by her on her arrival from Angouléme in 1821, and whom she introduced into Paris, showing her all the secrets of elegant life and taking her away from Lucien de Rubempré. Later, when the "Distinguished Provincial" had won his way into high society, she, at the instance of Mme. de Montcornet, enlisted him on the Royalist side. [A Distinguished Provincial at Paris.] In 1824 she was at an Opéra ball to which she had come through an anonymous note, and, leaning on the arm of Sixte du Châtelet, she met Lucien de Rubempré whose beauty struck her and whom she seemed, indeed, not to remember. The poet had his revenge for her former disdain, by means of some cutting phrases, and Jacques Collin—Vautrin—masked, caused her uneasiness by persuading her that Lucien was the author of the note and that he loved her. [Scenes from a Courtesan's Life.] The Chaulieus were intimate with her at the time when their daughter Louise was courted by Baron de Macumer. [Letters of Two Brides.] Despite the silent opposition of the Faubourg Saint-Germain, after the Revolution of 1830, the Marquise d'Espard did not close her salon, since she did not wish to renounce her Parisian prestige. In this she was seconded by one or two women in her circle and by Mlle. des Touches. [Another Study of Woman.] She was at home Wednesdays.

In 1833 she attended a soirée at the home of the Princess de Cadignan, where Marsay disclosed the mystery surrounding the abduction of Senator Malin in 1806. [The Gondreville Mystery.] Notwithstanding an evil report circulated against her by Mme. d'Espard, the princesse told Daniel d'Arthez that the marquise was her best friend; she was related to her. [The Secrets of a Princess.] A tuated by jealou y for Mme. Félix de Vandenesse, Mme. d'Espard fostered the growing intimacy between that young woman and Nathan the poet; she wished to see an apparent rival compromised. In 1835 the marquise defended vaudeville entertainments against Lady Dudley, who said she could not endure them. [A Daughter of Eve] In 1840, on leaving the Italiens, Mme. d'Espard humiliated Mme. de Rochefide by snubbing her; all the women followed her example, shunning the mistress of Calyste du Guénie. [Béatrix.] In short the Marquise d'Espard was one of the most snobbish people of her day. Her disposition was sour and malevolent, despite its elegant veneer.

Estival (Abbé d'), provincial priest and Lenten exhorter at the church of Saint-Jacques du Haut-Pas, Paris. According to Théodose de la Peyrade, who pointed him out to Mme. Colleville, he was devoted to predication in the interest of the poor. By spirituality and unction he redeemed a scarcely agreeable exterior. [The Middle Classes.]

Estorade (Baron, afterwards Comte de l'), a little Provincial gentleman, father of Louis de l'Estorade. A very religious and very miserly man who hoarded for his son. He lost his wife about 1814, who died of grief through lack of hope of ever seeing her son again—having heard nothing of him after the battle of Leipsic. M. de l'Estorade was an excellent grandparent. He died at the end of 1826. [Letters of Two Brides.]

Estorade (Louis, Chevalier, then Vicomte and Comte de l'), son of the preceding; peer of France; president of the Chamber in the Court of Accounts; grand officer of the Legion of Honor; born in 1787. After having been excluded from the conscription under the Empire, for a long time, he was enlisted in 1813, serving on the Guard of Honor. At Leipsic he was captured by the Russians and did not reappear in France until the Restoration. He suffered severely in Siberia; at thirty-seven he appeared to be fifty. Pale, lean, taciturn and somewhat deaf, he bore much resemblance to the Knight of the Rueful Countenance. He succeeded, however, in making himself agreeable to Renée de Maucombe whom he married, dowerless, in 1824. Urged on by his wife who became ambitious after becoming a mother, he left Crampade, his country estate, and although a mediocre he rose to the highest offices. [Letters of Two Brides. The Member for Arcis.]

Estorade (Madame de l'), born Renée de Maucombe in 1807, of a very old Provençal family, located in the Géménos Valley, twenty kilometres from Marseilles. She was educated at the Carmellite convent of Blois, where she was intimate with Louise de Chaulieu. The two friends always remained constant. For several years they corresponded, writing about life, love and marriage, when Renée the wise gave to the passionate Louise advice and prudent counsel not always followed. In 1836 Mme. de l'Estorade hastened to the country to be present at the death-bed of her friend, now become Mme. Marie Gaston. Renée de Maucombe was married at the age of seventeen, upon leaving the convent. She gave her husband three children, though she never loved him, devoting herself to the duties of motherhood. [Letters of Two Brides.] In 1838-39 the serenity of this sage person was disturbed by meeting Dorlange-Sallenauve. She believed he sought her, and she must needs fight an insidious liking for him. Mme. de Camps counseled and enlightened Mme. de l'Estorade, with considerable foresight, in this delicate crisis. Some time later, when a widow, Mme. de l'Estorade was on the point of giving her hand to Sallenauve, who became her son-in-law. [The Member for Arcis.] In 1841 Mme. de l'Estorade remarked of M. and Mme. Savinien de Portenduère: "Theirs is the most perfect happiness that I have ever seen!" [Ursule Mirouët.]

Estorade (Armand de l'), elder son of M. and Mme. de l'Estorade; godson of Louise de Chaulieu, who was Baronne de Macumer and afterwards Mme. Marie Gaston. Born in December, 1825; educated at the college of Henri IV. At first stupid and meditative, he awakened afterwards, was crowned at Sorbonne, having obtained first prize for a translation of Latin, and in 1845 made a brilliant showing in his thesis for the degree of doctor of laws. [Letters of Two Brides. The Member for Arcis.]

Estorade (René de l'), second child of M. and Mme. de l'Estorade. Bold and adventurous as a child. He had a will of iron, and his mother was convinced that he would be "the cunningest sailor afloat." [Letters of Two Brides.]

Estorade (Jeanne-Athénaïs de l'), daughter and third child of M. and Mme. de l'Estorade. Called "Naïs" for short. Married in 1847 to Charles de Sallenauve. (*See* Sallenauve, Mme. Charles de.)

Estourny (Charles d'), a young dandy of Paris who went to Havre during the Restoration to view the sea, obtained entrance into the Mignon household and eloped with Bettina-Caroline, the elder daughter. He afterwards deserted her and she died of shame. In 1827 Charles d'Estourny was sentenced by the police court for habitual fraud in gambling. [Modeste Mignon.] A Georges-Marie Destourny, who styled himself Georges d'Estourny, was the son of a bailiff, at Boulogne, near Paris, and was undoubtedly identical with Charles d'Estourny. For a time he was the protector of Esther van Gobseck, known as La Torpille. He was born about 1801, and, after having obtained a splendid education, had been left without resources by his father, who was forced to sell out under adverse circumstances. Georges d'Estourny speculated on the Bourse with money obtained from "kept" women who trusted in him. After his sentence he left Paris without squaring his accounts. He had aided Cérizet, who afterwards became his partner. He was a handsome fellow, open-hearted and generous as the chief of robbers. On account of the knaveries which brought him into court, Bixiou nick-named him "Tricks at Cards." [Scenes from a Courtesan's Life. A Man of Business.]

Etienne & Co., traders at Paris under the Empire. In touch with Guillaume, clothier of rue Saint-Denis, who foresaw their failure and awaited "with anxiety as at a game of cards." [At the Sign of the Cat and Racket.]

Eugène, Corsican colonel of the Sixth regiment of the line, which was made up almost entirely of Italians—the first to enter Tarragone in 1808. Colonel Eugéne, a second Murat, was extraordinarily brave. He knew how to make use of the species of bandits who composed his regiment. [The Maranas.]

Eugénie, assumed name of Prudence Servien, which name see.

Euphrasie, Parisian courtesan, timec of the Restoration and Louis Philippe. A pretty, winsome blonde with blue eyes and a melodious voice; she had an air of the utmost frankness, yet was profoundly depraved and expert in refined vice. In 1821 she transmitted a terrible and fatal disease to Crottat, the notary. At that time she lived on rue Feydeau. Euphrasie pretended that in her early youth she had passed entire days and nights trying to support a lover who had forsaken her for a heritage. With the brunette, Aquilina, Euphrasie took part in a famous orgy, at the home of Frédéric Taillefer, on rue Joubert, where were also Emile Blondet, Rastignac, Bixiou and Raphaél de Valentin. Later she is seen at the Théâtre-Italien, in company with the aged antiquarian, who had sold Raphaël the celebrated "magic skin"; she was running through with the old merchant's treasures. [Melmoth Reconciled. The Magic Skin.]

Europe, assumed name of Prudence Servien, which name see.

Evangélista (Madame), born Casa-Réal in 1781, of a great Spanish family collaterally descended from the Duke of Alva and related to the Claës of Douai; a creole who came to Bordeaux in 1800 with her husband, a large Spanish financier. In 1813 she was left a widow, with her daughter. She paid no thought to the value of money, never knowing how to resist a whim. So one morning in 1821 she was forced to call on the broker and expert, Elie Magus, to get an estimate on the value of her magnificent diamonds. She became wearied of life in the country, and therefore favored the marriage of her daughter with Paul de Manerville, in order that she might follow the young couple to Paris where she dreamed of appearing in grand style and of a further exercise of her power. For that matter she displayed much astuteness in arranging the details of this marriage, at which time Maitre Solonet, her notary, was much taken with her, desiring to wed her, and defending her warmly against Maitre Mathias the lawyer for the Manervilles. Beneath the exterior of an excellent woman she knew, like Catherine de Medicis, how to hate and wait. [A Marriage Settlement.]

Evangélista (Natalie), daughter of Mme. Evangélista; married to Paul de Manerville. (*See* that name.)

Evelina, young girl of noble blood, wealthy and cultured, of a strict Jansenist family; sought in marriage by Benassis, in the beginning of the Restoration. Evelina reciprocated Benassis' love, but her parents opposed the match. Evelina died soon after gaining her freedom and the doctor did not survive her long. [The Country Doctor.]

F

Faille & Bouchot, Parisian perfumers who failed in 1818. They gave an order for ten thousand phials of peculiar shape to hold a new cosmetic, which phials Anselme Popinot purchased for four sous each on six months' time, with the intention of filling them with the "Cephalic Oil" invented by César Birotteau. [César Birotteau.]

Falcon (Jean), alias Beaupied, or more often Beau-Pied, sergeant in the Seventy-second demi-brigade in 1799, under the command of Colonel Hulot. Jean Falcon was the clown of his company. Formerly he had served in the artillery. [The Chouans.] In 1808, still under the command of Hulot, he was one in the army of Spain and in the troops led by Murat.

In that year he was witness of the death of Béga, the French surgeon, assassinated by a Spaniard. [The Muse of the Department.] In 1841 he was body-servant of his old-time colonel, now become a marshal. For thirty years he had been in his employ. [Cousin Betty.]

Falcon (Marie-Cornélie), famous singer of the Opéra; born at Paris on January 28, 1812. On July 20, 1832, she made a brilliant début in the rôle of Alice, in "Robert le Diable." She also created with equal success the parts of Rachel in "La Juive" and Valentine in "The Huguenots." In 1836 the composer Conti declared to Calyste du Guénie that he was madly enamored of this singer, "the youngest and prettiest of her time." He even wished to marry her—so he said—but this remark was probably a thrust at Calyste, who was smitten with the Marquise de Rochefide, whose lover the musician was at this time. [Béatrix.] Cornélie Falcon disappears from the scene in 1840, after a famous evening when, before a sympathetic audience, she mourned on account of the ruin of her voice. She married a financier, M. Malençon, and is now a grandmother. Mme. Falcon has given, in the provinces, her name to designate tragic "sopranos." "La Vierge de l'Opéra," interestingly delineated by M. Emmanuel Gonzalés, reveals—according to him—certain incidents in her career.

Falleix (Martin), Auvergnat coppersmith on rue du Faubourg Saint-Antoine, Paris; born about 1796; he had come from the country with his kettle under his arm. He was patronized by Bidault, alias Gigonnet, who advanced him capital though at heavy interest. The usurer also introduced him to Saillard, the cashier of the Minister of Finance, who with his savings enabled him to open a foundry. Martin Falleix obtained a brevet for invention and a gold medal at the Exposition of 1824. Mme. Baudoyer undertook his education, deciding he would do for a son-in-law. On his side he worked for the interests of his future father-in-law. [The Government Clerks.] About 1826 he discussed on the Bourse, with Du Tillet, Werbrust and Claparon, the third liquidation of

Nucingen, which solidly established the fortune of that celebrated Alsatian banker. [The Firm of Nucingen.]

Falleix (Jacques), brother of the preceding; stock-broker, one of the shrewdest and richest, the successor of Jules Desmarets and stock-broker for the firm of Nucingen   On rue Saint-George he fitted up a most elegant little house for his mistress, Mme. du Val-Noble.   He failed in 1829, the victim of one of the Nucingen liquidations. [The Government Clerks.   The Thirteen.   Scenes from a Courtesan's Life.]

Fanchette, servant of Doctor Rouget at Issoudun, at the close of the eighteenth century; a stout Berrichonne who, before the advent of La Cognette, was thought to be the best cook in town.   [A Bachelor's Establishment.]

Fanjat, physician and something of an alienist; uncle of Comtesse Stéphanie de Vandiéres.   She was supposed to have perished in the disaster of the Russian campaign.   He found her near Strasbourg, in 1816, a lunatic, and took her to the ancient convent of Bon-Hommes, in the outskirts of l'Isle Adam, Seine-et-Oise, where he tended her with a tender care.   In 1819 he had the sorrow of seeing her expire as a result of a tragic scene when, recovering her reason all at once, she recognized her former lover Philippe de Sucy, whom she had not seen since 1812.   [Farewell.]

Fanny, aged servant in the employ of Lady Brandon, at La Grenadiére under the Restoration.   She closed the eyes of her mistress, whom she adored, then conducted the two children from that house to one of a cousin of hers, an old retired dressmaker of Tours, rue de la Guerche (now rue Marceau), where she intended to live with them; but the elder of the sons of Lady Brandon enlisted in the navy and placed his brother in college, under the guidance of Fanny. [La Grenadiére.]

Fanny, young girl of romantic temperament, fair and blonde, the only daughter of a banker of Paris.   One evening at her father's house she asked the Bavarian Hermann for a "dreadful German story," and thus innocently led to the death of Frédérie Taillefer who had in his youth committed a secret murder, now related in his hearing.   [The Red Inn.]

Fario, old Spanish prisoner of war at Issoudun during the Empire. After peace was declared he remained there making a small business venture in grains. He was of Grenada and had been a peasant   He was the butt of many scurvy tricks on the part of .the "Knights of Idlesse," and he avenged himself by stabbing their leader, Maxence Gilet. This attempted assassination was momentarily charged to Joseph Bridau. Fario finally obtained full satisfaction for his vindictive spirit by witnessing a duel where Gilet fell mortally wounded by the . hand of Philippe Bridau. Gilet had previously become disconcerted by the presence of the grain-dealer on the field of battle. [A Bachelor's Establishment.]

Farrabesche, ex-convict, now an estate-guard for Mme. Graslin, at Montégnac, time of Louis Philippe; of an old family of La Corréze; born about 1791. He had had an elder brother killed at Montebello, in 1800 a captain at twenty-two, who by his surpassing heroism had saved the army and the Consul Bonaparte. There was, too, a second brother who fell at Austerlitz in 1805, a sergeant in the First regiment of the Guard. Farrabesche himself had got it into his head that he would never serve, and when summoned in 1811 he fled to the woods. There he affiliated more or less with the Chauffeurs and, accused of several assassinations, was sentenced to death for contumacy. At the instance of Abbé Bonnet he gave himself up, at the beginning of the Restoration, and was sent to the bagne for ten years, returning in 1827. After 1830, re-established as a citizen, he married Catherine Curieux, by whom he had a child. Abbé Bonnet for one, and Mme. Graslin for another, proved themselves counselors and benefactors of Farrabesche. [The Country Parson.]

Farrabesche (Madame), born Catherine Curieux, about 1798; daughter of the tenants of Mme. Brézac, at Vizay, an important mart of La Corréze; mistress of Farrabesche in the last years of the Empire. She bore him a son, at the age of seventeen, and was soon separated from her lover on his imprisonment in the galleys. She returned to Paris and hired out. In her last place she worked for an old lady whom she tended devotedly, but who died leaving her nothing. · In 1833 she came back to the country; she was just out of a hospital, cured of a disease caused by fatigue, but still very feeble. Shortly after she married her former lover. Catherine Curieux was rather large, well-made, pale, gentle and refined by her visit to Paris, though she could neither read nor write. She had three married sisters, one at Aubusson, one at Limoges, and one at Saint-Léonard. [The Country Parson.]

Farrabesche (Benjamin), son of Farrabesche and Catherine Curieux; born in 1815; brought up by the relatives of his mother until 1827, then taken back by his father whom he dearly loved and whose energetic and rough nature he inherited. [The Country Parson.]

Faucombe (Madame de), sister of Mme. des Touches and aunt of Félicité des Touches—Camille Maupin;—an inmate of the convent of Chelles, to whom Félicité was confided by her dying mother, in 1793. The nun took her niece to Faucombe, a considerable estate near Nantes belonging to the deceased mother, where she (the nun) died of fear in 1794. [Béatrix.]

Faucombe (De), grand-uncle on the maternal side of Félicité des Touches. Born about 1734, died in 1814. He lived at Nantes, and in his old age had married a frivolous young woman, to whom he turned over the conduct of affairs. A passionate archæologist he gave little attention to the education of his grand-niece who was left with him in 1794, after the death of Mme. de Faucombe, the aged nun of Chelles. Thus it happened that Félicité grew up by the side of the old man and young woman, without guidance, and left entirely to her own devices. [Béatrix.]

Faustine, young woman of Argentan who was executed in 1813 at Mortagne for having killed her child. [Jealousies of a Country Town.]

Félicie, chambermaid of Mme. Diard at Bordeaux in 1823. [The Maranas.]

Félicité, a stout, ruddy, cross-eyed girl, the servant of Mme. Vauthier who ran a lodging-house on the corner of Notre-

Dame-des-Champs and Boulevard du Montparnasse, time of Louis Philippe. [The Seamy Side of History.]

Félix, office-boy for Attorney-General Granville, in 1830. [Scenes from a Courtesan's Life.]

Fendant, former head-clerk of the house of Vidal & Porchon; a partner with Cavalier. Both were book-sellers, publishers, and book-dealers, doing business on rue Serpente, Paris, about 1821. At this time they had dealings with Lucien Chardon de Rubempré. The house for social reasons was known as Fendant & Cavalier. Half-rascals, they passed for clever fellows. While Cavalier traveled, Fendant, the more wily of the two, managed the business. [A Distinguished Provincial at Paris.]

Ferdinand, real name of Ferdinand du Tillet.

Ferdinand, fighting name of one of the principal figures in the Breton uprising of 1799. One of the companions of MM. du Guénie, de la Billardière, de Fontaine and de Montauran. [The Chouans. Béatrix.]

Férédia (Count Bagos de), Spanish prisoner of war at the Vendôme under the Empire; lover of Mme. de Merret. Surprised one evening by the unexpected return of her husband, he took refuge in a closet which was ordered walled up by M. de Merret. There he died heroically without even uttering a cry. [La Grande Bretéche.]

Féret (Athanase), law-clerk of Maitre Bordin, procureur to the Châtelet in 1787. [A Start in Life.]

Ferragus XXIII. (*See* Bourignard.)

Ferraro (Count), Italian colonel whom Castanier had known during the Empire, and whose death in the Zembin swamps Castanier alone had witnessed. The latter therefore intended to assume Ferraro's personality in Italy after forging certain letters of credit. [Melmoth Reconciled.]

Ferraud (Comte), son of a retired councilor of the Parisian Parliament who had emigrated during the Terror, and who was ruined by these events. Born in 1781. During the Consulate he returned to France, at which time he declined certain offers made by Bonaparte. He remained ever true to the tenets of Louis XVIII. Of pleasing presence he won his way, and the Faubourg Saint-Germain regarded him as an ornament. About 1809 he married the widow of Colonel Chabert, who had an income of forty thousand francs. By her he had two children, a son and a daughter. He resided on rue de Varenne, having a pretty villa in the Montmorency Valley. During the Restoration he was made director-general in a ministry, and councilor of state. [Colonel Chabert.]

Ferraud (Comtesse), born Rose Chapotel; wife of Comte Ferraud. During the Republic, or at the commencement of the Empire, she married her first husband, an officer named Hyacinthe and known as Chabert, who was left for dead on the battlefield of Eylau, in 1807. About 1818 he tried to reassert his marital rights. Colonel Chabert claimed to have taken Rose Chapotel out of a questionable place at Palais-Royal. During the Restoration this woman was a countess and one of the queens of Parisian society. When brought face to face with her first husband she feigned at first not to recognize him, then she displayed such a dislike for him that he abandoned his idea of legal restitution. [Colonel Chabert.] The Comtesse Ferraud was the last mistress of Louis XVIII., and remained in favor at the court of Charles X. She and Mesdames de Listomère, d'Espard, de Camps and de Nucingen were invited to the select receptions of the Minister of Finance, in 1824. [The Government Clerks.]

Ferraud (Jules), son of Comte Ferraud and Rose Chapotel, the Comtesse Ferraud. While still a child, in 1817 or 1818, he was one day at his mother's home when Colonel Chabert called. She wept and he asked hotly if the officer was responsible for the grief of the countess. The latter with her two children then played a maternal comedy which was successful with the ingenuous soldier. [Colonel Chabert.]

Fessard, grocer at Saumur during the Restoration. Astonished one day by Nanon's, the servant's, purchase of a wax-candle, he asked if "the three magi were visiting them." [Eugénie Grandet.]

Fichet (Mademoiselle), the richest heiress of Issoudun during the Restoration. Godet, junior, one of the "Knights of Idlesse" paid court to her mother in the hope of obtaining, as a reward for his devotion, the hand of the young girl. [A Bachelor's Establishment.]

Finot (Andoche), managing-editor of journals and reviews, times of the Restoration and Louis Philippe. Son of a hatter of rue du Coq (now rue Marengo). Finot was abandoned by his father, a hard trader, and made a poor beginning. He wrote a bombastic announcement for Popinot's "Cephalic Oil." His first work was attending to announcements and personals in the papers. He was invited to the Birotteau ball. Finot was acquainted with Félix Gaudissart, who introduced him to little Anselme, as a great promoter. He was previously on the editorial staff of the "Courrier des Spectacles," and he had a piece performed at the Gaîté. [César Birotteau.] In 1820 he ran a little theatrical paper whose office was located on rue du Sentier. He was nephew of Giroudeau, a captain of dragoons; was witness of the marriage of Philippe Bridau with Flore Brazier, the widow of J.-J. Rouget. [A Bachelor's Establishment.] In 1821 Finot's paper was on rue Saint-Fiacre. Etienne Lousteau, Hector Merlin, Félicien Vernou, Nathan, F. du Bruel and Blondet all contributed to it. Then it was that Lucien de Rubempré made his reputation by a remarkable report of "L'Alcade dans l'embarras," a three act drama performed at the Panorama-Dramatique. Finot then lived on rue Feydeau. [A Distinguished Provincial at Paris.] In 1824 he was at the Opéra ball in a group of dandies and littérateurs, which surrounded Lucien de Rubempré, who was flirting with Esther Gobseck. [Scenes from a Courtesan's Life.] In this year Finot was guest at an entertainment at the home of Rabourdin, the chief of bureau, when he allowed himself to be won over to that official's cause by his friend Chardin des Lupeaulx, who had asked him to exert the voice of the press against Baudoyer, the rival of Rabourdin. [The Government Clerks.] In 1825 he was present at a breakfast given at the Rocher de Cancale, by Frédéric Marest in celebration of his entrance to the law office of Desroches; he was also at the orgy which followed at the home of Florine. [A Start in Life.] In 1831 Gaudissart said that his friend Finot had an income of thirty thousand francs, that he would be councilor of state, and was booked for a peer of France. He aspired to end up as his "shareholder." [Gaudissart the Great.] In 1836 Finot was dining with Blondet, his fellow-editor, and with Couture, a man about town, in a private room of a well-known restaurant, when he heard the story of the financial trickeries of Nucingen, wittily related by Bixiou. [The Firm of Nucingen.] Finot concealed "a brutal nature under a mild exterior," and his "impertinent stupidity was flecked with wit as the bread of a laborer is flecked with garlic." [Scenes from a Courtesan's Life.]

Firmiani, a respectable quadragenarian who in 1813 married the lady who afterwards became Mme. Octave de Camps. He was unable, so it was said, to offer her more than his name and his fortune. He was formerly receiver-general in the department of Montenotte. He died in Greece in 1823. [Madame Firmiani.]

Firmiani (Madame). (*See* Camps, Mme. de.)

Fischer, the name of three brothers, laborers in a village situated on the extreme frontiers of Lorraine, at the foot of the Vosges. They set out to join the army of the Rhine by reason of Republican conscriptions. The first, Pierre, father of Lisbeth—or "Cousin Betty"—was killed in 1815 in the Francstireurs. The second, André, father of Adeline who became the wife of Baron Hulot, died at Tréves in 1820. The third, Johann, having committed some acts of peculation, at the instigation of his nephew Hulot, while a commissary contractor in Algiers, province of Oran, committed suicide in 1841. He was over seventy when he killed himself. [Cousin Betty.]

Fischer (Adeline). (*See* Hulot d'Ervy, Baronne Hector.)

Fischer (Lisbeth), known as "Cousin Betty"; born in 1796; brought up a peasant. In her childhood she had to give way to her first cousin, the pretty Adeline, who was pampered by the whole family. In 1809 she was called to Paris by Adeline's husband and placed as an apprentice with the well-known Pons Brothers, embroiderers to the Imperial Court. She became a skilled workwoman and was about to set up for herself when the Empire was overthrown. Lisbeth was a Republican, of restive temperament, capricious, independent and unaccountably savage. She habitually declined to wed. She refused in succession a clerk of the minister of war, a major, an army-contractor, a retired captain and a wealthy lace-maker. Baron Hulot nick-named her the "Nanny-Goat." A resident of rue du Doyenné (which ended at the Louvre and was obliterated about 1855), where she worked for Rivet, a successor of Pons, she made the acquaintance of her neighbor, Wenceslas Steinbock, a Livonian exile, whom she saved from poverty and suicide, but whom she watched with a jealous strictness. Hortense Hulot sought out and succeeded in seeing the Pole; a wedding followed between the young people which caused Cousin Betty a deep resentment, cunningly concealed, but terrific in its effects. Through her Wenceslas was introduced to the irresistible Mme. Marneffe, and the happiness of a young household was quickly demolished. The same thing happened to Baron Hulot whose misconduct Lisbeth secretly abetted. Lisbeth died in 1844 of a pulmonary phthisis, principally caused by chagrin at seeing the Hulot family reunited. The relatives of the old maid never found out her evil actions. They surrounded her bedside, caring for her and lamenting the loss of "the angel of the family." Mlle. Fischer died on rue Louis-le-Grand, Paris, after having dwelt in turn on rues du Doyenné, Vaneau, Plumet (now Oudinot) and du Montparnasse, where she managed the household of Marshal Hulot, through whom she dreamed of wearing the countess' coronet, and for whom she donned mourning. [Cousin Betty.]

Fitz-William (Miss Margaret), daughter of a rich and noble Irishman who was the maternal uncle of Calyste du Guénie; hence the first cousin of that young man. Mme. du Guénie, the mother, was desirous of mating her son with Miss Margaret. [Béatrix.]

Flamet. (*See* la Billardière, Flamet de.)

Fleurant (Mother), ran a café at Croisic which Jacques Cambremer visited. [A Seaside Tragedy.]

Fleuriot, grenadier of the Imperial Guard, of colossal size, to whom Philippe de Sucy entrusted Stéphanie de Vandiéres, during the passage of the Bérésina in 1812. Unfortunately separated from Stéphanie, the grenadier did not find her again until 1816. She had taken refuge in an inn of Strasbourg, after escaping from an insane asylum. Both were then sheltered by Dr. Fanjat and taken to Auvergne, where Fleuriot soon died. [Farewell.]

Fleury, retired infantry captain, comptroller of the Cirque-Olympique, and employed during the Restoration in Rabourdin's bureau, of the minister of finance. He was attached to his chief, who had saved him from destitution. A subscriber, but a poor payer, to "Victories and Conquests." A zealous Bonapartist and Liberal. His three great men were Napoleon, Bolivar and Beranger, all of whose ballads he knew by heart, and sang in a sweet, sonorous voice. He was swamped with debt. His skill at fencing and small-arms kept him from Bixiou's jests. He was likewise much feared by Dutocq who flattered him basely. Fleury was discharged after the nomination of Baudoyer as chief of division in December, 1824. He did not take it to heart, saying that he had at his disposal a managing editorship in a journal. [The Government Clerks.] In 1840, still working for the above theatre, Fleury became manager of "L'Echo de la Biévre," the paper owned by Thuillier. [The Middle Classes.]

Flicoteaux, rival of Rousseau the Aquatic. Historic, legendary and strictly honest restaurant-keeper in the Latin quarter between rue de la Harpe and rue des Grés—Cujas—enjoying the custom, in 1821-22, of Daniel d'Arthez, Etienne Lousteau and Lucien Chardon de Rubempré. [A Distinguished Provincial at Paris.]

Florent, partner of Chanor; they were manufacturers and dealers in bronze, rue des Tournelles, Paris, time of Louis Philippe. [Cousin Betty. Cousin Pons.]

Florentine. (*See* Cabirolle, Agathe-Florentine.)

Florimond (Madame), dealer in linens, rue Vielle-du-Temple, Paris, 1844-45. Maintained by an "old fellow" who made her his heir, thanks to Fraisier, the man of business, whom she perhaps would have married through gratitude, had it not been for his physical condition. [Cousin Pons.]

Florine. (*See* Nathan, Mme. Raoul.)

Florville (La), actress at the Panorama-Dramatique in 1821. Among her contemporaries were Coralie, Florine and Bouffé, or Vignol. On the first night performance of "The Alcade," she played in a curtain-raiser, "Bertram." For a few days she was the mistress of a Russian prince who took her to Saint-Mandé, paying her manager a good sum for her absence from the theatre. [A Distinguished Provincial at Paris.]

Fœdora (Comtesse), born about 1805. Of Russian lower class origin and wonderfully beautiful. Espoused perhaps morganatically by a great lord of the land. Left a widow she reigned over Paris in 1827. Supposed to have an income of eighty thousand francs. She received in her drawing-rooms all the notables of the period, and there "appeared all the works of fiction that were not published anywhere else." Raphaél de Valentin was presented to the countess by Rastignac and fell desperately in love with her. But he left her house one day never to return, being definitely persuaded that she was "a woman without a heart." Her memory was cruel, and her address enough to drive a diplomat to despair. Although the Russian ambassador did not receive her, she had entry into the set of Mme. de Sérizy; visited with Mme. de Nucingen and Mme. de Restaud; received the Duchesse de Carigliano, the haughtiest of the Bonapartist clique. She had listened to many young dandies, and to the son of a peer of France, who had offered her their names in exchange for her fortune. [The Magic Skin.]

Fontaine (Madame), fortune-teller, Paris, rue Vielle-du-Temple, time of Louis Philippe. At one time a cook. Born in 1767. Earned a considerable amount of money, but previously had lost heavily in a lottery. After the suppression of this game of chance she saved up for the benefit of a nephew. In her divinations Mme. Fontaine made use of a giant toad named Astaroth, and of a black hen with bristling feathers, called Cleopatra or Bilonche. These two animals caught Gazonal's eye in 1845, when in company with De Lora and Bixiou he visited the fortune-teller's. The Southerner, however, asked only a five-franc divination, while in the same year Mme. Cibot, who came to consult her on an important matter, had to pay a hundred francs. According to Bixiou, " a third of the lorettes, a fourth of the statesmen and a half of the artists" consulted Mme. Fontaine. She was the Egeria of a minister, and also looked for "a tidy fortune," which Bilonche had promised her. [The Unconscious Humorists. Cousin Pons.]

Fontaine (Comte de), one of the leaders of the Vendée, in 1799, and then known as Grand-Jacques. [The Chouans.] One of the confidential advisers of Louis XVIII. Field marshal, councilor of state, comptroler of the extraordinary domains of the realm, deputy and peer of France under Charles X.; decorated with the cross of the Legion of Honor and the Order of Saint Louis. Head of one of the oldest houses of Poitou. Had married a Mlle. de Kergarouët, who had no fortune, but who came of a very old Brittany family related to the Rohans. Was the father of three sons and three daughters. The oldest son became president of a court, married the daughter of a multi-millionaire salt merchant. The second son, a lieutenant-general, married Mlle. Monegod, a rich banker's daughter whom the aunt of Duc d'Hérouville had refused to consider for her nephew. [Modeste Mignon.] The third son, director of a Paris municipality, then director-general in the Department of Finance, married the only daughter of M. Grossetéte, receiver-general at Bourges[1] Of the three daughters, the first married M. Planat de Baudry, receiver-general; the second married Baron de Villaine, a magistrate of bourgeois origin ennobled by the king; the third, Emilie, married her old uncle, the Comte de Kergarouët, and after his death, Marquis Charles de Vandenesse. [The

[1] [Le Curé de Village]

Ball at Sçeaux.] The Comte de Fontaine and his family were present at the Birotteau ball, and after the perfumer's bankruptcy procured a situation for him. [César Birotteau.] He died in 1824. [The Government Clerks.]

Fontaine (Baronne de), born Anna Grossetéte, only daughter of the receiver-general of Bourges. Attended the school of Mlles. Chamarolles with Dinah Piédefer, who became Mme. de la Baudraye. Thanks to her fortune she married the third son of the Comte de Fontaine. She removed to Paris after her marriage and kept up correspondence with her old school-mate who now lived at Sancerre. She kept her informed as to the prevailing styles. Later at the first performance of one of Nathan's dramas, about the middle of the reign of Louis Philippe, Anna de Fontaine affected not to recognize this same Mme. de la Baudraye, then the known mistress of Etienne Lousteau. [The Muse of the Department.]

Fontanieu (Madame), friend and neighbor of Mme. Vernier at Vouvray in 1831. The jolliest gossip and greatest joker in town. She was present at the interview between the insane Margaritis and Félix Gaudissart, when the drummer was so much at sea. [Gaudissart the Great.]

Fontanon (Abbé), born about 1770. Canon of Bayeux cathedral in the beginning of the nineteenth century when he "guided the consciences" of Mme. and Mlle. Bontems. In November, 1808, he got himself enrolled with the Parisian clergy, hoping thus to obtain a curacy and eventually a bishopric. He became again the confessor of Mlle. Bontems, now the wife of M. de Granville, and contributed to the trouble of that household by the narrowness of his provincial Catholicism and his inflexible bigotry. He finally disclosed to the magistrate's wife the relations of Granville with Caroline Crochard. He also brought sorrow to the last moments of Mme. Crochard, the mother, [A Second Home.] In December, 1824, at Saint-Roch he pronounced the funeral oration of Baron Flamet de la Billardière. [The Government Clerks.] Previous to 1824 Abbé Fontanon was vicar at the church of

Saint Paul, rue Saint-Antoine. [Honorine.] Confessor of
Mme. de Lanty in 1839, and always eager to pry into family .
secrets, he undertook an affair with Dorlange-Sallenauve
in the interest of Mariannina de Lanty. [The Member for
Arcis.]

Fortin (Madame), mother of Mme. Marneffe. Mistress of
General de Montcornet, who had lavished money on her during his visits to Paris which she had entirely squandered,
under the Empire, in the wildest dissipations. For twenty
years she queened it, but died in poverty though still believing herself rich. Her daughter inherited from her the tastes
of a courtesan. [Cousin Betty.]

Fortin (Valérie), daughter of preceding and of General de
Montcornet. (*See* Crevel, Madame.)

Fosseuse (La), orphan daughter of a grave-digger, whence
the nick-name. Born in 1807. Frail, nervous, independent,
retiring at first, she tried hiring out, but then fell into vagrant
habits. Reared in a village on the outskirts of Grenoble,
where Dr. Benassis came to live during the Restoration, she
became an object of special attention on the part of the
physician who became keenly interested in the gentle, loyal,
peculiar and impressionable creature. La Fosseuse though
homely was not without charm. She may have loved her
benefactor. [The Country Doctor.]

Fouché (Joseph), Duc d'Otrante, born near Nantes in 1753;
died in exile at Trieste in 1820. Oratorian, member of the
National Convention, councilor of state, minister of police
under the Consulate and Empire, also chief of the department of the Interior and of the government of the Illyrian
provinces; and president of the provisional government in
1815. In September, 1799, Colonel Hulot said: "Bernadotte,
Carnot, even citizen Talleyrand—all have left us. In a word
we have with us but a single good patriot, friend Fouché, who
holds everything by means of the police. There's a man for
you!" Fouché took especial care of Corentin who was perhaps his natural son. He sent him to Brittany during an
uprising in the year VIII, to accompany and direct Mlle. de

Verneuil, who was commissioned to betray and capture the Marquis de Montauran, the Chouan leader. [The Chouans.] In 1806 he caused Senator Malin de Gondreville to be kidnapped by masked men in order that the Château de Gondreville might be searched for important papers which, however, proved as compromising for Fouché as for the senator. This kidnapping, which was charged against Michu, the Simeuses and the Hauteserres, led to the execution of the first and the ruin of the others.   In 1833, Marsay, president of the ministerial chamber, while explaining the mysteries of the affair to the Princesse de Cadignan, paid this tribute to Fouché: "A genius dark, deep and extraordinary, little understood but certainly the peer of Philip II., Tiberius or Borgia." [The Gondreville Mystery.]   In 1809 Fouché and Peyrade saved France in connection with the Walcheren episode; but on the return of the Emperor from the Wagram campaign Fouché was rewarded by dismissal. [Scenes from a Courtesan's Life.]

Fouquereau, concierge to M. Jules Desmarets, stock-broker, rue Ménars in 1820.   Specially employed to look after Mme. Desmarets. [The Thirteen.]

Fourchon, retired farmer of the Ronquerolles estate, near the forest of Aigues, Burgundy.   Had also been a schoolmaster and a mail-carrier.   An old man and a confirmed toper since his wife's death.   At Blangy in 1823 he performed the three-fold duties of public clerk for three districts, assistant to a justice of the peace, and clarionet player.   At the same time he followed the trade of rope-maker with his apprentice Mouche, the natural son of one of his natural daughters.   But his chief income was derived from catching otters.   Fourchon was the father-in-law of Tonsard, who ran the Grand-I-Vert tavern. [The Peasantry.]

Foy (Maximilien-Sébastien), celebrated general and orator born in 1775 at Ham; died at Paris in 1825. [César Birotteau.]   In 1821, General Foy, while in the shop of Dauriat talking with an editor of the "Constitutionnel" and the manager of "La Minerve," noticed the beauty of Lucien de

Rubempré, who had come in with Lousteau to dispose of some sonnets. [A Distinguished Provincial at Paris.]

Fraisier, born about 1814, probably at Mantes. Son of a cobbler; an advocate and man of business at No. 9 rue de la Perle, Paris, in 1844-45. Began as copy-clerk at Couture's office. After serving Desroches as head-clerk for six years he bought the practice of Levroux, an advocate of Mantes, where he had occasion to meet Lebœuf, Vinet, Vatinelle and Bouyonnet. But he soon had to sell out and leave town on account of violating professional ethics. Whereupon he opened up a consultation office in Paris. A friend of Dr. Poulain who attended the last days of Sylvain Pons, he gave crafty counsel to Mme. Cibot, who coveted the chattels of the old bachelor. He also assured the Camusot de Marvilles that they should be the legatees of the old musician despite the faithful Schmucke. In 1845 he succeeded Vitel as justice of the peace; the coveted place being secured for him by Camusot de Marville, as a fee for his services. In Normandy he again acted successfully for this family. Fraisier was a dried-up little man with a blotched face and an unpleasant odor. At Mantes a certain Mme. Vatinelle nevertheless "made eyes at him"; and he lived at Marais with a servant-mistress, Dame Sauvage. But he missed more than one marriage, not being able to win either his client, Mme. Florimond,' or the daughter of Tabareau. To tell the truth De Marville advised him to leave the latter alone. [Cousin Pons.]

Franchessini (Colonel), born about **1789**, served in the Imperial Guard, and was one of the most dashing colonels of the Restoration, but was forced to resign on account of a slur on his character. In 1808, to provide for foolish expenditures into which a woman led him, he forged certain notes. Jacques Collin—Vautrin—took the crime to himself and was sent to the galleys for several years. In 1819 Franchessini killed young Taillefer in a duel, at the instigation of Vautrin. The following year he was with Lady Brandon—probably his mistress—at the grand ball given by the Vicomtesse de Beauséant, just before her flight. In 1839, Franchessini was a leading member of the Jockey club, and held the rank of colonel in the National Guard. Married a rich Irishwoman who was devout and charitable and lived in one of the finest mansions of the Bréda quarter. Elected deputy, and being an intimate friend of Rastignac, he evinced open hostility for Sallenauve and voted against his being seated in order to gratify Maxime de Trailles. [Father Goriot. The Member for Arcis.]

François (Abbé), curé of the parish at Alençon in 1816. "A Cheverus on a small scale" he had taken the constitutional oath during the Revolution and for this reason was despised by the "ultras" of the town although he was a model of charity and virtue. Abbé François frequented the homes of M and Mme. du Bousquier and M. and Mme. Granson; but M. du Bousquier and Athanase Granson were the only ones to give him cordial welcome. In his last days he became reconciled with the curate of Saint-Léonard, Alençon's aristocratic church, and died universally lamented. [Jealousies of a Country Town.]

François, head valet to Marshal de Montcornet at Aigues in 1823. Attached specially to Emile Blondet when the journalist visited there. Salary twelve hundred francs. In his master's confidence. [The Peasantry.]

François, in 1822, stage-driver between Paris and Beaumont-sur-Oise, in the service of the Touchard Company. [A Start in Life.]

Françoise, servant of Mme. Crochard, rue Saint-Louis in Marais in 1822. Toothless woman of thirty years' service. Was present at her mistress' death-bed. This was the fourth she had buried. [A Second Home.]

Frappart, in 1839, at Arcis-sur-Aube, proprietor of a dance-hall where was held the primary, presided over by Colonel Giguet, which nominated Sallenauve. [The Member for Arcis.]

Frappier, finest carpenter in Provins in 1827-28. It was to him that Jacques Brigant came as apprentice when he went to the town to be near his childhood's friend, Pierrette

Lorrain. Frappier took care of her when she left Rogron's house. Frappier was married. [Pierrette.]

Frédéric, one of the editors of Finot's paper in 1821, who reported the Théâtre-Français and the Odéon. [A Distinguish d Provincial at Paris.]

Frelu (La Grande), girl of Croisic who had a child by Simon Gaudry. Nurse to Pierrette Cambremer whose mother died when she was very young. [A Seaside Tragedy.]

Fresconi, an Italian who, during the Restoration and until 1828, ran a nursery on Boulevard du Montparnasse. The business was not a success. Barbet the book-seller was interested in it; he turned it into a lodging-house, where dwelt Baron Bourlac. [The Seamy Side of History.]

Fresquin, former supervisor of roads and bridges. Married and father of a family. Employed, time of Louis Philippe, by Grégoire Gérard in the hydraulic operations for Mme. Graslin at Montégnac. In 1843 Fresquin was appointed district tax collector. [The Country Parson.]

. **Frisch** (Samuel), Jewish jeweler on rue Saint-Avoie in 1829. Furnisher and creditor of Esther Gobseck. A general pawnbroker. [Scenes from a Courtesan's Life.]

Fritaud (Abbé), priest of Sancerre in 1836. [The Muse of the Department.]

Fritot, dealer in shawls on the stock exchange, Paris, time of Louis Philippe. Rival of Gaudissart. He sold an absurd shawl for six thousand francs to Mistress Noswell, an eccentric Englishwoman. Fritot was once invited to dine with the King. [Gaudissart II.]

Fritot (Madame), wife of preceding. [Gaudissart II.]

Froidfrond (Marquis de), born about 1777. Gentleman of Maine-et-Loire. While very young he became insolvent and sold his château near Saumur, which was bought at a low price for Félix Grandet by Cruchot the notary, in 1811. About 1827 the marquis was a widower with children, and was spoken of as a possible peer of France. At this time Mme. des Grassins tried to persuade Eugénie Grandet, now an orphan, that she would do well to wed the marquis, and that this marriage was a pet scheme of her father. And again in 1832 when Eugénie was left a widow by Cruchot de Bonfons, the family of the marquis tried to arrange a marriage with him. [Eugénie Grandet.]

Fromaget, apothecary at Arcis-sur-Aube, time of Louis Philippe. As his patronage did not extend to the Gondre-villes, he was disposed to work against Keller; that is why he probably voted for Giguet in 1839. [The Member for Arcis.]

Fromenteau, police-agent. With Contenson he had belonged to the political police of Louis XVIII. In 1845 he aided in unearthing prisoners for debt. Being encountered at the home of Théodore Gaillard, by Gazonal, he revealed some curious details concerning different kinds of police to the bewildered countryman. [The Unconscious Humorists.]

Funcal (Comte de), an assumed name of Bourignard, when he was met at the Spanish Embassy, Paris, about 1820, by Henri de Marsay and Auguste de Maulincour. There was a real Comte de Funcal, a Portuguese-Brazilian, who had been a sailor, and whom Bourignard duplicated exactly. He may have been "suppressed" violently by the usurper of his name. [The Thirteen.]

G

Gabilleau, deserter from the Seventeenth infantry; chauffeur executed at Tulle, during the Empire, on the very day when he had planned an escape. Was one of the accomplices of Farrabeschc who profited by a hole made in his dungeon by the condemned man to make his own escape. [The Country Parson.]

Gabriel, born about 1790; messenger at the Department of Finance, and check-receiver at the Theatre Royal, during the Restoration. A Savoyard, and nephew of Antoine, the oldest messenger in the department. Husband of a skilled lace-maker and shawl-mender. He lived with his uncle Antoine and another relative employed in the department, Laurent. [The Government Clerks.]

Gabusson, cashier in employ of Dauriat the editor in 1821. [A Distinguished Provincial at Paris.]

Gaillard (Th odore), journalist, proprietor or manager of newspapers. In 1822 he and Hector Merlin established a Royalist paper in which Rubempré, palinodist, aired opinions favorable to the existing government, and slashed a very good book of his friend Daniel d'Arthez. [A Distinguished Provincial at Paris.] Under Louis Philippe he was one of the owners of a very important political sheet. [Béatrix. Scenes from a Courtesan's Life.] In 1845 he ran a strong paper. At first a man of wit, "he ended by becoming stupid on account of staying in the same environment." He interlarded his speech with epigrams from popular pieces, pronouncing them with the emphasis given by famous actors. Gaillard was good with his Odry and still better with Lemaitre. He lived at rue Ménars. There he was met by Lora, Bixiou and Gazonal. [The Unconscious Humorists.]

Gaillard (Madame Théodore), born at Alençon about 1800. Given name Suzanne. "A Norman beauty, fresh, blooming, and sturdy." One of the employés of Mme. Lardot, the laundress, in 1816, the year when she left her native town after having obtained some money of M. du Bousquier by persuading him that she was with child by him. The Chevalier de Valois liked Suzanne immensely, but did not allow himself to be caught in this trap. Suzanne went to Paris and speedily became a fashionable courtesan. Shortly thereafter she reappeared at Alençon for a visit to attend Athanase Granson's funeral. She mourned with the desolate mother, saying to her on leaving: "I loved him!" At the same time she ridiculed the marriage of Mlle. Cormon with M. du Bousquier, thus avenging the deceased and Chevalier de Valois. [Jealousies of a Country Town.] Under the name of Mme. du Val-Noble she became noted in the artistic and fashionable set. In 1821–22, she was the mistress of Hector Merlin. [A Distinguished Provincial at Paris. A Bachelor's Establishment.] After having been maintained by Jacques Falleix, the broker who failed, she was for a short time in 1830 mistress of Peyrade, who was concealed under the name of Samuel Johnson, "the nabob." She was acquainted with Esther Gobseck, who lived on rue Saint-Georges in a mansion that had been fitted up for her—Suzanne—by Falleix, and obtained by Nucingen for Esther. [Scenes fr m a Courtesan's Life.] In 1838 she married Théodore Gaillard her lover since 1830. In 1845 she received Lora, Bixiou, and Gazonal. [Béatrix. The Unconscious Humorists.]

Gaillard, one of three guards who succeeded Courtecuisse, and under the orders of Michaud, in the care of the estate of General de Montcornet at Aigues. [The Peasantry.]

Galard, market-gardener of Auteuil; father of Mme. Lemprun, maternal grandfather of Mme. Jérôme Thuillier. He died, very aged, of an accident in 1817. [The Peasantry.]

Galard (Mademoiselle), old maid, landed proprietor at Besançon, rue du Perron. She let the first floor of her house to Albert Savarus, in 1834. [Albert Savarus.]

Galardon (Madame), née Tiphaine, elder sister of M. Tiphaine, president of the court at Provins. Married at first to a Guénée, she kept one of the largest retail dry-goods shops in Paris, on rue Saint-Denis. Towards the end of the year 1815 she sold out to Rogron and went back to Provins. She had three daughters whom she provided with husbands in the little town: the eldest married M. Lesourd, king's attorney; the second, M. Martener a physician; the third, M. Auffray a notary. Finally she herself married for her second husband, M. Galardon, receiver of taxes. She invariably added to her signature, "*née* Tiphaine." She defended Pierrette Lorrain, and was at outs with the Liberals of Provins, who were induced to persecute Rogron's ward. [Pierrette.]

Galathionne (Prince and Princess), Russians. The prince was one of the lovers of Diane de Maufrigneuse. [The Secrets of a Princess.] In September, 1815, he protected La Minoret a celebrated opera dancer, to whose daughter he gave a dowry. [The Middle Classes.] In 1819 Marsay, appearing in the box of the Princess Galathionne, at the Italiens, had Mme. de Nucingen at his mercy. [Father Goriot.] In 1821 Lousteau said that the story of the Prince Galathionne's diamonds, the Maubreuil affair and the Pombreton will, were fruitful newspaper topics. [A Distinguished

Provincial at Paris.] In 1834-35, the princess gave balls which the Comtesse Félix de Vandenesse attended. [A Daughter of Eve.] About 1840 the prince tried to get Mme. Schontz away from the Marquis de Rochefide; but she said: "Prince, you are no handsomer, but you are older than Rochefide. You would beat me, while he is like a father to me." [Béatrix.]

Galope-Chopine. (*See* Cibot.)

Gamard (Sophie), old maid; owner of a house at Tours on rue de la Psalette, which backed the Saint Gatien church. She let part of it to priests. Here lodged the Abbés Troubert, Chapeloud and François Birotteau. The house had been purchased during the Terror by the father of Mlle. Gamard, a dealer in wood, a kind of parvenu peasant. After receiving Abbé Birotteau most cordially she took a disliking to him which was secretly fostered by Troubert, and she finally dispossessed him, seizing the furniture which he valued so greatly. Mlle. Gamard died in 1826 of a chill. Troubert circulated the report that Birotteau had caused her death by the sorrow which he had caused the old maid. [The Vicar of Tours.]

Gambara (Paolo), musician, born at Crémona in 1791; son of an instrument-maker, a moderately good performer and a great composer who was driven from his home by the French and ruined by the war. These events consigned Paolo Gambara to a wandering existence from the age of ten. He found little quietude and obtained no congenial situation till about 1813 in Venice. At this time he put on an opera, "Mahomet," at the Fenice theatre, which failed miserably. Nevertheless he obtained the hand of Marianina, whom he loved, and with her wandered through Germany to settle finally in Paris in 1831, in a wretched apartment on rue Froidmanteau. The musician, an accomplished theorist, could not interpret intelligently any of his remarkable ideas, and he would play to his wondering auditors jumbled compositions which he thought to be sublime inspirations. However he enthusiastically analyzed "Robert le Diable," having heard Meyerbeer's masterpiece while a guest of Andréa Marcosini. In 1837 he was reduced to mending musical instruments, and occasionally he went with his wife to sing duets in the open air on the Champs-Elysées, to pick up a few sous. Emilio and Massimilla de Varése were deeply sympathetic of the Gambaras, whom they met in the neighborhood of Faubourg Saint-Honoré. Paolo Gambara had no commonsense except when drunk. He had invented an outlandish instrument which he called the "panharmonicon." [Gambara.]

Gambara (Marianina), Venetian, wife of Paolo Gambara. With him she led a life of almost continual poverty, and for a long time maintained them at Paris by her needle. Her clients on rue Froidmanteau were mostly profligate women, who however were kind and generous towards her. From 1831 to 1836 she left her husband, going with a lover, Andréa Marcosini, who abandoned her at the end of five years to marry a dancer; and in January, 1837, she returned to her husband's home emaciated, withered and faded, "a sort of nervous skeleton," to resume a life of still greater squalor. [Gambara.]

Gandolphini (Prince), Neapolitan, former partisan of King Murat. A victim of the last Revolution he was, in 1823, banished and poverty stricken. At this time he was sixty-five years old, though he looked eighty. He lived modestly enough with his young wife at Gersau—Lucerne—under the English name of Lovelace. He also passed for a certain Lamporani, who was at that time a well-known publisher of Milan. When in the · presence of Rodolphe the prince resumed his true self he said: "I know how to make up. I was an actor during the Empire with Bourrienne, Mme. Murat, Mme. d'Abrantès, and any number of others."— Character in a novel "L'Ambitieux par Amour," published by Albert Savarus, in the "Revue de l'Est," in 1834. Under this fictitious name the author related his own history: Rodolphe was himself, and the Prince and Princesse Gadolphini were the Duc and Duchesse d'Argaïolo. [Albert Savarus.]

Gandolphini (Princesse), née Francesca Colonna, a Roman of illustrious origin, fourth child of the Prince and Princess

Colonna. While very young she married Prince Gandolphini, one of the richest landed proprietors of Sicily. Under the name of Miss Lovelace, she met Rodolphe in Switzerland and he fell in love with her.—Heroine of a novel entitled "L'Ambitieux par Amour," by Albert Savarus. [Albert Savarus.]

Ganivet, bourgeois of Issoudun. In 1822, in a conversation where Maxence Gilet was discussed, Commandant Potel threatened to make Ganivet "swallow his tongue without sauce" if he continued to slander the lover of Flore Brazier. [A Bachelor's Establishment.]

Ganivet (Mademoiselle), a woman of Issoudun "as ugly as the seven capital sins." Nevertheless she succeeded in winning a certain Borniche-Héreau who in 1778 left her an income of a thousand crowns. [A Bachelor's Establishment.]

Gannerac, in transfer business at Angoulême. In 1821-22 he was involved in the affair of the notes endorsed by Rubempré in imitation of the signature of his brother-in-law Séchard. [Lost Illusions.]

Garangeot, in 1845 conducted the orchestra in a theatre run by Félix Gaudissart, succeeding Sylvain Pons to the baton. Cousin of Héloïse Brisetout, who obtained the place for him. [Cousin Pons.]

Garceland, mayor of Provins during the Restoration. Son-in-law of Guépin. Indirectly protected Pierrette Lorrain from the Liberals of the village led by Maitre Vinet, who acted for Rogron. [Pierrette.]

Garcenault (De), first president of the Court of Besançon in 1834. He got the chapter of the cathedral to secure Albert Savarus as counsel in a lawsuit between the chapter and the city. Savarus won the suit. [Albert Savarus.]

Garnery, one of two special detectives in May, 1830, authorized by the attorney-general, De Granville, to seize certain letters written to Lucien de Rubempré by Mme. de Sérizy, the Duchesse de Maufrigneuse and Mlle. Clotilde de Grandlieu. [Scenes from a Courtesan's Life.]

Gasnier, peasant living near Grenoble; born about 1789. Married and the father of several children whom he loved dearly. Inconsolable at the loss of the eldest. Doctor Benassis, mayor of the commune, mentioned this parental affection as a rare instance among tillers of the soil. [The Country Doctor.]

Gasselin, a Breton born in 1794; servant of the Guénics of Guérande, in 1836, having been in their employ since he was fifteen. A short, stout fellow with black hair, furrowed face; silent and slow. He took care of the garden and stables. In 1832 in the foolish venture of Duchesse de Berry, in which Gasselin took part with the Baron du Guénic and his son Calyste, the faithful servant received a sabre cut on the shoulder, while shielding the young man. This action seemed so natural to the family that Gasselin received small thanks. [Béatrix.]

Gaston (Louis), elder natural son of Lady Brandon, born in 1805. Left an orphan in the early years of the Restoration, he was, though still a child, like a father to his younger brother Marie Gaston, whom he placed in college at Tours; after which he himself shipped as cabin-boy on a man-of-war. After being raised to the rank of captain of an American ship and becoming wealthy in India, he died at Calcutta, during the first part of the reign of Louis Philippe, as a result of the failure of the "famous Halmer," and just as he was starting back to France, married and happy. [La Grenadiére. Letters of Two Brides.]

Gaston (Marie), second natural son of Lady Brandon; born in 1810. Educated at the college of Tours, which he quitted in 1827. Poet; protégé of Daniel d'Arthez, who often gave him food and shelter. In 1831 he met Louise de Chaulieu, the widow of Macumer, at the home of Mme. d'Espard. He married her in October, 1833, though she was older than he, and he was encumbered with debts amounting to 30,000 francs. The couple living quietly at Ville-d'Avray, were happy until a day when the jealous Louise conceived unjustifiable suspicions concerning the fidelity of her husband; on which account she died after they had been married two years. During these two years Gaston wrote at least four plays. One of them written in collaboration with his wife was presented with the greatest success under the names of Nathan and "others." [La Grenadiére. Letters of Two Brides.] In his early youth Gaston had published, at the expense of his friend Dorlange, a volume of poetry, "Les Perce-neige," the entire edition of which found its way, at three sous the volume, to a second-hand book-shop, whence, one fine day, it inundated the quays from Pont Royal to Pont Marie. [The Member for Arcis.]

Gaston (Madame Louis), an Englishwoman of cold, distant manners; wife of Louis Gaston; probably married him in India where he died as a result of unfortunate business deals. As a widow she came to France with two children, where without resource she became a charge to her brother-in-law who visited and aided her secretly. She lived in Paris on rue de la Ville-Evêque. The visits made by Marie Gaston were spoken of to his wife who became jealous, not knowing their object. Mme. Louis Gaston was thus in-nocently the cause of Mme. Marie Gaston's death. [Letters of Two Brides.]

Gaston (Madame Marie), born Armande-Louise-Marie de Chaulieu, in 1805. At first destined to take the veil; educated at the Carmellite convent of Blois with Renée de Maucombe who became Mme. de l'Estorade. She remained constant in her relations with this faithful friend—at least by letter—who was a prudent and wise adviser. In 1825 Louise married her professor in Spanish, the Baron de Macumer, whom she lost in 1829. In 1833 she married the poet Marie Gaston. Both marriages were sterile. In the first she was adored and believed that she loved; in the second she was loved as much as she loved, but her insane jealousy, and her horseback rides from Ville-d'Avray to Verdier's were her undoing, and she died in 1835 of consumption, contracted purposely through despair at the thought that she had been deceived. After leaving the convent she had lived successively at the following places: on Faubourg Saint-Germain, Paris, where she saw M. de Bonald; at Chantepleur, an estate in Burgundy; at La Crampade, in Provence, with Mme. de l'Estorade;

in Italy; at Ville-d'Avray, where she sleeps her last sleep in a park of her own planning. [Letters of Two Brides.]

Gatienne, servant of Mme. and Mlle. Bontems, at Bayeux, in 1805. [A Second Home.]

Gaubert, one of the most illustrious generals of the Republic; first husband of a Mlle. de Ronquerolles whom he left a widow at the age of twenty, making her his heir. She married again in 1806, choosing the Comte de Sérizy. [A Start in Life.]

Gaubertin (François), born about 1770; son of the ex-sheriff of Soulanges, Burgundy, before the Revolution. About 1791, after five years' clerkship to the steward of Mlle. Laguerre at Aigues, he succeeded to the stewardship. His father having become public prosecutor in the department, time of the Republic, he was made mayor of Blangy. In 1796 he married the "citizeness" Isaure Mouchon, by whom he had three children: a son, Claude, and two daughters, Jenny—Mme. Leclercq—and Elisa. He had also a natural son, Bournier, whom he placed in charge of a local newspaper. At the death of Mlle. Laguerre, Gaubertin, after twenty-five years of stewardship, possessed 600,000 francs. He ended by dreaming of acquiring the estate at Aigues; but the Comte de Montcornet purchased it, retained him in charge, caught him one day in a theft and discharged him summarily. Gaubertin received at that time sundry lashes with a whip of which he said nothing, but for which he revenged himself. The old steward became, nevertheless, a person of importance. In 1820 he was mayor of Ville-aux-Fayes, and supplied one-third of the Paris wood. Being general agent of this rural industry, he managed the forests, lumber and guards. Gaubertin was related throughout a whole district, like a "boa-constrictor twisted around a gigantic tree"; the church, the magistracy, the municipality, the government—all did his bidding. Even the peasantry served his interests indirectly. When the general, disgusted by the numberless vexations of his estate, wished to sell the property at Aigues, Gaubertin bought the forests, while his partners,

Rigou and Soudry, acquired the vineyards and other grounds. [The Peasantry.]

Gaubertin (Madame), born Isaure Mouchon in 1778. Daughter of a member of the Convention and friend of Gaubertin senior. Wife of François Gaubertin. An affected creature of Ville-aux-Fayes who played the great lady mightily. [The Peasantry.]

Gaubertin (Claude), son of François Gaubertin, godson of Mlle. Laguerre, at whose expense he was educated at Paris. The busiest attorney at Ville-aux-Fayes in 1823. After five years' practice he spoke of selling his office. He probably became judge. [The Peasantry.]

Gaubertin (Jenny), elder daughter of François Gaubertin. (*See* Leclercq, Madame.)

Gaubertin (Elisa or Elise), second daughter of François Gaubertin. Loved, courted and longed for since 1819 by the sub-prefect of Ville-aux-Fayes, M. des Lupeaulx— the nephew. M. Lupin, notary at Soulanges, sought on his part the young girl's hand for his only son Amaury. [The Peasantry.]

Gaubertin-Vallat (Mademoiselle), old maid, sister of Mme. Sibilet, wife of the clerk of the court at Ville-aux-Fayes, in 1823. She ran the town's stamp office. [The Peasantry.]

Gaucher was in 1803 a boy working for Michu. [The Gondreville Mystery.]

Gaudet, second clerk in Desroches' law office in 1824. [A Start in Life.]

Gaudin, chief of squadron in the mounted grenadiers of the Imperial Guard; made baron of the Empire, with the estate of Wistchnau. Made prisoner by Cossacks at the passage of the Bérésina, he escaped, going to India where he was lost sight of. However he returned to France about 1830, in bad health, but a multi-millionaire. [The Magic Skin.]

Gaudin (Madame), wife of foregoing, managed the Hôtel Saint-Quentin, rue des Cordiers, Paris, during the Resto-

ration. Among her guests was Raphaël de Valentin.
Her husband's return in 1830 made her wealthy and a baroness.
[The Magic Skin.]

Gaudin (Pauline), daughter of the foregoing. Was acquainted
with, loved, and modestly aided Raphaél de Valentin, a poor
lodger at Hôtel Saint-Quentin.   After the return of her
father she lived with her parents on rue Saint-Lazare.   For
a long time her whereabouts were unknown to Raphaél
who had quitted the hotel abruptly; then he met her again
one evening at the Italiens. They fell into each other's
arms, declaring their mutual love.   Raphaël who also had
become rich resolved to espouse Pauline; but frightened by
the shrinkage of the "magic skin" he fled precipitately
and returned to Paris.   Pauline hastened after him, only
to behold him die upon her breast in a transport of furious,
impotent love.   [The Magic Skin.]

Gaudissart (Jean-François), father of Félix Gaudissart.
[César Birotteau.]

Gaudissart (Félix), native of Normandy, born about 1792,
a "great" commercial traveler making a specialty of the
hat trade.   Known to the Finots, having been in the employ
of the father of Andoche.   Also handled all the "articles
of Paris."   In 1816 he was arrested on the denunciation
of Peyrade—Pére Canquoëlle.   He had imprudently con-
versed in the David café with a retired officer concerning a
conspiracy against the Bourbons that was about to break
out.   Thus the conspiracy was thwarted and two men were
sent to the scaffold.   Gaudissart being released by Judge
Popinot was ever after grateful to the magistrate and devoted
to the interests of his nephew.   When he became minister,
Anselme Popinot obtained for Gaudissart license for a large
theatre on the boulevard, which in 1834 aimed to supply
the demand for popular opera.   This theatre employed
Sylvain Pons, Schmucke, Schwab, Garangcot and Héloïse
Brisetout, Félix's mistress.   [Scenes from a Courtesan's
Life. Cousin Pons.]   "Gaudissart the Great," then a
young man, attended the Birotteau ball. About that time
he probably lived on rue des Deux-Ecus, Paris   César

Birotteau.] During the Restoration, a "pretended florist's agent" sent by Judge Popinot to Comte Octave de Bauvan, he bought at exorbitant prices the artificial flowers made by Honorine. [Honorine.] At Vouvray in 1831 this man, so accustomed to fool others, was himself mystified in rather an amusing manner by a retired dyer, a sort of "country Figaro" named Vernier. A bloodless duel resulted. After the episode, Gaudissart boasted that the affair had been to his advantage. He was "in this Saint-Simonian period". the lover of Jenny Courand. [Gaudissart the Great.]

Gaudron (Abbé), an Auvergnat; vicar and then curate of the church of Saint-Paul-Saint-Louis, rue Saint-Antoine, Paris, during the Restoration and the Government of July. A peasant filled with faith, square below and above, a "sacerdotal ox" utterly ignorant of the world and of literature. Being confessor of Isidore Baudoyer he endeavored in 1824 to further the promotion of that incapable chief of bureau in the Department of Finance. In the same year he was present at a dinner at the Comte de Bauvan's when were discussed questions relating to woman. [The Government Clerks. Honorine.] In 1826 Abbé Gaudron confessed Mme. Clapart and led her into devout paths; the former Aspasia of the Directory had not confessed for forty years. In February, 1830, the priest obtained the Dauphiness' protection for Oscar Husson, son of Mme. Clapart by her first husband, and that young man was promoted to a sub-lieutenancy in a regiment where he had been serving as subaltern. [A Start in Life.]

Gault, warden of the Conciergerie in May, 1830, when Jacques Collin and Rubempré were imprisoned there. He was then aged. [Scenes from a Courtesan's Life.]   .

Gay, boot-maker in Paris, rue de la Michodière, in 1821, who furnished the boots for Rubempré which aroused Matifat's suspicion. [A Distinguished Provincial at Paris.]

Gazonal (Sylvestre-Palafox-Castel), one of the most skillful weavers in the Eastern Pyrenees; commandant of the National Guard, September, 1795. On a visit to Paris in 1845 for the settlement of an important lawsuit he sought out his cousin, Léon de Lora, the landscape artist, who in one day, with Bixiou the caricaturist, showed him the under side of the city, opening up to him a whole gallery full of "unconscious humorists"—dancers, actresses, police-agents, etc. Thanks to his two cicerones, he won his lawsuit and returned home. [The Unconscious Humorists.]

Gendrin, caricaturist, tenant of M. Molineux, Cour Batave, in 1818. According to his landlord, the artist was a profoundly immoral man who drew caricatures against the government, brought bad women home with him and made the hall uninhabitable. [César Birotteau.]

Gendrin, brother-in-law of Gaubertin the steward of Aigues. He also had married a daughter of Mouchon. Formerly an attorney, then for a long time a judge of the Court of First Instance at Ville-aux-Fayes, he at last became president of the court, through the influence of Comte de Soulanges, under the Restoration. [The Peasantry.]

Gendrin, court counselor of a departmental seat in Burgundy, and a distant relative of President Gendrin. [The Peasantry.]

Gendrin. only son of President Gendrin; recorder of mortgages in that sub-prefecture in 1823. [The Peasantry.]

Gendrin-Wattebled (or Vatcbled), born about 1733. General supervisor of streams and forests at Soulanges, Burgundy, from the reign of Louis XV. Was still in office in 1823. A nonagenarian he spoke, in his lucid moments, of the jurisdiction of the Marble Table. He reigned over Soulanges before Mme. Soudry's advent. [The Peasantry.]

Genestas (Pierre-Joseph), cavalry officer, born in 1779. At first a regimental lad, then a soldier. Sub-lieutenant in 1802; officer of the Legion of Honor after the battle of Moskowa. chief of squadron in 1829. In 1814 he married the widow of his friend Renard, a subaltern. She died soon after, leaving a child that was legally recognized by Genestas, who entrusted him, then a young man, to the care of Dr. Benassis. In December, 1829, Genestas was promoted to be a lieutenant-colonel in a regiment quartered at Poitiers. [The Country Doctor.]

Genestas (Madame Judith), Polish Jewess, born in 1795. Married in 1812 after the Sarmatian custom to her lover Renard, a French quartermaster, who was killed in 1813. Judith gave him one son, Adrien, and survived the father one year. *In extremis* she married Genestas a former lover, who adopted Adrien. [The Country Doctor.]

Genestas (Adrien), adopted son of Commandant Genestas, born in 1813 to Judith the Polish Jewess and Renard who was killed before the birth of his son. Adrien was a living picture of his mother—olive complexion, beautiful black eyes of a spirituelle sadness, and a head of hair too heavy for his frail body. When sixteen he seemed but twelve. He had _fallen into bad habits, but after living with Dr. Benassis for eight months, he was cured and became robust. [The Country Doctor.]

Geneviève, an idiotic peasant girl, ugly and comparatively rich. Friend and companion of the Comtesse de Vandiéres, then insane and an inmate of the asylum of Bons-Hommes, near Isle-Adam, during the Restoration. Jilted by a mason, Dallot, who had promised to marry her, Geneviéve lost what little sense love had aroused in her. [Farewell.]

Genovese, tenor at the Fenice theatre, Venice, in 1820. Born at Bergamo in 1797. Pupil of Veluti. Having long loved La Tinti, he sang outrageously in her presence, so long as she resisted his advances, but regained all his powers after she yielded to him. [Massimilla Doni.] In the winter of 1823-24, at the home of Prince Gandolphini, in Geneva, Genovese sang with his mistress, an exiled Italian prince, and Princess Gandolphini, the famous quartette, "Mi manca la voce." [Albert Savarus.]

Gentil, old valet in service of Mme. de Bargeton, during the Restoration. During the summer of 1821, with Albertine and Lucien de Rubempré, he accompanied his mistress to Paris. [A Distinguished Provincial at Paris.]

Gentillet sold in 1835 an old diligence to Albert Savarus when the latter was leaving Besançon after the visit on the part of Prince Soderini. [Albert Savarus.]

Gentillet (Madame), maternal grandmother of Félix Grandet. She died in 1806 leaving considerable property. In Grandet's "drawing room" at Saumur was a pastel of Mme. Gentillet, representing her as a shepherdess. [Eugénie Grandet.]

Georges, confidential valet of Baron de Nucingen, at Paris, time of Charles X. Knew of his aged master's love affairs and aided or thwarted him at will. [Scenes from a Courtesan's Life.]

Gérard (François-Pascal-Simon, Baron), celebrated painter —1770-1837—procured for Joseph Bridau in 1818 two copies of Louis XVIII.'s portrait which were worth to the beginner, then very poor, a thousand francs, a tidy sum for the Bridau family. [A Bachelor's Establishment.] The Parisian salon of Gérard, much sought after, had a rival at Chaussée-d'Antin in that of Mlle. de Touches. [Béatrix.]

Gérard, adjutant-general of the Seventy-second demi-brigade, commanded by Hulot. A careful education had developed a superior intellect in Gérard. He was a staunch Republican. Killed by the Chouan, Pille-Miche, at Vivetière, December, 1799. [The Chouans.]

Gérard (Grégoire), born in 1802, probably in Limousin. Protestant of somewhat uncouth exterior, son of a journeyman carpenter who died when rather young; godson of F. Grossetête. From the age of twelve the banker had encouraged him in the study of the exact sciences for which he had natural aptitude. Studied at Ecole Polytechnique from nineteen to twenty-one; then entered as a pupil of engineering in the National School of Roads and Bridges, from which he emerged in 1826 and stood the examinations for ordinary engineer two years later. He was cool-headed and warm-hearted. He became disgusted with his profession when he ascertained its many limitations, and he plunged into the July (1830) Revolution. He was probably on the point of adopting the Saint-Simonian doctrine, when M. Grossetête prevailed upon him to take charge of some important works on the estate of Mme. Pierre Graslin in Haute-Vienne. Gérard wrought wonders aided by Fresquin and other capable men. He became mayor of Montégnac in 1838. Mme. Graslin died about 1844. Gérard followed out her final wishes, and lived in her château, assuming guardianship of Francis Graslin. Three months later, again furthering the desires of the deceased, Gérard married a native girl, Denise Tascheron, the sister of a man who had been executed in 1829. [The Country Parson.]

Gérard (Madame Grégoire), wife of foregoing, born Denise Tascheron, of Montégnac, Limousin; youngest child of a rather large family. She lavished her sisterly affection on her brother, the condemned Tascheron, visiting him in prison and softening his savage nature. With the aid of another brother, Louis-Marie, she made away with certain compromising clues of her eldest brother's crime, and restored the stolen money, afterwards she emigrated to America, where she became wealthy. Becoming homesick she returned to Montégnac, fifteen years later, where she recognized Francis Graslin, her brother's natural son, and became a second mother to him when she married the engineer, Gérard. This marriage of a Protestant with a Catholic took place in 1844. "In grace, modesty, piety and beauty, Mme. Gérard resembled the heroine of 'Edinburgh Prison.'" [The Country Parson.]

Gérard (Madame), widow, poor but honest, mother of several grown-up daughters; kept a furnished hôtel on rue Louis-le-Grand, Paris, about the end of the Restoration. Being under obligations to Suzanne du Va-Noble—Mme. Théodore Gaillard—she sheltered her when the courtesan was driven away from a fine apartment on rue Saint-Georges, following the ruin and flight of her lover, Jacques Falleix, the stockbroker. Mme. Gérard was not related to the other Gérards mentioned above. [Scenes from a Courtesan's Life.]

Giardini, Neapolitan cook somewhat aged. He and his wife ran a restaurant in rue Froidmanteau, Paris, in 1830-31. He had established, so he said, three restaurants in Italy: at Naples, Parma and Rome. In the first years of Louis Philippe's reign, his peculiar cookery was the fare of Paolo Gambara. In 1837 this crank on the subject of special dishes had fallen to the calling of broken food huckster on rue Froidmanteau. [Gambara.]

Giboulard (Gatienne), a very pretty daughter of a wealthy carpenter of Auxerre; vainly desired, about 1823, by Sarcus for wife, but his father, Sarcus the Rich, would not consent. Later the social set of Mme. Soudry, the leading one of a neighboring village, dreamed for a moment of avenging themselves on the people of Aigues by winning over Gatienne Giboulard. She could have embroiled M. and Mme. Montcornet, and perhaps even compromised Abbé Brossette. [The Peasantry.]

Gigelmi, Italian orchestra conductor, living in Paris with the Gambaras. After the Revolution of 1830, he dined at Giardini's on rue Froidmanteau. [Gambara.]

Gigonnet. (*See* Bidault.)

Giguet (Colonel), native probably of Arcis-sur-Aube, where he lived after retirement. One of Mme. Marion's brothers. One of the most highly esteemed officers of the Grand Army. Had a fine sense of honor; was for eleven years merely captain of artillery; chief of battalion in 1813; major in 1814. On account of devotion to Napoleon he refused to serve the Bourbons after the first abdication; and he gave such proofs of his fidelity in 1815, that he would have been exiled had it not been for the Comte de Gondreville, who obtained for him retirement on half-pay with the rank of colonel. About 1806 he married one of the daughters of a wealthy Hamburg banker, who gave him three children and died in 1814. Between 1818 and 1825 Giguet lost the two younger children, a son named Simon alone surviving. A Bonapartist and Liberal, the colonel was, during the Restoration, president of the committee at Arcis, where he came in touch with Grévin, Beauvisage and Varlet, notables of the same stamp. He abandoned active politics after his ideas triumphed, and, during the reign of Louis Philippe, he became a noted horticulturist, the creator of the famous Giguet rose. Nevertheless the colonel continued to be the god of his sister's very influential salon where he appeared at the time of the legislative elections of 1839.   In the first part of May of that year the little old man, wonderfully preserved, presided over an electoral convention at Frappart's, the candidates in the field being his own son, Simon Giguet, Philéas Beauvisage, and Sallenauve-Dorlange.   [The Member for Arcis.]

Giguet (Colonel), brother of the preceding and of Mme. Marion; was brigadier of gendarmes at Arcis-sur-Aube in 1803; promoted to a lieutenancy in 1806.   As brigadier Giguet was one of the most experienced men in the service.   The commandant of Troyes mentioned him especially to the two Parisian detectives, Peyrade and Corentin, entrusted with watching the actions of the Simeuses and the Hauteserres which resulted in the ruin of these young Royalists on account of the pretended seizure of Gondreville.   However, an adroit manœuvre on the part of François Michu at first prevented Brigadier Giguet from seizing these conspirators whom he had tracked to earth.   After his promotion to lieutenant he succeeded in arresting them.   He finally became colonel of the gendarmes of Troyes, whither Mme. Marion, then Mlle. Giguet, went with him.   He died before his brother and sister, and made her his heir.   [The Gondreville Mystery.   The Member for Arcis.]

Giguet (Simon), born during the first Empire, the oldest and only surviving child of Colonel Giguet of the artillery.   In 1814 he lost his mother, the daughter of a rich Hamburg banker, and in 1826 his maternal grandfather who left him an income of two thousand francs, the German having favored others of the large family.   He did not hope for any further inheritance save that of his father's sister, Mme. Marion, which had been augmented by the legacy of Colonel Giguet of the gendarmes.   Thus it was that, after studying law with the subprefect Antonin Goulard, Simon Giguet, deprived of a fortune which at first seemed assured to him, became a simple attorney in the little town of Arcis, where attorneys are of little service.   His aunt's and his father's position fired him with ambition for a political career.   Giguet ogled at the same time for the hand and dowry of Cécile Beauvisage.   Of mediocre ability; upheld the Left Centre, but failed of election in May, 1839, when he presented himself as candidate for Arcis-sur-Aube. [The Member for Arcis.]

Gilet (Maxence), born in 1789. He passed at Issoudun for the natural son of Lousteau, the sub-delegate. Others thought him the son of Dr. Rouget, a friend and rival of Lousteau. In short "fortunately for the child both claimed him"; though he belonged to neither. His true father was found to be a "charming officer of dragoons in the garrison at Bourges." His mother, the wife of a poor drunken cobbler of Issoudun, had the marvelous beauty of a Transteverin. Her husband was aware of his wife's actions and profited by them: through interested motives, Lousteau and Rouget were allowed to believe whatever they wished about the child's paternity, for which reason both contributed to the education of Maxence, usually known as Max. In 1806, at the age of seventeen, Max enlisted in a regiment going to Spain. In 1809 he was left for dead in Portugal in an English battery; taken by the English and conveyed to the Spanish prison-hulks at Cabrera. There he remained from 1810 till 1814. When he returned to Issoudun his father and his mother had both died in the hospital. On the return of Bonaparte, Max served as captain in the Imperial Guard. During the second Restoration he returned to Issoudun and became leader of the "Knights of Idlesse" which were addicted to nocturnal escapades more or less agreeable to the inhabitants of the town. "Max played at Issoudun a part almost identical with that of Smith in 'The Fair Maid of Perth'; he was the champion of Bonapartism and opposition. They relied upon him, as the citizens of Perth had relied upon Smith on great occasions." A possible Cæsar Borgia on more extensive ground, Gilet lived very comfortably, although without a personal income. And that is why Max with certain inherited qualities and defects rashly went to live with his supposed natural brother, Jean-Jacques Rouget, a rich and witless old bachelor who was under the thumb of a superb servant-mistress, Flore Brazier, known as La Rabouilleuse. After 1816 Gilet lorded t over the household; the handsome chap had won the heart

of Mlle. Brazier.   Surrounded by a sort of staff, Maxence contested the important inheritance of Rouget, maintaining his
ground with marvelous skill against the two lawful heirs,
Agathe and Joseph Bridau; and he would have appropriated
it but for the intervention of a third heir, Philippe Bridau.
Max was killed in a duel by Philippe in the early part of
December, 1822. [A Bachelor's Establishment.]

Gillé, once printer to the Emperor; owner of script letters which Jérôme-Nicolas Séchard made use of in 1819,
claiming for them that they were the ancestors of the English type of Didot. [Lost Illusions.]

Gina, character in "L'Ambitieux par Amour," autobiographical novel by Albert Savarus; a sort of "ferocious"
Sormano. Represented as a young Sicilian girl, fourteen
years old, in the services of the Gandolphinis, political refugees
at Gersau, Switzerland, in 1823. So devoted as to pretend
dumbness on occasion, and to wound more or less seriously
the hero of the romance, Rodolphe, who had secretly entered
the Gandolphini home. [Albert Savarus.]

Ginetta (La), young Corsican girl.   Very small and slender,
but no less clever.   Mistress of Théodore Calvi, and an
accomplice in the double crime committed by her lover,
towards the end of the Restoration, when she was able on
account of her small size to creep down an open chimney at
the widow Pigeau's, and thus to open the house door for
Théodore who robbed and murdered the two inmates, the
widow and the servant. [Scenes from a Courtesan's Life.]

Girard, banker and discounter at Paris during the Restoration; perhaps also somewhat of a pawnbroker; an acquaintance of Esther Gobseck's.   Like Palma, Werbrust and
Gigonnet, he held a number of notes signed by Maxime de
Trailles; and Gobseck who knew it used them against the
count, then the lover of Mme. de Restaud, when Trailles went
to the usurer in rue des Grés and besought assistance in vain.
[Gobseck.]

Girard (Mother), who ran a little restaurant at Paris in rue
de Tournon, prior to 1838, had a successor with whom Gode-

froid promised to board when he was inspecting the left bank of the Seine, and trying to aid the Bourlac-Mergis. [The Seamy Side of History.]

Girardet, attorney at Besançon, between 1830 and 1840. A talkative fellow and adherent of Albert Savarus, he followed, probably in the latter's interest, the beginning of the Watteville suit. When Savarus left Besançon suddenly, Girardet tried to straighten out his colleague's affairs, and advanced him five thousand francs. [Albert Savarus.]

Giraud (Léon), was at Paris in 1821 member of the Cénacle of rue des Quatre-Vents, presided over by Daniel d'Arthez. He represented the philosophical element. His "doctrines" predicted the end of Christianity and of the family. In 1821 he was also in charge of a "grave and dignified" opposition journal. He became the head of a moral and political school, whose "sincerity atoned for its errors." [A Distinguished Provincial at Paris.] About the same time Giraud frequented the home of the mother of his friend Joseph Bridau, and was going there at the time when the painter's elder brother, the Bonapartist Philippe, got into trouble. [A Bachelor's Establishment.] The Revolution of July opened the political career of Léon Giraud who became master of requests in 1832, and afterwards councilor of state. In 1845 Giraud was a member of the Chamber, sitting in the Left Centre. [The Secrets of a Princess. The Unconscious Humorists.]

Girel, of Troyes. According to Michu, Girel, a Royalist like himself, during the first Revolution, played the Jacobin in the interest of his fortune. From 1803 to 1806, at any rate, he was in correspondence with the Strasbourg house of Breintmayer, which dealt with the Simeuse twins when they were tracked by Bonaparte's police. [The Gondreville Mystery.]

Girodet (Anne-Louis), celebrated painter, born at Montargis, in 1767, died at Paris in 1824. Under the Empire he was on friendly terms with his colleague, Théodore de Sommervieux. One day in the latter's studio he greatly admired a portrait of Augustine Guillaume and an interior, which he advised him but in vain not to exhibit at the Salon, thinking the two works too true to nature to be appreciated by the public. [At the Sign of the Cat and Racket.]

Giroud (Abbé), confessor of Rosalie de Watteville at Besançon between 1830 and 1840. [Albert Savarus.]

Giroudeau, born about 1774. Uncle of Andoche Finot; began as simple soldier in the army of Sambre and Meuse; five years master-at-arms in the First Hussars—army of Italy; charged at Eylau with Colonel Chabert. He passed into the dragoons of the Imperial Guard, where he was captain in 1815. The Restoration interrupted his military career. Finot, manager of various Parisian papers and reviews, put him in charge of the cash and accounts of a little journal devoted to dramatic news, which he ran from 1821 to 1822. Giroudeau was also the editor, and his duty it was to wage the warfare; beyond that he lived a gay life. Although on the wrong side of forty and afflicted with catarrh he had for mistress Florentine Cabirolle of the Gaîté. He went with the high-livers—among others with his former mess-mate Philippe Bridau, at whose wedding with Flore Brazier he was present in 1824. In November, 1825, Frédéric Marest gave a grand breakfast to Desroches' clerks at the Rocher de Cancale, to which Giroudeau was invited. All spent the evening with Florentine Cabirolle who entertained them royally but involuntarily got Oscar Husson into trouble. Ex-Captain Giroudeau bore firearms during the "three glorious days," re-entered the service after the accession of citizen royalty and soon became colonel then general, 1834-35. At this time he was enabled to satisfy a legitimate resentment against his former friend, Bridau, and block his advancement. [A Distinguished Provincial at Paris. A Start in Life. A Bachelor's Establishment.]

Givry, one of several names of the second son of the Duc de Chaulieu, who became by his marriage with Madeleine de Mortsauf a Lenoncourt-Givry-Chaulieu. [Letters of Two Brides. The Lily of the Valley. Scenes from a Courtesan's Life.]

Gobain (Madame Marie), formerly cook to a bishop; lived during the Restoration in Paris on rue Saint-Maur, Popinot quarter, under very peculiar circumstances. She was in the service of Octave de Banvan. Was the maid and house-keeper of Comtes e Honorine when the latter left home and became a maker of artificial flowers. Mme. Gobain had been secretly engaged by M. de Bauvan, who through her was enabled to keep watch over his wife. Gobain displayed the greatest loyalty. At one time the comtesse took the servant's name. [Honorine.]

Gobenheim, brother-in-law of François and Adolphe Keller, whose name he added to his own. About 1819 in Paris he was at first made receiver in the César Birotteau bankruptcy, but was later replaced by Camusot. [César Birotteau.] Under Louis Philippe, Gobenheim, as broker for the Paris prosecuting office, invested the very considerable savings of Mme. Fabien du Ronceret. [Béatrix.]

Gobenheim, nephew of Gobenheim-Keller of Paris; young banker of Havre in 1829; visited the Mignons, but not as a suitor for the heiress' hand. [Modeste Mignon.]

Gobet (Madame), in 1829 at Havre made shoes for Mme. and Mlle. Mignon. Was scolded by the latter for lack of style. [Modeste Mignon.]

Gobseck (Jean-Esther Van), usurer, born in 1740 at Antwerp of a Jewess and a Dutchman. Began as a cabin-boy. Was only ten years of age when his mother sent him off to the Dutch possessions in India. There and in America he met distinguished people, also several corsairs; traveled all over the world and tried many trades. The passion for money took entire hold of him. Finally he came to Paris which became the centre of his operations, and established himself on rue des Grés. There Gobseck, like a spider in his web, crushed the pride of Maxime de Trailles and brought tears to the eyes of Mme. de Restaud and Jean-Joachim Goriot—1819. About this same time Ferdinand du Tillet sought out the money-lender to make some deals with him, and spoke of him as " Gobseck the Great, master of Palma, Gigonnet, Werbrust, Keller and Nucingen." Gobseck went every evening to the

Thémis café to play dominoes with his friend Bidault-Gigon-net. In December, 1824, he was found there by Elisabeth Baudoyer, whom he promised to aid; indeed, supported by Mitral, he was able to influence Lupeaulx to put in Isidore Baudoyer as chief of division succeeding La Billardière. In 1830, Gobseck, then an octogenarian, died in his wretched hole on rue des Grés though he was enormously wealthy. Der-ville received his last wishes. He had obtained a wife for the lawyer and entrusted him with several confidences. Fifteen years after the Dutchman's death, he was spoken of on the boulevard as the "Last of the Romans"—among the old-fashioned money-lenders like Gigonnet, Chaboisseau, and Samanon, against whom Lora and Bixiou set the modern Vauvinet. [Gobseck. Father Goriot. César Birotteau. The Government Clerks. The Unconscious Humorists.]

Gobseck (Sarah Van), called "La Belle Hollandaise." A peculiarity of this family—as well as the Maranas—that the female side always kept the family name. Thus Sarah Van Gobseck was the grand-niece of Jean-Esther Van Gob-seck. This prostitute, mother of Esther, who was also a courtesan, was a typical daughter of Paris. She caused the bankruptcy of Roguin, Birotteau's attorney, and was herself ruined by Maxime de Trailles whom she adored and main-tained when he was a page to Napoleon. She died in a house on Palais-Royal, the victim of a love-mad captain, December, 1818. The affair created a stir. Juan and Francis Diard had something to say about it. Esther's name lived after her. The Paris of the boulevards from 1824 to 1839 often mentioned her prodigal and stormy career. [Gobseck. César Birotteau. The Maranas. Scenes from a Courtesan's Life. The Mem-ber for Arcis.]

Gobseck (Esther Van), born in 1805 of Jewish origin; daughter of the preceding and great-grand-niece of Jean. For a long time in Paris she followed her mother's calling, and having begun it early in life she knew its varied phases. Was nick-named "La Torpille." Was for some time one of the "rats" of the Royal Academy of Music, and numbered among her protectors, Lupeaulx. In 1823 her reduced circumstances almost forced her to leave Paris for Issoudun, where, for a machiavellian purpose, Philippe Bridau would have made her the mistress of Jean-Jacques Rouget. The affair did not materialize. She went to Mme. Meynardie's house where she remained till about the end of 1823. One evening, while passing the Porte-Saint-Martin theatre, she chanced to meet Lucien de Rubempré, and they loved each other at first sight. Their passion led into many vicissitudes. The poet and the ex-prostitute were rash enough to attend an Opéra ball together in the winter of 1824. Unmasked and insulted Esther fled to rue de Langlade, where she lived in dire poverty. The dangerous, powerful and mysterious protector of Rubempré, Jacques Collin, followed her there, lectured her and shaped her future life, making her a Catholic, educating her carefully and finally installing her with Lucien on rue Taitbout, under the surveillance of Jacqueline Collin, Paccard and Prudence Servien. She could go out only at night. Nevertheless, the Baron de Nucingen discovered her and fell madly in love with her. Jacques Collin profited by the episode; Esther received the banker's attentions, to the enrichment of Lucien. In 1830 she owned a house on rue Saint-Georges which had belonged previously to several celebrated courtesans; there she received Mme. du Val-Noble, Tullia and Florentine—two dancers, Fanny Beaupré and Florine—two actresses. Her new position resulted in police intervention on the part of Lonchard, Contenson, Peyrade and Corentin. On May 13, 1830, unable longer to endure Nucingen, La Torpille swallowed a Javanese poison. She died without knowing that she had fallen heir to seven millions left by her great-grand-uncle. [Gobseck. The Firm of Nucingen. A Bachelor's Establishment. Scenes from a Courtesan's Life.]

Godain, born in 1796, in Burgundy, near Soulanges, Blangy and Ville-aux-Fayes; nephew of one of the masons who built Mme. Soudry's house. A shiftless farm laborer, exempt from military duty on account of smallness of stature; was at first the lover, then the husband, of Catherine Tonsard, whom he married about 1823. [The Peasantry.]

Godain (Madame Catherine), the eldest of the legitimate daughters of Tonsard, landlord of the Grand-I-Vert,
situated between Conches and Ville-aux-Fayes in Burgundy.
Of coarse beauty and by nature depraved; a hanger-on at
the Tivoli-Socquard, and a devoted sister to Nicolas Tonsard
for whom she tried to obtain Geneviéve Niseron.   Courted by
Charles, valet at Aigues.   Feared by Amaury Lupin.   Married Godain one of her lovers, giving a dowry of a thousand
francs cunningly obtained from Mme. Montcornet.   [The
Peasantry.]

Godard (Joseph), born in 1798, probably at Paris; related
slightly to the Baudoyers through Mitral.   Stunted and
puny; fifer in the National Guard; "crank" collector of
curios; a virtuous bachelor living with his sister, a florist on
rue Richelieu.   Between 1824 and 1825 a possible assistant
in the Department of Finance in the bureau managed by
Isidore Baudoyer, whose son-in-law he dreamed of becoming.
An easy mark for Bixiou's practical jokes.   With Dutocq he
was an unwavering adherent of the Baudoyers and their
relatives the Saillards. [The Government Clerks.   The
Middle Classes.]

Godard (Mademoiselle), sister of the foregoing, and lived on
rue Richelieu, Paris, where in 1824 she ran a florist's shop.
Mlle. Godard employed Zélie Lorain who became later the
wife of Minard.   She received him and Dutocq.   [The
Government Clerks.]

Godard (Manon), serving-woman of Mme. de la Chanterie;
arrested in 1809, between Alençon and Mortagne, implicated
in the Chauffeurs trial which ended in the capital punishment
of Mme. des Tours-Miniéres, daughter of Mme. de la Chanterie.
Manon Godard was sentenced by default to twenty-two years
imprisonment, and gave herself up in order not to abandon her
mistress.   A long time after the baroness was set free, time
of Louis Philippe, Manon was still living with her, on rue
Chanoinesse, in the house which sheltered Alain, Montauran
and Godefroid.   [The Seamy Side of History.]

Goddet, retired surgeon-major of the Third regiment of the line; the leading physician of Issoudun in 1823.   His son was one of the "Knights of Idlesse."   Goddet junior pretended to pay court to Mme. Fichet, in order to reach her daughter who had the best dowry in Issoudun.   [A Bachelor's Establishment.]

Godefroid, known only by his given name; born about 1806, probably at Paris; son of a wealthy merchant; educated at the Liautard Institution; naturally feeble, morally and physically; tried his hand at and made a failure of: law, governmental work, letters, pleasure, journalism, politics and marriage.   At the close of 1836 he found himself poor and forsaken; thereupon he tried to pay his debts and live economically.   He left Chaussée-d'Antin and took up his abode on rue Chanoinesse, where he became one of Mme. de la Chanteries' boarders, known as the "Brotherhood of the Consolation."   The recommendation of the Monegods, bankers, led to his admission.   Abbé de Véze, Montauran, Tresnes, Alain, and above all the baroness initiated him, coached him, and entrusted to him various charitable missions.   Among others, about the middle of the reign of Louis Philippe, he took charge of and relieved the frightful poverty of the Bourlacs and the Mergis, the head of which as an imperial judge in 1809 had sentenced Mme. de la Chanterie and her daughter.   After he succeeded with this generous undertaking, Godefroid was admitted to the Brotherhood.   [The Seamy Side of History.]

Godenars (Abbé de), born about 1795; one of the vicars-general of the archbishop of Besançon between 1830 and 1840. From 1835 on he tried to get a bishopric.   One evening he was present at the aristocratic salon of the Wattevilles, at the time of the sudden flight of Albert Savarus, caused by their young daughter.   [Albert Savarus.]

Godeschal (François-Claude-Marie), born about 1804.   In 1818, at Paris, he was third clerk in the law office of Derville, rue Vivienne, when the unfortunate Chabert appeared upon the scene.   [Colonel Chabert.]   In 1820, then an orphan and poor, he and his sister, the dancer Mariette, to whom he was devoted, lived on an eighth floor on rue Vielle-du-Temple.   He

had already given evidence of a practical temperament, independent and self-seeking, but upright and capable of generous
outbursts. [A Bachelor's Establishment.] In 1822, having
risen to second clerk, he left Maître Derville to become head-
clerk in Desroches' office, who was greatly pleased with him.
Godeschal even undertook to reform Oscar Husson. [A
Start in Life.] Six years later, while still Desroches' head-
clerk, he drew up a petition wherein Mme. d'Espard prayed a
guardian for her husband. [The Commission in Lunacy.]
Under Louis Philippe he became one of the advocates of Paris
and paid half his fees—1840--proposing to pay the other half
with the dowry of Céleste Colleville, whose hand was refused
him, despite the recommendation of Cardot the notary. Was
engaged for Peyrade, in the purchase of a house near the
Madeleine. [The Middle Classes.] About 1845 Godeschal
was still practicing, and numbered among his clients the
Camusots de Marville. [Cousin Pons.]

Godeschal (Marie), born about 1804. She maintained,
almost all her life, the nearest and most tender relations with
her brother Godeschal the notary. Without relatives or
means, she kept house with him in 1820, on the eighth floor
of a house on rue Vielle-du-Temple, Paris. Ambition and
love for her brother caused her to become a dancer. She
had studied her profession from her tenth year. The
famous Vestris instructed her and predicted great things for
her. Under the name of Mariette, she was engaged at the
Porte-Saint-Martin and the Royal Academy of Music. Her
success displeased the famous Bégrand. In January, 1821,
her angelic beauty, maintained despite her profession, opened
to her the doors of the Opéra. Then she had lovers. The aristocratic and elegant Maufrigneuse protected her for several years.
Mariette also favored Philippe Bridau and was the innocent
cause of a theft committed by him in order to enable him to
contend with Maufrigneuse. Four months later she went to
London, where she won the rich members of the House of
Lords, and returned as première to the Academy of Music.
She was intimate with Florentine Cabirolle, who often received
in the Marais. There it was that Mariette kept Oscar Husson

out of serious trouble. Mariette attended many festivities. And at the close of the reign of Louis Philippe, she was still a leading figure in the Opéra. [A Bachelor's Establishment. A Start in Life. Scenes from a Courtesan's Life. Cousin Pons.]

Godin, under Louis Philippe, a Parisian bourgeois engaged in a lively dispute with a friend of La Palférine's. [A Prince of Bohemia.]

Godin (La), peasant woman of Conches, Burgundy, about 1823, whose cow Vermichel threatened to seize for the Comte de Montcornet. [The Peasantry.]

Godivet, recorder of registry of Arcis-sur-Aube in 1839. Through the scheming of Pigoult he was chosen as one of the two agents for an electoral meeting called by Simon Giguet, one of the candidates, and presided over by Philéas Beau-visage. [The Member for Arcis.]

Godollo (Comtesse Torna de), probably a Hungarian; police spy reporting to Corentin. Was ordered to prevent the marriage of Théodose de la Peyrade and Céleste Colleville. To accomplish this she went to live in the Thuilliers' house, Paris, in 1840, cultivated them and finally ruled them. She sometimes assumed the name of Mme. Komorn. Her wit and beauty exercised a passing effect upon Peyrade. [The Middle Classes.]

Goguelat, infantryman of the first Empire, entered the Guard in 1812; was decorated by Napoleon on the battlefield of Valontina; returned during the Restoration to the village of Isére, of which Benassis was mayor, and became postman. [The Country Doctor.]

Gohier, goldsmith to the King of France in 1824; supplied Elisabeth Baudoyer with the monstrance with which she decorated the church of Saint Paul, in order to bring about Isidore Baudoyer's promotion in office. [The Government Clerks.]

Gomez, captain of the "Saint Ferdinand," a Spanish brig which in 1833 conveyed the newly-enriched Marquis d'Aigle-mont from America to France. Gomez was boarded by a

Columbian corsair whose captain, the Parisian, ordered him cast overboard. [A Woman of Thirty.]

Gondrand (Abbé), confessor, under the Restoration, at Paris, of the Duchesse Antoinette de Langeais, whose excellent dinners and petty sins he dealt with at his ease in her salon where Montriveau often found him. [The Thirteen.]

Gondreville (Malin, his real name; more frequently known as the Comte de), born in 1763, probably at Arcis-sur-Aube. Short and stout; grandson of a mason employed by Marquis de Simeuse in the building of the Gondreville château; only son of the owner of a house at Arcis where dwelt his friend Grévin in 1839. On the recommendation of Danton, he entered the office of the attorney at the châtelet, Paris, in 1787. Head clerk for Maitre Bordin in the same city, the same year. Returned to the country two years later to become a lawyer at Troyes. Became an obscure and cowardly member of the Convention. Acquired the friendship of Talleyrand and Fouché, in June, 1800, under singular and opportune circumstances. Successively and rapidly became tribune, councilor of state, count of the Empire—created Comte de Gondreville—and finally senator. As councilor of state, Gondreville devoted his attention to the preparation of the code. He cut a dash at Paris. He had purchased one of the finest mansions in Faubourg Saint-Germain and married the only daughter of Sibuelle, a wealthy contractor of "shady" character whom Gondreville made co-receiver of Aube, with Marion. The marriage was celebrated during the Directory or the Consulate. Three children were the result of this union: Charles de Gondreville, Maréchale de Garigliano, Mme. François Keller. In his own interest, Malin attached himself to Bonaparte. Later, in the presence of the Emperor and of Dubois, the prefect of police, Gondreville selfishly simulated a false generosity and asked that the Hauteserres and Simeuses be striken from the list of the proscribed. Afterwards they were falsely accused of kidnapping him. As senator in 1809, Malin gave a grand ball at Paris, when he vainly awaited the Emperor's appearance, and when Mme. de Lansac reconciled the Soulanges family. Louis XVIII.

made him peer of France. His wide experience and owner-
ship of many secrets aided Gondreville, whose counsels
hindered Decazes and helped Villèle. Charles X. disliked him
because he remained too intimate with Talleyrand. Under
Louis Philippe this bond was relaxed. The July monarchy
heaped honors upon him by making him peer once more.
One evening in 1833 he met at the home of the Princesse de
Cadignan, Henri de Marsay, the prime minister, who had an
inexhaustible fund of political stories, new to all the company
save Gondreville. He was much engrossed with the elections
of 1839, and gave his influence to his grandson, Charles
Keller, for Arcis. He concerned himself little with the candidates, who were finally elected; Dorlange-Sallenauve,
Philéas Beauvisage, Trailles and Giguet. [The Gondreville
Mystery. A Start in Life. Domestic Peace. The Member
for Arcis.]

Gondreville (Comtesse Malin de), born Sibuelle; wife of
foregoing; person whose complete insignificance was manifest at the great ball given in Paris by the count in 1809.
[Domestic Peace.]

Gondreville (Charles de), son of the preceding, and sub-
lieutenant of dragoons in 1818. Young and wealthy, he
died in the Spanish campaign of 1823. His death caused
great sorrow to his mistress, Mme. Colleville. [The Middle
Classes.]

Gondrin, born in 1774, in the department of Isére. Con-
scripted in 1792 and put in the artillery. Was in the Italian
and Egyptian campaigns under Bonaparte, as a private,
and returned east after the Peace of Amiens. Enrolled,
during the Empire, in the pontoon corps of the Guard, he
marched through Germany and Russia; was in the battle
at Bérésina aiding to build the bridge by which the remnant
of the army escaped; with forty-one comrades, received the
praise of General Eblé who singled him out particularly.
Returned to Wilna, as the only survivor of the corps after
the death of Eblé and in the beginning of the Restoration.
Unable to read or write, deaf and decrepit, Gondrin for-

lornly left Paris which had treated him inhospitably, and returned to the village in Dauphiné, where the mayor, Dr. Benassis, gave him work as a ditcher and continued to aid him in 1829. [The Country Doctor.]

Gondrin (Abbé), young Parisian priest about the middle of the reign of Louis Philippe. Exquisite and eloquent. Knew the Thuilliers. [The Middle Classes.]

Gondureau, assumed name of Bibi-Lupin.

Gonore (La), widow of Moses the Jew, chief of the southern *rouleurs*, in May, 1830; mistress of Dannepont the thief and assassin; ran a house of ill-repute on rue Sainte-Barbe for Mme. Nourrisson. [Scenes from a Courtesan's Life.]

Gordes (Mademoiselle de), at the head of an aristocratic salon of Alençon, about 1816, while her father, the aged Marquis de Gordes, was still living with her. [Jealousies of a Country Town.]

Gorenflot, mason of Vendôme, who walled up the closet concealing Mme. de Merret's lover, the Spaniard Bagos de Férédia. [La Grande Bretéche.]

Gorenflot, probably posed for Quasimodo of Hugo's "Notre-Dame." Decrepit, misshapen, deaf, diminutive, he lived in Paris about 1839, and was organ-blower and bell-ringer in the church of Saint-Louis en l'Ile. He also acted as messenger in the confidential financial correspondence between Bricheteau and Dorlange-Sallenauve. [The Member for Arcis.]

Goriot,[1] (Jean-Joachim), born about 1750; started as a porter in the grain market. During the first Revolution, although he had received no education, but having a trader's instinct, he began the manufacture of vermicelli and made a fortune out of it. Thrift and fortune favored him under the Terror. He passed for a bold citizen and fierce patriot. Prosperity enabled him to marry from choice the only daughter of a wealthy farmer of Brie, who died young

---

[1] Two Parisian theatres and five authors have depicted Goriot's life on the stage; March 6, 1835, at the Vaudeville, Ancelot and Paul Dupont; the same year, the month following, at the Variétés, Théaulon, Alexis de Comberousse and Jaime Père. Also the *Bœuf Gras* of a carnival in a succeeding year bore the name of Goriot.

and adored. Upon their two children, Anastasie and Delphine, he lavished all the tenderness of which their mother had been the recipient, spoiling them with fine things. Goriot's griefs date from the day he set each up in housekeeping in magnificent fashion on Chaussée-d'Antin. Far from being grateful for his pecuniary sacrifices, his sons-in-law, Restaud and Nucingen, and his daughters themselves, were ashamed of .his bourgeois exterior. In 1813 he had retired saddened and impoverished to the Vauquer boarding-house on rue Neuve-Sainte-Geneviéve. The quarrels of his daughters and the greedy demands for money increased and in 1819 followed him thither. Almost all the guests of the house and especially Mme. Vauquer herself—whose ambitious designs upon him had come to naught—united in persecuting Goriot, now well-nigh poverty-stricken. He found an agreeable respite when he acted as a go-between for the illicit love affair of Mme. de Nucingen and Rastignac, his fellow-lodger. The financial distress of Mme. de Restaud, Trailles' victim, gave Goriot the finishing blow. He was compelled to give up the final and most precious bit of his silver plate, and· beg the assistance of Gobseck the usurer. He was crushed. A serious attack of apoplexy carried him off. He died on rue Neuve-Sainte-Geneviéve. Rastignac watched over him, and Bianchon, then an interne, attended him. Only two men, Christophe, Mme. Vauquer's servant, and Rastignac, followed the remains to Saint-Etienne du Mont and to Pére-Lachaise. The empty carriages of his daughters followed as far as the cemetery. [Father Goriot.]

Goritza (Princesse), a charming Hungarian, celebrated for her beauty, towards the end of Louis XV.'s reign, and to whom the youthful Chevalier de Valois became so attached that he came near fighting on her account with M. de Lauzun; nor could he ever speak of her without emotion. From 1816 to 1830, the Alençon aristocracy were given glimpses of the princess's portrait, which adorned the chevalier's gold snuff-box. [Jealousies of a Country Town.]

Gorju (Madame), wife of the mayor of Sancerre, in 1836,

and mother of a daughter "whose figure threatened to change with her first child," and who sometimes came with her to the receptions of Mme. de la Baudraye, the "Muse of the Department." One evening, in the fall of 1836, she heard Lousteau reading ironically fragments of "Olympia." [The Muse of the Department.]

Gothard, born in 1788; lived about 1803 in Arcis-sur-Aube, where his courage and address obtained for him the place of groom to Laurence de Cinq-Cygne. Devoted servant of the countess; he ·was one of the principals acquitted in the trial which ended with the execution of Michu. [The Gondreville Mystery.] Gothard never left the service of the Cinq-Cygne family. Thirty-six years later he was their steward. With his brother-in-law, Poupard, the Arcis tavern-keeper, he electioneered for his masters. [The Member for Arcis.]

Goujet (Abbé), curé of Cinq-Cygne, Aube, about 1792, discovered for the son of Beauvisage the farmer, who were still good Catholics, the Greek name of Philéas, one of the few saints not abolished by the new régime. [The Member for Arcis.] Former abbé of the Minimes, and a friend of Hauteserre. Was the tutor of Adrien and Robert Hauteserre; enjoyed a game of boston with their parents—1803. His political prudence sometimes led him to censure the audacity of their kinswoman, Mlle. de Cinq-Cygne. Nevertheless, he held his own with the persecutor of the house, Corentin the police-agent; and attended Michu when that victim of a remarkable trial, known as "the abduction of Gondreville," went to the scaffold. During the Restoration he became Bishop of Troyes. [The Gondreville Mystery.]

Goujet (Mademoiselle), sister of the foregoing; good-natured old maid, ugly and parsimonious, who lived with her brother. Almost every evening she played boston at the Hauteserres and was terrified by Corentin's visits. [The Gondreville Mystery.]

Goulard, mayor of Cinq-Cygne, Aube, in 1803. Tall, stout and miserly; married a wealthy tradeswoman of Troyes, whose property, augmented by all the lands of the rich abbey of Valdes-Preux, adjoined Cinq-Cygne. Goulard lived in the old abbey, which was very near the château of Cinq-Cygne. Despite his revolutionary proclivities, he closed his eyes to the actions of the Hauteserres and Simeuses who were Royalist plotters. [The Gondreville Mystery.]

Goulard (Antonin), native of Arcis, like Simon Giguet. Born about 1807; son of the former huntsman of the Simeuse family, enriched by the purchase of public lands. (*See* preceding biography.) Early left motherless, he came to Arcis to live with his father, who abandoned the abbey of Valpreux. Went to the Imperial lyceum, where he had Simon Giguet for school-mate, whom he afterwards met again on the benches of the Law school at Paris. Obtained, through Gondreville, the Cross of the Legion of Honor. The royal government of 1830 opened up for him a career in the public service. In 1839 he became sub-prefect for Arcis-sur-Aube, during the electoral period. The delegate, Trailles, satisfied Antonin's rancor against Giguet: his official recommendations caused the latter's defeat. Both the would-be prefect and the sub-prefect vainly sought the hand of Cécile Beauvisage. Goulard cultivated the society of officialdom: Marest, Vinet, Martener, Michu. [The Member for Arcis.]

Gounod, nephew of Vatel, keeper of the Montcornet estate at Aigues, Burgundy. About 1823 he probably became assistant to the head-keeper, Michaud. [The Peasantry.]

Goupil (Jean-Sébastien-Marie), born in 1802; a sort of humpless hunchback; son of a well-to-do farmer. After running through with his inheritance, in Paris, he became head-clerk of the notary Crémière-Dionis, of Nemours— 1829. On account of François Minoret-Levrault, he annoyed in many ways, even anonymously, Ursule Mirouët, after the death of Dr. Minoret. Afterwards he repented his actions, repaid their instigator, and succeeded the notary, Crémière-Dionis. Thanks to his wit, he became honorable, straightforward and completely transformed. Once established, Goupil married Mlle. Massin, eldest daughter of Massin-Levrault junior, clerk to the justice of the peace at Nemours. She was homely, had a dowry of 80,000 francs, and gave him rickety, dropsical children. Goupil took part in the "three glorious days" and had obtained a July decoration. He was very proud of the ribbon. [Ursule Mirouët.]

Gouraud (General, Baron), born in 1782, probably at Provins. Under the Empire he commanded the Second regiment of hussars, which gave him his rank. The Restoration caused his impoverished years at Provins. He mixed in politics and the opposition there, sought the hand and above all the dowry of Sylvie Rogron, persecuted the apparent heiress of the old maid, Mlle. Pierrette Lorrain—1827—and, seconded by Vinet the attorney, reaped in July, 1830, the fruits of his cunning liberalism. Thanks to Vinet, the ambitious parvenu, Gouraud married, in spite of his gray hair and stout frame, a girl of twenty-five, Mlle. Matifat, of the well-known drug-firm of rue des Lombards, who brought with her fifty thousand crowns. Titles, offices and emoluments now flowed in rapidly. He resumed the service, became general, commanded a division near the capital and obtained a peerage. His conduct during the ministry of Casimir Perier was thus rewarded. Furthermore he received the grand ribbon of the Legion of Honor, after having stormed the barricades of, Saint-Merri, and was "delighted to thrash the bourgeois who had been an eye-sore to him" for fifteen years. [Pierrette.] About 1845 he had stock in Gaudissart's theatre. [Cousin Pons.]

Gourdon the elder, husband of the only daughter of the old head-keeper of streams and forests, Gendrin-Wattebled; was in 1823 physician at Soulanges and attended Michaud. Nevertheless he went among the best people of Soulanges, headed by Mme. Soudry, who regarded him in the light of an unknown and neglected savant, when he was but a parrot of Buffon and Cuvier, a simple collector and taxidermist. [The Peasantry.]

Gourdon the younger, brother of the preceding; wrote the poem of "La Bilboquéide" published by Bournier. Married the niece and only heiress of Abbé Tupin, curé of Soulanges, where he himself had been in 1823 clerk for Sarcus. He was wealthier than the justice. Mme. Soudry and her set gave admiring welcome to the poet, preferring him to Lamartine, with whose works they slowly became acquainted. [The Peasantry.]

Goussard (Laurent) was a member of the revolutionary municipality of Arcis-sur-Aube. Particular friend of Danton, he made use of the tribune's influence to save the head of the ex-superior of the Ursulines at Arcis, Mother Marie des Anges, whose gratitude for his generous and skillful action caused substantial enrichment to this purchaser of the grounds of the convent, which was sold as "public land." Thus it was that forty years afterwards this adroit Liberal owned several mills on the river Aube, and was still at the head of the advanced Left in that district. The various candidates for deputy in the spring of 1839, Keller, Giguet, Beauvisage, Dorlange-Sallenauve, and the government agent, Trailles, treated Goussard with the consideration he deserved. [The Member for Arcis.]

Grados had in his hands notes of Vergniaud the herder. By means of funds from Derville the lawyer, Grados was paid in 1818 by Colonel Chabert. [Colonel Chabert.]

Graff (Johann), brother of a tailor established in Paris under Louis Philippe. Came himself to Paris after having been head-waiter in the hotel of Gédéon Brunner at Frankfort; and ran the Hôtel du Rhin in rue du Mail where Frédéric Brunner and Wilhelm Schwab alighted penniless in 1835. The landlord obtained small positions for the two young men; for the former with Keller; for the latter with his brother the tailor. [Cousin Pons.]

Graff (Wolfgang), brother of the foregoing, and rich tailor of Paris, at whose shop in 1838 Lisbeth Fischer fitted out Wenceslas Steinbock. On his brother's recommendation, he employed Wilhelm Schwab, and, six years later, took him into the family by giving him Emilie Graff in marriage. [Cousin Betty. Cousin Pons.]

Grancey (Abbé de), born in 1764. Took orders because of a disappointment in love; became priest in 1786, and curé in 1788. A distinguished prelate who refused three bishoprics in order not to leave Besançon. In 1834 he became vicar-general of that diocese. The abbé had a handsome head. He gave free vent to cutting speeches. Was acquainted with Albert Savarus whom he liked and aided. A frequenter of the Watteville salon he found out and rebuked Rosalie, the singular and determined enemy of the advocate. He also intervened between Madame and Mademoiselle de Watteville. He died at the end of the winter of 1836-37. [Albert Savarus.]

Grancour (Abbé de), one of the vicars-general of the bishopric of Limoges, about the end of the Restoration; and the physical antithesis of the other vicar, the attenuated and moody Abbé Dutheil whose lofty and independent liberal doctrines he, with cowardly caution, secretly shared. Grancour frequented the Graslin salon and doubtless knew of the Tascheron tragedy. [The Country Parson.]

Grandemain was in 1822 at Paris clerk for Desroches. [A Start in Life.]

Grandet (Félix), of Saumur, born between 1745 and 1749. Well-to-do master-cooper, passably educated. In the first years of the Republic he married the daughter of a rich lumber merchant, by whom he had in 1796 one child, Eugénie. With their united capital, he bought at a bargain the best vineyards about Saumur, in addition to an old abbey and several farms. Under the Consulate he became successively member of the district government and mayor of Saumur. But the Empire, which supposed him to be a Jacobin, retired him from the latter office, although he was the town's largest tax-payer. Under the Restoration the despotism of his extraordinary avarice disturbed the peace of his family. His younger brother, Guillaume, failed and killed himself, leaving in Félix's hands the settlement of his affairs, and sending to him his son Charles, who had hastened to Saumur, not knowing his father's ruin. Eugénie loved her cousin and combated her father's niggardliness, which looked after his own interests to the neglect of his brother. The struggle between Eugénie and her father broke Mme. Grandet's heart. The phases of the terrible duel were violent and numerous. Félix Grandet's passion resorted to stratagem and stubborn force. Death alone could settle with this domestic tyrant. In 1827, an octogenarian and worth seventeen millions, he was carried off by a stroke of paralysis. [Eugénie Grandet.]

Grandet (Madame Félix), wife of preceding; born about 1770; daughter of a rich lumber merchant, M. de la Gaudiniére; married in the beginning of the Republic, and gave birth to one child, Eugénie, in 1796. In 1806 she added considerably to the combined wealth of the family through two large inheritances—from her mother and M. de la Bertellière, her maternal grandfather. A devout, shrinking, insignificant creature, bowed beneath the domestic yoke, Mme. Grandet never left Saumur, where she died in October, 1822, of lung trouble, aggravated by grief at her daughter's rebellion and her husband's severity. [Eugénie Grandet.]

Grandet (Victor-Ange-Guillaume), younger brother of Félix Grandet; became rich at Paris in wine-dealing. In 1815 before the battle of Waterloo, Frédéric de Nucingen bought of him one hundred and fifty thousand bottles of champagne at thirty sous, and sold them at six francs; the allies drank them during the invasion—1817-19. [The Firm of Nucingen.] The beginning of the Restoration favored Guillaume. He was the husband of a charming woman, the natural daughter of a great lord, who died young after giving him a child. Was colonel of the National Guard, judge of the Court of Commerce, governor of one of the arrondissements of Paris and deputy. Saumur accused him of aspiring still higher and wishing to become the father-in-law of a petty duchess of the imperial court. The bankruptcy of Maître Roguin was the partial cause of the ruin of Guillaume, who blew out his brains to avoid disgrace, in November, 1819. In his last requests, Guillaume implored his elder brother to care for Charles whom the suicide had rendered doubly an orphan. [Eugénie Grandet.]

Grandet (Charles), only lawful child of the foregoing; nephew of Félix Grandet; born in 1797. He led at first the gay life of a young gallant, and maintained relations with a certain Annette, a married woman of good society. The tragic death of his father in November, 1819, astounded him and led him to Saumur. He thought himself in love with his cousin Eugénie to whom he swore fidelity. Shortly thereafter he left for India, where he took the name of Carl Sepherd to escape the consequences of treasonable actions. He returned to France in 1827 enormously wealthy, debarked at Bordeaux in June of that year, accompanying the Aubrions whose daughter Mathilde he married, and allowed Eugénie Grandet to complete the settlement with the creditors of his father. [Eugénie Grandet.] By his marriage he became Comte d'Aubrion. [The Firm of Nucingen.]

Grandet (Eugénie).[1] (*See* Bonfons, Eugénie Cruchot de.)

Grandlieu (Comtesse de), related to the Herouvilles; lived in the first part of the seventeenth century; probable ancestress of the Grandlieus, well known in France two centuries later. [The Hated Son.]

Grandlieu (Mademoiselle), under the first Empire married an imperial chamberlain, perhaps also the prefect of Orne, and was received, alone, in Alençon among the exclusive and aristocratic set lorded over by the Esgrignons. [Jealousies of a Country Town.]

Grandlieu (Duc Ferdinand de), born about 1773; may have descended from the Comtesse de Grandlieu who lived early in the seventeenth century, and consequently connected with the old and worthy nobility of the Duchy of Brittany whose device was "Caveo non timeo." At the end

---

[1] The incidents of her life have been dramatized by Bayard for the Gymnase-Dramatique, under the title of "The Miser's Daughter."

of the eighteenth and the first half of the nineteenth centuries, Ferdinand de Grandlieu was the head of the elder branch, wealthy and ducal, of the house of Grandlieu. Under·the Consulate and the Empire his high and assured rank enabled him to intercede with Talleyrand in behalf of M. d'Hauteserre and M. de Simeuse, compromised in the fictitious abduction of Malin de Gondreville. Grandlieu by his marriage with an Ajuda of the elder branch, connected with the Barganzas and of Portuguese descent, had several daughters, the eldest of whom assumed the veil in 1822. His other daughters were Clotilde-Frédérique, born in 1802; Joséphine the third; Sabine born in 1809; Marie-Athenaïs, born about 1820. An uncle by marriage of Mme♦ de Langeais, he had at Paris, in Faubourg Saint-Germain, a hotel where, during the reign of Louis XVIII., the Princesse de Blamont-Chauvry, the Vidame de Pamiers and the Duc de Navarreins assembled to consider a startling escapade of Antoinette de Langeais. At least ten years later Grandlieu availed himself of his intimate friend Henri de Chaulieu and also of Corentin—Saint-Denis—in order to stay the suit against Lucien de Rubempré which was about to compromise his daughter Clotilde-Frédérique. [The Gondreville Mystery. The Thirteen. A Bachelor's Establishment. Modeste Mignon. Scenes from a Courtesan's Life.]

Grandlieu (Duchesse Ferdinand de), of Portuguese descent, born Ajuda and of the elder branch of that house connected with the Braganzas. Wife of Ferdinand de Grandlieu, and mother of several daughters. Of sedentary habits, proud, pious, good-hearted and beautiful, she wielded in Paris during the Restoration a sort of supremacy over the Faubourg Saint-Germain. The second and the next to the youngest of her children gave her much anxiety. Combating the hostility of those about her she welcomed Rubempré, the suitor of her daughter Clotilde-Frédérique—1829-30. The unfortunate results of the marriage of her other daughter Sabine, Baronne Calyste du Guénie, occupied Mme. de Grandlieu's attention in 1837, and she succeeded in reconciling the young couple, with the assistance of Abbé Brossette,

Maxime de Trailles, and La Palférine. Her religious scruples had made her halt a moment; but they fell like her political fidelity, and, with Mmes. d'Espard, de Listomère and des Touches, she tacitly recognized the bourgeois royalty, a few years after a new reign began, and re-opened the doors of her salon. [Scenes from a Courtesan's Life. Béatrix. A Daughter of Eve.]

Grandlieu (Mademoiselle de), eldest daughter of the Duc and Duchesse de Grandlieu, took the veil in 1822. [A Bachelor's Establishment. Scenes from a Courtesan's Life.]

Grandlieu (Clotilde-Frédérique de), born in 1802; second daughter of the Duc and Duchesse de Grandlieu; a long, flat creature, the caricature of her mother. She had no consent save that of her mother when she fell in love with and wished to marry the ambitious Lucien de Rubempré in the spring of 1830. She saw him for the last time on the road to Italy in the forest of Fontainebleu near Bouron and under very painful circumstances the young man was arrested before her very eyes. [Scenes from a Courtesan's Life.]

Grandlieu (Joséphine de). (*See* Ajuda-Pinto, Marquise Miguel d'.)

Grandlieu (Sabine de). (*See* Guénie, Baronne Calyste du.)

Grandlieu (Marie-Athénais de). (*See* Grandlieu, Vicomtesse Juste de.)

Grandlieu (Vicomtesse de), sister of Comte de Born; descended more directly than the duke from the countess of the seventeenth century. From 1813, the time of her husband's death, the head of the younger Grandlieu house whose device was "Grands faits, grand lieu." Mother of Camille and of Juste de Grandlieu, and the mother-in-law of Ernest de Restaud. Returned to France with Louis XVIII. At first she lived on royal bounty, but afterwards regained a considerable portion of her property through the efforts of Maitre Derville, about the beginning of the Restoration. She was very grateful to the lawyer, who also took her part against the Legion of Honor, was admitted to her confidential circle and told her the secrets of the Restaud household, one evening in the winter of 1830 when Ernest de Restaud, son of the Comtesse Anastasie, was paying court to Camille whom he finally married. [Scenes from a Courtesan's Life. Colonel Chabert. Gobseck.]

Grandlieu (Camille de). (*See* Restaud, Comtesse Ernest de.)

Grandlieu (Vicomte Juste de), son of Vicomtesse de Grandlieu; brother of Comtesse Ernest de Restaud; cousin and afterwards husband of Marie-Athénaïs de Grandlieu, combining by this marriage the fortunes of the two houses of Grandlieu and obtaining the title of duke. [Scenes from a Courtesan's Life. Gobseck.]

Grandlieu (Vicomtesse Juste de), born about 1820, Marie-Athénaïs de Grandlieu; last daughter of Duc and Duchesse de Grandlieu; married to her cousin, the Vicomte Juste de Grandlieu. She received at Paris in the first days of the July government, a young married woman like herself, Mme. Félix de Vandenesse, then in the midst of a flirtation with Raoul Nathan. [Scenes from a Courtesan's Life. Gobseck. A Daughter of Eve.]

Granet, deputy-mayor of the second arrondissement of Paris, in 1818, under La Billardière. With his homely wife he was invited to the Birotteau ball. [César Birotteau.]

Granet, one of the leading men of Besançon, under Louis Philippe. In gratitude for a favor done him by Albert Savarus he nominated the latter for deputy. [Albert Savarus.]

Granson (Madame), poor widow of a lieutenant-colonel of artillery killed at Jéna, by whom she had a son, Athanase. From 1816 she lived at No. 8 rue du Bercail in Alençon, where the benevolence of a distant relative, Mme. du Bousquier, put in her charge the treasury of a maternal society against infanticide, and brought her into contact, under peculiar circumstances, with the woman who afterwards became Mme. Théodore Gaillard. [Jealousies of a Country Town.]

Granson (Athanase), son of the preceding; born in 1793; subordinate in the mayor's office at Alençon in charge of registry. A sort of poet, liberal in politics and filled with ambition; weary of poverty and overflowing with grandiose sentiments. In 1816 he loved, with a passion that his common-sense combated, Mme. du Bousquier, then Mlle. Cormon, his senior by more than seventeen years. In 1816 the marriage dreaded by him took place. He could not brook the blow and drowned himself in the Sarthe. He was mourned only by his mother and Suzanne du Val-Noble. [Jealousies of a Country Town.] Nevertheless, eight years after it was said of him: "The Athanase Gransons must die, withered up, like the grains which fall on barren rock." [The Government Clerks.]

Granville (Comte de) had a defective civil status, the orthography of the name varying frequently through the insertion of the letter "d" between the "n" and "v." In 1805 at an advanced age he lived at Bayeux, where he was probably born. His father was a president of the Norman Parliament. At Bayeux the Comte married his son to the wealthy Angélique Bontems. [A Second Home.]

Granville (Vicomte de), son of Comte de Granville, and comte upon his father's death; born about 1779; a magistrate through family tradition. Under the guidance of Cambacérès he passed through all the administrative and judicial grades. He studied with Maitre Bordin, defended Michu in the trial resulting from the "Gondreville Mystery," and learned officially and officiously of one of its results a short time after his marriage with a young girl of Bayeux, a rich heiress and the acquirer of extensive public lands. Paris was generally the theatre for the brilliant career of Maître Granville who, during the Empire, left the Augustin quai where he had lived to take up his abode with his wife on the ground-floor of a mansion in the Marais, between rue Vielle-du-Temple and rue Neuve-Saint-François. He became successively advocate-general at the court of the Seine, and president of one of its chambers. At this time a domestic drama was being enacted in his life. Hampered in his open and broad-minded nature by the bigotry of Mme. de Granville, he sought domestic happiness outside his home, though he already had a family of four children. He had met Caroline Crochard on rue du Tourniquet-Saint-Jean. He installed her on rue Taitbout and found in this relation, though it was of brief duration, the happiness vainly sought in his proper home. Granville screened this fleeting joy under the name of Roger. A daughter Eugénie, and a son Charles, were born of this adulterous union which was ended by the desertion of Mlle. Crochard and the misconduct of Charles. Until the death of Mme. Crochard, the mother of Caroline, Granville was able to keep up appearances before his wife. Thus it happened that he accompanied her to the country, Seine-et-Oise, when he assisted M. d'Albon and M. de Sucy. The remainder of Granville's life, after his wife and his mistress left him, was passed in comparative solitude in the society of intimate friends like Octave de Bauvan and Sérizy. Hard work and honors partially consoled him. His request as attorney-general caused the reinstatement of César Birotteau, one of the tenants at No. 397 rue Saint-Honoré. He and his wife had been invited to the famous ball given by Birotteau more than three years previously. As attorney-general of the Court of Cassation, Granville secretly protected Rubempré during the poet's famous trial, thus drawing upon himself the powerful affection of Jacques Collin, counterbalanced by the enmity of Amélie Camusot. The Revolution of July upheld Granville's high rank. He was peer of France under the new régime, owning and occupying a small mansion on rue Saint-Lazare, or traveling in Italy. At this time he was one of Dr. Bianchon's patients. [The Gondreville Mystery. A Second Home. Farewell. César Birotteau. Scenes from a Courtesan's Life. A Daughter of Eve. Cousin Pons.]

Granville (Comtesse Angélique de), wife of preceding, and daughter of Bontems, a farmer and sort of Jacobin whom the Revolution enriched through the purchase of evacuated property at low prices. She was born at Bayeux in 1787, and received from her mother a very bigoted education.

At the beginning of the Empire she married the son of one of the neighbors of the family, then Vicomte and later Comte de Granville; and, under the influence of Abbé Fontanon, she maintained at Paris the manners and customs of an extreme devotee. She thus evoked the infidelity of her husband who had begun by simply neglecting her. Of her four children she retained charge of the education of her two daughters. She broke off entirely from her husband when she discovered the existence of her rival, Mlle. de Bellefeuille—Caroline Crochard—and returned to Bayeux to end her days, remaining to the last the austere, stingy sanctified creature who had formerly been scandalized by the openness of the affair of Montriveau and Mme. de Langeais. She died in 1822. [A Second Home. The Thirteen. A Daughter of Eve.]

Granville (Vicomte de), elder son of the preceding. Was reared by his father. In 1828 he was deputy-attorney at Limoges, where he afterwards became advocate-general. He fell in love with Véronique Graslin, but incurred her secret disfavor by his proceedings against the assassin Tascheron. The vicomte had a career almost identical with that of his father. In 1833 he was made first president at Orleans, and in 1844 attorney-general. Later near Limoges he came suddenly upon a scene which moved him deeply: the public confession of Véronique Graslin. The vicomte had unknowingly been the executioner of the châtelaine of Montégnac. [A Second Home. A Daughter of Eve. The Country Parson.]

Granville (Baron Eugéne de), younger brother of the foregoing. King's attorney at Paris from May, 1830. Three years later he still held this office, when he informed his father of the arrest of a thief named Charles Crochard, who was the count's natural son. [Scenes from a Courtesan's Life. A Second Home.]

Granville (Marie-Angélique de). (*See* Vandenesse, Comtesse Félix de.)

Granville (Marie-Eugénie de). (*See* Tillet, Madame Ferdinand du.)

Graslin (Pierre), born in 1775. An Auvergnat, compatriot and friend of Sauviat, whose daughter Véronique he married in 1822. He began as bank-clerk with Grosstête & Perret, a first-class firm of the town. A man of business and a hard worker he became successor to his employers. His fortune, increased by lucky speculations with Brézac, enabled him to buy one of the finest places in the chief city of Haute-Vienne. But he was not able to win his wife's heart. His physical unattractiveness, added to by his carelessness and grinding avarice, were complicated by a domestic tyranny which soon showed itself. Thus it was that he was only the legal father of a son named Francis, but he was ignorant of this fact, for, in the capacity of juror in the Court of Assizes dealing with the fate of Tascheron, the real father of the child, he urged but in vain the acquittal of the prisoner. Two years after the boy's birth and the execution of the mother's lover, in April, 1831, Pierre Graslin died of weakness and grief. The July Revolution suddenly breaking forth had shaken his financial standing, which was regained only with an effort. It was at the time when he had bought Montégnac from the Navarreins. [The Country Parson.]

Graslin (Madame Pierre), wife of preceding; born Véronique Sauviat, at Limoges in May, 1802; beautiful in spite of traces of small-pox; had had the spoiled though simple childhood of an only daughter. When twenty she married Pierre Graslin. Soon after marriage her ingenuous nature, romantic and refined, suffered in secret from the harsh tyranny of the man whose name she bore. Véronique, however, held aloof from the gallants who frequented her salon, especially the Vicomte de Granville. She had become the secret mistress of J.-F. Tascheron, a porcelain worker. She was on the point of eloping with him when a crime committed by him was discovered. Mme. Graslin suffered the most poignant anguish, giving birth to the child of the condemned man at the very moment when the father was led to execution. She inflicted upon herself the bitterest flagellations. She could devote herself more freely to penance after her husband's death, which occurred two years later. She left Limoges for Montégnac, where she made herself truly famous by charitable works on a huge scale. The sudden return of the sister of her lover dealt her the final blow. Still she had energy enough to bring about the union of Denise Tascheron and Grégoire Gérard, gave her son into their keeping, left important bequests destined to keep alive her memory, and died during the summer of 1844 after confessing in public in the presence of Bianchon, Dutheil, Granville, Mme. Sauviat and Bonnet who were all seized with admiration and tenderness for her. [The Country Parson.]

Graslin (Francis), born at Limoges in August, 1829. Only child of Véronique Graslin, legal son of Pierre Graslin, but natural son of J.-F. Tascheron. He lost his legal father two years after his birth, and his mother thirteen years later. His tutor M. Ruffin, his maternal grandmother Mme. Sauviat, and above all the Grégoire Gérards watched over his boyhood at Montégnac. [The Country Parson.]

Grasset, bailiff and successor of Louchard. On the demand of Lisbeth Fischer and by Rivet's advice, in 1838, he arrested W. Steinbock in Paris and took him to Clichy prison. [Cousin Betty.]

Grassins (Des), ex-quartermaster of the Guard, seriously wounded at Austerlitz, pensioned and decorated. Time of Louis XVIII. he became the richest banker in Saumur, which he left for Paris where he located with the purpose of settling the unfortunate affairs of the suicide, Guillaume Grandet and where he was later made a deputy. Although the father of a family he conceived a passion for Florine, a pretty actress of the Théâtre du Madame,[1] to the havoc of his fortune. [Eugénie Grandet.]

Grassins (Madame des), born about 1780; wife of foregoing, giving him two children; spent most of her life at Saumur. Her husband's position and sundry physical charms which she was able to preserve till nearly her fortieth year enabled her to shine somewhat in society. With

---

[1] The name of this theatre was changed, in 1830, to Gymnase-Dramatique.

the Gruchots she often visited the Grandets, and, like the family of the President de Bonfons, she dreamed of mating Eugénie with her son Adolphe. The dissipated life of her husband at Paris and the combination of the Gruchots upset her plans. Nor was she able to do much for her daughter. However, deprived of much of her property and making the best of things, Mme. des Grassins continued unaided the management of the bank at Saumur. [Eugénie Grandet.]

Grassins (Adolphe des), born in 1797, son of M. and Mme. des Grassins; studied law at Paris where he lived in a lavish way. A caller at the Nucingens where he met Charles Grandet. Returned to Saumur in 1819 and vainly courted Eugénie Grandet. Finally he returned to Paris and rejoined his father whose wild life he imitated. [Eugénie Grandet.]

Grassou (Pierre), born at Fougéres, Brittany, in 1795. Son of a Vendean peasant and militant Royalist. Removing at an early age to Paris he began as clerk to a paint-dealer who was from Mayenne and a distant relative of the Orgemonts. A mistaken idea led him toward art. His Breton stubbornness led him successively to the studios of Servin, Schinner and Sommervieux. He afterwards studied, but fruitlessly, the works of Granet and Drolling; then he completed his art studies with Duval-Lecamus. Grassou profited nothing by his work with these masters, nor did his acquaintance with Lora or Joseph Bridau assist him. Though he could understand and admire he lacked the creative faculty and the skill in execution. For this reason Grassou, usually called Fougéres by his comrades, obtained their warm support and succeeded in getting admission, into the Salon of 1829, for his "Toilet of a Condemned Chouan," a very mediocre painting palpably along the lines of Gerard Dow. The work obtained for him from Charles X. the cross of the Legion of Honor. At last his canvasses found purchasers. Elie Magus gave him an order for pictures after the Flemish school, which he sold to Vervelle as works of Dow or Téniers. At that time Grassou lived at No. 2 rue de Navarin. He became the son-in-law of Vervelle, in 1832, marrying Virginie Vervelle, the heiress of the family, who brought him a dowry of one hundred thousand francs, as well as country and city property. His determined mediocrity opened the doors of the Academy to him and made him an officer in the Legion of Honor in 1839, and major of a battalion in the National Guard after the riots of May 12. He was adored by the middle classes, becoming their accredited artist. Painted portraits of all the members of the Crevel and Thuillier families, and also of the director of the theatre who preceded Gaudissart. Left many frightful and ridiculous daubs, one of which found its way into Topinard's humble home. [Pierre Grassou. A Bachelor's Establishment. Cousin Betty. The Middle Classes. Cousin Pons.]

Grassou (Madame Pierre), born Virginie Vervelle; red-haired and homely; sole heiress of wealthy dealers in cork, on rue Boucherat. Wife of the preceding whom she married in Paris in 1832. There is a portrait of her painted in this same year before her marriage, which at first was a colorless study by Grassou, but was dexterously retouched by Joseph Bridau. [Pierre Grassou.]

Gravelot brothers, lumber-merchants of Paris, who purchased in 1823 the forests of Aigues, the Burgundy estate of General de Montcornet. [The Peasantry.]

Gravier, paymaster-general of the army during the first Empire, and interested at that time in large Spanish affairs with certain commanding officers. Upon the return of the Bourbons he purchased at twenty thousand francs of La Baudraye the office of tax-receiver for Sancerres, which office he still held about 1836. With the Abbé Duret and others he frequented the home of Mme. Dinah de la Baudraye. He was little, fat and common. His court made little way with the baroness, despite his talent and his worldly-wise ways of a bachelor. He sang ballads, told stories, and displayed pseudo-rare autographs. [The Muse of the Department.]

Gravier, of Grenoble; head of a family; father-in-law

of a notary; chief of division of the prefecture of Isére in 1829. Knew Genestas and recommended to him Dr. Benassis, the mayor of the village of which he himself was one of the benefactors, as the one to attend Adrien Genestas-Renard. [The Country Doctor.]

Grenier, known as Fleur-de-Genêt; deserter from the Sixty-ninth demi-brigade; chauffeur executed in 1809. [The Seamy Side of History.]

Grenouville, proprietor of a large and splendid notion store in Boulevard des Italiens, Paris, about 1840; a customer of the Bijous, embroiderers also in business at Paris. At this time an ardent admirer of Mlle. Olympe Bijou, former mistress of Baron Hulot and Idamore Chardin. He married her and gave an income to her parents. [Cousin Betty.]

Grenouville (Madame), wife of the preceding; born Olympe Bijou, about 1824. In the middle of the reign of Louis Philippe she lived in Paris near La Courtille, in rue Saint-Maur-du-Temple. Was a pretty but poor embroiderer surrounded by a numerous and poverty-stricken family when Josépha Mirah obtained for her old Baron Hulot and a shop. Having abandoned Hulot for Idamore Chardin, who left her, Olympe married Grenouville and became a well-known tradeswoman. [Cousin Betty.]

Grenville (Arthur-Ormond, Lord), wealthy Englishman; was being treated at Montpellier for lung trouble when the rupture of the treaty of peace of Amiens confined him to Tours. About 1814 he fell in love with the Marquise Victor d'Aiglemont, whom he afterwards met elsewhere. Posing as a physician he attended her in an illness and succeeded in curing her. He visited her also in Paris, finally dying to save her honor, after suffering his fingers to be crushed in a door—1823. [A Woman of Thirty.]

Grévin of Arcis, Aube, began life in the same way as his compatriot and intimate friend, Malin de Gondreville. In 1787, he was second clerk to Maitre Bordin, attorney of the Châtelet, Paris. Returned to Champagne at the outbreak of the Revolution. There he received the successive protection of Danton, Bonaparte and Gondreville. By virtue of them he became an oracle to the Liberals, was enabled to marry Mlle. Varlet, the only daughter of the best physician of the city, to purchase a notary's practice, and to become wealthy. A level-headed man, Grévin often advised Gondreville, and he directed the mysterious and fictitious abduction —1803 and the years following. Of his union with Mlle. Varlet, who died rather young, one daughter was born, Séverine, who became Mme. Philéas Beauvisage. In his old age he devoted a great deal of attention to his children and their brilliant future, especially during the election of May, 1839. [A Start in Life. The Gondreville Mystery. The Member for Arcis.]

Grévin (Madame), wife of foregoing; born Varlet; daughter of the best doctor of Arcis-sur-Aube; sister of another Varlet, a doctor in the same town; mother of Mme. Séverine Philéas Beauvisage. With Mme. Marion she was more or less implicated in the Gondreville mystery. She died rather young. [The Gondreville Mystery.]

Grévin, corsair, who served under Admiral de Simeuse in the Indies. In 1816, paralyzed and deaf, he lived with his granddaughter, Mme. Lardot, a laundress of Alençon, who employed Césarine and Suzanne and was patronized by the Chevalier de Valois. [Jealousies of a Country Town.]

Gribeaucourt (Mademoiselle de), old maid of Saumur and friend of the Cruchots during the Restoration. [Eugénie Grandet.]

Griffith (Miss), born in 1787; Scotch woman, daughter of a minister in straitened circumstances; under the Restoration she was governess of Louise de Chaulieu, whose love she won by reason of her kindliness and penetration. [Letters of Two Brides.]

Grignault (Sophie). (*See* Nathan, Mme. Raoul.)

Grimbert, held, in 1819, at Ruffec, Charente, the office of the Royal Couriers. At that time he received from Mlles. Laure and Agathe de Rastignac, a considerable sum of money addressed to their brother Eugéne, at the Pension Vauquer, Páris. [Father Goriot.]

Grimont, born about 1786; a priest of some capability; curé of Guérande, Brittany. In 1836, a constant visitor at the Guénics, he exerted a tardily acquired influence over Félicité des Touches, whose disappointments in love he fathomed and whom he determined to turn towards a religious life. Her conversion gave Grimont the vicar-generalship of the diocese of Nantes. [Béatrix.]

Grimpel, physician at Paris in the Panthéon quarter, time of Louis XVIII. Among his patients was Mme. Vauquer, who sent for him to attend Vautrin when the latter was overcome by a narcotic treacherously administered by Mlle. Michonneau. [Father Goriot.]

Grindot, French architect in the first half of the nineteenth century; won the Roman prize in 1814. His talent, which met the approval of the Academy, was heartily recognized by the masses of Paris. About the end of 1818 César Birotteau gave him carte-blanche in the remodeling of his apartments on rue Saint-Honoré, and invited him to his ball. Matifat, between the years 1821 and 1822, commissioned him to ornament the suite of Mme. Raoul Nathan on rue de Bondy. The Comte de Sérizy employed him likewise in 1822 in the restoration of his château of Presles near Beaumont-sur-Oise. About 1829 Grindot embellished a little house on rue Saint-Georges where successively dwelt Suzanne Gaillard and Esther van Gobseck. Time of Louis Philippe, Arthur de Rochefide, and M. and Mme. Fabien du Roncerct gave him contracts. His decline and that of the monarchy coincided. He was no longer in vogue during the July government. On motion of Chaffaroux he received twenty-five thousand francs for the decoration of four rooms of Thuillier's. Lastly Crevel, an imitator and grinder, utilized Grindot on rue des Saussaies, rue du Dauphin and rue Barbet-de-Jouy for his official and secret habitations. [César Birotteau. Lost Illusions. A Distinguished Provincial at Paris. A Start in Life. Scenes from a Courtesan's Life. Béatrix. The Middle Classes. Cousin Betty.]

Groison, non-commissioned officer of cavalry in the Imperial Guard; later, during the Restoration, estate-keeper of Blangy, where he succeeded Vaudoyer at a salary of three hundred francs. Montcornet, mayor of that commune, arranged a marriage between the old soldier and the orphan daughter of one of his farmers who brought him three acres of vineyards. [The Peasantry.]

Gros (Antoine-Jean), celebrated painter born in Paris in 1771, drowned himself June, 1835. Was the teacher of Joseph Bridau and, despite his parsimonious habits, supplied materials—about 1818—to the future painter of "The Venetian Senator and the Courtesan" enabling him to obtain five thousand francs from a double government position. [A Bachelor's Establishment.]

Groslier, police commissioner of Arcis-sur-Aube at the beginning of the electoral campaign of 1839. [The Member for Arcis.]

Grosmort, small boy of Alençon in 1816. Left the town in that year and went to Prébaudet, an estate of Mme. du Bousquier, to tell her of Troisville's arrival. [Jealousies of a Country Town.]

Gross-Narp (Comte de), son-in-law, no doubt fictitious, of a very great lady, invented and represented by Jacqueline Collin to serve the menaced interests of Jacques Collin in Paris about the end of the Restoration. [Scenes from a Courtesan's Life.]

Grosstête (F.), director, with Perret, of a Limoges banking-house, during the Empire and Restoration. His clerk and successor was Pierre Graslin. Retired from business, a married man, wealthy, devoted to horticulture, he spent much of his time in the fields in the outskirts of Limoges. Endowed with a superior intellect, he seemed to understand Véronique Graslin, whose society he sought and whose secrets he tried to fathom. He introduced his godson, Grégoire Gérard, to her. [The Country Parson.]

Grosstête (Madame F.), wife of preceding; a person of some importance in Limoges, time of the Restoration. [The Country Parson.]

Grosstête, younger brother of F. Grosstête. Receiver-general at Bourges during the Restoration. He had a large fortune which enabled his daughter Anna to wed a Fontaine about 1823. [The Country Parson. The Muse of the Department.]

Grozier (Abbé) was chosen, in the early part of the Restoration, to arbitrate the dispute of two proof-readers—one of whom was Saint-Simon—over Chinese paper. He proved that the Chinese make their paper from bamboo. [Lost Illusions.] He was librarian of the Arsenal at Paris. Was tutor of the Marquis d'Espard. Was learned in the history and manners of China. Taught this knowledge to his pupil. [The Commission in Lunacy.][1]

Gruget (Madame Etienne), born in the latter part of the eighteenth century. About 1820, lace-maker at No. 12 rue des Enfants-Rouges, Paris, where she concealed and cared for Gratien Bourignard, the lover of her daughter Ida, who drowned herself. Bourignard was the father of Mme. Jules Desmarets. [The Thirteen.] Becoming a nurse about the end of 1824, Mme. Gruget attended the division-chief, La Billardière, in his final sickness. [The Government Clerks.] In 1828 she followed the same profession for ten sous a day, including board. At that time she attended the last illness of Comtesse Flore Philippe de Brambourg, on rue Chaussée-d'Antin, before the invalid was removed to the Dubois hospital. [A Bachelor's Establishment.]

Gruget (Ida), daughter of the preceding. About 1820 was a corset-fitter at No. 14 rue de la Corderie-du-Temple, Paris; employed by Mme. Meynardie. She was also the mistress of Gatien Bourignard. Passionately jealous, she rashly made a scene in the home of Jules Desmarets, her lover's son-in-law. Then she drowned herself, in a fit of despair, and was buried in a little cemetery of a village of Seine-et-Oise. [The Thirteen.]

Gua Saint-Cyr (Madame du), in spite of the improbability

[1] Abbé Grosier, or Crosier (Jean Baptiste-Gabriel-Alexandre), born March 17, 1743, at Saint-Omer, died December 8, 1823, at Paris; collaborator of the "Literary Year" with Fréron and Geoffroy, and author of a "General History of China"—Paris 1777-1784, 12 vols.

aroused on account of her age, passed for a time, in 1799, as the mother of Alphonse de Montauran. She had been married and was then a widow; Gua was not her true name. She was the last mistress of Charette and, being still young, took his place with the youthful Alphonse de Montauran. She displayed a savage jealousy for Mlle. de Verneuil. One of the first Vendean sallies of 1799, planned by Mme. du Gua, was unsuccessful and absurd. The old "mare of Charette" caused the coach between Mayenne and Fougéres to be waylaid; but the money stolen was that which was being sent her by her mother. [The Chouans.]

Gua Saint-Cyr (Du), name assumed in Brittany, in 1799, by Alphonse de Montauran, the Chouan leader. [The Chouans.]

Gua Saint-Cyr (Monsieur and Madame du), son and mother; rightful bearers of the name were murdered, with the courier, in November by the Chouans. [The Chouans.]

Gudin (Abbé), born about 1759; was one of the Chouan leaders in 1799. He was a formidable fellow, one of the Jesuits stubborn enough, perhaps devoted enough, to oppose upon French soil the proscriptive edict of 1793. This firebrand of Western conflict fell, slain by the Blues, almost under the eyes of his patriot nephew, the sub-lieutenant, Gudin. [The Chouans.]

Gudin, nephew of the preceding, and nevertheless a patriot conscript from Fougéres, Brittany, during the campaign of 1799; successively corporal and sub-lieutenant. The former grade was obtained through Hulot. Was the superior of Beau-Pied. Gudin was killed near Fougéres by Marie de Verneuil, who had assumed the attire of her husband, Alphonse de Montauran. [The Chouans.]

Guénée (Madame). (*See* Galardon, Madame.) ·

Guénic (Gaudebert-Calyste-Charles, Baron du), born in 1763. Head of a Breton house of very ancient founding, he justified throughout his long life the device upon his coat-of-arms, which read: "Fac!" Without hope of reward he constantly defended, in Vendée and Brittany, his God and his king by service as private soldier and captain, with Charette, Cathelineau, La Rochejacquelein, Eibée, Bonchamp and the Prince of Loudon. Was one of the commanders of the campaign of 1799 when he bore the name of "L'Intimé," and was, with Banvan, a witness to the marriage *in extremis* of Alphonse de Montauran and Marie de Verneuil. Three years later he went to Ireland, where he married Miss Fanny O'Brien, of a noble family of that country. Events of 1814 permitted his return to Guérande, Loire-Inférieure, where his house, though impoverished, wielded great influence. In recognition of his unfaltering devotion to the Royalist cause, M. du Guénic received only the Cross of Saint-Louis. Incapable of protesting, he intrepidly defended his town against the battalions of General Travot, in the following year. The final Chouan insurrection, that of 1832, called him to arms once again. Accompanied by Calyste, his only son, and a servant, Gasselin, he returned to Guérande, lived there for some years, despite his numerous wounds, and died suddenly, at the age of seventy-four, in 1837. [The Chouans. Béatrix.]

Guénic (Baronne du), wife of the preceding; native of Ireland; born Fanny O'Brien, about 1793, of aristocratic lineage. Poor and surrounded by wealthy relatives, beautiful and distinguished, she married, in 1813, Baron du Guénie, following him the succeeding year to Guérande and devoting her life and youth to him. She bore one son, Calyste, to whom she was more like an elder sister. She watched closely the two mistresses of the young man, and finally understood Félicité des Touches; but she always was in a tremor on account of Béatrix de Rochefide, even after the marriage of Calyste, which took place in the year of the baron's death. [Béatrix.]

Guénic (Gaudebert-Calyste-Louis du), probably born in 1815, at Guérande, Loire-Inférieure; only son of the foregoing, by whom he was adored, and to whose dual influence he was subject. He was the physical and moral replica of his mother. His father wished to make him a gentleman of the old school. In 1832 he fought for the heir of the

Bourbons. He had other aspirations which he was able to satisfy at the home of an illustrious châtelaine of the vicinity, Mlle. Félicité des Touches. The chevalier was much enamored of the celebrated authoress, who had great influence over him, did not accept him and turned him over to Mme. de Rochefide. Béatrix played with the heir of the house of Guénie the same ill-starred comedy carried through by Antoinette de Langeais with regard to Montriveau. Calyste married Mlle. Sabine de Grandlieu, and took the title of baron after his father's death. He lived in Paris on Faubourg Saint-Germain, and between 1838 and 1840 was acquainted with Georges de Maufrigneuse, Savinien de Portenduère, the Rhétorés, the Lenoncourt-Chaulieus and Mme. de Rochefide—whose lover he finally became. The intervention of the Duchesse de Grandlieu put an end to this love affair. [Béatrix.]

Guénic (Madame Calyste du), born Sabine de Grandlieu; wife of the preceding, whom she married about 1837. Nearly three years later she was in danger of dying upon hearing, at her confinement, that she had a fortunate rival in the person of Béatrix de Rochefide. [Béatrix.]

Guénic (Zéphirine du), born in 1756 at Guérande; lived almost all her life with her younger brother, the Baron du Guénie, whose ideas, principles and opinions she shared. She dreamed of a rehabilitation of her impoverished house, and pushed her economy to the point of refusing to undergo an operation for cataract. For a long time she wished that Mlle. Charlotte de Kergarouët might become her niece by marriage. [Béatrix.]

Guépin, of Provins, located in Paris. He had at the "Trois Quenouilles" one of the largest draper's shops on rue Saint-Denis. His head-clerk was his compatriot, Jérôme-Denis Rogron. In 1815, he turned over his business to his grandson and returned to Provins, where his family formed a clan. Later Rogrou retired also and rejoined him there. [Pierrette.]

Guerbet, wealthy farmer in the country near Ville-aux-Fayes; married, in the last of the eighteenth or first of the nineteenth century, the only daughter of Mouchon junior, then postmaster of Conches, Burgundy. After the death of his father-in-law, about 1817, he succeeded to the office. [The Peasantry.]

Guerbet, brother of the foregoing, and related to the Gaubertins and Gendrins. Rich tax-collector of Soulanges, Burgundy. Stout, dumpy fellow with a butter face, wig, earrings, and immense collars; given to pomology; was the wit of the village and one of the lions of Mme. Soudry's salon. [The Peasantry.]

Guerbet, circuit judge of Ville-aux-Fayes, Burgundy, in 1823. Like his uncle, the postmaster, and his father, the tax-collector, he was entirely devoted to Gaubertin. [The Peasantry.]

Guillaume, in the course of, or at the end of the eighteenth century, began as clerk to Chevrel, draper, on rue Saint-Denis, Paris, "at the Sign of the Cat and Racket"; afterwards became his son-in-law, succeeded him, became wealthy and retired, during the first Empire, after marrying off his two daughters, Virginie and Augustine, in the same day. He became member of the Consultation Committee for the uniforming of the troops, changed his home, living in a house of his own on rue du Colombier, was intimate with the Ragons and the Birotteaus, being invited with his wife to the ball given by the latter. [At the Sign of the Cat and Racket. César Birotteau.]

Guillaume (Madame), wife of the preceding; born Chevrel; cousin of Mme. Roguin; a stiff-necked, middle-class woman, who was scandalized by the marriage of her second daughter, Augustine, with Théodore de Sommervieux. [At the Sign of the Cat and Racket.]

Guillaume, servant of Marquis d'Aiglemont in 1823. [A Woman of Thirty.]

Guinard (Abbé), priest of Sancerre in 1836. [The Muse of the Department.]

Gyas (Marquise de), lived at Bordeaux during the Restoration; gave much thought to marrying off her daughter, and, being intimate with Mme. Evangélista, felt hurt when Natalie Evangélista married Paul de Mancrville in 1822. However, the Marquis de Gyas was one of the witnesses at the wedding. [A Marriage Settlement.]

H

Habert (Abbé), vicar at Provins under the Restoration; a stern, ambitious prelate, a source of annoyance to Vinet; dreamed of marrying his sister Céleste to Jérôme-Denis Rogron. [Pierrette.]

Habert (Céleste), sister of the preceding; born about 1797; managed a girls' boarding-school at Provins, in the closing years of Charles X.'s reign. Visited at the Rogrons. Gouraud and Vinet shunned her. [Pierrette.]

Hadot (Madame), who lived at La Charité, Nièvre, in 1836, was mistaken for Mme. Barthélemy-Hadot, the French novelist, whose name was mentioned at Mme. de la Baudraye's, near Sancerre. [The Muse of the Department.]

Halga (Chevalier du), naval officer greatly esteemed by Suffren and Portenduère; captain of Kergarouët's flagship; lover of that admiral's wife, whom he survived. He served in the Indian and Russian waters, refused to take up arms against France, and returned with a petty pension after the emigration. Knew Richelieu intimately. Remained in Paris the inseparable friend and adherent of Kergarouët. Called near the Madeleine upon the Mesdames de Rouville, other protégées of his patron. The death of Louis XVIII. took Halga back to Guérande, his native town, where he became mayor and was still living in 1836. He was well acquainted with the Guénics and made himself ridiculous by his fancied ailments as well as by his solicitude for his dog, Thisbé. [The Purse. Béatrix.]

Halpersohn (Moses), a refugee Polish Jew, excellent physician, communist, very eccentric, avaricious, friend of Lelewel the insurrectionist. Time of Louis Philippe at Paris he attended Vanda de Mergi, given up by several doctors, and alone diagnosed her complicated disease. [The Seamy Side of History.]

Halpertius, assumed name of Jacques Collin.

Hannequin (Léopold), Parisian notary. The "Revue de l'Est," a paper published at Besançon, time of Louis Philippe, gave, in an autobiographical novel of its editor-in-chief, Albert Savarus, entitled "L'Ambitieux par Amour," the story of the boyhood of Léopold Hannequin, the author's inseparable friend. Savarus told of their joint travels, and of the quiet preparation made by his friend for a notary-ship during the time known as the Restoration. During the monarchy of the barricades Hannequin remained the stead-fast friend of Savarus, being one of the first to find his hiding-place. At that time the notary had an office in Paris. He married there to advantage, became head of a family, and deputy-mayor of a precinct, and obtained the decoration for a wound received at the cloister of Saint-Merri. He was welcomed and made use of in Faubourg Saint-Germain, the Saint-Georges quarter and the Marais. At the Grand-lieus' request he drew up the marriage settlement of their daughter Sabine with Calyste du Guénie—1837. Four years later he consulted with old Marshal Hulot, on rue du Montparnasse, regarding his will in behalf of Mlle. Fischer and Mme. Steinbock. About 1845, at the request of Héloïse Brisetout, he drew up Sylvain Pons' will. [Albert Savarus. Béatrix. Cousin Betty. Cousin Pons.]

Happe & Duncker, celebrated bankers of Amsterdam, amateur art-collectors, and snobbish parvenus, bought, in 1813, the fine gallery of Balthazar Claés, paying one hundred thousand ducats for it. [The Quest of the Absolute.]

Haudry, doctor at Paris during the first part of the nineteenth century. An old man and an upholder of old treatments; having a practice mainly among the middle class. Attended César Birotteau, Jules Desmarets, Mme. Descoings and Vanda de Mergi. His name was still cited at the end of Louis Philippe's reign. [César Birrotteau. The Thirteen.

A Bachelor's Establishment. The Seamy Side of History. Cousin Pons.]

Haugoult (Pére), oratorian and regent of the Vedôme college, about 1811. Stern and narrow-minded, he did not comprehend the budding genius of one of his pupils, Louis Lambert, but destroyed the "Treatise on the Will," written by the lad. [Louis Lambert.]

Hauteserre (D'), born in 1751; grandfather of Marquis de Cinq-Cygne; guardian of Laurence de Cinq-Cygne; father of Robert and Adrien d'Hauteserre. A gentleman of caution he would willingly have parleyed with the Revolution; he made this evident after 1803 in the Arcis precinct where he resided, and especially during the succeeding years marked by an affair which jeopardized the lives of some of his family. Gondreville, Peyrade, Corentin, Fouché and Napoleon were bugaboos to d'Hauteserre. He outlived his sons. [The Gondreville Mystery. The Member for Arcis.]

Hauteserre (Madame d'), wife of the preceding; born in 1763; mother of Robert and Adrien; showed throughout her wearied, saddened frame the marks of the old régime. Following Goujet's advice she countenanced the deeds of Mlle. de Cinq-Cygne, the bold, dashing counter-revolutionist of Arcis during 1803 and succeeding years. Mme. Hauteserre survived her sons. [The Gondreville Mystery.]

Hauteserre (Robert d'), elder son of the foregoing. Brusque, recalling the men of mediæval times, despite his feeble constitution. A man of honor, he followed the fortunes of his brother Adrien and his kinsmen the Simeuses. Like them, he emigrated during the first Revolution, and returned to the neighborhood of Arcis about 1803. Like them again he became enamored of Mlle. de Cinq-Cygne. Wrongly accused of having abducted the senator, Malin de Gondreville, and sentenced to ten years' hard labor, he obtained the Emperor's pardon and was made sub-lieutenant in the cavalry. He died as colonel at the storming of Moskowa, September 7, 1812. [The Gondreville Mystery.]

Hauteserre (Adrien d'), second son of M. and Mme. d'Hauteserre; was of different stamp from his older brother Robert, yet had many things in common with the latter's career. He also was influenced by honor. He also emigrated and, on his return, fell under the same sentence. He also obtained Napoleon's pardon and a commission in the army, taking Robert's place in the attack on Moskowa; and in recognition of his severe wounds became brigadier-general after the battle of Dresden, August 26, 27, 1813. The doors of the Château de Cinq-Cygne were opened to admit the mutilated soldier, who married its mistress, Laurence, though his affection was not requited. This marriage made Adrien Marquis de Cinq-Cygne. During the Restoration he was made a peer, promoted to lieutenant-general, and obtained the Cross of Saint-Louis. He died in 1829, lamented by his wife, his parents and his children. [The Gondreville Mystery.]

Hauteserre (Abbé d'), brother of M. d'Hauteserre; somewhat like his young kinsman in disposition; made some ado over his noble birth; thus it happened that he was killed, shot in the attack on the Hôtel de Cinq-Cygne by the people of Troyes, in 1792. [The Gondreville Mystery.]

Hautoy (Francis du), gentleman of Angouléme; was consul at Valence. Lived in the chief city of Charente between 1821 and 1824; frequented the Bargetons; was on the most intimate terms with the Senonches, and was said to be the father of Françoise de la Haye, daughter of Mme. de Senonches. Hautoy seemed slightly superior to his associates. [Lost Illusions.]

Henri, police-agent at Paris in 1840, given special assignments by Corentin, and placed as servant successively at the Thuilliers, and with Népomucéne Picot, with the duty of watching Théodose de la Peyrade. [The Middle Classes.]

Herbelot, notary of Arcis-sur-Aube during the electoral period of spring, 1839; visited the Beauvisages, Marions and Mollots. [The Member for Arcis.]

Herbelot (Malvina), born in 1809; sister of the preceding, whose curiosity she shared, when the Arcis elections were in progress. She also called on the Beauvisages and the Mollots, and, despite her thirty years, sought the society of the young women of these houses. [The Member for Arcis.]

Herbomez, of Mayenne, nick-named General Hardi; chauffeur implicated in the Royalist uprising in which Henriette Bryond took part, during the first Empire. Like Mme. de la Chanterie's daughter, Herbomez paid with his head his share in the rebellion. His execution took place in 1809. [The Seamy Side of History.]

Herbomez (D'), brother of the foregoing, but more fortunate, he ended by becoming a count and receiver-general. [The Seamy Side of History.]

Hérédia (Marie). (*See* Soria, Duchesse de.)

Hermann, a Nuremberg merchant who commanded a free company enlisted against the French, in October, 1799. Was arrested and thrown into a prison of Andernach, where he had for fellow-prisoner, Prosper Magnan, a young assistant surgeon, native of Beauvais, Oise. Hermann thus learned the terrible secret of an unjust detention followed by an execution equally unjust. Many years after, in Paris, he told the story of the martyrdom of Magnan in the presence of F. Taillefer, the unpunished author of the dual crime which had caused the imprisonment and death of an innocent man. [The Red Inn.]

Héron, notary of Issoudun in the early part of the nineteenth century, who was attorney for the Rougets, father and son. [A Bachelor's Establishment.]

Hérouville (Maréchal d'), whose ancestors' names were inscribed in the pages of French history, during the sixteenth and seventeenth centuries, replete with glory and dramatic mystery; was Duc de Nivron. He was the last governor of Normandy, returned from exile with Louis XVIII. in 1814, and died at an advanced age in 1819. [The Hated Son. Modeste Mignon.]

Hérouville (Duc d'), son of the preceding; born in 1796, at Vienna, Austria, during the emigration, "fruit of the matrimonial autumn of the last governor of Normandy"; descendant of a Comte d'Hérouville, a Norman free-lance who lived under Henri IV. and Louis XIII. He was Marquis de Saint-Sever, Duc de Nivron, Comte de Bayeux, Vicomte d'Essigny, grand equerry and peer of France, chevalier of the Order of the Spur and of the Golden Fleece, and grandee of Spain. A more modest origin, however, was ascribed to him by some. The founder of his house was supposed to have been an usher at the court of Robert of Normandy. But the coat-of-arms bore the device "Herns Villa"—House of the Chief. At any rate, the physical unattractiveness and comparative lack of means of D'Hérouville, who was a kind of dwarf, contrasted with his aristocratic lineage. However, his income allowed him to keep a house on rue Saint-Thomas du Louvre, Paris, and to keep on good terms with the Chaulieus. He maintained Fanny Beaupré, who apparently cost him dear; for, about 1829, he sought the hand of the Mignon heiress. During the reign of Louis Philippe, D'Hérouville, then a social leader, had acquaintance with the Hulots, was known as a celebrated art amateur, and resided on rue de Varenne, in Faubourg Saint-Germain. Later he took Josépha Mirah from Hulot, and installed her in fine style on rue Saint-Maur-du-Temple with Olympe Bijou. [The Hated Son. Jealousies of a Country Town. Modeste Mignon   Cousin Betty.]

Hérouville (Mademoiselle d'), aunt of the preceding; dreamed of a rich marriage for that stunted creature, who seemed a sort of reproduction of an evil Hérouville of past ages. She desired Modeste Mignon for him; but her aristocratic pride revolted at the thought of Mlle. Monegod or Augusta de Nucingen. [Modeste Mignon.]

Hérouville (Héléne d'), niece of the preceding; sister of Duc d'Hérouville; accompanied her relatives to Havre in 1829; afterwards knew the Mignons. [Modeste Mignon.]

Herrera (Carlos), unacknowledged son of the Duc d'Ossuna; canon of the cathedral of Toledo, charged with a political mission to France by Ferdinand VII. He was drawn into an ambush by Jacques Collin, who killed him, stripped him and then assumed his name until about 1830. [Lost Illusions. Scenes from a Courtesan's Life.]

Hiclar, Parisian musician, in 1845, who received from Dubourdieu, a symbolical painter, author of a figure of Harmony, an order to compose a symphony suitable of being played before the picture. [The Unconscious Humorists.]

Hiley, alias the Laborer, a chauffeur and the most cunning of minor participants in the Royalist uprising of Orne. Was executed in 1809. [The Seamy Side of History.]

Hippolyte, young officer, aide-de-camp to General Eblé in the Russian campaign; friend of Major Philippe de Sucy. Killed in an attack on the Russians near Studzianka, November 28, 1812. [Farewell.]

Hochon, born at Issoudun about 1738; was tax-receiver at Selles, Berry. Married Maximilienne, the sister of Sub-Delegate Lousteau. Had three children, one of whom became Mme. Borniche. Hochon's marriage and the change of the political horizon brought him back to his native town, where he and his family were long known as the Five Hochons. Mlle. Hochon's marriage and the death of her brothers made the jest still tenable; for M. Hochon, despite a proverbial avarice, adopted their posterity—François Hochon, Baruch and Adolphine Borniche. Hochon lived till an advanced age. He was still living at the end of the Restoration, and gave shrewd advice to the Bridaus regarding the Rouget legacy. [A Bachelor's Establishment.]

Hochon (Madame), wife of the preceding, born Maximilienne Lousteau about 1750; sister of the sub-delegate; also godmother of Mme. Bridau, *née* Rouget. During her whole life she displayed a sweet and resigned sympathy. The neglected and timorous mother of a family, she bore the matrimonial yoke of a second Félix Grandet. [A Bachelor's Establishment.]

Hochon, elder son of the foregoing; survived his brother and sister; married at an early age to a wealthy woman by whom he had one son; died a year before her, in 1813, slain at the battle of Hanau. [A Bachelor's Establishment.]

Hochon (François), son of the preceding, born in 1798. Left an orphan at sixteen he was adopted by his paternal grandparents and lived in Issoudun with his cousins, the Borniche children. He affiliated secretly with Maxence Gilet, being one of the "Knights of Idlesse," till his conduct was discovered. His stern grandfather sent the young man to Poitiers where he studied law and received a yearly allowance of six hundred francs. [A Bachelor's Establishment.]

Honorine. (*See* Banvan, Comtesse Octave de.)

Hopwood (Lady Julia), English; made a journey to Spain between 1818 and 1819, and had there for a time a chambermaid known as Caroline, who was none other than Antoinette de Langeais, who had fled from Paris after Montriveau jilted her. [The Thirteen.]

Horeau (Jacques), alias the Stuart, had been lieutenant in the Sixty-ninth demi-brigade. Became one of the associates of Tinténiac, known through his participation in the Quiberon expedition. Turned chauffeur and compromised himself in the Orne Royalist uprising. Was executed in 1809. [The Seamy Side of History.]

Hortense was, under Louis Philippe, one of the numerous mistresses of Lord Dudley. She lived on rue Tronchet when Cérizet employed Antonia Chocardelle to hoodwink Maxime de Trailles. [A Man of Business. The Member for Arcis.]

Hostal (Maurice de l'), born in 1802; living physical portrait of Byron; nephew and like an adopted son of Abbé Loraux. He became, at Marais, in rue Payenne, the secretary and afterwards the confidant of Octave de Banvan. Was acquainted with Honorine de Banvan on rue Saint-Maur-Popincourt and all but fell in love with her. Turned diplomat, left France, married the Italian, Onorina Pedrotti, and became head of a family. While consul to Genoa, about 1836, he again met Octave de Bàuvan, then a widower and near his end, who entrusted his son to him. M. de l'Hostal once entertained Claude Vignon, Léon de Lora and Félicité des Touches, to whom he related the marital troubles of the Bauvans. [Honorine.]

Hostal (Madame Maurice de l'), wife of the preceding, born Onorina Pedrotti. A beautiful and unusually rich Genoese; slightly jealous of the consul; perhaps overheard the story of the Bauvans. [Honorine.]

Hulot, born in 1766, served under the first Republic and Empire. Took an active part in the wars and tragedies of the time. Commanded the Seventy-second demi-brigade, called the Mayençaise, during the Chouan uprising of 1799. Fought against Montauran. His career as private and officer had been so filled that his thirty-three years seemed an age. He went out a great deal. Rubbed elbows with Montcornet; called on Mme. de la Baudraye. He remained a democrat during the Empire; nevertheless Bonaparte recognized him. Hulot was made colonel of the grenadiers of the Guard, Comte de Forzheim and marshal. Retired to his splendid home on rue du Montparnasse, where he passed his declining years simply, being deaf, remaining a friend of Cottin de Wissembourg, and often surrounded by the family of a brother whose misconduct hastened his end in 1841. Hulot was given a superb funeral. [The Chouans. The Muse of the Department. Cousin Betty.]

Hulot d'Ervy (Baron Hector), born about 1775; brother of the preceding; took the name of Hulot d'Ervy early in life in order to make a distinction between himself and his brother to whom he owed the brilliant beginning of a civil and military career. Hulot d'Ervy became ordonnance commissary during the Republic. The Empire made him a baron. During one of these periods he married Adeline Fischer, by whom he had two children. The succeeding governments, at least that of July, also favored Hector Hulot, and he became in turn intendant-general, director of the War Department, councilor of state, and grand officer of the Legion of Honor. His private misbehavior dated from these periods and gathered force while he lived at Paris. Each of his successive mistresses —Jenny Cadine, Josépha Mirah, Valérie Marneffe, Olympe Bijou, Elodie Chardin, Atala Judiei, Agathe Piquetard— precipitated his dishonor and ruin. He hid under various names, as Thoul, Thoree and Vyder, anagrams of Hulot, Hector and D'Ervy.. Neither the persecutions of the money-lender Samanon nor the influence of his family could reform him. After his wife's death he married, February 1, 1846, Agathe Piquetard, his kitchen-girl and the lowest of his servants. [Cousin Betty.]

Hulot d'Ervy (Baronne Hector), wife of the preceding; born Adeline Fischer, about 1790, in the village of Vosges; remarkable for her beauty; was married for mutual love, despite her inferior birth, and for some time lived caressed and adored by her husband and venerated by her brother-in-law. At the end of the Empire probably commenced her sorrows and the faithlessness of Hector, notwithstanding the two children born of their union, Victorin and Hortense. Had it not been for her maternal solicitude the baroness could have condoned the gradual degradation of her husband. The honor of the name and the future of her daughter gave her concern. No sacrifice was too great for her. She vainly offered herself to Célestin Crevel, whom she had formerly scorned, and underwent the parvenu's insults; she besought Josépha Mirah's aid, and rescued the baron from Atala Judici. The closing years of her life were not quite so miserable. She devoted herself to charitable offices, and lived on rue Louis-le-Grand with her married children and their reclaimed father. The intervention of Victorin, and the deaths of the Comte de Forzheim, of Lisbeth Fischer and of M. and Mme. Crevel, induced comfort and security that was often menaced. But the conduct of Hector with Agathe Piquetard broke the thread of Mme. Hulot d'Ervy's life; for some time she had had a nervous trouble. She died aged about fifty-six. [Cousin Betty.]

Hulot (Victorin), elder child of the foregoing. Married Mlle. Célestine Crevel and was father of a family. Became under Louis Philippe one of the leading attorneys of Paris. Was deputy, counsel of the War Department, consulting counsel of the police service and counsel for the civil list. His salary for the various offices came to eighteen thousand francs. He was seated at Palais-Bourbon when the election of Dorlange-Sallenauve was contested. His connection with the police enabled him to save his family from the clutches of Mme. Valérie Crevel. In 1834 he owned a house on rue Louis-le-Grand. Seven or eight years later he sheltered nearly all the Hulots and their near kindred, but he could not prevent the second marriage of his father. [The Member for Arcis. Cousin Betty.]

Hulot (Madame Victorin), wife of preceding, born Célestine Grevel; married as a result of a meeting between her father and her father-in-law, who were both libertines. She took part in the dissensions between the two families, replaced Lisbeth Fischer in the care of the house on rue Louis-le-Grand, and probably never saw the second Mme. Célestin Crevel, unless at the death-bed of the retired perfumer. [Cousin Betty.]

Hulot (Hortense). (*See* Steinbock, Comtesse Wenceslas.)

Hulot d'Ervy (Baronne Hector), *née* Agathe Piquetard of Isigny, where she became the second wife of Hector Hulot d'Ervy. Went to Paris as kitchen-maid for Hulot about December, 1845, and was married to her master, then a widower, on February 1, 1846. [Cousin Betty.]

Humann, celebrated Parisian tailor of 1836 and succeeding years. At the instance of the students Rabourdin and Juste he clothed the poverty-stricken Zephirin Marcas "as a politician." [Z. Marcas.]

Husson (Madame.) (*See* Mme. Clapart.)

Husson (Oscar), born about 1804, son of the preceding and of M. Husson—army-contractor; led a checkered career, explained by his origin and childhood. He scarcely knew his father, who made and soon lost a fortune. The previous fast life of his mother, who afterwards married again, gave rise to or upheld some more or less influential connections and made her, during the first Empire, the titular *femme de chambre* to Madame Mére—Letitia Bonaparte. Napoleon's fall marked the ruin of the Hussons. Oscar and his mother—now married to M. Clapart—lived in a modest apartment on rue de la Cerisaie, Paris. Oscar obtained a license and became clerk in Desroches' law office in Paris, being coached by Godeschal. During this time he became acquainted with two young men, his cousins the Marests. One of them had previously instigated an early escapade of Oscar's, and it was now followed by one much more serious, on rue de Vendôme at the house of Florentine Cabirolle, who was then maintained by Cardot, Oscar's wealthy uncle. Husson was forced to abandon law and enter military service. He was in the cavalry regiment of the Duc de Maufrigneuse and the Vicomte de Sérizy. The interest of the dauphiness and of Abbé Gaudron obtained for him promotion and a decoration. He became in turn aide-de-camp to La Fayette, captain, officer of the Legion of Honor and lieutenant-colonel. A noteworthy deed made him famous on Algerian territory during the affair of La Macta; Husson lost his left arm in the vain attempt to save Vicomte de Sérizy. Put on half-pay, he obtained the post of collector for Beaumont-sur-Oise. He then married—1838—Georgette Pierrotin and met again the accomplices or witnesses of his earlier escapades—one of the Marests, the Moreaus, etc. [A Start in Life.]

Husson (Madame Oscar), wife of the preceding; born Georgette Pierrotin; daughter of the proprietor of the stage-service of Oise. [A Start in Life.]

Hyde de Neuville (Jean-Guillaume, Baron)—1776-1857—belonged to the Martignac ministry of 1828; was, in 1797, one of the most active Bourbon agents. Kept civil war aflame in the West, and held a conference in 1799 with First Consul Bonaparte relative to the restoration of Louis XVIII. [The Chouans.]

I

Idamore, nick-name of Chardin junior while he was *claqueur* in a theatre on the Boulevard du Temple, Paris. [Cousin Betty.]

Isemberg (Maréchal, Duc d'), probably belonged to the Imperial nobility. He lost at the gaming table, in November, 1809, in a grand fête given at Paris at Senator Malin de Gondreville's home, while the Duchesse de Lansac was acting as peacemaker between a youthful married couple. [Domestic Peace.]

J

Jacmin (Philoxène), of Honfleur; perhaps cousin of Jean Butscha; maid to Eléonore de Chaulieu; in love with Germain Bonnet, valet of Melchior de Canalis. [Modeste Mignon.]

Jacométy, head jailer of the Conciergerie, at Paris, in May, 1830, during Rubempré's imprisonment. [Scenes from a Courtesan's Life.]

Jacquelin, born in Normandy about 1776; in 1816 was employed by Mlle. Cormon, an old maid of Alençon. He married when she espoused M. du Bousquier. After the double marriage Jacquelin remained for some time in the service of the niece of the Abbé de Sponde. [Jealousies of a Country Town.]

Jacques, for a considerable period butler of Claire de Beauséant, following her to Bayeux. Essentially "aristocratic, intelligent and discreet," he understood the sufferings of his mistress. [Father Goriot. The Deserted Woman.]

Jacquet (Claude-Joseph), a worthy bourgeois of the Restoration; head of a family, and something of a crank. He performed the duties of a deputy-mayor in Paris, and also had charge of the archives in the Department of Foreign Affairs. Was greatly indebted to his friend Jules Desmarets; so he deciphered for him, about 1820, a code letter of Gratien Bourignard. When Clémence Desmarets died, Jacquet comforted the broker in the Saint-Roch church and in the Pére-Lachaise cemetery. [The Thirteen.]

Jacquinot, said to have succeeded Cardot as notary at Paris, time of Louis Philippe [The Middle Classes]; but since Cardot was succeeded by Berthier, his son-in-law, a discrepancy is apparent.

Jacquotte, left the service of a curé for that of Dr. Benassis, whose house she managed with a devotion and care not unmixed with despotism. [The Country Doctor.]

Jan,[1] a painter who cared not a fig for glory. About 1838 he covered with flowers and decorated the door of a bed-chamber in a suite owned by Crevel on rue du Dauphin, Paris. [Cousin Betty.]

Janvier, priest in a village of Isére in 1829, a "veritable Fénelon shrunk to a curé's proportions"; knew, understood and assisted Benassis. [The Country Doctor.]

Japhet (Baron), celebrated chemist who subjected to hydrofluoric acid, to chloride of nitrogen, and to the action of the voltaic battery the mysterious "magic skin" of Raphaél de Valentin. To his stupefaction the savant wrought no change on the tissue. [The Magic Skin.]

Jean, coachman and trusted servant of M. de Merret, at Vendôme, in 1816. [La Grande Bretêche. Another Study of Woman.]

Jean, landscape gardener and farm-hand for Félix Grandet, engaged about November, 1819, in a field on the bank of the Loire, filling holes left by removed poplars and planting other trees. [Eugénie Grandet.]

Jean, one of the keepers of Pérc-Lachaise cemetery in 1820-1821; conducted Desmarets and Jacquet to the tomb of Clémence Bourignard, who had recently been interred.[2] [The Thirteen.]

---

[1] Perhaps the fresco-painter, Laurent-Jan, author of "Unrepentant Misanthropy," and the friend of Balzac, to whom the latter dedicated his drama, "Vautrin."

[2] In 1868, at Paris, MM Ferdinand Dugué and Peaucellier presented a play at the Gaîté theatre, where one of the chief characters was Clémence Bourignard-Desmarets.

Jean, lay brother of an abbey until 1791, when he found a home with Niseron, curé of Blangy, Burgundy; seldom left Grégoire Rigou, whose factotum he finally became. [The Peasantry.]

· **Jeannette,** born in 1758; cook for Ragon at Paris in 1818, in rue du Petit-Lion-Saint-Sulpice; distinguished herself at the Sunday receptions. [César Birotteau.]

Jeanrenaud (Madame), a Protestant, widow of a salt barge-man, by whom she had a son. A stout, ugly and vulgar woman, who recovered, during the Restoration, a fortune that had been stolen by the Catholic ancestors of D'Espard and was restored by him despite a suit to restrain him by injunction. Mme. Jeanrenaud lived at Villeparisis, and then at Paris, where she dwelt successively on rue de la Vrillière —No. 8—and on Grand rue Verte. [The Commission in Lunacy.]

Jeanrenaud, son of the preceding, born about 1792. He served as officer in the Imperial Guard, and, through the influence of D'Espard-Négrepelisse, became, in 1828, chief of squadron in the First regiment of the Cuirassiers of the Guard. Charles X. made him a baron. He then married a niece of Monegod. His beautiful villa on Lake Geneva is mentioned by Albert Savarus in "L'Ambitieux par Amour," published in the reign of Louis Philippe. [The Commission in Lunacy. Albert Savarus.]

Jenny was, during the Restoration, maid and confidante of Aquilina de la Garde; afterwards, but for a very brief time, mistress of Castanier. [Melmoth Reconciled.]

Jérôme (Pére), second-hand book-seller on Pont Notre-Dame, Paris, in 1821, at the time when Rubempré was making a start there. [A Distinguished Provincial at Paris.]

Jérôme, valet successively of Galard and of Albert Savarus at Besançon. He may have served the Parisian lawyer less sedulously because of Mariette, a servant at the Watte-villes, whose dowry he was after. [Albert Savarus.]

Johnson (Samuel), assumed name of the police-agent, Peyrade.

Jolivard, clerk of registry, rue de Normandie, Paris, about the end of Louis Philippe's reign. He lived on the first floor of the house owned by Pillerault, attended by the Cibots and tenanted by the Chapoulots, Pons and Schmucke. [Cousin Pons.]

Jonathas, valet of M. de Valentin senior; foster-father of Raphaël de Valentin, whose steward he afterwards became when the young man was a multi-millionaire. He served him faithfully and survived him. [The Magic Skin.]

Jordy (De) had been successively captain in a regiment of Royal-Suédois and professor in the Ecole Militaire. He had a refined nature and a tender heart; was the type of a poor but uncomplaining gentleman. His soul must have been the scene of sad secrets. Certain signs led one to believe that he had had children whom he had adored and lost. M. de Jordy lived modestly and quietly at Nemours. A similarity of tastes and character drew him toward Denis Minoret whose intimate friend he became, and at whose home he conceived a liking for the doctor's young ward—Mme. Savinien de Portenduère. He had great influence over her, and left her an income of fourteen hundred francs when he died in 1823. [Ursule Mirouët.]

Joseph, with Charles and François, was of the establishment of Montcornet at Aigues, Burgundy, about 1823. [The Peasantry.]

Joseph, faithful servant of Rastignac at Paris, under the Restoration. In 1828 he carried to the Marquise de Listomère a letter written by his master to Mme. de Nucingen. This error, for which Joseph could hardly be held responsible, caused the scorn of the marquise when she discovered that the missive was intended for another. [The Magic Skin. A Study of Woman.]

Joseph, in the service of F. du Tillet, Paris, when his

master was fairly launched in society and received Birotteau in state. [César Birotteau.]

Joseph, given name of a worthy chimney-builder of rue Saint-Lazare, Paris, about the end of the reign of Louis Philippe. Of Italian origin, the head of a family, saved from ruin by Adeline Hulot, who acted for Mme. de la Chanterie. Joseph was in touch with the scribe, Vyder, and when he took Mme. Hulot to see the latter she recognized in him her husband. [Cousin Betty.]

Josépha. (*See* Mirah, Josépha.)

Josette, cook for Claës at Douai; greatly attached to Joséphine, Marguerite and Félicie Claés. Died about the end of the Restoration. [The Quest of the Absolute.]

Josette, old housekeeper for Maître Mathias of Bordeaux during the Restoration. She accompanied her master when he bade farewell to Paul de Manerville the emigrant. [A Marriage Settlement.]

Josette, in and previous to 1816 chambermaid of Victoire-Rose Cormon of Alençon. She married Jacquelin when her mistress married du Bousquier. [Jealousies of a Country Town.]

Judici (Atala), born about 1829, of Lombard descent; had a paternal grandfather, who was a wealthy chimney-builder of Paris during the first Empire, an employer of Joseph; he died in 1819. Mlle. Judiei did not inherit her grandfather's fortune, for it was run through with by her father. In 1844 she was given by her mother—so the story goes—to Hector Hulot for fifteen thousand francs. She then left her family, who lived on rue de Charonne, and lived maritally with her protector, who had turned public scribe on Passage du Soleil. The pretty Atala was obliged to leave Hulot when his wife found him. Mme. Hulot promised her a dowry and to wed her to Joseph's oldest son. She was sometimes called Judix, which is a French corruption of the Italian name. [Cousin Betty.]

Judith. (*See* Mme. Genestas.)

Julien, one of the turnkeys of the Conciergerie in 1830, during the trial of Herrera—Vautrin—and Rubempré. [Scenes from a Courtesan's Life.]

Julien, probably a native of Champagne; a young man in 1839, and in the service of Sub-Prefect Goulard, in Arcis-sur-Aube. He learned through Anicette, and revealed to the Beauvisages and Mollots, the Legitimist plots of the Château de Cinq-Cygne, where lived Georges de Maufrigneuse, Daniel d'Arthez, Laurence de Cinq-Cygne, Diane de Cadignan and Berthe de Maufrigneuse. [The Member for Arcis.]

Julliard, head of the firm of Julliard in Paris, about 1806. At the "Ver Chinois," rue Saint-Denis, he sold silk in bolls. Sylvie Rogron was assistant saleswoman. Twenty years later he met her again in their native country of Provins, where he had retired in 1815, the head of a family grouped about the Guépins and the Guénées, thus forming three great clans. [Pierrette.]

Julliard, elder son of the preceding; married the only daughter of a rich farmer and also conceived a platonic affection at Provins for Mélanie Tiphaine, the most beautiful woman of the official colony during the Restoration. Julliard followed commerce and literature; he maintained a stage line, and a journal christened "La Ruche," in which latter he burned incense to Mme. Tiphaine. [Pierrette.]

Jussieu (Julien), youthful conscript in the great draft of 1793. Sent with a note for lodgment to the home of Mme. de Dey at Carentan, where he was the innocent cause of that woman's sudden death; she was just then expecting the return of her son, a Royalist hunted by the Republican troops. [The Conscript.]

Juste, born in 1811, studied medicine in Paris, and afterwards went to Asia to practice. In 1836 he lived on rue Corneille with Charles Rabourdin, when they helped the poverty-stricken Zéphirin Marcas. [Z. Marcas.]

Justin, old and experienced valet of the Vidame de Pamiers; was secretly slain by order of Bourignard because he had discovered the real name, but carefully concealed, of the father of Mme. Desmarets. [The Thirteen.]

Justine, was maid to the Comtesse Foedora, in Paris, when her mistress received calls from M. de Valentin. [The Magic Skin.]

K

Katt, a Flemish woman, the nurse of Lydie de la Peyrade, whom she attended constantly in Paris on rue des Moineaux about 1829, and during her mistress' period of insanity on rue Honoré Chevalier in 1840. [Scenes from a Courtesan's Life. The Middle Classes.]

Keller (François), one of the influential and wealthy Parisian bankers, during a period extending perhaps from 1809 to 1839. As such, in November, 1809, under the Empire, he was one of the guests at a fine reception, given by Comte Malin de Gondreville, meeting there Isemberg, Montcornet, Mesdames de Lansac and de Vaudemont, and a mixed company composed of members of the aristocracy and people illustrious under the Empire. At this time, moreover, François Keller was in the family of Malin de Gondreville, one of whose daughters he had married. This marriage, besides making him the brother-in-law of the Maréchal de Carigliano, gave him assurance of the deputyship, which he obtained in 1816 and held until 1836. The district electors of Arcis-sur-Aube kept him in the legislature during that long period. François Keller had, by his marriage with Mademoiselle de Gondreville, one son, Charles, who died before his parents in the spring of 1839. As deputy, François Keller became one of the most noted orators of the Left Centre. He shone as a member of the opposition, especially from 1819 to 1825. Adroitly he drew about himself the robe of philanthropy. Politics never turned his attention from finance. In 1819, on rue du Houssay, while Decazes awaited him, François Keller, seconded by his brother and partner, Adolphe Keller, refused to aid the needy perfumer, César Birotteau. Between 1821 and 1823 the creditors of Guillaume Grandet, the bankrupt, unanimously selected him and M. des Grassins of Saumur as adjusters. Despite his display of Puritanical virtues, the private career of François Keller was not spotless. In 1825 it was known that he had an illegitimate and costly liaison with Flavie Colleville. Rallying to the support of the new monarchy from 1830 to 1836, François Keller saw his Philippist zeal rewarded in 1839. He exchanged his commission at the Palais-Bourbon for a peerage, and received the title of count. [Domestic Peace. César Birotteau. Eugénie Grandet. The Government Clerks. The Member for Arcis.]

Keller (Madame François), wife of the preceding; daughter of Malin de Gondreville; mother of Charles Keller, who died in 1839. Under the Restoration, she inspired a warm passion in the heart of the son of the Duchesse de Marigny. [Domestic Peace. The Member for Arcis. The Thirteen.]

Keller (Charles), born in 1809, son of the preceding couple, grandson of the Comte de Gondreville, nephew of the Maréchale de Carigliano; his life was prematurely ended in 1839, at a time when a brilliant future seemed before him. As a major of staff at the side of the Prince Royal, Ferdinand d'Orléans, he took the field in Algeria. His bravery urged him on in pursuit of the Emir Abd-el-Kader, and he gave up his life in the face of the enemy. Becoming viscount as a result of the knighting of his father, and assured of the favors of the heir presumptive to the throne, Charles Keller, at the moment when death surprised him, was on the point of taking his seat in the Lower Chamber; for the body of electors of the district of Arcis-sur-Aube were almost sure to elect a man whom the Tuileries desired so ardently. [The Member for Arcis.]

Keller (Adolphe), brother—probably younger—of François and his partner; a very shrewd man, who was really in charge of the business, a "regular lynx." On account of his intimate relations with Nucingen and F. du Tillet, he flatly refused to aid César Birotteau, who implored his assistance. [The Middle Classes. Pierrette. César Birotteau.]

Kergarouët (Comte de), born about the middle of the

eighteenth century; of the Bretagne nobility; entered the navy, served long and valiantly upon the sea, commanded the "Belle-Poule," and died a vice-admiral. Possessor of a great fortune, by his charity he made amends for the foulness of some of his youthful love affairs (1771 and following), and at Paris, near the Madeleine, towards the beginning of the nineteenth century, with much delicacy, he helped the Baronne Leseigneur de Rouville. A little later, at the age of seventy-two, having for a long time been a widower and retired from the navy, while enjoying the hospitality of his relatives, the Fontaines and the Planat de Bandrys, who lived in the neighborhood of Sçeaux, Kergarouët married his niece, one of the daughters of Fontaine. He died before her. M. de Kergarouët was also a relative of the Portenduères and did not forget them. [The Purse. The Ball at Sçeaux. Ursule Mirouët.]

Kergarouët (Comtesse de). (*See* Vandenesse, Marquise Charles de.)

Kergarouët (Vicomte de), nephew of the Comte de Kergarouët, husband of a Pen-Hoél, by whom he had four daughters. Evidently lived at Nantes in 1836. [Béatrix.]

Kergarouët (Vicomtesse de), wife of the preceding, born at Pen-Hoél in 1789; younger sister of Jacqueline; mother of four girls; very affected woman and looked upon as such by Félicité des Touches and Arthur de Rochefide. Lived in Nantes in 1836. [Béatrix.]

Kergarouët (Charlotte de), born in 1821, one of the daughters of the preceding, grand-niece of the Comte de Kergarouët; of his four nieces she was the favorite of the wealthy Jacqueline de Pen-Hoél; a good-hearted little country girl; fell in love with Calyste du Guénie in 1836, but did not marry him. [Béatrix.]

Kolb, an Alsatian, served as "man of all work" at the home of the Didots in Paris; had served in the cuirassiers. Under the Restoration he became "printer's devil" in the establishment of David Séchard of Angoulême, for whom he showed an untiring devotion, and whose servant, Marion, he married. [Lost Illusions.]

Kolb (Marion), wife of the preceding, with whom she became acquainted while at the home of David Séchard. She was, at first, in the service of the Angouléme printer, Jérôme-Nicolas Séchard, for whom she had less praise than for David. Marion Kolb was like her husband in her constant, childlike devotion. [Lost Illusions.]

Kouski, Polish lancer in the French Royal Guards, lived very unhappily in 1815-16, but enjoyed life better the following year. At that time he lived at Issoudun in the home of the wealthy Jean-Jacques Rouget, and served the commandant, Maxence Gilet. The latter became the idol of the grateful Kouski. [A Bachelor's Establishment.]

Kropoli (Zéna), Montenegrin of Zahara, seduced in 1809 by the French gunner, Auguste Niseron, by whom she had a daughter, Geneviéve. One year later, at Vincennes, France, she died as a result of her confinement. The necessary marriage papers, which would have rendered valid the situation of Zéna Kropoli, arrived a few days after her death. [The Peasantry.]

L

La Bastie (Monsieur, Madame and Mademoiselle de). (*See* Mignon.)

La Bastie **la Brière** (Ernest de), member of a good family of Toulouse, born in 1802; very similar in appearance to Louis XIII.; from 1824 to 1829, private secretary to the minister of finances. On the advice of Madame d'Espard, and thus being of service to Eléonore de Chaulieu, he became secretary to Melchior de Canalis and, at the same time, referendary of the Cour des Comptes. He became a chevalier of the Legion of Honor. In 1829 he conducted for Canalis a love romance by correspondence, the heroine of the affair being Marie-Modeste-Mignon de la Bastie (of Havre). He played his part so successfully that she fell in love and marriage was agreed upon. This union, which made him the wealthy Vicomte de la Bastie la Brière, was effected the following February in 1830. Canalis and the minister of 1824 were witnesses for Ernest de la Briére, who fully deserved his good fortune. [The Government Clerks. Modeste Mignon.]

La Bastie la Brière (Madame Ernest de), wife of the preceding, born Marie-Modeste Mignon about 1809, younger daughter of Charles Mignon de la Bastie and of Bettina Mignon de la Bastie—born Wallenrod. In 1829, while living with her family at Havre, with the same love, evoked by a passion for literature, which Bettina Brentano d'Arnim conceived for Goethe, she fell in love with Melchior de Canalis; she wrote frequently to the poet in secret, and he responded through the medium of Ernest de la Briére; thus there sprang up between the young girl and the secretary a mutual love which resulted in marriage. The witnesses for Marie-Modeste Mignon were the Duc d'Hérouville and Doctor Desplein. As one of the most envied women in Parisian circles, in the time of Louis Philippe, she became the close friend of Mesdames de l'Estorade and Popinot. [Modeste Mignon. The Member for Arcis. Cousin Betty.] La Bastie is sometimes written La Bâtie.

La **Baudraye**[1] (Jean-Athanase-Polydore Miland de), born in 1780 in Berry, descended from the simple family of Milaud, recently ennobled. M. de la Baudraye's father was a good financier of pleasing disposition; his mother was a Castéran la Tour. He was in poor health, his weak constitution being the heritage left him by an immoral father. His father, on dying, also left him a large number of notes to which were affixed the noble signatures of the emigrated aristocracy. His avarice aroused, Polydore de la Baudraye occupied himself, at the time of the Restoration, with collecting these notes; he made frequent trips to Paris; negotiated with Clément Chardin des Lupeaulx at the Hôtel de Mayence; obtained, under a promise, afterwards executed, to sell them profitably, some positions and titles, and became successively auditor of the seals, baron, officer

[1] The motto on the Baudraye coat-of-arms was: "Deo patet sic fides et hominibus."

of the Legion of Honor and master of petitions. The individual receivership of Sancerre, which became his also, was bought by Gravier. M. de la Baudraye did not leave Sancerre; he married towards 1823 Mademoiselle Dinah Piédefer, became a person of large property following his acquisition to the castle and estate of Anzy, settled this property with the title upon a natural son of his wife; he so worked upon her feelings as to get from her the power of attorney and signature, sailed for America, and became rich through a large patrimony left him by Silas Piédefer—1836-42. At that time he owned in Paris a stately mansion, on rue de l'Arcade, and upon winning back his wife, who had left him, he placed her in it as mistress. He now became count, commander of the Legion of Honor, and peer of France. Frédéric de Nucingen received him as such and served him as sponsor, when, in the summer of 1842, the death of Ferdinand d'Orléans necessitated the presence of M. de la Baudraye at Luxembourg. [The Muse of the Department.]

La Baudraye (Madame Polydore Milaud de), wife of the preceding, born Dinah Piédefer in 1807 or 1808 in Berry; daughter of the Calvinist, Moise Piédefer; niece of Silas Piédefer, from whom she inherited a fortune. She was brilliantly educated at Bourges, in the Chamarolles boarding-school, with Anna deFontaine, born Grosstête—1819. Five years later, through personal ambition, she gave up Protestantism, that she might gain the protection of the Cardinal-Archbishop of Bourges, and a short time after her conversion she was married, about 1823. For thirteen consecutive years, at least, Madame de la Baudraye reigned in the city of Sancerre and in her country-house, Château d'Anzy, at Saint-Satur near by. Her court was composed of a strange mixture of people: the Abbé Duret and Messieurs Clagny, Gravier, Gatien Boirouge. At first, only Clagny and Duret knew of the literary attempts of Jan Diaz, pseudonym of Madame de la Baudraye, who had just bought the artistic furniture of the Rougets of Issoudun, and who invited and received two " Parisiens de Sancerre,"

Horace Bianchon and Etienne Lousteau, in September, 1836. A liaison followed with Etienne Lousteau, with whom Madame de la Baudraye lived on rue des Martyrs in Paris from 1837 to 1839. As a result of this union she had two sons, recognized later by M. de la Baudraye. Madame de la Baudraye now putting into use the talent, neglected during her love affair, became a writer. She wrote "A Prince of Bohemia," founded on an anecdote related to her by Raoul Nathan, and probably published this novel. The fear of endless scandal, the entreaties of husband and mother, and the unworthiness of Lousteau, finally led Dinah de la Baudraye to rejoin her husband, who owned an elegant mansion on rue de l'Arcade. This return, which took place in May, 1842, surprised Madame d'Espard, a woman who was not easily astonished. Paris of the reign of Louis Philippe often quoted Dinah de la Baudraye and paid considerable attention to her. During this same year, 1842, she assisted in the first presentation of Léon Gozlan's drama, "The Right Hand and the Left Hand," given at the Odéon. [The Muse of the Department. A Prince of Bohemia. Cousin Betty.]

La Berge (De), confessor of Madame de Mortsauf at Cloche-gourde, strict and virtuous. He died in 1817, mourned on account of his "apostolic strength," by his patron, who appointed as his successor the over-indulgent François Birotteau. [The Lily of the Valley.]

La Bertellière, father of Madame la Gaudinière, grand-father of Madame Félix Grandet, was lieutenant in the French Guards; he died in 1806, leaving a large fortune. He considered investments a "waste of money." Nearly twenty years later his portrait was still hanging in the hall of Félix Grandet's house at Saumur. [Eugénie Grandet.]

La Billardière (Athanase-Jean-François-Michel, Baron Flamet de), son of a counselor in the Parliament of Bretagne, took part in the Vendean wars as a captain under the name of Nantais, and as negotiator played a singular part at Quiberon. The Restoration rewarded the services of this unintelligent member of the petty nobility, whose Catholicism was more lukewarm than his love of monarchy. He became mayor of the second district of Paris, and division-chief in the Bureau of Finances, thanks to his kinship with a deputy on the Right. He was one of the guests at the famous ball given by his deputy, César Birotteau, whom he had known for twenty years. On his death-bed, at the close of December, 1824, he had designated, although without avail, as his successor, Xavier Rabourdin, one of the division-chiefs and real director of the bureau of which La Billardière was the nominal head. The newspapers published obituaries of the deceased. The short notice prepared jointly by Chardin des Lupeaulx, J.-J. Bixiou and F. du Bruel, enumerated the many titles and decorations of Flamet de la Billardière, gentleman of the king's bedchamber, etc., etc. [The Chouans. César Birotteau. The Government Clerks.]

La Billardière (Benjamin, Chevalier de), son of the preceding, born in 1802. He was a companion of the young Vicomte de Portenduère in 1824, being at the time a rich supernumerary in the office of Isidore Baudoyer under the division of his father, Flamet de la Billardière. His insolence and foppishness gave little cause for regret when he left the Bureau of Finances for the Department of Seals in the latter part of the same year, 1824, that marked the expected and unlamented death of Baron Flamet de la Billardière. [The Government Clerks.]

La Blottière (Mademoiselle Merlin de), under the Restoration, a kind of dowager and canoness at Tours; in company with Mesdames Pauline Salomon de Villenoix and de Listomére, upheld, received and welcomed François Birotteau. [The Vicar of Tours.]

Labranchoir (Comte de), owner of an estate in Dauphiné, under the Restoration, and, as such, a victim of the depredations of the poacher, Butifer. [The Country Doctor.]

La Brière (Ernest de). (*See* La Bastie la Briére.)

Lacépède (Comte de), a celebrated naturalist, born at

Agen in 1756, died at Paris in 1825. Grand chancelor of the Legion of Honor for several years towards the beginning of the nineteenth century. This well-known philosopher was invited to César Birotteau's celebrated ball, December 17, 1818. [César Birotteau.]

La Chanterie (Le Chantre de), of a Norman family dating from the crusade of Philippe Auguste, but which had fallen into obscurity by the end of the eighteenth century; he owned a small fief between Caen and Saint-Lô.   M. le Chantre de la Chanterie had amassed in the neighborhood of three hundred thousand crowns by supplying the royal armies during the Hanoverian war. He died during the Revolution, but before the Terror. [The Seamy Side of History.]

La Chanterie (Baron Henri Le Chantre de), born in 1763, son of the preceding, shrewd, handsome and seductive. When master of petitions in the Grand Council of 1788, he married Mademoiselle Barbe-Philiberte de Champignelles. Ruined during the Restoration through having lost his position and thrown away his inheritance, Henri Le Chantre de la Chanterie became one of the most cruel presidents of the revolutionary courts and was the terror of Normandie. Imprisoned after the ninth Thermidor, he owed his escape to his wife, by means of an exchange of clothing. He did not see her more than three times during eight years, the last meeting being in 1802, when, having become a bigamist, he returned to her home to die of a disgraceful disease, leaving, at the same time, a second wife likewise ruined. This last fact was not made public until 1804. [The Seamy Side of History.]

La Chanterie (Baronne Henri Le Chantre de), wife of the preceding, born Barbe-Philiberte de Champignelles in 1772, a descendant of one of the first families of Lower Normandie.   Married in 1788, she received in her home, fourteen years later, the dying man whose name she bore, a bigamist fleeing from justice.   By him she had a daughter, Henriette, who was executed in 1809 for having been connected with the Chauffeurs in Orne   Unjustly accused herself, and imprisoned in the frightful Bicêtre of Rouen, the baroness began to instruct in morals the sinful women among whom she found herself thrown. The fall of the Empire was her deliverance. Twenty years later, being part owner of a house in Paris, Madame de la Chanterie undertook the training of Godefroid. She was then supporting a generous private philanthropic movement, with the help of Manon Godard and Messieurs de Véze, de Montauran, Mongenod and Alain. Madame de la Chanterie aided the Bourlacs and the Mergis, an impoverished family of magistrates who had persecuted her in 1809. Her Christian works were enlarged upon. In 1843 the baroness became head of a charitable organization which was striving to consecrate, according to law and religion, the relations of those living in free union. To this end she selected one member of the society, Adeline Hulot d'Ervy, and sent her to Passage du Soleil, then a section of Petite-Pologne, to try to bring about the marriage of Vyder—Hector Hulot d'Ervy—and Atala Judiei. [The Seamy Side of History. Cousin Betty]. The Revolution having done away with titles, Madame de la Chanterie called herself momentarily Madame, or Citizeness, Lechantre.

Lacroix, restaurant-keeper on Place du Marché, Issoudun, 1822, in whose house the Bonapartist officers celebrated the crowning of the Emperor. On December 2, of the same year, the duel between Philippe Bridau and Maxence took place after the entertainment. [A Bachelor's Establishment.]

Laferté (Nicolas). (*See* Cochegrue, Jean.)

La Garde (Madame de). (*See* Aquilina.)

La Gaudinière (Madame), born La Bertellière, mother of Madame Félix Grandet; very avaricious; died in 1806; leaving the Félix Grandets an inheritance, "the amount of which no one knew." [Eugénie Grandet.]

Laginski (Comte Adam Mitgislas), a wealthy man who had been proscribed, belonged to one of the oldest and most illustrious families of Poland, and counted among his relations the Sapiéhas, the Radziwills, the Mniszechs, the Rezwuskis, the Czartoriskis, the Lecszinskis, and the Lubomirskis.

He had relations in the German nobility and his mother was a Radziwill. Young, plain, yet with a certain distinguished bearing, with an income of eighty thousand francs, Laginski was a leading light in Paris, during the reign of Louis Philippe. After the Revolution of July, while still unsophisticated, he attended an entertainment at the home of Félicité des Touches in Chaussée-d'Antin on rue du Mont-Blanc, and had the opportunity of listening to the delightful chats between Henri de Marsay and Emile Blondet. Comte Adam Laginski, during the autumn of 1835, married the object of his affections, Mademoiselle Clémentine du Rouvre, niece of the Ronquerolles. The friendship of his steward, Paz, saved him from the ruin into which his créole-like carelessness, his frivolity and his recklessness were dragging him. He lived in perfect contentment with his wife, ignorant of the domestic troubles which were kept from his notice. Thanks to the devotion of Paz and of Madame Laginska, he was cured of a malady which had been pronounced fatal by Doctor Horace Bianchon. Comte Adam Laginski lived on rue de la Pépiniére, now absorbed in part by rue de la Boétie. He occupied one of the most palatial and artistic houses of the period, so called, of Louis Philippe. He attended the celebration given in 1838 at the first opening of Josépha Mirah's residence on rue de la Ville-l'Evêque. In this same year he attended the wedding of Wenceslas Steinbock. [Another Study of Woman. The Imaginary Mistress. Cousin Betty.]

Laginska (Comtesse Adam), born Clémentine du Rouvre in 1816, wife of the preceding, niece, on her mother's side, of the Marquis de Ronquerolles and of Madame de Sérizy. She was one of the charming group of young women, which included Mesdames de l'Estorade, de Portenduère, Marie de Vandenesse, du Guénie and de Maufrigneuse. Captain Paz was secretly in love with the countess, who, becoming aware of her steward's affection, ended by having very nearly the same kind of feeling for him. The unselfish virtue of Paz was all that saved her, not only at this juncture, but in another more dangerous one, when he rescued her from

M. de la Palférine, who was escorting her to the Opéra ball and who was on the point of taking her to a private room in a restaurant—January, 1842. [The Imaginary Mistress.]

Lagounia (Perez de), woolen-draper at Tarragone in Catalonia, in the time of Napoleon, under obligations to La Marana. He reared as his own daughter, in a very pious manner, Juana, a child of the celebrated Italian courtesan, until her mother visited her, during the time of the French occupation in 1808. [The Maranas.]

Lagounia (Donna de), wife of the preceding, divided with him the care of Juana Marana until the girl's mother came to Tarragone at the time it was sacked by the French. [The Maranas.]

La Grave (Mesdemoiselles), kept a boarding-house in 1824 on rue Notre-Dame-des-Champs in Paris. In this house M. and Madame Phellion gave lessons. [The Government Clerks.]

Laguerre (Mademoiselle), given name, probably, Sophie, born in 1740, died in 1815, one of the most celebrated courtesans of the eighteenth century; opera singer, and fervent follower of Piccini. In 1790, frightened by the march of public affairs, she established herself at the Aigues, in Bourgogne, property procured for her by Bouret, from its former owner. Before Bouret, the grandfather of La Palférine, entertained her, and she brought about his ruin. The recklessness of this woman, surrounded as she was by such notorious knaves as Gaubertin, Fourchon, Tonsard, and Madame Soudry, prepared no little trouble for Montcornet, the succeeding proprietor. Sophie Laguerre's fortune was divided among eleven families of poor farmers, all living in the neighborhood of Amiens, who were ignorant of their relationship with her. [The Peasantry. A Prince of Bohemia.] M. H. Gourdon de Genouillac wrote a biography of the singer, containing many details which are at variance with the facts here cited. Among other things we are told that the given name of Mademoiselle Laguerre was Joséphine and not Sophie.

La Haye (Mademoiselle de).   (*See* Petit-Claud, Madame.)

Lamard, probably a rival of Félix Gaudissart. In a café in Blois, May, 1831, he praised the well-known commercial traveler, who treated him, nevertheless, as a "little cricket." [Gaudissart the Great.]

Lambert (Louis), born in 1797 at Montoire in Loire-et-Cher. Only son of simple tanners, who did not try to counteract his inclination, shown when a mere child, for study. He was sent in 1807 to Lefebvre, a maternal uncle, who was vicar of Mer, a small city on the Loire near Blois. Under the kindly care of Madame de Staël, he was a student in the college of Vendôme from 1811 to 1814. Lambert met there Barchon de Penhoën and Jules Dufaure. He was apparently a poor scholar, but finally developed into a prodigy; he suffered the persecutions of Father Haugoult, by whose brutal hands his "Treatise on the Will," composed during class hours, was seized and destroyed. The mathematician had already doubled his capacity by becoming a philosopher. His comrades had named him Pythagoras. His course completed, and his father being dead, Louis Lambert lived for two years at Blois, with Lefebvre, until, growing desirous of seeing Madame de Staël, he journeyed to Paris on foot, arriving July 14, 1817. Not finding his illustrious benefactress alive, he returned home in 1820. During these three years Lambert lived the life of a workman, became a close friend of Meyraux, and was cherished and admired as a member of the Cénacle on rue des Quatre-Vents, which was presided over by Arthez. Once more he went to Blois, journeyed over Touraine, and became acquainted with Pauline Salomon de Villenoix, whom he loved with a passion that was reciprocated. He had suffered from brain trouble previous to their engagement, and as the wedding day approached the disease grew constantly worse, although occasionally there were periods of relief. During one of these good periods, in 1822, Lambert met the Cambremers at Croisic, and on the suggestion of Pauline de Villenoix, he made a study of their history. The malady returned, but was interrupted occasionally by outbursts of beautiful thought, the fragments of which were collected by Mademoiselle Salomon. Louis had likewise occasional fits of insanity. He believed himself powerless and wished, one day, to perform on his own body Origène's celebrated operation. Lambert died September 25, 1824, the day before the date selected for his marriage with Pauline. [Louis Lambert. A Distinguished Provincial at Paris. A Seaside Tragedy.]

Lambert (Madame), lived in Paris in 1840. She was then at a very pious age, "played the saint," and performed the duties of housekeeper for M. Picot, professor of mathematies, No. 9, rue du Val-de-Grâce. In the service of this old philosopher she reaped enormous profits. Madame Lambert hypocritically took advantage of her apparent devotion to him. She sought Théodose de la Peyrade, and begged him to write a memorial to the Academy in her favor, for she longed to receive the reward offered by Montyon. At the same time she put into La Peyrade's keeping twenty-five thousand francs, which she had accumulated by her household thefts. On this occasion, Madame Lambert seems to have been the secret instrument of Corentin, the famous police-agent. [The Middle Classes.]

Langeais (Duc de), a refugee during the Restoration, who planned, at the time of the Terror, by correspondence with the Abbé de Marolles and the Marquis de Beauséant to help escape from Paris, where they were in hiding, two nuns, one of whom, Sister Agathe, was a Langeais. [An Episode Under the Terror.] In 1812 Langeais married Mademoiselle Antoinette de Navarreins, who was then eighteen years old. He allowed his wife every liberty, and, neither abandoning any of his habits, nor giving up any of his pleasures, he lived, indeed, apart from her. In 1818 Langeais commanded a division in the army and occupied a position at court. He died in 1823. [The Thirteen.]

Langeais (Duchesse Antoinette de),[1] wife of the preceding,

[1] At the Vaudeville and Caîté theatres in Paris, Ancelot and Alexis Decomberousse at the former, and Messieurs Ferdinand Dugué and Peaucellier at the latter, brought out plays founded on the life of Antoinette de Langeais, in 1834 and 1868 respectively.

daughter of the Duc de Navarreins; born in 1794; reared by the Princesse de Blamont-Chauvry, her aunt; grand-niece of the Vidame de Pamiers; niece of the Duc de Grandlieu by her marriage. Very beautiful and intelligent, Madame de Langeais reigned in Paris at the beginning of the Restoration. In 1819 her best friend was the Vicomtesse Claire de Beauséant, whom she wounded cruelly, for her own amusement, calling on her one morning for the express purpose of announcing the marriage of the Marquis d'Ajuda-Pinto. Of this pitiless proceeding she repented later, and asked pardon, moreover, of the forsaken woman. Soon afterwards the Duchesse de Langeais had the pleasure of captivating the Marquis de Montriveau, playing for him the rôle of Célimène and making him suffer greatly. He had his revenge, however, for, scorned in her turn, or believing herself scorned, she suddenly disappeared from Paris, after having scandalized the whole Saint-Germain community by remaining in her carriage for a long time in front of the Montriveau mansion. Some bare-footed Spanish Car-melites received her on their island in the Mediterranean, where she became Sister Thérése. After prolonged searching Montriveau found her, and, in the presence of the mother-superior, had a conversation with her as she stood behind the grating. Finally he managed to carry her off—dead. In this bold venture the marquis was aided by eleven of The Thirteen, among them being Ronquerolles and Marsay. The duchess, having lost her husband, was free at the time of her death in 1824. [Father Goriot. The Thirteen.]

Langeais (Mademoiselle de). (*See* Agathe, Sister.)

Langlumé, miller, a jolly impulsive little man, in 1823 deputy-mayor of Blangy in Bourgogne, at the time of the political, territorial and financial contests of which the country was the theatre, with Rigou and Montcornet as actors. He was of great service to Geneviéve Niseron's paternal grandfather. [The Peasantry.]

Languet, vicar, built Saint-Sulpice, and was an acquaint-ance of Toupillier, who asked alms in 1840 at the doors of this church in Paris, which since 1860 has been one of the sixth ward parish churches. [The Middle Classes.]

Lansac (Duchesse de), of the younger branch of the Parisian house of Navarreins, 1809, the proud woman who shone under Louis XV. The Duchesse de Lansac, in November of the same year, consented, one evening, to meet Isemberg, Montcornet, and Martial de la Roche-Hugon in Malin de Gondreville's house, for the purpose of conciliating her nephew and niece in their domestic quarrel. [Domestic Peace.]

Lantimèche, born in 1770. In 1840, at Paris, a penniless journeyman locksmith and inventor, he went to the money-lender, Cérizet, on rue des Poules, to borrow a hundred francs. [The Middle Classes.]

Lanty (Comte de), owner of an expensive mansion near the Elysée-Bourbon, which he had bought from the Maréchal de Garigliano. He gave there under the Restoration some magnificent entertainments, at which were present the upper classes of Parisian society, ignorant, though they were, of the count's lineage. Lanty, who was a mysterious man, passed for a clever chemist. He had married the rich niece of the peculiar eunuch, Zambinella, by whom he had two children, Marianina and Filippo. [Sarrasine. The Member for Arcis.]

Lanty (Comtesse de), wife of the preceding, born in 1795, niece and likewise adopted daughter of the wealthy eunuch, Zambinella, was the mistress of M. de Maucombe, by whom she had a daughter, Marianina de Lanty. [Sarrasine. The Member for Arcis.]

Lanty (Marianina de), daughter of the preceding and according to law of the Comte de Lanty, although she was in reality the daughter of M. de Maucombe; born in 1809. She bore a striking resemblance to her sister, Renée de l'Estorade, born Maucombe. In 1825 she concealed, and lavished care on her great-uncle, Zambinella. During her parents' sojourn in Rome she took lessons in sculpture of Charles Dorlange, who afterwards, in 1839, became a member for Arcis, under the name of Comte de Sallenauve. [Sarrasine. The Member for Arcis.]

Lanty (Filippo de), younger brother of the preceding, second child of the Comte and the Comtesse de Lanty. Being young and handsome he was an attendant at the fêtes given by his parents during the Restoration. By his marriage, which took place under Louis Philippe, he became allied with the family of a German grand duke. [Sarrasine. The Member for Arcis.]

La Palférine (Gabriel-Jean-Anne-Victor-Benjamin-Georges-Ferdinand-Charles-Edouard-Rusticoli, Comte de), born in 1802; of an ancient Italian family which had become impoverished; grandson on the paternal side of one of the protectors of Joséphine-Sophie Laguerre; descended indirectly from the Comtesse Albany—whence his given name of Charles-Edouard.   He had in his veins the mixed blood of the condottiere and the gentleman. Under Louis Philippe, idle and fast going to ruin, with his Louis XIII. cast of countenance, his evil-minded wit, his lofty independent manners, insolent yet winning, he was a type of the brilliant Bohemian of the Boulevard de Gand; so much so, that Madame de la Baudraye, basing her information on points furnished her by Nathan, one day drew a picture of him, writing a description in which artificiality and artlessness were combined.   In this were many interesting touches: La Palférine's strange servant, the little Savoyard—Father Anchise; the contempt shown at all times for the bourgeois class and forms of government; the request for the return of his toothbrush, then in the possession of a deserted mistress, Antonia Chocardelle; his relations with Madame du Bruel, whom he laid siege to, won, and neglected—a yielding puppet, of whom, strange to say, he broke the heart and made the fortune.   He lived at that time in the Roule addition, in a plain garret, where he was in the habit of receiving Zéphirin Marcas. The wretchedness of his quarters did not keep La Palférine out of the best society, and he was the guest of Josépha Mirah at the first entertainment given in her house on rue de la Ville-l'Evêque. By a strange order of events, Comte Rusticoli became Béatrix de Rochefide's lover, a few years after the events just narrated, at a time when the Débats published a novel by him which was spoken of far and wide. Nathan laid the foundation for this affair. Trailles, Charles-Edouard's master, carried on the negotiations and brought the intrigue to a consummation, being urged on by the Abbé Brossette's assent and the Duchesse de Grandlieu's request. La Palférine's liaison with Madame de Rochefide effected a reconciliation between Calyste du Guénie and his wife. In the course of time, however, Comte Rusticoli deserted Béatrix and sent her back to her husband, Arthur de Rochefide. During the winter of 1842 La Palférine was attracted to Madame de Laginska, had some meetings with her, but failed in this affair through the intervention of Thaddée Paz. [A Prince of Bohemia. A Man of Business. Cousin Betty. Béatrix: The Imaginary Mistress.]

La Peyrade (Charles-Marie-Théodose de), born near Avignon in 1813, one of eleven children of the police-agent Peyrade's youngest brother, who lived in poverty on a small estate called Canquoëlle; a bold Southerner of fair skin; given to reflection; ambitious, tactful and astute. In 1829 he left the department of Vaucluse and went to Paris on foot in search of Peyrade who, he had reason to believe, was wealthy, but of whose business he was ignorant. Théodose departed through the Barriére d'Enfer, which has been destroyed since 1860, at the moment when Jacques Collin murdered his uncle. At that time he entered a house of ill-fame, where he had unwittingly for mistress Lydie Peyrade, his full-blooded cousin. Théodose then lived for three years on a hundred louis which Corentin had secretly given to him. On giving him the money, the national chief of police quietly advised him to become an attorney. Journalism, however, at first, seemed a tempting career to M. de la Peyrade, and he went into politics, finally becoming editor of a paper managed by Cérizet. The failure of this journal left Théodose once more very poor. Nevertheless, through Corentin, who secretly paid the expenses of his studies, he was able to begin and continue a course in law.   Once licensed, M. de la Peyrade became a barrister and professing to be entirely converted to Socialism, he freely pleaded the cause of the poor before the magistrate of the eleventh or twelfth district.   He occupied the third story of the Thuillier house on rue Saint-Dominique-d'Enfer. He fell into the hands of Dutocq and Cérizet and suffered under the pressure of these grasping creditors.   Théodose now decided that he would marry M. Thuillier's natural daughter, Mademoiselle Céleste Colleville, but, with Félix Phellion's love to contend with, despite the combined support, gained with difficulty, of Madame Colleville and of M. and Mademoiselle Thuillier, he failed through Corentin's circumvention.   His marriage with Lydie Peyrade repaired the wrong which he had formerly done unwittingly.   As successor to Corentin he became national chief-of-police in 1840.   [Scenes from a Courtesan's Life.   The Middle Classes.]

La Peyrade (Madame de), first cousin and wife of the preceding, born Lydie Peyrade in 1810, natural daughter of the police officer Peyrade and of Mademoiselle Beaumesnil; passed her childhood successively in Holland and in Paris, on rue des Moineaux, whence, Jacques Collin, thirsting for revenge, abducted her during the Restoration. Being somewhat in love, at that time, with Lucien de Rubempré she was taken to a house of ill-fame, Peyrade being at the time very ill.   Upon her departure she was insane.   Her own cousin, Théodose de la Peyrade, had been her lover there, fortuitously and without dreaming that they were blood relatives.   Corentin adopted this insane girl, who was a talented musician and singer, and at his home on rue Honoré-Chevalier, in 1840, he arranged for both the cure and the marriage of his ward.   [Scenes from a Courtesan's Life.   The Middle Classes.]

La Pouraille, usual surname of Dannepont.

Laravinière, tavern-keeper in Western France, lodged "brigands" who had armed themselves as Royalists under the first Empire.   He was condemned, either by **Bourlac**

or Mergi, to five years in prison. [The Seamy Side of History.]

Lardot (Madame), born in 1771, lived in Alençon in 1816 on rue du Cours—a street still bearing the same name. She was a laundress, and took as boarders a relative named Grévin and the Chevalier de Valois. She had among her employés Césarine and Suzanne, afterwards Madame Théodore Gaillard. [Jealousies of a Country Town.]

Laroche, born in 1763 at Blangy in Bourgogne, was, in 1823, an aged vine-dresser, who felt a calm, relentless hatred for the rich, especially the Montcornets, occupants of Aigues. [The Peasantry.]

La Roche (Sébastien de), born early in the nineteenth century, was probably the son of an unpretentious, retired Treasury clerk. In December, 1824, he found himself in Paris, poor, but capable and zealous, as a supernumerary in the office of Xavier Rabourdin of the Department of Finance. He lived with his widowed mother in the busiest part·of Marais on rue du Roi-Doré. M. and Madame Rabourdin received and gave him assistance. M. de la Roche showed them his great appreciation by preparing a copy of a rare and mysterious government work. The discovery of this book by Dutocq unfortunately resulted in the discharge of both chief and clerk. [The Government Clerks.]

La Roche-Guyon (De), the eldest of one of the oldest families in the section of Orne, at one time connected with the Esgrignons, who visited them frequently. In 1805 he sued vainly, through Maitre Chesnel, for the hand of Armande d'Esgrignon. [Jealousies of a Country Town.]

La Roche-Hugon (Martial de), shrewd, turbulent and daring Southerner, had a long and brilliant administrative career in politics. Even in 1809 the Council of State employed him as one of the masters of petitions. Napoleon Bonaparte was patron of this young Provençal. Also, in November of the same year, Martial was invited to the fête given by

Malin de Gondreville—a celebration which the Emperor was vainly expected to attend. Montcornet was present, also the Duchesse de Lansac, who succeeded in bringing about a reconciliation between her nephew and niece, M. and Madame de Soulanges. M. de la Roche-Hugon's mistress, Madame de Vaudremont, was also in attendance at this ball. For five years he had enjoyed a close friendship with Montcornet, and this bond was lasting. In 1815 the securing of Aigues for Montcornet was undertaken by Martial, who had served as prefect under the Empire, and retained his office under the Bourbons. Thus from 1821 to 1823 M. de la Roche-Hugon was at the head of the department in Bourgogne, which contained Aigues and Ville-aux-Fayes, M. des Lupeaulx's sub-prefecture. A dismissal from this office, to which the Comte de Casteran succeeded, threw Martial into the opposition among the Liberalists, but this was for a short time, as he soon accepted an embassy. Louis Philippe's government honored M. de la Roche-Hugon by making him minister, ambassador, and counselor of state. Eugéne de Rastignac, who had favored him before, now gave him one of his sisters in marriage. Several children resulted from this union. Martial continued to remain influential, and associated with the popular idols of the time, M. and Madame de l'Estorade. His relations with the national chief of police, Corentin, in 1840, were also indicative of his standing. As a deputy the next year M. de la Roche-Hugon probably filled the directorship in the War Department, left vacant by Hector Hulot. [Domestic Peace. The Peasantry. A Daughter of Eve. The Member for Arcis. The Middle Classes. Cousin Betty.]

La Roche-Hugon (Madame Martial de). (See Rastignac, Mesdemoiselles de.)

La Rodière (Stéphanie de). (See Nueil, Madame Gaston de.)

La Roulie (Jacquin), chief huntsman of the Prince de Cadignan, took part with his master, in 1829, in the exciting hunt given in Normandie, in which as spectators or riders were the Mignons de la Bastie, the Maufrigneuscs, the Hérouvilles, M. de Canalis, Eléonore de Chaulieu and Ernest de la Briére. Jacquin la Roulie was at that time an old man and a firm believer in the French school; he had an argument with John Barry, another guest, who defended English principles. [Modeste Mignon.]

Larsonnière (M. and Madame de), formed the aristocracy of the little city of Saumur, of which Félix Grandet had been mayor in the years just previous to the First Empire. [Eugénie Grandet.]

La Thaumassière (De), grandson of the Berry historian, a young land-owner, the dandy of Sancerre. While present in Madame de la Baudraye's parlor, he had the misfortune to yawn during an exposition which she was giving, for the fourth time, of Kant's philosophy; he was henceforth looked upon as a man completely lacking in understanding and in soul. [The Muse of the Department.]

Latournelle (Simon-Babylas), born in 1777, was notary at Havre, where he had bought the most extensive practice for one hundred thousand francs, lent him in 1817 by Charles Mignon de la Bastie. He married Mademoiselle Agnés Labrosse, having by her one son, Exupére. He remained the intimate friend of his benefactors, the Mignons. [Modeste Mignon.]

Latournelle (Madame), wife of the preceding, born Agnés Labrosse, daughter to the clerk of the court of first instance at Havre. Tall and ungainly of figure, a bourgeoise of rather ancient tastes, at the same time good-hearted, she had somewhat late in life, by her marriage, a son whose given name was Exupére. She entertained Jean Butscha. Madame Latournelle was a frequent visitor of the Mignons de la Bastie, and at all times testified her affection for them. [Modeste Mignon.]

Latournelle (Exupére), son of the preceding couple, went with them often to visit the Mignons de la Bastie, towards the end of the Restoration.   He was then a tall, insignificant young man.   [Modeste Mignon.]

Laudigeois, married, head of a family, typical petty bourgeois, employed during the Restoration by the mayor of the eleventh or twelfth ward in Paris, a position from which he was unjustly expelled by Colleville in 1840.   In 1824 an intimate neighbor of the Phellions, and exactly like them in morals, he attended their informal card-party on Thursday evening.   Laudigeois, introduced by the Phellions, finally became a close friend of the Thuilliers, during the reign of Louis Philippe.   His civil statistical record should be corrected, as his name in several of the papers is spelled Leudigeois.   [The Government Clerks.   The Middle Classes.]

Laure, given name of a sweet and charming young peasant girl, who took Servin's course in painting at Paris in 1815. She protected Ginevra di Piombo, an affectionate friend, who was her elder.   [The Vendetta.]

Laurent, a Savoyard, Antoine's nephew; husband of an expert laundress of laces, mender of cashmeres, etc.   In 1824 he lived with them and their relative, Gabriel, in Paris. In the evening he was door-keeper in a subsidized theatre; in the daytime he was usher in the Bureau of Finance.   In this position Laurent was first to learn of the worldly and official success attained by Célestine Rabourdin, when she attempted to have Xavier appointed successor to Flamet de la Billardière.   [The Government Clerks.]

Laurent, Paris, 1815, M. Henri de Marsay's servant, equal to the Frontins of the old régime; was able to obtain for his master, through the mail-carrier, Moinot, the address of Paquita Valdés and other information about her.   [The Thirteen.]

Lavienne, Jean-Jules Popinot's servant in Paris, rue du Fouarre, 1828; "made on purpose for his master," whom he aided in his active philanthropy by redeeming and renewing pledges given to the pawnbrokers.   He took the place of his master in Palais de Justice during the latter's absence. [The Commission in Lunacy.]

Lavrille, famous naturalist, employed in the Jardin des Plantes, and dwelling on rue de Buffon, Paris, 1831. Consulted as to the shagreen, the enlargment of which was so passionately desired by Raphaël de Valentin, Lavrille could do nothing more than talk on the subject and sent the young man to Planchette, the professor of mechanics. Lavrille, "the grand mogul of zoölogy," reduced science to a catalogue of names. He was then preparing a monograph on the duck family. [The Magic Skin.]

Lebas (Joseph), born in 1779, a penniless orphan, he was assisted and employed in Paris, first by the Guillaumes, cloth-merchants on rue Saint-Denis, at the Cat and Racket. Under the First Empire he married Virginie,[1] the elder of his employer's daughters, although he was in love with the younger, Mademoiselle Augustine. He succeeded the Guillaumes in business. [At the Sign of the Cat and Racket.] During the first years of the Restoration he presided over the Tribunal of Commerce. Joseph Lebas, who was intimate with M. and Madame Birotteau, attended their ball with his wife. He also strove for César's rehabilitation. [César Birotteau.] During the reign of Louis Philippe, having for an intimate friend Célestin Crevel, he retired from business and lived at Corbeil. [Cousin Betty.]

Lebas (Madame Joseph), wife of the preceding, born Virginie Guillaume in 1784, elder of Guillaume's daughters, lived at the Cat and Racket; the counterpart, physically and morally, of her mother. Under the First Empire, at the parish church of Saint-Leu, Paris, her marriage took place on the same day that her younger sister, Augustine de Sommervieux, was wedded. The love which she felt for her husband was not reciprocated. She viewed with indifference her sister's misfortunes, became intimate in turn with the Birotteaus and the Crevels; and, having retired from business, spent her last days in the middle of Louis Philippe's reign at Corbeil. [At the Sign of the Cat and Racket. César Birotteau. Cousin Betty.]

---

[1] The names of Virginie and Augustine are confused in the original text.

Lebas, probably a son of the preceding. In 1836 first assistant of the king's solicitor at Sancerre; two years later counselor to the court of Paris. In 1838 he would have married Hortense Hulot if Crevel had not prevented the match. [The Muse of the Department. Cousin Betty.]

Lebœuf, for a long time connected with the prosecuting attorney at Nantes, being president of the court there in the latter part of Louis Philippe's reign. He was well acquainted with the Camusot de Marvilles, and knew Maitre Fraisier, who claimed his acquaintance in 1845. [Cousin Pons.]

Lebrun, sub-lieutenant, then captain in the Seventy-second demi-brigade, commanded by Hulot during the war against the Chouans in 1799. [The Chouans.]

Lebrun, division-chief in the War Department in 1838. Marneffe was one of his employés. [Cousin Betty.]

Lebrun, protégé, friend and disciple of Doctor Bouvard. Being a physician at the prison in May, 1830, he was called upon to establish the death of Lucien de Rubempré. [Scenes from a Courtesan's Life.] In 1845 Lebrun was chief physician of the Parisian boulevard theatre, managed by Félix Gaudissart. [Cousin Pons.]

Lecamus (Baron de Tresnes), counselor to the royal court of Paris, lived, in 1816, rue Chanoinesse, with Madame de la Chanterie. Known there by the name of Joseph, he was a Brother of Consolation in company with Montauran, Alain, Abbé de Véze and Godefroid. [The Seamy Side of History.]

Lechesneau, through the influence of Cambacérés and Bonaparte, appointed attorney-general in Italy, but as a result of his many disreputable love-affairs, despite his real capacity for office-holding, he was forced to give up his position. Between the end of the Republic and the beginning of the Empire he became head of the grand jury at Troyes. Lechesneau, who had been repeatedly bribed by Senator Malin, had to occupy himself in 1806 with the Hauteserre-Simeuse-Michu affair. [The Gondreville Mystery.]

Leclerq, native of Bourgogne, commissioner for the vintners in the department to which Ville-aux-Fayes, a sub-prefecture of this same province, belonged. He was of service to Gaubertin, Madame Soudry, also Rigou, perhaps, and was in turn under obligations to them. Having arranged a partnership he founded the house of "Leclerq & Company," on Quai de Béthune, Ile Saint-Louis, Paris, in competition with the well-known house of Grandet. In 1815 Leclerq married Jenny Gaubertin. As a banker he dealt in wine commissions, and became regent of the National Bank. During the Restoration he represented as deputy on the Left Centre the district of Ville-aux-Fayes, and not far from the sub-prefecture, in 1823, bought a large estate, which brought thirty thousand francs rental. [The Peasantry.]

Leclerq (Madame), wife of the preceding, born Jenny Gaubertin, eldest daughter of Gaubertin, steward of Aigues in Bourgogne, received two hundred thousand francs as dowry. [The Peasantry.]

Leclerq, brother-in-law of the preceding, during the Restoration was special collector at Ville-aux-Fayes, Bourgogne, and joined the other members of his family in worrying, more or less, the Comte de Montcornet. [The Peasantry.]

Lecocq, a trader, whose failure was very cleverly foretold by Guillaume at the Cat and Racket. This failure was Guillaume's Battle of Marengo. [At the Sign of the Cat and Racket.]

Lefebvre, Louis Lambert's uncle, was successively oratorian, sworn priest and curé of Mer, a small city near Blois. Had a delightful disposition and a heart of rare tenderness. He exercised a watchful care over the childhood and youth of his remarkable nephew. The Abbé Lefebvre later on lived at Blois, the Restoration having caused him to lose his position. In 1822, under form of a letter sent from Croisic, he was the first to receive information concerning the Cambremers. The next year, having become much older in appearance, while riding in a stage-coach he told of the frightful state of suffering, sometimes mingled with remarkable dis-

plays of intellect, which preceded the death of Louis Lambert.
[Louis Lambert.   A Seaside Tragedy.]

Lefebvre (Robert), well-known French painter of the First
Empire.   In 1806, at the expense of Laurence de Cinq-
Cygne, he painted Michu's portrait.   [The Gondreville Mystery.]   Among the many paintings executed by Robert
Lefebvre is a portrait of Hulot d'Ervy dressed in the uniform
of chief commissary of the Imperial Guard.   This is dated
1810.   [Cousin Betty.]

Léganès (Marquis de), Spanish grandee, married, father
of two daughters, Clara and Mariquita, and of three sons,
Juanito, Philippe and Manuel.   He manifested a spirit of
patriotism in the war carried on against the French during
the Empire and died then under the most tragic circumstances,
in which Mariquita was an unwilling abettor.   The Marquis
de Léganés died by the hand of his eldest son, who had been
condemned to be his executioner.   [El Verdugo.]

Léganès (Marquise de), wife of the preceding and condemned to die with the other members of the family by
the hand of her eldest son.   She spared him the necessity
of doing this horrible deed of war by committing suicide.
[El Verdugo.]

Léganès (Clara de), daughter of the preceding couple;
also shared the condemnation of the Marquis de Léganés
and died by the hand of Juanito.   [El Verdugo.]

Léganès (Mariquita de), sister of the preceding, had rescued
Major Victor Marchand of the French infantry from danger
in 1808.   In testimony of his gratitude he was able to obtain
pardon for one member of the Léganés family, but with the
horribly cruel provision that the one spared should become
executioner of the rest of the family.   [El Verdugo.]

Léganès (Juanito de), brother of the last-named, born
in 1778.   Small and of poor physique, of gentlemanly
manners, yet proud and scornful, he was gifted with that
delicacy of feeling which in the olden times caused Spanish

gallantry to be so well known. Upon the earnest request of his proud-spirited family he consented to execute his father, his two sisters and his two brothers. Juanito only was saved from death, that his family might not become extinct. [El Verdugo.]

Léganès (Philippe de), younger brother of the preceding, born in 1788, a noble Spaniard condemned to death; executed by his elder brother in 1808, during the war waged against the French. [El Verdugo.]

Léganès (Manuel de), born in 1800, youngest of the five Léganés children, suffered, in 1808, during the war waged by the French in Spain, the fate of his father, the marquis, and of his elder brother and sisters. The youngest scion of this noble family died by the hand of Jnanito de Léganés. [El Verdugo.]

Léger, extensive farmer of Beaumont-sur-Oise, married daughter of Reybert, Moreau's successor as exciseman of the Presles estate, belonging to the Comte de Sérizy; had by his wife a daughter who became, in 1838, Madame Joseph Bridau. [A Start in Life.]

Legrelu, a bald-headed man, tall and good-looking; in 1840 became a vintner in Paris on rue des Canettes, corner of rue Guisarde. Toupillier, Madame Cardinal's uncle, the "pauper of Saint-Sulpice," was his customer. [The Middle Classes.]

Lelewel, a nineteenth century revolutionist, head of the Polish Republican party in Paris in 1835. One of his friends· was Doctor Moïse Halpersohn. [The Imaginary Mistress. The Seamy Side of History.]

Lemarchand. (*See* Tours, Miniéres des.)

Lemire, professor of drawing in the Imperial Lyceum, Paris, in 1812; foresaw the talent of Joseph Bridau, one of his pupils, for painting, and threw the future artist's mother into consternation by telling her of this fact. [A Bachelor's Establishment.]

Lempereur, in 1819, Chaussée-d'Antin, Paris, clerk to Charles Claparon, at that time "straw-man" of Tillet, Roguin & Company. [César Birotteau.]

Lemprun, born in 1745, son-in-law of Galard, market-gardener of Auteuil. Employed, in turn, in the houses of Thélusson and of Keller in Paris, he was probably the first messenger in the service of the Bank of France, having entered that establishment when it was founded. He met Mademoiselle Brigitte Thuillier during this period of his life, and in 1814 gave Céleste, his only daughter, in marriage to Brigitte's brother, Louis-Jérôme Thuillier. M. Lemprun died the year following. [The Middle Classes.]

Lemprun (Madame), wife of the preceding, daughter of Galard, the market-gardener of Auteuil, mother of one child— Madame Céleste Thuillier. She lived in the village of Auteuil from 1815 until the time of her death in 1829. She reared Céleste Phellion, daughter of L.-J. Thuillier and of Madame de Colleville. Madame Lemprun left a small fortune inherited from her father, M. Galard, which was administered by Brigitte Thuillier. This Lemprun estate consisted of twenty thousand francs, saved by the strictest economy, and of a house which was sold for twenty-eight thousand francs. [The Middle Classes.]

Lemulquinier, a native of Flanders, owed his name to the linen-yarn dealers of that province, who are called *mulquiniers.* He lived in Douai, was the valet of Balthazar Claés, and encouraged and aided his master in his foolish investigations, despite the extreme coldness of his own nature and the opposition of Josette, Martha, and the women of the Claés family. Lemulquinier even went so far as to give all of his personal property to M. Claés. [The Quest of the Absolute.]

Lenoncourt (De), born in 1708, marshal of France, marquis at first, then duke, was the friend of Victor-Amédée de Verneuil, and adopted Marie de Verneuil, the acknowledged natural daughter of his old comrade, when the latter died.

Suspected unjustly of being this young girl's lover, the septuagenarian refused to marry her, and leaving her behind, he changed his place of residence to Coblentz. [The Chouans.]

Lenoncourt (Duc de), father of Madame de Mortsauf. The early part of the Restoration was the brilliant period of his career. He obtained a peerage, owned a house in Paris on rue Saint-Dominique-Saint-Germain, looked after Birotteau and found him a situation just after his failure. Lenoncourt played for the favor of Louis XVIII., was first gentleman in the king's chamber, and welcomed Victurnien d'Esgrignon, with whom he had some relationship. The Duc de Lenoncourt was, in 1835, visiting the Princesse de Cadignan, when Marsay explained the reasons the political order had for the mysterious kidnapping of Gondreville. Three years later he died a very old man. [The Lily of the Valley. César Birotteau. Jealousies of a Country Town. The Gondreville Mystery. Béatrix.]

Lenoncourt (Duchesse de), wife of the preceding, born in 1758, of a cold, severe, insincere, ambitious nature, was almost always unkind to her daughter, Madame de Mortsauf. [The Lily of the Valley.]

Lenoncourt-Givry (Duc de), youngest son of M. and Madame de Chaulieu, at first followed a military career. Titles and names in abundance came to him. In 1827 he married Madeleine de Mortsauf, the only heir of her parents. [Letters of Two Brides.] The Duc de Lenoncourt-Givry was a man of some importance in the Paris of Louis Philippe and was invited to the festival at the opening of Josépha Mirah's new house, rue de la Ville-l'Evêque. [Cousin Betty.] The year following attention was still turned towards him indirectly, when Sallenauve was contending in defence of the duke's brother-in-law. [The Member for Arcis.]

Lenoncourt-Givry (Duchesse de), wife of the preceding, bore the first name of Madeleine. Madame de Lenoncourt-Givry was one of two children of the Comte and Comtesse de Mortsauf. She lived almost alone in her family, having lost at an early age her mother, then her brother Jacques. While passing her girlhood in Touraine, she met Félix de Vandenesse, from whom she knew how to keep aloof on becoming an orphan. Her inheritance of names, titles and wealth brought about her marriage with the youngest son of M. and Madame de Chaulieu in 1827, and established for her a friendship with the Grandlieus, whose daughter, Clotilde, accompanied her to Italy about 1830. During the first day of their journey the arrest of Lucien Chardon de Rubempré took place under their eyes near Bouron, Seine-et-Marne. [The Lily of the Valley. Letters of Two Brides. Scenes from a Courtesan's Life.]

Lenormand was court registrar at Paris during the Restoration, and did Comte Octave de Bauvan a service by passing himself off as owner of a house on rue Saint-Maur, which belonged in reality to the count and where the wife of that high magistrate lived, at that time being separated from her husband. [Honorine.]

Léopold, a character in " L'Ambitieux par Amour," a novel by Albert Savarus, was Maitre Léopold Hannequin. The author pictured him as having a strong passion—imaginary or true—for the mother of Rodolphe, the hero of this autobiographical novel, published by the "Revue de l'Est" under the reign of Louis Philippe. [Albert Savarus.]

Lepas (Madame de), for a long time keeper of a tavern at Vendôme, of Flemish physique; acquainted with M. and Madame de Merret, and furnished information about them to Doctor Horace Bianchon; Comte Bagos de Férédia, who died so tragically, having been a lodger in her house. She was also interviewed by the author, who, under the name of Valentine, gave on the stage of the Gymnase-Dramatique the story of the incontinence and punishment of Joséphine de Merret. This Vendôme tavern-keeper pretended also to have lodged some princesses, M. Decazes, Général Bertrand, the King of Spain, and the Duc and Duchesse d'Abrantès. [La Grande Bretéche. Another Study of Woman.]

Lepître, strong Royalist, had some relations with M. de Vandenesse, when.they wished to rescue Marie-Antoinette from the Temple. Later, under the Empire, having become head of an academy, in the old Joyeuse house, Quartier Saint-Antoine, Paris, Lepître counted among his pupils a son of M. de Vandenesse, Félix. Lepître was fat, like Louis XVIII., and club-footed. [The Lily of the Valley.]

Lepître (Madame), wife of the preceding, reared Félix de Vandenesse. [The Lily of the Valley.]

Leprince (Monsieur and Madame). M. Leprince was a Parisian auctioneer towards the end of the Empire and at the beginning of the Restoration. He finally sold his business at a great profit; but being injured by one of Nucingen's failures, he lost in some speculations on the Bourse some of the profits that he had realized. He was the father-in-law of Xavier Rabourdin, whose fortune he risked in these dangerous speculations, that his son-in-law's domestic comfort might be increased. Crushed by misfortune he died under Louis XVIII., leaving some rare paintings which beautified the parlor of his children's home on rue Duphot. Madame Leprince, who died before the bankrupt auctioneer, a distinguished woman and a natural artist, worshiped and, consequently, spoiled her only child, Célestine, who became Madame Xavier Rabourdin. She communicated to her daughter some of her own tastes, and thoughtlessly, perhaps, developed in her a love of luxury, intelligent and refined. [The Government Clerks.]

Leroi (Pierre), called also Marche-à-terre, a Fougéres Chouan, who played an important part during the civil war of 1799 in Bretagne, where he gave evidence of courage and heartlessness. He survived the tragedy of this period, for he was seen on the Place d'Alençon in 1809 when Cibot —Pille-Miche—was tried at the bar as a chauffeur and attempted to escape. In 1827, nearly twenty years later, this same Pierre Leroi was known as a peaceable cattle-trader in the markets of his province. [The Chouans. The Seamy Side of History. Jealousies of a Country Town.]

Leroi (Madame), mother of the preceding, being ill, was cured on coming to Fougéres to pray under the oak of the Patte-d'Oie. This tree was decorated with a beautiful wooden image of the Virgin, placed there in memory of Sainte-Anne d'Auray's appearance in this place. [The Chouans.]

Leseigneur de Rouville (Baronne), pensionless widow of a sea-captain who had died at Batavia, under the Republic, during a prolonged engagement with an English vessel; mother of Madame Hippolyte Schinner. Early in the nineteenth century she lived at Paris with her unmarried daughter, Adélaïde. On the fourth story of a house belonging to Molineux, on rue de Surène, near the Madeleine, Madame Leseigneur occupied unadorned and gloomy apartments. There she frequently received Hippolyte Schinner, Messieurs du Halga and de Kergarouët. She received from two of these friends many delicate marks of sympathy, despite the gossip of the neighbors who were astonished that Madame de Rouville and her daughter should have different names, and shocked by their very suspicious behavior. The manner in which Mesdames Leseigneur recognized the good offices of Schinner led to his marriage with Mademoiselle de Rouville. [The Purse.]

Leseigneur (Adélaïde). (*See* Schinner, Madame Hippolyte.)

Lesourd, married the eldest daughter of Madame Guénée of Provins, and toward the end of the Restoration presided over the justice court of that city, of which he had first been king's attorney. In 1828 he was able, indeed, to defend Pierrette Lorrain, thus showing his opposition to the local Liberalist leadérs, represented by Rogron, Vinet and Gourand. [Pierrette.]

Lesourd (Madame), wife of the preceding and eldest daughter of Madame Guénée; for a long time called in Provins, "the little Madame Lesourd." [Pierrette.]

Léveillé (Jean-François), notary in Alençon, inflexible

correspondent of the Royalists of Normandie under the Empire. He issued arms to them, received the surname of Confesseur, and, in 1809, was put to death with others as the result of a judgment rendered by Bourlac. [The Seamy Side of History.]

Levrault, enriched by the iron industry in Paris, died in 1813; former owner of the house in Nemours which came into the possession finally of Doctor Minoret, who lived there in 1815. [Ursule Mirouët.]

Levrault-Crémière, related to the preceding, an old miller, who became a Royalist under the Restoration; he was mayor of Nemours from 1829 to 1830, and was replaced after the Revolution of July by the notary, Crémière-Dionis. [Ursule Mirouët.]

Levrault-Levrault, eldest son, thus named to distinguish him from his numerous relatives of the same name; he was a butcher in Nemours in 1829, when Ursule Mirouët was undergoing persecution. [Ursule Mirouët.]

Liautard (Abbé), in the first years of the nineteenth century was at the head of an institution of learning in Paris; had among his pupils Godefroid, Madame de la Chanterie's lodger in 1836 and the future Brother of Consolation. [The Seamy Side of History.]

Lina (Duc de), an Italian, at Milan early in the century, one of the lovers of La Marana, the mother of Madame Diard. [The Maranas.]

Lindet (Jean-Baptiste-Robert, called Robert), member of the Legislature and of the Convention, born at Bernay in 1743, died at Paris in 1825; minister of finance under the Republic, weakened Antoine and the Poiret brothers by giving them severe work, although twenty-five years later they were still laboring in the Treasury. [The Government Clerks.]

Lisieux (François), called the Grand-Fils (grandson), a rebel of the department of Mayenne; chauffeur under the

First Empire and connected with the Royalist insurrection in the West, which caused Madame de la Chanterie's imprisonment. [The Seamy Side of History.]

Listomère (Marquis de), son of the "old Marquise de Listomère"; deputy of the majority under Charles X., with hopes of a peerage; husband of Mademoiselle de Vandenesse the elder, his cousin. One evening in 1828, in his own house on rue Saint-Dominique, he was quietly reading the "Gazette de France" without noticing the flirtation carried on at his side by his wife and Eugéne de Rastignac, then twenty-five years old. [The Lily of the Valley. A Distinguished Provincial at Paris. A Study of Woman.]

Listomère (Marquise de), wife of the preceding, elder of M. de Vandenesse's daughters, and sister of Charles and Félix. Like her husband and cousin, during the early years of the Restoration, she was a brilliant type of the period, combining, as she did, godliness with worldliness, occasionally figuring in politics, and concealing her youth under the guise of austerity. However, in 1828, her mask seemed to fall at the moment when Madame de Mortsauf died; for, then, she wrongly fancied herself the object of Eugéne de Rastignac's wooing. Under Louis Philippe she took part in an intrigue formed for the purpose of throwing her sister-in-law, Marie de Vandenesse, into the power of Raoul Nathan. [The Lily of the Valley. Lost Illusions. A Distinguished Provincial at Paris. A Study of Woman. A Daughter of Eve.]

Listomère (Marquis de), mother-in-law of the preceding, born Grandlieu. She lived in Paris at an advanced age in Ile Saint-Louis, during the early years of the nineteenth century; received on his holidays her grand-nephew, Félix de Vandenesse, then a student, and frightened him by the solemn or frigid appearance of everything about her. [The Lily of the Valley.]

Listomère (Baronne de), had been the wife of a lieutenant-general. As a widow she lived in the city of Tours under the Restoration, assuming all the grand airs of the past centuries. She helped the Birotteau brothers. In 1823 she received the army paymaster, Gravier, and the terrible Spanish husband who killed the French surgeon, Béga. Madame de Listomère died, and her wish to make François Birotteau her partial heir was not executed. [The Vicar of Tours. César Birotteau. The Muse of the Department.]

Listomère (Baron de), nephew of the preceding, born in 1791; was in turn lieutenant and captain in the navy. During a leave of absence spent with his aunt at Tours he began to intervene in favor of the persecuted abbé, François Birotteau, but finally opposed him upon learning of the power of the Congregation, and that the priest's name figured in Baronne de Listomère's will. [The Vicar of Tours.]

Listomère (Comtesse de), old, lived in Saint-Germain suburbs of Paris, in 1839. At the Austrian embassy she became acquaintéd with Rastignac, Madame de Nucingen, Ferdinand du Tillet and Maxime de Trailles. [The Member for Arcis.]

Listomère-Landon (Marquise de), born in Provence, 1744; lady of the eighteenth century aristocracy, had been the friend of Duclos and Maréchal de Richelieu. Later she lived in the city of Tours, where she tried to help by unbiased counsel her unsophisticated niece by marriage, the Marquise Victor d'Aiglemont. Gout and her happiness over the return of the Duc d'Angoulême caused Madame de Listomère's death in 1814. [A Woman of Thirty.]

Lolotte. (*See* Topinard, Madame.)

Longueville (De), noble and illustrious family, whose last scion, the Duc de Rostein-Limbourg, executed in 1793, belonged to the younger branch. [The Ball at Sçeaux.]

Longueville, deputy under Charles X., son of an attorney, without authority placed the particle *de* before his name. M. Longueville was connected with the house of Palma, Werbrust & Co.; he was the father of Auguste, Maximilien and Clara; desired a peerage for himself and a minister's daughter for his elder son, who had an income of fifty thousand francs. [The Ball at Sçeaux.]

Longueville (Auguste), son of the preceding, born late in the eighteenth century, possessed an income of fifty thousand francs; married, probably a minister's daughter; was secretary of an embassy; met Madame Emilie de Vandenesse during a vacation which he was spending in Paris, and told her the secret of his family. Died young, while employed in the Russian embassy. [The Ball at Sçeaux.]

Longueville (Maximilien), one of Longueville's three children, sacrificed himself for his brother and sister; entered business, lived on rue du Sentier—then no longer called rue du Groschenet; was employed in a large linen establishment, situated near rue de la Paix; fell passionately in love with Emilie de Fontaine, who became Madame Charles de Vandenesse. She ceased to reciprocate his passion upon learning that he was merely a novelty clerk. However, M. Longueville, as a result of the early death of his father and of his brother, became a banker, a member of the nobility, a peer, and finally the Vicomte "Guiraudin de Longueville." [The Ball at Sçeaux.]

Longueville (Clara), sister of the preceding; she was probably born during the Empire; was a very refined young woman of frail constitution, but good complexion; lived in the time of the Restoration; was companion and protégée of her elder brother, Maximilien, future Vicomte Guiraudin, and was cordially received at the Planat de Baudry's pavilion, situated in the valley of Sçeaux, where she was a good friend of the last unmarried heiress of Comte de Fontaine. [The Ball at Sçeaux.]

Lora (Léon de), born in 1806, descendant of a noble family of Roussillon, of Spanish origin; penniless son of Comte Fernand Didas y Lora and Léonie de Lora, born Gazonal; younger brother of Juan de Lora, nephew of Mademoiselle Urraca y Lora; he left his native country at an early age. His family, with the exception of his mother, who died, remained at home long after his departure, but he never inquired concerning them.   He went to Paris, where, having entered the artist, Schinner's, studio, under the name of Mistigris, he became celebrated for his animation and repartée. From 1820 he shone in this way, rarely leaving Joseph Bridau —a friend whom he accompanied to the Comte de Sérizy's at Presles in the valley of Oise.   Later Léon protected his very sympathetic but commonplace countryman, Pierre Grassou. In 1830 he became a celebrity.   Arthez entrusted to him the decoration of a castle, and Léon de Lora forthwith showed himself to be a master.   Some years later he took·a tour through Italy with Félicité des Touches and Claude Vignon. Being present when the domestic troubles of the Bauvans were recounted, Lora was able to give a finished analysis of Honorine's character to M. de l'Hostal.   Being a guest at all the social feasts and receptions he was in attendance at one of Mademoiselle Brisetout's gatherings on rue Chauchat.   There he met Bixiou, Etienne· Lousteau, Stidmann and Vernisset.   He visited the Hulots frequently and their intimate friends.   With the aid of Joseph Bridau he rescued W. Steinbock from Clichy, saw him marry Hortense, and was invited to the second marriage of Valérie Marneffe.   He was then the greatest living painter of landscapes and sea-pieces, a prince of repartée and dissipation, and dependent on Bixiou.   Fabien du Ronceret gave to him the ornamentation of an apartment on rue Blanche. Wealthy, illustrious, living on rue Berlin, the neighbor of Joseph Bridau and Schinner, member of the Institute, officer of the Legion of Honor, Léon, assisted by Bixiou, received his cousin Palafox Gazonal, and pointed out to him many well-known people about town.   [The Unconscious Humorists.   A Bachelor's Establishment.   A Start in Life.   Pierre Grassou.   Honorine.   Cousin Betty.   Béatrix.]

Lora (Don Juan de), elder brother of the preceding, spent his whole life in Roussillon, his native country; in the presence of their cousin, Palafox Gazonal, denied that his younger brother, "le petit Léon," possessed great artistic ability. [The Unconscious Humorists.]

Loraux (Abbé), born in 1752, of unattractive bearing, yet the very soul of tenderness. Confessor of the pupils of the Lycée Henry IV., and of Agathe Bridau, for twenty-two years vicar of Saint-Sulpice at Paris; in 1818 confessor of César Birotteau; became in 1819 curé of the Blancs-Manteaux in Marais parish. He thus became a neighbor of Octave de Bauvan, in whose home he placed in 1824 M. de l'Hostal, his nephew and adopted son. Loraux, who was the means of restoring to Banvan the Comtesse Honorine, received her confessions. He died in 1830, she being his nurse at the time. [A Start in Life. A Bachelor's Establishment. César Birotteau. Honorine.]

Lorrain, petty merchant of Pen-Hoël in the beginning of the nineteenth century; married and had a son, whose wife and child, Pierrette, he took care of after his son's death. Lorrain was completely ruined later, and took refuge in a home for the old and needy, confiding Pierrette, both of whose parents were now dead, to the care of some near relatives, the Rogrons of Provins. Lorrain's death took place previously to that of his wife. [Pierrette.]

Lorrain (Madame), wife of the preceding, and grandmother of Pierrette; born about 1757; lived the simple life of her husband, to whom she bore some resemblance. A widow towards the end of the Restoration, she became comfortably situated after the return of Collinet of Nantes. Upon going to Provins to recover her granddaughter, she found her dying; went into retirement in Paris, and died soon after, making Jacques Brigaut her heir. [Pierrette.]

Lorrain, son of the preceding couple, Bretagne; captain in the Imperial Guard; major in the line; married the second daughter of a Provins grocer, Auffray, through whom he had Pierrette; died a poor man, on the battlefield of Montereau, February 18, 1814. [Pierrette.]

Lorrain (Madame), wife of the preceding and mother of Pierrette; born Auffray in 1793; half sister to the mother of Sylvie and Denis Rogrou of Provins. In 1814, a poor widow, still very young, she lived with the Lorrains of Pen-Hoël, a town in the Vendéan Marais. It is said that she was consoled by the ex-major, Brigaut, of the Catholic army, and survived the unfortunate marriage of Madame Néraud, widow of Auffray, and maternal grandmother of Pierrette, only three years. [Pierrette.]

Lorrain (Pierrette), daughter of the preceding, born in the town of Pen-Hoél in 1813; lost her father when fourteen months old and her mother when six years old; lovable disposition, delicate and unaffected. After a happy childhood, spent with her excellent maternal grandparents and a playmate, Jacques Brigaut, she was sent to some first maternal cousins of Provins, the wealthy Rogrons, who treated her with pitiless severity. Pierrette died on Easter Tuesday, March, 1828, as the result of sickness brought on by the brutality of her cousin, Sylvie Rogron, who was extremely envious of her. A trial of her persecutors followed her death, and, despite the efforts of old Madame Lorrain, Jacques Brigant, Martener, Desplein and Bianchon, her assailants escaped through the craftily exerted influence of Vinet. [Pierrette.]

Louchard, the craftiest bailiff of Paris; undertook the recovery of Esther van Gobseck, who had escaped from Frédéric de Nucingen; did business with Maître Fraisier. [Scenes from a Courtesan's Life. Cousin Pons.]

Louchard (Madame), wife of the preceding, did not live with him; acquainted with Madame Komorn de Godollo and, in 1840, furnished her information about Théodose de la Peyrade. [The Middle Classes.]

Loudon (Prince de), general in the Vendéan cavalry, lived at Le Mans during the Terror. He was brother of a Verneuil who was guillotined, was noted for "his boldness and the martyrdom of his punishment." [The Chouans. Modeste Mignon.]

Loudon (Prince Gaspard de), born in 1791, third and only surviving son of the Duc de Verneuil's four children; fat and commonplace, having, very inappropriately, the same name as the celebrated Vendéan cavalry general; became probably Desplein's son-in-law. He took part in 1829 in a great hunt given in Normandie, in company with the Hérouvilles, the Cadignans and the Mignons. [Modeste Mignon.]

Louis XVIII. (Louis-Stanislas-Xavier), born at Versailles, November 16, 1754, died September 16, 1824, King of France. He was in political relations with Alphonse de Montauran, Malin de Gondreville, and some time before this, under the name of the Comte de Lille, with the Baronne de la Chanterie. He considered Peyrade an able officer and was his patron. King Louis XVIII., friend of the Comte de Fontaine, engaged Félix de Vandenesse as secretary. His last mistress was the Comtesse Ferraud. [The Chouans. The Seamy Side of History. The Gondreville Mystery. Scenes from a Courtesan's Life. The Ball at Sçeaux. The Lily of the Valley. Colonel Chabert. The Government Clerks.]

Louise, during the close of Louis Philippe's reign, was Madame W. Steinbock's waiting-maid at Paris, rue Louis-le-Grand, and was courted by Hulot d'Ervy's cook, at the time when Agathe Piquetard, who was destined to become the second Baronne Hulot, was another servant. [Cousin Betty.]

Lourdois, during the Empire wealthy master-painter of interiors; contractor with thirty thousand francs income; of Liberal views. Charged an enormous sum for the famous decorations in César Birotteau's apartments, where he was a guest with his wife and daughter at the grand ball of December 17, 1818. After the failure of the perfumer, a little later, he treated him somewhat slightingly. [At the Sign of the Cat and Racket. César Birotteau.]

Lousteau, sub-delegate at Issoudun and afterwards the intimate friend of Doctor Rouget, at that time his enemy, because the doctor was possibly the father of Mademoiselle Agathe Rouget, then become Madame Bridau. Lousteau died in 1800. [A Bachelor's Establishment.]

Lousteau (Etienne), son of the preceding, born at Sancerre in 1799, nephew of Maximilienne Hochon, born Lousteau, school-mate of Doctor Bianchon. Urged on by his desire for a literary vocation, he entered Paris without money, in 1819, made a beginning with poetry, was the literary partner of Victor Ducange in a melodrama played at the Gaitè in 1821, undertook the editing of a small paper devoted to the stage, of which Andoche Finot was proprietor. He had at that time two homes, one in the Quartier Latin, rue de la Harpe, above the Servel café, another on rue de Bondy, with Florine his mistress. Not having a better place, he became at times Flicoteaux's guest, in company with Daniel d'Arthez and especially Lucien de Rubempré, whom he trained, piloted, and introduced to Dauriat, in fact, whose first steps he aided, not without feeling regret later in life. For one thousand francs per month, Lousteau rid Philippe Bridau of his wife, Flore, placing her in a house of ill-fame. He was at the Opéra, the evening of the masque ball of the year 1824, where Blondet, Bixiou, Rastignac, Jacques Collin, Châtelet and Madame d'Espard discovered Lucien de Rubempré with Esther Gobseck. Lousteau wrote criticisms, did work for various reviews, and for Raoul Nathan's gazette. He lived on rue des Martyrs, and was Madame Schontz's lover. He obtained by some little intrigue a deputyship at Sancerre; carried on a long liaison with Dinah de la Baudraye; just escaped a marriage with Madame Berthier, then Félicie Cardot; was father of Madame de la Baudraye's children, and spoke as follows concerning the birth of the eldest: "Madame la Baronne de la Baudraye is happily delivered of a child; M. Etienne Lousteau has the honor of announcing it." During this liaison, Lousteau, for the sum of five hundred francs, gave to Fabien du Roncerct a discourse to be read at a horticultural exhibition, for which the latter was decorated. He attended a house-warming at Mademoiselle Brisetout's, rue Chauchat; asked Dinah and Nathan for the purpose or moral of the "Prince of Bohemia." Loustean's manner of living underwent little change when Madame de la Baudraye left him. He heard Maitre Desroches recount one of Cérizet's adventures, saw Madame Marneffe marry Crevel, took charge of the "Echo de la Biévre," and undertook the managment of a theatre with Ridal, the author of vaudevilles. [A Distinguished Provincial at Paris. A Bachelor's Establishment. Scenes from a Courtesan's Life. A Daughter of Eve. Béatrix. The Muse of the Department. Cousin Betty. A Prince of Bohemia. A Man of Business. The Middle Classes. The Unconscious Humorists.]

Luigia, young and beautiful Roman girl of the suburbs, wife of Benedetto, who claimed the right of selling her. She tried to kill herself at the same time she killed him, but did not succeed. Charles de Sallenauve—Dorlange—protected her, taking care of her when she became a widow, and made her his housekeeper in 1839. Luigia soon left her benefactor, the voice of slander having accused them in their mutually innocent relations. [The Member for Arcis.]

Lupeaulx (Clément Chardin des), officer and politician, born about 1785; left in good circumstances by his father; who was ennobled by Louis XV., his coat-of-arms showing "a ferocious wolf of sable. bearing a lamb in its jaws," with this motto: "En lupus in historia." A shrewd and ambitious man, ready for all enterprises, even the most compromising, Clément des Lupeaulx knew how to make himself of service to Louis XVIII. in several delicate undertakings. Many influential members of the aristocracy placed in his hands their difficult business and their lawsuits. He served thus as mediator between the Duc de Navarreins and Polydore Milaud de la Baudraye, and attained a kind of mightiness that Annette seemed to fear would be disastrous to Charles Grandet. He accumulated duties and ranks, was master of petitions in the Council of State, secretary-general to the minister of finance, colonel in the National Guard, government commissioner in a joint-stock company; also provided with an inspectorship in the king's house, he became Chevalier de Saint-Louis and officer of the Legion of Honor. An open follower of Voltaire, but an attendant at mass, at all times a Bertrand in pursuit of a Raton, egotistic and vain, a glutton and a libertine, this man of intellect, sought after in all social circles, a kind of minister's "household drudge," openly lived, until 1825, a life of pleasure and anxiety, striving for political success and love conquests. As mistresses he is known to have had Esther van Gobseck, Flavie Colleville; perhaps, even, the Marquise d'Espard. He was seen at the Opéra ball in the winter of 1824, at which Lucien de Rubempré reappeared. The close of this year brought about considerable change in the Secretary-General's affairs. Crippled by debt, and in the power of Gobseck, Bidault and Mitral, he was forced to give up one of the treasury departments to Isidore Baudoyer, despite his personal liking for Rabourdin. He gained as a result of this stroke a coronet and a deputy-ship. He had ambitions for a peerage, the title of gentleman of the king's chamber, a membership in the Academy of Inscriptions and Belles-lettres, and the commander's cross. [The Muse of the Department. Eugénie Grandet. A Bachelor's Establishment. A Distinguished Provincial at Paris. The Government Clerks. Scenes from a Courtesan's Life. Ursule Mirouët.]

Lupeaulx (Des), nephew of the preceding, and, thanks to him, appointed sub-prefect of Ville-aux-Fayes, Bourgogne, in 1821, in the department presided over successively by Martial de la Roche-Hugon and Casteran. As Gaubertin's prospective son-in-law, M. des Lupeaulx, espousing the cause of his fiancée's family, was instrumental in disgusting Montcornet, owner of Aigues, with his property. [The Peasantry.]

Lupin, born in 1778, son of the last steward of the Soulanges in Bourgogne; in time he became manager of the domain, notary and deputy mayor of the city of Soulanges. Although married and a man of family, M. Lupin, still in excellent physical condition, was, in 1823, a brilliant figure in Madame Soudry's reception-room, where he was known for his tenor voice and his extreme gallantries—the latter characteristic being proved by two liaisons carried on with two middle-class women, Madame Sarcus, wife of Sarcus the Rich, and Euphémie Plissoud. [The Peasantry.]

Lupin (Madame), wife of the preceding, called "Bebelle;" only daughter of a salt-merchant enriched by the Revolution; had a platonic affection for the chief clerk, Bonnac. Madame Lupin was fat, awkward, of very ordinary appearance, and weak intellectually. On account of these characteristics Lupin and the Soudry adherents neglected her. [The Peasantry.]

Lupin (Amaury), only son of the preceding couple, perhaps the lover of Adéline Sarcus, who became Madame Adolphe Sibilet; was on the point of marrying one of Gaubertin's daughters, the same one, doubtless, that was wooed and won by M. des Lupeaulx. In the midst of this liaison and of these matrimonial designs, Amaury Lupin was sent to Paris in 1822 by his father to study the notary's profession with Maitre Crottat, where he had for a companion another clerk, Georges Marest, with whom he committed some indiscretions and went into debt. Amaury went with his friend to the Lion d'Argent, rue d'Enghien in the Saint-Denis section, when Marest took Pierrotin's carriage to Isle-Adam. On the way they met Oscar Husson, and made fun of him. The following year Amaury Lupin returned to Soulanges in Bourgogne. [The Peasantry. A Start in Life.]

M

Machillot (Madame), kept in Paris, in 1838, in the Notre Dame-des-Champs neighborhood, a modest restaurant, which was patronized by Godefroid on account of its nearness to Bourlac's house. [The Seamy Side of History.]

Macumer (Felipe Hénarez, Baron de), Spanish descendant of the Moors, about whom much information has been furnished by Talleyrand; had a right to names and titles as follows: Hénarez, Duc de Soria, Baron de Macumer. He never used all of them; for his entire youth was a succession of sacrifices, misfortunes and undue trials. Macumer, a leading Spanish revolutionist of 1823, saw fortune turn against him. Ferdinand VII., once more enthroned, recognized him as constitutional minister, but never forgave him for his assumption of power. Seeing his property confiscated and himself banished, he took refuge in Paris, where he took poor lodgings on rue Hillerin-Bertin and began to teach Spanish for a living, notwithstanding he was Baron de Sardaigne with large estates and a palace at Sassari. Macumer also suffered many heart-aches. He vainly loved a woman who was beloved by his own brother. His brother's passion being reciprocated, Macumer sacrificed himself for their happiness. Under the simple name of Hénarez, Macumer was the instructor of Armande-Marie-Louise de Chaulieu, whom he did not woo in vain. He married her, March, 1825. At various times the baron occupied or owned Chantepleurs, a château Nivernais, a house on rue du Bac, and La Crampade, Louis de l'Estorade's residence in Provençe. The foolish, annoying jealousy of Madame de Macumer embittered his life and was responsible for his physical break-down. Idolized by his wife, in spite of his marked plainness, he died in 1829. [Letters of Two Brides.]

Macumer (Baronne de). (*See* Gaston, Madame Marie.)

Madeleine, first name of Madeleine Vinet, by which she was called while employed as a domestic. [Scenes from a Courtesan's Life. Cousin Pons.]

Madou (Angélique), woman of the masses, fat but spry; although ignorant, very shrewd in her business of selling dried fruit. At the beginning of the Restoration she lived in Paris on rue Perrin-Gasselin, where she fell prey to the usurer Bidault—Gigonnet. Angélique Madou at first dealt harshly with César Birotteau, when he was unable to pay his debts; but she congratulated him, later on, when, as a result of his revived fortunes, the perfumer settled every obligation. Angélique Madou had a little godchild, in whom she occasionally showed much interest. [César Birotteau.]

Magnan (Prosper), of Beauvais, son of a widow; chief-surgeon's assistant; executed in 1799 at Andernach on the banks of the Rhine, being the innocent victim of circumstantial evidence, which condemned him for the double crime of robbery and murder—this crime having, in reality, been committed by his comrade, Jean-Frédéric-Taillefer, who escaped punishment. [The Red Inn.]

Magnan (Madame), mother of the preceding, lived at Beauvais, where she died a short time after her son's death, and previous to the arrival of Hermann, who was bringing her a letter from Prosper. [The Red Inn.]

Magus (Elie), Flemish Jew, Dutch-Belgian descent, born in 1770. He lived now at Bordeaux, now at Paris; was a merchant of costly articles, such as pictures, diamonds and curiosities. By his influence Madame Luigi Porta, born Ginevra di Piombo, obtained from a print-seller a position as colorist. Madame Evangélista engaged him to estimate the value of her jewels. He bought a copy of Rubens from Joseph Bridau and some Flemish subjects from Pierre Grassou, selling them later to Vervelli as genuine Rembrandts or Téniers; he arranged for the marriage of the artist with a cork-maker's daughter. Very wealthy, and having retired from business in 1835, he left his house on the Boulevard Bonne-Nouvelle to occupy an old dwelling on Chaussée des Minimes, now called rue de Béarn. He took with him his treasures, his daughter, Noémi, and Abramko as a guard for his property. Elie Magus was still living in 1845, when he had just acquired, in a somewhat dishonorable manner, a number of superb paintings from Sylvain Pons' collection. [The Vendetta. A Marriage Settlement. A Bachelor's Establishment. Pierre Grassou. Cousin Pons.]

Mahoudeau (Madame), in 1840, in company with Madame Cardinal, her friend, created a disturbance during one of Bobino's performances at a small theatre near the Luxembourg, where Olympe Cardinal was playing. While playing the "jeune premiére" she was recognized by her mother. [The Middle Classes.]

Mahuchet (Madame), women's shoemaker, "a very foulmouthed woman," in the language of Madame Nourrisson;

mother of seven children. After having dunned a countess, to no avail, for a hundred francs that was due her, she conceived the idea of carrying off the silverware, on display at a grand dinner to be given by her debtor one evening, as a pledge. She promptly returned, however, the silver she had taken, upon finding that it was white metal. [The Unconscious Humorists.]

Malaga, surname of Marguerite Turquet.

Malassis (Jeanne), from the country, a servant of Pingret, who was an avaricious and wealthy old peasant of the suburbs of Limoges. Mortally injured while hastening to the assistance of her master, who was robbed and murdered, she was the second victim of J.-F. Tascheron. [The Country Parson.]

Malfatti, Venetian doctor; in 1820 called into consultation with one of his fellow-physicians in France, concerning the sickness of the Duc Cataneo. [Massimilla Doni.]

Malin. (*See* Gondreville.)

Mallet, policeman in the department of Orne in 1809. Ordered to find and arrest Madame Bryond des Miniéres, he let her escape, by means of an agreement with his comrade, Ratel, who was to have aided in her capture. Having been imprisoned for this deed, Mallet was declared by Bourlac deserving of capital punishment, and was put to death the same year. [The Seamy Side of History.]

Malvaut (Jenny). (*See* Derville, Madame.)

Mancini (De), Italian, fair, effeminate, madly beloved by La Marana, who had by him a daughter, Juan-Pepita-Maria de Mancini, later Madame Diard. [The Maranas.]

Mancini (Juana-Pepita-Maria de). (*See* Diard, Madame.)

Manerville (De), born in 1731; Norman gentleman to whom the governor of Guyenne, Richelieu, married one of the wealthiest Bordeaux heiresses. He purchased a commission as major of the Gardes de la Porte, in the latter part of Louis

XV.'s reign; had by his wife a son, Paul, who was reared with austerity; emigrated, at the outbreak of the Revolution, to Martinique, but managed to save his property, Lanstrac, etc., thanks to Maitre Mathias, head-clerk of the notary. He became a widower in 1810, three years before his death. [A Marriage Settlement.]

Manerville (Paul François-Joseph, Comte de), son of the preceding, born in 1794, received his education in the college at Vendôme, finishing his work there in 1810, the year of his mother's death. He passed three years at Bordeaux with his father, who had become overbearing and avaricious; when left an orphan, he inherited a large fortune, including Lanstrac in Gironde, and a house in Paris, rue de la Pépiniére. He spent six years in Europe as a diplomat, passing his vacations in Paris, where he was intimate with Henri de Marsay, and was a lover of Paquita Valdés. There he was subject to the trifling of Madame Charles de Vandenesse, then Emilie de Fontaine; also, perhaps, met Lucien de Rubempré. In the winter of 1821 he returned to Bordeaux, where he was a social leader. Paul de Manerville received the appropriate nick-name of "le fleur des pois." Despite the good advice of his two devoted friends, Maitre Mathias and Marsay, he asked, through the instrumentality of his great-aunt, Madame de Maulincour, for the hand of Natalie Evangélista in marriage, and obtained it. After being wedded five years, he was divorced from his wife and sailed for Calcutta under the name of Camille, one of his mother's given names. [The Thirteen. The Ball at Sceaux. Lost Illusions. A Distinguished Provincial at Paris. A Marriage Settlement.]

Manerville (Comtesse Paul de), wife of the preceding, born Mademoiselle Natalie Evangélista, non-lineal descendant of the Duke of Alva, related also to the Claés. Having been spoiled as a child, and being of a sharp, domineering nature, she robbed her husband without impoverishing him. She was a leader at Paris as well as at Bordeaux. As the mistress of Félix de Vandenesse she disliked his dedication to a story, for in it he praised Madame de Mortsauf. Later, in company with Lady Dudley and Mesdames d'Espard, Charles de Vandenesse and de Listomère, she attempted to compromise the Comtesse Félix de Vandenesse, recently married, with Raoul Nathan. [A Marriage Settlement. The Lily of the Valley. A Daughter of Eve.]

Manette, under the Restoration at Clochegourde in Touraine, the Comtesse de Mortsauf's housekeeper, taking her mother's place in the care of her young master and mistress, Jacques and Madeleine de Mortsauf. [The Lily of the Valley.]

Manon. (*See* Godard, Manon.)

Manon-la-Blonde, during the last years of the Restoration a Paris prostitute, who fell violently in love with Théodore Calvi, became a receiver of stolen goods, brought to her by the companion of Jacques Collin, who committed murder also, at the time of the robbery; she thus became the indirect or,involuntary cause of the Corsican's arrest. [Scenes from a Courtesan's Life.]

Manseau (Pére), tavern-keeper at Echelles, a town in Savoie, gave aid to La Fosseuse, in her poverty, and sheltered this unfortunate woman in a barn. La Fosseuse became the protégée of Doctor Benassis. [The Country Doctor.]

Marana (La), the last of a long series of prostitutes bearing the same name; natural descendant of the Hérouvilles. She was known to have had more than one distinguished lover: Mancini, the Duc de Lina, and a king of Naples. She was notorious in Venice, Milan and Naples. She had by Mancini one child, whom he acknowledged, Juan-Pepita-Maria, and had her reared in good morals by the Lagounias, who were under obligations to her. Upon going to seek her daughter in Tarragone, Spain, she surprised the girl in company with Montefiore, but scorned to take vengeance upon him. She accepted as husband of the young girl M. Diard, who had asked for her hand. In 1823, when she was dying in the hospital at Bordeaux, Marana once more saw her daughter, still virtuous, although unhappy. [The Hated Son. The Maranas.]

Marcas (Zéphirin), born about 1803 in a Brétagne family at Vitré. In after life he supported his parents who were in poor circumstances. He received a free education in a seminary, but had no inclination for the priesthood. Carrying hardly any money he went to Paris, in 1823 or 1824, and after studying with a lawyer became his chief clerk. Later he studied men and objects in five capitals: London, Berlin, Vienna, St. Petersburg and Constantinople. For five years he was a journalist, and reported the proceedings of the "Chambres." He often visited R. de la Palférine. With women he proved to be of the passionate-timid kind. With the head of a lion, and a strong voice, he was equal as an orator to Berryer, and the superior of M. Thiers. For a long time he supplied the political ability needed by a deputy who had become a minister, but, convinced of his disloyalty, he overthrew him, only to restore him for a short time. He once more entered into polemical controversy; saw the news-papers which had sparkled with his forceful, high-minded criticism die; and lived miserably upon a daily allowance of thirty sous, earned by copying for the Palais. Marcas lived at that time, 1836, in the garret of a furnished house on rue Corneille. His thankless debtor, become minister again, sought him anew. Had it not been for the hearty attention of his young neighbors, Rabourdin and Juste, who furnished him with some necessary clothing, and aided him at Humann's expense, Marcas would not have taken advantage of the new opportunity that was offered him. His new position lasted but a short time. The third fall of the government hastened that of Marcas. Lodged once more on rue Corneille he was taken with a nervous fever. The sickness increased and finally carried away this unrecognized genius. Z. Marcas was buried in a common grave in Montparnasse cemetery, January, 1838. [A Prince of Bohemia. Z. Marcas.]

Marchand (Victor), son of a Parisian grocer, infantry-major during the campaign of 1808, a lover of Clara Léganés, to whom he was under obligation; tried, without success, to marry this girl of the Spanish nobility, who preferred to suffer the most horrible of deaths, decapitation by the hand of her own brother. [El Verdugo.]

Marche-à-Terre. (*See* Leroi, Pierre.)

Marcillac (Madame de). Thanks to some acquaintances of the old régime, whom she had kept, and to her relationship with the Rastignacs, with whom she lived quietly, she found the means of introducing to Claire de Beauséant, Chevalier de Rastignac, her well-beloved grand-nephew—about 1819. [Father Goriot.]

Marcosini (Count Andrea), born in 1807 at Milan; although an aristocrat he took temporary refuge in Paris as a liberal; a wealthy and handsome poet; took his period of exile in 1834 in good spirits. He was received on terms of friendship by Mesdames d'Espard and Paul de Manerville. On the rue Froidmanteau he was constantly in pursuit of Marianina Gambara; at the Italian Giardini's "table-d'hôte" he discussed musical topics and spoke of "Robert le Diable." For five years he kept Paolo Gambara's wife as his mistress; then he gave her up to marry an Italian dancer. [Gambara.]

Maréchal, under the Restoration an attorney at Ville-aux-Fayes, Bourgogne, Montcornet's legal adviser, helped by his recommendation to have Sibilet appointed steward of Aigues in 1817. [The Peasantry.]

Mareschal, supervisor in the college of Vendôme in 1811, when Louis Lambert became a student in this educational institution. [Louis Lambert.]

Marest (Frédéric), born about 1802, son of a rich lumber-merchant's widow, cousin of Georges Marest; attorney's clerk in Paris, November, 1825; lover of Florentine Cabirolle, who was maintained by Cardot; made the acquaintance at Maitre Desroches' of Oscar Husson, and took him to a fête given by Mademoiselle Cabirolle on rue de Vendôme, where his friend foolishly compromised himself. [A Start in Life.] Frédéric Marest, in 1838, having become an examining magistrate in the public prosecutor's office in Paris, had to examine Auguste de Mergi, who was charged with having committed robbery to the detriment of Doctor Halpersohn. [The Seamy Side of History.] The following year, while acting as king's solicitor at Arcis-sur-Aube, Frédéric Marest, still unmarried and very corpulent, became acquainted with Martener's sons, Goulard, Michu and Vinet, and visited in the Beauvisage and Mollot families. [The Member for Arcis.]

Marest (Georges), cousin of the preceding, son of the senior member of a large Parisian hardware establishment on rue Saint-Martin. He became, in 1822, the second clerk of a Parisian notary, Maitre A. Crottat. He had then as a comrade in study and in pleasure Amaury Lupin. At this time Marest's vanity made itself absurdly apparent in Pierrotin's coach, which did service in the valley of Oise; he hoaxed Husson, amused Bridau and Lora, and vexed the Comte de Sérizy. Three years later Georges Marest had become the chief clerk of Léopold Hannequin. He lost by debauchery a fortune amounting to thirty thousand francs a year, and died a plain insurance-broker. [The Peasantry. A Start in Life.]

Margaritis, of Italian origin, took up his residence in Vouvray in 1831, an old man of deranged mind, most eccentric of speech, and who pretended to be a vine-grower. He was induced by Vernier to hoax the famous traveler, Gaudissart, during a business trip of the latter. [Gaudissart the Great.]

Margaritis (Madame), wife of the insane Margaritis. She kept him near her for the sake of economy, and made amends to the deceived Gaudissart. [Gaudissart the Great.]

Margueron, wealthy citizen of Beaumont-sur-Oise, under Louis XVIII., wished his son to be tax-collector of the district in which he himself owned the farm lying next to the property of Sérizy at Presles, and which he had leased to Léger. [A Start in Life.]

Marianne, during the Restoration, servant of Sophie Gamard at Tours. [The Vicar of Tours.]

Marianne, served with Gaucher in Michu's house, October, 1803, in the district of Arcis-sur-Aube, at Cinq-Cygne. **She**

served her master with discretion and fidelity. [The Gondreville Mystery.]

Mariast, owned No. 22 rue de la Montagne-Sainte-Geneviéve, Paris, and let it to Messieurs d'Espard during nearly the whole period of the Restoration. [The Commission in Lunacy.]

Marie des Anges (Mére), born in 1762, Jacques Bricheteau's aunt, superior of the Ursuline convent at Arcis-sur-Aube, saved from the guillotine by Danton, had the fifth of April of each year observed with a mass in her nephew's behalf, and, under Louis Philippe, protected the descendant of a celebrated Revolutionist, Charles de Sallenauve; her influence gave him the position of deputy of the district. [The Member for Arcis.]

Mariette. (*See* Godeschal, Marie.)

Mariette, born in 1798; from 1817 in the service of the Wattevilles of Besançon; was under Louis Philippe, despite her extreme homeliness, and on account of the money she had saved, courted by Jérôme, a servant of Albert Savarus. Mademoiselle de Watteville, who was in love with the lawyer, used Mariette and Jérôme to her own advantage. [Albert Savarus.]

Mariette, in 1816, cook in the employ of Mademoiselle Cormon, of Alençon; sometimes received advice from M. du Ronceret; an ordinary kitchen-maid in the same household, when her mistress became Madame du Bousquier. [Jealousies of a Country Town.]

Mariette, was in the employ of La Fosseuse, towards the end of the Restoration, in the village over which Benassis was mayor. [The Country Doctor.]

Marigny (Duchesse de), much sought after in the Saint-Germain section; related to the Navarreins and the Grandlieus; a woman of experience and good at giving advice; real head of her house; died in 1810. [The Thirteen.]

Marigny[1] (De), son of the preceding, harebrained, but attractive, had an attachment for Madame Keller, a middle-class lady of the Chaussée-d'Antin. [The Thirteen.]

Marin, in 1839, at Cinq-Cygne, in the district of Arcis-sur-Aube, first valet of Georges de Maufrigneuse and protector of Anicette. [The Member for Arcis.]

Marion of Arcis, grandson of a steward in the employ of Simeuse; brother-in-law of Madame Marion, born Giguet. He had the confidence of Malin, acquired for him the Gondreville property, and became a lawyer in Aube, then president of an Imperial court. [The Gondreville Mystery. The Member for Arcis.]

Marion, brother of the preceding and brother-in-law of Colonel Giguet, whose sister became his wife. Through Malin's influence, he became co-receiver-general of Aube, with Sibuelle as his colleague. [The Gondreville Mystery. The Member for Arcis.]

Marion (Madame), wife of the preceding, Colonel Giguet's sister. She was on intimate terms with Malin de Gondreville. After her husband's death she returned to her native country, Arcis, where her parlor was frequented by many guests. Under Louis Philippe, Madame Marion exerted her powers in behalf of Simon Giguet, the Colonel's son. [The Member for Arcis.]

Marion. (*See* Kolb, Madame.)

Mariotte, of Auxerre, a rival of the wealthy Gaubertin in contracting for the forest lands of that portion of Bourgogne in which Aigues, the large estate of Montcornet, was situated. [The Peasantry.]

Mariotte (Madame), of Auxerre, mother of the preceding, in 1823, had Mademoiselle Courtecuisse in her service. [The Peasantry.]

Marius, the cognomen, become hereditary, of a native of

---

[1] During the last century the Marignys owned, before the Verneuils, Rosembray, an estate where a great hunt brought together, 1829, Cadignan, Chaulieu, Canals, Mignon, etc.

Toulouse, who established himself as a Parisian hair-dresser, and was thus nick-named by the Chevalier de Parny, one of his patrons, in the early part of the nineteenth century. He handed down this name of Marius as a kind of permanent property to his successors. [The Unconscious Humorists.]

Marmus (Madame), wife of a savant, who was an officer in the Legion of Honor and a member of the Institute. They lived together on rue Duguay-Trouin in Paris, and were (in 1840) on intimate terms with Zélie Minard. [The Middle Classes.]

Marmus, husband of the preceding and noted for his absent-mindedness. [The Middle Classes.]

Marneffe (Jean-Paul-Stanislas), born in 1794, employed in the War Department. In 1833, while a mere clerk living on twelve hundred francs a year, he married Mademoiselle Valérie Fortin. Having become as unprincipled as a convict, under the patronage of Baron Hulot, his wife's paramour, he left rue du Doyenné to install himself in luxury in the Saint-Germain section, and later became head-clerk, assistant chief, and chief of the bureau, chevalier, then officer of the Legion of Honor. Jean-Paul-Stanislas Marneffe, decayed physically as well as morally, died in May, 1842. [Cousin Betty.]

Marneffe[1] (Madame). (*See* Crevel, Madame Célestin.)

Marneffe (Stanislas), legal son of the preceding couple, suffered from scrofula, much neglected by his parents. [Cousin Betty.]

Marolles (Abbé de), an old priest, who lived towards the close of the eighteenth century. Having escaped in September, 1792, from the massacre of the Carmelite convent, now a small chapel on rue de Vaugirard, he concealed himself in the upper Saint-Martin district, near the German highway. He had under his protection, at this time, two

---

[1] In 1849, at Paris, Clairville produced upon the stage of the Gymnase-Dramatique, the episodes in the life of Madame Marneffe, somewhat modified, under the double title, "Madame Marneffe, or the Prodigal Father" (a vaudeville drama in five acts).

nuns, who were in as great danger as he, Sister Marthe and Sister Agathe. On January 22, 1793, and on January 21, 1794, the Abbé de Marolles, in their presence, said masses for the repose of Louis XVI.'s soul, having been asked to do so by the executioner of the "martyr-king," whose presence at mass the Abbé knew nothing of until January 25, 1794, when he was so informed at the corner of rue des Frondeurs by Citizen Ragou. [An Episode under the Terror.]

Maronis (Abbé de), a priest of great genius, who would have been another Borgia, had he worn the tiara. He was Henri de Marsay's teacher, and made of him a complete skeptic, in a period when the churches were closed. The Abbé de Maronis died a bishop in 1812. [The Thirteen.]

Marron, under the Restoration, a physician at Marsac, Charente; nephew of the Curé Marron. He married his daughter to Postel, a pharmacist of Angouléme. He was intimate with the family of David Séchard. [Lost Illusions. Scenes from a Courtesan's Life.]

Marsay (De), immoral old gentleman. To oblige Lord Dudley he married one of the former's mistresses and recognized their son as his own. For this favor he received a hundred thousand francs per year for life, money which he soon threw away in evil company. He confided the child to his old sister, Mademoiselle de Marsay, and died, as he had lived, away from his wife. [The Thirteen.]

Marsay (Madame de). (*See* Vordac, Marquise de.)

Marsay (Mademoiselle de), sister-in-law of the preceding, took care of her son, Henri, and treated him so well that she was greatly mourned by him when she died advanced in years. [The Thirteen.]

Marsay (Henri de), born between 1792 and 1796, son of Lord Dudley and the celebrated Marquise de Vordac, who was first united in marriage to the elder De Marsay. This gentleman adopted the boy, thus becoming, according to law, his father. The young Henri was reared by Mademoiselle de Marsay and the Abbé de Maronis. He was on intimate terms, in 1815, with Paul de Manerville, and was already one of the all powerful Thirteen, with Bourignard, Montriveau and Ronquerolles. At that time he found on rue Saint-Lazare a girl from Lesbosen, Paquita Valdés, whom he wished to make his mistress. He met at the same time his own natural sister, Madame de San-Réal, of whom he became the rival for Paquita's love. At first Marsay had been the lover of the Duchesse Charlotte, then of Arabelle Dudley, whose children were his very image. He was also known to be intimate with Delphine de Nucingen up to 1819, then with Diane de Cadignan. In his position as member of the Thirteen Henri was in Montriveau's party when Antoinette de Langeais was stolen from the Carmelites. He bought Coralie for sixty thousand francs. He passed the whole of his time during the Restoration in the company of young men and women. He was the companion and counselor of Victurnien d'Esgrignon, Savinien de Portenduère and above all of Paul de Manerville, whose course he vainly tried to direct after an ill-appointed marriage, and to whom he announced, as possible, his own union. Marsay aided Lucien de Rubempré and served for him, with Rastignac, as second in a duel with Michel Chrestien. The Chaulieu and Fontaine women feared or admired Henri de Marsay— a man who was slighted by M. de Canalis, the much toasted poet. The Revolution of July, 1830, made Marsay a man of no little importance. He, however, was content to tell over his old love affairs gravely in the home of Félicité des Touches. As prime minister from 1832 to 1833, he was an habitué of the Princesse de Cadignan's Legitimist salon, where he served as a screen for the last Vendean insurrection. There, indeed, Marsay brought to light the secrets, already old, of Malin's kidnapping. Marsay died in 1834, a physical wreck, having but a short time before, when Nathan was courting Marie de Vandenesse, taken part in the intrigue, although he was disgusted with the author. [The Thirteen. The Unconscious Humorists. Another Study of Woman. The Lily of the Valley. Father Goriot. Jealousies of a Country Town. Ursule Mirouët. A Marriage Settlement. Lost

Illusions. A Distinguished Provincial at Paris. Letters of
Two Brides. The Ball at Sçeaux. Modeste Mignon. The
Secrets of a Princess. The Gondreville Mystery. A Daughter
of Eve.]

Martainville (Alphonse-Louis-Dieudonné), publicist and
dramatic writer, born at Cadiz, in 1776, of French parents,
died August 27, 1830. He was an extreme Royalist and,
as such, in 1821 and 1822, threw away his advice and support
on Lucien de Rubempré, then a convert to Liberalism. [A
Distinguished Provincial at Paris.]

Martener, well-educated old man who lived in Provins
under the Restoration. He explained to the archæologist,
Desfondrilles, who consulted him, the reason why Europe, dis-
daining the waters of Provins, sought Spa, where the waters
were less efficacious, according to French medical advice.
[Pierrette.]

Martener, son of the preceding; physician at Provins in
1827, capable man, simple and gentle. He married Madame
Guénée's second daughter. When consulted one day by
Mademoiselle Habert, he spoke against the marriage of
virgins of forty, and thus filled Sylvie Rogron with despair.
He protected and cared for Pierrette Lorrain, the victim
of this same old maid. [Pierrette.]

Martener (Madame), wife of the preceding, second daughter
of Madame Guénée, and sister of Madame Auffray. Having
taken pity on Pierrette Lorrain in her sickness, she gave to
her, in 1828, the pleasures of music, playing the compositions
of Weber, Beethoven or Hérold. [Pierrette.]

Martener, son of the preceding couple, protégé of Vinet the
elder, honest and thick-headed. He was, in 1839, examining
magistrate at Arcis-sur-Aube and caucused, during the
election season in the spring of this same year, with the
officers, Michu, Goulard, O. Vinet and Marest. [The Member
for Arcis.]

Martha was for a long time the faithful chambermaid of

Joséphine Claés; she died in old age between 1828 and 1830. [The Quest of the Absolute.]

Marthe (Sister), a Gray sister of Auvergne; from 1809 to 1816 instructed Véronique Sauviat—Madame Graslin—in reading, writing, sacred history, the Old and the New Testaments the Catechism, the elements of arithmetic. [The Country Parson.]

Marthe (Sister), born Beauséant, in 1730, a nun in the Abbey of Chelles, fled with Sister Agathe (*née* Langeais) and the Abbé de Marolles to a poor lodging in the upper Saint-Martin dis rict. On January 22, 1793, she went to a pastry-cook near Saint Laurent to get the wafers necessary for a mass for the repose of Louis XVI.'s soul. At this ceremony she was present, as was also the man who had executed the King. The following year, January 21, 1794, this same ceremony was repeated exactly. She passed these two years of the Terror under Mucins Scoevola's protection. [An Episode under the Terror.]

Marthe (Sister), in the convent of the Carmelites at Blois, knew two young women, Mesdames de l'Estorade and Gaston. [Letters of Two Brides.]

Martin, a woman of a Dauphiné village, of which Doctor Benassis was mayor, kept the hospital children for three francs and a bar of soap each month. She was, possibly, the first person in the country seen by Genestas-Bluteau, and also the first to impart knowledge to him. [The Country Doctor.]

Martineau, name of two brothers employed by M. de Mortsauf in connection with his farms in Touraine. The elder was at first a farm-hand, then a steward; the younger, a warden. [The Lily of the Valley.]

Martineau, son of one of the two Martineau brothers. [The Lily of the Valley.]

Marty (Jean-Baptiste), actor of melodrama, employé or manager of the Gaîté, before and after the Paris fire of

1836; born in 1779, celebrated during the Restoration; in 1819 and 1820 he played in "Mont-Sauvage," a play warmly applauded by Madame Vauquer. This woman was accompanied to the theatre on the Boulevard du Crime, by her rue Neuve-Sainte-Geneviéve lodger, Jacques Collin, called also Vautrin, on the evening before his arrest. [Father Goriot.] Marty died, at an advanced age, in 1868, a chevalier in the Legion of Honor, after having been for many years mayor of Charenton.

Marville (De).   (*See* Camusot.)

Mary, an Englishwoman in the family of Louis de l'Estorade during the Restoration and under Louis Philippe. [Letters of Two Brides.   The Member for Arcis.]

Massin-Levrault, junior, son of a poor locksmith of Montargis, grand-nephew of Doctor Denis Minoret, as a result of his marriage with a Levrault-Minoret; father of three girls, Paméla, Aline, and Madame Goupil. He bought the office of clerk to the justice of peace in Nemours, January, 1815, and lived at first with his family in the good graces of Doctor Minoret, through whom his sister became postmistress at Nemours. Massin-Levrault, junior, was one of the indirect persecutors of Ursule de Portenduère. He became a municipal councilor after July, 1830, began to lend money to the laboring people at exorbitant rates of interest, and finally developed into a confirmed usurer. [Ursule Mirouët.]

Massin-Levrault (Madame), wife of the preceding, born Levrault-Minoret in 1793, grand-niece of Doctor Denis Minoret on the maternal side; her father was a victim of the campaign in France. She strove in every way possible to win the affections of her wealthy uncle, and was one of Ursule de Portenduère's persecutors. [Ursule Mirouët.]

Massol, native of Carcassonne, licentiate in law and editor of the "Gazette des Tribunaux" in May, 1830. Without knowing their relationship he brought together Jacqueline and Jacques Collin, a boarder at the Concierge, and, acting under Granville's orders, in his journal attributed Lucien de Rubempré's suicidal death to the rupture of a tumor. A Republican, through the lack of the particle *de* before his name, and very ambitious, he was, in 1834, the associate of Raoul Nathan in the publication of a large journal, and sought to make a tool of the poet-founder of this paper. In company with Stidmann, Steinbock and Claude Vignon, Massol was a witness of the second marriage of Valérie Marneffe.   In 1845, having become a councilor of state and president of a section, he supported Jenny Cadine. He was then charged with the administrative lawsuit of S.-P. Gazonal. [Scenes from a Courtesan's Life. The Magic Skin. A Daughter of Eve. Cousin Betty. The Unconscious Humorists.]

Masson, friend of Maitre Desroches, an attorney, to whom, upon the latter's advice, Lucien de Rubempré hastened, when Coralie's furniture was attached, in 1821. [A Distinguished Provincial at Paris.]

Masson (Publicola), born in 1795, the best known chiropodist in Paris, a radical Republican of the Marat type, even resembled the latter physically; counted Léon de Lora among his customers. [The Unconscious Humorists.]

Mathias, born in 1753. He started as third clerk to a Bordeaux notary, Chesneau, whom he succeeded. He married, but lost his wife in 1826. He had one son on the bench, and a married daughter. He was a good example of the old-fashioned country magistrate, and gave out his enlightened opinions to two generations of Manervilles.   [A Marriage Settlement.]

Mathilde (La Grande), on terms of friendship with Jenny Courand in Paris, under the reign of Louis Philippe. [Gaudissart the Great.]

Mathurine, a cook, spiritual and upright, first in the employ of the Bishop of Nancy, but later given a place on rue Vancau, Paris, with Valérie Marneffe, by Lisbeth, a relative of the former on her mother's side. [Cousin Betty.]

Matifat, a wealthy druggist, on rue des Lombards, Paris,

at the beginning of the nineteenth century; kept the "Reine des Roses," which later was handled by Ragon and Birotteau; typical member of the middle classes, narrow in views and pleased with himself, vulgar in language and, perhaps, in action. He married and had a daughter, whom he took, with his wife, to the celebrated ball tendered by César Birotteau on rue Saint-Honoré, Sunday, December 17, 1818. As a friend of the Collevilles, Thuilliers and Saillards, Matifat obtained for them invitations from César Birotteau. In 1821 he supported on rue de Bondy an actress, who was shortly transferred from the Panorama to the Gymnase-Dramatique. Although called Florine, her true name was Sophie Grignault, and she became subsequently Madame Nathan. J.-J. Bixiou and Madame Desroches visited Matifat frequently during the year 1826, sometimes on rue du Cherche-Midi, sometimes in the suburbs of Paris. Having become a widower, Matifat remarried under Louis Philippe, and retired from business. He was a silent partner in the theatre directed by Gaudissart. [César Birotteau. A Bachelor's Establishment. Lost Illusions. A Distinguished Provincial at Paris. The Firm of Nucingen. Cousin Pons.]

Matifat (Madame), first wife of the preceding, a woman who wore a turban and gaudy colors. She shone, under the Restoration, in bourgeois circles and died probably during the reign of Louis Philippe. [César Birotteau. The Firm of Nucingen.]

Matifat (Mademoiselle), daughter of the preceding couple, attended the Birotteau ball, was sought in marriage by Adolphe Cochin and Maitre Desroches; married General Baron Gouraud, a poor man much her elder, bringing to him a dowry of fifty thousand crowns and expectations of an estate on rue du Cherche-Midi and a house at Luzarches. [César Birotteau. The Firm of Nucingen. Pierrette.]

Maucombe (Comte de), of a Provençal family already celebrated under King René. During the Revolution he "clothed himself in the humble garments of a provincial proof-reader," in the printing-office of Jérôme-Nicolas

Séchard at Angoulême. He had a number of children: Renée, who became Madame de l'Estorade; Jean, and Marianina, a natural daughter, claimed by Lanty. He was a deputy by the close of 1826, sitting between the Centre and the Right. [Lost Illusions. Letters of Two Brides.]

· **Maucombe** (Jean de), son of the preceding, gave up his portion of the family inheritance to his older sister, Madame de l'Estorade, born Renée de Maucombe [Letters of Two Brides.]

Maufrigneuse (Duc de), born in 1778, son of the Prince de Cadignan, who died an octogenarian towards the close of the Restoration, leaving then as eldest of the house the Prince de Cadignan. The prince was in love with Madame d'Uxelles, but married her daughter, Diane, in 1814, and afterwards lived unhappily with her. He supported Marie Godeschal; was a cavalry colonel during the reigns of Louis XVIII. and Charles X.; had under his command Philippe Bridau, the Vicomte de Sérizy, Oscar Husson. He was on intimate terms with Messieurs de Grandlieu and d'Espard. [The Secrets of a Princess. A Start in Life. A Bachelor's Establishment. Scenes from a Courtesan's Life.]

Maufrigneuse (Duchesse de), wife of the preceding, born Diane d'Uxelles in 1796, married in 1815. She was in turn the mistress of Marsay, Miguel d'Ajuda-Pinto, Victurnien d'Esgrignon, Maxime de Trailles, Eugéne de Rastignac, Armand de Montriveau, Marquis de Ronquerolles, Prince Galathionne, the Duc de Rhétoré, a Grandlieu, Lucien de Rubempré, and Daniel d'Arthez. She lived at various times in the following places: Anzy, near Sancerre; Paris, on rue Saint-Honoré in the suburbs and on rue Miromesnil; Cinq-Cygne in Champagne; Geneva and the borders of Léman. She inspired a foolish platonic affection in Michel Chrestien, and kept at a distance the Duc d'Hérouville, who courted her towards the end of the Restoration, by sarcasm and brilliant repartee. Her first and last love affairs were especially well known. For her the Marquis Miguel d'Ajudo-Pinto gave up Berthe de Rochefide, his wife, avenging thus a former mistress, Claire de Beauséant. Her liaison with Victurnien d'Esgrignon became the most stormy of romances. Madame de Maufrigneuse, disguised as a man and possessed of a passport, bearing the name of Félix de Vandenesse, succeeded in rescuing from the Court of Assizes the young man who had compromised himself in yielding to the foolish extravagance of his mistress. The duchesse received even her tradesmen in an angelic way, and became their prey. She scattered fortunes to the four winds, and her indiscretions led to the sale of Anzy in a manner advantageous to Polydore Miland de la Baudraye. Some years later she made a vain attempt to rescue Lucien de Rubempré, against whom a criminal charge was pending. The Restoration and the Kingdom of 1830 gave to her life a different lustre. Having fallen heir to the worldly sceptre of Mesdames de Langeais and de Beauséant, both of whom she knew socially, she became intimate with the Marquise d'Espard, a lady with whom in 1822 she disputed the right to rule the "fragile kingdom of fashion." She visited frequently the Chaulieus, whom she met at a famous hunt near Havre. In July, 1830, reduced to poor circumstances, abandoned by her husband, who had then become the Prince de Cadignan, and assisted by her relatives, Mesdames d'Uxelles and de Navarreins, Diane operated as it were a kind of retreat, occupied herself with her son Georges, and strengthening herself by the memory of Chrestien, also by constantly visiting Madame d'Espard, she succeeded, without completely foregoing society, in making captive the celebrated deputy of the Right, a man of wealth and maturity, Daniel Arthez himself. In her own home and in that of Félicité des Touches she heard, between 1832 and 1835, anecdotes of Marsay. The Princesse de Cadignan had portraits of her numerous lovers. She had also one of the *Madame* whom she had attended, and upon meeting him, showed it to Marsay, minister of Louis Philippe. She owned also a picture of Charles X. which was thus inscribed, "Given by the King." After the marriage of her son to a Cinq-Cygne, she visited often at the estate of that name, and was there in 1839, during the regular election. [The Secrets of a Princess. Modeste Mignon. Jealousies of a Country Town. The Muse of the Department. Scenes from a Courtesan's Life. Letters of Two Brides. Another Study of Woman. The Gondreville Mystery. The Member for Arcis.]

Maufrigneuse (Georges de), son of the preceding, born in 1814, had successively in his service Toby and Marin, took the title of duke towards the close of the Restoration, was in the last Vendéan uprising. Through his mother's instrumentality, who paved the way for the match in 1833, he married Mademoiselle Berthe de Cinq-Cygne in 1838, and became heir to the estate of the same name the following year during the regular election. [The Secrets of a Princess. The Gondreville Mystery. Béatrix. The Member for Arcis.]

Maufrigneuse (Berthe de), wife of the preceding, daughter of Adrien and Laurence de Cinq-Cygne, married in 1838, although she had been very nearly engaged in 1833; she lived with all of her family on their property at Aube during the spring of 1839. [Béatrix. The Gondreville Mystery. The Member for Arcis.]

Maugredie, celebrated Pyrrhonic physician, being called into consultation, he gave his judgment on the very serious case of Raphaël de Valentin. [The Magic Skin.]

Maulincour[1] (Baronne de), born Rieux, an eighteenth century woman who "did not lose ·her head" during the Revolution; intimate friend of the Vidame de Pamiers. At the beginning of the Restoration she spent half of her time in the suburbs of Saint-Germain, where she managed to educate her grandson, Auguste Carbonnon de Maulincour, and the remainder on her estates at Bordeaux, where she demanded the hand of Natalie Evangélista in marriage for her grand-nephew, Paul de Manerville. Of the family of this girl she had an unfavorable, but just opinion. The Baronne de Maulincour died a short time before her grandson of the

[1] Some Maulincourts had, during the last century, a place of residence on Chausée des Minimes, in the Marais, of which Élie Magus subsequently became proprietor.

chagrin which she felt on account of this young man's unhappy experiences. [A Marriage Settlement. The Thirteen.]

Maulincour (Auguste Carbonnon de), born in 1797, grandson of the preceding, by whom he was reared; moulded by the Vidame de Pamiers, whom he left but rarely; lived on rue de Bourbon in Paris; had a short existence, under Louis XVIII., which was full of brilliance and misfortune. Having embraced a military career he was decorated, becoming major in a cavalry regiment of the Royal Guard, and afterwards lieutenant-colonel of a company of body-guards. He vainly courted Madame de Langeais, fell in love with Clémence Desmarets, followed her, compromised her, and persecuted her. By his indiscretions he drew upon himself the violent enmity of Gratien Bourignard, father of Madame Desmarets. In this exciting struggle Maulincour, having neglected the warnings that many self-imposed accidents had brought upon him, also a duel with the Marquis de Ronquerolles, was fatally poisoned and soon after followed the old baroness, his grandmother, to Pére-Lachaise. [The Thirteen.]

Mauny (Baron de), was killed during the Restoration, or after 1830, in the suburbs of Versailles, by Victor (the Parisian), who struck him with a hatchet. The murderer finally took refuge at Aiglemont in the family of his future mistress, Héléne. [A Woman of Thirty.]

Maupin (Camille). (*See* Touches, Félicité des.)

Maurice, valet, employed by the Comte and Comtesse de Restaud, during the Restoration. His master believed his servant to be faithful to his interests, but the valet, on the contrary, was true to those of the wife who opposed her husband in everything. [Father Goriot. Gobseck.]

Médal (Robert), celebrated and talented actor, who was on the Parisian stage in the last years of Louis Philippe, at the time when Sylvain Pons directed the orchestra in Gaudissart's theatre. [Cousin Pons.]

Melin, inn-keeper or "cabaretier" in the west of France,

furnished lodging in 1809 to the Royalists who were afterwards condemned by Mergi, and himself received five years
of confinement. [The Seamy Side of History.]

Melmoth (John), an Irishman of pronounced English
characteristics, a Satanical character, who made a strange
agreement with Rodolphe Castanier, Nucingen's faithless
cashier, whereby they were to make a reciprocal exchange
of personalities; in 1821, he died in the odor of holiness, on
rue Férou, Paris. [Melmoth Reconciled.]

Memmi (Emilio). (*See* Varése, Prince de.)

Mène-à-Bien, cognomen of Coupiau.

Mergi (De), magistrate during the Empire and the Restoration, whose activity was rewarded by both governments,
inasmuch as he always struck the members of the party out
of power. In 1809 the court over which he presided was
charged with the cases of the " Chauffeurs of Mortagne."
Mergi showed great hatred in his dealings with Madame de
la Chanterie. [The Seamy Side of History.]

Mergi (De), son of the preceding, married Vanda de Bourlac.
[The Seamy Side of History.]

Mergi (Baronne Vanda de), born Bourlac, of Polish
origin on her mother's side, belonged to the family of Tarlowski, married the son of Mergi, the celebrated magistrate,
and, having survived him, was condemned to poverty and
sickness; was aided in Paris by Godefroid, a messenger from
Madame de la Chanterie, and attended by her father and
Doctors Bianchon, Desplein, Haudry and Moïse Halpersohn,
the last of whom finally saved her. [The Seamy Side of
History.]

Mergi (Auguste de), during the last half of Louis Philippe's
reign was in turn a collegian, university student and humble
clerk in the Palais at Paris; looked after the needs of his
mother, Vanda de Mergi, with sincerest devotion. For her
sake he stole four thousand francs from Moïse Halpersohn,
but remained unpunished, thanks to one of the Brothers

of Consolation, who boarded with Madame de la Chanterie. [The Seamy Side of History.]

Merkstus, banker at Douai, under the Restoration had a bill of exchange for ten thousand francs signed by Balthazar Claés, and, in 1819, presented it to the latter for collection. [The Quest of the Absolute.]

Merle, captain in the Seventy-second demi-brigade; jolly and careless. Killed at La Vivetière in December, 1799, by Pille-Miche (Cibot). [The Chouans.]

Merlin, of Douai, belonged to the convention, of which he was, for two years, one of the five directors; attorney-general in the court of appeal; in September, 1805, rejected the appeal of the Simeuses, of the Hauteserres, and of Michu, men who had been condemned for kidnapping Senator Malin. [The Gondreville Mystery.]

Merlin (Hector), came to Paris from Limoges, expecting to become a journalist; a Royalist; during the two years in which Lucien de Rubempré made his literary and political beginning, Merlin was especially noted. At that time he was Suzanne du Val-Noble's lover, and a polemical writer for a paper of the Right-Centre; he also brought honor to Andoche Finot's little gazette by his contributions. As a journalist he was dangerous, and could, if necessary, fill the chair of the editor-in-chief. In March, 1822, with Théodore Gaillard, he established the "Réveil," another kind of "Drapeau Blanc." Merlin had an unattractive face, lighted by two pale-blue eyes, which were fearfully sharp; his voice had in it something of the mewing of a cat, something of the hyena's asthmatic gasping. [A Distinguished Provincial at Paris.]

Merlin de la Blottière (Mademoiselle), of a noble family of Tours (1826); François Birotteau's friend. [The Vicar of Tours.]

Merret (De), gentleman of Picardie, proprietor of the Grande-Bretéche, near Vendôme, under the Empire; had the room walled up, where he knew the Spaniard Bagos de Férédia, lover of his wife, was in hiding. He died in

1816 at Paris as the result of excesses. [Another Study of Woman. La Grande Bretéche.]

Merret (Madame Joséphine de), wife of the preceding, mistress of Bagos de Férédia, whom she saw perish almost under her eyes, after she had refused to give him up to her husband. She died in the same year as Merret, at La Grande Bretéche, as a result of the excitement she had undergone. The story of Madame de Merret was the subject of a vaudeville production given at the Gymnase-Dramatique theatre, under the title of "Valentine." [Another Study of Woman. La Grande Bretéche.]

Métivier, paper merchant on rue Serpente in Paris, under the Restoration; correspondent of David Séchard, friend of Gobseck and of Bidault, accompanying them frequently to the café Thémis, between rue Dauphine and the Quai des Augustins. Having two daughters, and an income of a hundred thousand francs, he withdrew from business. [Lost Illusions. The Government Clerks. The Middle Classes.]

Métivier, nephew and successor of the preceding, one of whose daughters he married. He was interested in the book business, in connection with Morand and Barbet; took advantage of Bourlac in 1838; lived on rue Saint-Dominique d'Enfer, in the Thuillier house in 1840; engaged in usurious transactions with Jeanne-Marie-Brigitte, Cérizet, Dutocq, discounters of various kinds and titles. [The Seamy Side of History. The Middle Classes.]

Meynardie (Madame), at Paris, under the Restoration, in all probability, had an establishment or shop in which Ida Gruget was employed; undoubtedly controlled a house of ill-fame, in which Esther van Gobseck was a boarder. [The Thirteen. Scenes from a Courtesan's Life.]

Meyraux, medical doctor; a scholarly young Parisian, with whom Louis Lambert associated, November, 1819. Until his death in 1832 Meyraux was a member of the rue des Quatre-Vents Cénacle, over which Daniel d'Arthez presided. [Louis Lambert. A Distinguished Provincial at Paris.]

Michaud (Justin), an old chief quartermaster to the cuirassiers of the Imperial Guard, chevalier of the Legion of Honor. He married one of the Montcornet maids, Olympe Charel, and became, under the Restoration, head warden of the Montcornet estates at Blangy in Bourgogne. Unknown to himself he was secretly beloved by Geneviéve Niseron. His military frankness and loyal devotion succumbed before an intrigue formed against him by Sibilet, steward of Aigues, and by the Rigous, Soudrys, Gaubertins, Fourchons and Tonsards. On account of the complicity of Courtecuisse and Vaudoyer the bullet fired by François Tonsard, in 1823, overcame the vigilance of Michaud. [The Peasantry.]

Michaud (Madame Justin), born Olympe Charel, a virtuous and pretty farmer's daughter of Le Perche; wife of the preceding; chambermaid of Madame de Montcornet—born Troisville—before her marriage and induction to Aigues in Bourgogne. Her marriage to Justin Michaud was the outcome of mutual love. She had in her employ Cornevin, Juliette and Gounod; sheltered Geneviéve Niseron, whose strange disposition she seemed to understand. For her husband, who was thoroughly hated in the Canton of Blangy, she often trembled, and on the same night that Michaud was murdered she died from overanxiety, soon after giving birth to a child which did not survive her. [The Peasantry.]

Michel, waiter at Socquard's café and coffee-house keeper at Soulanges in 1823. He also looked after his patron's vineyard and garden. [The Peasantry.]

Michonneau (Christine-Michelle). (*See* Poiret, the elder, Madame.)

Michu, during the progress of and after the French Revolution he played a part directly contrary to his regular political affiliations. His lowly birth, his harsh appearance, and his marriage with the daughter of a Troyes tanner of advanced opinion, all helped to make his pronounced Republicanism seem in keeping, although beneath it he hid his Royalist faith and an active devotion to the Simeuses, the **Hauteserres**

and the Cinq-Cygnes. Michu controlled the Gondreville
estate between 1789 and 1804, after it was snatched from
its rightful owners, and under the Terror he presided over the
Jacobin club at Arcis. As a result of the assassination
of the Duc d'Enghien March 21, 1804, he lost his position
at Gondreville. Michu then lived not far from there, near
Laurence de Cinq-Cygne, to whom he made known his secret
conduct, and, as a result, became overseer of all the estate
attached to the castle. Having publicly shown his opposition to Malin, he was thought guilty of being leader in a
plot to kidnap the new Seigneur de Gondreville, and was
consequently condemned to death, a sentence which was
executed, despite his innocence, October, 1806. [The Gondreville Mystery.]

Michu (Marthe), wife of the preceding, daughter of a
Troyes tanner, "the village apostle of the Revolution,"
who, as a follower of Baboeuf, a believer in racial and social
equality, was put to death. A blonde with blue eyes, and
of perfect build, in accordance with her father's desire,
despite her modest innocence, posed before a public assembly
as the Goddess of Liberty. Marthe Michu adored her husband, by whom she had a son, François, but being ignorant
for a long time of his secret, she lived in a manner separated
from him, under her mother's wing. When she did learn of
her husband's Royalist actions, and that he was devoted
to the Cinq-Cygnes, she assisted him, but falling into a skilfully contrived plot, she innocently brought about her husband's execution. A forged letter having attracted her to
Malin's hiding-place, Madame Michu furnished all the necessary evidence to make the charge of kidnapping seem plau-
sible. She also was cast into prison and was awaiting trial
when death claimed her, November, 1806. [The Gondreville
Mystery.]

Michu (François), son of the preceding couple, born in 1793.
In 1803, while in the service of the house of Cinq-Cygne,
he ferreted out the police-system that Giguet represented.
The tragic death of his parents (a picture of one of them

hung on the wall at Cinq-Cygne) caused his adoption in some way or other by the Marquise Laurence, whose efforts afterwards paved the way for his career as a lawyer from 1817 to 1819, an occupation which he left, only to become a magistrate. In 1824 he was associate judge of the Alençon court. Then he was appointed attorney of the king and received the cross of the Legion of Honor, after the suit against Victurnien d'Esgrignon by M. du Bosquier and the Liberals. Three years later he performed similar duties at the Arcis court, over which he presided in 1839. Already wealthy, and receiving an income of twelve thousand francs granted him in 1814 by Madame de Cinq-Cygne, François Michu married a native of Champagne, Mademoiselle Girel, a Troyes heiress. In Arcis he attended only the social affairs given by the Cinq-Cygnes, then become allies of the Cadignans, and in fact never visited any others. [The Gondreville Mystery. Jealousies of a Country Town. The Member for Arcis.]

Michu (Madame François), wife of the preceding, born Girel. Like her husband, she rather looked with scorn upon Arcis society, in 1839, and departed little from the circle made up of government officers' families and the Cinq-Cygnes. [The Gondreville Mystery. The Member for Arcis.]

Migeon, in 1836, porter in the rue des Martyrs house in which Etienne Lousteau lived for three years; he was commissioned for nine hundred francs by Mme. de la Baudraye, who then lived with the writer, to carry her jewelry to the pawn-broker. [The Muse of the Department.]

Migeon (Paméla), daughter of the preceding, born in 1823; in 1837, the intelligent little waiting-maid of Madame de la Baudraye, when he baronne lived with Lousteau. [The Muse of the Department.]

Mignon de la Bastie (Charles), born in 1773 in the district of Var, "last member of the family to which Paris is indebted for the street and the house built by Cardinal Mignon"; went to war under the Republic; was closely associated with Anne Dumay. At the beginning of the Empire, as the result of mutual affection, his marriage with Bettina Wallenrod, only daughter of a Frankfort banker, took place. Shortly before the return of the Bourbons, he was appointed lieutenant-colonel, and became commander of the Legion of Honor. Under the Restoration Charles Mignon de la Bastie lived at Havre with his wife, and acquired forthwith, by means of banking, a large fortune, which he shortly lost. After absenting himself from the country, he returned, during the last year of Charles X.'s reign, from the Orient, having become a multi-millionaire. Of his four children, he lost three, two having died in early childhood, while Bettina Caroline, the third, died in 1827, after being misled and finally deserted by M. d'Estourny. Marie-Modeste was the only child remaining, and she was confided during her father's journeys to the care of the Dumays, who were under obligations to the Mignons; she married Ernest de la Bastie-La Brière (also called La Brière-la Bastie). The brilliant career of Charles Mignon was the means of his reassuming the title, Comte de la Bastie. [Modeste Mignon.]

Mignon (Madame Charles), wife of the preceding, born Bettina Wallenrod-Tustall-Bartenstild, indulged daughter of a banker in Frankfort-on-the-Main. She became blind soon after her elder daughter, Bettina-Caroline's troubles and early death, and had a presentiment of the romance connected with her younger daughter, Marie-Modeste, who became Madame Ernest de la Bastie-La Briére. Towards the close of the Restoration, Madame Charles Mignon, as the result of an operation by Desplein, recovered her sight and was a witness of Marie-Modeste's happiness. [Modeste Mignon.]

Mignon (Bettina-Caroline), elder daughter of the preceding couple; born in 1805, the very image of her father; a typical Southern girl; was favored by her mother over her younger sister, Marie-Modeste, a kind of "Gretchen," who was similar in appearance to Madame Mignon. Bettina-Caroline was seduced, taken away and finally deserted by a "gentleman of fortune," named D'Estourny, and shortly sank at Havre under the load of her sins and suffering, surrounded by nearly all of her family.   Since 1827 there has been inscribed on her tomb in the little Ingouville cemetery the following inscription: "Bettina Caroline Mignon, died when twenty-two years of age.   Pray for her!"   [Modeste Mignon.]

Mignon (Marie-Modeste).   (*See* La Bastie-La Briére, Madame Ernest de.)

Mignonnet, born in 1782, graduate of the military schools, was an artillery captain in the Imperial Guard, but resigned under the Restoration and lived at Issoudun.   Short and thin, but of dignified bearing; much occupied with science; friend of the cavalry officer Carpentier, with whom he joined the citizens against Maxence Gilet.   Gilet's military partisans, Commandant Potel and Captain Renard, lived in the Faubourg of Rome, Belleville of the coporation of Berry. [A Bachelor's Establishment.]

Milaud, handsome representative of the self-enriched plebeian branch of Milauds; relative of Jean-Athanase-Polydore Milaud de la Baudraye, in whose marriage he put no confidence, and from whom he expected to receive an inheritance.   Under the favor of **Marchangy,** he undertook the career of a public prosecutor.   Under Louis XVIII. he was a deputy at Angouléme, a position to which he was succeeded by Maitre Petit-Claud.   Milaud eventually performed the same duties at Nevers, which was probably his native country. [Lost Illusions.   The Muse of the Department.]

Milaud de la Baudraye.   (*See* La Baudraye.)

Millet, Parisian grocer, on rue Chanoinesse, in 1836 attended to the renting of a small, unfurnished room in Madame de la Chanterie's house; gave Godefroid information, after having submitted him to a rigid examination.   [The Seamy Side of History.]

Minard (Louis), refractory "chauffeur," connected with the Royalist insurrection in western France, 1809, was tried at the bar of justice, where Bourlac and Mergi presided; he was executed the same year that he was condemned to death.   [The Seamy Side of History.]

Minard (Auguste-Jean-François), as clerk to the minister of finances he received a salary of fifteen hundred francs. In the florist establishment of a fellow-workman's sister, Mademoiselle Godard, of rue Richelieu, he met a clerk, Zélie Lorain, the daughter of a porter. He fell in love with her, married her, and had by her two children, Julien and Prudence. He lived near the Courcelles gate, and as an economical worker of retiring disposition he was made the butt of J.-J. Bixiou's jests in the Treasury Department. Necessity gave him fortitude and originality. After giving up his position in December, 1824, Minard opened a trade in adulterated teas and chocolates, and subsequently became a distiller. In 1835 he was the richest merchant in the vicinity, having an establishment on the Place Maubert and one of the best houses on the rue des Maçons-Sorbonne. In 1840 Minard became mayor of the eleventh district, where he lived, judge of the tribunal of commerce, and officer of the Legion of Honor. He frequently met his former colleagues of the period of the Restoration: Colleville, Thuillier, Dutocq, Fleury, Phellion, Xavier Rabourdin, Saillard, Isidore Baudoyer and Godard. [The Government Clerks. The Firm of Nucingen. The Middle Classes.]

Minard (Madame), wife of the preceding, born Zélie Lorain, daughter of a porter. On account of her cold and prudent disposition, she did not persist long in her trial at the Conservatory, but became florist's girl in Mademoiselle Godard's establishment on rue Richelieu. After her marriage to François Minard she gave birth to two children, and, with the help of Madame Lorain, her mother, reared them comfortably near the Courcelles gate. Under Louis Philippe, having become rich, and living in that part of the Saint-Germain suburbs which lies next to Saint-Jacques, she showed, as did her husband, the silly pride of the enriched mediocrity. [The Government Clerks. The Middle Classes.]

Minard (Julien), son of the preceding couple, attorney; at first considered "the family genius." In 1840 he committed some indiscretions with Olympe Cardinal, creator of

"Love's Telegraphy," played at Mourier's small theatre[1] on the Boulevard. His dissipation ended in a separation brought about by Julien's parents, who contributed to the support of the actress, then become Madame Cérizet. [The Middle Classes.]

Minard (Prudence), sister of the preceding, was sought in marriage by Félix Gaudissart towards the end of Louis Philippe's réign. [The Middle Classes. Cousin Pons.]

Minette,[2] vaudeville actress on rue de Chartres, during the Restoration, died during the first part of the Second Empire, lawful wife of a director of the Gaz; was well known for her brilliancy, and was responsible for the saying that "Time is a great faster," quoted sometimes before Lucien de Rubempré in 1821-22. [A Distinguished Provincial at Paris.]

Minorets (The), representatives of the well-known "company of army contractors," in which Mademoiselle Sophie Laguerre's steward, who preceded Gaubertin at Aigues, in Bourgogne, acquired a one-third share, after giving up his stewardship. [The Peasantry.] The relatives of Madame Flavie Colleville, daughter of a ballet-dancer, who was supported by Galathionne and, perhaps, by the contractor, Du Bourguier, were connected with the Minorets, probably the army contractor Minorets. [The Government Clerks.]

Minoret (Doctor Denis), born in Nemours in 1746, had the support of Dupont, deputy to the States-General in 1789, who was his fellow-citizen; he was intimate with the Abbé Morellet, also the pupil of Rouelle the chemist, and an ardent admirer of Diderot's friend, Bordeu, by means of whom, or his friends, he gained a large practice. Denis Minoret invented the Lelièvre balm, became an acquaintance and protector of Robespierre, married the daughter of the celebrated harpsichordist, Valentin Mirouët, died suddenly,

[1] This theatre was built in 1831 on the Boulevard du Temple, where the first Ambigu had been situated; it was afterwards moved to No. 40, rue de Bondy, December 30, 1862.

[2] Minette married M. Marguerite; she lived in Paris during the last years of her life in the large house at the corner of rue Saint-Georges and rue Provence.

soon after the execution of Madame Roland. The Empire, like the former governments, recompensed Minoret's ability, and he became consulting physician to His Imperial and Royal Majesty, in 1805, chief hospital physician, officer of the Legion of Honor, chevalier of Saint-Michel, and member of the Institute. Upon withdrawing to Nemours, January, 1815, he lived there in company with his ward, Ursule Mirouët, daughter of his brother-in-law, Joseph Mirouët, later Madame Savinien de Portenduère, a girl whom he had taken care of since she had become an orphan. As she was the living image of the late Madame Denis Minoret, he loved her so devotedly that his lawful heirs, Minoret-Levrault, Massin, Crémière, fearing that they would lose a large inheritance, mistreated the adopted child. Doctor Minoret, at the time when he was worried over their plotting, saw Bouvard, a fellow-Parisian with whom he had formerly associated, and through his influence interested himself greatly in the subject of magnetism. In 1835, surrounded by some of his nearest relatives, Minoret died at an advanced age, having been converted from the philosophy of Voltaire through the influence of Ursule, whom he remembered substantially in his will. [Ursule Mirouët.]

Minoret-Levrault (François), son of the oldest brother of the preceding, and his nearest heir, born in 1769, strong but uncouth and illiterate, had charge of the post-horses and was keeper of the best tavern in Nemours, as a result of his marriage with Zélie Levrault-Crémière, an only daughter. After the Revolution of 1830 he became deputy-mayor. As principal heir to Doctor Minoret's estate he was the bitterest persecutor of Ursule Mirouët, and made way with the will which favored the young girl. Later, being compelled to restore her property, overcome by remorse, and sorrowing for his son, who was the victim of a runaway, and for his insane wife, François Minoret-Levrault became the faithful keeper of the property of Ursule, who had then become Madame Savinien de Portenduère. [Ursule Mirouët.]

Minoret-Levrault (Madame François), wife of the preceding, born Zélie Levrault-Crémière, physically feeble, sour of countenance and action, harsh, greedy, as illiterate as her husband, brought him as dower half of her maiden name (a local tradition) and a first-class tavern. She was, in reality, the manager of the Nemours post-house. She worshiped her son Désiré, whose tragic death was sufficient punishment for her avaricious persecutions of Ursule de Portenduère. She died insane in Doctor Blanche's sanitarium in the village of Passy[1] in 1841. [Ursule Mirouët.]

Minoret (Désiré), son of the preceding couple, born in 1805. Obtained a half scholarship in the Louis-le-Grand lyceum in Paris, through the instrumentality of Fontanes, an acquaintance of Dr. Minoret; finally studied law. Under Goupil's leadership he became somewhat dissipated as a young man, and loved in turn Esther van Gobseck and Sophie Grignault—Florine—who, after declining his offer of marriage, became Madame Nathan. Désiré Minoret was not actively associated with his family in the persecution of Ursule de Portenduère. The Revolution of 1830 was advantageous to him. He took part during the three glorious days of fighting, received the decoration, and was selected to be deputy attorney to the king at Fontainebleau. He died as a result of the injuries received in a runaway, October, 1836. [Ursule Mirouët.]

Mirah (Josépha) born in 1814. Natural daughter of a wealthy Jewish banker, abandoned in Germany, although she bore as a sign of her identity an anagram of her Jewish name, Hiram. When fifteen years old and a working girl in Paris, she was found out and misled by Célestin Crevel, whom she left eventually for Hector Hulot, a more liberal man. The munificence of the commissary of stores exalted her socially, and gave her the opportunity of training her voice. Her vocal attainments established her as a prima donna, first at the Italiens, then on rue le Peletier. After Hector Hulot became a bankrupt, she abandoned him and his house on rue Chauchat, near the Royal Academy, where,

[1] Since 1860 a suburb of Paris

at different times, had lived Tullia, Comtesse du Bruel and Héloïse Brisetout. The Duc d'Hérouville became Mademoiselle Mirah's lover. This affair led to an elegant reception on rue de la Ville-l'Evêque to which all Paris received invitation. Josépha had at all times many followers. One of the Kellers and the Marquis d'Esgrignon made fools of themselves over her. Eugéne de Rastignac, at that time minister, invited her to his home, and insisted upon her singing the, celebrated cavatina from " La Muette." Irregular in her habits, whimsical, covetous, intelligent, and at times good-natured, Josépha Mirah gave some proof of generosity when she helped the unfortunate Hector Hulot, for whom she went so far as to get Olympe Grenouville. She finally told Madame Adeline Hulot of the baron's hiding-place on the Passage du Soleil in the Petite-Pologne section. [Cousin Betty.]

Mirault, name of one branch of the Bargeton family, merchants in Bordeaux during the eighteenth and nineteenth centuries. [Lost Illusions.]

Mirbel (Madame de), well-known miniature-painter from 1796 to 1849; made successively the portrait of Louise de Chaulieu, given by this young woman to the Baron de Macumer, her future husband; of Lucien de Rubempré for Esther Gobseck; of Charles X. for the Princess of Cadignan, who hung it on the wall of her little salon on rue Miromesnil, after the Revolution of 1830. This last picture bore the inscription, "Given by the King." [Letters of Two Brides. Scenes from a Courtesan's Life. The Secrets of a Princess.]

Mirouët (Ursule). (*See* Portenduère, Vicomtesse Savinien de.)

Mirouët (Valentin), celebrated harpsichordist and instrument-maker; one of the best known French organists; father-in-law of Doctor Minorct; died in 1785. His business was bought by Erard. [Ursule Mirouët.]

Mirouët (Joseph), natural son of the preceding and brother-in-law of Doctor Denis Minorct. He was a good musician and of a Bohemian disposition. He was a regiment musician during the wars in the latter part of the eighteenth and the beginning of the nineteenth centuries. He passed through Germany, and while there married Dinah Gröllman, by whom he had a daughter, Ursule, later the Vicomtesse de Portenduère, who had been left a penniless orphan in her early youth. [Ursule Mirouët.]

Mitant (La), a very poor woman of Conches in Bourgogne, who was condemned for having let her cow graze on the Montcornet estate. In 1823 the animal was seized by the deputy, Brunet, and his assistants, Vermichel and Fourchon. [The Peasantry.]

Mitouflet, old grenadier of the Imperial Guard, husband of a wealthy vineyard proprietress, kept the tavern Soleil d'Or at Vouvray in Touraine. After 1830 Félix Gaudissart lived there and Mitouflet served as his second in a harmless duel brought on by a practical joke played on the illustrious traveling salesman, dupe of the insane Margaritis. [Gaudissart the Great.]

Mitouflet, usher to the minister of war under Louis Philippe, in the time of Gottin de Wissembourg, Hulot d'Ervy and Marneffe. [Cousin Betty.]

Mitral, a bachelor, whose eyes and face were snuff-colored, a bailiff in Paris during the Restoration, also at the same time a money-lender. He numbered among his patrons Molineux and Birotteau. He was invited to the celebrated ball given in December, 1818, by the perfumer. Being a maternal uncle of Isidore Baudoyer, connected in a friendly way with Bidault—Gigonnet—and Esther-Jean van Gobseck, Mitral, by their good-will, obtained his nephew's appointment to the Treasury, December, 1824. He spent his time then in Isle-Adam, the Marais and the Saint-Marceau section, places of residence of his numerous family. In possession of a fortune, which undoubtedly would go later to the Isidore Baudoyers, Mitral retired to the Seine-et-Oise division. [César Birotteau. The Government Clerks.]

Mizerai, in 1836 a restaurant-keeper on rue Michel-le-Comte, Paris. Zéphirin Marcas took his dinners with him at the rate of nine sous. [Z. Marcas.]

Modinier, steward to Monsieur de Watteville; "governor" of Rouxey, the patrimonial estate of the Wattevilles. [Albert Savarus.]

Moinot, in 1815 mail-carrier for the Chaussée-d'Antin; married and the father of four children; lived in the fifth story at 11, rue des Trois-Fréres, now known as rue Taitbout. He innocently exposed the address of Paquita Valdés to Laurent, a servant of Marsay, who artfully tried to obtain it for him. "My name," said the mail-carrier to the servant, "is written just like *Moineau* (sparrow)—M-o-i-n-o-t." "Certainly," replied Laurent. [The Thirteen.]

Moïse, Jew, who was formerly a leader of the *rouleurs* in the South. His wife, La Gonore, was a widow in 1830. [Scenes from a Courtesan's Life.]

Moïse, a Troyes musician, whom Madame Beauvisage thought of employing in 1839 as the instructor of her daughter, Cécile, at Arcis-sur-Aube. [The Member for Arcis.]

Molineux (Jean-Baptiste), Parisian landlord, miserly and selfish. Mesdames Crochard lived in one of his houses between rue du Tourniquct-Saint-Jean and rue la Tixeranderie, in 1815. Mesdames Leseigneur de Rouville and Hippolyte Schinner were also his tenants, at about the same time, on rue de Surène. Jean-Baptiste Molineux lived on Cour-Batave during the first part of Louis XVIII.'s reign. He then owned the house next to César Birotteau's shop on rue Saint-Honoré. Molineux was one of the many guests present at the famous ball of December 17, 1818, and a few months later was the annoying assignee connected with the perfumer's failure. [A Second Home. The Purse. César Birotteau.]

Mollot, through the influence of his wife Sophie, appointed clerk to the justice of the peace at Arcis-sur-Aube; often visited Madame Marion, and saw at her home Goulard, Beauvisage, Giguet, and Herbelot. [The Member for Arcis.]

Mollot (Madame Sophie), wife of the preceding, a prying, prating woman, who disturbed herself greatly over Maxime de Trailles during the electoral campaign in the division of Arcis-sur-Aube, April, 1839. [The Member for Arcis.]

Mollot (Ernestine), daughter of ʳthe preceding couple, was, in 1839, a young girl of marriageable age. [The Member for Arcis.]

Mongenod, born in 1764; son of a grand council attorney, who left him an income of five or six thousand. Becoming bankrupt during the Revolution, he became first a clerk with Frédéric Alain, under Bordin, the solicitor. He was unsuccessful in several ventures: as a journalist with the "Sentinelle," started or built up by him; as a musical composer with the "Péruviens," an opéra-comique given in 1798 at the Feydau theatre.[1] His marriage and the family expenses attendant rendered his financial condition more and more embarrassing. Mongenod had lent money to Frédéric Alain, so that he might be present at the opening performance of the "Mariage de Figaro." He borrowed, in turn, from Alain a sum of money which he was unable to return at the time agreed. He set out thereupon for America, made a fortune, returned January, 1816, and reimbursed Alain. From this time dates the opening of the celebrated Parisian banking-house of .Mongenod & Co. The firm-name changed to Mongenod & Son, and then to Mongenod Brothers. In 1819 the bankruptcy of the perfumer, César Birotteau, having taken place, Mongenod became personally interested at the Bourse,[2] in the affair, negotiating with merchants and discounters. Mongenod died in 1827. [The Seamy Side of History. César Birotteau.]

Mongenod (Madame Charlotte), wife of the preceding,

[1] The Feydau theatre, with its dependencies on the thoroughfare of the same name, existed in Paris until 1826 on the site now taken by the rue de la Bourse.

[2] The Bourse temporarily occupied a building on rue Feydau, while the present palace was building.

in the year 1798 bore up bravely under her poverty, even selling her hair for twelve francs that her family might have bread. Wealthy, and a widow after 1827, Madame Mongenod remained the chief adviser and support of the bank, operated in Paris on rue de la Victoire, by her two sons, Frédéric and Louis. [The Seamy Side of History.]

Mongenod (Frédéric), eldest of the preceding couple's three children, received from his thankful parents the given name of M. Alain and became, after 1827, the head of his father's banking-house on rue de la Victoire. His honesty is shown by the character of his patrons, among whom were the Marquis d'Espard, Charles Mignon de la Bastie, the Baronne de la Chanterie and Godefroid. [The Commission in Lunacy. The Seamy Side of History.]

Mongenod (Louis), younger brother of the preceding, with whom he had business association on rue de la Victoire, where he was receiving the prudent advice of his mother, Madame Charlotte Mongenod, when Godefroid visited him in 1836. [The Seamy Side of History.]

Mongenod (Mademoiselle), daughter of Frédéric and Charlotte Mongenod, born in 1799; she was offered in marriage, January, 1816, to Frédéric Alain, who would not accept this token of gratitude from the wealthy Mongenods. Mademoiselle Mongenod married the Vicomte de Fontaine. [The Seamy Side of History.]

Monistrol, native of Auvergne, a Parisian broker, towards the last years of Louis Philippe's reign, successively on rue de Lappe and the new Beaumarchais boulevard. He was one of the pioneers in the curio business, along with the Popinots, Ponses, and the Rémoncncqs. This kind of business afterwards developed enormously. [Cousin Pons.]

Montauran (Marquis Alphonse de), was, in the closing years of the eighteenth century, connected with nearly all of the well-known Royalist intrigues in France and elsewhere. He frequently visited, along with Flamet de la Billardière and the Comte de Fontaine, the home of Ragon, the perfumer, who was proprietor of the "Reine des Roses," from which went forth the Royalist correspondence between the West and Paris. Too young to have been at Versailles, Alphonse de Montauran had not "the courtly manners for which Lauzun, Adhémar, Coigny, and so many others were noted." His education was incomplete. Towards the autumn of 1799 he especially distinguished himself. His attractive appearance, his youth, and a mingled gallantry and authoritativeness, brought him to the notice of Louis XVIII., who appointed him governor of Bretagne, Normandie, Maine and Anjou. Under the name of Gars, having become commander of the Chouans, in September, the marquis conducted them in an attack against the Blues on the plateau of La Pélerine, which extends between Fougéres, Ille-et-Vilaine, and Ernée, Mayenne. Madame du Gua did not leave him even then. Alphonse de Montauran sought the hand of Mademoiselle d'Uxelles, after leaving this, the last mistress of Charette. Nevertheless, he fell in love with Marie de Verneuil, the spy, who had entered Bretagne with the express intention of delivering him to the Blues. He married her in Fougères, but the Republicans murdered him and his wife a few hours after their marriage. [César Birotteau. The Chouans.]

Montauran (Marquise Alphonse de), wife of the preceding; born Marie-Nathalie de Verneuil at La Chanterie near Alençon, natural daughter of Mademoiselle Blanche de Casteran, who was abbess of Notre-Dame de Séez at the time of her death, and of Victor-Amédée, Duc de Verneuil, who owned her and left her an inheritance, at the expense of her legitimate brother. A lawsuit between brother and sister resulted. Marie-Nathalie lived then with her guardian, the Maréchal Duc de Lenoncourt, and was supposed to be his mistress. After vainly trying to bring him to the point of marriage she was cast off by him. She passed through divers political and social paths during the Revolutionary period. After having shone in court circles she had Danton for a lover. During the autumn of 1799 Fouché hired Marie de Verneuil to betray Alphonse de Montauran, but the lovely spy and the chief of the Chouans fell in love with each other. They were united in marriage a few hours before their death towards the end of that year, 1799, in which Jacobites and Chouans fought on Bretagne soil. Madame de Montauran was attired in her husband's clothes when a Republican bullet killed her. [The Chouans.]

Montauran (Marquis de), younger brother of Alphonse de Montauran, was in London, in 1799, when he received a letter from Colonel Hulot containing Alphonse's last wishes. Montauran complied with them; returned to France, but did not fight against his country. He kept his wealth through the intervention of Colonel Hulot and finally served the Bourbons in the gendarmerie, where he himself became a colonel. When Louis Philippe came to the throne, Montauran believed an absolute retirement necessary. Under the name of M. Nicolas, he became one of the Brothers of Consolation, who met in Madame de la Chanterie's home on rue Chanoinesse. He saved M. Auguste de Mergi from being prosecuted. In 1841 Montauran was seen on rue du Montparnasse, where he assisted at the funeral of the elder Hulot. [The Chouans. The Seamy Side of History. Cousin Betty.]

Montbauron (Marquise de), Raphaél de Valentin's aunt, died on the scaffold during the Revolution. [The Magic Skin.]

Montcornet (Maréchal, Comte de), Grand Cross of the Legion of Honor, Commander of Saint-Louis, born in 1774, son of a cabinet-maker in the Faubourg Saint-Antoine, "child of Paris," mingled in almost all of the wars in the latter part of the eighteenth and beginning of the nineteenth centuries. He commanded in Spain and in Pomerania, and was colonel of cuirassiers in the Imperial Guard. He took the place of his friend, Martial de la Roche-Hugon in the affections of Madame de Vaudremont. The Comte de Montcornet was in intimate relations with Madame or Mademoiselle Fortin, mother of Valérie Crevel. Towards 1815, Montcornet bought, for about a hundred thousand francs, the Aigues, Sophie Laguerre's old estate, situated between

Conches and Blangy, near Soulanges and Ville-aux-Fayes. The Restoration allured him. He wished to have his origin overlooked, to gain position under the new régime, to efface all memory of the expressive nick-name received from the Bourgogne peasantry, who called him the "Upholsterer." In the early part of 1819 he married Virginie de Troisville. His property, increased by an income of sixty thousand francs, allowed him to live in state. In winter he occupied his beautiful Parisian mansion on rue Neuve-des-Mathurins, now called rue des Mathurins, and visited many places, especially the homes of Raoul Nathan and of Esther Gobseck. During the summer the count, then mayor of Blangy, lived at Aigues. His unpopularity and the hatred of the Gaubertins, Rigous, Sibilets, Soudrys, Tonsards, and Fourchons rendered his sojourn there unbearable, and he decided to dispose of the estate. Montcornet, although of violent disposition and weak character, could not avoid being a subordinate in his own family. The monarchy of 1830 overwhelmed Montcornet, then lieutenant-general unattached, with gifts, and gave a division of the army into his command. The count, now become marshal, was a frequent visitor at the Vaudeville.[1] Montcornet died in 1837. He never acknowledged his daughter, Valérie Grevel, and left her nothing. He is probably buried in Père-Lachaise cemetery, where a monument was to be raised for him under W. Steinbock's supervision. Maréchal de Montcornet's motto was: "Sound the Charge." [Domestic Peace. Lost Illusions. A Distinguished Provincial at Paris. Scenes from a Courtesan's Life. The Peasantry. A Man of Business. Cousin Betty.]

Montcornet (Comtesse de.)   (*See* Blondet, Madame Emile.)

Montefiore, Italian of the celebrated Milanese family of Montefiore, commissary in the Sixth of the line under the Empire; one of the finest fellows in the army; marquis, but unable under the laws of the kingdom of Italy to use his

---

[1] A Parisian theatre, situated until 1838 on rue de Chartres. Rue de Chartres, which also disappeared, although later, was located between the Palais-Royal square and the Place du Carrousel.

title. Thrown by his disposition into the "mould of the Rizzios," he barely escaped being assassinated, in 1808 in the city of Tarragone by La Marana, who surprised him in company with her daughter, Juana-Pepita-Maria de Mancini, afterwards François Diard's wife. Later, Montefiore himself married a celebrated Englishwoman. In 1823 he was killed and plundered in a deserted alley in Bordeaux by Diard, who found him, after being away many years, in a gambling-house at a watering-place. [The Maranas.]

Montès de Montejanos (Baron), a rich Brazilian of wild and primitive disposition; towards 1840, when very young, was one of the first lovers of Valérie Fortin, who became in turn Madame Marneffe and Madame Célestin Crevel. He saw her again at the Faubourg Saint-Germain and at the Place or Pâté des Italiens, and had occasion for being envious of Hector Hulot, W. Steinbock and still others. He had revenge on his mistress by communicating to her a mysterious disease from which she died in the same manner as Célestin Crevel. [Cousin Betty.]

Montpersan (Comte de), nephew of a canon of Saint-Denis, upon whom he called frequently; an aspiring rustic, grown sour on account of disappointment and deceit; married, and head of a family. At the beginning of the Restoration he owned the Château de Montpersan, eight leagues from Moulins in Allier, where he lived. In 1819 he received a call from a young stranger who came to inform him of the death of Madame de Montpersan's lover. [The Message.]

Montpersan (Comtesse Juliette de), wife of the preceding, born about 1781, lived at Montpersan with her family, and while there learned from her lover's fellow-traveler of the former's death as a result of an overturned carriage. The countess rewarded the messenger of misfortune in a delicate manner. [The Message.]

Montpersan (Mademoiselle dc), daughter of the preceding couple, was but a child when the sorrowful news arrived which caused her mother to leave the table. The child, thinking only of the comical side of affairs, remarked upon her father's gluttony, suggesting that the countess' abrupt departure had allowed him to break the rules of diet imposed by her presence. [The Message.]

Montriveau (Général Marquis de), father of Armand de Montriveau. Although a knighted chevalier, he continued to hold fast to the exalted manners of Bourgogne, and scorned the opportunities which rank and wealth had offered in his birth. Being an encyclopædist and "one of those already mentioned who served the Republic nobly," Montriveau was killed at Novi near Joubert's side. [The Thirteen.]

Montriveau (Comte de), paternal uncle of Armand de Montriveau. Corpulent, and fond of oysters. Unlike his brother he emigrated, and in his exile met with a cordial reception by the Dulmen branch of the Rivaudoults of Arschoot, a family with which he had some relationship. He died at St. Petersburg. [The Thirteen.]

Montriveau (Général Marquis Armand de), nephew of the preceding and only son of Général de Montriveau. As a penniless orphan he was entered by Bonaparte in the school of Châlons. He went into the artillery service, and took part in the last campaigns of the Empire, among others that in Russia. At the battle of Waterloo he received many serious wounds, being then a colonel in the Guard. Montriveau passed the first three years of the Restoration far away from Europe. He wished to explore the upper sections of Egypt, and Central Africa. After being made a slave by savages he escaped from their hands by a bold ruse and returned to Paris, where he lived on rue de Seine near the Chamber of Peers. Despite his poverty and lack of ambition and influential friends, he was soon promoted to a general's position. His association with The Thirteen, a powerful and secret band of men, who counted among their members Ronquerolles, Marsay and Bourignard, probably brought him this unsolicited favor. This same freemasonry aided Montriveau in his desire to have revenge on Antoinette de Langeais for her delicate flirtation; also later, when still feeling for her the

same passion, he seized her body from the Spanish Carmelites. About the same time the general met, at Madame
de Beauséant's, Rastignac, just come to Paris, and told him
about Anastasie de Restaud. Towards the end of 1821, the
general met Mesdames d'Espard and de Bargeton, who were
spending the evening at the Opéra. Montriveau was the
living picture of Kleber, and in a kind of tragic way became a
widower by Antoinette de Langeais. Having become celebrated for a long journey fraught with adventures, he was the
social lion at the time he ran across a companion of his Egyptian travels, Sixte du Châtelet. Before a select audience of
artists and noblemen, gathered during the first years of the
reign of Louis Philippe at the home of Mademoiselle des
Touches, he told how he had unwittingly been responsible
for the vengeance taken by the husband of a certain Rosina,
during the time of the Imperial wars. Montriveau, now admitted to the peerage, was in command of a department.
At this time, having become unfaithful to the memory of
Antoinette de Langeais, he became enamored of Madame
Rogron, born Bathilde de Chargeboeuf, who hoped soon to
bring about their marriage. In 1839, in company with M.
de Ronquerolles, he became second to the Duc de Rhétoré,
elder brother of Louise de Chaulieu, in his duel with Dorlange-
Sallenauve, brought about because of Marie Gaston. [The
Thirteen. Father Goriot. Lost Illusions. A Distinguished
Provincial at Paris. Another Study of Woman. Pierrette.
The Member for Arcis.]

Morand, formerly a clerk in Barbet's publishing-house,
in 1838 became a partner; along with Métivier tried to take
advantage of Baron de Bourlac, author of "The Spirit of
Modern Law." [The Seamy Side of History.]

Moreau, born in 1772; son of a follower of Danton, pro-
curcur-syndic at Versailles during the Revolution; was Madame
Clapart's devoted lover, and remained faithful almost all
the rest of his life. After a very adventurous life Moreau,
about 1805, became manager of the Presles estate, situated
in the valley of the Oise, which was the property of the

Comte de Sérizy. He married Estelle, maid of Léontine
de Sérizy, and had by her three children. After serving
as manager of the estate for seventeen years, he gave up his
position, when his dishonest dealings with Léger were exposed by Reybert, and retired a wealthy man. A silly
deed of his godson, Oscar Husson, was, more than anything
else, the cause of his dismissal from his position at Presles.
Moreau attained a lofty position under Louis Philippe,
having grown wealthy through real-estate, and became
the father-in-law of Constant-Cyr-Melchior de Canalis.
At last he became a prominent deputy of the Centre under
the name of Moreau of the Oise. [A Start in Life.]

Moreau (Madame Estelle), fair-skinned wife of the preceding, born of lowly origin at Saint-Lô, became maid to
Léontine de Sérizy. Her fortune made, she became overbearing and received Oscar Husson, son of Madame Clapart
by her first husband, with unconcealed coldness. She bought
the flowers for her coiffure from Nattier, and, wearing some
of them, she was seen, in the autumn of 1822, by Joseph
Bridau and Léon de Lora, who had just arrived from Paris
to do some decorating in the château at Sérizy. [A Start in
Life.]

Moreau (Jacques), eldest of the preceding couple's three
children, was the agent between his mother and Oscar Husson
at Presles. [A Start in Life.]

Moreau, the best upholsterer in Alençon, rue de la Porte-
de-Séez, near the church; in 1816 furnished Madame du
Bousquier, then Mademoiselle Rose Cormon, the articles
of furniture made necessary by M. de Troisville's unlooked-
for arrival at her home on his return from Russia. [Jealousies
of a Country Town.]

Moreau, an aged workman at Dauphiné, uncle of little
Jacques Colas, lived, during the Restoration, in poverty
and resignation, with his wife, in the village near Grenoble—
a place which was completely changed by Doctor Benassis.
[The Country Doctor.]

Moreau-Malvin, " a prominent butcher," died about 1820. His beautiful tomb of white marble ornaments rue du Maréchal-Lefebvre at Pére-Lachaise, near the burial-place of Madame Jules Desmarets and Mademoiselle Raucourt of the Comédie-Française. [The Thirteen.]

Morillon (Pére), a priest, who had charge, for some time under the Empire, of Gabriel Claës' early education. [The Quest of the Absolute.]

Morin (La), a very poor old woman who reared La Fosseuse, an orphan, in a kindly manner, in a market-town near Grenoble, but who gave her some raps on the fingers with her spoon when the child was too quick in taking soup from the common porringer. La Morin tilled the soil like a man, and murmured frequently at the miserable pallet on which she and La Fosseuse slept. [The Country Doctor.]

Morin (Jeanne-Marie-Victoire Tarin, veuve), accused of trying to obtain money by forging signatures to promissory-notes, also of the attempted assassination of Sieur Ragoulleau; condemned by the Court of Assize at Paris on January 11, 1812, to twenty years of hard labor. The elder Poiret, a man who never thought independently, was a witness for the defence, and often thought of the trial. The widow Morin, born at Pont-sur-Seine, Aube, was a fellow-country-woman of Poiret, who was born at Troyes. [Father Goriot.] Many extracts have been taken from the items published about this criminal case.

Morisson, an inventor of purgative pills, which were imitated by Doctor Poulain, physician to Pons and the Cibots, when, as a beginner, he wished to make his fortune rapidly. [Cousin Pons.]

Mortsauf (Comte de), head of a Touraine family, which owed to an ancestor of Louis XI.'s reign—a man who had escaped the gibbet—its fortune, coat-of-arms and position. The count was the incarnation of the "refugee." Exiled, either willingly or unwillingly, his banishment made him weak of mind and body. He married Blanche-Henriette de Lenoncourt, by whom he had two children, Jacques and Madeleine. On the accession of the Bourbons he was breveted field-marshal, but did not leave Clochegourde, a castle brought to him in his wife's dowry and situated on the banks of the Indre and the Cher. [The Lily of the Valley.]

Mortsauf (Comtesse de),[1] wife of the preceding; born Blanche-Henriette de Lenoncourt, of the "house of Lenon-court-Givry, fast becoming extinct," towards the first years of the Restoration; was born after the death of three brothers, and thus had a sorrowful childhood and youth; found a good foster-mother in her aunt, a Blamont-Chauvry; and when married found her chief pleasure in the care of her children. This feeling gave her the power to repress the love which she felt for Félix de Vandenesse, but the effort which this hard struggle caused her brought on a severe stomach disease of which she died in 1820. [The Lily of the Valley.]

Mortsauf (Jacques de), elder child of the preceding couple, pupil of Dominis, most delicate member of the family, died prematurely. With his death the line of Lenoncourt-Givrys proper passed away, for he would have been their heir. [The Lily of the Valley.]

Mortsauf (Madeleine de), sister of the preceding; after her mother's death she would not receive Félix de Vandenesse, who had been Madame de Mortsauf's lover. She became in time Duchesse de Leoncourt-Givry (see that name). [The Lily of the Valley.]

Mouche, born in 1811, illegitimate son of one of Fourchon's natural daughters and a soldier who died in Russia; was given a home, when an orphan, by his maternal grandfather, whom he aided sometimes as ropemaker's apprentice. About 1823, in the district of Ville-aux-Fayes, Bourgogne, he profited by the credulity of the strangers whom he was supposed to teach the art of hunting otter. Mouche's attitude and conversation, as he came in the autumn of 1823 to the Aigues, scandalized the Montcornets and their guests. [The Peasautry.]

---

[1] Beauplan and Barrière presented a play at the Comedie-Française, having for a heroine Madame de Mortsauf, June 14, 1853.

Mouchon, eldest of three brothers who lived in 1793 in the Bourgogne valley of Avonne or Aigues; managed the estate of Ronquerolles; became deputy of his division to the Convention; had a reputation for uprightness; preserved the property and the life of the Ronquerolles; died in the year 1804, leaving two daughters, Mesdames Gendrin and Gaubertin. [The Peasantry.]

Mouchon, brother of the preceding, had charge of the relay post-house at Conches, Bourgogne; had a daughter who married the wealthy farmer Guerbet; died in 1817. [The Peasantry.]

Mouchon, brother of the preceding, born in 1756; priest, who had, before the Revolution, the curacy of Ville-aux-Fayes, and knew how to keep it during the Restoration. This sharpness illustrates his character. He was in high favor with the Rigous, Soudrys, Gaubertins, Sibilets, Fourchons and Tonsards. They called him sometimes by the name of "Moucheron." [The Peasantry.]

Mougin, born about 1805 in Toulouse, fifth of the Parisian hair-dressers who, under the name of Marius, successively owned the same business. In 1845, a wealthy married man of family, captain in the Guard and decorated after 1832, an elector and eligible to office, he had established himself on the Place de la Bourse as capillary artist emeritus, where his praises were sung by Bixiou and Lora to the wondering Gazonal. [The Unconscious Humorists.]

Mouilleron, king's attorney at Issoudun in 1822, cousin to every person in the city during the quarrels between the Rouget and Bridau families. [A Bachelor's Establishment.]

Murat (Joachim, Prince). In October, 1800, on the day in which Bartolomeo di Piombo was presented by Lucien Bonaparte, he was, with Lannes and Rapp, in the rooms of Bonaparte, the First Consul. He became Grand Duke of Berg in 1806, the time of the well-known quarrel between the Simeuses and Malin de Gondreville. Murat came to the rescue of Colonel Chabert's cavalry regiment at the battle of Eylau, February 7 and 8, 1807. "Oriental in tastes," he exhibited, even before acceding to the throne of Naples in 1808, a foolish love of luxury for a modern soldier. Twenty years later, during a village celebration in Dauphiné, Benassis and Genestas listened to the story of Bonaparte, as told by a veteran, then become a laborer, who mingled with his narrative a number of entertaining stories of the bold Murat. [The Vendetta. The Gondreville Mystery. Colonel Chabert. Domestic Peace. The Country Doctor.]

Muret gave information about Jean-Joachim Goriot, his predecessor in the manufacture of "pâtes alimentaires." [Father Goriot.]

Musson, well-known hoaxer in the early part of the nine-teenth century. The policeman, Peyrade, imitated his crafti-ness in manner and disguise twenty years later, while acting as an English nabob keeping Suzanne Gaillard. [Scenes from a Courtesan's Life.]

N

Nanon, called Nanon the Great from her height (6 ft. 4 in.); born about 1769. First she tended cows on a farm that she was forced to leave after a fire; turned away on every side, because of her appearance, which was repulsive, she became, about 1791, at the age of twenty-two, a member of Félix Grandet's household at Saumur, where she remained the rest of her life. She always showed gratitude to her master for having taken her in. Brave, devoted and serious-minded, the only servant of the miser, she received as wages for very hard service only sixty francs a year. However, the ac-cumulations from even so paltry an income allowed her, in 1819, to make a life investment of four thousand francs with Monsieur Cruchot. Nanon had also an annuity of twelve hundred francs from Madame de Bonfons, lived near the daughter of her former master, who was dead, and, about 1827, being almost sixty years of age, married Antoine Cornoiller. With her husband, she continued her work of devoted service to Eugénie de Bonfons. [Eugénie Grandet.]

Napolitas, in 1830, secretary of Bibi-Lupin, chief of the secret police. Prison spy at the Conciergerie, he played the part of a son in a family accused of forgery, in order to observe closely Jacques Collin, who pretended to be Carlos Herrera. [Scenes from a Courtesan's Life.]

Narzicof (Princess), a Russian; had left to the merchant Fritot, according to his own account, as payment for supplies, the carriage in which Mistress Noswell, wrapped in the shawl called Sélim, returned to the Hotel Lawson. [Gaudissart II.]

Nathan (Raoul), son of a Jew pawn-broker, who died in bankruptcy a short while after marrying a Catholic, was for twenty-five years (1820-45) one of the best known writers in Paris. Raoul Nathan touched upon many branches: the journal, romance, poetry and the stage. In 1821, Dauriat published for him an imaginative work which Lucien de Rubempré alternately praised and criticized. The harsh criticism was meant for the publisher only. Nathan then put on the stage the "Alcade dans l'Embarras"—a comedie called an "imbroglio" and presented at the Panorama-Dramatique. He signed himself simply "Raoul"; he had as collaborator Cursy—M. du Bruel. The play was a distinct success. About the same time, he supplanted Lousteau, lover of Florine, one of his leading actresses. About this time also Raoul was on terms of intimacy with Emile Blondet, who wrote him a letter dated from Aigues (Bourgogne) in which he described the Montcornets, and related their local difficulties. Raoul Nathan, a member of all the giddy and dissipated social circles, was with Giroudeau, Finot and Bixiou, a witness of Philip Bridau's wedding to Madame J.-J. Rouget. He visited Florentine Cabirolle, when the Marests and Oscar Husson were there, and appeared often on the rue Saint-Georges, at the home of Esther van Gobseck, who was already much visited by Blondet, Bixiou and Lousteau. Raoul, at this time, was much occupied with the press, and made a great parade of Royalism. The accession of Louis Philippe did not diminish the extended circle of his relations. The Marquise d'Espard received him. It was at her house that he heard evil reports of Diane de Cadignan, greatly to the dissatisfaction of Daniel d'Arthez, also present. Marie de Vandenesse, just married, noticed Nathan, who was handsome by reason of an artistic, uncouth ugliness, and elegant irregularity of features, and in the full glory of his renown as a writer and a gallant. Raoul resolved to make the most of the situation. Although turned Republican, he took very readily to the idea of winning a lady of the aristocracy. The conquest of Madame the Comtesse de Vandenesse would have revenged him for the contempt shown him by Lady Dudley, but, fallen into the hands of usurers, fascinated with Florine, living in pitiable style in a passage between the rue Basse-du-Rempart and the rue Neuve-des-Mathurins, and being often detained on the rue Feydau, in the offices of a paper he had founded, Raoul failed in his scheme in connection with the countess, whom Vandenesse even succeeded in restoring to his own affections, by very skilful play with Florine. During the first years of Louis Philippe's reign, Nathan presented a flaming and brilliant drama, the two collaborators in which were Monsieur and Madame Marie Gaston, whose names were indicated on the hand-bills by stars only. In his younger days he had had a play of his put on at the Odéon, a romantic work after the style of "Pinto,"[1] at a time when the classic was dominant, and the stage had been so greatly stirred up for three days that the play was prohibited. At another time he presented at the Théâtre-Français a great drama that fell "with all the honors of war, amid the roar of news-paper cannon." In the winter of 1837-38, Vanda de Mergi read a new romance of Nathan's, entitled "La Perle de Dol." The memory of his social intrigues still haunted Nathan when he returned so reluctantly to M. de Clagny, who demanded it of him, a printed note, announcing the birth of Melchior de la Baudraye, as follows: "Madame la Baronne de la Baudraye is happily delivered of a child; M. Etienne Lousteau has the honor of announcing it to you." Nathan

[1] A drama by Népomucène Lemercier; according to Labitte, "the first work of the renovated stage."

sought the society of Madame de la Baudraye, who got from him, in the rue de Chartres-du-Roule, at the home of Béatrix de Rochefide, a certain story, to be arranged as a novel, related more or less after the style of Sainte-Beuve, concerning the Bohemians and their prince, Rusticoli de la Palférine. Raoul cultivated likewise the society of the Marquise de Rochefide, and, one evening of October, 1840, a proscenium box at the Variétés was the means of bringing together Canalis, Nathan and Béatrix. Received everywhere, perfectly at home in Marguerite Turquet's boudoir, Raoul, as a member of a group composed of Bixiou, La Palférine and Maitre Cardot, heard Maitre Desroches tell how Cérizet made use of Antonia Chocardelle, to "get even" with Maxime de Trailles. Nathan afterwards married his mistress, Florine, whose maiden name was really Sophie Grignault. [Lost Illusions. A Distinguished Provincial at Paris. Scenes from a Courtesan's Life. The Secrets of a Princess. A Daughter of Eve. Letters of Two Brides. The Seamy Side of History. The Muse of the Department. A Prince of Bohemia. A Man of Business. The Unconscious Humorists.]

Nathan[1] (Madame Raoul), wife of the preceding, born Sophie Grignault, in 1805, in Bretagne. She was a perfect beauty, her foot alone left something to be desired. When very young she tried the double career of pleasure and the stage, under the now famous name of Florine. The details of her early life are rather obscure: Madame Nathan, as supernumerary of the Gaîté, had six lovers, before choosing Etienne Lousteau in that relation in 1821. She was at that time closely connected with Florentine Cabirolle, Claudine Chaffaroux, Coralie and Marie Godeschal. She had also a supporter in Matifat, the druggist, and lodged on the rue de Bondy, where, after a brilliant success at the Panorama-Dramatique, with Coralie and Bouffé, she received in magnificent style the diplomatists, Lucien de Rubempré, Camusot and others. Florine soon made an advantageous change in lover, home, theatre and protector; Nathan, whom she afterwards married,

---

[1] On the stage of the Boulevard du Temple Madame Nathan (Florine) henceforth made a salary of eight thousand francs.

supplanted Lousteau about the middle of Louis Philippe's reign. Her home was on rue Hauteville instead of rue de Bondy; and she had moved from the stage of the Panorama to that of the Gymnase. Having made an engagement at the theatre of the Boulevard Bonne-Nouvelle, she met there her old rival, Coralie, against whom she organized a cabal; she was distinguished for the brilliancy of her costumes, and brought into her train of followers successively the opulent Dudley, Désiré Minoret, M. des Grassins, the banker of Saumur, and M. du Rouvre; she even ruined the last two. Florine's fortune rose during the monarchy of July. Her association with Nathan subserved, moreover, their mutual interests; the poet won respect for the actress, who knew moreover how to make herself formidable by her spirit of intrigue and the tartness of her sallies of wit. Who did not know her mansion on the rue Pigalle? Indeed, Madame Nathan was an intimate acquaintance of Coralie, Esther la Torpille, Claudine du Bruel, Euphrasie, Aquilina, Madame Théodore Gaillard, and Marie Godeschal; entertained Emile Blondet, Andoche Finot, Etienne Lousteau, Félicien Vernou, Couture, Bixiou, Rastignac, Vignon, F. du Tillet, Nucingen, and Conti. Her apartments were embellished with the works of Bixiou, F. Souchet, Joseph Bridau, and H. Schinner. Madame de Vandenesse, being somewhat enamored of Nathan, would have destroyed these joys and this splendor, without heeding the devotion of the writer's mistress, on the one hand, or the interference of Vandenesse on the other. Florine, having entirely won back Nathan, made no delay in marrying him. [The Muse of the Department. Lost Illusions. A Distinguished Provincial at Paris. Scenes from a Courtesan's Life. The Government Clerks. A Bachelor's Establishment. Ursule Mirouët. Eugénie Grandet. The Imaginary Mistress. A Prince of Bohemia. A Daughter of Eve. The Unconscious Humorists.]

Navarreins (Duc de), born about 1767, son-in-law of the Prince de Cadignan, through his first marriage; father of Antoinette de Langeais, kinsman of Madame d'Espard, and cousin of Valentin; accused of "haughtiness." He was patron of M. du Bruel—Cursy—on his entrance into the government service; had a lawsuit against the hospitals, which he entrusted to the care of Maitre Derville. He had Polydore de la Baudraye dignified to the appointment of collector, in consideration of his having released him from a debt contracted during the emigration; held a family council with the Grandlieus and Chaulieus when his daughter compromised her reputation by accepting an invitation to the house of Montriveau; was the patron of Victurnien d'Esgrignon; owned near Ville-aux-Fayes, in the sub-prefecture of Auxerrois, extensive estates, which were respected by Montcornet's enemies, the Gaubertins, the Rigous, the Soudrys, the Fourchons, and the Tonsards; accompanied Madame d'Espard to the Opéra ball, when Jacques Collin and Lucien de Rubempré mystified the marchioness; for five hundred thousand francs sold to the Graslins his estates and his Montégnac forest, near Limoges; was an acquaintance of Foedora through Valentin; was a visitor of the Princesse de Cadignan, after the death of their common father-in-law, of whom he had little to make boast, especially in matters of finance. The Duc de Navarrein's mansion at Paris was on the rue du Bac. [A Bachelor's Establishment. Colonel Chabert. The Muse of the Department. The Thirteen. Jealousies of a Country Town. The Peasantry. Scenes from a Courtesan's Life. The Country Parson. The Magic Skin. The Gondreville Mystery. The Secrets of a Princess. Cousin Betty.]

Négrepelisse (De), a family dating back to the Crusades, already famous in the times of Saint-Louis, the name of the younger branch of the "renowned family" of Espard, borne during the Restoration in Angoumois, by M. de Bargeton's father-in-law, M. de Négrepelisse, an imposing looking old country gentleman, and one of the last representatives of the old French nobility, mayor of Escarbes, peer of France, and commander of the Order of Saint-Louis. Négrepelisse survived by several years his son-in-law, whom he took under his roof when Anaïs de Bargeton went to Paris in the summer of 1821. [The Commission in Lunacy. Lost Illusions. A Distinguished Provincial at Paris.]

Négrepelisse (Comte Clément de), born in 1812; cousin of the preceding, who left him his title. He was the elder of the two legitimate sons of the Marquis d'Espard. He studied at College Henri IV., and lived in Paris during the Restoration, as did also his brother, under their father's roof, on the rue de la Montagne-Sainte-Geneviéve. The Comte de' Négrepelisse seldom visited his mother, the Marquise d'Espard, who lived apart from her family in the Faubourg Saint-Honoré. [The Commission in Lunacy.]

Negro (Marquis di), a Genoese noble, "Knight Hospitaller endowed with all known talents," was a visitor, in 1836, of the consul-general of France, at Genoa, when Maurice de l'Hostal gave before Damaso Pareto, Claude Vignon, Léon de Lora, and Félicité des Touches, a full account of the separation, the reconciliation, and, in short, the whole history of Octave de Bauvan and his wife. [Honorine.]

Népomucène, a foundling; servant-boy of Madame Vauthier, manager and door-keeper of the house on the Boulevard Montparnasse, which was occupied by the families of Bourlac and Mergi. Népomucène usually wore a ragged blouse and, instead of shoes, gaiters or wooden clogs. To his work with Madame Vauthier was added daily work in the wood-yards of the vicinity, and, on Sundays and Mondays, during the summer, he worked also with the wine-merchants at the barrier. [The Seamy Side of History.]

Néraud, a physician at Provins during the Restoration. He ruined his wife, who was the widow of a grocer named Auffray, and who had married him for love. He survived her. Being a man of doubtful character and a rival of Dr. Martener, Nérand attached himself to the party of Gouraud and Vinet, who represented Liberal ideas; he failed to uphold Pierrette Lorrain, the granddaughter of Auffray, against her guardians, the Rogrons. [Pierrette.]

Néraud (Madame), wife of the preceding. Married first to Auffray, the grocer, who was sixty years old; she was only thirty-eight at the beginning of her widowhood; she married

Dr. Néraud almost immediately after the death of her first husband. By her first marriage she had a daughter, who was the wife of Major Lorrain, and the mother of Pierrette. Madame Néraud died of grief, amid squalid surroundings, two years after her second marriage. The Rogrons, descended from old Auffray by his first marriage, had stripped her of almost all she had. [Pierrette.]

Nicolas. (*See* Montauran, Marquis de.)

Ninette, born in 1832, "rat" at the Opéra in Paris, was acquainted with Léon de Lora and J.-J. Bixiou, who called Gazonal's attention to her in 1845. [The Unconscious Humorists.]

Niolland (Abbé), the promising pupil of Abbé Roze. Concealed during the Revolution at the house of M. de Négrepelisse, near Barbezieux, he had in charge the education of Marie-Louise-Anaïs (afterwards Madame de Bargeton), and taught her music, Italian and German. He died in 1802. [Lost Illusions.]

Niseron, curate of Blangy (Bourgogne) before the Revolution; predecessor of Abbé Brossette in this curacy; uncle of Jean-François Niseron. He was led by a childish but innocent indiscretion on the part of his great-niece, as well as by the influence of Dom Rigou, to disinherit the Niserons in the interests of the Mesdemoiselles Pichard, house-keepers in his family. [The Peasantry.]

Niseron (Jean-François), beadle, sacristan, chorister, bell-ringer, and grave-digger of the parish of Blangy (Bourgogne), during the Restoration; nephew and only heir of Niseron the curé; born in 1751. He was delighted at the Revolution, was the ideal type of the Republican, a sort of Michel Chrestien of the fields; treated with cold disdain the Pichard family, who took from him the inheritance, to which he alone had any right; lived a life of poverty and sequestration; was none the less respected; was of Montcornet's party represented by Brossette; their opponent, Grégoire Rigou, felt for him both esteem and fear. Jean-François Niseron lost, one after another, his wife and his two children, and had by his side, in his old days, only Geneviéve, natural daughter of his deceased son, Auguste. [The Peasantry.]

Niseron (Auguste), son of the preceding; soldier of the Republic and of the Empire; while an artilleryman in 1809, he seduced, at Zahara, a young Montenegrin, Zéna Kropoli, who died, at Vincennes, early in the year 1810, leaving him an infant daughter. Thus he could not realize his purpose of marrying her. He himself was killed, before Montereau, during the year 1814, by the bursting of a shell. [The Peasantry.]

Niseron (Geneviève), natural daughter of the preceding and the Montenegrin woman, Zéna Kropoli; born in 1810, and named Geneviéve after a paternal aunt; an orphan from the age of four, she was reared in Bourgogne by her grandfather, Jean-François Niseron. She had her father's beauty and her mother's peculiarities. Her patronesses, Madame de Montcornet and Madame de Michaud, bestowed upon her the surname Péchina, and, to guard her against Nicholas Tonsard's attentions, placed her in a convent at Auxerre, where she might acquire skill in sewing and forget Justin Michaud, whom she loved unconsciously. [The Peasantry.]

Noël, book-keeper for Jean-Jules Popinot of Paris, in 1828, at the time that the judge questioned the Marquis d'Espard, whose wife tried to deprive him of the right to manage his property. [The Commission in Lunacy.]

Noswell (Mistress), a rich and eccentric Englishwoman, who was in Paris at the Hotel Lawson about the middle of Louis Philippe's reign; after much mental debate she bought of Fritot the shawl called Sélim, which he said at first it was "impossible" for him to sell. [Gaudissart II.]

Nouastre (Baron de), a refugee of the purest noble blood. A ruined man, he returned to Alençon in 1800, with his daughter, who was twenty-two years of age, and found a home with the Marquis d'Esgrignon, and died of grief two months later. Shortly afterwards the marquis married the orphan daughter. [Jealousies of a Country Town.]

Nourrisson (Madame), was formerly, under the Empire, attached to the service of the Prince d'Ysembourg in Paris. The sight of the disorderly life of a "great lady" of the times decided Madame Nourrisson's profession. She set up shop as a dealer in old clothes, and was also known as mistress of various houses of shame. Intimate relations with Jacqueline Collin, continued for more than twenty years, made this two-fold business profitable. The two matrons willingly exchanged, at times, names and business signs, resources and profits. It was in the old clothes shop, on the rue Neuve-Saint-Marc, that Frédéric de Nucingen bargained for Esther van Gobseck. Towards the end of Charles X.'s reign, one of Madame Nourrisson's establishments, on the rue Saint-Barbe, was managed by La Conore; in the time of Louis Philippe another—a secret affair—existed at the so-called "Pâté des Italiens"; Valérie Marneffe and Wenceslas Steinbock were once caught there together. Madame Nourrisson, first of the name, evidently continued to conduct her business on the rue Saint-Marc, since, in 1845, she narrated the minutiæ of it to Madame Mahuchet before an audience composed of the well-known trio, Bixiou, Lora and Gazonal, and related to them her own history, disclosing to them the secrets of her own long past beginnings in life. [Scenes from a Courtesan's Life. Cousin Betty. The Unconscious Humorists.]

Nouvion (Comte de), a noble refugee, who had returned in utter poverty; chevalier of the Order of Saint-Louis; lived in Paris in 1828, subsisting on the delicately disguised charity of his friend, the Marquis d'Espard, who made him superintendent of the publication, at No. 22 rue de la Montagne-Sainte-Geneviéve, of the "Picturesque History of China," and offered him a share in the possible profits of the work. [The Commission in Lunacy.]

Noverre, a celebrated dancer, born in Paris 1727; died in 1807; was the rather unreliable customer of Chevrel the draper, father-in-law and predecessor of Guillaume at the Cat and Racket. [At the Sign of the Cat and Racket.]

Nucingen (Baron Frédéric de), born, probably at Strasbourg, about 1767. At that place he was formerly clerk
to M. d'Aldrigger, an Alsatian banker. Of better judgment
than his employer, he did not believe in the success of the
Emperor in 1815 and speculated very skilfully on the battle of
Waterloo. Nucingen now carried on business alone, and on
his own account, in Paris and elsewhere; he thus prepared by
degrees the famous house of the rue Saint-Lazare, and laid
the foundation of a fortune, which, under Louis Philippe,
reached almost eighteen million francs. At this period he
married one of the two daughters of a rich vermicelli-maker,
Mademoiselle Delphine Goriot, by whom he had a daughter,
Augusta, eventually the wife of Eugéne de Rastignac.
From the first years of the Restoration may be dated the
real brilliancy of his career, the result of a combination with
the Kellers, Ferdinand du Tillet, and Eugéne de Rastignac
in the successful manipulation of schemes in connection with
the Wortschin mines, followed by opportune assignments
and adroitly managed cases of bankruptcy. These various
combinations ruined the Ragons, the Aiglemonts, the Ald-
riggers, and the Beaudenords. At this time, too, Nucingen,
though clamorously declaring himself an out-and-out Bour-
bonist, turned a deaf ear to César Birotteau's appeals for
credit, in spite of knowing of the latter's consistent Royalism.
There was a time in the baron's life when he seemed to change
his nature; it was when, after giving up his hired dancer,
he madly entered upon an amour with Esther van Gobseck,
alarmed his physician, Horace Bianchon, employed Corentin,
Georges, Lonchard, and Peyrade, and became especially the
prey of Jacques Collin. After Esther's suicide, in May, 1830,
Nucingen abandoned "Cythera," as Chardin des Lupeaulx
had done before, and became again a man of figures, and was
overwhelmed with favors: insignia, the peerage, and the
cross of grand officer of the Legion of Honor. Nucingen,
being respected and esteemed, in spite of his blunt ways
and his German accent, was a patron of Beaudenord, and a
frequent guest of Cointet, the minister; he went everywhere,
and, at the mansion of Mademoiselle des Touches, heard Mar-

say give an account of some of his old love-affairs; witnessed, before Daniel d'Arthez, the calumniation of Diane de Cadignan by every one present in Madame d'Espard's parlor; guided Maxime de Trailles between the hands, or, rather, the clutches of Claparon-Cérizet; accepted the invitation of Josépha Mirah to her reception on the rue Ville-l'Evêque. When Wenceslas Steinbock married Hortense Hulot, Nucingen and Cottin de Wissembourg were the bride's witnesses. Furthermore, their father, Hector Hulot d'Ervy, borrowed of him more than a hundred thousand francs. The Baron de Nucingen acted as sponsor to Polydore de la Baudraye when he was admitted to the French peerage. As a friend of Ferdinand du Tillet, he was admitted on most intimate terms to the boudoir of Carabine, and he was seen there, one evening in 1845, along with Jenny Cadine, Gazonal, Bixiou, Léon de Lora, Massol, Claude Vignon, Trailles, F. du Bruel, Vauvinet, Marguerite Turquet, and the Gaillards of the rue Ménars. [The Firm of Nucingen. Father Goriot. Pierrette. César Birotteau. Lost Illusions. A Distinguished Provincial at Paris. Scenes from a Courtesan's Life. Another Study of Woman. The Secrets of a Princess. A Man of Business. Cousin Betty. The Muse of the Department. The Unconscious Humorists.]

Nucingen (Baronne Delphine de), wife of the preceding, born in 1792; of fair complexion; the spoiled daughter of the opulent vermicelli-maker, Jean-Joachim Goriot; on the side of her mother, who died young, the granddaughter of a farmer. In the latter period of the Empire she contracted, greatly to her taste, a marriage for money. Madame de Nucingen formerly had as her lover Henri de Marsay, who finally abandoned her most cruelly. Reduced, at the time of Louis XVIII., to the society of the Chaussée-d'Antin, she was ambitious to be admitted to the Faubourg Saint-Germain, a circle of which her elder sister, Madame de Restaud, was a member. Eugéne de Rastignac opened to her the parlor of Madame de Beauséant, his cousin, rue de Grcville, in 1819, and, at about the same time, became her lover. Their liaison lasted more than fifteen years. An apartment on the rue d'Artois, fitted up by Jean-Joachim Goriot, sheltered their early love. Having entrusted to Rastignac a certain sum for play at the Palais-Royal, the baroness was able with the proceeds to free herself of a humiliating debt to Marsay. Meanwhile she lost her father. The Nucingen carriage, without an occupant, however, followed the hearse. [Father Goriot.] Madame de Nucingen entertained a great deal on the rue Saint-Lazare. It was there that Auguste de Maulincour saw Clémence Desmarets, and Adolphe des Grassins met Charles Grandet. [The Thirteen. Eugénie Grandet.] César Birotteau, on coming to beg credit of Nucingen, as also did Rodolphe Castanier, immediately after his forgery, found themselves face to face with the baroness. [César Birotteau. Melmoth Reconciled.] At this period, Madame de Nucingen took the box at the Opéra which Antoinette de Langeais had occupied, believing undoubtedly, said Madame d'Espard, that she would inherit her charms, wit and success. [Lost Illusions. A Distinguished Provincial at Paris. The Commission in Lunacy.] According to Diane de Cadignan, Delphine had a horrible journey when she went to Naples by sea, of which she brought back a most painful reminder. The baroness showed a haughty and scornful indulgence when her husband became enamored of Esther van Gobseck. [Scenes from a Courtesan's Life.] Forgetting her origin she dreamed of seeing her daughter Augusta become Duchesse d'Hérouville; but the Hérouvilles, knowing the muddy source of Nucingen's millions, declined this alliance. [Modeste Mignon. The Firm of Nucingen.] Shortly after the year 1830, the baroness was invited to the house of Félicité des Touches, where she saw Marsay once more, and heard him give an account of an old love-affair. [Another Study of Woman.] Delphine aided Marie de Vandenesse and Nathan to the extent of forty thousand francs during the checkered course of their intrigues. She remembered indeed having gone through with similar experiences. [A Daughter of Eve.] About the middle of the monarchy of July, Madame de Nucingen, as mother-in-law of Eugéne de Rastignac, visited Madame d'Espard and met Maxime de Trailles and Ferdinand du Tillet in the Faubourg Saint-Germain. [The Member for Arcis.]

Nueil (De), proprietor of the domain of the Manervilles, which, doubtless, descended to the younger son, Gaston. [The Deserted Woman.]

Nueil (Madame de), wife of the preceding, survived her husband, and her eldest son, became the dowager Comtesse de Nueil, and afterwards owned the domain of Manerville, to which she withdrew in retirement. She was the type of the scheming mother, careful and correct, but worldly. She matched off Gaston, and was thereby involuntarily the cause of his death. [The Deserted Woman.]

Nueil (De), eldest son of the preceding, died of consumption in the reign of Louis XVIII., leaving the title of Comte de Nueil to his younger brother, Baron Gaston. [The Deserted Woman.]

Nueil (Gaston de), son of the Nueils and brother of the preceding, born about 1799, of good extraction and with fortune suitable to his rank. He went, in 1822, to Bayeux, where he had family connections, in order to recuperate from the wearing fatigues of Parisian life; had an opportunity to force open the closed door of Claire de Beauséant, who had been living in retirement in that vicinity ever since the marriage of Miguel d'Ajuda-Pinto to Berthe de Rochefide; he fell in love with her, his love was reciprocated, and for nearly ten years he lived with her as her husband in Normandie and Switzerland. Albert Savarus, in his autobiographical novel, "L'Ambitieux par Amour," made a vague reference to them as living together on the shore of Lake Geneva. After the Revolution of 1830, Gaston de Nueil, already rich from his Norman estates that afforded an income of eighteen thousand francs, married Mademoiselle Stéphanie de la Rodière. Wearying of the marriage tie, he wished to renew his former relations with Madame de Beauséant. Exasperated by the haughty repulse at the hands of his former mistress, Nueil killed himself. [The Deserted Woman. Albert Savarus.]

Nueil (Madame Gaston de), born Stéphanie de la Rodière, about 1812, a very insignificant character, married, at the beginning of Louis Philippe's reign, Gaston de Nucil, to whom she brought an income of forty thousand francs a year. She was enceinte after the first month of her marriage. Having become Comtesse de Nueil, by succession, upon the death of her brother-in-law, and being deserted by Gaston, she continued to live in Normandie. Madame Gaston de Nneil survived her husband. [The Deserted Woman.]

O

O'Flaharty (Major), maternal uncle of Raphaël de Valentin, to whom he bequeathed ten millions upon his death in Calcutta, August, 1828. [The Magic Skin.]

Oignard, in 1806 was chief clerk to Maitre Bordin, a Parisian lawyer. [A Start in Life.]

Olga, daughter of the Topinards, born in 1840. She was not a legitimate child, as ‘ parents were not married at the time when Schmucke saw her with them in 1845. He loved her for the beauty of her light Teutonic hair. [Cousin Pons.]

Olivet, an Angouléme lawyer, succeeded by Petit-Claud. [Lost Illusions.]

Olivier was in the service of the policemen, Corentin and Peyrade, when they found the Hauteserres and the Simeuses with the Cinq-Cygne family in 1803. [The Gondreville Mystery.]

Olivier (Monsieur and Madame),first in the employ of Charles X. as outrider and laundress; had charge of three children, of whom the eldest became an under notary's clerk; were finally, under Louis Philippe, servants of the Marneffes and of Mademoiselle Fischer, to whom, through craftiness or gratitude, they devoted themselves exclusively. [Cousin Betty.]

Orfano (Duc d'), title of Maréchal Cottin.

Orgemont (D'), wealthy and avaricious banker, proprietor at Fougéres, bought the Abbaye de Juvigny's estate. He remained neutral during the Chouan insurrection of 1799 and came into contact with Coupiau, Galope-Chopine, and Mesdames du Gua-Saint-Cyr and de Montauran. [The Chouans.]

Orgemont (D'), brother of the preceding, a Breton priest who took the oath of allegiance. He died in 1795 and was buried in a secluded spot, discovered and preserved by M. d'Orgemont, the banker, as a place of hiding from the fury of the Vendeans. [The Chouans.]

Origet, famous Tours physician; known to the Mortsaufs, châtelains of Clochegourde. [The Lily of the Valley.]

Orsonval (Madame d'), frequently visited the Cruchot and Grandet f milies at Saumur. [Eugénie Grandet.᾽

Ossian, valet in the service of Mougin, the well-known hair-dresser on the Place de la Bourse, in 1845. Ossian's duty was to show the patrons out, and in this capacity he attended Bixiou, Lora and Gazonal. [The Unconscious Humorists.]

Ottoboni, an Italian conspirator who hid in Paris. In 1831, on dining at the Giardinis on rue Froidmanteau, he became acquainted with the Gambaras. [Gambara.]

P

Paccard, released convict, in Jacques Collin's clutches, well known as a thief and drunkard. He was Prudence Servien's lover, and both were employed by Esther van Gobseck at the same time, Paccard being a footman; lived with a carriage-maker on rue de Provence, in 1829. After stealing seven hundred and fifty thousand francs, which had been left by Esther van Gobseck, he was obliged to give up seven hundred and thirty thousand of them. [Scenes from a Courtesan's Life.]

Paccard (Mademoiselle), sister of the preceding, in **the**

power of Jacqueline Collin. [Scenes from a Courtesan's Life.]

Palma, Parisian banker of the Poissonière suburbs; had, during the régime of the Restoration and of July, great fame as a financier. He was "private counsel for the Keller establishment." Birotteau, the perfumer, at the time of his financial troubles, vainly asked him for help. [The Firm of Nucingen. César Birotteau.] With Werbrust as a partner he dealt in discounts as shrewdly as did Gobseck and Bidault, and thus was in a position to help Lucien de Rubempré. [Gobseck. Lost Illusions. A Distinguished Provincial at Paris.] He was also M. Werbrust's associate in the muslin, calico and oil-cloth establishment at No. 5 rue du Sentier, when Maximilien was so friendly with the Fontaines. [The Ball at Sçeaux.]

Pamiers (Vidame de), "oracle of Faubourg Saint-Germain at the time of the Restoration," a member of the family council dealing with Antoinette de Langeais, who was accused of compromising herself with Montriveau. Past-commander of the Order of Malta, prominent in both the eighteenth and nineteenth centuries, old and confidential friend of the Baronne de Maulincour. Palmiers reared the young Baron Auguste de Maulincour, defending him with all his power against Bourignard's hatred. [The Thirteen.] As a former intimate friend of the Marquis d'Esgrignon, the vidame introduced the Vicomte d'Esgrignon—Victurnien—to Diane de Maufrigneuse. An intimate friendship between the young man and the future Princess de Cadignan was the result. [Jealousies of a Country Town.]

Pannier, merchant and banker after 1794; treasurer of the "brigands"; connected with the uprising of the Chauffeurs of Mortagne in 1809. Having been condemned to twenty years of hard labor, Pannier was branded and placed in the galleys. Appointed lieutenant-general under Louis XVIII., he governed a royal castle. He died without children. [The Seamy Side of History.]

Paradis, born in 1830; Maxime de Trailles' servant-boy or "tiger"; quick and bold; made a tour, during the election period in the spring of 1839, through the Arcis-sur-Aube district, with his master, meeting Goulard, the sub-prefect, Poupart, the tavern-keeper, and the Maufrigneuses and Mollots of Cinq-Cygne. [The Member for Arcis.]

· **Parquoi** (François), one of the Chouans, for whom Abbé Gudin held a funeral mass in the heart of the forest, not far from Fougéres, in the autumn of 1799. François Parquoi died, as did Nicolas Laferté, Joseph Brouet and Sulpice Coupiau, of injuries received at the battle of La Pélerine and at the siege of Fougéres. [The Chouans.]

Pascal, porter of the Thuilliers in their Place de la Madeleine house; acted also as beadle at La Madeleine church. [The Middle Classes.]

Pascal (Abbé), chaplain at Limoges prison in 1829; gentle old man. He tried vainly to obtain a confession from Jean-François Tascheron, who had been imprisoned for robbery followed by murder. [The Country Parson.]

Pastelot, priest in 1845, in the Saint-François church in the Marais, on the street now called rue Charlot; watched over the dead body of Sylvain Pons. [Cousin Pons.]

Pastureau (Jean François), in 1829, owner of an estate in Isére, the value of which was said to have been impaired by the passing by of Doctor Benassis' patients. [The Country Doctor.]

Patrat (Maitre), notary at Fougéres in 1799, an acquaintance of D'Orgemont, the banker, and introduced to Marie de Verneuil by the old miser. [The Chouans.]

Patriote, a monkey, which Marie de Verneuil, its owner, had taught to counterfeit Danton. The craftiness of this animal reminded Marie of Corentin. [The Chouans.]

Pauline, for a long time Julie d'Aiglemont's waiting-maid. [A Woman of Thirty.]

Paulmier, employed under the Restoration in the Ministry

of Finance in Isidore Baudoyer's bureau of Flamet de la
Billardière's division.   Paulmier was a bachelor, but quarreled
continually with his married colleague, Chazelles. [The Government Clerks.]

Paz (Thaddée), Polish descendant of a distinguished
Florentine family, the Pazzi, one of whose members had become a refugee in Poland. Living contemporaneously
with his fellow-citizen and friend, the Comte Adam Mitgislas
Laginski, like him Thaddée Paz fought for his country,
later on following him into exile in Paris, during the reign
of Louis Philippe. Bearing up bravely in his poverty, he
was willing to become steward to the count, and he made
an able manager of the Laginski mansion. He gave up
this position, when, having become enamored of Clémentine
Laginska, he saw that he could no longer control his passion
by means of a pretended mistress, Marguerite Turquet,
the horsewoman. Paz (pronounced Pac), who had willingly
assumed the title of captain, had seen the Steinbocks married. His departure from France was only feigned, and he
once more saw the Comtesse Laginska, during the winter
of 1842. At Rusticoli he took her from La Palférine, who
was on the point of carrying her away. [The Imaginary
Mistress.   Cousin Betty.]

Péchina (La), nick-name of Geneviève Niseron.

Pederotti (Signor), father of Madame Maurice de l'Hostal.
He was a Genoa banker; gave his only daughter a dowry of a
million; married her to the French consul, and left her, on dying six months later in January, 1831, a fortune made in grain
and amounting to two millions. Pederotti had been made
count by the King of Sardinia, but, as he left no male heir,
the title became extinct. [Honorine.]

Pelletier, one of Benassis' patients in Isére, who died in
1829, was buried on the same day as the last " cretin," which
had been kept on account of popular superstition. Pelletier
left a wife, who saw Genestas, and several children, of whom
the eldest, Jacques, was born about 1807. [The Country
Doctor.]

Pen-Hoël (Jacqueline de), of a very old Breton family, lived at Guérande, where she was born about 1780. Sister-in-law of the Kergarouëts of Nantes, the patrons of Major Brigant, who, despite the displeasure of the people, did not themselves hesitate to assume the name of Pen-Hoël. Jacqueline protected the daughters of her younger sister, the Vicomtesse de Kergarouët. She was especially attracted to her eldest niece, Charlotte, to whom she intended to give a dowry, as she desired the girl to marry Calyste du Guénic, who was in love with Félicité des Touches. [Béatrix.]

Péroux (Abbé), brother of Madame Julliard; vicar of Provins during the Restoration. [Pierrette.]

Perrache, small hunchback, shoemaker by trade, and, in 1840, porter in a house belonging to Corentin on rue Honoré-Chevalier, Paris. [The Middle Classes.]

Perrache (Madame), wife of the preceding, often visited Madame Cardinal, niece of Toupillier, one of Corentin's renters. [The Middle Classes.]

Perret, with his partner, Grosstête, preceded Pierre Graslin in a banking-house at Limoges, in the early part of the nineteenth century. [The Country Parson.] .

Perret (Madame), wife of the preceding, an old woman in 1829, disturbed herself, as did every one in Limoges, over the assassination committed by Jean-François Tascheron. [The Country Parson.]

Perrotet, in 1819, laborer on Félix Grandet's farm in the suburbs of Saumur. [Eugénie Grandet.]

Petit-Claud, son of a very poor tailor of L'Houmeau, a suburb of Angoulême, where he pursued his studies in the town lyceum, becoming acquainted at the same time with Lucien de Rubempré. He studied law at Poitiers. On going back to the chief city of La Charente, he became clerk to Maitre Olivet, an attorney whom he succeeded. Now began Petit-Claud's period of revenge for the insults which his poverty and homeliness had brought on. He met

Cointet, the printer, and went into his employ, although at the same time he feigned allegiance to the younger Séchard, also a printer. This conduct paved the way for his accession to the magistracy. He was in turn deputy and king's procureur. Petit-Claud did not leave Angouléme, but made a profitable marriage in 1822 with Mademoiselle Françoise de la Haye, natural daughter of Francis du Hautoy and of Madame de Senonches. [Lost Illusions.]

Petit-Claud (Madame), wife of the preceding, natural daughter of Francis du Hautoy and of Madame de Senonches; born Françoise de la Haye, given into the keeping of old Madame Cointet; married through the instrumentality of Madame Cointet's son, the printer, known as Cointet the Great. Madame Petit-Claud, though insignificant and forward, was provided with a very substantial dowry. [Lost Illusions.]

Peyrade, born about 1758 in Provence, Comtat, in a large family of poor people who eked out a scant subsistence on a small estate called Canquoëlle. Peyrade, paternal uncle of Théodose de la Peyrade, was of noble birth, but kept the fact secret. He went from Avignon to Paris in 1776, where he entered the police force two years later. Lenoir thought well of him. Peyrade's success in life was impaired only by his immoralities; otherwise it would have been much more brilliant and lasting. He had a genius for spying, also much executive ability. Fouché employed him and Corentin in connection with the affair of Gondreville's imaginary abduction. A kind of police ministry was given to him in Holland. Louis XVIII. counseled with him and gave him employment, but Charles X. held aloof from this shrewd employé. Peyrade lived in poverty on rue des Moineaux with an adored daughter, Lydie, the child of La Beaumesnil of the Comédie-Française. Certain events brought him into the notice of Nucingen, who employed him in the search for Esther Gobseck, at the same time warning him against the courtesan's followers. The police department, having been told of this arrangement by the so-called Abbé Carlos

Herrera, would not permit him to enter into the employ of a private individual. Despite the protection of his friend, Corentin, and the talent as a policeman, which he had shown under the assumed names of Canquoëlle and Saint-Germain, especially in connection with F. Gaudissart's seizure, Peyrade failed in his struggle with Jacques Collin. His excellent transformation into a nabob defender of Madame Théodore Gaillard made the former convict so angry that, during the last years of the Restoration, he took revenge on him by making way with him. Peyrade's daughter was abducted and he died from the effects of poison. [The Gondreville Mystery. Scenes from a Courtesan's Life.]

Peyrade (Lydie).[1] (*See* La Peyrade, Madame Théodose de.)

Phellion, born in 1780, husband of a Le Perche woman, who bore him three children, two of whom were sons, Félix and Marie-Théodore, and one a daughter, who became Madame Barniol; clerk in the Ministry of Finance, Xavier Rabourdin's bureau, division of Flamet de la Billardière, a position which he held until the close of 1824. He upheld Rabourdin, who, in turn, often defended him. While living on rue du Faubourg-Saint-Jacques near the Sourds-Muets, he taught history, literature and elementary ethics to the students of Mesdemoiselles La Grave. The Revolution of July did not affect him; even his retirement from service did not cause him to give up the home in which he remained for at least thirty years. He bought for eighteen thousand francs a small house on Feuillantines lane, now rue des Feuillantines, which he occupied, after he had improved it, in a serious Bourgeois manner. Phellion was a major in the National Guard. For the most part he still had the same friends, meeting and visiting frequently Baudoyer, Dutocq, Fleury, Godard, Laudigeois, Rabourdin, Madame Poiret the elder, and especially the Colleville, Thuillier and Minard families. His leisure time was occupied with politics and art. At the

---

[1] Under the title of "Lydie" a portion of the life of Peyrade's daughter was used in a play presented at the Théâtre des Nations, now Théâtre de Paris, but the author did not publish his play.

Odéon he was on a committee of classical reading. His political influence and vote were sought by Théodose de la Peyrade in the interest of Jérôme Thuillier's candidacy for the General Council; for Phellion favored another candidate, Horace Bianchon, relative of the highly-honored J.-J. Popinot. [The Government Clerks. The Middle Classes.]

Phellion (Madame), wife of the preceding; belonged to a family who lived in a western province. Her family being so large that the income of more than nine thousand francs, pension and rentals, was insufficient, she continued, under Louis Philippe, to give lessons in harmony to Mesdemoiselles La Grave, as in the Restoration, with the strictness observed in her every-day life.

Phellion (Félix), eldest son of the preceding couple, born in 1817; professor of mathematics in a Royal college at Paris, then a member of the Academy of Sciences, and chevalier of the Legion of Honor. By his remarkable works and his discovery of a star, he was thus made famous before he was twenty-five years old, and married, after this fame had come to him, Céleste-Louise-Caroline-Brigitte Colleville, the sister of one of his pupils and a woman for whom his love was so strong that he gave up Voltairism for Catholicism. [The Middle Classes.]

Phellion (Madame Félix), wife of the preceding; born Céleste-Louise-Caroline-Brigitte Colleville. Although M. and Madame Colleville's daughter, she was reared almost entirely by the Thuilliers. Indeed, M. L.-J. Thuillier, who had been one of Madame Flavie Colleville's lovers, passed for Céleste's father. M., Madame and Mademoiselle Thuillier were all determined to give her their Christian names and to make up a large dowry for her. Olivier Vinet, Godeschal, Théodose de la Peyrade, all wished to marry Mademoiselle Colleville. Nevertheless, although she was a devoted Christian, she loved Félix Phellion, the Voltairean, and married him after his conversion to Catholicism. [The Middle Classes.]

Phellion (Marie-Théodore), Félix Phellion's younger brother, in 1840 pupil at the Ecole des Ponts et Chaussées. [The Middle Classes.]

Philippart (Messieurs), owners of a porcelain manufactory at Limoges, in which was employed Jean-François Tascheron, the murderer of Pingret and Jeanne Malassis. [The Country Parson.]

Philippe, employed in Madame Marie Gaston's family; formerly an attendant of the Princesse de Vaurémont; later became the Duc Henri de Chaulieu's servant; finally entered Marie Gaston's household, where he was employed after his wife's decease. [Letters of Two Brides. The Member for Arcis.]

Pichard (Mademoiselle), house-keeper of Niseron, vicar of Blangy in Bourgogne. Prior to 1789 she brought her niece, Mademoiselle Arséne Pichard, to his house. [The Peasantry.]

Pichard (Arséne), niece of the preceding. (*See* Rigou, Madame Grégoire.) [The Peasantry.]

Picot (Népomucène), astronomer and mathematician, friend of Biot after 1807, author of a "Treatise on Differential Logarithms," and especially of a "Theory of Perpetual Motion," four volumes, quarto, with engravings, Paris, 1825; lived, in 1840, No. 9 rue du Val-de-Grâce. Being very near-sighted and erratic, the prey of his thieving servant, Madame Lambert, his family thought that he needed a protector. Being instructor of Félix Phellion, with whom he took a trip to England, Picot made known his pupil's great ability, which the boy had modestly kept secret, at the home of the Thuilliers, Place de la Madeleine, before an audience composed of the Collevilles, Minards and Phellions. Celeste Colleville's future was thus determined. As Picot was decorated late in life, his marriage to a wealthy and eccentric Englishwoman of forty was correspondingly late. After passing through a successful operation for a cancer, he returned, "a new man," to the home of the Thuilliers. He was led through gratitude to leave to the Félix Phellions the wealth brought him by Madame Picot. [The Middle Classes.]

Picquoiseau (Comtesse), widow of a colonel. She and Madame de Vaumerland boarded with one of Madame Vauquer's rivals, according to Madame de l'Ambermcsnil. [Father Goriot.]

Pius VII. (Barnabas Chiaramonti), lived from 1740 till 1823; pope. Having been asked by letter in 1806, if a woman might go *décolleté* to the ball or to the theatre, without endangering her welfare, he answered his correspondent, Madame Angélique de Granville, in a manner befitting the gentle Fénelon. [A Second Home.]

Piédefer (Abraham), descendant of a middle class Calvinist family of Sancerre, whose ancestors in the sixteenth century were skilled workmen, and subsequently woolendrapers; failed in business during the reign of Louis XVI.; died about 1786, leaving two sons, Moïse and Silas, in poverty. [The Muse of the Department.]

Piédefer (Moïse), elder son of the preceding, profited by the Revolution in imitating his forefathers; tore down abbeys and churches; married the only daughter of a Convention member who had been guillotined, and by her had a child, Dinah, later Madame Milaud de la Baudraye; compromised his fortune by his agricultural speculations; died in 1819. [The Muse of the Department.]

Piédefer (Silas), son of Abraham Piédefer, and younger brother of the preceding; did not receive, as did Moïse Piédefer, his part of the small paternal fortune; went to the Indies; died, about 1837, in New York, with a fortune of twelve hundred thousand francs. This money was inherited by his niece, Madame de la Baudraye, but was seized by her husband. [The Muse of the Department.]

Piédefer (Madame Moïse), sister-in-law of the preceding, unaffable and excessively pious; pensioned by her son-in-law; lived successively in Sancerre and at Paris with her daughter, Madame de la Baudraye, whom she managed to separate from Etienne Lousteau. [The Muse of the Department.]

Pierquin, born about 1786, successor to his father as notary in Douai; distant cousin of the Molina-Claës of rue de Paris, through the Pierquins of Antwerp; self-interested and positive by nature; aspired to the hand of Marguerite Claés, eldest daughter of Balthazar, who afterwards became Madame Emmanuel de Solis; finally married Félicie, a younger sister of his first choice, in the second year of Charles X.'s reign. [The Quest of the Absolute.]

Pierquin (Madame), wife of the preceding, born Félicie Claés, found, as a young girl, a second mother in her elder sister, Marguerite. [The Quest of the Absolute.]

Pierquin, brother-in-law of the preceding; physician who attended the Claés at Douai. [The Quest of the Absolute.]

Pierrot, assumed name of Charles-Amédée-Louis-Joseph Rifoël, Chevalier du Vissard. [The Seamy Side of History.]

Pierrotin, born in 1781. After having served in the cavalry, he left the service in 1815 to succeed his father as manager of a stage-line between Paris and Isle-Adam—an undertaking which, though only moderately successful, finally flourished. One morning in the autumn of 1822, he received as passengers, at the Lion d'Argent, some people, either famous or of rising fame, the Comte Hugret de Sérizy, Léon de Lora and Joseph Bridau, and took them to Presles, a place near Beaumont. Having . become "coach-proprietor of Oise," in 1838 he married his daughter, Georgette, to Oscar Husson, a high officer, who, upon retiring, had been appointed to a collectorship in Beaumont, and who, like the Canalises and the Moreaus, had for a long time been one of Pierrotin's customers. [A Start in Life.]

Pietro, Corsican servant of the Bartolomeo di Piombos, kinsmen of Madame Luigi Porta. [The Vendetta.]

Pigeau, during the Restoration, at one time head-carrier and afterwards owner of a small house, which he had built with his own hands and on a very economical basis, at Nanterre (between Paris and Saint-Germain-in-Laye.) [Scenes from a Courtesan's Life.]

Pigeau (Madame), wife of the preceding; belonged to a family of wine merchants. After her husband's death, about the end of the Restoration, she inherited a little property, which caused her much unhappiness, in consequence of her avarice and distrust. Madame Pigeau was planning to remove from Nanterre to Saint-Germain with a view to living there on her annuity, when she was murdered, with her servant and her dogs, by Théodore Calvi, in the winter of 1828-29. [Scenes from a Courtesan's Life.]

Pigeron, of Auxerre, was murdered, it is said, by his wife; be that as it may, the autopsy, entrusted to Vermut, a druggist of Soulanges, in Bourgogne, proved the use of poison. [The Peasantry.]

Pigoult, was head clerk in the office where Malin de Gondreville and Grévin studied pettifogging; was, about 1806, first justice of the peace at Arcis, and then president of the tribunal of the same town, at the time of the lawsuit in connection with the abduction of Malin, when he and Grévin were the prosecuting attorneys.   [The Gondreville Mystery.] In the neighborhood of 1839, Pigoult was still living, having his home in the ward.   At that time he made public recognition of Pantaléon, Marquis de Sallenauve, and supposed father of Charles Dorlange, Comte de Sallenauve, thus serving the interests, or rather the ambitions, of the deputy. .[The Member for Arcis.]

Pigoult, son of the preceding, acquired the hat manufactory of Philéas Beauvisage, made a failure of the undertaking, and committed suicide; but appeared to have had a natural, though sudden, death. [The Member for Arcis.]

Pigoult (Achille), son of the preceding and grandson of the next preceding, born in 1801. A man of unattractive personality, but of great intelligence, he supplanted Crévin, and, in 1819, was the busiest notary of Arcis. Gondreville's influence, and his intimacy with Beauvisage and Giguet, were the causes of his taking a prominent part in the political contests of that period; he opposed Simon Giguet's candidacy, and successfully supported the Comte de Sallenauve. The introduction of the Marquis Pantaléon de Sallenauve to old Pigoult was brought about through Achille Pigoult, and assured a triumph for the sculptor, Sallenauve-Dorlange. [The Member for Arcis.]

Pillerault (Claude-Joseph), a very upright Parisian trader, proprietor of the Cloche d'Or, a hardware establishment on the Quai de la Ferraille; made a modest fortune, and retired from business in 1814. After losing, one after another, his wife, his son, and an adopted child, Pillerault devoted his life to his niece, Constance-Barbe-Joséphine, of whom he was guardian and only relative. Pillerault lived on the rue des Bourdonnais, in 1818, occupying a small apartment let to him by Camusot of the Cocon d'Or. During that period, Pillerault was remarkable for the intelligence, energy and courage displayed in connection with the unfortunate Birotteaus, who were falling into bad repute. He found out Claparon, and terrified Molineux, both enemies of the Birotteaus. Politics and the Café David, situated between the rue de la Monnaie and the rue Saint-Honoré, consumed the leisure hours of Pillerault, who was a stoical and staunch Republican; he was exceedingly considerate of Madame Vaillant, his house-keeper, and treated Manuel, Foy, Perier, Lafayette and Courier as gods. [César Birotteau.] Pillerault lived to a very advanced age. The Anselme Popinots, his grand-nephew and grand-niece, paid him a visit in 1844. Poulain cured the old man of an illness when he was more than eighty years of age; he then owned an establishment (rue de Normandie, in the Marais), managed by the Cibots, and counting among its occupants the Chapoulot family, Schmucke and Sylvain Pons. [Cousin Pons.]

Pillerault (Constance-Barbe-Joséphine). (*See* Birotteau, Madame César.)

Pimentel (Marquis and Marquise de), enjoyed extended influence during the Restoration, not only with the society element of Paris, but especially in the department of Charente, where they spent their summers. They were reputed to be the wealthiest land-owners around Angouléme, were on intimate terms with their peers, the Rastignacs, together with whom they composed the shining lights of the Bargeton circle. [Lost Illusions.]

Pinaud (Jacques), a "poor linen-merchant," the name under which M. d'Orgemont, a wealthy broker of Fougéres, tried to conceal his identity from the Chouans, in 1799, to avoid being a victim of their robbery. [The Chouans.]

Pingret, uncle of Monsieur and Madame des Vauneaulx; a miser, who lived in an isolated house in the Faubourg Saint-Etienne, near Limoges; robbed and murdered, with his servant Jeanne Malassis, one night in March, 1829, by Jean-François Tascheron. [The Country Parson.]

Pinson, long a famous Parisian restaurant-keeper of the rue de l'Ancienne-Comédie, at whose establishment Théodose de la Peyrade, reduced, in the time of Louis Philippe, to the uttermost depths of poverty, dined, at the expense of Cérizet and Dutocq, at a cost of forty-seven francs; there also these three men concluded a compact to further their mutual interests. [The Middle Classes.]

Piombo (Baron Bartolomeo di), born in 1738, a fellow-countryman and friend of Napoleon Bonaparte, whose mother he had protected during the Corsican troubles. After a terrible vendetta, carried out in Corsica against all the Portas except one, he had to leave his country, and went in great poverty to Paris with his family. Through the intercession of Lucien Bonaparte, he saw the First Consul (October, 1800) and obtained property, titles and employment. Piombo was not without gratitude; the friend of Daru, Drouot, and Carnot, he gave evidence of devotion to his benefactor until the latter's death. The return of the Bourbons did not deprive him entirely of the resources that he had acquired. For his Corsican property Bartolomeo received of Madame Letitia Bonaparte a sum which allowed him to purchase and occupy the Portenduère mansion. The marriage of his adored daughter, Ginevra, who, against her father's will, became the wife of the last of the Portas, was a source of vexation and grief to Piombo, that nothing could diminish. [The Vendetta.]

Piombo (Baronne Elisa di), born in 1745, wife of the preceding and mother of Madame Porta, was unable to obtain from Bartolomeo the pardon of Ginevra, whom he would not see after her marriage. [The Vendetta.]

Piombo (Ginevra di). (*See* Porta, Madame Luigi.)

Piombo (Gregorio di), brother of the preceding, and son of Bartolomeo and Elisa di Piombo; died in his infancy, a victim of the Portas, in the vendetta against the Piombos. [The Vendetta.]

Piquetard (Agathe). (*See* Hulot d'Ervy, Baronne Hector.)

Piquoizeau, porter of Frédéric de Nucingen, when Rodolphe Castanier was cashier at the baron's bank. [Melmoth Reconciled.]

Plaisir, an "illustrious hair-dresser" of Paris; in September, 1816, on the rue Taitbout, he waited on Caroline Crochard de Bellefeuille, at that time mistress of the Comte de Granville. [A Second Home.]

Planchette, an eminent professor of mechanics, consulted by Raphaël de Valentin on the subject of the wonderful piece of shagreen that the young man had in his possession; he took him to Spieghalter, the mechanician, and to Baron Japhet, the chemist, who tried in vain to stretch this skin. The failure of science in this effort was a cause of amazement to Planchette and Japhet. "They were like Christians come from the tomb without finding a God in heaven." Planchette was a tall, thin man, and a sort of poet always in deep contemplation. [The Magic Skin.]

Plantin, a Parisian publicist, was, in 1834, editor of a review, and aspired to the position of master of requests in the Council of State, when Blondet recommended him to Raoul Nathan, who was starting a great newspaper. [A Daughter of Eve.]

Plissoud, like Brunet, court-crier at Soulanges (Bourgogne), and afterwards Brunet's unfortunate competitor. He belonged, during the Restoration, to the "second" society of his village, witnessed his exclusion from the "first" by reason of the misconduct of his wife, who was born Euphémie Wattebled. Being a gambler and a drinker, Plissoud did not save any money; for, though he was appointed to many offices, they were all lacking in lucrativeness; he was insurance agent, as well as agent for a society that insured against the chances for conscription. Being an enemy of Soudry's party, Maitre Plissoud might readily have served, especially for pecuniary considerations, the interests of Montcornet, proprietor at Aigues. [The Peasantry.]

Plissoud (Madame Euphémie), wife of the preceding and daughter of Wattebled; ruled the "second" society of Soulanges, as Madame Soudry did the first, and though married to Plissoud, lived with Lupin as if she were his wife. [The Peasantry.]

Poidevin was, in the month of November, 1806, second clerk of Maitre Bordin, a Paris attorney. [A Start in Life.]

Poincet, an old and unfortunate public scribe, and interpreter at the Palais de Justice of Paris; about 1815, he went with Christemio to see Henri de Marsay, in order to translate the words of the messenger of Paquita Valdés. [The Thirteen.]

Poirel (Abbé), a priest of Tours; advanced to the canonry at the time that Monseigneur Troubert and Mademoiselle Gamard persecuted Abbé François Birrotteau. [The Vicar of Tours.]

Poiret, the elder, born at Troyes. He was the son of a clerk and of a woman whose wicked ways were notorious, and who died in a hospital. Going to Paris with a younger brother, they became clerks in the Department of Finance under Robert Lindet; there he met Antoine, the office boy; he left this department, in 1816, with a retiring pension, and was replaced by Saillard. [The Government Clerks.]

Afflicted with cretinism he remained a bachelor because of the horror inspired by the memory of his mother's immoral life; he was a confirmed *idémiste*, repeating, with slight variation, the words of those with whom he was conversing. Poiret established himself on the rue Neuve-Sainte-Geneviéve, at Madame Vauquer's private boarding-house; he occupied the second story at the widow's house, became intimate with Christine-Michelle Michonneau and married her, when Horace Bianchon demanded the exclusion of this young woman from the house for denouncing Jacques Collin (1819). [Father Goriot.] Poiret often afterwards met M. Clapart, an old comrade whom he had found again on the rue de la Cerisaïe; had apartments on the rue des Poules and lost his health. [A Start in Life. Scenes from a Courtesan's Life.] He died during the reign of Louis Philippe. [The Middle Classes.]

Poiret (Madame), wife of the preceding, born Christine-Michelle Michonneau, in 1779, doubtless had a stormy youth. Pretending to have been persecuted by the heirs of a rich old man for whom she had cared, Christine-Michelle Michonneau went, during the Restoration, to board with Madame Vauquer, the third floor of the house on rue Neuve-Sainte-Geneviéve; made Poiret her squire; made a deal with Bibi-Lupin—Gondureau—to betray Jacques Collin, one of Madame Vauquer's guests. Having thus sated her cupidity and her bitter feelings, Mademoiselle Michonneau was forced to leave the house on rue Neuve-Sainte-Geneviéve, at the formal demand of Bianchon, another of the guests. [Father Goriot.] Accompanied by Poiret, whom she afterwards married, she moved to the rue des Poules and rented furnished rooms. Being summoned before the examining magistrate Camusot (May,.1830), she recognized Jacques Collin in the pseudo Abbé Carlos Herrera. [Scenes from a Courtesan's Life.] Ten years later, Madame Poiret, now a widow, was living on a corner of the rue des Postes, and numbered Cérizet among her lodgers. [The Middle Classes.]

Poiret the younger, brother of Poiret the elder, and brother-in-law of the preceding, born in 1771; had the same start, the same instincts, and the same weakness of intellect as the elder; ran the same career, overwhelmed with work under Lindet; remained at the Treasury as copying clerk ten years longer than Poiret the elder; was also book-keeper for two merchants, one of whom was Camusot of the Cocon d'Or; he lived on the rue du Martroi; dined regularly at the Veau qui Tette, on the Place du Châtelet; bought his hats of Tournan, on rue Saint-Martin; and, a victim of J.-J. Bixiou's practical jokes, he wound up by being business clerk in the office of Xavier Rabourdin. Being retired on January 1, 1825, Poiret the younger counted on living at Madame Vauquer's boarding-house. [The Government Clerks.]

Polissard, appraiser of the wood of the Ronquerolles estate in 1821; at this time, probably on the recommendation of Gaubertin, he employed as agent for the wood-merchant, Vaudoyer, a peasant of Ronquerolles, who had shortly before been discharged from the post of forest-keeper of Blangy (Bourgogne). [The Peasantry.]

Pollet, book-publisher in Paris, in 1821; a rival of Doguereau; published "Léonide ou La Vieille de Suresnes," a romance by Victor Ducange; had business relations with Porchon and Vidal; was at their establishment, when Lucien de Rubempré presented to them his "Archer de Charles IX." [A Distinguished Provincial at Paris.]

Pombreton (Marquis de), a genuine anomaly; lieutenant of the black musketeers under the old régime, friend of the Chevalier de Valois, who prided himself on having lent him for assistance in leaving the country, twelve hundred pistoles. Pombreton returned this loan afterwards, almost beyond a question of doubt, but the fact of the case always remained unknown, for M. de Valois, an unusually successful gamester, was interested in spreading a report of the return of this loan, to shadow the resources that he derived from the gaming table; and so, five years later, about 1821, Etienne Lousteau declared that the Pombreton succession and the Maubreuil[1] affair were

---

[1] Maubreuil died at the end of the Second Empire.

among the most profitable "stereotypes" of journalism. Finally, Le Courrier de l'Orne of M. du Bousquier published, about 1830, these lines: " A certificate for an income of a thousand francs a year will be awarded to the person who can show the existence of a M. de Pombreton before, during, or after the emigration." [Lost Illusions. A Distinguished Provincial at Paris. Jealousies of a Country Town.]

Pomponne (La). (*See* Toupinet, Madame.)

Pons (Sylvain)[1], born about 1785; son of the old age of Monsieur and Madame Pons, who, before 1789, founded the famous Parisian house for the embroidery of uniforms that was bought, in 1815, by M. Rivet, first cousin of the first Madame Camusot of the Cocon d'Or, sole heir of the famous Pons brothers, embroiderers to the Court; under the Empire, he won the Prix de Rome for musical composition, returned to Paris about 1810, and was for many years famous for his romances and melodies which were full of delicacy and good taste. From his stay in Italy, Pons brought back the tastes of the bibliomaniac and a love for works of art. His passion for collecting consumed almost his entire patrimony. Pons became Sauvageot's rival. Monistrol and Elie Magus felt a hidden but envious appreciation of the artistic treasures ingeniously and economically collected by the musician. Being ignorant of the rare value of his museum, he went from house to house, giving private lessons in harmony. This lack of knowledge proved his ruin afterwards, for he became all the more fond of paintings, stones and furniture, as lyric glory was denied him, and his ugliness, coupled with his supposed poverty, kept him from getting married. The pleasures of a gourmand replaced those of the lover; he likewise found some consolation for his isolation in his friendship with Schmucke. Pons suffered from his taste for high living; he grew old, like a parasitic plant, outside the circle of his family, only tolerated by his distant cousins, the Camusot de Marvilles, and their connections, Cardot, Berthier and

[1] M. Alphonse de Launay has derived from the life of Sylvain Pons a drama that was presented at the Cluny theatre, Paris, about 1873.

Popinot. In 1834, at the awarding of prizes to the young
ladies of a boarding-school, he met the pianist Schmucke,
a teacher as well as himself, and in the strong intimacy that
grew up between them, he found some compensation for
the blighted hopes of his existence. Sylvain Pons was
director of the orchestra at the theatre of which Félix Gaudissart was manager during the monarchy of July. He had
Schmucke admitted there, with whom he passed several
happy years, in a house, on the rue de Normandie, belonging
to C.-J. Pillerault. The bitterness of Madeleine Vivet and
Amélie Camusot de Marville, and the covetousness of Madame
Gibot, the door-keeper, and Fraisier, Magus, Poulain and
Rémonencq were perhaps the indirect causes of the case
of hepatitis of which Pons died (in April, 1845), appoint-
ing Schmucke his residuary legatee before Maitre Léopold
Hannequin, who had been hastily summoned by Héloïse
Brisetout. Pons was on the point of being employed to com-
pose a piece of ballet music, entitled "Les Mohicans." This
work most likely fell to his successor, Garangeot. [Cousin
Pons.]

Popinot, alderman of Sancerre in the eighteenth century;
father of Jean-Jules Popinot and Madame Ragon (born
Popinot). He was the officer whose portrait, painted by
Latour, adorned the walls of Madame Ragon's parlor, during
the Restoration, at her home in the Quartier Saint-Sulpice,
Paris. [César Birotteau.]

Popinot (Jean-Jules), son of the preceding, brother of
Madame Ragon, and husband of Mademoiselle Bianchon
—of Sancerre—embraced the profession of law, but did not
attain promptly the rank which his powers and integrity
deserved. Jean-Jules Popinot remained for a long time a
judge of a lower court in Paris. He took a deep interest in
the fate of the young orphan Anselme Popinot, his nephew,
and a clerk of César Birotteau; and was invited with Madame
Jean-Jules Popinot to the perfumer's famous ball, on Sunday,
December 17, 1818. Nearly eighteen months later, Jean-
Jules Popinot once more saw Anselme, who was set up as a

druggist on the rue des Cinq-Diamants, and met Félix Gaudissart, the commercial-traveler, and tried to excuse certain imprudent utterances of his on the political situation, that had been reported by Canquoëlle-Peyrade, the police-agent. [César Birotteau.] Three years later he lost his wife, who had brought him, for dowry, an income of six thousand francs, representing exactly twice his personal assets. Living from this time at the rue du Fouarre, Popinot was able to give free rein to the exercise of charity, a virtue that had become a passion with him. At the urgent instance of Octave de Bauvan, Jean-Jules Popinot, in order to aid Honorine, the count's wife, sent her a pretended commission-merchant, probably Félix Gaudissart, offering a more than generous price for the flowers she made. [Honorine.] Jean-Jules Popinot eventually established a sort of benevolent agency. Lavienne, his servant, and Horace Bianchon, his wife's nephew aided him. He relieved Madame Toupinet, a poor woman on the rue du Petit-Banquier, from want (1828). Madame d'Espard's request for a guardian for her husband served to divert Popinot from his rôle of Saint Vincent de Paul; a man of rare delicacy hidden beneath a rough and uncultured exterior, he immediately discovered the injustice of the wrongs alleged by the marchioness, and recognized the real victim in M. d'Espard, when he cross-questioned him at No. 22 rue de la Montagne-Sainte-Geneviéve, in an apartment, the good management of which he seemed to envy, though the rooms were simply furnished, and in striking contrast with the splendor of which he had been a witness, at the home of the marchioness in the Faubourg Saint-Honoré. A delay caused by a cold in the head, and especially the influence of Madame d'Espard's intrigues, removed Popinot from the cause, in which Camusot was substituted. [The Commission in Lunacy.] We have varying accounts of Jean-Jules Popinot's last years. Madame de la Chanterie's circle mourned the death of the judge in 1833 [The Seamy Side of History] and Phellion in 1840. J.-J. Popinot probably died at No. 22 rue de la Montagne-Sainte-Geneviève, in the apartment that he had already coveted, being the counselor to the court, municipal counselor of Paris, and a member of the General Council of the Seine. [The Middle Classes.]

Popinot (Anselme), a poor orphan, and nephew of the preceding and of Madame Ragon (born Popinot), who took charge of him in his infancy. Small of stature, red-haired, and lame, he gladly became clerk to César Birotteau, the Paris perfumer of the Reine des Roses, the successor of Ragon, with whom he did a great deal of work, in order to be able to show appreciation for the favor shown a part of his family, that was well-nigh ruined as a result of some bad investments (the Wortschin mines, 1818-19). Anselme Popinot, being secretly in love with Césarine Birotteau, his employer's daughter—the feeling being reciprocated, more-over—brought about, as far as his means allowed, the re-habilitation of César, thanks to the profits of his drug business, established on the rue des Cinq-Diamants, between 1819 and 1820. The beginning of his great fortune and of his domestic happiness dated from this time. [César Birotteau.] After Birotteau's death, about 1822, Popinot married Mademoiselle Birotteau, by whom he had three children, two sons and a daughter. The consequences of the Revolution of 1830 brought Anselme Popinot in the way of power and honors; he was twice deputy after the beginning of Louis Philippe's reign, and was also minister of commerce. [Gaudissart the Great.] Anselme Popinot, twice secretary of state, had finally been made a count, and a peer of France. He owned a mansion on the rue Basse du Rempart. In 1834 he rewarded Félix Gaudissart for services formerly rendered on the rue des Cinq-Diamants, and entrusted to him the management of a boulevard theatre, where the opera, the drama, the fairy spectacle, and the ballet took turn and turn. [Cousin Pons.] Four years later the Comte Popinot, again minister of commerce and agriculture, a lover of the arts and one who gladly acted the part of the refined Mæcenas, bought for two thousand francs a copy of Steinbock's "Groupe de Samson" and stipulated that the mould should be destroyed that there might be only two copies, his own and the one belonging to Madcmoiselle Hortense Hulot, the artist's fiancée.

When Wenceslas married Mademoiselle Hulot, Popinot and Eugéne de Rastignac were the Pole's witnesses. [Cousin Betty.]

Popinot (Madame Anselme), wife of the preceding, born Césarine Birotteau, in 1801. Beautiful and attractive, though, at one time, almost promised to Alexandre Crottat, she married, about 1822, Anselme Popinot, whom she loved and by whom she was loved. [César Birotteau.] After her marriage, though in the midst of splendor, she remained the simple, open, and even artless character that she was in the modest days of her youth.[1] The transformation of the dancer Claudine du Bruel, the whilom Tullia of the Royal Academy of Music, to a moral bourgeois matron, surprised Madame Anselme, who became intimate with her. [A Prince of Bohemia.] The Comtesse Popinot rendered aid, in a delicate way, in 1841, to Adeline Hulot d'Ervy. Her influence, with that of Mesdames de Rastignac, de Navarreins, d'Espard, de Grandlieu, de Carigliano, de Lenoncourt, and de la Bastie, procured Adeline's appointment as salaried inspector of charities. [Cousin Betty.] Three years later, when one of her three children married Mademoiselle Camusot de Marville, Madame Popinot, although she appeared at the most exclusive social gatherings, imitated modest Anselme, and, unlike Amélie Camusot, received Pons, a tenant of her maternal great-uncle, C.-J. Pillerault. [Cousin Pons.]

Popinot (Vicomte), the eldest of the three children of the preceding couple, married, in 1845, Cécile Camusot de Marville. [Cousin Pons.] During the course of the year 1846, he questioned Victorin Hulot about the remarkable second marriage of Baron Hector Hulot d'Ervy, which was solemnized on the first of February of that year. [Cousin Betty.]

Popinot (Vicomtesse), wife of the preceding; born Cécile Camusot in 1821, before the name Marville was added to Camusot through the acquisition of a Norman estate. Redhaired and insignificant looking, but very pretentious, she

---

[1] In 1838, the little theatre Panthéon, destroyed in 1846, gave a vaudeville play, by M. Eugène Cormon, entitled "César Birotteau," of which Madame Anselme Popinot was one of the heroines.

persecuted her distant kinsman Pons, from whom she afterwards inherited; from lack of sufficient fortune she failed of
more than one marriage, and was treated with scorn by the
wealthy Frédéric Brunner, especially because of her being
an only daughter and the spoiled child. [Cousin Pons.]

Popinot-Chandier (Madame and Mademoiselle), mother
and daughter; of the family of Madame Boirouge; hailing
from Sancerre; frequent visitors of Madame de la Baudraye,
whose superiority of manner they ridiculed in genuine bourgeois fashion. [The Muse of the Department.]

Porchon. (*See* Vidal.)

Porraberil (Euphémie). (*See* San-Réal, Marquise de.)

Porriquet, an elderly student of the classics, was teacher
of Raphaél de Valentin, whom he had as a pupil in the sixth
class, in the third class, and in rhetoric. Retired from the
university without a pension after the Revolution of July,
on suspicion of Carlism, seventy years of age, without means,
and with a nephew whose expenses he was paying at the
seminary of Saint-Sulpice, he went to solicit the aid of his
dear "foster-child," to obtain the position of principal of a
provincial school, and suffered rough treatment at the
hands of the *carus alumnus*, every act of whose shortened Valentin's existence. [The Magic Skin.]

Porta (Luigi), born in 1793, strikingly like his sister Nina.
He was the last member that remained, at the beginning
of the nineteenth century, of the Corsican family of Porta,
by reason of a bloody vendetta between his kinspeople and
the Piombos. Luigi Porta alone was saved, by Elisa Vanni,
according to Giacomo; he lived at Genoa, where he enlisted,
and found himself, when quite young, in the affair of the
Bérésina. Under the Restoration he was already an officer
of high rank; he put an end to his military career and was
hunted by the authorities at the same time as Labédoyère.
Luigi Porta found Paris a safe place of refuge. Servin,
the Bonapartist painter, who had opened a studio of drawing,
where he taught his art to young ladies, concealed the officer.

One of his pupils, Ginevra di Piombo, discovered the outlaw's hiding-place, aided him, fell in love with him, made him fall in love with her, and married him, despite the opposition of her father, Bartolomeo di Piombo. Luigi Porta chose as a witness, when he was married, his former comrade, Louis Vergniaud, also known to Hyacinthe-Chabert. He lived from hand to mouth by doing secretary's work, lost his wife, and, crushed by his poverty, went to tell the Piombos of her death. He died almost immediately after her (1820). [The Vendetta.]

Porta (Madame Luigi), wife of the preceding, born Ginevra di Piombo about 1790; shared, in Corsica as in Paris, the stormy life of her father and mother, whose adored child she was. In Servin's, the painter's, studio, where with her talent she shone above the whole class, Ginevra knew Mesdames Tiphaine and Camusot de Marville, at that time Mesdemoiselles Roguin and Thirion. Defended by Laure alone, she endured the cruelly planned persecution of Amélie Thirion, a Royalist, and an envious woman, especially when the favorite drawing pupil discovered and aided Luigi Porta, whom she married shortly afterwards, against the will of Bartolomeo di Piombo. Madame Porta lived most wretchedly; she resorted to Magus to dispose of copies of paintings at a meagre price; brought a son into the world, Barthélemy; could not nurse him, lost him, and died of grief and exhaustion in the year 1820. [The Vendetta.]

Portail (Du), name assumed by Corentin, when as "prefect of secret police of diplomacy and political affairs," he lived on the rue Honoré-Chevalier, in the reign of Louis Philippe. [The Government Clerks.]

Portenduère (Comte Luc-Savinien de), grandson of Admiral de Portenduère, born about 1788, represented the elder branch of the Portenduères, of whom Madame de Portenduère and her son Savinien represented the younger branch. Under the Restoration, being the husband of a rich wife, the father of three children and member for Isére, he lived, according to the season of the year, in the château of Portenduère or the Portenduère mansion, which were situated, the one in Dauphiné, and the other in Paris, and extended no aid to the Vicomte Savinien, though he was harassed by his creditors. [Ursule Mirouët.]

Portenduère (Madame de), born Kergarouët, a Breton, proud of her noble descent and of her race. She married a post-captain, nephew of the famous Admiral de Portenduère, the rival of the Suffrens, the Kergarouëts, and the Simeuses; bore him a son, Savinien; she survived her husband; was on intimate terms with the Rouvres, her country neighbors; for, having but little means, she lived, during the Restoration, in the little village of Nemours, on the rue des Bourgeois, where Denis Minoret was domiciled. Savinien's prodigal dissipation and the long opposition to his marriage to Ursule Mirouët saddened, or at least disturbed, Madame de Portenduère's last days. [Ursule Mirouët.]

Portenduère (Vicomte Savinien de), son of preceding, born in 1806; cousin of the Comte de Portenduère, who was descended from the famous admiral of this name, and greatnephew of Vice-Admiral Kergarouët. During the Restoration he left the little town of Nemours and his mother's society to go and try the life of Paris, where, in spite of his relationship with the Fontaines, he fell in love with Emilie de Fontaine, who did not reciprocate his love, but married first Admiral de Kergarouët, and afterwards the Marquis de Vandenesse. [The Ball at Sçeaux.] Savinien also became enamored of Léontine de Sérizy; was on intimate terms with Marsay, Rastignac, Rubempré, Maxime de Trailles, Blondet and Finot; soon lost a considerable sum of money, and, laden with debts, became a boarder at Sainte-Pélagie; he then received Marsay, Rastignac and Rubempré, the latter wishing to relieve his distress, much to the amusement of Florine, afterwards Madame, Nathan. [Scenes from a Courtesan's Life.] Urged by Ursule Mirouët, his ward, Denis Minoret, who was one of Savinien's neighbors at Nemours, raised the sum necessary to liquidate young Portenduère's debt, and freed him of its burden. The viscount enlisted in the marine service, and retired with the rank and insignia of an ensign, two years after the Revolution of July, and five years before being able to marry Ursule Mirouët. [Ursule Mirouët.] The Vicomte and Vicomtesse de Portenduère made a charming couple, recalling two other happy families of Paris, the Laginskis and the Ernest de la Basties. In 1840 they lived on the rue Saint-Pères, became the intimate friends of the Calyste du Guénics, and shared their box at the Italiens. [Béatrix.]

Portenduère (Vicomtesse Savinien de), wife of the preceding, born in 1814. The orphan daughter of an unfortunate artist, Joseph Mirouët, the military musician, and Dinah Grollman, a German; natural granddaughter of Valentin Mirouët, the famous harpsichordist, and consequently niece of the rich Dr. Denis Minoret; she was adopted by the last-named, and became his ward, so much the more adored as, in appearance and character, she recalled Madame Denis Minoret, deceased. Ursule's girlhood and youth, passed at Nemours, were marked alternately by joy and bitterness. Her guardian's servants, as well as his intimate friends, overwhelmed her with indications of interest. A distinguished performer, the future viscountess received lessons in harmony from Schmucke, the pianist, who was summoned from Paris. Being of a religious nature, she converted Denis Minoret, who was an adherent of Voltaire's teachings; but the influence she acquired over him called forth against the young girl the fierce animosity of Minoret-Levrault, Massin, Crémière, Dionis and Goupil, who, foreseeing that she would be the doctor's residuary legatee, abused her, slandered her, and persecuted her most cruelly. Ursule was also scornfully treated by Madame de Portenduère, with whose son, Savinien, she was in love. Later, the relenting of Minoret-Levrault and Goupil, shown in various ways, and her marriage to the Vicomte de Portenduère, at last approved by his mother, offered Ursule some consolation for the loss of Denis Minoret. [Ursule Mirouët.] Paris adopted her, and made much of her; she made a glorious success in society as a singer. [Another Study of Woman.] Amid her own great happiness, the viscountess showed herself the devoted friend, in 1840, of Madame Calyste du Guénie, just after her confinement, who was almost dying of grief over the treachery of her husband. [Béatrix.]

Postel was pupil and clerk of Chardon the druggist of L'Houmeau, a suburb of Angouléme; succeeded Chardon after his death; was kind to his former patron's unfortunate family; desired, but without success, to marry Eve, who was afterwards Madame David **Séchard**, and became the husband of Léonie Marron, by whom he had several sickly children. [Lost Illusions.]

Postel (Madame), wife of the preceding, born Léonie Marron, daughter of Doctor Marron, a practitioner in Marsac (Charente); through jealousy she was disagreeable to the beautiful Madame Séchard; through cupidity she fawned upon the Abbé Marron, from whom she hoped to inherit. [Lost Illusions.]

Potasse, sobriquet of the **Protez** family, manufacturers of chemicals, as associates of Cochin; known by Minard, Phellion, Thuillier and Colleville, types of Parisians of the middle class, about 1840. [The Middle Classes.]

Potel, former officer of the Imperial forces, retired, during the Restoration, to Issoudun, with Captain Renard; he took sides with Maxence Gilet against the officers, Mignonnet and Carpentier, declared enemies of the chief of the "Knights of Idlesse." [A Bachelor's Establishment.]

Poulain (Madame), born in 1778. She married a trousers-maker, who died in very reduced circumstances; for from the sale of his business she received only about eleven hundred francs for income. She lived then, for twenty years, on work which some fellow-countrymen of the late Poulain gave to her, and the meagre profits of which afforded her the opportunity of starting in a professional career her son, the future physician, whom she dreamed of seeing gain a rich marriage settlement. Madame Poulain, though deprived of an education, was very tactful, and she was in the habit of retiring when patients came to consult her son. This she did when Madame Cibot called at the office on rue d'Orléans, late in 1844 or early in 1845. [Cousin Pons.]

Poulain (Doctor), born about 1805, friendless and without fortune; strove in vain to gain the patronage of the Paris "four hundred" after 1835. He kept constantly near him his mother, widow of a trousers-maker. As a poor-neighborhood physician he afterwards lived with his mother on rue d'Orléans at the Marais. He became acquainted with Madame Cibot, door-keeper at a house on rue de Normandie, the proprietor of which, C.-J. Pillerault, uncle of the Popinots and ordinarily under Horace Bianchon's treatment, he cured. By Madame Cibot, Poulain was called also to attend Pons in a case of inflammation of the liver. Aided by his friend Fraisier, he arranged matters to suit the Camusots de Marville, the rightful heirs of the musician. Such a service had its reward. In 1845, following the death of Pons, and that of his residuary legatee, Schmucke, soon after, Poulain was given an appointment in the Quinze-Vingts hospital as head physician of this great infirmary. [Cousin Pons.]

Poupart, or Poupard, from Arcis-sur-Aube, husband of Gothard's sister; one of the heroes of the Simeuse affair; proprietor of the Mulet tavern. Being devoted to the interest of the Cadignans, the Cinq-Cygnes and the Hauteserres, in 1839, during the electoral campaign, he gave lodging to Maxime de Trailles, a government envoy, and to Paradis, the count's servant. [The Member for Arcis.]

Poutin, colonel of the Second lancers, an acquaintance of Maréchal Cottin, minister of war in 1841, to whom he told that many years before this one of his men at Severne, having stolen money to buy his mistress a shawl, repented of his deed and ate broken glass so as to escape dishonor. The Prince of Wissembourg told this story to Hulot d'Ervy, while upbraiding him for his dishonesty. [Cousin Betty.]

Prélard (Madame), born in 1808, pretty, at first mistress of the assassin Auguste, who was executed. She remained con-

stantly in the clutches of Jacques Collin, and was married by
Jacqueline Collin, aunt of the pseudo-Herrera, to the head
of a Paris hardware-house on Quai aux Fleurs, the Bouclier
d'Achille. [Scenes from a Courtesan's Life.]

Prévost (Madame), well-known florist, whose store still
remains in the Palais-Royal. Early in 1830, Frédéric de
Nucingen bought a ten louis bouquet there for Esther van
Gobseck. [Scenes from a Courtesan's Life.]

Prieur (Madame), laundress at Angouléme, for whom
Mademoiselle Chardon, afterwards Madame David Séchard,
worked. [Lost Illusions.]

Pron (Monsieur and Madame), both teachers. M. Pron
taught rhetoric in 1840 at a college in Paris directed by priests.
Madame Pron, born Barniol, and therefore sister-in-law of
Madame Barniol-Phellion, succeeded Mesdemoiselles La Grave,
about the same time, as director of their young ladies' board-
ing-school. M. and Madame Pron lived in the Quartier
Saint-Jacques, and frequently visited the Thuilliers. [The
Middle Classes.]

Protez and Chiffreville, manufactured chemicals; sold a
hundred thousand francs' worth to the inventor, Balthazar
Claés, about 1812. [The Quest of the Absolute.] On account of their friendly relations with Cochin, of the Treasury,
all the Protezes and the Chiffrevilles were invited to the
celebrated ball given by César Birotteau, Sunday, December 17, 1818, on rue Saint Honoré. [César Birotteau.]

Proust, clerk to Maitre Bordin, a Paris attorney, in November, 1806; this fact became known a few years later
by Godeschal, Oscar Husson and Marest, when they re-
viewed the books of the attorneys who had been employed
in Bordin's office. [A Start in Life.]

Provençal (Le), born in 1777, undoubtedly in the vicinity
of Arles. A common soldier during the wars at the close
of the eighteenth century, he took part in the expedition
of General Desaix into upper Egypt. Having been taken
prisoner by the Maugrabins he escaped only to lose himself

in the desert, where he found nothing to eat but dates. Reduced to the dangerous friendship of a female panther, he tamed her, singularly enough, first by his thoughtless caresses, afterwards by premeditation. He ironically named her Mignonne, as he had previously called Virginie, one of his mistresses. Le Provençal finally killed his pet, not without regret, having been moved to great terror by the wild animal's fierce love. About the same time the soldier was discovered by some of his own company. Thirty years afterwards, an aged ruin of the Imperial wars, his right leg gone, he was one day visiting the menagerie of Martin the trainer, and recalled his adventure for the delectation of a young spectator. [A Passion in the Desert.]

Q

Quélus (Abbé), priest of Tours or of its vicinity, called frequently on the Chessels, neighbors of the Mortsaufs, at the beginning of the century. [The Lily of the Valley.]

Queverdo, faithful steward of the immense domain of Baron de Macumer, in Sardinia. After the defeat of the Liberals in Spain, in 1823, he was told to look out for his master's safety. Some fishers for coral agreed to pick him up on the coast of Andalusia and set him off at Macumer. [Letters of Two Brides.]

Quillet (François), office-boy employed by Raoul Nathan's journal on rue Feydau, Paris, 1835. He aided his employer by lending him the name of François Quillet. Raoul, in great despair, while occupying a furnished room on rue du Mail, threw several creditors off his track by the use of this assumed name. [A Daughter of Eve.]

R

Rabouilleuse (La), name assumed by Flore Brazier, who became in turn Madame Jean-Jacques Rouget and Madame Philippe Bridau. (See this last name.)

Rabourdin (Xavier), born in 1784; his father was unknown to him. His mother, a beautiful and fastidious woman, who lived in luxury, left him a penniless orphan of sixteen. At this time he left the Lycée Napoleon and became a supernumerary clerk in the Treasury Department. He was soon promoted, becoming second head clerk at twenty-two and head clerk at twenty-five An unknown, but influential friend, was responsible for this progress, and also gave him an introduction into the home of M. Leprince, a wealthy widower, who had formerly been an auctioneer. Rabourdin met, loved and married this man's only daughter. Beginning with this time, when his influential friend probably died, Rabourdin saw the end of his own rapid progress. Despite his faithful, intelligent efforts, he occupied at forty the same position. In 1824 the death of M. Flamet de la Billardière left open the place of division chief This office, to which Rabourdin had long aspired, was given to the incapable Baudoyer, who had been at the head of a bureau, through the influence of money and the Church. Disgusted, Rabourdin sent in his resignation. He had been responsible for a rather remarkable plan for executive and social reform, and this possibly contributed to his overthrow. During his career as a minister Rabourdin lived on rue Duphot. He had by his wife two children, Charles, born in 1815, and a daughter, born two years later. About 1830 Rabourdin paid a visit to the Bureau of Finances, where he saw once more his former pages, nephews of Antoine, who had retired from service by that time. From these he learned that Colleville and Baudoyer were tax-collectors in Paris. [The Government Clerks.] Under the Empire he was a guest at the evening receptions given by M. Guillaume, the cloth-dealer of rue Saint-Denis. [At the Sign of the Cat and Racket.] Later he and his wife were invited to attend the famous ball tendered by César Birotteau, December 17, 1818. [César Birotteau.] In 1840, being still a widower, Rabourdin was one of the directors of a proposed railway. At this time he began to lodge in a house on the Place de la Madeleine, which had been recently bought by the Thuilliers, whom he had known in the Bureau of Finance. [The Middle Classes.]

Rabourdin (Madame), born Célestine Leprince, in 1796; beautiful, tall and of good figure; reared by an artistic mother; a painter and a good musician; spoke many tongues and even had some knowledge of science. She was married when very young through the instrumentality of her father, who was then a widower. Her reception-rooms were not open to Jean-Jacques Bixiou, but she was frequently visited by the poet Canalis, the painter Schinner, Doctor Bianchon, who was especially fond of her company; Lucien de Rubempré, Octave de Camps, the Comte de Granville, the Vicomte de Fontaine, F. du Bruel, Andoche Finot, Derville, Châtelet, then deputy; Ferdinand du Tillet, Paul de Manerville, and the Vicomte de Portenduère. A rival, Madame Colleville, had dubbed Madame Rabourdin "The Célimène of rue Duphot." Having been over-indulged by her mother, Célestine Leprince thought herself entitled to a man of high rank. Consequently, although M. Rabourdin pleased her, she hesitated at first about marrying him, as she did not consider him of high enough station. This did not prevent her loving him sincerely. Although she was very extravagant, she remained always strictly faithful to him. By listening to the demands of Chardin des Lupeaulx, secretary-general in the Department of Finance, who was in love with her, she might have obtained for her husband the position of division chief. Madame Rabourdin's reception days were Wednesdays and Fridays. She died in 1840. [The Commission in Lunacy. The Government Clerks.]

Rabourdin (Charles), law-student, son of the preceding couple, born in 1815, lived from 1836 to 1838 in a house on rue Corneille, Paris. There he became acquainted with Z. Marcas, helped him in his distress, attended him on his death-bed, and, with Justi, a medical student, as his only companion, followed the body of this great, but unknown man to the beggar's grave in Montparnasse cemetery. After having told some friends the short, but pitiful story of Z. Marcas, Charles Rabourdin, following the advice of the deceased, left the country, and sailed from Havre for the

Malayan islands; for he had not been able to gain a foothold in France. [Z. Mareas.]

Racquets (Des).   (*See* Raquets, des.)

Ragon born about 1748; a perfumer on rue Saint-Honoré, between Saint-Roche and rue des Frondeurs, Paris, towards the close of the eighteenth century; small man, hardly five feet tall, with a face like a nut-cracker, self-important and known for his gallantry.   He was succeeded in his business, the "Reine des Roses," by his chief clerk, César **Birotteau**, after the eighteenth Brumaire.   As a fo mer perfumer to Her Majesty Queen Marie-Antoinette, M. Ragon always showed Royalist zeal, and, under the Republic, the Vendeans used him to communicate between the princes and the Royalist committee of Paris.   He received at that time the Abbé de Marolles, to whom he pointed out and revealed the person of Louis XVI.'s executioner.   In 1818, being a loser in the Nucingen speculation in Wortschin mining stock, Ragon lived with his wife in an apartment on rue du Petit-Bourbon-Saint-Sulpice. [César Birotteau.   An Episode under the Terror.]

Ragon (Madame), born Popinot; sister of Judge Popinot, wife of the preceding, being very nearly the same age as her husband, was in 1818 "a tall slender woman of wrinkled face, sharp nose, thin lips, and the artificial manner of a marchioness of the old line." [César Birotteau.]

Ragoulleau[1] (Jean-Antoine), a Parisian lawyer, whose signature the widow Morin tried to extort.   She also attempted his assassination, and was condemned, January 11, 1812, on the evidence of a number of witnesses, among others that of Poiret, to twenty years of hard labor. [Father Goriot.]

Raguet working boy in the establishment of César Birottcau, the perfumer, in 1818. [César Birotteau.]

Raparlier, a Douai notary; drew up marriage con-

---

[1] The real spelling of the name, as shown by some authentic papers, is Ragoulleau.

tracts in 1825 for Marguerite Claés and Emmanuel de Solis, for Félicie Claés and Pierquin the notary, and for Gabriel Claës and Mademoiselle Conyncks. [The Quest of the Absolute.]

Raparlier, a Douai auctioneer, under the Restoration; nephew of the preceding; took an inventory at the Claës house after the death of Madame Balthazar Claés in 1816 [The Quest of the Absolute.]

Rapp, French general, born at Colmar in 1772; died in 1821. As aide-de-camp of the First Consul, Bonaparte, he found himself one day in October serving near his chief at the Tuileries,. when the proscribed Corsican, Bartolomeo di Piombo, came up rather unexpectedly. Rapp, who was suspicious of this man, as he was of all Corsicans, wished to stay at Bonaparte's side during the interview, but the Consul good-naturedly sent him away. [The Vendetta.] On October 13, 1806, the day before the battle of Jéna, Rapp had just made an important report to the Emperor at the moment when Napoleon was receiving on the next day's battlefield Mademoiselle Laurence de Cinq-Cygne and M. de Chargeboeuf, who had come from France to ask for the pardon of the two Hauteserres and the two Simeuses, people affected by a political suit and condemned to hard labor. [The Gondreville Mystery.]

Raquets (Des), lived at Douai, of Flemish descent, and devoted to the traditions and customs of his province; very wealthy uncle of the notary Pierquin, his only heir, who received his inheritance towards the close of the Restoration. [The Quest of the Absolute.]

Rastignac (Chevalier de), great-uncle of Eugéne de Rastignac; as vice-admiral was commander of the "Vengeur" before 1789, and lost his entire fortune in the service of the king, as the revolutionary government did not wish to satisfy his demands in the adjusting of the Compagnic des Indes affairs. [Father Goriot.]

Rastignac (Baron and Baronne de) had, near Ruffec,

Charente, an estate, where they lived in the latter part of the eighteenth and the beginning of the nineteenth centuries, and where were born to them five children: Eugéne, Laure-Rose, Agathe, Gabriel and Henri. They were poor, and lived in close retirement, keeping a dignified silence, and like their neighbors, the Marquis and Marquise de Pimentel, exercised, through their connection with court circles, a strong influence over the entire province, being invited at various times to the home of Madame de Bargeton, at Angoulême, where they met Lucien de Rubempré and were able to understand him. [Father Goriot. Lost Illusions.]

Rastignac(Eugéne de),[1] eldest son of the Baron and Baronne de Rastignac, born at Rastignac near Ruffec in 1797. He came to Paris in 1819 to study law; lived at first on the third floor of the Vauquer lodging-house, rue Neuve-Sainte-Geneviéve, having then some association with Jacques Collin, called Vautrin, who was especially interested in him and wanted him to marry Victorine Taillefer. Rastignac became the lover of Madame de Nucingen, second daughter of Joachim Goriot, an old vermicelli-maker, and, in February, 1820, lived on rue d'Artois in pretty apartments, rented and furnished by the father of his mistress. Goriot died in his arms. The servant, Christophe, and Rastignac were the only attendants in the good man's funeral procession. At the Vauquer lodging-house he was intimate with Horace Blanchon, a medical student. [Father Goriot.] In 1821, at the Opéra, young Rastignac made fun for the occupants of two boxes over the provincialisms of Madame de Bargeton and Lucien de Rubempré, "young Chardon." This led Madame d'Espard to leave the theatre with her relative, thus publicly and in a cowardly way abandoning the distinguished provincial. Some months later Rastignac sought the favor of this same Lucien de Rubempré, who was by that time an influential citizen. He agreed to act with Marsay as the poet's witness in the duel which he fought with Michel Chrestien, in regard to Daniel d'Arthez. [A Dis-

[1] In a recent publication of Monsieur S. de Lovenjoul, he speaks of a recent abridged biography of Eugène de Rastignac.

tinguished Provincial at Paris.] At the last masquerade ball of 1824 Rastignac found Rubempré, who had disappeared from Paris some time before. Vautrin, recalling his memories of the Vauquer lodging-house, urged him authoritatively to treat Lucien as a friend. Shortly after, Rastignac became a frequenter of the sumptuous mansion furnished by Nucingen for Esther van Gobseck on rue Saint-Georges. Rastignac was present at Lucien de Rubempré's funeral in May, 1830. [Scenes from a Courtesan's Life.] About the same time the Comte de Fontaine asked his daughter Emilie what she thought of Rastignac—among several others —as a possible husband for her. But, knowing the relations of this youthful aspirant with Madame de Nucingen, she saved herself by replying maliciously. [The Ball at Sçeaux.] In 1828 Rastignac sought to become Madame d'Espard's lover, but was restrained by his friend, Doctor Bianchon. [The Interdiction.] During the same year Rastignac was treated slightingly by Madame de Listomère, because he asked her to return a letter, which through mistake had been sent to her, but which he had meant for Madame de Nucingen. [A Study of Woman.] After the Revolution of July he was a guest at Mademoiselle des Touchès's evening party, where Marsay told the story of his first love. [Another Study of Woman.] At this time he was intimate with Raphaél de Valentin, and expected to marry an Alsatian. [The Magic Skin.] In 1832, Rastignac, having been appointed a baron, was under-secretary of state in the department of which Marsay was the minister. [The Secrets of a Princess.] In 1833-1834, he volunteered as nurse at the bedside of the dying minister, in the hope of being remembered in his will. One evening about this same time he took Raoul Nathan and Emile Blondet, whom he had met in society, to supper with him at Véry's. Ile then advised Nathan to profit by the advances made him by the Comtesse Félix de Vandenesse. [A Daughter of Eve.] In 1833, at the Princesse de Cadignan's home, in the presence of the Marquise d'Espard, the old Ducs de Lenoncourt and de Navarreins, the Comte and the Comtesse de Vandenesse, D'Arthez, two ambassadors, and

two well-known orators of the Chamber of Peers, Rastignac
heard his minister reveal the secrets of the abduction of
Senator Malin, an affair which took place in 1806. [The
Gondreville Mystery.] In 1836, having become enriched by the
third Nucingen failure, in which he was more or less a willing
accomplice, he became possessed of an income of forty thousand francs. [The Firm of Nucingen.] In 1838 he attended
the opening reception given at Josépha's mansion on rue
de la Ville-l'Evêque. He was also a witness at Hortense
Hulot's marriage to Wenceslas Steinbock. He married
Augusta de Nucingen, daughter of Delphine de Nucingen,
his former mistress, whom he had quitted five years previously. In 1839, Rastignac, minister once more, and
this time of public works, was made count almost in spite
of himself. In 1845 he was, moreover, made a peer. He
had then an income of 300,000 francs. He was in the habit
of saying: " There is no absolute virtue, all things are dependent on circumstances." [Cousin Betty. The Member for
Arcis. The Unconscious Humorists.]

Rastignac (Laure-Rose and Agathe de),[1] sisters of Eugéne de
Rastignac; second and third children of the Baron and Baronne
de Rastignac; Laure, the elder, born in 1801; Agathe, the
second, born in 1802; both were reared unostentatiously in the
Rastignac château. In 1819 they sent what they had saved
by economy to their brother Eugéne, then a student. Several
years after, when he was wealthy and powerful, he married one
of them to Martial de la Roche-Hugon, the other to a minister.
In 1821, Laure, with her father and mother, was present at
a reception of M. de Bargeton's, where she admired Lucien de
Rubempré. [Father Goriot. Lost Illusions.] Madame de
la Roche-Hugon in 1839 took her several daughters to a
children's dance at Madame de l'Estorade's in Paris. [The
Member for Arcis.]

Rastignac (Monseigneur Gabriel de), brother of Eugéne
de Rastignac; one of the youngest two children of the Baron
and Baronne de Rastignac; was private secretary to the

---

[1] The Mesdemoiselles de Rastignac are here placed together under their maiden
name, as it is not known which one married Martial de la Roche-Hugon.

Bishop of Limoges towards the end of the Restoration, during the trial of Tascheron. In 1832 he became, when only a young man of thirty, a bishop. He was consecrated by the Archbishop Dutheil. [Father Goriot. The Country Parson. A Daughter of Eve.]

Rastignac (Henri de), the fifth child, probably, of the Baron de Rastignac and his wife. Nothing is known of his life. [Father Goriot.]

Ratel, gendarme in the Orne district; in 1809, along with his fellow-officer, Mallet, was charged with the capture of "Lady" Bryond des Miniares, who was implicated in the affair known as the "Chauffeurs de Mortagne." He found the fugitive, but, instead of arresting her, allowed himself to be unduly influenced by her, and then protected her and let her escape. This action on his part was known to Mallet. Ratel, when imprisoned, confessed all, and committed suicide before the time assigned for trial. [The Seamy Side of History.]

Ravenouillet, porter in Bixiou's house, at No. 112 rue Richelieu, in 1845; son of a Carcassonne grocer; a steward throughout his life and owed his first position to his fellow-countryman, Massol. Ravenouillet, although uneducated, was not unintelligent. According to Bixiou, he was the "Providence at thirty per cent" of the seventy-one lodgers in the house, through whom he netted in the neighborhood of six thousand francs a month. [The Unconscious Humorists.]

Ravenouillet (Madame), wife of the preceding. [The Unconscious Humorists.]

Ravenouillet (Lucienne), daughter of the preceding couple, was in 1845 a pupil the Paris Conservatory of Music. [The Unconscious Humorists.]

Regnauld (Baron) (1754-1829), celebrated artist, member of the Institute. Joseph Bridau, when fourteen, was a frequent visitor at his studio, in 1812-1813. [A Bachelor's Establishment.]

Regnault, former chief clerk to Maitre Roguin, a Paris notary; came to Vendôme in 1816 and purchased there a notaryship. He was called by Madame de Merret to her death-bed, and was made her executor. In this position, some years later, he urged Doctor Bianchon to respect one of the last wishes of the deceased by discontinuing his promenades in the Grande Bretéche garden, as she had wished this property to remain entirely unused for half a century. Maitre Regnault married a wealthy cousin of Vendôme. Regnault was tall and slender, with sloping forehead, small pointed head and wan complexion. He frequently used the expression, "One moment." [La Grande Bretéche.]

Regnier (Claude-Antoine), Duc de Massa, born in 1746, died 1814; an advocate, and afterwards deputy to the Constituency; was high justice—justice of the peace—during the celebrated trial of the Simeuses and Hauteserres, accused of the abduction of Senator Malin. He noticed the talent displayed by Granville for the defendants, and a little later, having met him at Archchancelor Cambacérès's house, he took the young barrister into his own carriage, setting him down on the Quai des Augustins, at the young man's door, after giving him some practical advice and assuring him of his protection. [The Gondreville Mystery. A Second Home.]

Rémonencq, an Auvergnat, dealer in old iron, established on rue de Normandie, in the house in which Pons and Schmucke lived, and where the Cibots were porters. Rémonencq, who had come to Paris with the intention of being a porter, ran errands between 1825 and 1831 for the dealers in curiosities on Boulevard Beaumarchais and the coppersmiths on rue de Lappe, then opened in this same quarter a small shop for odds and ends. He lived there in sordid economy. He had been in Sylvain Pons's house, and had fully recognized the great value of the aged collector's treasures. His greed urged him to crime, and he instigated Madame Cibot in her theft at the Pons house. After receiving his share of the property, he poisoned the husband of the portress, in order to marry the widow, with whom he established à curiosity shop in an excellent building on the Boulevard de la Madeleine. About 1846 he unwittingly poisoned himself with a glass of vitriol, which he had placed near his wife. [Cousin Pons.]

Rémonencq (Mademoiselle), sister of the preceding, "a kind of idiot with a vacant stare, dressed like à Japanese idol." She was her brother's house-keeper. [Cousin Pons.]

Rémonencq (Madame), born in 1796, at one time a beautiful oyster-woman of the "Cadran Bleu" in Paris; married for love the porter-tailor, Gibot, in 1828, and lived with him in the porter's lodge of a house on rue de Normandie, belonging to Claude-Joseph Pillerault. In this house the musicians, Pons and Schmucke, lived. She busied herself for some time with the management of the house and the cooking for these two celibates. At first she was faithful, but finally, moved by Rémonencq, and encouraged by Fontaine, the necromancer, she robbed the ill-fated Pons. Her husband having been poisoned, without her knowledge, by Rémonencq, she married the second-hand dealer, now a dealer in curiosities, and proprietor of the beautiful shop on the Boulevard de la Madeleine. She survived her second husband. [Cousin Pons.]

Rémy or Remy (Jean), peasant of Arcis-sur-Aube, against whom a neighbor lost a lawsuit concerning a boundary line. This neighbor, who was given to drink, used strong language in speaking against Jean Rémy in a session of the electors who had organized in the interest of Dorlange-Sallenauve, a candidate, in the month of April, 1839. If we may believe this neighbor, Jean Rémy was a wife-beater, and had a daughter who had obtained, through the influence of a deputy, and apparently without any claim, an excellent tobacco-stand on rue Mouffetard. [The Member for Arcis.]

Renard, former captain in the Imperial army, withdrew to Issoudun during the Restoration; one of the officers in the Faubourg de Rome, who were hostile to the "pékins" and partisans of Maxence (Max) Gilet. Renard and Commandant

Potel were seconds for Maxence in his duel with Philippe
Bridau—a duel which resulted in the former's death. [A
Bachelor's Establishment.]

Renard, regimental quartermaster in the cavalry, 1812.
Although educated as a notary he became an under officer.
He had the face of a girl and was considered a "wheedler."
He saved the life of his friend, Genestas, several times, but
enticed away from him a Polish Jewess, whom he loved,
married in Sarmatian fashion, and left enceinte. When
fatally wounded in the battle against the Russians, just
before the battle of Lutzen, in his last hours, to Genestas,
he acknowledged having betrayed the Jewess, and begged
this gentleman to marry her and claim the child, which
would soon be born. This was done by the innocent
officer. Renard was the son of a Parisian wholesale
grocer, a "toothless shark," who would not listen to
anything concerning the quartermaster's offspring. [The
Country Doctor.]

Renard (Madame). (*See* Genestas, Madame.)

Renard (Adrien). (*See* Genestas, Adrien.)

René, the only servant to M. du Bousquier of Alençon,
in 1816; a silly Breton servant, who, although very greedy,
was perfectly reliable. [Jealousies of a Country Town.]

Restaud (Comte de), a man whose sad life was first brought
to the notice of Barchou de Penhöen, a school-mate of Dufaure
and Lambert; born about 1780; husband of Anastasie Goriot,
by whom he was ruined; died in December, 1824, while trying
to adjust matters favorably for his eldest son, Ernest, the only
one of Madame de Restaud's three children whom he recognized as his own. To this end he had pretended that, having
been very extravagant, he was greatly in debt to Gobseck.
He assured his son by another letter of the real condition of his
estate. M. de Restaud was similar in appearance to the
Duc de Richelieu, and had the proud manners of the statesman of the aristocratic faubourg. [Gobseck. Father Goriot.]

Restaud (Comtesse Anastasie de), wife of the preceding; elder daughter of the vermicelli-maker, Jean-Joachim Goriot; a beautiful brunette of queenly bearing and manners. Like the fair and gentle Madame de Nucingen, her sister, she showed herself severe and ungrateful towards the kindliest and weakest of fathers. She had three children, two boys and a girl; Ernest, the eldest, being the only legitimate one. She ruined herself for Trailles, her lover's, benefit, selling her jewels to Gobseck and endangering her children's future. As soon as her husband had breathed his last, in a moment anxiously awaited, she took from under his pillow and burned the papers which she believed contrary to her own interests and those of her two natural children. It thus followed that Gobseck, the fictitious creditor, gained a claim on all of the remaining property. [Gobseck. Father Goriot.]

Restaud (Ernest de), 'eldest child of the preceding, and their only legitimate one, as the other two were natural children of Maxime de Trailles. In 1824, while yet a child, he received from his dying father instruction to hand to Derville, the attorney, a sealed package which contained his will; but Madame de Restaud, by means of her maternal authority, kept Ernest from carrying out his promise. On attaining his majority, after his fortune had been restored to him by his father's fictitious creditor, Gobseck, he married Camille de Grandlieu, who reciprocated his love for her. As a result of this marriage Ernest de Restaud became connected with the Legitimists, while his brother Félix, who had almost attained the position of minister under Louis Philippe, followed the opposite party. [Gobseck. The Member for Arcis.]

Restaud (Madame Ernest de), born Camille de Grandlieu in 1813, daughter of the Vicomtesse de Grandlieu. During the first years of Louis Philippe's reign, while very young, she fell in love with and married Ernest de Restaud, who was then a minor. [Gobseck. The Member for Arcis.]

Restaud (Félix-Georges de), one of the younger children of the Comte and Comtesse de Restaud; probably a natural son of Maxime de Trailles. In 1839, Félix de Restaud was chief secretary to his cousin Eugéne de Rastignac, minister of public works. [Gobseck. The Member for Arcis.]

Restaud (Pauline de), legal daughter of the Comte and Comtesse de Restaud, but probably the natural daughter of Maxime de Trailles. We know nothing of her life. [Gobseck.]

Reybert (De), captain in the Seventh regiment of artillery under the Empire; born in the Messin country. During the Restoration he lived in Presles, Seine-et-Oise, with his wife and daughter, on only six hundred francs pension. As a neighbor of Moreau, manager of the Comte de Sérizy's estate, he detected the steward in some extortions, and sending his wife to the count, denounced the guilty man. He was chosen as Moreau's successor. Reybert married his daughter, without furnishing her a dowry, to the wealthy farmer Léger. [A Start in Life.]

Reybert (Madame de), born Corroy, in Messin, wife of the preceding, and like him of noble family. Her face was pitted by small-pox until it looked like a skimmer; her figure was tall and spare; her eyes were bright and clear; she was as straight as a stick; she was a strict Puritan, and subscribed to the Courrier Français. She paid a visit to the Comte de Sérizy, and unfolded to him Moreau's extortions, thus obtaining for her husband the stewardship of Presles. [A Start in Life.]

Rhétoré (Duc Alphonse de), eldest son of the Duc and Duchesse de Chaulieu, he became an ambassador in the diplomatic service. For many years during the Restoration he kept Claudine Chaffaroux, called Tullia, the star dancing-girl at the Opéra, who married Bruel in 1824. He became acquainted with Lucien de Rubempré, both in his own circle of acquaintance and in the world of gallantry, and entertained him one evening in his box at a first performance at the Ambigu in 1821. He reproached his guest for having wounded Châtelet and Madame de Bargeton by his newspaper satire, and at the same time, while addressing him continually as Chardon, he counseled the young man to become a Royalist, in order that Louis XVIII. might restore to him the title and name of the Rubemprés, his maternal ancestors. The Duc de Rhétoré, however, disliked Lucien de Rubempré, and a little later at a performance in the Italiens, he traduced him to Madame de Sérizy, who was really in love with the poet. [A Bachelor's Establishment. A Distinguished Provincial at Paris. Scenes from a Courtesan's Life. Letters of Two Brides.] In 1835, he married the Duchesse d'Argaïolo, born the Princesse Soderini, a woman of great beauty and fortune. [Albert Savarus.] In 1839, he had a duel with Dorlange-Sallenauve, having provoked the latter, by speaking in a loud voice, which he knew could be easily understood, and slandering Marie Gaston, second husband of Dorlange's sister, Louise de Chaulieu. Dorlange was wounded. [The Member for Arcis.

Rhétoré (Duchesse de), born Francesca Soderini in 1802; a very beautiful and wealthy Florentine; married, when very young, by her father, to the Duc d'Argaïolo, who was also very rich and much older than herself. In Switzerland or Italy she became acquainted with Albert Savarus, when, as a result of political events, she and her husband were proscribed and deprived of their property. The Duchesse d'Argaïolo and Albert Savarus loved platonically, and Francesca-like she promised her hand to her François whenever she should become a widow. In 1835, having been widowed for some time, and, as a result of Rosalie de Watteville's plots, believing herself forgotten and betrayed by Savarus, from whom she had received no news, she gave her hand to the Duc de Rhétoré, the ex-ambassador. The marriage took place in the month of May at Florence and was celebrated with much pomp. The Duchesse d' Argaïolo is pictured under the name of the Princesse Gandolphini in "L'Ambitieux par Amour," published in 1834 by the Revue de l'Est. Under Louis Philippe, the Duchesse de Rhétoré became acquainted with Mademoiselle de Watteville at a charity entertainment. On their second meeting, which took place at the Opéra ball,

Mademoiselle de Watteville revealed her own ill-doings and vindicated Savarus. [Albert Savarus.]

Richard (Veuve), a Nemours woman from whom Ursule Mirouët, afterwards Vicomtesse de Portenduère, after the death of Doctor Minoret, her guardian, purchased a house to occupy. [Ursule Mirouët.]

Ridal (Fulgence), dramatic author, member of the Cénacle, which held its sessions at D'Arthez's home on rue des Quatre-Vents, during the Restoration. He disparaged Léon Giraud's beliefs, went under a Rabelaisian guise, careless, lazy and skeptical, also inclined to be melancholy and happy at the same time; nick-named by his friends the "Regimental Dog." Fulgence Ridal and Joseph Bridau, with other members of the Cénacle, were present at an evening party given by Madame Veuve Bridau, in 1819, to celebrate the return of her son Philippe from Texas. [A Bachelor's Establishment. A Distinguished Provincial at Paris.] In 1845, having been a vaudevillist, he was given the direction of a theatre in association with Lousteau. He had influential government friends. [The Unconscious Humorists.]

Riffé, copying-clerk in the Financial Bureau, who had charge of the "personnel." [The Government Clerks.]

Rifooël. (*See* Vissard, Chevalier du.)

Riganson, called Biffon, also Chanoine, constituted with La Biffe, his mistress, one of the most important couples in his class of society. When a convict he met Jacques Collin, called Vautrin, and in May, 1830, saw him once more at the Conciergerie, at the time of the judical investigation succeeding Esther Gobseck's death. Riganson was short of stature, fat, and with livid skin, and an eye black and sunken. [Scenes from a Courtesan's Life.]

Rigou (Grégoire), born in 1756; at one time a Benedictine friar. Under the Republic he married Arséne Pichard, only heir of the rich Curé Niseron. He became a money-lender; filled the office of mayor of Blangy, Bourgogne, up to 1821, when he was succeeded by Montcornet. On **the**

arrival of the general in the country Rigou endeavored to be friendly with him, but having been quickly slighted, he became one of the Montcornets' most dangerous enemies, along with Gaubertin, mayor of Ville-aux-Fayes, and Soudry, mayor of Soulanges. This triumvirate succeeded in arousing the peasants against the owner of Aigues, and the local citizens having become more or less opposed to him, the general sold his property, and it fell ⁺o the three associates. Rigou was selfish, avaricious but pleasure-loving; he looked like a condor. His name was often the subject of a pun, and he was called Grigou (G. Rigou—a miserly man). " Deep as a monk, silent as a Benedictine, crafty as a priest, this man would have been a Tiberius in Rome, a Richelieu under Louis XIII. or a Fouché under the Convention." [The Peasantry.]

Rigou (Madame), born Arséne Pichard, wife of the preceding, niece of a maid named Pichard, who was house-keeper for Curé Niseron under the Revolution, and whom she succeeded as house-keeper. She inherited, together with her aunt, some money from the wealthy priest. She was known while young by the name of La Belle Arséne. She had great influence over the curé, although she could neither read nor write. After her marriage with Rigou, she became the old Benedictine's slave. She lost her Rubens-like freshness, her magical figure, her beautiful teeth and the lustre of her eyes when she gave birth to her daughter, who eventually became the wife of Soudry (fils). Madame Rigou quietly bore the continued infidelity of her husband, who always had pretty maids in his household. [The Peasantry.]

Rivaudoult d'Arschoot, of the Dulmen branch of a noted family of Galicia or Russic-Rouge; heirs, through their grandfather, to this family, and also, in default of the direct heirs, successors to the titles. [The Thirteen.]

Rivet (Achille), maker of lace and embroidery on rue des Mauvaises-Paroles, in the old Langeais house, built by the illustrious family at the time when the greatest lords were clustered around the Louvre. In 1815 he succeeded the Pons Brothers, embroiderers to the Court, and was judge in the tribunal of commerce. He employed Lisbeth Fischer, and, despite their quarrel, rendered this spinster some service. Achille Rivet worshiped Louis Philippe, who was to him the "noble representative of the class out of which he constructed his dynasty." He loved the Poles less, at the time they were preventing European equilibrium. He was willing to aid Cousin Betty in the revenge against Wenceslas, which she once contemplated, as a result of her jealousy. [Cousin Betty. Cousin Pons.]

Robert, a Paris restaurant-keeper, near Frascati. Early in 1822 he furnished a banquet lasting nine hours, at the time of the founding of the Royalist journal, the "Réveil." Théodore Gaillard and Hector Merlin, founders of the paper, Nathan and Lucien de Rubempré, Martainville, Auger, Destains and many authors who "were responsible for monarchy and religion," were present. "We have enjoyed an excellent monarchical and religious feast!" said one of the best known romanticists as he stood on the threshold. This sentence became famous and appeared the next morning in the "Miroir." Its repetition was wrongly attributed to Rubempré, although it had been reported by a book-seller who had been invited to the repast. [A Distinguished Provincial at Paris.]

Rochefide (Marquis Arthur de), one of the later nobility; married through his father's instrumentality, in 1828, Béatrix de Casteran, a descendant of the more ancient nobility. His father thought that by doing this his son would obtain an appointment to the peerage, an honor which he himself had vainly sought. The Comtesse de Montcornet was interested in this marriage. Arthur de Rochefide served in the Royal Guards. He was a handsome man, but not especially worthy. He spent much of his time at his toilet, and it was known that he wore a corset. He was everybody's friend, as he joined in with the opinions and extravagances of everybody. His favorite amusement was horse-racing, and he supported a journal devoted to the subject of horses. Having been deserted by his wife, he mourned without becoming the object of ridicule, and passed for a "jolly, good fellow." Made rich by the death of his father and of his elder sister, who was the wife of D'Ajuda-Pinto, he inherited, among other things, a splendid mansion on rue d'Anjou-Saint-Honoré. He slept and ate there only occasionally and was very happy at not having the marital obligations and expense customary with married men. At heart he was so well satisfied at having been deserted by his wife, that he said to his friends, "I was born lucky." For a long time he supported Madame Schontz, and then they lived together maritally. She reared his legitimate son as carefully as though he were her own child. After 1840 she married Du Ronceret, and Arthur de Rochefide was rejoined by his wife. He soon communicated to her a peculiar disease, which Madame Schontz, angered at having been abandoned, had given to him, as well as to Baron Calyste du Guénic. [Béatrix.] In 1838, Rochefide was present at the house-warming given by Josépha in her mansion on rue de la Ville-l'Evêque. [Cousin Betty.]

Rochefide (Marquise de), wife of the preceding, younger daughter of the Marquis de Casteran; born Béatrix-Maximilienne-Rose de Casteran, about 1808, in the Casteran Castle, department of Orne. After being reared there she became the wife of the Marquis de Rochefide in 1828. She was fair of skin, but a flighty, vain coquette, without heart or brains—a second Madame d'Espard, except for her lack of intelligence. About 1832 she left her husband to flee into Italy with the musician, Gennaro Conti, whom she took from her friend, Mademoiselle des Touches. · Finally she allowed Calyste du Guénie to pay her court. She had met him also at her friend's house, and at first resisted the young man. Afterwards, when he was married, she abandoued herself to him. This liaison filled Madame du Guénie with despair, but was ended after 1840 by the crafty manœuvres of the Abbé Brossette. Madame de Rochefide then rejoined her husband in the elegant mansion on rue d'Anjou-Saint-Honoré, but not until she had retired with him to Nogent-sur-Marne, to care for her health which had been

injured during the resumption of marital relations.   Before
this reconciliation she lived in Paris on rue de Chartres-du-
Roulc, near Monceau Park.   The Marquise de Rochefide had,
by her husband, a son, who was for some time under the care
of Madame Schontz.   [Béatrix.   The Secrets of a Princess.]
In 1834, in the presence of Madame Félix de Vandenesse,
then in love with the poet Nathan, the Marquise Charles de
Vandenesse, sister-in-law of Madame Félix, Lady Dudley,
Mademoiselle des Touches, the Marquise d'Espard, Madame
Moïna de Saint Héreen and Madame de Rochefide expressed
their ideas on love and marriage.   "Love is heaven," said
Lady Dudley.   "It is hell!" cried Mademoiselle des Touches.
"But it is a hell where there is love," replied Madame de
Rochefide.   "There is often more pleasure in suffering than
in happiness; remember the martyrs!"   [A Daughter of Eve.]
The history of Sarrasine was told her about 1830.   The
marquise was acquainted with the Lantys, and at their house
saw the strange Zambinella.   [Sarrasine.]   One afternoon,
in the year 1836 or 1837, in her house on rue des Chartres,
Madame de Rochefide heard the story of the "Prince of
Bohemia" told by Nathan.   After this narrative she became
wild over La Palférine.   [A Prince of Bohemia.]

Rochegude (Marquis de), an old man in 1821, possessing
an income of six hundred thousand francs, offered a brougham
at this time to Coralie, who was proud of having refused it,
being "an artist, and not a prostitute."   [A Distinguished
Provincial at Paris.]   This Rochegude was apparently a
Rochefide.   The change of names and confusion of families
was corrected eventually by law.

Rodolphe, natural son of an intelligent and charming Parisian and of a Barbançon gentleman who died before he was able
to arrange satisfactorily for his sweetheart.   Rodolphe was a
fictitious character in "L'Ambitieux par Amour," by Albert
Savarus in the "Revue de l'Est" in 1834, where. under this
assumed name, he recounted his own adventures.   [Albert
Savarus.]

Roger, general, minister and director of personnel in the

War Department in 1841. For thirty years a comrade of Baron Hulot. At this time he enlightened his friend on the administrative situation, which was seriously endangered at the time he asked for an appointment for his sub-chief, Marneffe. This advancement was not merited, but became possible through the dismissal of Coquet, the chief of bureau. [Cousin Betty.]

Rogron, Provins tavern-keeper in the last half of the eighteenth century and the beginning of the nineteenth. He was at first a carter, and married the daughter of M. Auffray, a Provins grocer, by his first wife. When his father-in-law died, Rogron bought his house from the widow for a song, retired from business and lived there with his wife. He possessed about two thousand francs in rentals, obtained from twenty-seven pieces of land and the interest on the twenty thousand francs raised by the sale of his tavern. Having become in his old age a selfish, avaricious drunkard and shrewd as a Swiss tavern-keeper, he reared coarsely and without affection the two children, Sylvie and Jérôme-Denis, whom he had by his wife. He died, in 1822, a widower. [Pierrette.]

Rogron (Madame), wife of the preceding; daughter, by his first wife, of M. Auffray, a Provins grocer; paternal aunt of Madame Lorrain, the mother of Pierrette; born in 1743; very homely; married at the age of sixteen; left her husband a widower. [Pierrette.]

Rogron (Sylvie), elder child of the preceding; born between 1780 and 1785 at Provins; sent to the country to be nursed. When thirteen years old she was placed in a store on rue Saint-Denis, Paris. When twenty years old she was second clerk in a silk-store, the Ver Chinois, and towards the end of 1815, bought with her own savings and those of her brother the property of the Sœur de Famille, one of the best retail haberdasher's establishments and then kept by Madame Guénée. Sylvie and Jérôme-Denis, partners in this establishment, retired to Provins in 1823. They lived there in their father's house, he having been dead several months, and received their cousin, the young Pierrette Lorrain, a fatherless and motherless child of a delicate nature, whom they treated harshly, and who died as a result of the brutal treatment of Sylvie, an envious spinster. This woman had been sought in marriage, on account of her dowry, by Colonel Gouraud, and she believed herself deserted by him for Pierrette. [Pierrette.]

Rogron (Jérôme-Denis), two years younger than his sister Sylvie, and like her sent to Paris by his father. When very young he entered the establishment of one of the leading haberdashers on rue Saint-Denis, the firm of Guépin at the Trois Quenouilles. He became first clerk there at eighteen. Finally associated with Sylvie in the haberdasher's establishment, the Sœur de Famille, he withdrew with her in 1823 to Provins. Jérôme-Denis Rogron was ignorant and did not amount to much, but depended on his sister in everything, for Sylvie had "good sense and was sharp at a bargain." He allowed his sister to maltreat Pierrette Lorrain, and, when called before the Provins court as responsible for the young girl's death, was acquitted. In his little city, Rogron, through the influence of the attorney, Vinet, opposed the government of Charles X. After 1830 he was appointed receiver-general. The former Liberal, who was one of the masses, said that Louis Philippe would not be a real king until he could create noblemen. In 1828, although homely and unintelligent, he married the beautiful Bathilde de Chargeboeuf, who inspired in him an old man's foolish passion. [Pierrette.]

Rogron (Madame Denis), born Bathilde de Chargeboeuf, about 1803, one of the most beautiful young girls of Troyes, poor but noble and ambitious. Her relative, Vinet the attorney, had made "a little Catherine de Médicis" of her, and married her to Denis Rogron. Some years after this marriage she desired to become a widow as soon as possible, so that she might marry Général Marquis de Montriveau, a peer of France, who was very attentive to her. Montriveau controlled the department in which Rogrou had a receivership. [Pierrette.]

Roguin, born in 1761; for twenty-five years a Paris notary; tall and heavy; black hair and high forehead; of somewhat distinguished appearance; affected with ozœna. This affection caused his ruin, for, having married the only daughter of the banker, Chevrel, he disgusted his wife very soon, and she was untrue to him. On the other hand, he had paid mistresses, and kept and was fleeced by Sarah van Gobseck— "La Belle Hollandaise"—mother of Esther. He had met her about 1815. In 1818 and 1819 Roguin, seriously compromised by careless financial ventures as well as by dissipation, disappeared from Paris; and thus brought about the ruin of Guillaume Grandet, César Birotteau, and Mesdames Descoings and Bridau. [César Birotteau. Eugénie Grandet. A Bachelor's Establishment.] Roguin had by his wife a daughter, whom he married to the president of the Provins tribunal. She was called in that city "the beautiful Madame Tiphaine." [Pierrette.] In 1816 he made, for Ginevra di Piombo, a respectful request of her father that he would allow his daughter to marry Luigi Porta, an enemy of the family. [The Vendetta.]

Roguin (Madame), born Chevrel between the years 1770 and 1780; only daughter of Chevrel, the banker; wife of the preceding; cousin of Madame Guillaume of The Cat and Racket, and fifteen years her junior; aided her relative's daughter, Augustine, in her love affair with the painter, Sommervieux; pretty and coquettish; for a long time the mistress of Tillet, the banker; was present with her husband at the famous ball given by César Birotteau, December 17, 1818. She had a country-house at Nogent-sur-Marne, in which she lived with her lover after Roguin's departure. [César Birotteau. At the Sign of the Cat and Racket. Pierrette.] In 1815 Caroline Crochard, then an embroiderer, worked for Madame Roguin, who made her wait for her wages. [A Second Home.] In 1834 and 1835 Madame Roguin, then more than fifty years of age, still posed as young and dominated Du Tillet, who was married to the charming Marie-Eugénie de Granville. [A Daughter of Eve.]

Roguin (Mathilde-Mélanie). (*See* Tiphaine, Madame.)

Romette (La). (*See* Paccard, Jéromette.)

Ronceret (Du), president of the Alençon tribunal under the Restoration; was then a tall man, very thin, with forehead sloping back to his thin chestnut hair; eyes of different colors, and compressed lips. Not having been courted by the nobility, he turned his attention to the middle classes, and then in the suit against Victurnien d'Esgrignon, charged with forgery, he immediately took part in the prosecution. That a preliminary trial might be avoided he kept away from Alençon, but a judgment which acquitted Victurnien was rendered during his absence. M. du Ronceret, in Machiavelli fashion, manœuvred to gain for his son Fabien the hand of a wealthy heiress of the city, Mademoiselle Blandureau, who had also been sought by Judge Blondet for his son Joseph. In this contest the judge won over his chief. [Jealousies of a Country Town.] M. du Ronceret died in 1837, while holding the presidency of chamber at the Royal Court of Caen. The Du Roncerets, ennobled under Louis XV., had arms bearing the word "Servir" as a motto and a squire's helmet. [Béatrix.]

Ronceret (Madame du), wife of the preceding, tall and ill-formed; of serious disposition; dressed herself in the most absurd costumes of gorgeous colors; spent much time at her toilet, and never went to a ball without first decorating her head with a turban, such as the English were then wearing. Madame du Ronceret received each week, and each quarter gave a great three-course dinner, which was much spoken of in Alençon, for the president then endeavored, with his miserly abundance, to compete with M. du Bousquier's elegance. In the Victurnien d'Esgrignon affair, Madame du Ronceret, at the instigation of her husband, urged the deputy, Sauvages, to work against the young nobleman. [Jealousies of a Country Town.]

Ronceret (Fabien-Félicien du), or Duronceret, son of the preceding couple; born about 1802, educated at Alençon;

was here the companion in dissipation of Victurnien d'Esgrignon, whose evil nature he stimulated at M. du Bousquier's instigation. [Jealousies of a Country Town.] At first a judge in Alençon, Du Ronceret resigned after the death of his father and went to Paris in 1838, with the intention of pushing himself into notice by first causing an uproar. He became acquainted in Bohemian circles where he was called " The Heir," on account of some prodigalities. Having made the acquaintance of Couture, the journalist, he was presented by him to Madame Schontz, a popular courtesan of the day, and became his successor in an elegantly furnished establishment in a first floor on rue Blanche. He there began as vice-president of a horticultural society. After an opening session, during which he delivered an address which he had paid Lousteau five hundred francs to compose, and where he made himself noticed by a flower given him by Judge Blondet, he was decorated. Later he married Madame Schontz, who wished to enter middle-class society. Ronceret expected, with her influence, to become president of the court and officer of the Legion of Honor. [Béatrix.] While purchasing a shawl for his wife at M. Fritot's, in company with Bixiou, Fabien du Ronceret was present about 1844 at the comedy which took place when the Sélim shawl was sold to Mistress Noswell. [Gaudissart II.]

Ronceret (Madame Fabien du), born Joséphine Schiltz in 1805, wife of the preceding, daughter of a colonel under the Empire; fatherless and motherless, at nine years of age she was sent to Saint-Denis by Napoleon in 1814, and remained in that educational institution, as assistant-mistress, until 1827. At this time Joésphine Schiltz, who was a god-child of the Empress, began the adventurous life of a courtesan, after the example of some of her companions who were, like her, at the end of their patience. She now changed her name from Schiltz to Schontz, and she was also known under the assumed name of Little Aurélie. Animated, intelligent and pretty, after having sacrificed herself to true love, after having known "some poor but dishonorable writers," after having tried intimacy with several rich simpletons, she was

met in a day of distress, at Valentino Mussard's, by Arthur de
Rochefide, who loved her madly. Having been abandoned
by his wife for two years, he lived with her in free union.
This evil state of affairs existed until the time when Joséphine
Schiltz was married by Fabien du Ronceret. In order to
have revenge on the Marquis de Rochefide for abandoning her,
she gave him a peculiar disease, which she had made Fabien
du Ronceret contract, and which also was conveyed to
Calyste du Guénie. During her life as a courtesan, her rivals
were Suzanne de Val-Noble, Fanny Beaupré, Mariette,
Antonia, and Florine. She was intimate with Finot, Nathan,
Claude Vignon, to whom she probably owed her critical
mind, Bixiou, Léon de Lora, Victor de Vernisset, La Palférine, Gobenheim, Vermanton the cynical philosopher, etc.
She even hoped to marry one of these. In 1836 she lived
on rue Fléchier, and was the mistress of Lousteau, to whom
she wished to marry Félicie Cardot, the notary's daughter.
Later she belonged to Stidmann. In 1838 she was present at
Josépha's house-warming on rue de la Ville-l'Evêque. In
1840, at a first performance at the Ambigu, she met Madame
de la Baudraye, then Lousteau's mistress. Joséphine Schiltz
finally became the wife of President du Ronceret. [Béatrix.
The Muse of the Department. Cousin Betty. The Unconscious Humorists.]

Ronquerolles (Marquis de), brother of Madame de Sérizy;
uncle of the Comtesse Laginska; one of "The Thirteen,"
and one of the most efficient governmental diplomats under
Louis Philippe; next to the Prince de Talleyrand the shrewdest ambassador; was of great service to Marsay during his
service as a minister; was sent to Russia in 1838 on a secret
mission. Having lost his two children during the cholera
scourge of 1832, he was left without a direct heir. He had
been a deputy on the Right Centre under the Restoration,
representing a department in Bourgogne, where he was
proprietor of a forest and of a castle next to the Aigues in the
commune of Blangy. When Gaubertin, the steward, was
discharged by the Comte de Montcornet, Soudry spoke as follows: "Patience! We have Messieurs de Soulanges and de

Ronquerolles." [The Imaginary Mistress. The Peasantry. Ursule Mirouët.] M. de Ronquerolles was an intimate friend of the Marquis d'Aiglemont; they even addressed each other familiarly as *thou* instead of *you*. [A Woman of Thirty.] He alone knew of Marsay's first love and the name of "Charlotte's" husband. [Another Study of Woman.] In 1820 the Marquis de Ronquerolles, while at a ball at the Elysée-Bourbon, in the Duchesse de Berri's house, provoked Auguste de Maulincour, of whom Ferragus Bourignard had complained, to a duel. Also, as a result of his membership in the Thirteen, Ronquerolles, along with Marsay, helped General de Montriveau abduct the Duchesse de Langeais from the convent of bare-footed Carmelites, where she had taken refuge. [The Thirteen.] In 1839 he was M. de Rhétoré's second in a duel fought with Dorlange-Sallenauve, the sculptor, in connection with Marie Gaston. [The Member for Arcis.]

Rosalie, rosy-cheeked and buxom, waiting-maid to Madame de Merret at Vendôme; then, after the death of her mistress, servant employed by Madame Lepas, tavern-keeper in that town. She finally told Horace Bianchon the drama of La Grande Bretéche and the misfortunes of the Merrets. [Another Study of Woman. La Grande Bretéche.]

Rosalie, chambermaid to Madame Moreau at Presles in 1822. [A Start in Life.]

Rose, maid in the service of Armande-Louise-Marie de Chaulieu in 1823, at the time when this young lady, having left the Carmelites of Blois, came to live with her father on the Boulevard des Invalides in Paris. [Letters of Two Brides.]

Rosina, an Italian from Messina, wife of a Piedmont gentleman, who was captain in the French army under the Empire; mistress of her husband's colonel. She died with her lover near Bérésina in 1812, her jealous husband having set fire to the hut which she and the colonel were occupying. [Another Study of Woman.]

Roubaud, born about 1803 was declared doctor by the Paris medical school, a pupil of Desplein; practiced medicine at Montégnac, Haute-Vienne, under Louis Philippe; small man of fair skin and very insipid appearance, but with gray eyes which betrayed the depth of a physiologist and the tenacity of a student. Rubaud was introduced to Madame Graslin by the Curé Bonnet, who was in despair at **Rubaud's** religious indifference. The young physician admired and secretly loved this celebrated Limousinese, and became converted suddenly to Catholicism on seeing the saintly death of Madame Graslin. When dying she made him head-physician in a hospital founded by her at the Tascherons near Montégnac. [The Country Parson.]

Rouget (Doctor), an Issoudun physician under Louis XVI. and the Republic; born in 1737; died in 1805; married the most beautiful girl of the city, whom, it is said, he made very unhappy. He had by her two children: a son, Jean-Jacques; and, ten years later, a daughter, Agathe, who became Madame Bridau. The birth of this daughter brought about a rupture between the doctor and his intimate friend, the subdelegate Lousteau, whom Rouget, doubtless wrongly, accused of being the girl's father. Each of these men charged the other with being the father of Maxence Gilet, who was in reality the son of a dragoon officer, stationed at Bourges. Doctor Rouget, who passed for a very disagreeable, unaccommodating man, was selfish and spiteful. He quickly got rid of his daughter, whom he hated. After his wife, his mother-in-law and his father-in-law had died, he was very rich, and although his life was apparently regular and free from scandal, he was in reality very dissipated. In 1799, filled with admiration for the beauty of the little Rabouilleuse, Flore Brazier, he received her into his own home, where she stayed, becoming first the mistress, and afterwards the wife of his son, Jean-Jacques, and eventually Madame Philippe Bridau, Comtesse de Brambourg. [A Bachelor's Establishment.]

Rouget (Madame), born Descoings, wife of the preceding,

daughter of rich and avaricious wool-dealers at Issoudun, elder sister of the grocer, Descoings, who married the widow of M. Bixiou and afterwards died with André Chénier, July 25, 1794, on the scaffold. As a young woman, although in very poor health, she was celebrated for her beauty. Not being gifted with a very sound intellect, when married it was thought that she was very badly treated by Doctor Rouget. Her husband believed that she was unfaithful to him for the sake of the sub-delegate, Lousteau. Madame Rouget, deprived of her dearly-beloved daughter, and finding her son lacking altogether in affection for her, declined rapidly and died early in 1799, unwept by her husband, who had counted correctly on her early death. [A Bachelor's Establishment.]

Rouget (Jean-Jacques), born at Issoudun in 1768, son of the preceding couple, brother of Madame Bridau, who was ten years his junior. Entirely lacking in intellect, he became wildly in love with Flore Brazier, whom he knew as a child in his father's house. He made this girl his servant-mistress soon after the doctor's death, and allowed her lover, Maxence Gilet, near her. He finally married her in 1823, being urged to do so by his nephew, Philippe Bridau, who soon took Rouget to Paris, and there arranged for the old man's early death by starting him into dissipation. [A Bachelor's Establishment.] After the death of J.-J. Rouget, the Baudrayes of Sancerre bought part of his furniture, and had it removed from Issoudun to Anzy, where they placed it in their castle, which had formerly belonged to the Cadignans. [The Muse of the Department.]

Rouget (Madame Jean-Jacques). (*See* Bridau, Madame Philippe.)

Rousse (La), significant name given Madame Prélard. (*See* this last name.)

Rousseau, driver of the public hack which carried the taxes collected at Caen. This conveyance was attacked and plundered by robbers in May, 1809, in the forest of

Chesnay, near Mortagne, Orne. Rousseau, being looked upon as an accomplice of the robbers, was included in the prosecution which took place soon after; but he was acquitted. [The Seamy Side of History.]

Roustan, Mameluke, in the service of Napoleon Bonaparte. He was with his master on the eve of the battle of Jéna, October 13, 1806, when Laurence de Cinq-Cygne and M. de Chargeboeuf observed him holding the Emperor's horse as Napoleon dismounted. This was just before these two approached the Emperor to ask pardon for the Hauteserres and the Simeuses, who had been condemned as accomplices in the abduction of Senator Malin. [The Gondreville Mystery.]

Rouville (de). (*See* Leseigneur, Madame.)

Rouvre (Marquis du), father of the Comtesse Clémentine Laginska; threw away a considerable fortune, by means of which he had brought about his marriage with a Ronquerolles maiden. This fortune was partly eaten up by Florine, "one of the most charming actresses of Paris." [The Imaginary Mistress.] M. du Rouvre was the brother-in-law of the Comte de Sérizy, who, like him, had married a Ronquerolles. Having been a marquis under the old régime, M. du Rouvre was created count and made chamberlain by the Emperor. [A Start in Life.] In 1829, M. du Rouvre, then ruined, lived at Nemours. He had near this city a castle which he sold at great loss to Minoret-Levrault. [Ursule Mirouët.]

Rouvre (Chevalier du), younger brother of the Marquis du Rouvre; an eccentric old bachelor, who became wealthy by dealing in houses and real estate, and is supposed to have left his fortune to his niece, the Comtesse Clémentine Laginska. [The Imaginary Mistress. Ursule Mirouët.]

Rouzeau, an Angouléme printer, predecessor and master of Jérôme-Nicolas Séchard, in the eighteenth century. [Lost Illusions.]

Rubempré (Lucien-Chardon de), born in 1800 at Angouléme;

son of Chardon, a surgeon in the armies of the Republic who became an apothecary in that town, and of Mademoiselle de Rubempré, his wife, the descendant of a very noble family. He was a journalist, poet, romance writer, author of "Les Marguerites," a book of sonnets, and of the "Archer de Charles IX.," a historical romance. He shone for a time in the salon of Madame de Bargeton, born Marie-Louise-Anaïs de Négrepelisse, who became enamored of him, enticed him to Paris, and there deserted him, at the instigation of her cousin, Madame d'Espard. He met the members of the Cénacle on rue des Quatre-Vents, and became well acquainted with D'Arthez. Etienne Lousteau, who revealed to him the shameful truth concerning literary life, introduced him to the well-known publisher, Dauriat, and escorted him to an opening night at the Panorama-Dramatique theatre, where the poet saw the charming Coralie. She loved him at first sight, and he remained true to her until her death in 1822. Started by Lousteau into undertaking Liberal journalism, Lucien de Rubempré passed over suddenly to the Royalist side, founding the "Reveil," an extremely partisan organ, with the hope of obtaining from the King the right to adopt the name of his mother. At this time he frequented the social world and thus brought to poverty his mistress. He was wounded in a duel by Michel Chrestien, whom he had made angry by an article in the "Reveil," which had severely criticised a very excellent book by Daniel d'Arthez. Coralie having died, he departed for Angoulême on foot, with no resources except twenty francs that Bérénice, the cousin and servant of her mistress, had received from chance lovers. He came near dying of exhaustion and sorrow, very near the city of his birth. He found there Madame de Bargeton, then the wife of Comte Sixte du Châtelet, prefect of Charente and a state councilor. Despite the warm reception given him, first by a laudatory article in a local newspaper, and next by a serenade from his young fellow-citizens, he left Angouléme hastily, desperate at having been responsible for the ruin of his brother-in-law, David Séchard, and contemplating suicide. While walking along he chanced upon Canon Carlos Herrera (Jacques Collin—Vautrin), who took him to Paris and became the guardian of his future career. In 1824, while passing an evening at the theatre Porte-Saint-Martin, Rubempré became acquainted with Esther Van Gobseck, called La Torpille, a courtesan. They were both seized at once with a violent love. A little later, at the last Opéra ball of the winter of 1824, they would have compromised their security and pleasure if it had not been for the interference of Jacques Collin, called Vautrin, and if Lucien had not denied certain people the pleasure of satisfying their ill-willed curiosity, by agreeing to take supper at Lointier's.[1] Lucien de Rubempré sought to become the son-in-law of the Grandlieus; he was welcomed by the Rabourdins; he became protector of Savinien de Portenduère; he became the lover of Mmes. Maufrigneuse and Sérizy, and the beloved of Lydie Peyrade. His life of ambition and of pleasure ended in the Conciergerie, where he was imprisoned unjustly, charged with robbing and murdering Esther, or with being an accomplice. He hanged himself while in prison, May 15, 1830. [Lost Illusions. A Distinguished Provincial at Paris. The Government Clerks. Ursule Mirouët. Scenes from a Courtesan's Life.] Lucien de Rubempré lived in turn in Paris at the Hôtel du Gaillard-Bois, rue de l'Echelle, in a room in the Quartier Latin, in the Hôtel de Cluny on the street of the same name, in a lodging-house on rue Charlot, in another on rue de la Lune in company with Coralie, in a little apartment on rue Cassette with Jacques Collin, who followed him at least to one of his two houses on the Quai Malaquais and on rue Taitbout, the former home of Beaudenord and of Caroline de Bellefeuille. He is buried in Pére-Lachaise in a costly tomb which contains also the body of Esther Gobseck, and in which there is a place reserved for Jacques Collin. A series of articles, sharp and pointed, on Rubempré is entitled "Les Passants de Paris."

Ruffard, called Arrachelaine, a robber and at the same time employed by Bibi-Lupin, chief of secret police in 1830; connected, with Godet, in the assassination of the Crottats,

---

[1] The Lointier restaurant, on rue Richelieu, opposite rue de la Bourse, was very popular about 1846 with the "four hundred."

husband and wife, committed by Dannepont, called La Pouraille. [Scenes from a Courtesan's Life.]

Ruffin, born in 1815, the instructor of Francis Graslin after 1840. Ruffin was a professional teacher, and was possessed of a wonderful amount of information. His extreme tenderness "did not exclude from his nature the severity necessary on the part of one who wishes to govern a child." He was of pleasing appearance, known for his patience and piety. He was taken to Madame Graslin from his diocese by the Archbishop Dutheil, and had, for at least nine years, the direction of the young man who had been put in his charge. [The Country Parson.]

Rusticoli. (*See* La Palférine.)

S

Sabatier, police-agent; Corentin regretted not having had his assistance in the search with Peyrade, at Gondreville, in 1803. [The Gondreville Mystery.]

Sabatier (Madame), born in 1809. She formerly sold slippers in the trade gallery of the Palais de Justice, in Paris; widow of a man who killed himself by excessive drinking, became a trained nurse, and married a man whom she had nursed and had cured of an affection of the urinary ducts ("lurinary," according to Madame Cibot), and by whom she had a fine child. She lived in rue Barre-du-Bec. Madame Bordevin, a relative, wife of a butcher of the rue Charlot, was god-mother of the child. [Cousin Pons.]

Sagredo, a very wealthy Venetian senator, born in 1730, husband of Bianca Vendramini; was strangled, in 1760, by Facino Cane, whom he had found with Bianca, conversing on the subject of love, but in an entirely innocent way. [Facino Cane.]

Sagreda (Bianca), wife of the preceding, born Vendramini, about 1742; in 1760, she undeservingly incurred the suspicion, in the eyes of her husband, of criminal relations with Facino Cane, and was unwilling to follow her platonic friend away from Venice after the murder of Sagredo. [Facino Cane.]

Saillard, a clerk of mediocre talent in the Department of Finance, during the reigns of Louis XVIII. and of Charles X.; formerly book-keeper at the Treasury, where he is believed to have succeeded the elder Poiret;[1] he was afterwards appointed chief cashier, and held that position a long while. Saillard married Mademoiselle Bidault, a daughter of a furniture merchant, whose establishment was under the pillars of the Paris market, and a niece of the bill-discounter on rue Greneta; he had by her a daughter, Elisabeth, who became by marriage Madame Isidore Baudoyer; owned an old mansion on Place Royale, where he lived together with the family of Isidore Baudoyer; he became mayor of his ward during the monarchy of July, and renewed then his acquaintance with his old comrades of the department, the Minards and the Thuilliers. [The Government Clerks. The Middle Classes.]

Saillard (Madame), wife of the preceding, born Bidault, in 1767; niece of the bill-discounter called Gigonnet; was the leading spirit of the household on Place Royale, and, above all, the counselor of her husband; she reared her daughter Elisabeth, who became Madame Baudoyer, very strictly. [César Birotteau. The Government Clerks.]

Sain, shared with Augustin the sceptre of miniature painting under the Empire. In 1809, before the Wagram campaign, he painted a miniature of Montcornet, then young and handsome; this painting passed from the hands of Madame Fortin, mistress of the future marshal, to the hands of their daughter, Madame Valérie Crevel (formerly Marneffe). [Cousin Betty.]

Saint-Denis (De), assumed name of the police-agent, Corentin.

Sainte-Beuve (Charles-Augustin), born at Boulogne-sur-

[1] The Compilers subsequently dispute this.

Mer in 1805; died in Paris in 1869; an academician and senator under the Second Empire. An illustrious Frenchman of letters whom Raoul Nathan imitated poorly enough before Béatrix de Rochfide in his account of the adventures of Charles-Edouard Rusticoli de la Palférine. [A Prince of Bohemia.]

Sainte-Sévère (Madame de), cousin to Gaston de Nueil, lived in Bayeux, where she received, in 1822, her young kinsman, just convalescing from some inflammatory disorder caused by excess in study or in pleasure. [The Deserted Woman.]

Saint-Estève (De), name of Jacques Collin as chief of the secret police.

Saint-Estève (Madame de), an assumed name, shared by Madame Jacqueline Collin and Madame Nourrisson.

Saint-Foudrille (De), a "brilliant scholar," lived in Paris, and most likely in the Saint-Jacques district, at least about 1840, the time when Thuillier wished to know him. [The Middle Classes.]

Saint-Foudrille (Madame de), wife of the preceding, received, about 1840, a very attentive visit from the Thuillier family. [The Middle Classes.]

Saint-Georges (Chevalier de), 1745-1801, a mulatto, of superb figure and features, son of a former general; captain of the guards of the Duc d'Orléans; served with distinction under Dumouriez; arrested in 1794 on suspicion, and released after the 9th Thermidor; he became distinguished in the pleasing art of music, and especially in the art of fencing. The Chevalier de Saint-Georges traded at the Cat and Racket on the rue Saint-Denis, but did not pay his debts. Monsieur Guillaume had obtained a judgment of the consular government against him. [At the Sign of the Cat and Racket.] Later he was made popular by a production of a comédie-vaudeville of Roger de Beauvoir, at the Variétées under Loüis Philippe, with the comedian Lafont[1] as interpreter.

---

[1] Complimented in 1836, at the chateau of Madame de la Baudraye, by Etienne Lousteau and Horace Bianchon.

Saint-Germain (De), one of the assumed names of police-agent Peyrade.

Saint-Héreen (Comte de), husband of Moïna d'Aiglemont, was heir of one of the most illustrious houses of France. He lived with his wife and mother-in-law in a house belonging to the former, on the rue Plumet (now rue Oudinot), adjoining the Boulevard des Invalides; about the middle of December, 1843, he left this house alone to go on a political mission; during this time his wife received too willingly the frequent and compromising visits of young Alfred de Vandenesse, and his mother-in-law died suddenly. [A Woman of Thirty.]

Saint-Héreen (Comtesse Moïna de), wife of the preceding; of five children she was the only one that survived Monsieur and Madame d'Aiglemont, in the second half of Louis Philippe's reign. Blindly spoiled by her mother, she repaid that almost exclusive affection by coldness only, or even disdain. By a cruel word Moïna caused the death of her mother; she dared, indeed, to recall to her mother her former relations with Marquis Charles de Vandenesse, whose son Alfred· she herself was receiving with too much pleasure in the absence of Monsieur de Saint-Héreen. [A Woman of Thirty.] In a conversation concerning love with the Marquise de Vandenesse, Lady Dudley, Mademoiselle des Touches, the Marquise of Rochefide, and Madame d'Espard, Moïna laughingly remarked: "A lover is forbidden fruit, a statement that sums up the whole case with me." [A Daughter of Eve.] Madame Octave de Camps, referring to Naïs de l'Estorade, then a child, made the following cutting remark: "That little girl makes me anxious; she reminds me of Moïna d'Aiglemont." [The Member for Arcis.]

Saint-Martin (Louis-Claude de), called the "Unknown Philosopher," was born on the 18th of January, 1743, at Amboise, and died Ocober 13, 1803; he was very often received at Clochegourde by Madame de Verneuil, an aunt of Madame de Mortsauf, who knew him there. At Clochegourde, Saint-Martin superintended the publication of his last books, which were printed at Letourmy's in Tours. [The Lily of the Valley.]

Saint-Vier (Madame de). (*See* Gentillet.)

Saintot (Astolphe de), one of the frequenters of the Bargeton salon at Angouléme; president of the society of agriculture of his town; though "ignorant as a carp," he passed for a scholar of the first rank; and, though he did nothing, he let it be believed that he had been occupied for several years with writing a treatise on modern methods of cultivation. His success in the world was due, for the most part, to quotations from Cicero, learned by heart in the morning and recited in the evening. Though a tall, stout, red-faced man, Saintot seemed to be ruled by his wife. [Lost Illusions.]

Saintot (Madame de), wife of the preceding. Her Christian name was Elisa, and she was usually called Lili, a childish designation that was in strong contrast with the character of this lady, who was dry and solemn, extremely pious, and a cross and quarrelsome card-player. [Lost Illusions.]

Sallenauve (François-Henri-Pantaléon-Dumirail, Marquis de), a noble of Champagne, lost and ruined by cards, in his old age was reduced to the degree of a street-sweep, under the service of Jacques Bricheteau. [The Member for Arcis.]

Sallenauve (Comte de), legal son of the preceding, was born in 1809 of the relations of Catherine-Antoinette Goussard and Jacques Collin; grandson of Danton through his mother; school-mate of Marie Gaston, whose friend he continued to be, and for whom he fought a duel. For a long time he knew nothing of his family, but lived almost to the age of thirty under the name of Charles Dorlange. [The Member for Arcis.]

Sallenauve (Comtesse de), wife of the preceding, born Jeanne-Athenaïs de l'Estorade (Naïs, by familiar abbreviation) in February, 1827; the precocious and rather spoilt child of the Comte and Comtesse Louis de l'Estorade. [Letters of Two Brides. The Member for Arcis.]

Salmon, formerly expert in the museum at Paris. In 1826, while on a visit at Tours, whither he had gone to see his mother-in-law, he was engaged to assess a "Virgin" by Valentin and a "Christ" by Lebrun, paintings which Abbé François Birotteau had inherited from Abbé Chapeloud, having left them in an apartment recently occupied by himself at Mademoiselle Sophie Gamard's. [The Vicar of Tours.]

Salomon (Joseph), of Tours, or near Tours, uncle and guardian to Pauline Salomon de Villenoix, a very rich Jewess. He was deeply attached to his niece and wished a brilliant match for her. Louis Lambert, who was engaged to Pauline, said: "This terrible Salomon freezes me; this man is not of our heaven." [Louis Lambert.]

Samanon, a squint-eyed speculator, followed the various professions of a money-handler during the reigns of Louis XVIII., Charles X., and Louis Philippe. In 1821, Lucien de Rubempré, still a novice, visited Samanon's establishment in the Faubourg Poissonniére, where he was then engaged in the numerous trades of dealing in old books and old clothes, of brokerage, and of discount. There he found a certain great man of unknown identity, a Bohemian and cynic, who had come to borrow his own clothes that he had left in pawn. [A Distinguished Provincial at Paris.] Nearly three years later, Samanon was the man of straw of the Gobseck-Bidault (Gigonnet) combination, who were persecuting Chardin des Lupeaulx for the payment of debts due them. [The Government Clerks.] After 1830, the usurer joined with the Cérizets and the Claparons when they tried to circumvent Maxime de Trailles. [A Man of Business.] The same Samanon, about 1844, had bills to the value of ten thousand francs against Baron Hulot d'Ervy, who was seeking refuge under the name of Father Vyder. [Cousin Betty.]

San-Esteban (Marquise de), a foreign and aristocratic sounding assumed name, under which Jacqueline Collin disguised herself when she visited the Conciergerie, in May,

1830, to see Jacques Collin, himself under the incognito of Carlos Herrera. [Scenes from a Courtesan's Life.]

San-Réal (Don Hijos, Marquis de), born about 1735, a powerful nobleman; he enjoyed the friendship of Ferdinand VII., King of Spain, and married a natural daughter of Lord Dudley, Margarita-Euphémia Porrabéril (born of a Spanish mother), with whom he lived in Paris, in 1815, in a mansion on the rue Saint-Lazare, near Nucingen. [The Thirteen.]

San-Réal (Marquise de), wife of the preceding, born Margarita-Euphémia Porrabéril, natural daughter of Lord Dudley and a Spanish woman, and sister of Henri de Marsay; had the restless energy of her brother, whom she resembled also in appearance. Brought up at Havana, she was then taken back to Madrid, accompanied by a creole girl of the Antilles, Paquita Valdés, with whom she maintained passionate unnatural relations, that marriage did not interrupt and which were being continued in Paris in 1815, when the marquise, meeting a rival in her brother, Henri de Marsay, killed Paquita. After this murder, Madame de San Réal retired to Spain to the convent of Los Dolorés. [The Thirteen.]

Sanson (Charles-Henri), public executioner in the period of the Revolution, and beheader of Louis XVI.; he attended two masses commemorating the death of the King, celebrated in 1793 and 1794, by the Abbé de Marolles, to whom his identity was afterwards disclosed by Ragon. [An Episode under the Terror.]

Sanson, son of the preceding, born about 1770, descended, as was his father, from headsmen of Rouen. After having been captain of cavalry he assisted his father in the execution of Louis XVI.; was his agent when scaffolds were operated at the same time in the Place Louis XV. and the Place du Trône, and eventually succeeded him. Sanson was prepared to "accommodate" Théodore Calvi in May, 1830; he awaited the condemning order, which was not issued. He had the appearance of a rather distinguished Englishman. At least Sanson gave Jacques Collin that impression, when he met the ex-convict, then confined at the Conciergerie. [Scenes from a Courtesan's Life.] Sanson lived in the rue des Marais (the district of the Faubourg Saint-Martin), which is a much shorter street now than formerly.

Sarcus was justice of the peace, in the reign of Louis XVIII., at Soulanges (Bourgogne), where he lived on his fifteen hundred francs, together with the rent of a house in which he lived, and three hundred francs from the public funds. Sarcus married the elder sister of Vermut, the druggist of Soulanges, by whom he had a daughter, Adeline, afterwards Madame Adolphe Sibilet. This functionary of inferior order, a handsome little old man with iron-gray hair, was none the less the politician of the first order in the society of Soulanges, which was completely under Madame Soudry's sway, and which counted almost all Montcornet's enemies. [The Peasantry.]

Sarcus, cousin in the third degree of the preceding; called Sarcus the Rich; in 1817 a counselor at the prefecture of the department of Bourgogne, which Monsieur de la Roche-Hugon and Monsieur de Casteran governed successively under the Restoration, and which included as dependencies Ville-aux-Fayes, Soulanges, Blangy, and Aigues. He recommended Sibilet as steward for Aigues, which was Montcornet's estate. Sarcus the Rich was a member of the Chamber of Deputies; he was also said to be right-hand man to the prefect. [The Peasantry.]

Sarcus (Madame), wife of the preceding; born Vallat, in 1778, of a family connected with the Gaubertins, was supposed in her youth to have favored Monsieur Lupin, who, in 1823, was still paying devoted attentions to this woman of forty-five, the mother of an engineer. [The Peasantry.]

Sarcus, son of the preceding couple, became, in 1823, general engineer of bridges and causeways of Ville-aux-Fayes, thus completing the group of powerful native families hostile to the Montcornets. [The Peasantry.]

Sarcus-Taupin, a miller at Soulanges, who enjoyed an

income of fifty thousand francs; the Nucingen of his town; was father of a daughter whose hand was sought by Lupin, the notary, and by President Gendrin for their respective sons. [The Peasantry.]

Sarrasine (Matthieu or Mathieu), a laborer in the neighborhood of Saint-Dié, father of a rich lawyer of Franche-Comté, and grandfather of the sculptor, Ernest-Jean Sarrasine. [Sarrasine.]

Sarrasine, a rich lawyer of Franche-Comté in the eighteenth century, father of the sculptor, Ernest-Jean Sarrasine. [Sarrasine.]

Sarrasine (Ernest-Jean), a famous French sculptor, son of the preceding and grandson of Matthieu Sarrasine. When quite young he showed a calling for art strong enough to combat the will of his father, who wished him to adopt the legal profession; he went to Paris, entered Bouchardon's studio, found a friend and protector in this master; became acquainted with Madame Geoffrin, Sophie Arnould, the Baron d'Holbach, and J.-J. Rousseau. Having become the lover of Clotilde, the famous singer at the Opéra, Sarrasine won the sculptor's prize founded by Marigny, a brother of La Pompadour, and received praise from Diderot. He then went to Rome to live (1758); became intimate with Vien, Louthrebourg,[1] Allegrain, Vitagliani, Cicognara, and Chigi. He then fell madly in love with the eunuch Zambinella, uncle of the Lanty-Duvignons; believing him to be a woman, he made a magnificent bust of the singular singer, who was kept by Cicognara, and, having carried him off, was murdered at the instigation of his rival in the same year, 1758. The story of Sarrasine's life was related, during the Restoration, to Béatrix de Rochefide. [Sarrasine. The Member for Arcis.]

Sauteloup, familiarly called "Father Sautcloup," had the task, in May, 1830, of reading to Théodore Calvi, who was condemned to death and a prisoner in the Conciergerie, the

---

[1] Or Louthrebourg, and also Lauterbourg, intentionally left out in the Repertory because of the various ways of spelling the name

denial of his petition for appeal.   [Scenes from a Courtesan's Life.]

Sauvage (Madame), a person of repulsive appearance, and of doubtful morality, the servant-mistress of Maitre Fraisier; on the death of Pons, kept house for Schmucke, who inherited from Pons to the prejudice of the Camusot de Marvilles.   [Cousin Pons.]

Sauvage, first deputy of the king's attorney at Alençon; a young magistrate, married, harsh, stiff, ambitious, and selfish; took sides against Victurnien d'Esgrignon in the notorious affair known as the D'Esgrignon-Du-Bousquier case; after the famous lawsuit he was sent to Corsica.   [Jealousies of· a Country Town.]

Sauvagnest, successor of the attorney Bordin, and predecessor of Maitre Desroches; was an attorney in Paris. [A Start in Life.]

Sauvaignou (of Marseilles), a head carpenter, had a hand in the sale of the house on the Place de la Madeleine which was bought in 1840, by the Thuilliers at the urgent instance of Cérizet, Claparon, Dutocq, and especially Théodose de la Peyrade.   [The Middle Classes.]

Sauviat (Jérôme-Baptiste), born in Auvergne, about 1747; a traveling tradesman from 1792 to 1796; of commercial tastes, rough, energetic, and avaricious; of a profoundly religious nature; was imprisoned during the Terror; barely escaped being beheaded for abetting the escape of a bishop; married Mademoiselle Champagnac at Limoges in 1797; had by her a daughter, Véronique (Madame Pierre Graslin); after the death of his father-in-law, he bought, in the same town, the house which he was occupying as tenant and where he sold old iron; he continued his business there; retired from business in wealth, but still, at a later period, went as superintendent into a porcelain factory with J.-F. Tascheron; gave his attention to that work for at least three years, and died then through an accident in 1827.   [The Country Parson.]

Sauviat (Madame), wife of the preceding; born Champagnac, about 1767; daughter of a coppersmith of Limoges, who became a widower in 1797, and from whom she afterwards inherited. Madame Sauviat lived, in turn, near the rue de la Vieille-Poste, a suburb of Limoges, and at Montégnac. Like Sauviat, she was industrious, rough, grasping, economical, and hard, but pious withal; and like him, too, she adored Véronique, whose terrible secret she knew,—a sort of Marcellange affair.[1] [The Country Parson.]

Savaron de Savarus, a noble and wealthy family, whose various members known in the eighteenth century were as follows: Savaron de Savarus (of Tournai), a Fleming, true to Flemish traditions, with whom the Claés and the Pierquins seem to have had transactions. [The Quest of the Absolute.] Mademoiselle Savarus, a native of Brabant, a wealthy unmarried heiress; Savarus (Albert), a French attorney, descended, but not lineally, from the Comte de Savarus. [Albert Savarus.]

Savarus (Albert Savaron de), of the family of the preceding list, but natural son of the Comte de Savarus, was born about 1798; was secretary to a minister of Charles X., and was also Master of Requests. The Revolution of 1830 fatally interrupted a very promising career; a deep love, which was reciprocated, for the Duchesse d'Argaïolo (afterwards Madame Alphonse de Rhétoré) restored to Savarus his energetic and enterprising spirit; he succeeded in being admitted to the bar of Besançon, built up a good practice, succeeded brilliantly, founded the "Revue de l'Est," in which he published an autobiographic novel, "L'Ambitieux par Amour," and met with warm support in his candidacy for the Chamber of Deputies (1834). Albert Savarus, with his mask of a deep thinker, might have seen all his dreams realized, but for the romantic and jealous fancies of Rosalie de Watteville, who discovered and undid the advocate's plans, by bringing about the second marriage of Madame d'Argaïolo. His hopes thus baffled, Albert Savarus became a friar of the

---

[1] A famous criminal case of the time.

parent institution of the Carthusians, which was situated near Grenoble, and was known as Brother Albert. [The Quest of the Absolute. Albert Savarus.]

Scherbelloff, Scherbellof, or Sherbelloff (Princesse), maternal grandmother of Madame de Montcornet. [The Peasantry. Jealousies of a Country Town.]

Schiltz married a Barnheim (of Baden), and had by her a daughter, Joséphine, afterwards Madame Fabien du Ronceret; was "an intrepid officer, a chief among those bold Alsatian partisans who almost saved the Emperor in the campaign of France." He died at Metz, despoiled and ruined. [Béatrix.]

Schiltz (Joséphine), otherwise known as Madame Schontz. (*See* Ronceret, Madame Fabien du.)

Schinner (Mademoiselle), mother of Hippolyte Schinner, the painter, and daughter of an Alsatian farmer; being seduced by a coarse but wealthy man, she refused the money offered as compensation for refusing to legitimize their liaison, and consoled herself in the joys of maternity, the duties whereof she fulfilled with the most perfect devotion. At the time of her son's marriage she was living in Paris, and shared with him an apartment situated near the artist's studio, and not far from the Madeleine, on the rue des Champs-Elysées. [The Purse.]

Schinner (Hippolyte), a painter, natural son of the preceding; of Alsatian origin, and recognized by his mother only; a pupil of Gros, in whose studio he formed a close intimacy with Joseph Bridau. [A Bachelor's Establishment.] He was married during the reign of Louis XVIII.; he was at that time a knight of the Legion of Honor, and was already a celebrated character. While working in Paris, near the Madeleine, in a house belonging to Molineux, he met the other occupants, Madame and Mademoiselle Leseigneur de Rouville, and seems to have imitated with respect to them the delicate conduct of their benefactor and friend, Kergarouët; was touched by the cordiality extended to him by the baroness in spite of his poverty; he loved Adelaïde de Rouville, and, the passion being reciprocated, he married her. [The Purse.] Being associated with Pierre Grassou, he gave him excellent advice, which this indifferent artist was scarcely able to profit by. [Pierre Grassou.] In 1822, the Comte de Sérizy employed Schinner to decorate the château of Presles; Joseph Bridau, who was trying his hand, completed the master's work, and even, in a passing fit of levity, appropriated his name. [A Start in Life.] Schinner was mentioned in the autobiographical novel of Albert Savarus, "L'Ambitieux par Amour." [Albert Savarus.] He was the friend of Xavier Rabourdin. [The Government Clerks.] He drew vignettes for the works of Canalis. [Modeste Mignon.] To him we owe the remarkable ceilings of Adam Laginski's house situated on the rue de la Pépiniére. [The Imaginary Mistress.] About 1845, Hippolyte Schinner lived not far from the rue de Berlin, near Léon de Lora, to whom he had been first instructor. [The Unconscious Humorists.]

Schinner (Madame), wife of Hippolyte Schinner, born Adelaïde Leseigneur de Rouville, daughter of the Baron and Baronne de Rouville, her father being a naval officer; lived during the Restoration in Paris with her mother, boarding at a house situated on the rue de Surène and belonging to Molineux. Bereft of her father, the future Madame Schinner would then have found it difficult to await the slow adjustment of her father's pension, had not their old friend, Admiral de Kergarouët, come in his unobtrusive way to the assistance of herself and her mother. About the same time she nursed their neighbor, Hippolyte Schinner, who was suffering from the effects of a fall, and conceived for him a love that was returned; the gift of a little embroidered purse on the part of the young woman brought about the marriage. [The Purse.]

Schmucke (Wilhelm), a German Catholic, and a man of great musical talent; open-hearted, absent-minded, kind, sincere, of simple manners, of gentle and upright bearing. Originally he was precentor to the Margrave of Anspach;

he had known Hoffman, the eccentric writer of Berlin, in whose memory he afterwards had a cat named Mürr. Schmucke then went to Paris; in 1835-36, he lived there in a small apartment on the Quai Conti, at the corner of the rue de Nevers.[1] Previous to this, in the Quartier du Marais, he gave lessons in harmony, that were much appreciated, to the daughters of the Granvilles, afterwards Mesdames de Vandenesse and du Tillet; at a later period the former lady asked him to endorse some notes of hand for Raoul Nathan's benefit. [A Daughter of Eve.] Schmucke was also instructor of Lydie Peyrade before her marriage with Théodose de la Peyrade. [Scenes from a Courtesan's Life]; but those whom he regarded as his favorite pupils were Mesdames de Vandenesse and du Tillet, and the future Vicomtesse de Portenduère,Mademoiselle Mirouët of Nemours, the three "Saint-Cecilias" who combined to pay him an annuity. [Ursule Mirouët.] The former precentor, now of ugly and aged appearance, readily obtained a welcome with the principals of boarding-schools for young ladies. At a distribution of prizes he was brought in contact with Sylvain Pons for whom he immediately felt an affection that proved to be mutual (1834). Their intimacy brought them under the same roof, rue de Normandie, as tenants of C.-J. Pillerault (1836). Schmucke lived for nine years in perfect happiness. Gaudissart, having become manager of a theatre, employed him in his orchestra, entrusted him with the work of making copies of the music, and employed him to play the piano and various instruments that were not used in the boulevard theatres: the viol d'amore, English horn, violoncello, harp, castanets, bells, saxhorns, etc. Pons made him his residuary legatee (April, 1845); but the innocent German was not strong enough to contend with Maitre Fraisier, agent of the Camusot de Marvilles, who were ignored in this will. In spite of Topinard, to whom, in despair at the death of his friend, he went to demand hospitality, in the Bordin district, Schmucke allowed himself to be swindled, and was soon carried off by apoplexy. [Cousin Pons.]

[1] Perhaps the former lodging place of Napoleon Bonaparte.

Schontz (Madame), name borne by Mademoiselle Schiltz, afterwards Madam Fabien du Ronceret. (*See* this last name.)

Schwab (Wilhelm), born at Strasbourg in the early part of the nineteenth century, of the German family of Kehl, had Frédéric (Fritz) Brunner as his friend, whose follies he shared, whose poverty he relieved, and with whom he went to Paris; there they went to the Hotel du Rhin, rue du Mail, kept by Johann Graff, father of Emilie, and brother of the famous tailor, Wolfgang Graff. Schwab kept books for this rival of Humann and Staub. Several years later he played the flute at the theatre at which Sylvain Pons directed the orchestra. During an intermission at the first brilliant performance of "La Fiancée du Diable," presented in the fall of 1844, Schwab invited Pons through Schmucke to his approaching wedding; he married Mademoiselle Emilie Graff— a love-match—and joined in business with Frédéric Brunner, who was a banker and enriched by the inheritance of his father's property. [Cousin Pons.]

Schwab (Madame Wilhelm), wife of the preceding; born Mademoiselle Emilie Graff; an accomplished beauty; niece of Wolfgang Graff, the wealthy tailor, who provided her with dowry. [Cousin Pons.]

Scio (Madame), a prominent singer of the Théâtre Feydeau in 1798, was very beautiful in "Les Péruviens," a comic opera by Mongenod, produced with very indifferent success. [The Seamy Side of History.]

Scœvola (Mucius). Under this assumed name was concealed, during the Terror, a man who had been huntsman to the Prince de Conti, to whom he owed his fortune. A plasterer, and proprietor of a small house in Paris, on about the highest point of the Faubourg Saint-Martin,[1] near the rue d'Allemagne, he affected an exaggerated civism, which masked an unfailing fidelity to the Bourbons, and he in some mysterious way afforded protection to Sisters Marthe and Agathe (Mesdemoiselles de Beauséant and de Langeais),

---

[1] His parish was the Saint-Laurent church, which for a while during the Revolution had the name of Temple of Fidelity.

nuns who had escaped from the Abbey of Chelles, and were, with Abbé de Marolles, taking refuge under his roof. [An Episode under the Terror.]

Séchard (Jérôme-Nicolas), born in 1743. After having been a workman in a printer's shop of Angouléme situated on the Place du Mûrier, though very illiterate, he became its owner at the beginning of the Revolution; was acquainted at that time with the Marquis de Maucombe, married a woman that was provided with a certain competency, but soon lost her, after having by her a son, David. In the reign of Louis XVIII., fearing the competition of Cointet, J.-N. Séchard retired from active life, selling his business to his son, whom he intentionally deceived in the trade, and moved to Marsac, near Angouléme, where he raised grapes, and drank to excess. During all the latter part of his life, Séchard mercilessly aggravated the commercial difficulties which his son David was struggling against. The old miser died about 1829, leaving property of some value. [Lost Illusions.]

Séchard (David), only son of the preceding, school-mate and friend of Lucien de Rubempré, learned the art of printing from the Didots of Paris. On one occasion, upon his return to his native soil, he gave many evidences of his kindness and delicacy; having purchased his father's printing shop, he allowed himself to be deliberatly cheated and duped by him; employed as proof-reader Lucien de Rubempré, whose sister, Eve Chardon, he adored with a passion that was fully reciprocated; he married her in spite of the poverty of both parties, for his business was on the decline. The expense involved, the competition of the Cointets, and especially his experiments as inventor in the hope of finding the secret of a particular way of making paper, reduced him to very straitened circumstances. Indeed, everything combined to destroy Séchard; the cunning and power of the Cointet house, the spying of the ungrateful Cérizet, formerly his apprentice, the disorderly life of Lucien de Rubempré, and the jealous greed of his father. A victim of .the wiles of

Cointet, Séchard abandoned his discovery, resigned himself to his fate, inherited from his father, and, cheered by the devotion of the Kolbs, dwelt in Marsac, where Derville, led by Corentin, hunted him out with a view to gaining information as to the origin of Lucien de Rubempré's million. [Lost Illusions. A Distinguished Provincial at Paris. Scenes from a Courtesan's Life.]

Séchard (Madame David), wife of the preceding, born Eve Chardon in 1804, daughter of a druggist of L'Houmeau (a suburb of Angoulême), and of a member of the house of Rubempré; worked first at the house of Madame Prieur, a laundress, for the consideration of fifteen sous a day; manifested great devotion to her brother Lucien, and on marrying David Séchard, in 1821, transferred her devotion to him; having undertaken to manage the printing shop, she competed with Cérizet, Cointet, and Petit-Claud, and almost succeeded in softening Jérôme-Nicholas Séchard. Madame Séchard shared with her husband the inheritance of old J.-N. Séchard, and was then the modest châtelaine of La Verberie, at Marsac. By her husband she had at least one child, named Lucien. Madame Séchard was tall and of dark complexion, with blue eyes. [Lost Illusions. A Distinguished Provincial at Paris. Scenes from a Courtesan's Life.]

Séchard (Lucien), son of the preceding couple. [Lost Illusions.]

Ségaud, solicitor at Angoulême, was successor to Petit-Claud, a magistrate, about 1824. [Lost Illusions.]

Sélérier, called the Auvergnat, Père Ralleau, Le Rouleur, and especially Fil-de-Soie, belonged to the aristocracy of the galleys, and was a member of the group of "Ten Thousand," whose chief was Jacques Collin; the latter, however, suspected him of having sold him to the police, about 1819, when Bibi-Lupin arrested him at the Vauquer boarding-house. [Father Goriot.] In his business Sélérier always avoided bloodshed. He was of philosophical turn, very selfish, incapable of love, and ignorant of the meaning of friendship. In May, 1830, when being a prisoner at the Conciergerie, and about to be condemned to fifteen years of forced labor, he saw and recognized Jacques Collin, the pseudo-Carlos Herrera, himself incriminated. [Scenes from a Courtesan's Life.]

Senonches (Jacques de), a noble of Angouléme, a great huntsman, stiff and haughty, a sort of wild boar; lived on very good terms with his wife's lover, François du Hautoy, and attended Madame de Bargeton's receptions. [Lost Illusions.]

Senonches (Madame Jacques de), wife of the preceding, bore the given name of Zéphirine, which was abbreviated to Zizine. By François du Hautoy, her adored lover, she had a daughter, Françoise de la Haye, who was presented as her ward, and who became Madame Petit-Claud. [Lost Illusions.]

Sepherd (Carl), name assumed by Charles Grandet in the Indies, the United States, Africa, etc., while he was in the slave-trading business. [Eugénie Grandet.]

Sérizy, or Sérisy (Comte Hugret de), born in 1765, descended in direct line from the famous President Hugret, ennobled under François I. The motto of this family was "I, semper melius eris," so that the final s of melius, the word eris, and the I of the beginning, represented the name (Sérizy) of the estate that had been made a county. A son of a first president of Parliament (who died in 1794), Sérizy was himself, as early as 1787, a member of the Grand Council; he did not emigrate during the Revolution, but remained in his estate of Sérizy, near Arpajon; became a member of the Council of Five Hundred, and afterwards of the Council of State. The Empire made him a count and a senator. Hugret de Sérizy was married, in 1806, to Léontine de Ronquerolles, the widow of Général Gaubert. This union made him the brother-in-law of the Marquis de Ronquerolles, and the Marquis du Rouvre. Every honor was alloted to him in course; chamberlain under the Empire, he afterwards became vice-president of the Council of State, peer of France, Grand Cross of the Legion of Honor, and member of the Privy Council. The glorious career of Sérizy, who was an unusually industrious person, did not offer compensation for his domestic misfortunes. Hard work and protracted vigils soon aged the high functionary, who was ever unable to win his wife's heart; but he loved her and sheltered her none the less constantly. It was chiefly to avenge her for the indiscretion of the volatile young Oscar Husson, Morean's godson, that he discharged the not overhonest steward of Presles. [A Start in Life.] The system of government that succeeded the Empire increased Sérizy's influence and renown; he was an intimate friend of the Bauvans and the Grandvilles. [A Bachelor's Establishment. Honorine. Modeste Mignon.] His weakness in matters concerning his wife was such that he assisted her in person, when, in May, 1830, she hastened to the Conciergerie in the hope of saving her lover, Lucien de Rubempré, and entered the cell where the young man had just committed suicide. Sérizy even consented to be executor of the poet's will. [Scenes from a Courtesan's Life.]

Sérizy (Comtesse de), wife of the preceding, born Léontine de Ronquerolles about 1784, sister of the Marquis du Ronquerolles; married, as her first husband, Général Gaubert, one of the most illustrious soldiers of the Republic; married a second time, when quite young, but could never entertain any feeling stronger than that of respect for M. de Sérizy, her second husband, by whom, however, she had a son, an officer, who was killed during the reign of Louis Philippe. [A Start in Life.] Worldly and brilliant, and a worthy rival of Mesdames de Beauséant, de Langeais, de Maufrigneuse, de Carigliano, and d'Espard, Léontine de Sérizy had several lovers, among them being Auguste de Maulincour, Victor d'Aiglemont and Lucien de Rubempré. [The Thirteen. Ursule Mirouët. A Woman of Thirty.] This last liaison was a very stormy one. Lucien acquired considerable influence over Madame de Sérizy, and made use of it to reach the Marquise d'Espard, by effecting an annulment of the decree which she had obtained against her husband, the Marquis d'Espard, placing him under guardianship. And so it was that, during Rubempré's imprisonment and after his suicide, she suffered the bitterest anguish. Léontine de Sérizy almost broke the bars of the Conciergerie, insulted Camusot, the examining magistrate, and seemed to be beside herself. The intervention of Jacques Collin saved her and cured her, when three famous physicians, Messieurs Bianchon, Desplein, and Sinard declared themselves powerless to relieve her. [Scenes from a Courtesan's Life.] During the winter the Comtesse de Sérizy lived on the Chaussée-d'Antin; during the summer at Sérizy, her favorite residence, or still more at Presles, and sometimes near Nemours in Le Rouvre, the seat of the family of that name. Being a neighbor, in Paris, of Félicité des Touches, she was a frequent visitor of that emulator of George Sand, and was at her house when Marsay related the story of his first love-affair, taking part herself in the conversation. [Another Study of Woman.] Being a maternal aunt of Clémentine du Rouvre, Madame de Sérizy gave her a handsome dowry when she married Laginski; with her brother Ronquerolles, at his home on the rue de la Pépiniére, she met Thaddée Paz, the Pole's comrade. [The Imaginary Mistress.]

Sérizy (Vicomte de), only son of the preceding couple, graduated from the Ecole Polytechnique in 1825, and entered the cavalry regiment of the Garde Royale, by favor, as sub-lieutenant, under command of the Duc de Maufrigneuse; at this time Oscar Husson, nephew of Cardot, entered the same regiment as a private. [A Start in Life.] In October, 1829, Sérizy, being an officer in the company of the guards stationed at Havre, was instructed to inform M. de Verneuil, proprietor of some well-stocked Norman "preserves," that Madame could not participate in the chase that he had organized. Having become enamored of Diane de Maufrigneuse, the viscount found her at Verneuil's house; she received his attentions, as a means of avenging herself on Léontine de Sérizy, then mistress of Lucien de Rubempré. [Modeste Mignon.] Being advanced to the rank of lieutenant-colonel of a cavalry regiment, he was severely wounded at the disastrous battle of Macta, in Africa (June 26, 1835), and died at Toulon as a result of his wounds. [The Imaginary Mistress. A Start in Life.]

Servais, the only good gilder in Paris, according to Elie Magus, whose advice he heeded; he had the good sense to use English gold, which is far better than the French. Like the book-binder, Thouvenin, he was in love with his own work. [Cousin Pons.]

Servien (Prudence), born, in 1806, at Valenciennes, daughter of very poor weavers, was employed, from the age of seven years, in a spinning-mill; corrupted early by her life in the work-room, she was a mother at the age of thirteen; having had to testify in the court of assizes against Jean-François Durut, she made of him a formidable enemy, and fell into the power of Jacques Collin, who promised to shelter her from the resentment of the convict. She was at one time a ballet-girl, and afterwards served as Esther van Gobseck's chamber-maid, under the names of Eugénie and Europe; was the mistress of Paccard, whom she very probably married afterwards; aided Vautrin in fooling Nucingen and getting money from him. [Scenes from a Courtesan's Life.]

Servin, born about 1775, a distinguished painter, made a love-match with the daughter of a penniless general; in 1815 was manager of a studio in Paris, which was frequented by Mademoiselle Laure, and Mesdemoiselles Mathilde-Mélanie Roguin, Amélie Thirion and Ginevra di Piombo, the last three of whom were afterwards, respectively, Mesdames Tiphaine, Camusot de Marville, and Porta. Servin at that time was concealing an exile who was sought by the police, namely Luigi Porta, who married the master's favorite pupil, Mademoiselle Ginevra di Piombo. [The Vendetta.]

Servin (Madame), wife of the preceding, remembering that the romance of Porta and Ginevra's love had been the cause of all his pupils' leaving her husband's studio, refused to shelter Mademoiselle de Piombo when driven from her father's home. [The Vendetta.]

Sévérac (De), born in 1764, a country gentleman, mayor of a village in the canton of Angouléme, and author of an article on silkworms, was received at Madame de Bargeton's in 1821. A widower, without children, and doubtless very rich, but not knowing the ways of the world, one evening on the rue du Minage, he found as ready listeners only the poor but aristocratic Madame du Brossard and her daughter Camille, a young woman of twenty-seven years. [Lost Illusions.]

Sibilet, clerk of the court at Ville-aux-Fayes (Bourgogne), distant cousin of François Gaubertin, married a Mademoiselle Gaubertin-Vallat, and had by that marriage six children. [The Peasantry.]

Sibilet (Adolphe), eldest of the six children of the preceding, - born about 1793; was, at first, clerk to a notary, then an unimportant employé in the land-registry office; and then, in the latter part of the year 1817, succeeded his cousin, François Gaubertin, in the administration of Aigues, Général de Montcornet's estate, in Bourgogne. Sibilet had married Mademoiselle Adeline Sarcus (of the poor branch), who bore him two children in three years; his selfish interest and his personal obligations led him to gratify the ill-feeling of his predecessor, by being disloyal to Montcornet. [The Peasantry.]

Sibilet (Madame Adolphe), wife of the preceding, born Adeline Sarcus, only daughter of a justice of the peace, rich with beauty as her sole fortune, she was reared by her mother, in the little village of Soulanges (Bourgogne), with all possible care. Not having been able to marry Amaury Lupin (son of Lupin the notary), with whom she was in love, in despair she allowed herself, three years after her mother's death, to be married, by her father, to the disagreeable and repulsive Adolphe Sibilet. [The Peasantry.]

Sibilet, son of the court clerk, and police commissioner at Ville-aux-Fayes. [The Peasantry.]

Sibilet (Mademoiselle), daughter of the court clerk, afterwards Madame Hervé. [The Peasantry.]

Sibilet, son of the court clerk, first clerk of Maître Corbinet, notary at Ville-aux-Fayes, to whom he was the appointed successor. [The Peasantry.]

Sibilet, son of the court clerk, and clerk in the Department of Public Lands, presumptive successor of the registrar of documents at Ville-aux-Fayes. [The Peasantry.]

Sibilet (Mademoiselle), daughter of the court clerk, born about 1807, postmistress at Ville-aux-Fayes; betrothed to Captain Corbinet, brother of the notary. [The Peasantry.]

Sibuelle, a wealthy contractor of somewhat tarnished reputation during the Directory and the Consulate, gave his daughter in marriage to Malin de Gondreville, and through the credit of his son-in-law became, with Marion, co-receiver-general of the department of Aube. [The Gondreville Mystery.]

Sibuelle (Mademoiselle), only daughter of the preceding, became Madame Malin de Gondreville. [The Gondreville Mystery.]

Siéyès (Emmanuel-Joseph), born in 1748 at Fréjus, died in Paris in 1836, was successively vicar-general of Chartres, deputy to the States-General and the Convention, member of the Committee of Public Safety, member of the Five Hundred, member of the Directory, consul, and senator; famous also as a publicist. In June, 1800, he might have been found in the Office of Foreign Relations, in the rue du Bac, where he took part with Talleyrand and Fouché, in a secret council, in which the subject of overthrowing Bonaparte, then First Consul, was discussed. [The Gondreville Mystery.]

Signol (Henriette), a beautiful girl; of a good family of farmers, in the employ of Basine Clerget, a laundress at Angoulême; was the mistress of Cérizet, whom she loved and trusted; served as a tool against David Séchard, the printer. [Lost Illusions.]

Simeuse (Admiral de), father of Jean de Simeuse, was one of the most eminent French seamen of the eighteenth century. [Béatrix. The Gondreville Mystery. Jealousies of a Country Town.]

Simeuse (Marquis Jean de), whose name, "Cy meurs" or "Si meurs," was the motto of the family crest, was descended from a noble family of Bourgogne, who were formerly owners of a Lorrain fief called Ximeuse, corrupted to Simeuse. M. de Simeuse counted a number of illustrious men among his ancestors; he married Berthe de Cinq-Cygne; he was father of twins, Paul-Marie and Marie-Paul. He was guillotined at Troyes during the Terror; Michu's father-in-law presided over the Revolutionary tribunal that passed the death-sentence. [The Gondreville Mystery.]

. **Simeuse** (Marquise de), wife of the preceding, born Berthe de Cinq-Cygne, was executed at Troyes at the same time with her husband. [The Gondreville Mystery.]

Simeuse (Paul-Marie and Marie-Paul), twin sons of the preceding couple, born in 1773; grandsons on the father's side of the admiral who was as famous for his dissipation as for his valor; descended from the original owners of the famous Gondreville estate in Aube, and belonged to the noble Champagne family of the Chargeboeufs, the younger branch of which was represented by their mother, Berthe de Cinq-Cygne. Paul-Marie and Marie-Paul were among the emigrants; they returned to France about 1803. Both being in love with their cousin, Laurence de Cinq-Cygne, an ardent Royalist, they cast lots to decide which should be her husband; fate favored Marie-Paul, the younger, but circumstances prevented the consummation of the marriage. The twins differed only in disposition, and there in only one point: Paul-Marie was melancholy, while Marie-Paul was of a bright disposition. Despite the advice of their elderly relative, M. de Chargeboeuf, Messieurs de Simeuse compromised themselves with the Hauteserres; being watched by Fouché, who sent Peyrade and Corentin to keep an eye on them, they were accused of the abduction of Malin, of which they were not guilty, and sentenced to twenty-four years of penal servitude; were pardoned by Napoleon, entered as sub-lieutenants the same cavalry regiment, and were killed together in the battle of Sommo-Sierra (near Madrid, November 30, 1808). [The Gondreville Mystery.]

Simonin let carriages on the rue du Faubourg Saint-Honoré, Cour des Coches, Paris; about 1840, he let a berlin to Madame de Godollo, who, in accordance with the instructions of Corentin, the police-agent, was pretending to be taking a journey, but went no further than the Bois de Boulogne. [The Middle Classes.]

Simonnin, in the reign of Louis XVIII., was "errand-boy" to Maitre Derville on the rue Vivienne, Paris, when that advocate received Hyacinthe-Chabert. [Colonel Chabert.]

Sinard, a Paris physician, was called, in May, 1830, together with Messieurs Desplein and Bianchon, to the bedside of Léontine de Sérizy, who had lost her reason after the tragic end of her lover, Lucien de Rubempré. [Scenes from a Courtesan's Life.]

Sinet (Séraphine), a celebrated lorette, born in 1820, known by the sobriquet of Carabine, was present at Josépha Mirah's house-warming on the rue de la Ville-l'Evêque, in 1838. Five years later, being then mistress of the wealthy F. du Tillet, Mademoiselle Sinet supplanted the vivacious Marguerite Turquet as queen of the lorettes. [Cousin Betty.] A woman of splendid appearance, Séraphine was one of the marching chorus at the Opéra, and occupied the fine apartment on the rue Saint-Georges, where before her Suzanne du Val-Noble, Esther van Gobseck, Florine, and Madame Schontz had reigned. Of ready wit, dashing manners, and impish brazenness, Carabine held many successful receptions. Every day her table was set in magnificent style for ten guests. Artists, men of letters, and society favorites were among her frequent visitors. S.-P. Gazonal was taken to see her, in 1845, by Léon de Lora and Bixiou, together with Jenny Cadine of the Théâtre du Gymnase; and there he met Massol, Claude Vignon, Maxime de

Trailles, Nucingen, F. du Bruel, Malaga, Monsieur and Madame Gaillard, and Vauvinet, with a multitude of others, to say nothing of F. du Tillet. [The Unconscious Humorists.]

Sinot, attorney at Arcis-sur-Aube, commanded the patronage of the "Henriquinquistes" (partisans of Henri V.) in 1839, when the district had to elect a deputy to replace M. François Keller. [The Member for Arcis.]

Socquard, during the Empire and the Restoration, kept the Café de la Paix at Soulanges (Bourgogne). The Milo of Crotona of the Avonne Valley, a stout little man, of placid countenance, and a high, clear voice. He was manager of the Tivoli, a dancing-hall adjoining the café. Monsieur Vermichel, violin, and Monsieur Fourchon, clarinet, constituted the orchestra. Plissoud, Bonnébault, Viallet, and Amaury Lupin were steady patrons of his establishment, which was long famous for its billiards, its punch, and its mulled wine. In 1823, Socquard lost his wife. [The Peasantry.]

Socquard (Madame Junie), wife of the preceding, had many thrilling love-affairs during the Empire. She was very beautiful, and her luxurious mode of living, to which the leading men of Soulanges contributed, was notorious in the Avonne Valley. Lupin, the notary, had been guilty of great weakness in her direction, and Gaubertin, who took her away from him, unquestionably had by her a natural son, little Bournier. Junie was the secret of the prosperity of the Socquard house. She brought her husband a vineyard, the house he lived in, and the Tivoli. She died in the reign of Louis XVIII. [The Peasantry.]

Socquard (Aglaé), daughter of the preceding couple, born in 1801, inherited her father's ridiculous obesity. Being sought in marriage by Bonnébault, whom her father esteemed highly as a customer, but little as a son-in-law, she excited the jealousy of Marie Tonsard, and was always at daggers drawn with her. [The Peasantry.]

Soderini (Prince), father of Madame d'Argaïolo, who was

afterwards the Duchesse Alphonse de Rhétoré; at Besançon, in 1834, he demanded of Albert Savarus his daughter's letters and portrait. His sudden arrival caused a hasty departure on the part of Savarus, then a candidate for election to the Chamber of Deputies, and ignorant of Madame d'Argaïolo's approaching second marriage. [Albert Savarus.]

Solis (Abbé de), born about 1733, a Dominican, grand penitentiary of Toledo, vicar-general of the Archbishopric of Malines; a venerable priest, unassuming, kindly and large of person. He adopted Emmanuel de Solis, his brother's son, and, retiring to Douai, under the acceptable protection of the Casa-Réals, was confessor and adviser of their last descendant, Madame Balthazar Claës. The Abbé de Solis died in December, 1818. [The Quest of the Absolute.]

Solis (Emmanuel), nephew and adopted son of the preceding. Poor, and of a family originally from Granada, he responded well to the excellent education that he received, followed the teacher's calling, taught the humanities at the lyceum at Douai, of which he was afterwards principal, and gave lessons to the brothers of Marguerite Claës, whom he loved, the feeling being reciprocated. He married her in 1825; the more fully to enjoy his good fortune, he resigned the position as inspector of the University, which he then held. Shortly afterwards he inherited the title of Comte de Nourho, through the house of Solis. [The Quest of the Absolute.]

Solis (Madame Emmanuel de), wife of the preceding, born Marguerite Claés, in 1796, elder sister of Madame Félicie Pierquin, whose husband had first sought her hand, received from her dying mother the injunction to contend respectfully, but firmly, against her father's foolish efforts as inventor; and, in compliance with her mother's injunctions, by dint of great perseverance, succeeded in restoring the family fortunes that had been more than endangered. Madame de Solis gave birth to a child, in the course of a trip to Spain, where she was visiting Casa-Réal, the cradle of her mother's family. [The Quest of the Absolute.]

Solonet, born in 1795, obtained the decoration of the Legion of Honor for having made very active contribution to the second return of the Bourbons; was the youthful and worldly notary of Bordeaux; in the drawing up of the marriage contract between Natalie Evangélista and Paul de Manerville, he triumphed over the objections raised by his colleague, Mathias, who was defender of the Manerville interests. Solonet paid the most devoted attentions of a lover to Madame Evangélista, but his love was not returned, and he sought her hand in vain. [A Marriage Settlement.]

Solvet, a handsome youth, but addicted to gaming and other vices, loved by Caroline Crochard de Bellefeuille and preferred by her to Monsieur de Granville, her generous protector. Solvet made Mademoiselle Crochard very unhappy, ruined her, but was none the less adored by her. These facts were known to Bianchon, and related by him to the Comte de Granville, whom he met, one evening, in the reign of Louis Philippe, near the rue Gaillon. [A Second Home.]

Sommervieux (Théodore de), a painter, winner of the prix de Rome, knight of the Legion of Honor, was particularly successful in interiors; and excelled in chiaro-oscuro effects, in imitation of the Dutch. He made an excellent reproduction of the interior of the Cat and Racket, on the rue Saint-Denis, which he exhibited at the Salon at the same time with a fascinating portrait of his future wife, Mademoiselle Guillaume, with whom he fell madly in love, and whom he married about 1808, almost in spite of her parents, and thanks to the kind offices of Madame Roguin, whom he knew in his society life. The marriage was not a happy one; the daughter of the Guillaumes adored Sommervieux without understanding him. The painter often neglected his rooms on the rue des Trois-Fréres (now a part of the rue Taitbout) and transferred his homage to the Maréchale de Carigliano. He had an income of twelve thousand francs; before the Revolution his father was called the Chevalier de Sommervieux. [At he Sign of the Cat and Racket.] Théodore de Sommervieux designed a monstrance for Gohier, the king's goldsmith; this monstrance was bought by Madame Baudoyer and given to the church of Saint-Paul, at the time of the death of F. de la Billardière, head clerk of the administration, whose position she desired for her husband. [The Government Clerks.] Sommervieux also drew vignettes for the works of Canalis. [Modeste Mignon.]

Sommervieux (Madame Théodore de), wife of the preceding, born Augustine Guillaume, about 1792, second daughter of the Guillaumes of the Cat and Racket (a drapery establishment on the rue Saint-Denis, Paris), had a sad life that was soon wrecked; for, with the exception of Madame Roguin, her family never understood her aspirations to a higher ideal, or the feeling that prompted her to choose Théodore de Sommervieux. Mademoiselle Guillaume was married about the middle of the Empire, at her parish church, Saint-Leu, on the same day that her sister was married to Lebas, the clerk, and immediately after the ceremony referred to. A little less coarse in her feelings than her parents and their associates, but insignificant enough at best, without being aware of it she displeased the painter, and chilled the enthusiasm of her husband's studio friends, Schinner, Bridau, Bixiou, and Lora. Grassou, who was very much of a countryman, was the only one that refrained from laughing at her. Worn out at last, she tried to win back the heart that had become the possession of Madame de Carigliano; she even went to consult her rival, but could not use the weapons supplied her by the coquettish wife of the marshal, and died of a broken heart shortly after the famous ball given by César Birotteau, to which she was invited. She was buried in Montmartre cemetery. [At the Sign of the Cat and Racket. César Birotteau.]

Sonet, marble-worker and contractor for tombstones, at Paris, during the Restoration and Louis Philippe's reign. When Pons died, the marble-worker sent his agent to Schmucke to solicit an order for statues of Art and Friendship grouped together. Sonet had the draughtsman Vitelot as partner. The firm name was Sonet & Co. [Cousin Pons.]

Sonet (Madame), wife of the preceding, knew how to lavish attentions no less zealous than selfish on W. Schmucke, when he returned, broken-hearted, from Pére-Lachaise, in April, 1845, and suggested to him, with some modifications how-ever, to take certain allegorical monuments which the families of Marsay and Keller had formerly refused, preferring to apply to a genuine artist, the sculptor Stidmann. [Cousin Pons.]

Sophie, rival, namesake and contemporary of the famous Sophie, Doctor Véron's "blue ribbon," about 1844, was cook to the Comte Popinot on the rue Basse-du-Rempart, Paris. She must have been a remarkable culinary artist, for Sylvain Pons, reduced, in consequence of breaking with the Camusots, to dining at home, on the rue de Normandie, every day, often exclaimed in fits of melancholy, "O Sophie!" [Cousin Pons.]

Sorbier, a Parisian notary, to whom Chesnel (Choisnel) wrote, in 1822, from Normandie, to commend to his care the rattle-brained Victurnien d'Esgrignon. Unfortunately Sorbier was dead, and the letter was sent to his widow. [Jeal-ousies of a Country Town.]

Sorbier (Madame), wife of the preceding, mentioned in Chesnel's (or Choisnel's) letter of 1822, concerning Victurnien d'Esgrignon. She scarcely read the note, and simply sent it to her deceased husband's successor, Maitre Cardot. Thus the widow unwittingly served M. du Bousquier (du Croisier), the enemy of the D'Esgrignons. [Jealousies of a Country Town.]

Soria (Don Ferdinand, Duc de), younger brother of Don Felipe de Macumer, overwhelmed with kindness by his elder brother, owing him the duchy of Soria as well as the hand of Marie-Héréda, both being voluntarily renounced by the elder brother. Soria was not ungrateful; he hastened to his dying brother's bedside in 1829. The latter's death made Don Ferdinand Baron de Macumer. [Letters of Two Brides.]

Soria (Duchesse de), wife of the preceding, born Marie Hérédia, daughter of the wealthy Comte Hérédia, was loved by two brothers, Don Ferdinand, Duc de Soria, and Don

Felipe de Macumer. Though betrothed to the latter, she married the former, in accordance with her wishes, the Baron de Macumer having generously renounced her hand in favor of Don Ferdinand. The duchess retained a feeling of deep gratitude to him for his unselfishness, and at a later time bestowed every care on him in his last illness (1829). [Letters of Two Brides.]

Sormano, the "shy" servant of the Argaïolos, at the time of their exile in Switzerland, figures, as a woman, under the name of Gina, in the autobiographical novel of Albert Savarus, entitled "L'Ambitieux par l'Amour." [Albert Savarus.]

Souchet, a broker at Paris, whose failure ruined Guillaume Grandet, brother of the well-known cooper of Saumur. [Eugénie Grandet.]

Souchet (François), winner of the prix de Rome for his sculpture, about the beginning of Louis XVIII.'s reign; an intimate friend of Hippolyte Schinner, who confided to him his love for Adelaïde Lescigneur de Rouville, and was rallied on it by him. [The Purse.] About 1835, with Steinbock's assistance, Souchet carved the panels over the doors and mantels of Laginski's magnificent house on the rue de la Pépiniére, Paris. [The Imaginary Mistress.] He had given to Florine (afterwards Madame Raoul Nathan) a plaster cast of a group representing an angel holding an aspersorium, which adorned the actress's sumptuous apartments in 1834. [A Daughter of Eve.]

Soudry, born in 1773, a quartermaster, secured a valuable friend in M. de Soulanges, then adjutant-general, by saving him at the peril of his own life. Having become brigadier of gendarmes at Soulanges (Bourgogne), Soudry, in 1815, married Mademoiselle Cochet, Sophie Laguerre's former lady's-maid. Six years later, he was put on the retired list, at the request of Montcornet, and replaced in his brigade by Viallet; but, supported by the influence of François Gaubertin, he was elected mayor of Soulanges, and became the formidable enemy of the Montcornets. Like Grégoire

Rigou, his son's father-in-law, the old gendarme kept as
his mistress, under the same roof with his wife, his servant
Jeannette, who was younger than Madame Soudry. [The
Peasantry.]

Soudry (Madame), wife of the preceding, born Cochet
in 1763. Lady's-maid to Sophie Laguerre, Montcornet's
predecessor at Aigues, she had an understanding with François
Gaubertin, the steward of the estate, to make a victim of the
former opera singer. Twenty days after the burial of her
mistress, La Cochet married the brigadier, Soudry, a superb
specimen of manhood, though pitted with small-pox. During
the reign of Louis XVIII., Madame Soudry, who tried awk-
wardly enough to imitate her late mistress, Sophie Laguerre,
reigned supreme in the society of Soulanges, in her parlor
which was the meeting ground of Montcornet's enemies.
[The Peasantry.]

Soudry, natural son of Soudry, the brigadier of gendarmes;
legitimized at the time of his father's marriage to Mademoiselle
Cochet, in 1815. On the day on which Soudry became legally
possessed of a mother, he had just finished his course at Paris.
There he knew Gaubertin's son, during a stay which he had
at first intended to make long enough to entitle him to be
registered as an advocate, and eventually to enter the legal
profession; but he returned to Bourgogne to take charge
of an attorney's practice for which his father paid thirty
thousand francs. However, abandoning pettifoggery, Soudry
soon found himelf deputy king's attorney in a department
of Bourgogne, and, in 1817, king's attorney under Attorney-
General Bourlac, whom he replaced in 1821, thanks to the
influence of François Gaubertin. He then married Mademoiselle Rigou. [The Peasantry.]

Soudry (Madame), wife of the preceding, born Arséne Rigou,
the only daughter of wealthy parents, Grégoire Rigou and
Arséne Pichard; resembled her father in cunningness of character, and her mother in beauty. [The Peasantry.]

Soulanges (Comte Léon de), born in 1777, was colonel

of the artillery guard in 1809. In the month of November of that year, he found himself the guest of the Malin de Gondrevilles, in their mansion in Paris, on the evening of a great party; he met there Montcornet, a friend of his in the regiment; Madame de Vaudremont, who had once been his mistress, accompanied by Martial de la Roche-Hugon, her new lover; and finally his deserted wife, Madame de Soulanges, who had abandoned society, but who had come to the senator's house at the instigation of Madame de Lansac, with a view to a reconciliation, which was successfully carried out. [Domestic Peace.] Léon de Soulanges had several children as a result of his marriage; a son and some daughters; having refused one of his daughters in marriage to Montcornet, on the ground that she was too young, he made an enemy of that general. The count, remaining faithful to the Bourbons during the Hundred Days, was made a peer of France and a general in the artillery corps. Enjoying the favor of the Duc d'Angoulême, he was allowed a command during the Spanish war (1823), gained prominence at the siege of Cadiz and attained the highest degrees in the military hierarchy. Monsieur de Soulanges, who was very rich, owned, in the territory of the commune of Blangy (Bourgogne), a forest and a château adjoining the Aigues estate, which had itself once belonged to the house of Soulanges. At the time of the Crusades, an ancestor of the count had created this domain. Soulanges's motto was: "Je soule agir." Like M. de Ronquerolles he got on badly enough with his neighbor Montcornet. and seemed to favor François Gaubertin, Grégoire Rigou and Soudry, in their opposition to the future marshal. [The Peasantry.]

Soulanges (Comtesse Hortense de), wife of the preceding, and niece of the Duchesses de Lansac and de Marigny. In November, 1809, at a ball given by Malin de Gondreville, acting on the advice of Madame de Lansac, the countess, then on bad terms with her husband, conquered her proud timidity, and demanded of Martial de la Roche-Hugon a ring that she had received originally from her husband; M. de Soulanges had afterwards passed it on to his mistress, Madame de Vaudremont, who had given it to her lover, M. de la Roche-Hugon; this restitution effected the reconciliation of the couple. [Domestic Peace.] Hortense de Soulanges inherited from Madame de Marigny (who died about 1820) the Guébriant estate, with its encumbrance of an annuity. [The Thirteen.] Madame de Soulanges followed her husband to Spain at the time of the war of 1823. [The Peasantry.]

Soulanges (Amélie de), youngest daughter of the preceding couple, would have married the Comte Philippe de Brambourg, in 1828, but for the condemning revelations made by Bixiou concerning Joseph Bridau's brother. [A Bachelor's Establishment.]

Soulanges (Vicomte de), probably a brother of the preceding, was, in 1836, commander of a squad of hussars at Fontainebleau; then, in company with Maxime de Trailles, he was going to be second to Savinien de Portenduère in a duel with Désiré Minoret, but the duel was prevented by the unforeseen death of the latter; the underlying cause was the disgraceful conduct of the Minoret-Levraults towards Ursule Mirouët, future Vicomtesse de Portenduère. [Ursule Mirouët.]

Soulas (Amédée-Sylvain-Jacques de), born in 1809, a gentleman of Besançon, of Spanish origin (the name was written Souleyas, when Franche-Comté belonged to Spain), succeeded in shining brightly in the capital of Doubs on an income of four thousand francs, which allowed him to employ the services of "Babylas, the tiger." Such discrepancy betwen his means and his manner of living may well conyey an idea of this fellow's character, seeing that he sought in vain the hand of Rosalie de Watteville, but married, in the month of August, 1837, Madame de Watteville, her widowed mother. [Albert Savarus.]

Soulas (Madame Amédée de), born Clotilde-Louise de Rupt in 1798, stern in features and in character, a blonde of the extreme type, was married, in 1815, to the Baron de Watteville, whom she managed with little difficulty. She did not find it so easy, however, to govern her daughter,

Rosalie, whom she vainly tried to force to marry M. de Soulas. The presence, at Bensançon, of Albert Savarus, who was secretly loved by Mademoiselle de Watteville, gave a political significance to the salon of Rosalie's parents during the reign of Louis Philippe. Tired of her daughter's obstinacy, Madame de Watteville, now a widow, herself married M. de Soulas; she lived in Paris, in the winter at least, and knew how to be mistress of her house there, as she always had been elsewhere. [Albert Savarus.]

Sparchmann, hospital surgeon at Heilsberg, attended Colonel Chabert after the battle of Eylau. [Colonel Chabert.]

Spencer (Lord), about 1830, at Balthazar Claës's sale, bought some magnificent wainscoting that had been carved by Van Huysum, as well as the portrait of President Van Claés, a Fleming of the sixteenth century,—family treasures which the father of Mesdames de Solis and Pierquin was obliged to give up. [The Quest of the Absolute.]

Spieghalter, a German mechanician, who lived in Paris on the rue de la Santé, in the early part of Louis Philippe's reign, made unsuccessful efforts, with the aid of pressure, hammering and rolling, to stretch the anomalous piece of shagreen submitted to him by Raphaél de Valentin, at the suggestion of Planchette, professor of mechanics. [The Magic Skin.]

Sponde (Abbé de), born about 1746, was grand vicar of the bishopric of Séez. Maternal uncle, guardian, guest, and boarder of Madame du Bousquier—née Cormon—of Alençon; he died in 1819, almost blind, and strangely depressed by his niece's recent marriage. Entirely removed from worldly interests, he led an ascetic life, and an uneventful one, entirely consumed in thoughts of salvation, mortifications of the flesh, and secret works of charity. [Jealousies of a Country Town.]

Staël-Holstein (Anne-Louise-Germaine Necker, Baronne de), daughter of the famous Necker of Geneva, born in Paris in 1766; became the wife of the Swiss minister to France; author of "L'Allemagne," of "Corinne," and of "Delphine"; noted for her struggle against Napoleon Bonaparte; mother-in-law of the Duc Victor de Broglie and grandmother of the generation of the Broglies of the present day; died in the year 1817. At various times she lived in the Vendômois in temporary exile. During one of her first stays on the Loire, she was greeted with the singular formula of admiration, "Fameuse garce!" [The Chouans.] At a later period, Madame de Staël came upon Louis Lambert, then a ragged urchin, absorbed in reading a translation of Swedenborg's "Heaven and Hell." She was struck with him, and had him educated at the college of Vendôme, where he had the future minister, Jules Dufaure, as his boon companion; but she forgot her protégé, who was ruined rather than benefited by this passing interest. [Louis Lambert.] About 1823 Louise de Chaulieu (Madame Marie-Gaston) believed that Madame de Staël was still alive, though she died in 1817. [Letters of Two Brides.]

Stanhope (Lady Esther), niece of Pitt, met Lamartine in Syria, who described her in his "Voyage en Orient"; had sent Lady Dudley an Arabian horse, that the latter gave to Félix de Vandenesse in exchange for a Rembrandt. [The Lily of the Valley.] Madame de Bargeton, growing weary of Angoulême in the first years of the Restoration, was envious of this "blue-stocking of the desert." Lady Esther's father, Earl Charles Stanhope, Viscount Mahon, a peer of England, and a distinguished scholar, invented a printing press, known to fame as the Stanhope press, of which the miserly and mechanical Jérôme-Nicholas Séchard expressed a contemptuous opinion to his son. [Lost Illusions.]

Staub, a German, and a Parisian tailor of reputation; in 1821, made for Lucien de Rubempré, presumably on credit, some garments that he went in person to try on the poet at the Hôtel du Gaillard-Bois, on the rue de l'Echelle. Shortly afterwards, he again favored Lucien, who was brought to his establishment by Coralie. [A Distinguished Provincial at Paris.]

Steibelt, a famous musician, during the Empire was the instructor of Félicité des Touches at Nantes. [Béatrix.]

Steinbock (Count Wenceslas), born at Prélie (Livonia) in 1809; great-nephew of one of Charles XII.'s generals. An exile from his youth, he went to Paris to live, and, from inclination as much as on account of his poverty, he became a carver and sculptor. As assistant to François Souchet, a fellow-countryman of Laginski's, Wenceslas Steinbock worked on the decorations of the Pole's mansion, on the rue de la Pépiniére. [The Imaginary Mistress.] Living amid squalor on the rue du Doyenné, he was saved from suicide by his spinster neighbor, Lisbeth Fischer, who restored his courage and determination, and aided him with her resources. Wenceslas Steinbock then worked and succeeded. A chance that brought one of his works to the notice of the Hulot d'Ervys brought him into connection with these people; he fell in love with their daughter, and, the love being returned, he married her. Orders then came in quick succession to Wenceslas, living, as he did, on the rue Saint-Dominique-Saint-Germain, near the Esplanade des Invalides, not far from the marble stores, where the government had allowed him a studio. His services were secured for the work of the monument to be erected to the Maréchal de Montcornet. But Lisbeth Fischer's vindictive hatred, as well as his own weakness of character, caused him to fall beneath the fatal dominion of Valérie Marneffe, whose lover he became; with Stidmann, Vignon, and Massol, he witnessed that woman's second marriage. Steinbock returned to the conjugal domicile on the rue Louis-le-Grand, towards the latter part of Louis Philippe's reign. An exhansted artist, he confined himself to the barren rôle of critic; idle reverie replaced power of conception. [Cousin Betty.]

Steinbock (Countess Wenceslas), wife of the preceding; born Hortense Hulot d'Ervy in 1817; daughter of Hector Hulot d'Ervy and Adeline Fischer; younger sister of Victorin Hulot. Beautiful, and occupying a brilliant position in society through her parents, but lacking dowry, she made choice of husband for herself. Endowed with enduring pride of spirit, Madame Steinbock could with difficulty excuse Wenceslas for being unfaithful, and pardoned his disloyalty only after a long while. Her trials ended with the last years of Louis Philippe's reign. The wisdom and foresight of her brother Victorin, coupled with the results of the wills of the Maréchal Hulot, Lisbeth Fischer, and Valérie Crevel, at last brought wealth to the countess's household, who lived successively on the rue Saint-Dominique-Saint-Germain, the rue Plumet, and the rue Louis-le-Grand. [Cousin Betty.]

Steinbock (Wenceslas), only son of the preceding couple, born when his parents were living together, stayed with his mother after their separation. [Cousin Betty.]

Steingel, an Alsatian, natural son of General Steingel, who fell at the beginning of the Italian campaigns during the Republic; was, in Bourgogne, about 1823, under head-keeper Michaud, one of the three keepers of Montcornet's estates. [The Gondreville Mystery. The Peasantry.]

Stevens (Miss Dinah), born in 1791, daughter of an English brewer, ugly enough, saving, and puritanical, had an income of two hundred and forty thousand francs and expectations of as much more at her father's death; the Marquise de Vordac, who met her at some watering-place in 1827, spoke of her to her son Marsay, as a very fine match, and Marsay pretended that he was to marry the heiress; which he probably did, for he left a widow that erected to him, at Père-Lachaise, a superb monument, the work of Stidmann. [A Marriage Settlement. Cousin Pons.]

Stidmann, a celebrated carver and sculptor of Paris at the times of the Restoration and Louis Philippe; Wenceslas Steinbock's teacher; he carved, for the consideration of seven thousand francs, a representation of a fox-chase on the ruby-set gold handle of a riding whip that Ernest de la Briére gave to Modeste Mignon. [Modeste Mignon.] At the request of Fabien de Ronceret, Stidmann undertook to decorate an apartment for him on the rue Blanche [Béatrix]; he made the originals of a chimney-piece for the Hulot d'Ervys; was among the guests invited by Mademoiselle Brisetout at her little house-warming on the rue Chauchat (1838); the same year he was present at the celebration of Wenceslas Steinbock's marriage with Hortense Hulot; knew Dorlange-Sallenauve; with Vignon, Steinbock and Massol, he was a witness of Valérie Marneffe's second marriage to Célestin Crevel: entertained a secret love for Madame Steinbock when she was neglected by her husband [The Member for Arcis. Cousin Betty]; executed the work of Charles Keller's and Marsay's monuments. [Cousin Pons.] In 1845 Stidmann entered the Institute. [The Unconscious Humorists.]

Stopfer (Monsieur and Madame), formerly coopers at Neuchâtel, in 1823; were proprietors of an inn at Gersau (canton of Lucerne), near the lake, to which Rodolphe came. The same village sheltered the Gandolphinis, disguised under the name of Lovelace. [Albert Savarus.]

Sucy (Général Baron Philippe de), born in 1789, served under the Empire; on one occasion, at the crossing of the Bérésina, he tried to assure the safety of his mistress, Stéphanie de Vandiéres, a general's wife, of whom he afterwards lost all trace. Seven years later, however, being a colonel and an officer in the Legion of Honor, while hunting with his friend, the Marquis d'Albon, near the Isle-Adam, Sucy found Madame de Vandiéres insane, under the charge of the alienist Fanjat, and he undertook to restore her reason. With this end in view, he arranged an exact reproduction of the parting scenes of 1812, on an estate of his at Saint-Germain. The mad-woman recognized him indeed, but she died immediately. Having gained the promotion of general, Sucy committed suicide, the prey of incurable despair. [Farewell.]

Suzanne, real given name of Madame Théodore Gaillard.

Suzannet was, with the Abbé Vernal, the Comte de Fontaine, and M. de Châtillon, one of the four Vendean chiefs at the time of the uprising in the West in 1799. [The Chouans.]

Suzette, during the first years of Louis **XVIII.**'s reign, was lady's-maid to Antoinette de Langeais, in Paris, about the time that the duchess was receiving attentions from Montriveau. [The Thirteen.]

Suzon was for a long time valet de chambre for Maxime de Trailles. [A Man of Business. The Member for Arcis.]

Sylvie, cook for Madame Vauquer, the widow, on the rue Neuve-Saint-Geneviéve, during the years 1819 and 1820, at the time when Jean-Joachim Goriot, Eugéne de Rastignac, Jacques Collin, Horace Bianchon, the Poirets, Madame Couture, and Victorine Taillefer boarded there. [Father Goriot.]

T

Tabareau, bailiff of the justice of the peace in the eighth ward of Paris in 1844-1845. He was on good terms with Fraisier, the business agent. Madame Cibot, door-keeper, on the rue de Normandie, retained Tabareau to make a demand for her upon Schmucke for the payment of three thousand one hundred and ninety-two francs, due her from the German musician and Pons, for board, lodging, taxes, etc. [Cousin Pons.]

Tabareau (Mademoiselle), only child of Tabareau, the bailiff; a large, red-haired consumptive; was heir, through her mother, of a house on the Place Royale; a fact which made her hand sought by Fraisier, the business agent. [Cousin Pons.]

Taboureau, formerly a day-laborer, and afterwards, during the Restoration, a grain-dealer and money-lender in the commune of Isére, of which Doctor Benassis was mayor. He was a thin man, very wrinkled, bent almost double, with thin lips, and a hooked chin that almost made connection with his nose, little gray eyes spotted with black, and as sly as a horse-trader. [The Country Doctor.]

Taillefer (Jean-Frédéric), born about 1779 at Beauvais; by means of a crime, in 1799, he laid the foundations of his fortune, which was considerable. In an inn near Andernach,

Rhenish Prussia, Jean-Frédéric Taillefer, then a surgeon in the army, killed and robbed, one night, a rich native tradesman, Monsieur Walhenfer, by name; however, he was never incommoded by this murder; for accusing appearances pointed to his friend, colleague and fellow-countryman, Prosper Magnan, who was executed.   Returning to Paris, J.-F. Taillefer was from that time forth a wealthy and honored personage.   He was captain of the first company of grenadiers of the National Guard, and an influencial banker; received much attention during the funeral obsequies of J.-B. d'Aldrigger; made successful speculations in Nucingen's third venture.   He was married twice, and was brutal in his treatment of his first wife (a relative of Madame Couture) who bore him two children, Frédéric-Michel and Victorine. He was owner of a magnificent mansion on the rue Joubert. In Louis Philippe's reign he entertained in this mansion with one of the most brilliant affairs ever known, according to the account of the guests present, among whom were Blonde, Rastignac, Valentin, Cardot, Aquilina de la Garde, and Euphrasie.   M. Taillefer suffered, nevertheless, morally and physically; in the first place because of the crime that he had previously committed, for remorse for this deed came over him every fall, that being the time of its perpetration; in the second place, because of gout in the head, according to Doctor Brousson's diagnosis.   Though well cared for by his second wife, and by his daughter of the first wife, Jean-Frédéric died some time after a sumptuous feast given at his house.   An evening passed in the salon of a banker, father of Mademoiselle Fanny, hastened Taillefer's end; for there he was obliged to listen to Hermann's story about the unjust martyrdom of Magnan.   The funeral notice read as follows: "You are invited to be present at the funeral services of M. Jean-Frédéric Taillefer, of the firm Taillefer & Company, formerly contractor for supplies, in his life-time Knight of the Legion of Honor and of the Golden Spur, Captain of the First Company of Grenadiers of the Second Legion of the National Guard of Paris, died May 1st, at his mansion, rue Joubert.   The services will be conducted at—, etc. In behalf of——," etc. [The Firm of Nucingen. Father Goriot. The Magic Skin. The Red Inn.]

Taillefer (Madame), first wife of the preceding, and mother of Frédéric-Michel and Victorine Taillefer. As the result of the harsh treatment by her husband, who unjustly sus- pected her of being unfaithful, she died of a broken heart, presumably at quite an early age. [Father Goriot.]

Taillefer (Madame), second wife of Jean-Frédéric Taillefer, who married her as a speculation, but even then made her happy. She seemed to be devoted to him. [The Red Inn.]

Taillefer (Frédéric-Michel), son of Jean-Frédéric Taillefer by his first wife, did not even try to protect his sister, Vic- torine, from her father's unjust persecutions. Designated heir of the whole of his father's great fortune, he was killed, in 1819, near Clignancourt, by a dexterous and unerring stroke, in a duel with Colonel Franchessini, the duel being instigated by Jacques Collin, in the interest of Eugéne de Rastignac, though the latter knew nothing of the matter. [Father Goriot.]

Taillefer (Victorine), sister of the preceding, and daughter of Jean-Frédéric Taillefer by his first wife; a distant cousin of Madame Couture; her mother having died in 1819, she wrongfully passed in her father's opinion for "the child of adulterous connections"; was turned away from her father's house, and sought protection with her kinswoman, Madame Couture, the widow of Couture the ordainer, on the rue Neuve- Sainte-Geneviéve, in Madame Vauquer's boarding-house; there she fell in love with Eugéne de Rastignac; by the death of her brother she became heir to all the property of her father, Jean-Frédéric Taillefer, whose death-bed she com- forted in every way possible. Victorine Taillefer probably remained single. [Father Goriot. The Red Inn.]

Talleyrand-Périgord (Charles-Maurice de), Prince de Béné- vent, Bishop of Autun, ambassador and minister, born in Paris, in 1754, died in 1838, at his home on the rue Saint-

Florentin.[1] Talleyrand gave attention to the insurrectional stir that arose in Bretagne, under the direction of the Marquis de Montauran, about 1799. [The Chouans.] The following year (June, 1800), on the eve of the battle of Marengo, M. de Talleyrand conferred with Malin de Gondreville, Fouché, Carnot, and Siéyés, about the political situation. In 1804 he received M. de Chargeboeuf, M. d'Hauteserre the elder, and the Abbé Goujet, who came to urge him to have the names of Robert and Adrien d'Hauteserre and Paul-Marie and Marie-Paul de Simeuse erased from the list of emigrants; some time afterwards, when these latter were condemned, despite their innocence, as guilty of the abduction and detention of Senator Malin, he made every effort to secure their pardon, at the earnest instance of Maitre Bordin, as well as the Marquis de Chargeboeuf. At the hour of the execution of the Duc d'Enghien, which he had perhaps advised, he was found with Madame de Luynes in time to give her the news of it, at the exact moment of its happening. M. de Talleyrand was very fond of Antoinette de Langeais. A frequent visitor of the Chaulieus, he was even more intimate with their near relative, the elderly Princesse de Vaurémont, who made him executor of her will. [The Gondreville Mystery. The Thirteen. Letters of Two Brides.] Fritot, in selling his famous "Sélim" shawl to Mistress Noswell, made use of a cunning that certainly would not have deceived the illustrious diplomat; one day, indeed, on noticing the hesitation of a fashionable lady as between two bracelets, Talleyrand asked the opinion of the clerk who was showing the jewelry, and advised the purchase of the one rejected by the latter. [Gaudissart II.]

Tarlowski, a Pole; colonel in the Imperial Guard; ordnance officer under Napoleon Bonaparte; friend of Poniatowski; made a match between his daughter and Bourlac. [The Seamy Side of History.]

Tascheron, born about 1799; a very upright farmer, in a small way, in the market town of Montégnac, nine leagues

---

[1] Alexander I., Czar of Russia, once stayed at this house, which is now owned and occupied by the Baron Alphonse de Rothschild.

distant from Limoges; left his village in August, 1829, immediately after the execution of his son, Jean-François. With his wife, parents, children and grandchildren, he sailed for America, where he prospered and founded the town of Tascheronville in the State of Ohio. [The Country Parson.]

Tascheron (Jean-François), one of the sons of the preceding, born about 1805, a porcelain maker, working successively with Messieurs Graslin and Philippart; at the end of Charles X.'s reign, he committed a triple crime which, owing to his excellent character and antecedents, seemed for a long time inexplicable. Jean-François Tascheron fell in love with the wife of his first employer, Pierre Graslin, and she reciprocated the passion; to prepare a way for them to escape together, he went one night to the house of Pingret, a rich and miserly husbandman in the Faubourg Saint-Etienne, robbed him of a large sum of money, and, thinking to assure his safety, murdered the old man and his servant, Jeanne Malassis. Being arrested, despite his precautions, Jean-François Tascheron made especial effort not to compromise Madame Graslin. Condemned to death, he refused to confess, and was deaf to the prayers of Pascal, the chaplain, yielding somewhat, however, to his other visitors, the Abbé Bonnet, his mother, and his sister Denise; as a result of their influence he restored a considerable portion of the hundred thousand francs stolen. He was executed at Limoges, in August, 1829. He was the natural father of François Graslin. [The Country Parson.]

Tascheron (Louis-Marie), a brother of the preceding; with Denise Tascheron (afterwards Denise Gérard) he fulfilled a double mission: he destroyed the traces of the crime of Jean-François, that might betray Madame Graslin, and restored the rest of the stolen money to Pingret's heirs, Monsieur and Madame de Vanneaulx. [The Country Parson.]

Tascheron (Denise), a sister of the preceding. (*See* Gérard, Madame Grégoire.)

Taupin, curé of Soulanges (Bourgogne), cousin of **the**

Sarcus family and Sarcus-Taupin, the miller. He was a man of ready wit, of happy disposition, and on good terms with all his parishioners. [The Peasantry.]

Ternninck (De), Duc de Casa-Réal, which name see.

Terrasse and Duclos, keepers of records at the Palais, in 1822; consulted at that time with success by Godeschal. [A Start in Life.]

Thélusson, a banker, one of whose clerks was Lemprun before he entered the Banque de France as messenger. [The Middle Classes.]

Thérèse, lady's-maid to Madame de Nucingen during the Restoration and the reign of Louis Philippe. [Father Goriot. A Daughter of Eve.]

Thérèse, lady's-maid to Madame Xavier Rabourdin, on the rue Duphot, Paris, in 1824. [The Government Clerks.]

Thérèse, lady's-maid to Madame de Rochfide in the latter part of Charles X.'s reign, and during the reign of Louis Philippe. [Béatrix.]

Thérèse (Sister), the name under which Antoinette de Langeais died, after she had taken the veil, and retired to the convent of bare-footed Carmelites on an island belonging to Spain, probably the island of Léon. [The Thirteen.]

Thibon (Baron), chief of the Comptoir d'Escompte, in 1818, had been a colleague of César Birroteau, the perfumer. [César Birroteau.]

Thirion, usher to the closet of King Louis XVIII., was on terms of intimacy with the Ragons, and was invited to César Birotteau's famous ball on December 17, 1818, together with his wife and his daughter Amélie, one of Servin's pupils who married Camusot de Marville. [The Vendetta. César Birotteau.] The emoluments of his position, obtained by the patronage that his zeal deservedly acquired, enabled him to lay by a considerable sum, which the Camusot de Marvilles inherited. [Jealousies of a Country Town.]

Thomas was owner of a large house in Bretagne, that Marie de Verneuil (Madame Alphonse de Montauran) bought for Francine de Cottin, her lady's-maid, and a niece of Thomas. [The Chouans.]

Thomas (Madame) was a milliner in Paris towards the latter part of the reign of Charles X.; it was to her establishment that Frédéric de Nucingen, after being driven to the famous pastry shop of Madame Domas, an error arising from his Alsatian pronunciation, betook himself in quest of a black satin cape, lined with pink, for Esther van Gobseck. [Scenes from a Courtesan's Life.]

Thomire contributed to the material splendors of the famous entertainment given by Frédéric Taillefer, about 1831, at his mansion on the rue Joubert, Paris. [The Magic Skin.]

Thorec, an anagram of Hector, and one of the names successively assumed by Baron Hector Hulot d'Ervy, after deserting his conjugal roof. [Cousin Betty.]

Thorein, a carpenter, was employed in making changes in César Birotteau's apartments some days before the famous ball given by the perfumer on December 17, 1818. [César Birotteau.]

Thoul, anagram of the word Hulot, and one of the names successively assumed by Baron Hector Hulot d'Ervy, after his desertion of the conjugal roof. [Cousin Betty.]

Thouvenin, famous in his work, but an unreliable tradesman, was employed, in 1818, by Madame Anselme Popinot (then Mademoiselle Birotteau) to rebind for her father, the perfumer, the works of various authors. [César Birotteau.] Thouvenin, as an artist, was in love with his own works— like Servais, the favorite gilder of Elie Magus. [Cousin Pons.]

Thuillier was first door-keeper of the minister of finance in the second half of the eighteenth century; by furnishing meals to the clerks he realized from his position a regular annual income of almost four thousand francs; being married and the father of two children, Marie-Jeanne-Brigitte and Louis-Jérôme, he retired from active duties about 1806, and, losing his wife in 1810, himself died in 1814. He was commonly called "Stout Father Thuillier.'' [The Government Clerks. The Middle Classes.]

Thuillier (Marie-Jeanne-Brigitte), daughter of the preceding, born in 1787, of independent disposition and of obstinate will, chose the single state to become, as it were, the ambitious mother of Louis-Jérôme, a brother younger than herself by four years. She began life by making coin-bags at the Bank of France, then engaged in money-lending; took every advantage of her debtors, among others Fleury, her father's colleague at the Treasury. Being now rich, she met the Lempruns and the Galards; took upon herself the management of the small fortune of their heir, Céleste Lemprum, whom she had selected specially to be the wife of her brother; after their marriage she lived with her brother's family; was also one of Mademoiselle Colleville's god-mothers. On the rue Saint-Dominique-d'Enfer, and on the Place de la Madeleine, she showed herself many times to be the friend of Théodose de la Peyrade, who vainly sought the hand of the future Madame Phellion. [The Government Clerks. The Middle Classes.]

Thuillier (Louis-Jérôme), younger brother of the preceding, born in 1791. Thanks to his father's position, he entered the Department of Finance as clerk at an early age. Louis-Jérôme Thuillier, being exempted from military service on account of weak eyes, married Céleste Lemprun, Galard's wealthy granddaughter, about 1814. Ten years later he had reached the advancement of reporting clerk, in Xavier Rabourdin's office, Flamet de la Billardière's division. His pleasing exterior gave him a series of successes in love affairs, that was continued after his marriage, but cut short by the Restoration, bringing back, as it did, with peace, the gallants escaped from the battlefield. Among his amorous conquests may be counted Madame Flavie Colleville, wife of his intimate friend and colleague at the Treasury;

of their relations was born Céleste Colleville—Madame **Félix** Phellion. Having been deputy-chief for two years (since January 5, 1828), he left the Treasury at the outbreak of the Revolution of 1830. In him the office lost an expert in equivocal jests. Having left the department, Thuillier turned his energies in another direction. Marie-Jeanne-Brigitte, his elder sister, turning him to the intricacies of real estate, made him leave their lodging-place on the rue d'Argenteuil, to purchase a house on the rue Saint-Dominique-d'Enfer, which had formerly belonged to President Lecamus and to Petitot, the artist. Thuillier's conceit and vanity, now that he had become a well-known and important citizen, were greatly flattered when Théodose de la Peyrade hired apartments from him. M. Thuillier was manager of the "Echo de la Biévre," signed a certain pamphlet on political economy, was candidate for the Chamber of Deputies, purchased a second house, in 1840, on the Place de la Madeleine, and was chosen to succeed J.-J. Popinot as member of the General Council of the Seine. [The Government Clerks. The Middle Classes.]

Thuillier (Madame), wife of the preceding; born Céleste Lemprun, in 1794; only daughter of the oldest messenger in the Bank of France, and, on her mother's side, grand-daughter of Galard, a well-to-do truck-gardener of Auteuil; a transparent blonde, slender, sweet-tempered, religious, and barren. In her married life, Madame Thuillier was swayed beneath the despotism of her sister-in-law, Marie-Jeanne-Brigitte, but derived some consolation from the affection of Céleste Colleville, and, about 1841, contributed, as far as her influence permitted, to the marriage of this her god-daughter. [The Middle Classes.]

Tiennette, born in 1769, a Breton who wore her native costume, was, in 1829, the devoted servant of Madame de Portenduère the elder, on the rue des Bourgeois (now Bezout), Nemours. [Ursule Mirouët.]

Tillet (Ferdinand du), had legally a right only to the first part of his name, which was given him on the morning of

Saint-Ferdinand's day by the curate of the church of Tillet, a town near Andelys (Eure). Ferdinand was the son of an unknown great nobleman and a poor countrywoman of Normandie, who was delivered of her son one night in the curate's garden, and then drowned herself. The priest took in the new born son of the betrayed mother and took care of him. His protector being dead, Ferdinand resolved to make his own way in the world, took the name of his village, was first commercial traveler, and, in 1814, he became head clerk in Birotteau's perfumery establishment on the rue Saint-Honoré, Paris. While there he tried, but without success, to win Constance Birotteau, his patron's wife, and stole three thousand francs from the cash drawer. They discovered the theft and forgave the offender, but in such a way that Du Tillet himself was offended. He left the business and started a bank; being the lover of Madame Roguin, the notary's wife, he became involved in the business scheme known as "the lands of the Madeleine," the original cause of Birotteau's failure and of his own fortune (1818). Ferdinand du Tillet, now a lynx of almost equal prominence with Nucingen, with whom he was on very intimate terms, being loved by Mademoiselle Malvina d'Aldrigger, being looked up to by the Kellers also, and being further the patron of Tiphaine, the Provins Royalist, was able to crush Birotteau, and triumphed over him, even on December 17, 1818, the evening of the famous ball given by the perfumer; Jules Desmarets, Benjamin de la Billardière, and he were the only perfect types present of worldly propriety and distinction. [César Birotteau. The Firm of Nucingen. The Middle Classes. A Bachelor's Establishment. Pierrette.] Once started, M. du Tillet seldom left the Chaussée d'Antin, the financial quarter of Paris, during the Restoration and the reign of Louis Philippe. It was there that he received Birotteau, imploring aid, and gave him a letter of recommendation for Nucingen, the result of which was quite different from what the unfortunate merchant had anticipated. Indeed, it was agreed between the two business men, if the i's in the letter in question were not dotted, to give a negative answer; by this intentional omission, Du Tillet ruined the unfortunate Birotteau. He had his bank on the rue Joubert when Rodolphe Castanier, the dishonest cashier, robbed Nucingen. [Melmoth Reconciled.] Ferdinand du Tillet was now a consequential personage, when Lucien de Rubempré was making his start in Paris (1821). [A Distinguished Provincial at Paris.] Ten years later he married the last daughter of the Comte de Granville, a peer of France, and "one of the most illustrious names of the French magistracy." He occupied one of the elegant mansions on the rue Neuve-des-Mathurins, now rue des Mathurins; for a long time he kept Madame Roguin as his mistress; was often seen, in the Faubourg Saint-Honoré, with the Marquise d'Espard, being found there on the day that Diane de Cadignan was slandered in the presence of Daniel d'Arthez, who was very much in love with her. With Massol and Raoul Nathan he founded a prominent newspaper, which he used for his financial interests. He did not hesitate to get rid of Nathan, who was loaded down with debts; but he found Nathan before him once more, however, as candidate for the Chamber of Deputies, to succeed Nucingen, who had been made a peer of France; this time, also, he triumphed over his rival, and was elected. [The Secrets of a Princess. A Daughter of Eve.] M. du Tillet was no more sparing of Maxime de Trailles, but harassed him pitilessly, when the count was sent into Champagne as electoral agent of the government. [The Member for Arcis.] He was present at the féte given by Josépha Mirah, by way of a house-warming, in her mansion on the rue de la Ville-l'Evêque; Célestin Crevel and Valérie Marneffe invited him to their wedding. [Cousin Betty.] At the end of the monarchy of July, being a deputy, with his seat in the Left Centre, Ferdinand du Tillet kept in the most magnificent style Séraphine Sinet, the Opéra girl, more familiarly called Carabine. [The Unconscious Humorists.] There is a biography of Ferdinand du Tillet, elaborated by the brilliant pen of Jules Claretie, in "Le Temps" of September 5, 1884, under title of "Life in Paris."

Tillet (Madame Ferdinand du), wife of the preceding, born Marie-Eugénie de Granville in 1814, on of the four children of the Comte and Comtesse de Granville, and younger sister of Madame Félix de Vandenesse; a blonde like her mother; in her marriage, which took place in 1831, was a renewal of the griefs that had sobered the years of her youth. Eugénie du Tillet's natural playfulness of spirit could find vent only with her eldest sister, Angélique-Marie, and their harmony teacher, W. Schmucke, in whose company the two sisters forgot their father's neglect and the convent-like rigidness of a devotee's home. Poor in the midst of wealth, deserted by her husband, and bent beneath an inflexible yoke, Madame du Tillet could lend but too little aid to her sister—then Madame de Vandenesse—in the trouble caused by a passion she had conceived for Raoul Nathan. However, she supplied her with two powerful allies—Delphine de Nucingen and W. Schmucke. As a result of her marriage Madame du Tillet had two children. [A Daughter of Eve.]

Tinténiac, known for his part in the Quiberon affair, had among his confederates Jacques Horeau, who was executed in 1809 with the Chauffeurs of Orne. [The Seamy Side of History.]

Tinti (Clarina), born in Sicily about 1803; was maid in an inn, when her glorious voice came under the notice of a great nobleman, her fellow-countryman, the Duke Cataneo, who had her educated. At the age of sixteen, she made her début with brilliant success at several Italian theatres. In 1820, she was "prima donna assoluta" of the Fenice theatre, Venice. Being loved by Genovese, the famous tenor, Tinti was usually engaged with him. Of a passionate nature, beautiful and capricious, Clarina became enamored of Prince Emilio du Varese, at that time the lover of the Duchesse Cataneo, and became, for a while, the mistress of that descendant of the Memmis: the ruined palace of Varese, which Cataneo hired for Tinti, was the scene of these ephemeral relations. [Massimilla Doni.] In the winter of 1823-1824, at the home of Prince Gandolphini, in Geneva, with Genovese,

Princesse Gandolphini, and an exiled Italian prince, she sang the famous quartette, "Mi manca la voce." [Albert Savarus.]

Tiphaine, of Provins, brother of Madame Guénée-Galardon, rich in his own right, and expecting something more by way of inheritance from his father, adopted the legal profession; married a granddaughter of Chevrel, a prominent banker of Paris; had children by his marriage; presided over the court of his native town in the latter part of Charles X.'s reign. At that time an ardent Royalist, and resting secure under the patronage of the well-known financiers, Ferdinand du Tillet and Frédéric de Nucingen, M. Tiphaine contended against Gouraud, Vinet, and Rogron, the local representatives of the Liberal party, and for a considerable time upheld the cause of Mademoiselle Pierrette Lorrain, their victim. Tiphaine, however, suited himself to the cirumstances, and came over to Louis Philippe, the "revolutionist," under whose reign he became a member of the Chamber of Deputies; he was "one of the most esteemed orators of the Centre"; secured his appointment to the judgeship of the court of first instance of the Seine, and still later he was made president of the royal court. [Pierrette.]

Tiphaine (Madame), wife of the preceding, born Mathilde-Mélanie Roguin, in the early part of the nineteenth century; the only daughter of a wealthy notary of Paris, noted for his fraudulent failure in 1819; on her mother's side, granddaughter of Chevrel, the banker, and also distant cousin of the Guillaumes, and the families of Lebas and Sommervieux. Before her marriage she was a freqeunt visitor at the studio of Servin, the artist; she was there "the malicious oracle" of the Liberal party, and, with Laure, took sides with Ginevra di Piombo against Amélie Thirion, leader of the aristocratic group. [The Vendetta.] Clever, pretty, coquettish, correct, and a real Parisian, and protected by Madame Roguin's lover, Ferdinand du Tillet, Mathilde-Mélanic Tiphaine reigned supreme in Provins, in the midst of the Guénéc family, represented by Mesdames Galardon, Lessourd, Martcner, and Auffray; took in, or, rather, defended Pierrette Lorrain; and overwhelmed the Rogron salon with her spirit of raillery. [Pierrette.]

Tissot (Pierre-François), born March 10, 1768, at Versailles, died April 7, 1854; general secretary of the Maintenance Commission in 1793, successor to Jacques Delille in the chair of Latin poetry in the Collége de France; a member of the Academy in 1833, and the author of many literary and historical works; under the Restoration he was managing editor of the "Pilote," a radical sheet that published a special edition of the daily news for the provinces, a few hours after the morning papers. Horace Bianchon, the house-surgeon, there learned of the death of Frédéric-Michel Taillefer, who had been killed in a duel with Franchessini. [Father Goriot.] In the reign of Louis Philippe, when Charles-Edouard Rusticoli de la Palférine's burning activity vainly sought an upward turn, Tissot, from the professor's chair, pleaded the cause of the rights and aspirations of youth that had been ignored and despised by the power surrendered into the hands of superannuated mossbacks. [A Prince of Bohemia.]

Tito, a young and handsome Italian, in 1823, brought "la liberta e denaro" to the Prince and Princess Gandolphini, who were at that time impoverished outlaws, living in concealment at Gersau (canton of Lucerne) under the English name of Lovelace—"L'Ambitieux par Amour." [Albert Savarus.]

Toby, born in Ireland about 1807; also called Joby, and Paddy; during the Restoration, Beaudenord's "tiger" on the Quai Malaquais, Paris; a wonder of precocity in vice; acquired a sort of celebrity in exercise of his duties, a celebrity that was even reflected on Madame d'Aldrigger's future son-in-law. [The Firm of Nucingen.] During Louis Philippe's reign, Toby was a servant in the household of the Duc Georges de Maufrigneuse on the rue Miromesnil. [The Secrets of a Princess.]

Tonnelet (Maitre), a notary, and son-in-law of M. Gravier of Isère, whose intimate friend was Benassis, and who was

one of the co-workers of that beneficent physician. Tonnelet was thin and pale, and of medium height; he generally
dressed in black, and wore spectacles. [The Country Doctor.]

Tonsard (Mére), a peasant woman of Bourgogne, born in
1745, was one of the most formidable enemies of Montcornet,
the owner of Aigues, and of his head-keeper, Justin Michaud.
She had killed the keeper's favorite hound and she encroached
upon the forest trees, so as to kill them and take the dead
wood off.   A reward of a thousand francs having been offered
to the person who should discover the perpetrator of these
wrongs, Mére Tonsard had herself denounced by her granddaughter, Marie Tonsard, in order to secure this sum of
money to her family, and she was sentenced to five years'
imprisonment, though she probably did not serve her term.
Mére Bonnébault committed the same offences as Mére
Tonsard; they had had a quarrel, each wishing to profit by the
advantages of a denunciation, and had ended by referring
the matter to the casting of lots, which resulted in favor of
Mére Tonsard.   [The Peasantry.]

Tonsard (François), son of the preceding, born about
1773, was a country laborer, skilled more or less in everything;
he possessed a hereditary talent, attested, moreover, by
his name, for trimming trees, and various kinds of hedges.
Lazy and crafty, François Tonsard secured from Sophie
Laguerre, Montcornet's predecessor at Aigues, an acre of
land, on which he built, in 1795, the wine-shop known as
the Grand-I-Vert.   He was saved from conscription by
François Gaubertin, at that time steward of Aigues, at the
urgent request of Mademoiselle Cochet, their common mistress.   Being then married to Philippine Fourchon, and
Gaubertin having become his wife's lover, he could poach
with freedom, and so it was that the Tonsard family made
regular levies on the Aigues forest with impunity: they supplied themselves entirely from the wood of the forest, kept
two cows at the expense of the landlord, and were represented
at the harvest by seven gleaners.   Being incommoded by
the active watch kept over them by Justin Michaud, Gauber-

tin's successor, Tonsard killed him, one night in 1823. Afterwards in the dismemberment of Montcornet's estate, Tonsard got his share of the spoils. [The Peasantry.]

Tonsard (Madame), wife of the preceding; born Philippe Fourchon; daughter of the Fourchon who was the natural grandfather of Mouche; large, and of a good figure, with a sort of rustic beauty; lax in morals; extravagant in her tastes, none the less she assured the prosperity of the Grand-I-Vert, by reason of her talent as a cook, and her free coquetry. By her marriage she had four children, two sons and two daughters. [The Peasantry.]

Tonsard (Jean-Louis), born about 1801, son of the preceding, and perhaps also of François Gaubertin, to whom Philippe Tonsard was mistress. Exempted from military service in 1821 on account of a pretended disorder in the muscles of his right arm, Jean-Louis Tonsard posed, under the protection of Soudry, Rigou and Gaubertin, in a circumspect way, as the enemy of the Montcornets and Michaud. He was a lover of Annette, Rigou's servant girl. [The Peasantry.]

Tonsard (Nicolas), younger brother of the preceding, and the male counterpart of his sister Catherine; brutally persecuted, with his sister's connivance, Niscron's granddaughter, Geneviéve, called La l'échina, whom he tried to outrage. [The Peasantry.]

Tonsard (Catherine). (*See* Godain, Madame.)

Tonsard (Marie), sister of the preceding; a blonde; had the loose and uncivilized morals of her family. While mistress of Bonnébault, she proved herself, on one occasion at the Café de la Paix of Soulanges, to be fiercely jealous of Aglaé Socquard, whom he wished to marry. [The Peasautry.]

Tonsard (Reine), without any known relationship to all the preceding, was, in spite of being very ugly, the mistress of the son of the Oliviers, porters to Valérie Marneffe-Crevel; and she remained for a long time the confidential lady's-maid of that married courtesan; but, being bought over by Jacques Collin, she eventually betrayed and ruined the Crevel family. [Cousin Betty.]

Tony, coachman to Louis de l'Estorade, about 1840. [The Member for Arcis.]

Topinard, born about 1805; officer in charge of the property of the theatre managed by Félix Gaudissart; in charge also of the lamps and fixtures; and, lastly, he had the task of placing the copies of the music on the musicians' stands. He went every day to the rue Normandie to get news of Sylvain Pons, who was suffering from a fatal attack of hepatitis; in the latter part of April, 1845, he was, with Fraisier, Villemot and Sonet's agent, one of the pall-bearers at the funeral of the cousin of the Camusot de Marvilles. On leaving the Pére-Lachaise, Topinard, who was living in the Cité Bordin, was moved to compassion for Schmucke, brought him home, and finally received him under his roof. Topinard then secured the position of cashier with Gaudissart, but he almost lost his position for trying to defend the interests of Schmucke, of whom the heirs-at-law of Pons had undertaken to rid themselves. Even under these circumstances Topinard aided Schmucke in his distress; he alone followed the German's body to the cemetery, and took pains to have him buried beside Sylvain Pons. [Cousin Pons.]

Topinard (Madame Rosalie), wife of the preceding, born about 1815, called Lolotte; she was a member of the choir under the direction of Félix Gaudissart's predecessor, whose mistress she was. A victim of her lover's failure, she became box-opener of the first tier, and also quite a dealer in costumes during the following administration (1834-1845). She had first lived as Topinard's mistress, but he afterwards married her; she had three children by him. She took part in the funeral mass of Pons; when Schmucke was taken in by her husband in the Cité Bordin, she nursed the musician in his last illness. [Cousin Pons.]

Topinard, eldest son of the preceding couple, was a supernumerary in Gaudissart's company. [Cousin Pons.]

Topinard (Olga), sister of the preceding; a blonde of the German type; when quite young, she won the warmest affection of Schmucke, who was making his home with the employés of Gaudissart's theatre. [Cousin Pons.]

Torlonia (Duc), a name mentioned, in December, 1829, by the Baron Frédéric de Nucingen, as that of one of his friends, and pronounced by him "Dorlonia." The d ke had ordered a magnificent carpet, the price of which he considered exorbitant, but the baron bought it for Esther van Gobseck's "leedle balace" on the rue Saint-Georges. The Duc Torlonia belonged to the famous family of Rome, that was so hospitable to strangers, and was of French origin. The original name was Tourlogne. [Scenes from a Courtesan's Life.]

Torpille (La), sobriquet of Esther van Gobseck.

Touchard father and son, ran a line of stages, during the Restoration, to Beaumont-sur-Oise. [A Start in Life.]

Touches (Mademoiselle Félicité des), born at Guérande in 1791; related to the Grandlieus; not connected with the Touches family of Touraine, to which the regent's ambassador, more famous as a comic poet, belonged; became an orphan in 1793; her father, a major in the Gardes de la Porte, was killed on the steps of the Tuileries August 10, 1792, and her only brother, a younger member of the guard, was massacred at the Carmelite convent; lastly, her mother died of a broken heart a few days after this last catastrophe. Entrusted then to the care of her maternal aunt, Mademoiselle de Faucombe, a nun of Chelles,[1] she was taken by her to Faucombe, a considerable estate situated near Nantes, and soon afterwards she was put in prison along with her aunt on the charge of being an emissary of Pitt and Cobourg. The 9th Thermidor found them released; but Mademoiselle de Faucombe died of fright, and Félicité was sent to M. de Faucombe, an archæologist of Nantes, being her maternal great-uncle and her nearest relative. She grew up by her-

---

[1] It was perhaps at Chelles that Mademoiselle de Faucombe became acquainted with Mesdemoiselles de Beauséant and de Langeais.

self, "a tom-boy"; she had at her command an enormous library, which allowed her to acquire, at a very early age, a great mass of information. The literary spirit being developed in her, Mademoiselle des Touches began by assisting her aged uncle; wrote three articles that he believed were his own work, and, in 1822, made her beginning in literature with two volumes of dramatic works, after the fashion of Lope de Vega and Shakespeare, which produced a sort of artistic revolution. She then assumed as a permanent appellation, the pseudonym of Camille Maupin, and led a bright and independent life. Her income of eighty thousand livres, her castle of Les Touches, near Guérande— Loire-Inférieure— her Parisian mansion on the rue de Mont-Blanc—now rue de la Chaussée-d'Antin,—her birth, and her connections, had their power of influence. Her irregularities were covered as with a veil, in consideration of her genius. Indeed, Mademoiselle des Touches had more than one lover: a gallant about 1817; then an original mind, a sceptic, the real creator of Camille Maupin; and next Gennaro Conti, whom she knew in Rome, and Claude Vignon, a critic of reputation. [Béatrix. Lost Illusions. A Distinguished Provincial at Paris.] Félicité was a patron of Joseph Bridau, the romantic painter, who was despised by the bourgeois [A Bachelor's Establishment]; she felt a liking for Lucien de Rubempré, whom, indeed, she came near marrying; though this circumstance did not pevent her from aiding the poet's mistress, Coralie, the actress; for, at the time of their amours, Félicité des Touches was in high favor at the Gymnase. She was the anonymous collaborator of a comedy into which Léontine Volnys—the little Fay of that time—was introduced; she had intended to write another vaudeville play, in which Coralie was to have made the principal rôle. When the young actress took to her bed and died, which occurred under the Poirson-Cerfberr[1] management, Félicité paid the expenses of her burial, and was present at the funeral services, which were conducted at Notre-Dame de Bonne-Nouvelle.

---

[1] Delestre-Poirson, the vaudeville man, together with A. Cerfberr, established the Gymnase-Dramatique, December 20, 1820; with the Cerfberr Brothers, Delestre-Poirson continued the management of it until 1844.

She gave dinner-parties on Wednesdays; Levasseur, Conti, Mesdames Pasta, Cinti, Fodor, De Bargeton, and d'Espard, attended her receptions. [A Distinguished Provincial at Paris.] Although a Legitimist, like the Marquise d'Espard, Félicité, after the Revolution of July, kept her salon open, where were frequently assembled her neighbor Léontine de Sérizy, Lord Dudley and Lady Barimore, the Nucingens, Joseph Bridau, Mesdames de Cadignan and de Montcornet, the Comtesse de Vandenesse, Daniel d'Arthez, and Madame Rochegude, otherwise known as Rochefide. Canalis, Rastignac, Laginski, Montriveau, Bianchon, Marsay, and Blondet rivaled each other in telling piquant stories and passing caustic remarks under her roof. [Another Study of Woman.] Furthermore, Mademoiselle des Touches shortly afterwards gave advice to Marie de Vandenesse and condemned free love. [A Daughter of Eve.] In 1836, while traveling through Italy, which she was showing to Claude Vignon and Léon de Lora, the landscape painter, she was present at an entertainment given by Maurice de l'Hostal, the French consul at Genoa; on this occasion he gave an account of the ups and downs of the Bauvan family. [Honorine.] In 1837, after having appointed as her residuary legatee Calyste du Guénie, whom she adored, but to whom she refused to give herself over, Félicité des Touches retired to a convent in Nantes of the order of Saint-François. Among the works left by this second George Sand, we may mention "Le Nouveau Prométhée," a bold attempt, standing alone among her works, and a short autobiographical romance, in which she described her betrayed passion for Conti, an admirable work, which was regarded as the counterpart of Benjamin Constant's "Adolphe." [Béatrix. The Muse of the Department.]

Toupillier, born about 1750; of a wretchedly poor family, consisting of three sisters and five brothers, one of whom was father of Madame Cardinal. From drum-major in the Gardes-Françaises, Toupillier became beadle in the church of Saint-Sulpice, Paris; then dispenser of holy water, having been an artist's model in the meantime. Toupillier, at the beginning of the Restoration, suspected either of being a Bonapartist, or of being unfit for his position, was discharged from the service of the church, and had only the right to stand at the threshold as a privileged beggar; however, he profited greatly by his new position, for he knew how to arouse the compassionate feelings of the faithful in every possible way, chiefly by passing as a centenarian. Having been entrusted with the diamonds that Charles Crochard had stolen fom Mademoiselle Beaumesnil and which the young thief wished to get off his hands for the time being, Toupillier denied having received them and remained possessor of the stolen jewels. But Corentin, the famous police-agent, followed the pauper of Saint-Sulpice to the rue du Coeur-Volant, and surprised that new Cardillac engrossed in the contemplation of the diamonds. He, however, left them in his custody, on condition of his leaving by will all his property to Lydie Peyrade, Corentin's ward and Mademoiselle Beaumesnil's daughter. Corentin further required Toupillier to live in his house and under his surveillance on the rue Honoré-Chévalier. At that time Toupillier had an income of eighteen hundred francs, and a house on the rue Notre-Dame de Nazareth, a piece of property that was bought for forty-eight thousand francs; he might be seen, at the church, munching wretched crusts; but, the church once closed, he went to dine at the Lathuile restaurant, situated on the Barriére de Clichy, and at night he got drunk on the excellent Rousillon wines. Notwithstanding an attack made by Madame Cardinal and Cérizet on the closet containing the diamonds, when the pauper of Saint-Sulpice died in 1840, Lydie Peyrade, now Madame Théodose de la Peyrade, inherited all that Toupillier possessed. [The Middle Classes.]

Toupinet, a Parisian mechanic, at the time of the Restoration, being married and father of a family, he stole his wife's savings, the fruit of arduous labor; he was imprisoned, about 1828, probably for debts. [The Commission in Lunacy.]

Toupinet (Madame), wife of the preceding; known under the name Pomponne; kept a fruit-stand; lived, in 1828, on the rue du Petit-Banquier, Paris; unhappy in her married life; obtained from the charitable J.-J. Popinot, under the name of a loan, ten francs for purchasing stock. [The Commission in Lunacy.]

Tournan, a hatter of the rue Saint-Martin, Paris; among his customers was young Poiret, who, on July 3, 1823, brought him his head-covering, all greased, as a result of J.-J. Bixiou's practical joking. [The Government Clerks.]

Tours-Minières (Bernard-Polydor Bryond, Baron des), a gentleman of Alençon; born about 1772; in 1793, was one of the most active emissaries of the Comte de Lille (Louis XVIII.), in his conspiracy against the Republic. Having received the King's thanks, he retired to his estate in the department of Orne, which had long been burdened with mortgages; and, in 1807, he married Henriette Le Chantre de la Chanterie, with the concurrence of the Royalists, whose "pet" he was. He pretended to take part in the reactionary revolutionary movement of the West in 1809, implicated his wife in the matter, compromised her, ruined her, and then disappeared. Returning in secrecy to his country, under the assumed name of Lemarchand, he aided the authorities in getting at the bottom of the plot, and then went to Paris, where he became the celebrated police-agent Contenson. [The Seamy Side of History.] He knew Peyrade, and received from Lenoir's old pupil the significant sobriquet of "Philosopher." Being agent for Fouché during the period of the Empire, he abandoned himself in the most sensual way to his passions, and lived a life of irregularity and vice. During the time of the Restoration Lonchard had him employed by Nucingen at the time of the latter's amours with Esther van Gobseck. In the service of this noted banker, Coutenson (with Peyrade and Corentin) tried to protect him from the snares of Jacques Collin, and followed the pseudo-Carlos Herrera to his place of refuge on a house-top; but being hurled from the roof by his intended victim, he was instantly killed during the winter of 1829-1830. [Scenes from a Courtesan's Life.]

Tours-Minières (Baronne Bryond des), wife of the preceding; born Henriette Le Chantre de la Chanterie, in 1789; only daughter of Monsieur and Madame Le Chantre de la Chanterie; was married after her father's death. Through the machinations of Tours-Miniéres she was brought into contact with Charles-Amédée-Louis-Joseph Rifoël, Chevalier du Vissard, became his mistress, and took the field for him in the Royalist cause, in the department of Orne, in 1809. Betrayed by her husband, she was executed in 1810, in accordance with a death-sentence of the court presided over by Mergi, Bourlac being attorney-general. [The Seamy Side of History.]

Trailles (Comte Maxime de), born in 1791, belonged to a family that was descended from an attendant to Louis XI., and raised to the nobility by François I. This perfect example of the Parisian *condottieri* made his beginning in the early part of the nineteenth century as a page to Napoleon. Being loved, in turn, by Sarah Gobseck and Anastasie de Restaud, Maxime de Trailles, himself already ruined, ruined both of these; gaming was his master passion, and his caprices knew no bounds. [César Birotteau. Father Goriot. Gobseck.] He took under his attention the Vicomte Savinien de Portenduère, a novice in Parisian life, whom also he would have served later as his second against Désiré Minoret, but for the latter's death by accident. [Ursule Mirouët.] His ready wit usually saved him from the throng of creditors that swarmed about him, but even thus he once paid a debt due Cérizet, in spite of himself. Maxime de Trailles, at that time, was keeping, in a modest way, Antonia Chocardelle, who had a newsstand on the rue Coquenard, near the rue Pigalle, on which Trailles lived; and, at the same time, a certain Hortense, a protégée of Lord Dudley, was seconding the genius of that excellent comedian, Cérizet. [A Man of Business. The Member for Arcis.] The dominant party of the Restoration accused Maxime de Trailles of being a Bonapartist, and rebuked him for his shameless corruption of life; but the citizen monarchy extended him a cordial welcome. Marsay was the chief promoter of the count's fortunes; he moulded him, and sent him on delicate political missions, which he managed with marvelous success. [The Secrets of a Princess.] And so the Comte de Trailles was widely known in social circles: as the guest of Josépha Mirah, by his presence he honored the house-warming in her new apartments on the rue de la Ville-l'Evêque. [Cousin Betty.] Marsay being dead, he lost the power of his prestige. Eugéne de Rastignac, who had become somewhat of a Puritan, showed but slight esteem for him. However, Maxime de Trailles was on easy terms with one of the minister's intimate friends, the brilliant Colonel Franchessini. Nucingen's son-in-law—Eugéne de Rastignac—perhaps recalled Madame de Restaud's misfortunes, and doubtless entertained no good feeling for the man who was responsible for them all. None the less, he employed the services of M. de Trailles—who was always at ease in the Marquise d'Espard's salon, in the Faubourg Saint-Honoré, though a man over forty years of age, painted and padded and bowed down with debts—and sent him to look after the political situation in Arcis before the spring election of 1839. Trailles worked his wires with judgment; he tried to override the Cinq-Cygnes, partisans of Henri V.; he supported the candidacy of Philéas Beauvisage, and sought the hand of Cécile-Rénée Beauvisage, the wealthy heiress, but was unsuccessful on all sides. [The Member for Arcis.] M. de Trailles, furthermore, excelled in the adjustment of private difficulties. M. d'Ajuda-Pinto, Abbé Brossette, and Madame de Grandlieu called for his assistance, and, with the further aid of Rusticoli de la Palférine, effected the reconciliation of the families of Calyste du Guénie and Arthur de Rochefide. [Béatrix.] He became a member of the Chamber of Deputies, succeeding Philéas Beauvisage, who had replaced Charles de Sallenauve, at the Palais-Bourbon; here he was pointed out to S.-P. Gazonal. [The Unconscious Humorists.]

Trans (Mademoiselle), a young unmarried woman of Bordeaux, who, like Mademoiselle de Belor, was on the lookout for a husband when Paul de Mancrville married Natalie Evangélista. [A Marriage Settlement.]

Transon (Monsieur and Madame), wholesale dealers in earthenware goods on the rue des Lesdiguières, were on intimate terms, about 1824, with their neighbors, the Baudoyers and the Saillards. [The Government Clerks.]

Travot (Général), with his command, conducted, in 1815, the siege of Guérande, a fortress defended by the Baron du Guénie, who finally evacuated it, but who reached the wood with his Chouans and remained in possession of the country until the second return of the Bourbons. [Béatrix.]

Trognon (Maitre), a Parisian notary, wholly at the disposal of his neighbor, Maitre Fraisier; during the years 1844-1845 he lived on the rue Saint-Louis-au-Marais—now rue de Turenne—and reached the death-bed of Sylvain Pons before his colleague, Maitre Léopold Hannequin, though the latter actually received the musician's last wishes. [Cousin Pons.]

Troisville (Guibelin, Vicomte de), whose name is pronounced Tréville, and who, as well as his numerous family, bore simply the name Guibelin during the period of the Empire; he belonged to a noble line of ardent Royalists well known in Alençon. [The Seamy Side of History.] Very probably several of the Troisvilles, as well as the Chevalier de Valois and the Marquis d'Esgrignon, were among the correspondents of the Vendean chiefs, for it is well known that the department of Orne was counted among the centres of the anti-revolutionary uprising (1799). [The Chouans.] Furthermore, the Bourbons, after their restoration, overwhelmed the Troisvilles with honors, making several of them members of the Chamber of Deputies or peers of France. The Vicomte Guibelin de Troisville served during the emigration in Russia, where he married a Muscovite girl, daughter of the Princesse Scherbeloff; and, during the year 1816, he returned to establish himself permanently among the people of Alençon. Accepting temporarily the hospitality of Rose-Victoire Cormon (eventually Madame du Bousquier), he innocently inspired her with false hopes; the viscount, naturally reserved, failed to inform her of his being son-in-law of Scherbeloff, and legitimate father of the future Maréchale de Montcornet. Guibelin de Troisville, a loyal social friend of the Esgrignons, met in their salon the Roche-Guyons and the Castérans, distant cousins of his, but the intimate relations almost came to an end, when Mademoiselle Virginie de Troisville became Madame de Montcornet. [Jealousies of a Country Town.] However, in spite of this union, which he looked upon as a mésalliance, the viscount was never cool towards his daughter and her husband, but was their guest at Aigues, in Bourgogne. [The Peasantry.]

Trompe-la-Mort, a sobriquet of Jacques Collin.

Troubert (Abbé Hyacinthe), favorite priest of M. de Bourbonne; rose rapidly during the Restoration and Louis‧Philippe's reign; canon and vicar-general, in turn, of Tours, he was afterwards bishop of Troyes. His early career in Touraine showed him to be a deep, ambitious, and dangerous man, knowing how to remove from his path those that impeded his advance, and knowing how to conceal the full power of his animosity. The secret support of the Congregation and the connivance of Sophie Gamard allowed him to take advantage of Abbé François Birotteau's unsuspecting good nature, and to rob him of all the inheritance of Abbé Chapeloud, whom he had hated in his lifetime, and over whom he triumphed thus again, despite the shrewdness of the deceased priest. Abbé Troubert even won over to his side the Listomères, defenders of François Birotteau. [The Vicar of Tours.] About 1839, at Troyes, Monseigneur Troubert was on terms of intimacy with the Cinq-Cygnes, the Hauteserres, the Cadignans, the Maufrigneuses, and Daniel d'Arthez, who were more or less concerned in the matter of the Champagne elections. [The Member for Arcis.]

Troussenard (Doctor), a physician of Havre, during the Restoration, at the time that the Mignon de la Bastie family lived in that sub-prefecture of the Seine-Inférieure. [Modeste Mignon.]

Trudon, in 1818, a grocer of Paris, in the same quarter as César Birotteau, whom he furnished, on December 17th of that year, with nearly two hundred francs' worth of **wax** candies. [César Birotteau.]

Tullia, professional sobriquet of Madame du Bruel.

Tulloye, the name of the owner of a small estate near Angouléme, where M. de Bargeton, in the autumn of 1821, severely wounded M. de Chandour, an unsophisticated hot-head, whom he had challenged to a duel. The name Tulloye furnished a good opportunity in the affair for a play on words. [Lost Illusions.]

Turquet (Marguerite), born about 1816, better known under the sobriquet of Malaga, having the further appellation of the "Aspasia of the Cirque-Olympique," was originally a rider in the famous Bouthor Traveling Hippodrome, and was later a Parisian star at the Franconi theatre, in the summer on the Champs-Elysées, in the winter on the Boulevard du Crime. In 1837, Mademoiselle Turquet was living in the fifth story of a house on the rue des Fosses-du-Temple— a thoroughfare that has been built up since 1862—when Thaddée Paz set her up in sumptuous style elsewhere. But she wearied of the rôle of supposed mistress of the Pole. [The Imaginary Mistress.] Nevertheless, this position had placed Marguerite in a prominent light, and she shone thence-forth among the artists and courtesans. She had in Maitre Cardot, a notary on the Place du Châtelet, an earnest pro-tector; and as her lover she had a quite young musician. [The Muse of the Department.] A shrewd girl, she held on to Maitre Cardot, and made a popular hostess, in whose salon Desroches, about 1840, gave an entertaining account of a strange battle between two roués, Trailles and Cérizet, debtor and creditor, that resulted in a victory for Cérizet. [A Man of Business.] In 1838, Malaga Turquet was present at Josépha Mirah's elegant house-warming in her gorgeous new apartments on the rue de la Ville-l'Evéque. [Cousin Betty.]

U

Urbain, servant of Soudry, mayor of Soulanges, Bourgogne, during the Restoration; was at one time a cavalry soldier, who entered into the service of the mayor, an ex-brigadier of gendarmes, after failing to receive an appointment as gendarme. [The Peasantry.]

Urraca, aged Spanish woman, nurse of Baron de Macumer; the only family servant kept by her master after his ruin and during his exile in France. Urraca prepared the baron's chocolate in the very best style. [Letters of Two Brides.]

Urraca y **Lora** (Mademoiselle), paternal aunt of Léon de Lora, remained a spinster. As late as 1845 this quasi-Spaniard was still living in poverty in a commune of the Pyrénées-Orientales, with the father and elder brother of the artist. [The Unconscious Humorists.]

Ursule, servant employed by the Abbé Bonnet, curé of Montégnac, in 1829; a woman of canonical age. She received the Abbé de Rastignac, who had been sent by the Bishop of Limoges to bring the village curate to Jean-François Tascheron. It was desired that this man, although he was condemned to death, should be brought back within the "pale of the Church." Ursule learned from the Abbé de Rastignac of the reprieve that had been given the murderer, and being not only inquisitive, but also a gossip, she spread it throughout the whole village, during the time that she was buying the articles necessary for the preparation of breakfast for the Curé Bonnet and the Abbé de Rastignac. [The Village Parson.]

Ursule, from Picardie, very large; cook employed by Ragon, perfumer on rue Saint-Honoré, Paris, towards the end of the eighteenth century; about 1793 she took in hand the amorous education of César Birotteau, a little Tourraine peasant, just employed by the Ragons as errand-boy. Ill-natured, wanton, wheedling, dishonest, selfish and given to drink, Ursule did not suit the candid César, whom she abandoned, moreover, two years later, for a young Picardie rebel, who owned a few acres of land. He found concealment in Paris, and let her marry him. [César Birotteau.]

Uxelles (Marquise d'), related to the Princesse de Blamont-

Chauvry, and to the Duc and Duchesse de Lenoncourt; god-mother of César Birotteau. [César Birotteau.]

Uxelles (Duchesse d'), born about 1769, mother of Diane d'Uxelles; beloved by the Duc de Maufrigneuse, and about 1814 gave him her daughter in marriage; ten years later she withdrew to her Uxelles estate, where she lived a life of piety and selfishness. [The Secrets of a Princess.]

V

Vaillant (Madame), wife of a cabinet-maker in the Faubourg Saint-Antoine; mother of three children. In 1819 and 1820, for forty sous per month, she kept house for a young author,[1] who lived in a garret in rue Lesdiguières. She utilized her remaining time in turning the crank for a mechanic, and received only ten sous a day for this hard work. This woman and her husband were perfectly upright. At the wedding of Madame Vaillant's sister, the young writer became acquainted with Pére Canet—Facino Cane—clarinetist at the Quinze-Vingts—who told him his strange story. [Facino Cane.] In 1818, Madame Vaillant, already aged, kept house for Claude-Joseph Pillerault, the former Republican, on rue des Bourdonnais. The old merchant was good to his servant and did not let her shine his shoes. [César Birotteau.]

Valdès (Paquita), born in the West Indies about 1793, daughter of a slave bought in Georgia on account of her great beauty; lived in the early part of the Restoration and during the Hundred Days in Hôtel San-Réal, rue Saint-Lazare, Paris, with her mother and her foster-father, Christemio. In April, 1815, in the Jardin des Tuileries, she was met by Henri de Marsay, who loved her. She agreed to receive him secretly in her own home. She gave up everything for his sake, but in a transport of love, she cried out from force of habit: "O Mariquita!" This put her lover in such a fury that he tried to kill her. Not being able to do this, he returned, accompanied by some other members of "The Thir-

[1] Honoré de Balzac. He employed Madame Vaillant as a servant.

teen," only to find Paquita murdered; for, the Marquise de San-Réal, Marsay's own sister, who was very jealous of the favors granted the man by this girl, had slashed her savagely with a dagger. Having been kept in retirement since she was twelve years old, Paquita Valdés knew neither how to read nor to write. She spoke only English and Spanish. On account of the peculiar color of her eyes she was known as "the girl with the golden eyes," by some young men, one of whom was Paul de Manerville, who had noticed her during his promenades. [The Thirteen.]

Valdez, a Spanish admiral, constitutional minister of King Ferdinand VII. in 1820; was obliged to flee at the time of the reaction, and embarked on an English vessel. His escape was due to the warning given him by Baron de Macumer, who told him in time. [Letters of Two Brides.]

Valentin (De), head of a historic house of Auvergne, which had fallen into poverty and obscurity; cousin of the Duc de Navarreins; came to Paris under the monarchy, and made for himself an excellent place at the "very heart of power." This he lost during the Revolution. Under the Empire he bought many pieces of property given by Napoleon to his generals; but the fall of Napoleon ruined him completely. He reared his only son, Raphaël, with great harshness, although he expected him to restore the house to its former position. In the autumn of 1826, six months after he had paid his creditors, he died of a broken heart. The Valentins had on their arms: an eagle of gold in a field of sable, crowned with silver, beak and talons with gules, with this device: "The soul has not perished." [The Magic Skin.]

Valentin (Madame de), born Barbe-Marie O'Flaharty, wife of the preceding; heiress of a wealthy house; died young, leaving to her only son an islet in the Loire. [The Magic Skin.]

Valentin (Marquis Raphaël de),[1] only son of the preceding

[1] During the year 1851, at the Ambigu-Comique, was performed a drama by Alphonse Arnault and Louis Judicis, in which the life of Raphaël Valentin was reproduced.

couple, born in 1804, and probably in Paris, where he was reared; lost his mother when he was very young, and, after an unhappy childhood, received on the death of his father the sum of eleven hundred and twelve francs. On this he lived for nearly three years, boarding at the rate of a franc per day at the Hôtel de Saint-Quentin, rue des Cordiers. He began two great works there: a comedy, which was to bring him fame in a day, and the "Theory of the Will," a long work, like that of Louis Lambert, meant to be a continuation of the books by Mesmer, Lavater, Gall and Bichat. Raphaël de Valentin as a doctor of laws was destined by his father for the life of a statesman. Reduced to extreme poverty, and deprived of his last possession, the islet in the Loire, inherited from his mother, he was on the point of committing suicide, in 1830, when a strange dealer in curiosities of the Quai Voltaire, into whose shop he had entered by chance, gave him a strange piece of shagreen, the possession of which assured him the gratification of every desire, although his life would be shortened by each wish. Shortly after this he was invited to a sumptuous feast at Frédéric Taillefer's. On the next morning Raphaël found himself heir to six million francs. In the autumn of 1831 he died of consumption in the arms of Pauline Gaudin; they were mutual lovers. He tried in vain to possess himself of her, in a supreme effort. As a millionaire, Raphaël de Valentin lived in friendship with Rastignac and Blondet, looked after by his faithful servant, Jonathas, in a house on rue de Varenne. At one time he was madly in love with a certain Comtesse Foedora. Neither the waters of Aix, nor those of Mont-Dore, both of which he tried, were able to give him back his lost health. [The Magic Skin.]

Valentine, given name and title of the heroine of a vaudeville play[1] in two acts, by Scribe and Mélesville, which was performed at the Gymnase-Dramatique, January 4, 1836. This was more than twenty years after the death of M. and Madame de Merret, whose lives and tragic adventures were

---

[1] Madame Eugénie Savage played the principal part.

more or less vividly pictured in the play. [The Muse of the Department.]

Vallat (François), deputy to the king's attorney at Ville-aux-Fayes, Bourgogne, under the Restoration, at the time of the peasant uprising against General de Montcornet. He was a cousin of Madame Sarcus, wife of Sarcus the Rich. He sought promotion through Gaubertin, the mayor, who was influential throughout the entire district. [The Peasantry.]

Vallet, haberdasher in Soulanges, Bourgogne, during the Restoration, at the time of General de Montcornet's struggle against the peasants. The Vallet house was next to Socquard's Café de la Paix. [The Peasantry.]

Val-Noble (Madame du). (*See* Gaillard, Madame Théodore.)

Valois (Chevalier de), born about 1758; died, as did his friend and fellow-countryman, the Marquis d'Esgrignon, with the legitimate monarchy, August, 1830. This poor man passed his youth in Paris, where he was surprised by the Revolution. He was finally a Chouan, and when the western Whites arose in arms against the Republic, he was one of the members of the Alençon royal committee. At the time of the Restoration he was living in this city very modestly, but received by the leading aristocracy of the province as a true Valois. The chevalier carried snuff in an old gold snuffbox, ornamented with the picture of the Princess Coritza, a Hungarian, celebrated for her beauty, under Louis XV. He spoke only with emotion of this woman, for whom he had battled with Lauzun. The Chevalier de Valois tried vainly to marry the wealthy heiress of Alençon, Rose-Victoire Cormon, a spinster, who had the misfortune to become the wife, platonically speaking, of M. du Bousquier, the former contractor. In his lodging at Alençon with Madame Lardot, a laundress, the chevalier had as mistress one of the working women, Césarine, whose child was usually attributed to him. Césarine was, as a result, the sole legatee of her lover. The chevalier also took some liberties with another employé of Madame Lardot, Suzanne, a very beautiful Norman girl, who was afterwards known at Paris as a courtesan, under the name of Val-Noble, and who still later married Théodore Gaillard. M. de Valois, although strongly attached to this girl, did not allow her to defraud him. He was intimate with Messieurs de Lenoncourt, de Navarreins, de Verneuil, de Fontaine, de la Billardière, de Maufrigneuse and de Chaulieu. Valois made a living by gambling, but pretended to gain his modest livelihood from a Maitre Bordin, in the name of a certain M. de Pombreton. [The Chouans. Jealousies of a Country Town.]

Vandenesse (Marquis de), a gentleman of Tours; had by his wife four children: Charles, who married Emilie de Fontaine, widow of Kergarouët; Félix, who married Marie-Angélique de Granville; and two daughters, the elder of whom was married to her cousin, the Marquis de Listomère. The Vandnesse motto was: "Ne se vend." [The Lily of the Valley.]

Vandenesse (Marquise de), born Listomère, wife of the preceding; tall, slender, emaciated, selfish and fond of cards; " insolent, like all the Listomères, with whom insolence always counts as a part of the dowry." She was the mother of four children, whom she reared harshly, keeping them at a distance, especially her son Félix. She had something of a weakness for her son Charles, the elder. [The Lily of the Valley.]

Vandenesse (Marquis Charles de), son of the preceding, born towards the close of the eighteenth century; shone as a diplomatist under the Bourbons; during this period was the lover of Madame Julie d'Aiglemont, wife of Général d'Aiglemont; by her he had some natural children. With Desroches as his attorney, Vandenesse entered into a suit with his younger brother, Comte Félix, in regard to some financial matters. He married the wealthy widow of Kergarouët, born Emilie de Fontaine. [A Woman of Thirty. A Start in Life. A Daughter of Eve.]

Vandenesse (Marquise Charles de), born Emilie de Fontaine about 1802; the youngest of the Comte de Fontaine's daughters; having been overindulged as a child, her insolent bearing, a distinctive trait of character, was made manifest at the famous ball of César Birotteau, to which she accompanied her parents. [César Birotteau.] She refused Paul de Manerville, and a number of other excellent offers, before marrying her mother's uncle, Admiral Comte de Kergarouët. This marriage, which she regretted later, was resolved upon during a game of cards with the Bishop of Persépolis, as a result of the anger which she felt on learning that M. Longueville, on whom she had centred her affections, was only a merchant. [The Ball at Sçeaux.] Madame de Kergarouët scorned her nephew by marriage, Savinien de Portenduère, who courted her. [Ursule Mirouët.] Having become a widow, she married the Marquis de Vandenesse. A little later she endeavored to overthrow her sister-in-law, the Comtesse Félix de Vandenesse, then in love with Raoul Nathan. [A Daughter of Eve.]

Vandenesse (Comte Félix de), brother-in-law of the preceding, born late in the eighteenth century, bore the title of vicomte until the death of his father; suffered much in childhood and youth, first in his home life, then as a pupil in a boarding-school at Tours and in the Oratorien college at Pontlevoy. He was unhappy also at the Lepître school in Paris, and during his holidays spent on Ile Saint-Louis with one of the Listomères, a kinswoman. Félix de Vandenesse at last found happiness at Frapesle, a castle near Clochegourde. It was then that his platonic liaison with Madame de Mortsauf began—a union which occupied an important place in his life. He was, moreover, the lover of Lady Arabelle Dudley, who called him familiarly Amédée, pronounced "my dee." Madame de Mortsauf, having died, he was subjected to the secret hatred of her daughter Madeleine, later Madame de Lenoncourt-Givry-Chaulieu. About this time began his career in public life. During the "Hundred Days" Louis XVIII, entrusted to him a mission in Vendee. The King received him into favor, and finally employed him as private secretary. He was also appointed master of petitions in the State Council. Vandenesse frequently visited the Lenoncourts. He excited admiration, mingled with envy, in the mind of Lucien de Rubempré, who had recently arrived in Paris. Acting for the King, he helped César Birotteau. He was acquainted with the Prince de Talleyrand, and asked of him information about Macumer, for Louise de Chaulieu. [The Lily of the Valley. Lost Illusions. A Distinguished Provincial at Paris. César Birotteau. Letters of Two Brides.] After his father's death, Félix de Vandenesse assumed the title of count, and probably won a suit in regard to a land-sale against his brother, the marquis, who had been badly served by a rascally clerk of Maitre Desroches, Oscar Husson. [A Start in Life.] At this time, Comte Félix de Vandenesse began a very close relationship with Natalie de Manerville. She herself broke this off as a result of the detailed description that he gave her of the love which he had formerly felt for Madame de Mortsauf. [The Marriage Settlement.] The year following, he married Angélique-Marie de Granville, elder daughter of the celebrated magistrate of that name, and began to keep house on rue du Rocher, where he had a house, furnished with the best of taste.   At first he was not able to gain his wife's affection, as his known profligacy and his patronizing manners filled her with fear. She did not go with him to the evening entertainment given by Madame d'Espard, where he found himself with his elder brother, and where many gossiping tongues directed their speech against Diane de Cadignan, despite the presence of her lover, Arthez. Félix de Vandenesse went with his wife to a rout at the home of Mademoiselle des Touches, where Marsay told the story of his first love. The Comte and Comtesse de Vandenesse, who, under Louis Philippe, still frequented the houses of the Cadignans and the Montcornets, came very near having serious trouble. Madame de Vandenesse, had foolishly fallen in love with Raoul Nathan, but was kept from harm by her husband's skillful management. [The Secrets of a Princess. Another Study of Woman. The Gondreville Mystery. A Daughter of Eve.]

Vandenesse (Comtesse Félix de), wife of the preceding;

born Angélique-Marie de Granville in 1808; a brunette like her father. In bearing the cruel treatment of her prejudiced mother, in the Marais house, where she spent her youth, the Comtesse Félix was consoled by the tender affection of a younger sister, Marie-Eugénie, later Madame F. du Tillet The lessons in harmony given them by Wilhelm Schmucke afforded them some diversion. Married about 1828, and dowered handsomely, to the detriment of Marie-Eugénie, she underwent, when about twenty-five years old, a critical experience. Although mother of at least one child, becoming suddenly of a romantic turn of mind, she narrowly escaped becoming the victim of a worldly conspiracy formed against her by Lady Dudley and by Mesdames Charles de Vandenesse and de Manerville. Marie, moved by the strength of her passion for the writer, Raoul Nathan, and wishing to save him from financial trouble, appealed to the good offices of Madame de Nucingen and to the devotion of Schmucke. The proof furnished to her by her husband of the debasing relations and the extreme Bohemian life of Raoul, kept Madame Félix de Vandenesse from falling. [A Second Home. A Daughter of Eve.] Afterwards, her adventure, the dangers which she had run, and her rupture with the poet, were all recounted by M. de Clagny, in the presence of Madame de la Baudraye, Lousteau's mistress. [The Muse of the Department.]

Vandenesse (Alfred de), son of the Marquis Charles de Vandenesse, a coxcomb who, under the reign of Louis Philippe, at the Faubourg Saint-Germain, compromised the reputation of the Comtesse de Saint-Héreen, despite the presence of her mother, Madame d'Aiglemont, the former mistress of the marquis. [A Woman of Thirty.]

Vandières (Général, Comte de), old, feeble and childish, when, with his wife and a large number of soldiers, November 29, 1812, he started on a raft to cross the Bérésina. When the boat struck the other bank the shock threw the count into the river. His head was severed from his body by a cake of ice, and went down the river like a cannon-ball. [Farewell.]

Vandières (Comtesse Stéphanie de), wife of the preceding, niece of the alienist, Doctor Fanjat; mistress of Major de Sucy, who was afterwards a general. In 1812, during the campaign in Russia, she shared with her husband all the dangers, and managed to cross the Bérésina with her lover's aid, although she was unable to rejoin him. She wandered for a long time in northern or eastern Europe. Having become insane, she could say nothing but the word "Farewell"! She was found later at Strasbourg by the grenadier, Fleuriot. Having been taken to the Bons-Hommes near the Isle-Adam, she was attended by Fanjat. She there had as a companion an idiot by the name of Geneviéve. In September, 1819, Stéphanie again saw Philippe de Sucy, but did not recognize him. She died not far from Saint-Germain-cn-Laye, January, 1820, soon after the reproduction of the scene on the Bérésina, arranged by her lover. Her sudden return of reason killed her. [Farewell.]

Vanière, gardener to Raphaël de Valentin; obtained from the well, into which his frightened employer had thrown it, the wonderful piece of shagreen, which no weight, no reagent, and no pounding could either stretch or injure, and which none of the best known scientists could explain. [The Magic Skin.]

Vanneaulx (Monsieur and Madame des), small renters at Limoges, living with their two children on rue des Cloches towards the end of Charles X.'s reign. They inherited in the neighborhood of a hundred thousand francs from Pingret, of whom Madame des Vanneaulx was the only niece. This was after their uncle's murderer, J.-F. Tascheron, having been urged by the Curé Bonnet, restored a large portion of the money stolen in Faubourg Saint-Etienne. M. and Madame des Vanncaulx, who had accused the murderer of "indelicacy," changed their opinion entirely when he made this restitution. [The Country Parson.]

Vanni (Elisa), a Corsican woman who, according to one Giacomo, rescued a child, Luigi Porta, from the fearful vendetta of Bartolomeo di Pombo. [The Vendetta.]

Vannier, patriot, conscript of Fougéres, Bretagne, during the autumn of 1799 received an order to convey marching orders to the National Guard of his city—a body of men who were destined to aid the Seventy-second demi-brigade in its engagements with the Chouans. [The Chouans.]

Varese (Emilio Memmi, Prince of), of the Cane-Memmis, born in 1797, a member of the greater nobility, descendant of the ancient Roman family of Memmius, received the name of Prince of Varese on the death of Facino Cane, his relative. During the time of Austrian rule in Venice, Memmi lived there in poverty and obscurity. In the early part of the Restoration he was on friendly terms with Marco Vendramini, his fellow-countryman. His poverty would not permit of his keeping more than one servant, the gondolier, Carmagnola. For Massimilla Doni, wife of the Duke Cataneo, he felt a passion, which was returned, and which for a long time remained platonic, despite its ardor. He was unfaithful to her at one time, not being able to resist the unforeseen attractions of Clarina Tinti, a lodger in the Memmi palace, and unrivaled prima donna at the Fenice. Finally, conquering his timidity, and breaking with the "ideal," he rendered Massimilla Cataneo a mother, and married her when she became a widow. Varese lived in Paris under the reign of Louis Philippe, and, having been enriched by his marriage, one evening at the Champs-Elysées, aided certain destitute artists, the Cambaras, who were obliged to sing in the open air. He asked for the story of their misfortunes, and Marianina told it to him without bitterness. [Massimilla Doni. Gambara.]

Varese (Princess of), wife of the preceding, born Massimilla Doni, about 1800, of an ancient and wealthy Florentine family of the nobility; married, at first, the Duke Cataneo, a repulsive man who lived in Venice at the time of Louis XVIII. She was an enthusiastic attendant at the Fenice theatre during the winter when "Moses" and the "Semiramide" were given by a company, in which were found Clarina Tinti, Genovese and Carthagenova. Massimilla conceived a violent but at first a platonic love for Emilio Memmi, Prince of Varese, married him after Cataneo's death, following him to Paris, during the time of Louis Philippe, where she met with him the Gambaras and helped them in their poverty. [Massimilla Doni. Gambara.]

Varlet, an Arcis physician, early in the nineteenth century, at the time of the political and local quarrels of the Gondre-villes, Cinq-Cygnes, Simeuses, Michus, and Hauteserres; had a daughter who afterwards became Madame Grévin. [The Gondreville Mystery. The Member for Arcis.]

Varlet, son of the preceding, brother-in-law of Grévin; like his father, later a physician. [The Member for Arcis.]

Vassal, in 1822 at Paris, third clerk of Maitre Desroches, an advocate, by whom were employed also Marest, Husson and Godeschal. [A Start in Life.]

Vatel, formerly an army child, then corporal of the Vol-tigeurs, became, during the Restoration, one of the three guards of Montcornet's estate in Aigues, Bourgogne, under head-keeper Michaud; he detected Mére Tonsard in her trespassing. He was a valuable servant; gay as a lark, rather loose in his conduct with women, without any religious principles, and brave unto rashness. [The Peasantry.]

Vatinelle (Madame), a pretty and rather loose woman of Mantes, courted at the same time by Maitre Fraisier and the king's attorney, Olivier Vinet; she was "kind" to the former, thereby causing his ruin; the attorney soon found a means of compelling Fraisier, who was representing both sides in a lawsuit, to sell his practice and leave town. [Cousin Pons.]

Vauchelles (De), maintained relations of close friendship, about 1835, at Besançon, with Amédée de Soulas, his fellow-countryman, and Chavoncourt, the younger, a former college-mate. Vauchelles was of equally high birth with Soulas, and was also equally poor. He sought the hand of Made-moiselle Victoire, Chavoncourt's eldest sister, on whom a god-mother aunt had agreed to settle an estate yielding an income of seven thousand francs, and a hundred thousand francs in cash, in the marriage contract. To Rosalie de Watteville's satisfaction, he opposed Albert Savarus, the rival of the elder Chavoncourt, in his candidacy for a seat in the Chamber of Deputies. [Albert Savarus.]

Vaudoyer, a peasant of Ronquerolles, Bourgogne, appointed forest-keeper of Blangy, but discharged about 1821, in favor of Groison, by Montcornet, at that time mayor of the commune; supported G. Rigou and F. Gaubertin as against the new owner of Aigues. [The Peasantry.]

Vaudremont (Comtesse de), born in 1787; being a wealthy widow of twenty-two years in 1809, she was considered the most beautiful Parisian of the day, and was known as the "Queen of Fashion." In the month of November of the same year, she attended the great ball given by the Malin de Gondrevilles, who were disappointed at the Emperor's failure to appear on that occasion. Being the mistress of the Comte de Soulanges and Martial de la Roche-Hugon, Madame de Vaudremont had received from the former a ring taken from his wife's jewel-casket; she made a present of it to Martial, who, happening to be wearing it on the evening of the Gondreville ball, gave it to Madame de Soulanges, without once suspecting that he was restoring it to its lawful owner. Madame de Vaudremont's death followed shortly after this incident, which brought about the reconciliation of the Soulanges couple, urged by the Duchesse de Lansac; the countess perished in the famous fire that broke out at the Austrian embassy during the party given on the occasion of the wedding of the Emperor and the Archduchess Marie-Louise. [Domestic Peace.] The embassy was located on the part of the rue de la Chaussée-d'Antin (at that time rue du Mont-Blanc) comprised between the rue de la Victoire and the rue Saint-Lazare.

Vaumerland (Baronne de), a friend of Madame de l'Ambermesnil's, boarded with one of Madame Vauquer's rivals in the Marais, and intended, as soon as her term expired, to become a patron of the establishment on the rue Neuve-

Sainte-Geneviève; at least, so Madame de l'Ambermesnil declared. [Father Goriot.]

Vauquelin (Nicolas-Louis), a famous chemist, and a member of the Institute; born at Saint-André d'Hébertot, Calvadts, in 1763, died in 1829; son of a peasant; praised by Fourcroy; in turn, pharmacist in Paris, mine-inspector, professor at the School of Pharmacy, the School of Medicine, the Jardin des Plantes, and the Collége de France.   He gave César Birotteau the formula for a cosmetic for the hands, that the perfumer called "la double pâte des Sultanes," and, being consulted by him on the subject of "cephalic oil," he denied the possibility of restoring a suit of hair.   Nicolas Vauquelin was invited to the perfumer's great ball, given on December 17, 1818.   In recognition of the good advice received from the scientist, César Birotteau offered him a proof, before the time of printing, on China paper, of Muller's engraving of the Dresden Virgin, which proof had been found in Germany after two years of searching, and cost fifteen hundred francs. [César Birotteau.]

Vauquer (Madame), a widow, born Conflans about 1767. She claimed to have lost a brilliant position through a series of misfortunes, which, by the way, she never detailed specifically.   For a long time she kept a bourgeois boarding-house on the rue Neuve-Sainte-Geneviéve (now rue Tournefort), near the rue de l'Arbalète.   In 1819-1820, Madame Vauquer, a short, stout, languid woman, but rather well preserved in spite of being a little faded, had Horace Bianchon as tableboarder, and furnished with board and lodging the following: On the first floor of her house, Madame Couture and Mademoiselle Victorine Taillefer; on the second floor, Poiret, the elder, and Jacques Collin; on the third, Christine-Michelle Michonneau—afterwards Madame Poiret,—Joachim Goriot, whom she looked upon as a possible husband for herself, and Eugéne de Rastignac.   She was deserted by her various boarders shortly after the arrest of Jacques Collin. [Father Goriot.]

Vaurémont (Princesse de), one of the most prominent figures of the eighteenth century; grandmother of Madame Marie Gaston, who adored her; she died in 1817, the year of Madame de Staël's death, in a mansion belonging to the Chaulieus and situated near the Boulevard des Invalides. Madame de Vaurémont, at the time of her death, was occupying a suite of apartments in which she was shortly afterwards succeeded by Louise de Chaulieu (Madame Marie Gaston). Talleyrand, an intimate friend of the princess, was executor of her will. [Letters of Two Brides.]

Vauthier, commonly called Vieux-Chêne, former servant of the famous Longuy; hostler at the Ecu de France, Mortagne, in 1809; was implicated in the affair of the Chauffeurs, and condemned to twenty years of penal servitude, but was afterwards pardoned by the Emperor. During the Restoration he was murdered in the streets of Paris by an obscure and devoted countryman of the Chevalier du Vissard. [The Seamy Side of History.]

Vauthier (Madame), originally, in 1809, kitchen-girl in the household of the Prince de Wissembourg, on the rue Louis-le-Grand; then cook to Barbet, the publisher, owner of a lodging-house on the Boulevard Montparnasse; still later, about 1833, she managed this establishment for him, serving the same time as door-keeper in the house mentioned. At that time Madame Vauthier employed Népomucène and Félicité for the house-work; as lodgers she had Bourlac, Vanda and Auguste Mergi, and Godefroid. [The Seamy Side of History.]

Vautrin,[1] the most famous of Jacques Collin's assumed names.

Vauvinet, born about 1817, a money-lender of Paris, was of the elegant modern type, altogether different from Chaboisseau-Gobseck; he made the Boulevard des Italiens the centre of his operations; was a creditor of the Baron Hulot, first

---

[1] On March 14, 1840, a Parisian theatre, the Porte-Saint-Martin, presented a play in which the famous convict was a principal character. Although Frédéric Lemaître took the leading rôle, the play was presented only once. In April, 1868, however, the Ambigu-Comique revived it, with Frédéric Lemaître again in the leading rôle. (The play is printed among Balzac's Dramas.)

in the sum of seventy thousand francs; and then in an additional sum of forty thousand, really lent by Nucingen. [Cousin Betty.] In 1845, Léon de Lora and J.-J. Bixiou called S.-P. Gazonal's attention to him. [The Unconscious Humorists.]

Vavasseur, clerk in the Treasury Department, during the Empire, in Clergeot's division. He was succeeded by E.-L.-L.-E.-Cochin. [The Government Clerks.]

Védie (La), born in 1756, a homely spinster, her face being pitted with small-pox; a relative of La Cogñette, a distinguished cook; on the rcommendation of Flore Brazier and Maxence Gilet, she was employed as cook by J.-J. Rouget, after the death of a curate, whom she had served long, and who died without leaving her anything. She was to receive a pension of three hundred livres a year, after ten years of competent, faithful and loyal service. [A Bachelor's Establishment.]

Vendramini (Marco), whose name is also pronounced Vendramin;[1] probably a descendant of the last Doge of Venice; brother of Bianca Sagredo, born Vendramini; a Venetian patriot; an intimate friend of Memmi-Cane, Prince of Varese. In the intoxication caused by opium, his great resource about 1820, Marco Vendramini dreamed that his dear city, then under Austrian dominion, was free and powerful once more. He talked with Memmi of the Venice of his dreams, and of the famous Procurator Florain, now in in modern Greek, now in their native tongue; sometimes as they walked together, sometimes before La Vulpato and the Catancos, during a presentation of "Sémiramide," "Il Barbiere," or "Moses," as interpreted by La Tinti and Genovese. Vendramini died from excessive use of opium, at quite an early age, during the reign of Louis XVIII., and was greatly mourned by his friends. [Facino Cane. Massimilla Doni.]

Vergniaud (Louis), who made the Egyptian campaign

[1] The palace in Venice formerly owned by the Duchesse de Berri and the Comte de Chambord, in which Wagner, the musician, died, is even now called the Vendramin Palace. It is on the Grand-Canal, quite near the Justiniani Palace (now the Hôtel de-l'Europe.)

with Hyacinthe-Chabert and Luigi Porta, was quarter-master of hussars when he left the service. During the Restoration he was, in turn, cow-keeper on the rue du Petit-Banquier, keeper of a livery-stable, and cabman. As cow-keeper, Vergniaud, having a wife and three sons, being in debt to Grados, and giving too generously to Chabert, ended in insolvency; even then he aided Luigi Porta, again in trouble, and was his witness when that Corsican married Mademoiselle di Piombo. Louis Vergniaud, being a party to the conspiracies against Louis XVIII., was imprisoned for his share in these crimes. [Colonel Chabert. The Vendetta.]

Vermanton, a cynic philosopher, and a habitué of Madame Schontz's salon, between 1835 and 1840, when she was keeping house with Arthur de Rochefide. [Béatrix.]

Vermichel, common nick-name of Vert (Michel-Jean-Jérôme.)

Vermut, a druggist of Soulanges, in Bourgogne, during the Restoration; brother-in-law of Sarcus, the Soulanges justice of the peace, who had married his eldest sister. Though quite a distinguished chemist, Vermut was the object of the pleasantries and contemptuous remarks of the Soudry salon, especially at the hands of the Gourdons. Despite the slight esteem "of the first society of Soulanges," Vermut gave evidence of ability, when he disturbed Madame Pigeron by finding traces of poison in the body of her dead husband. [The Peasantry.]

Vermut (Madame), wife of the preceding; life and soul of the salon of Madame Soudry, who, however, declared that she was "bad form," and reproached her for flirting with Gourdon, author of "La Bilboquéide." [The Peasantry.]

Vernal (Abbé,) one of the four Vendean leaders, in 1799, when Montauran was opposing Hulot, the other three being Châtillon, Suzannet, and the Comte de Fontaine. [The Chouans.]

Vernet (Joseph), born in 1714, died in 1789, a famous French

artist; patronized the Cat and Racket, a drapery establishment on the rue Saint-Denis, of which M. Guillaume, father-
in-law of Sommervieux, was proprietor. [At the Sign of the
Cat and Racket.]

Verneuil (Marquis de), member of a historic family, and
probably an ancestor of the Verneuils of the eighteenth and
nineteenth centuries. In 1591, he was on intimate terms,
with the Norman Comte d'Hérouville, ancestor of the keeper
of Josépha Mirah, star of the Royal Academy of Music,
about 1838. The relations between the two families con-
tinned unbroken through the centuries. [The Hated Son.]

Verneuil (Victor-Amédée, Duc de), probably descended
from the preceding, died before the Revolution; by Mademoiselle Blanche de Casteran, he had a daughter, Marie-
Nathalie—afterwards Madame Alphonse de Montauran. He
acknowledged his natural daughter at the close of his life,
and almost disinherited his legitimate son in her favor.
[The Chouans.]

Verneuil (Mademoiselle de), probably a relative of the
preceding; sister of the Prince de Loudon, the Vendean
cavalry general; she went to Mans to save her brother, and
died on the scaffold in 1793, after the Savenay affair. [The
Chouans.]

Verneuil (Duc de), son of the Duc Victor-Amédée de
Verneuil, and brother of Madame Alphonse de Montauran,
with whom he had a lawsuit over the inheritance left by their
father; during the Restoration he lived in the town of Alençon
and was on intimate terms with the D'Esgrignons of that
place. He took Victurnien d'Esgrignon under his protection,
and introduced him to Louis XVIII. [The Chouans.
Jealousies of a Country Town.]

Verneuil (Duc de), of the family of the preceding, was
present at the entertainment given by Josépha Mirah, the
mistress of the Duc d'Hérouville, when she opened her
sumptuous suite of apartments on the rue de la Ville-l'Evêque,
Paris, in Louis Philippe's reign. [Cousin Betty.]

Verneuil (Duc de), a good-natured great nobleman, son-in-law of a wealthy first president of a royal court, who died in 1800; he was the father of four children, among them being Mademoiselle Laure and the Prince Gaspard de Loudon; owned the historic château of Rosembray, in the vicinity of Havre, and close by the forest of Brotonne; there he received, one day in October, 1829, the Mignon de la Basties, accompanied by the Hérouvilles, Canalis, and Ernest de la Briére, all of whom were at that time desirous to marry Modeste Mignon, soon to become Madame de la Briére de la Bastie. [Modeste Mignon.]

Verneuil (Duchesse Hortense de), wife of the preceding, a haughty and pious personage, daughter of a wealthy first president of a royal court, who died in 1800. Of her four children, only two lived—her daughter Laure and the Prince Gaspard de Loudon; she was on very intimate terms with the Hérouvilles, and especially with the elderly Mademoiselle d'Hérouville, and received a visit from them, one day in October, 1829, with the Mignon de la Basties, followed by Melchior de Canalis and Ernest de la Briére. [Modeste Mignon.]

Verneuil (Laure de), daughter of the preceding couple. At the entertainment at Rôsembray in October, 1829, Eléonore de Chaulieu gave her advice on the subject of tapestry and embroidery. [Modeste Mignon.]

Verneuil (Duchesse de), sister of the Prince de Blamont-Chauvry; an intimate friend of the Duchesse de Bourbon; sorely tried by the disasters of the Revolution; aunt and, in a way, mother by adoption of Blanche-Henriette de Mortsauf (born Lenoncourt). She belonged to a society of which Saint-Martin was the soul. The Duchesse de Verneuil, who owned the Clochegourde estate in Touraine, gave it, in her lifetime, to Madame de Mortsauf, reserving for herself only one room of the mansion. Madame de Verneuil died in the early part of the nineteenth century. [The Lily of the Valley.]

Verneuil (Marie-Nathalie de).[1] (*See* Montauran, Marquise Alphonse de.)

Vernier (Baron), intendant-general, under obligations to Hector Hulot d'Ervy, whom he met, in 1843, at the Ambigu theatre, as escort of a gloriously handsome woman. He afterwards received a visit from the Baronne Adeline Hulot, coming for information. [Cousin Betty.]

Vernier, formerly a dyer, who lived on his income at Vouvray (Touraine), about 1821; a cunning countryman, father of a marriageable daughter named Claire; was challenged by Félix Gaudissart in 1831, for having played a practical joke on that illustrious traveling merchant, and fought a bloodless pistol duel. [Gaudissart the Great.]

Vernier (Madame), wife of the preceding, a stout little woman, of robust health; a friend of Madame Margaritis; she gladly contributed her share to the mystification of Gaudissart as conceived by her husband. [Gaudissart the Great.]

Vernisset (Victor de), a poet of the "Angelic School," at the head of which stood Canalis, the academician; a contemporary of Béranger, Delavigne, Lamartine, Lousteau, Nathan, Vigny, Hugo, Barbier, Marie-Gaston and Gautier, he moved in various Parisian circles; he was seen at the Brothers of Consolation on the rue Chanoinesse, and he received pecuniary assistance from the Baronne de la Chanterie, president of the above-mentioned association; he was to be found, with Héloïse Brisetout, on the rue Chauchat, at the time of her house-warming in the apartments in which she succeeded Josépha Mirah; there he met J.-J. Bixiou, Léon de Lora, Etienne Lousteau, and Stidmann; he fell madly in love with Madame Schontz. He was invited to the marriage of Célestin Crevel and Valérie Marneffe. [The Seamy Side of History. Béatrix. Cousin Betty.]

Vernon (Maréchal), father of the Duc de Vissembourg and the Prince Chiavari. [Béatrix.]

[1] On June 23, 1837, under the title of *Le Gars*, the Ambigu-Comique presented a drama of Antony Béraud's in five acts and six tableaux, which was a modified reproduction of the adventures of Marie-Nathalie de Montauran.

Vernou (Félicien), a Parisian journalist. He used his influence in starting Marie Godeschal, usually called Mariette, at the Porte Saint-Martin. The husband of an ugly, vulgar, and crabbed woman, he had by her children that were by no means welcome. He lived in wretched lodgings on the rue Mandar, when Lucien de Rubempré was presented to him. Vernou was a caustic critic on the side of the opposition. The uncongeniality of his domestic life embittered his character and his genius. He was a finished specimen of the envious man, and pursued Lucien de Rubempré with an alert and malicious jealousy. [A Bachelor's Establishment. Lost Illusions. A Distinguished Provincial at Paris. Scenes from a Courtesan's Life.] In 1834, Blondet recommended him to Nathan as a "Handy Andy" for a newspaper. [A Daughter of Eve.] Célestin Crevel invited him to his marriage with Valérie Marneffe. [Cousin Betty.]

Vernou (Madame Félicien), wife of the preceding, whose vulgarity was one of the causes of her husband's bitterness, revealed herself in her true light to Lucien de Rubempré, when she mentioned a certain Madame Mahoudeau as one of her friends. [A Distinguished Provincial at Paris.]

Vert (Michel-Jean-Jérôme), nick-named Vermichel, formerly violinist in the Bourgogne regiment, was occupied, during the Restoration, with the various callings of fiddler, door-keeper of the Hôtel de Ville, drum-beater of Soulanges, jailer of the local prison, and finally bailiff's deputy in the service of Brunet. He was intimate friend of Fourchon, with whom he was in the habit of getting on sprees, and whose hatred for the Montcornets, owners of Aigues, he shared. [The Peasantry.]

Vert (Madame Michel), wife of the preceding, commonly called Vermichel, as was the case with her husband; a mustached virago, a metre in width, and of two hundred and forty pounds weight, but active in spite of this; she ruled her husband absolutely. [The Peasantry.]

Vervelle (Anténor), an eccentric bourgeois of Paris, made his fortune in the cork business. Retiring from the trade,

Vervelle became, in his own way, an amateur artist; wished to form a gallery of paintings, and believed that he was collecting Flemish specimens, works of Ténier, Metzu, and Rembrandt; employed Elie Magus to form the collection, and, with that Jew as go-between, married his daughter Virginie to Pierre Grassou. Vervelle, at that time, was living in a house of his own on the rue Boucherat, a part of the rue Saint-Louis (now rue de Turenne), near the rue Charlot. He also owned a cottage at Ville-d'Avray, in which the famous Flemish collection was stored—pictures really painted by Pierre Grassou. [Pierre Grassou.]

Vervelle (Madame Anténor), wife of the preceding, gladly accepted Pierre Grassou for a son-in-law, as soon as she found out that Maitre Cardot was his notary. Madame Vervelle, however, was horrified at the idea of Joseph Bridau's bursting in Pierre's studio, and "touching up" the portrait of Mademoiselle Virginie, afterwards Madame Grassou. [Pierre Grassou.]

Vervelle (Virginie). (*See* Grassou, Madame Pierre.)

Vèze (Abbé de), a priest of Mortagne, during the Empire, administered the last sacrament to Madame Bryond des Tours-Miniéres just before her execution in 1810; he was afterwards one of the Brothers of Consolation, installed in the home of the Baronne de la Chanterie on the rue Chanoinesse, Paris. [The Seamy Side of History.]

Viallet, an excellent gendarme, appointed brigadier at Soulanges, Bourgogne; replaced Soudry, retired. [The Peasantry.]

Victoire, in 1819, a servant of Charles Claparon, a banker on the rue de Provence, Paris; "a real Léonarde bedizened like a fish-huckster." [César Birotteau.]

Victor, otherwise known as the Parisian, a mysterious personage who lived in marital relations with the Marquis d'Aiglemont's eldest daughter, and made her the mother of several children. Victor, while dodging the pursuit of the police, who were on his track for the murder of Mauny, had found refuge for two hours in Versailles, on Christmas night of one of the last years of the Restoration, in a house near the Barriére de Montreuil (57, Avenue de Paris), with the parents of Héléne d'Aiglemont, the last named of whom fled with him. During Louis Philippe's reign, Victor was captain of the " Othello," a Colombian pirate, and lived very happily with his family—Mademoiselle d'Aiglemont and the children he had by her. He met with Général d'Aiglemont, his mistress's father, who was at that time a passenger on board the "Saint-Ferdinand," and saved his life. Victor perished at sea in a shipwreck. [A Woman of Thirty.]

Victorine, a celebrated seamstress of Paris, had among her customers the Duchesse Cataneo, Louise de Chaulieu, and, probably, Madame de Bargeton [Massimilla Doni. Lost Illusions. Letters of Two Brides.] Her successors assumed and handed down her name; Victorine IV.'s "intelligent scissors" were praised in the latter part of Louis Philippe's reign, when Fritot sold Mistress Noswell the Sélim shawl. [Gaudissart II.]

Vidal & Porchon, book-sellers on commission, Quai des Augustins, Paris, in 1821. Lucien de Rubempré had an opportunity to judge of their method of doing business, when his "Archer of Charles IX." and a volume of poems were brutally refused by them. Vidal & Porchon had in stock at that time the works of Kératry, Arlincourt, and Victor Ducange. Vidal was a stout, blunt man, who traveled for the firm. Porchon, colder and more diplomatic, seemed to have special charge of negotiations. [A Distinguished Provincial at Paris.]

Vien (Joseph-Marie), a celebrated painter, born at Montpellier in 1716, died at Rome in 1809. In 1758, with Allegrain and Loutherbourg, he aided his friend Sarrasine in abducting Zambinella, with a view to taking him to the apartments of the sculptor, who was madly in love with the eunuch, believing him to be a woman. At a later period, Vien made for Madame de Lanty a copy of the statue modeled by Sarrasine after Zambinella, and it was from this picture of Vien's that Girodet, the signer of "Endymion," received his inspiration. This statue of Sarrasine's was, long afterwards, reproduced by the sculptor Dorlange-Sallenauve. [Sarrasine. The Member for Arcis.]

Vieux-Chapeau, a soldier in the Seventy-second demibrigade, known to Jean Falcon, commonly called Beau-Pied; was killed in an engagement with the Chouans, in September, 1799. [The Chouans.]

Vigneau, of the commune of Isére, of which Benassis was creator, so to speak; he courageously took charge of an abandoned tile-factory, made a successful business of it, and lived with his family around him, which consisted of his mother, his mother-in-law, and his wife, who had formerly been in the service of the Graviers of Grenoble. [The Country Doctor.]

Vigneau (Madame), wife of the preceding, a perfect housekeeper; she received Genestas cordially, when brought to call by Benassis; Madame Vigneau was then on the point of becoming a mother. [The Country Doctor.]

Vignol. (See Bouffé.)

Vignon (Claude), a French critic, born in 1799, brought a remarkable power of analysis to the study of all questions of art, literature, philosophy, or political problems. A clear, deep, and unerring judge of men, a strong psychologist, he was famous in Paris as early as 1821, and was present, at the apartments of Florine, then acting at the Panorame-Dramatique, at the supper following the presentation of the "Alcade dans l'Embarras," and had a brilliant conversation on the subject of the press with Emile Blondet, in the presence of a German diplomatist. [A Distinguished Provincial at Paris.] In 1834, Claude Vignon was entrusted with the haute critique of the newspaper founded by Raoul Nathan. [A Daughter of Eve.] For quite a period Vignon had Félicité des Touches (Camille Maupin) as his mistress. In 1836, he brought her back from Italy, accompanied by Lora, when he heard the story of the domestic difficulties of the

Bauvans from Maurice de l'Hostal, French consul at Genoa. [Honorine.] Again, in 1836, at Les Touches, Vignon, on the point of giving up Camille Maupin, delivered to his former mistress a veritable dissertation, of surprising insight, on the subject of the heart, with reference to Calyste du Guénie, Gennaro Conti, and Béatrix de Rochefide. Such intimate knowledge of the human heart had gradually saddened and wearied him; he sought relief for his ennui in debauchery; he paid attention to La Schontz, really a courtesan of superior stamp, and moulded her. [Béatrix.] Afterwards, he became ambitious, and was secretary to Cottin de Wissembourg, minister of war; this position brought him into contact with Valérie Marneffe, whom he secretly loved; he, Stidmann, Steinbock, and Massol, were witnesses of her marriage to Crevel, this being the second time she had been led to the altar. He was counted among the habitués of Valérie's salon, when "Jean-Jacques Bixiou was going . . . to cozen Lisbeth Fischer.". [Cousin Betty.] He rallied to the support of Louis Philippe, and as editor of the Journal des Débats, and master of requests in the Council of State, he gave his attention to the lawsuit pending between S.-P. Gazonal and the prefect of the Pyrénées-Orientales; a position as librarian, a chair at the Sorbonne, and the decoration bore further testimony to the favor that he enjoyed. [The Unconscious Humorists.] Vignon's reputation remained undiminished, and, even in our own time, Madame Noémi Rouvier, sculptor and novelist, signs the critic's name to her works.

Vigor, manager of the post-station at Ville-aux-Fayes, during the Restoration; officer in the National Guard of that sub-prefecture of Bourgogne; brother-in-law of Leclercq, the banker, whose sister he had married. [The Peasantry.]

Vigor, manager of the post-station at Ville-aux-Fayes, during the Restoration; officer in the National Guard of that sub-prefecture of Bourgogne; brother-in-law of Leclercq, the banker, whose sister he had married. [The Peasantry.]

Vigor, son of the preceding. and, like the rest of his family, interested in protecting François Gaubertin from Montcornet; he was deputy judge of the court of Ville-aux-Fayes, in 1823. [The Peasantry.]

Villemot, head-clerk of Tabareau, the bailiff, was entrusted, in April, 1845, with the work of superintending the details of the interment of Sylvain Pons, and also to look after the interests of Schmucke, who had been appointed residuary legatee by the deceased. Villemot was entirely under the influence of Fraisier, business agent of the Camusot de Marvilles. [Cousin Pons.]

Villenoix (Salomon de), son of a wealthy Jew named Salomon, who in his old age had married a Catholic. Brought up in his mother's religion; he raised the Villenoix estate to a barony. [Louis Lambert.]

Villenoix (Pauline Salomon de), born about 1800; natural daughter of the preceding. During the Restoration, she was made to feel her origin. Her character and her superiority made her an object of envy in her provincial circle. Her meeting with Louis Lambert at Blois was the turning point in her life. Community of age, country, disappointments, and pride of spirit brought them in touch—a reciprocated passion was ·the result. Mademoiselle Salomon de Villenoix was going to marry Lambert, when the scholar's terrible mental malady asserted itself. She was frequently able to avert the sick man's paroxysms; she nursed him, advised him, and guided him, notably at Croisic, where at her suggestion Lambert related in letter-form the tragic misfortunes of the Cambremers, which he had just learned. On her return to Villenoix, Pauline took her fiancé with her, where she noted down and understood his last thoughts, sublime in their incoherence; he died in her arms, and from that time forth she considered herself the widow of Louis Lambert, whom she had buried in one of the islands of the lake park at Villenoix. [Louis Lambert. A Seaside Tragedy.] Two years later, being sensibly aged, and living in almost total retirement from the world at the town of Tours, but full of sympathy for weak mortals, Pauline de Villenoix protected the Abbé François Birotteau, the victim of Troubert's hatred. [The Vicar of Tours.]

Vilquin, the richest ship-owner of Havre, during the Restoration, purchased the estates of the bankrupt Charles Mignon, with the exception of a châlet given by Mignon to Dumay; this dwelling, being in close proximity to the millionaire's superb villa, and being occupied by the families of Mignon and Dumay, was the despair of Vilquin, Dumay obstinately refusing to sell it. [Modeste Mignon.'

Vilquin (Madame), wife of the preceding, had G.-C. d'Estourny as lover, previous to his amour with Bettina-Caroline Mignon; by her husband she had three children, two of whom were girls. The eldest of these, being richly endowed, was eventually Madame Francisque Althor. [Modeste Mignon.]

Vimeux, in 1824, an unassuming justice of the peace in a department of the North, rebuked his son Adolphe for the kind of life he was leading in Paris. [The Government Clerks.]

Vimeux (Adolphe), son of the preceding, in 1824, was copyist emeritus in Xavier Rabourdin's bureau in the Finance Department. A great dandy, he thought only of his dress, and was satisfied with meagre fare at the Katcomb's restaurant; he became a debtor of Antoine, the messenger boy; secretly his ambition was to marry a rich old lady. [The Government Clerks.]

Vinet had a painful career to start with; a disappointment crossed his path at the very outset. He had seduced a Mademoiselle de Chargeboeuf, and he supposed that her parents would acknowledge him as son-in-law, and endow their daughter richly; so he married her, but her family disowned her, and he therefore had to rely on himself entirely. As an attorney at Provins, Vinet made his mark by degrees; as head of the local opposition, with the aid of Goraud, he succeeded in making use of Denis Rogrou, a wealthy retired merchant, established the "Courrier de Provins," a Liberalist paper, adroitly defended the Rogrons against the charge of

killing Pierrette Lorrain by slow degrees, was elected to the
Chamber of Deputies about 1830, and became also attorney-
general, and probably minister of justice. [Pierrette. The
Member for Arcis. The Middle Classes. Cousin Pons.]

Vinet (Madame), wife of the preceding, born Chargeboeuf,
and therefore one of the descendants of the "noble family
of La Brie, a name derived from the exploit of a knight
in the expedition of Saint-Louis," was mother of two children,
who sufficed for her happiness. Absolutely controlled by
her husband, rejected and sacrificed by her family from
the time of her marriage, Madame Vinet scarcely dared in
the Rogrons' salon to speak in defence of Pierrette Lorrain
their victim. [Pierrette.]

Vinet (Olivier), son of the preceding couple, born in 1816.
A magistrate, like his father, began his career as deputy
king's attorney at Arcis, advanced to the position of king's
attorney in the town of Mantes, and, still further, was deputy
king's attorney, but now in Paris. Supported by his father's
influence, and being noted for his independent raillery,
Vinet was dreaded everywhere. Among the people of Arcis,
he mixed only with the little coterie of government officials,
composed of Goulard, Michu, and Marest. [The Member
for Arcis.] Being a rival of Maitre Fraisier in the affections
of Madame Vatinelle of Mantes, he resolved to destroy this
contestant in the race, and so thwarted his career. [Cousin
Pons.] At the Thuilliers', on the rue Saint-Dominique-
d'Enfer, Paris, where he displayed his usual impertinence,
Vinet was an aspirant to the hand of Céleste Colleville, the
heiress, who was eventually Madame Félix Phellion. [The
Middle Classes.]

Violette, a husbandman, tenanted in the department of
Aube, near Arcis, the Grouage farm, that was a part of the
Gondreville estate, at the time that Peyrade and Corentin,
in accordance with Fouché's instructions, undertook the
singular abduction of Senator Malin de Gondreville. A
miserly and deceitful man, this fellow Violette secretly
sided with Malin de Gondreville and the powers of the day

against Michu, the mysterious agent of the Cinq-Cygne, Hauteserre, and Simeuse families.   [The Gondreville Mystery.]

Violette (Jean), a descendant of the preceding; hosier of Arcis in 1837; took in hand Pigoult's business, as successor to Philéas Beauvisage.   In the electoral stir of 1839, Jean Violette seemed to be entirely at the disposal of the Goudreville faction.   [The Member for Arcis.]

Virginie, cook in the household of César Birotteau, the perfumer, in 1818.   [César Birotteau.]

Virginie, during the years 1835-1836, lady's-maid, on the rue Neuve-des-Mathurins (at present rue des Mathurins), Paris, to Marie-Eugénie du Tillet, who was at that time engrossed in righting the imprudent conduct of Angélique-Marie de Vandenesse.   [A Daughter of Eve.]

Virginie, mistress of a Provençal soldier, who, at a later period, during Bonaparte's campaign in Egypt, was lost for some time in a desert, where he lived with a female panther. The jealous mistress was constantly threatening to stab her lover, and he dubbed her Mignonne, by antiphrasis; in memory of her he gave the same name to the panther. [A Passion in the Desert.]

Virginie, a Parisian milliner. whose hats were praised, for a consideration, by Andoche Finot in his newspaper in 1821.   [A Distinguished Provincial at Paris.]

Virlaz, a rich furrier of Leipsic, from whom his nephew, Frédéric Brunner, inherited, about the middle of Louis Philippe's reign.   In his lifetime this Jew, head of the house of Virlaz & Co., suspecting Brunner, pére, the tavern-keeper of Frankfort, had the fortune of Madame Brunner (first of the name) placed in the coffers of the Al-Sartchild bank. [Cousin Pons.]

Vissard (Marquis du), in memory of his younger brother, the Chevalier Rifoël du Vissard, was created a peer of France by Louis XVIII., who entered him as a lieutenant in the Maison-Rouge, and made him a prefect upon the dissolution of the Maison-Rouge. [The Seamy Side of History.]

Vissard (Charles-Amédée-Louis-Joseph Rifoël, Chevalier du), noble and headstrong gentleman; played an important part, after 1789, in the various anti-revolutionary insurrections of western France. In December, 1799, he was at the Vivetière, and his impulsiveness was a contrast with the coolness of Marquis Alphonse de Montauran, also called Le Gars. [The Chouans.] He took part in the battle of Quiberon, and, in company with Boislaurier, took a leading part in the uprising of the Chauffeurs of Mortagne. Several circumstances, indeed, helped to strengthen his Royalist inclinations. Fergus found in Henriette Bryond des Tours-Miniéres a second Diana Vernon and became her lover. His monarchical zeal was enflamed by Bryond des Tours-Miniéres (Contenson, the spy), who secretly betrayed him. Like his accomplices, Rifoël du Vissard was executed in 1809. At times during his anti-revolutionary campaigns he assumed the name of Pierrot. [The Seamy Side of History.]

Vissembourg (Duc de), son of Maréchal Vernon; brother of the Prince de Chiavari; between 1835 and 1840 presided over a horticultural society, the vice-president of which was Fabien du Ronceret. [Béatrix.]

Vitagliani, tenor at the Argentina, Rome, when Zambinella took the soprano parts in 1758. Vitagliani was acquainted with J.-E. Sarrasine. [Sarrasine.]

Vital, born about 1810, a Parisian hatter, who succeeded Finot pére, whose store on rue du Coq was very popular about 1845, and deservedly so, apparently. He amused J.-J. Bixiou and Léon de Lora by his ridiculous pretensions. They wished him to supply S.-P. Gazonal with a hat, and he proposed to sell him a hat like that of Lousteau. On this occasion Vital showed them the head-covering that he had devised for Claude Vignon, who was undecided in politics. Vital really pretended to make each hat according to the personality of the person ordering it. He praised the Prince de Béthune's hat and dreamed of the time when high hats would go out of style. [The Unconscious Humorists.]

Vital (Madame), wife of the preceding, believed in her husband's genius and greatness. She was in the store when the hatter received a call from Bixiou, Lora and Gazonal. [The Unconscious Humorists.]

Vitel, born in 1776, Paris justice of the peace in 1845, an acquaintance of Doctor Poulain; was succeeded by Maitre Fraisier, a protégé of the Camusot de Marvilles. [Cousin Pons.]

Vitelot, partner of Sonet, the marble-cutter; designed tombstones. He failed to obtain the contract for monuments to Marsay, the minister, and to Keller, the officer. It was given to Stidmann. The plans made by Vitelot having been retouched, were submitted to Wilhelm Schmucke for the grave of Sylvain Pons, who was buried in Père-Lachaise. [Cousin Pons.]

Vitelot (Madame), wife of the preceding, severely rebuked an agent of the firm for bringing in as a customer W. Schmucke, heir-contestant to the Pons property. [Cousin Pons.]

Vivet (Madeleine), servant to the Camusot de Marvilles; during nearly twenty-five years was their feminine Maitre-Jacques. She tried in vain to gain Sylvain Pons for a husband, and thus to become their cousin. Madeleine Vivet, having failed in her matrimonial attempts, took a dislike for Pons, and persecuted him in a thousand ways. [Scenes from a Courtesan's Life. Cousin Pons.]

Volfgang,[1] cashier of Baron du Saint-Empire, F. de Nucingen, when this well-known Parisian banker of rue Saint-Lazare fell madly in love with Esther van Gobseck, and when Jacques Falleix's discomfiture occurred. [Scenes from a Courtesan's Life.]

Vordac (Marquise de), born in 1769, mistress of the rich Lord Dudley; she had by him a son, Henry. To legitimize this child she arranged a marriage with Marsay, a bankrupt old gentleman of tarnished reputation. He demanded payment of the interest on a hundred thousand francs as a reward for his marriage, and he died without having known

[1] He lived on rue de l'Arcade, near rue des Mathurins, Paris.

his wife. The widow of Marsay became by her second marriage the well-known Marquise de Vordac. She neglected her duties as mother until late in life, and paid no attention to Henri de Marsay except to propose Miss Stevens as a suitable wife for him. [The Thirteen.]

Vulpato (La), noble Venetian, very frequently present in Fenice; about 1820 tried to interest Emilio Memmi, Prince of Varese, and Massimilla Doni, Duchesse Cataneo, in each other. [Massimilla Doni.]

Vyder, anagram formed from d'Ervy, and one of the three names taken successively by Baron Hector Hulot d'Ervy, after deserting his wife. He hid under this assumed name, when he became a petition-writer in Paris, in the lower part of Petite Pologne, opposite rue de la Pépiniére, on Passage du Soleil, to-day called Galerie de Cherbourg. [Cousin Betty.]

W

Wadmann, an Englishman who owned, near the Marville estate in Normandie, a cottage and pasture-lands, which Madame Camusot de Marville talked of buying in 1845, when he was about to leave for England after twenty years' sojourn in France. [Cousin Pons.]

Wahlenfer or Walhenfer, wealthy German merchant who was murdered at the "Red Inn," near Andernach, Rhenish Prussia, October, 1799. The deed was done by Jean-Frédéric Taillefer, then a surgeon and under-assistant-major in the French army, who suffered his comrade, Prosper Magnan, to be executed for the crime. Wahlenfer was a short, heavy-set man of rotund appearance, with frank and cordial manners. He was proprietor of a large pin-manu-factory on the outskirts of Neuwied. He was from Aix-la-Chapelle. Possibly Wahlenfer was an assumed name. [The Red Inn.]

Wallenrod-Tustall-Bartenstild (Baron de), born in 1742, banker at Frankfort-on-the-Main; married in 1804, his only daughter, Bettina, to Charles Mignon de la Bastie, then only a lieutenant in the French army; died in 1814, following some disastrous speculations in cotton. [Modeste Mignon.]

Watschildine, a London firm which did business with F. de Nucingen, the banker. On a dark autumn evening in 1821, the cashier, Rodolphe Castanier, was surprised by the satanic John Melmoth, while he was in the act of forging the name of his employer on some letters of credit drawn on the Watschildine establishment. [Melmoth Reconciled.]

Wattebled, grocer in Soulanges, Bourgogne. in 1823; father of the beautiful Madame Plissoud; was in middle class society; kept a store on the first floor of a house belonging to Soudry, the mayor. [The Peasantry.]

Watteville (Baron de), Besançon gentleman of Swiss descent; last descendant of the well-known Dom Jean de Watteville, the renegade Abbé of Baumes (1613-1703); small and very thin, rather deficient mentally; spent his life in a cabinet-maker's establishment "enjoying utter ignorance"; collected shells and geological specimens; usually in good humor. After living in the Comté, "like a bug in a rug," in 1815 he married Clotilde-Louise de Rupt, who domineered over him completely. As soon as her parents died, about 1819, he lived with her in the beautiful Rupt house on rue de la Préfecture, a piece of property which included a large garden extending along the rue du Perron. By his wife, the Baron de Watteville had one daughter, whom he loved devotedly, so much, indeed, that he lost all authority over her. M. de Watteville died in 1836, as a result of his fall into the lake on his estate of Rouxey, near Besançon. He was buried on an islet in this same lake, and his wife, making great show of her sorrow, had erected thereon a Gothic monument of marble like the one to Héloïse and Abélard in the Pére-Lachaise. [Albert Savaraus.]

Watteville (Baronne de), wife of the preceding, and after his death of Amédée de Soulas (*See* Soulas, Madame A. de.)

Watteville (Rosalie de), only daughter of the preceding couple; born in 1816; a blonde with colorless cheeks and pale-blue eyes; slender and frail of body; resembled one of Albert Dürer's saints. Reared under her mother's stern oversight, accustomed to the most rigid religious observances, kept in ignorance of all worldly matters, she entirely concealed under her modesty of manner and retiring disposition her iron character, and her romantic audacity, so like that of her great-uncle, the Abbé de Watteville; and which was increased by the resoluteness and pride of the Rupt blood; although destined to marry Amédée de Soulas, "la fleur des pois"[1] of Besançon, she became enamored of the attorney, Albert Savaron de Savarus. By successfully carrying out her schemes she separated him from the Duchesse d'Argaïolo, although these two were mutually in love—a separation which caused Savarus great despair. He never knew of Rosalie's affection for him, and withdrew to the Grande Chartreuse. Mademoiselle de Watteville then lived for some time in Paris with her mother, who was then the wife of Amédée de Soulas. She tried to see the Duchesse d'Argaïolo, who, believing Savarus faithless, had given her hand to the Duc de Rhétoré. In February, 1838, on meeting her at a charity ball given for the benefit of the former civil pensioners, Rosalie made an appointment with her for the Opéra ball, when she told her former rival the secret of her manœuvres against Madame de Rhétoré, and of her conduct as regards the attorney. Mademoiselle de Watteville retired finally to Rouxey—a place which she left, only to take a trip in 1841 on an unknown mission, from which she came back seriously crippled, having lost an arm and a leg in a boiler explosion on a steamboat. Henceforth she devoted her life to the exercises of religion, and left her retreat no more. [Albert Savarus.]

Welff (called Welff the Great), after eleven years of cavalry service on the Rhine, in Italy and in Egypt under General Bonaparte, he was a gendarme at Arcis-sur-Aube in 1803, at the time of the police raid on Cinq-Cygne. He helped Corentin and Peyrade in their vain undertaking, and became the enemy of Michu, the Hauteserres, and the Simeuses, against whom

---

[1] Title of one of the first editions of "A Marriage Settlement."

he acted about 1806, when Senator Malin de Gondreville mysteriously disappeared. At that time Welff was a sub-lieutenant. [The Gondreville Mystery.]

Werbrust, associated with Palma, Parisian discounter on rue Saint-Denis and rue Saint-Martin, during the Restoration; knew the story of the glory and decay of César Birotteau, the perfumer, who was mayor of the second district; was the friend of the banker, Jean-Baptiste d'Aldrigger, at whose burial he was present; carried on business with the Baron de Nucingen, making a shrewd speculation when the latter settled for the third time with his creditors in 1836. [César Birotteau. The Firm of Nucingen.]

Werchauffen (Baron de), one cf Schirmer's aliases. (*See* Schirmer.)

Wierzchownia (Adam de), Polish gentleman, who, after the last division of Poland, found refuge in Sweden, where he sought consolation in the study of chemistry, a study for which he had always felt a strong liking. Poverty compelled him to give up this study, and he joined the French army. In 1809, while on the way to Douai, he was quartered for one night with M. Balthazar Claës. During a conversation with his host, he explained to him his ideas on the subject of "identity of matter" and the absolute, thus bringing misfortune on a whole family, for from that moment Balthazar Claés devoted time and money to his quest of the absolute. Adam de Wierzchownia, while dying at Dresden, in 1812, of a wound received during the last wars, wrote a final letter to Balthazar Claés, informing him of the different thoughts relative to the search in question, which had been in his mind since their first meeting. By this writing he increased the misfortunes of the Claés family. Adam de Wierzchownia had an angular wasted countenance, large head which was bald, eyes like tongues of fire, a large mustache. His calmness of manner frightened Madame Balthazar Claés.[1] [The Quest of the Absolute.]

[1] Under the title of *Gold, or the Dream of a Savant*, there is a play by Bayard and Biéville, which presents the misfortunes of the Claés. This was given at the Gymnase, November 11, 1837, by M. Bouffé and Madame E. Sauvage, both of whom are still alive.

Willemsens (Marie-Augusta). (*See* Brandon,[1] Comtesse de.)

Wimphen (De), married a friend of Madame d'Aiglemont's childhood. [A Woman of Thirty.]

Wimphen (Madame Louisa de), childhood friend of Madame Julie d'Aiglemont in school at Ecouen. In 1814, Madame d'Aiglemont wrote to her companion, who was then on the point of marrying, of her own disillusionment, and confidentially advised her to remain single. This letter, however, was not sent, for the Comtesse de Listomère-Landon, aunt of Julie d'Aiglemont by marriage, having found out about it, discouraged such an impropriety on the part of her niece. Unlike her friend, Madame de Wimphen married happily. She retained the confidence of Madame d'Aiglemont, and was present, indeed, at the important interview between Julie and Lord Grenville. After M. de Wimphen's arrival to accompany his wife home, these two lovers were left alone, until the unexpected arrival of M. d'Aiglemont made it necessary for Lord Grenville to conceal himself. The Englishman died shortly after this as a result of the night's exposure, when he was obliged to stay in the cold on the outside of a window-sill. This happened also immediately after his fingers were bruised by a rapidly closed door. [A Woman of Thirty.]

Wirth, valet of the banker, J.-B. d'Aldrigger; remained in the service of Mesdames d'Aldrigger, mother and daughters, after the death of the head of the family. He showed them the same devotion, of which he had often given proof. Wirth was a kind of Alsatian Caleb or Gaspard, aged and serious, but with much of the cunning mingled with his simple nature. Seeing in Godefroid de Beaudenord a good husband for Isaure d'Aldrigger, he was able to entrap him easily, and thus was partly responsible for their marriage. [The Firm of Nucingen.]

Wisch (Johann). Fictitious name given in a newspaper for Johann Fischer, when he had been accused of peculation. [Cousin Betty.]

---

[1] Lady Brandon was the mother of Louis Gaston and Marie Gaston.

Wissembourg (Prince de), one of the titles of Maréchal Cottin, the Duc d'Orfano. [Cousin Betty.]

Witschnau.   (*See* Gaudin.)

X

Ximeuse, fief situated in Lorraine; original spelling of the name Simeuse, which came to be written with an S on account of its pronunciation.   [The Gondreville Mystery.]

Y

Ysembourg (Prince d'), marshal of France, the Condé of the Republic. Madame Nourrisson, his confidential servant, looked upon him as a "simpleton," because he gave two thousand francs to one of the most renowned countesses of the Imperial Court, who came to him one day, with streaming eyes, begging him to give her the assistance upon which her children's life depended. She soon spent the money for a robe, which she needed to wear so as to be dressed stylishly at an embassy ball. This story was told by Madame Nourrisson, in 1845, to Léon de Lora, Bixiou, and Gazonal. [The Unconscious Humorists.]

Z

Zambinella, a eunuch, who sang at the Théâtre Argentina, Rome, the leading soprano parts; he was very beautiful. Sarassine, a French sculptor, believing him to be a woman, became enamored of him, and used him as a model for an excellent statue of Adonis, which may still be seen at the Musée d'Albani, and which Dorlange-Sallenauve copied nearly a century later. When he was over eighty years old and very wealthy, Zambinella lived, under the Restoration, with his niece, who was wife of the mysterious Lanty. While residing with the Lantys Zambinella died in Rome, 1830. The early life of Zambinella was unknown to the Parisian world. A mesmerist believed the old man, who was a sort of traveling mummy, to be the famous Balsamo, also known as Cagliostro, while the Bailli de Ferette took him to be the Comte de Saint-Germain. [Sarrasine. The Member for Arcis.]

Zarnowicki (Roman[1]), Polish general who, as a refugee in Paris, lived on the ground floor of the little two-story house on rue de Marbeuf, of which Doctor Halpersohn occupied the other floor in 1836. [The Seamy Side of History.]

NOTE.

The *Repertory of the Comédie Humaine*, as the reader can see for himself, should include only those episodes introducing characters inter-related and continually recurring. Consequently, the stories entitled *The Exiles, About Catherine de Médici, Maître Cornelius, The Unknown Masterpiece, The Elixir of Life, Christ in Flanders*, which antedate the eighteenth century, and *Seraphita*, which deals with the supernatural, are omitted, together with the *Analytical Studies*. But *The Hated Son* furnishes some indispensable information concerning a few biographies. The *Dramas* are outside the action of the *Comédie*, so contribute no names.

According to Théophile Gautier, *The Comédie Humaine* embraces two thousand characters. His reckoning is nearly exact; but as a result of cross-references, surnames, assumed names and the like, that number is far exceeded in this work, which, nevertheless, omits many characters outside the action, as: Chevet, Decamps, Delacroix, Finot Sr., the child of Calyste and Sabine du Guénic, Noémi Magus, Meyerbeer, Herbaut, Houbigant, Tanrade, Mousqueton, Arnal, Barrot, Bonald, Berryer, Gautier, Gozlan, Hugo, Hyacinthe, Lafont, Lamartine, Lassailly, F. Lemaître, Charles X., Louis Philippe, Odry, Talma, Thiers, Villèle, Rossini, Rousseau, Mlle. Déjazet, Mlle. Georges, etc.

---

[1] Probably a given name.